THE PRINCIPLES OF

PSYCHOLOGY

BY

HERBERT SPENCER

VOLUME II

NEW YORK
D. APPLETON AND COMPANY
1897

Authorized Edition.

PREFACE TO VOL. II.

OF this second volume, as of the first volume, it may be said that it is more a new work than a new edition. The only one of its several divisions which retains substantially its original shape, is Part VI., Special Analysis. In this, such changes of significance as will be found, have arisen by the addition of §§ 302—305, showing that the subject-matter of Logic is objective, and by the further developments given to the chapters on " The Perception of Body as Presenting Statical Attributes," " The Perception of Space," and " The Perception of Motion,"—developments by which the doctrine set forth in those chapters, has been more fully harmonized with the Doctrine of Evolution. Part VIII., General Analysis, though it contains fragments of the Part which bore that title in the First Edition, is mainly new in substance and wholly new in organization; and to Part IX., Corollaries, there was nothing answering in the First Edition. In round numbers, 350 pages of fresh matter are added to 300 pages of matter that has appeared before.

The instalments of which this volume consists, were issued to the subscribers at the following dates:—No. 27 (pp. 1—80) in March, 1871; No. 28 (pp. 81—160) in April, 1871; No. 29 (pp. 161—240) in June, 1871; No. 30 (pp. 241—320) in July, 1871; No. 31 (pp. 321—400) in October, 1871; No. 32 (pp. 401—480) in February, 1872; No. 33 (pp. 481—560) in June, 1872; and No. 34 (pp. 561—648) in October, 1872.

London, October, 1872.

CONTENTS OF VOL. II.

PART VI.—SPECIAL ANALYSIS.

PART VII.—GENERAL ANALYSIS.

PART VIII.—CONGRUITIES.

PART IX.—COROLLARIES.

PART VI.

SPECIAL ANALYSIS.

CHAPTER I.

LIMITATION OF THE SUBJECT.

§ 274. Unless he is warned against doing so, the reader will expect to find in the following chapters analyses of states of consciousness of all orders. The phenomena presented by the emotions, as well as those presented by the intellect, will be assumed to fall within the scope of the inquiry. A resolution into their components, not only of thoughts, but also of sentiments, will be looked for.

On comparing these two orders of our mental states, however, it will be seen that though one of them promises to yield satisfactory results under analysis, the other does not. Anything that is to be explained by separation of its parts and examination of the modes in which they are joined to one another, must be something which presents distinguishable parts united in definable ways. And when we have before us something which, though obviously composite, has its heterogeneous elements so mingled and fused together that they cannot be severally identified with clearness, we may conclude that an attempted analysis, if not absolutely fruitless, will bring us to conclusions that are doubtful or incomplete, or both. Now these contrasted characters are possessed by the modes of consciousness we class respectively as intellectual and emotional. A thought, no matter how simple or how complex, contains more or less definable and nameable elements, having connexions that may be described with distinctness. But a sentiment is altogether vague in its outlines, and has a structure which continues indistinct even under the most patient introspection. Dim traces of different components may be discerned; but the limitations both of the whole and of its parts are so faintly marked, and at the same time so entangled, that none but very general results can be reached. And this is a character which the genesis of the emotions, as we have traced it, necessarily implies. Whoever recalls §§ 214, 247 in Parts IV. and V., will see that emotions, having been evolved by the consolidation of clusters upon clusters of heterogeneous simple feelings, and the consolidation of such compound clusters into still larger and more heterogeneous ones, will see that analysis must fail to resolve them into their components.

Passing over the emotions, therefore, as not admitting of further interpretations than those which we reached synthetically in the last volume, we will here limit our analyses to the phenomena classed as intellectual.

§ 275. An analysis conducted in a systematic manner, must begin with the most complex phenomena of the series to be analyzed. After resolving them into phenomena that stand next in order of complexity, it must proceed similarly with these components; and so, by successive decompositions, must descend to the simpler and more general, reaching at last the simplest and most general. Consistently to pursue this method throughout Subjective Psychology is difficult. The commonest operations of consciousness are perplexing to persons unaccustomed to introspection, and its highly-involved operations, if dealt with at the outset, may be expected to tax the powers even of the habitual student.

Disadvantageous, however, in this respect, as such an arrangement of the subject may be, it is so much the best fitted for exhibiting the general law which it is the object of this Special Analysis to disclose, that I do not hesitate to adopt it. A little patience only is asked during the perusal of the next few chapters. What he finds in them that is not very comprehensible, the reader must pass over until subsequent chapters give the key to it. Should some of the matters discussed seem to him unimportant, perhaps he will suspend his judgment until their bearing on the doctrine at large becomes visible. And if he should not perceive the reason for interpreting certain mental phenomena after a particular manner, he is requested to take the analyses upon trust, in the belief that they will eventually be justified.

CHAPTER II.

§ 276. Of intellectual acts the highest are those which constitute Conscious Reasoning—reasoning called conscious to distinguish it from the unconscious or automatic reasoning that forms so large an element in ordinary perception. Of conscious reasoning the kind containing the greatest number of components definitely combined is Quantitative Reasoning. And of this, again, there is a division, more highly involved that the rest, which we may class apart as Compound Quantitative Reasoning. With it, then, we must set out.

Even in Compound Quantitative Reasoning itself there are degrees of composition, and to initiate our analysis rightly we must take first the most composite type. Let us contemplate an example of it.

§ 277. Suppose an engineer has constructed an iron tubular bridge, and finds that it is just strong enough to bear the strain it is subject to—a strain resulting mainly from its own weight. Suppose further that he is required to construct another bridge of like kind, but of double the span. Possibly it will be concluded that for this new bridge he might simply magnify the previous design in all its particulars—make the tube double the depth, double the width, and double the thickness, as well as double the length. But he sees that a bridge so proportioned would not support itself—he infers that the depth or the thickness must be more than double.

By what acts of thought does he reach this conclusion? He knows, in the first place, that the bulks of similar masses of matter are to each other as the cubes of the linear dimensions; and that, consequently, when the masses are not only similar in form but of the same material, the weights also are as the cubes of the linear dimensions. He knows, too, that in similar masses of matter which are subject to compression or tension, or, as in this case, to the transverse strain, the power of resistance varies as the squares of the linear dimensions.* Hence he sees that if another bridge be built proportioned in all respects exactly like the first but of double the size, the weight of it—that is, the gravitative force, or force tending to make it bend and break—will have increased as the *cubes* of the dimensions; while the sustaining force or force by which breaking is resisted, will have increased only as the *squares* of the dimensions, and that the bridge must therefore give way. Or, to present the reasoning in a formal manner, he sees that the—

$$\left.\begin{array}{l}\text{Sustaining force}\\\text{in the small tube}\end{array}\right\} \quad : \quad \left\{\begin{array}{l}\text{Sustaining force}\\\text{in the large tube}\end{array}\right\} : : 1^2 : 2^2$$

whilst at the same time he sees that the—

$$\left.\begin{array}{l}\text{Destroying force}\\\text{in the small tube}\end{array}\right\} \quad : \quad \left\{\begin{array}{l}\text{Destroying force}\\\text{in the large tube}\end{array}\right\} : : 1^3 : 2^3$$

Whence he infers that as the destroying force has increased in a much greater ratio than the sustaining force, the larger

---

* For simplicity's sake, I here state the law in its unqualified form—a form implying that the sides of the tube retain their original attitudes when exposed to the strain. In fact, however, the tendency to twist or warp, technically called "buckling," more difficult to prevent as the tube is increased in size, will imply a diminution in the ratio of increasing strength. But that the strength will increase in a smaller ratio than the squares of the dimensions, makes the engineer's inference all the more certain.

tube cannot sustain itself; seeing that the smaller one has
no excess of strength.

But now, leaving out of sight the various acts by which
the premisses are reached and the final inference is drawn,
let us consider the nature of the cognition that the ratio between the sustaining forces in the two tubes, must differ
from the ratio between the destroying forces; for this cognition it is which here concerns us, as exemplifying the most
complex ratiocination. There is, be it observed, no direct
comparison between these two ratios. How then are they
known to be unlike? Their unlikeness is known through
the intermediation of two other ratios to which they are
severally equal.

The ratio between the sustaining forces *equals* the ratio
$1^2 : 2^2$. The ratio between the destroying forces *equals* the
ratio $1^3 : 2^3$. And as it is seen that the ratio $1^2 : 2^2$ is unequal to the ratio $1^3 : 2^3$; it is by implication seen, that the
ratio between the sustaining forces is unequal to the ratio
between the destroying forces. What is the nature of this
implication? or rather—What is the mental act by which
this implication is perceived? It is manifestly not decomposable into steps. Though involving many elements, it is
a single intuition; and if expressed in an abstract form
amounts to the axiom—Ratios which are severally equal to
certain other ratios that are unequal to each other, are themselves unequal.

I do not propose here to analyze this highly complex intuition. I simply present it as an example of the more
intricate acts of thought which occur in Compound Quantitative Reasoning—an example to which the reader may
hereafter recur if he pleases. A nearly allied but somewhat
simpler intuition will better serve to initiate our analysis.

§ 278. This intuition is embodied in an axiom which
has not, I think, been specifically stated; though it is taken
for granted in Proposition XI. of the fifth book of Euclid;

where, as we shall presently see, the avowed reason for the inference, has this unavowed implication. This proposition, which is to the effect that " Ratios which are equal to the same ratio are equal to one another," it will be needful to quote in full.* It is as follows:—

" Let A be to B as C is to D; and as C is to D so let E be to F. Then A shall be to B as E to F.

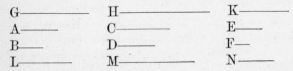

Take of A, C, E, any equimultiples whatever G, H, K; and of B, D, F, any equimultiples whatever L, M, N.† Therefore since A is to B as C to D, and G, H, are taken equimultiples of A, C, and L, M, of B, D; if G be greater than L, H is greater than M; and if equal, equal; and if less, less. Again, because C is to D as E to F, and H, K, are equimultiples of C, E; and M, N, of D, F; if H be greater than M, K is greater than N, and if equal, equal; and if less, less. But if G be greater than L, it has been shown that H is greater than M; and if equal, equal; and if less, less; therefore, of G be greater than L, K is greater than N; and if equal, equal; and if less, less. And G, K are any equimultiples whatever of A, E; and L, N, any whatever of B, F; therefore as A is to B so is E to F."

* In some editions the enunciation runs,—" Ratios which are the same to the same ratio are the same to each other ; " but the above is much the better.

† For the aid of those who have not lately looked into Euclid, it will be well to append the definition of proportionals, which is as follows:— " If there be four magnitudes, and if any equimultiples whatsoever be taken of the first and third, and any equimultiples whatsoever of the second and fourth, and if, according as the multiple of the *first* is greater than the multiple of the *second*, equal to it or less, the multiple of the *third* is also greater than the multiple of the *fourth*, equal to it or less; then, the *first* of the magnitudes is said to have to the *second* the *same ratio* that the *third* has to the *fourth*."

For the sake of simplicity, let us neglect such parts of this demonstration as consist in taking equimultiples and drawing the immediate inferences, and ask by what process is established that final relation among these equimultiples which serves as premiss for the desired conclusion. And to make the matter clearer, we will separate these equimultiples from the original magnitudes; and consider by itself the argument concerning them.

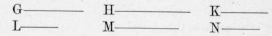

From the hypothesis and the construction, it is proved that if G be greater than L, H is greater than M; and if equal, equal; and if less, less. So, too, it is proved that if H be greater than M, K is greater than N; and if equal, equal; and if less, less. Whence it is inferred that if G be greater than L, K is greater than N; and if equal, equal; and if less, less. In general language then, the fact established is, that whatever relation subsists between G and L, the same relation subsists between H and M: whether it be a relation of superiority, of equality, or of inferiority. *So far as they are defined*, the relations G to L and H to M are known to be equal. Similarly with the relations H to M and K to N, which are known to be equal in respect to the characteristics predicated of them. And then, when it has been shown that the relation G to L equals the relation H to M; and that the relation K to N also equals it; it is said that *therefore* the relation G to L equals the relation K to N. Which *therefore*, involves the assumption that relations which are equal to the same relation, are equal to each other.

Perhaps the rejoinder will be this:—" In asserting that if G be greater than L, H is greater than M; and if equal, equal; and if less, less; it is *not* asserted that the relation G to L *equals* the relation H to M. Without negativing the assertion, G may be supposed to exceed L in a greater proportion than H exceeds M; and, in this case, the relations will not be equal." It might, I think, be argued that the possibility of this supposition arises from the vagueness of the definition of proportional magnitudes; and that it needs only to seize the true meaning of that definition, to see that no such supposition is permissible. Not to dwell on this, however, it will suffice to point out, that though the relations G to L, and H to M, are left to some extent indeterminate, and cannot therefore be called equal in an absolute sense, yet, *so far as they are determinate*, they are equal. Consider the proposition under one of its concrete aspects. Suppose it has been shown that if G be greater than L, H is greater than M; and that if H be greater than M, K is greater than N; then it is said that if G be greater than L, K is greater than N. What are here the premisses and inference? It is argued that the first relation being like the second in a certain particular (the superiority of its first magnitude); and the third relation being also like the second in this particular; the first relation must be like the third in this particular. The same argument is applicable to any other particular; and therefore to all particulars. Whence the implication is that relations that are like the same relation in all particulars, or are equal to it, are like each other in all particulars, or are equal.

Thus the general truth that relations which are equal to the same relation are equal to each other—a truth of which the foregoing proposition concerning ratios is simply one of the more concrete forms—must be regarded as an axiom. Like its analogue—things that are equal to the same thing are equal to each other—it is incapable of proof. Seeing how closely, indeed, the two are allied, some may contend that the one is but a particular form of the other, and should be included under it. They may say that a *relation* considered quantitatively is a species of *thing;* and that what is true of all things is, by implication, true of relations. Even were this satisfactorily shown, however, it would be needful, as will presently be seen, to enunciate this general law in respect to relations. At the same time the criticism serves to bring into yet clearer view the axiomatic nature of the law. For whether a quantified relation be or be not rightly regarded as a thing, it is unquestionably true that in the intellectual process by which relations that are equal to the same relation are perceived to be equal to each other, the concepts dealt with are the relations, and not the objects between which the relations subsist; that the equality of these relations can be perceived only by making *them* the objects of thought; and that hence the axiom, being established by the comparison of three concepts, is established by the same species of mental act as that which has for its terms substantive things instead of relations.

The truth—Relations that are equal to the same relation are equal to each other—which we thus find is known by an intuition,* and can only so be known, underlies important

* Here, and throughout, I use this word in its common acceptation, as meaning any cognition reached by an undecomposable mental act; whether the terms of that cognition be *presented* or *represented* to consciousness. Sir William Hamilton, in classing knowledge as *representative* and *presentative* or *intuitive*, restricts the meaning of intuition to that which is known by external perception. If, when a dog and a horse are looked at, it is seen that the one is less than the other, the cognition is intuitive; but if a dog and a horse are imagined, and the inferior size of the dog perceived in thought, the cognition is not intuitive in Sir William Hamilton's sense of the word. As, however, the act by which the relation of inferiority is established in consciousness, is alike in the two cases, the same term may properly be applied to it in either case. And I draw further reason for using the word in its common acceptation, from the fact that a definite line between presentative and representative *knowledge* cannot be drawn; though it can be drawn between presentative and representative *feelings*. Though there is much knowledge that it is purely representative, there is none that is purely presentative. Every perception whatever involves more or less of representation. And this is asserted by Sir William Hamilton himself, when, in opposition to Royer Collard's doctrine, that perception excludes memory, he writes—"On the contrary, I hold, that as memory, or a certain continuous representation, is a condition of consciousness, it is a condition of perception."

parts of geometry. An examination of the first proposition
in the sixth book of Euclid, and of the deductions made from
it in succeeding propositions, will show that many theorems
have this axiom for their basis.

§ 279. But on this axiom are built far wider and far more
important conclusions. It is the foundation of all Mathematical analysis. Alike in working out the simplest algebraical question, and in performing those higher analytical
processes of which algebra is the root, it is the one thing
taken for granted at every step. The successive transformations of an equation are linked together by acts of
thought, of which this axiom expresses the most general
form. True, the assumption of it is limited to that particular case in which its necessity is so self-evident as to be
almost unconsciously recognized; but it is not the less true
that this assumption cannot be made without involving the
axiom in its entire extent. Let us analyze an example—

$$x^2 + 2\,x = 8$$
$$x^2 + 2\,x + 1 = 9$$
$$x + 1 = \pm\,3$$
$$x = 2 \text{ or } -4.$$

Now it may seem that the only assumptions involved in
these three steps are—first, that if equals be added to
equals, the sums are equal; second, that the square roots
of equals are equals; and third, that if equals be taken from
equals, the remainders are equal. But a further all-
important assumption has been tacitly made. As at present written, there is nothing to mark any connexion
between the first form of the equation and the last.
Manifestly, however, the validity of the inference $x = 2$,
depends on the existence of some perfectly specific connexion between it and the original premiss $x^2 + 2\,x = 8$;
and this connexion implies connexions between the inter-

mediate steps. These connexions will be at once recognized on inserting the required symbols, thus:—

$$
\begin{array}{rcl}
x^2 \quad 2\,x & = & 8 \\
& \| & \\
x^2 + 2\,x + 1 & = & 9 \\
& \| & \\
x + 1 & = & 3 \\
& \| & \\
x & = & 2.
\end{array}
$$

Only through the successive cognitions represented by these signs of equality placed vertically, does the conclusion follow from the original premiss. The argument is worthless unless the value of x in the last form of the equation, is the same as its value in the first form; and this implies the preservation throughout, of an equality between the function of x and the function of its value. But now, in virtue of what assumption is it that the final relation between the two sides of the equation is asserted to be equal to the initial relation? On this assumption it is that the worth of the conclusion depends; and for this assumption no warrant is assigned. I answer, the warrant for this assumption is the axiom—Relations that are equal to the same relation are equal to each other. To make it clear that this axiom is involved, it needs but to simplify the consideration of the matter.   Suppose we represent the successive forms of the equation by the letters A, B, C, D. If A, B, C, D had represented substantive things; and if, when it had been shown that A was equal to B, and B was equal to C, and C was equal to D, it had been concluded that A was equal to D; what would have been assumed? There would have been two assumptions of the axiom—Things that are equal to the same thing are equal to each other: one to establish the equality of A and C by the intermediation of B; and one to establish the equality of A and D by the intermediation of C. Now the fact that A, B, C, D, do not stand for things, but stand for relations between things, cannot fundamentally alter the mental act by which the equality of the first and last is recognized. If, when A, B, C, D, are things, the equality of the first and last can be shown only by means of the axiom—Things that are equal to the same thing are equal to each other; then, when A, B, C, D, are relations, the equality of the first and last can be shown only by means of the axiom—Relations that are equal to the same relation are equal to each other.

It is true that in this case the relations dealt with are relations of equality; and the great simplification hence resulting may raise a doubt whether the process of thought really is the one described. Perhaps it will be argued that the successive forms of the equation being all relations of equality, it is known by an act of direct intuition that any one of them is equal to any other; or that if an axiom be implied, it is the axiom—All relations of equality are equal to each other. Doubtless relations of equality, unlike all other relations and unlike all magnitudes, are in their very expression so defined that the equality of any one of them to any other may be foreknown. But conceding this, the objection may still be met. For how is the relation between the two sides of an equation when reduced to its final form, known to be a relation of equality? Only through its affiliation on the original relation of equality, by means of all the intermediate relations. Strike out in the foregoing case the several transformations which link the first and last forms of the equation together, and it cannot be inferred that x equals 2. If, then, this ultimate relation is known to equal the first, only because it is known to equal the penultimate relation, and the penultimate relation to equal the antepenultimate, and so on; it is clear that the affiliation of the last relation on the first, involves the axiom—Relations that are equal to the same relation are equal to each other.

It must be admitted that in cases like these, where this general axiom is applied to relations of equality, it seems a superfluity. The alleged cognition here merges into a simpler order of cognitions, from which it is with difficulty distinguishable. Nevertheless, I think the arguments adduced warrant the belief that the mental process described is gone through; though perhaps almost automatically. And for this belief further warrant will be found when, under another head, we come to consider the case of inequations—a case in which no such source of difficulty exists, and yet in which the process of thought is unquestionably of like nature.

§ 280. Leaving here its several applications, and passing to the axiom itself, we have now to inquire by what mental act it is known that relations which are equal to the same relations are equal to each other. We have seen that this truth is not demonstrable, but can be reached only by direct intuition. What is the character of this intuition?

If the equality of the first and third relations is not proved but internally perceived, the internal perception must be one in which the first and third relations are in some way brought together before consciousness. Yet any direct comparison of the first and third without intermediation of the second would avail nothing; and any intermediation of the second would seem to imply a thinking of the three in serial order—first, second, third; third, second, first—which would not bring the first and third into the immediate connexion required. Hence, as neither a direct comparison of the first and third, nor a serial comparison of the three, can fulfil the requirement, it follows that they must be compared in couples. By the premises it is known that the first and second relations are equal, and that the second and third relations are equal. Consequently, there are presented to consciousness, two relations of equality between relations. The direct intuition is that these two relations of equality are themselves equal. And as these two relations of equality possess a common term, the intuition that they are equal *involves* the equality of the remaining terms. The nature of this intuition will, however, be best shown by symbols. Suppose the several relations to stand thus—A : B = C : D = E : F; then the act of thought by which the equality of the first and third relations is recognized, may be symbolized thus—*

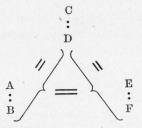

Introspection will, I think, confirm the inference that this represents the mental process gone through—that the first and second relations, contemplated as equal, form together one concept; that the third and second, similarly contemplated, form together another concept; and that, in the intuition of the equality of these concepts, the equality of the terminal relations is implied: or that, to define its nature abstractedly—the axiom expresses an intuition of the equality of two relations between relations.

To the minds of some readers this analysis will not at once commend itself. Indeed, as at first remarked, one inconvenience attendant on beginning with the most complex intellectual processes, is that the propriety of formulating them after a certain manner cannot be clearly

* The sign (:) used in mathematics to express a ratio, is, in this formula, as in many that follow, placed somewhat unusually in respect to the letters it connects, with a view to convenience of reading. It may here be added, in preparation for succeeding chapters, that this sign though here marking, as it commonly does, a ratio, or *quantitative relation*, will hereafter be used to mark *any relation.*

seen till analysis of the simpler intellectual processes has shown why they must be thus formulated. After reading the next few chapters, the truth of the above conclusion will become manifest. Meanwhile, though it may not be positively recognized as true by its perceivable correspondence with the facts of consciousness, it may be negatively recognized as true by observing the impossibility, lately shown, of establishing the equality of the first and last relations by any other intellectual act.

Before ending the chapter it should be noted that the relations thus far dealt with are relations of magnitudes, and, properly speaking, relations of homogeneous magnitudes; or, in other words, *ratios*. In the geometrical reasoning quoted from the fifth book of Euclid, this fact is definitely expressed. In the algebraical reasoning, homogeneity of the magnitudes dealt with seems, at first, not implied; since the same equation often includes at once magnitudes of space, time, force, value. But on remembering that these magnitudes can be treated algebraically, only by reducing them to the common denomination of *number*, and considering them as abstract magnitudes of the same order, we see that the relations dealt with are really those between homogeneous magnitudes—are really *ratios*. The motive for constantly speaking of them under the general name *relations* of which ratios are but one species, is that only when they are so classed, can the intellectual processes by which they are co-ordinated be brought under the same category with other acts of reasoning.

CHAPTER III.

§ 281. The results just reached do not, apparently, help us very far on the way to a theory of Compound Quantitative Reasoning. Such an intuition as that expressed in the axiom educed, can be but one among the many intuitions which, joined together, form a mathematical argument. However many times quoted, or applied in thought, the axiom—Relations which are equal to the same relation are equal to each other, can never do anything else than establish the equality of some two relations by the intermediation of a series of relations severally equal to both; and it is but in a moiety of cases that the equality of two relations is the fact to be arrived at. The proposition—" If two circles touch each other externally, the straight line which joins their centres shall pass through the point of contact," is one with which such an axiom can have no concern; and the same is manifestly the case with most geometrical truths. Some more general cognition, then, has to be found.

Guidance in the search for such a cognition, may be drawn from the consideration that it must be involved not only in all other kinds of quantitative reasoning, but *also* in the kind exemplified in the preceding chapter. This being an *à priori* necessity, it follows that as, in the case of algebraic reasoning, the foregoing axiom expresses the sole cognition by which the successive steps are rationally co-ordinated, the required fundamental cognition must be involved in it. Evidently, our best course will be to continue the line of analysis already commenced.

If, then, ceasing to consider in its totality the complex axiom—Relations which are equal to the same relation are equal to each other, we inquire what are the elements of thought into which it is proximately decomposable; we at once see that it twice over involves a recognition of the equality of two relations. Before it can be seen that the relations A : B and E : F, being severally equal to the relation C : D, are equal to each other; it must be seen that the relation A : B *is* equal to the relation C : D, and that the relation C : D *is* equal to the relation E : F. And this is the intellectual act of which we are in search. An intuition of the equality of two relations is implied in every step of quantitative reasoning—both that which deals with homogeneous magnitudes and that which deals with magnitudes not homogeneous. Let us take as our first field for the exemplification of this fact, the demonstration of geometrical theorems.

§ 282. We will begin by looking at the substance of a proposition; and will consider by what process the mind advances from that particular case of it which the demonstration establishes, to the recognition of its general truth. Let us take as an example, the proposition—" The angles at the base of an isosceles triangle are equal to each other."

To prove this, the abstract terms are forthwith abandoned, and the proposition is re-stated in a concrete form. " Let A B C be an isosceles triangle, of which the side A B is equal to the side A C; then the angle A B C shall be equal to the angle A C B." By a series of steps which need not be here specified, the way is found from these premisses to this conclusion. But now mark what takes place. As soon as this particular fact has been proved, the general fact is immediately re-enunciated and held to be proved. We pass directly from the concrete inference—the angle A B C *is* equal to the angle A C B—to the abstract inference: we say—therfore the angles at the base of an isosceles triangle are equal to each other. Q.E.D. Be the cogency of every step in the demonstration what it may, the truth of the proposition at large hinges entirely on the cognition that what holds in one case holds in all cases. What is the nature of this cognition? It is a consciousness of the equality of two relations—on the one hand, the relation between the sides and angles of the triangle A B C; and on the other hand, the relation between the sides and angles of another isosceles triangle, of any isosceles triangle, of all isosceles triangles. Whatever may be the way in which we figure to ourselves a class, this conclusion holds. Whether in the present case the abstract truth be recognized only after it has been seen to hold in this isosceles triangle, and in this, and in this; or whether after it has been seen to hold in some ideal type of an isosceles triangle; it is alike certain that the thing discerned is the equality of the relations presented in successive concepts. If we use the letter A to symbolize the premised fact (viz. that in the triangle A B C the sides A B and A C are equal), and the letter B to symbolize the fact asserted (viz. that the angle A B C is equal to the angle A C B); then, after establishing a certain relation (of coexistence) between A and B in this one case, we go on to affirm that the same relation holds between some other A and B, and between every A and every B: or, strictly speaking, not the *same* relation but an *equal* relation. And as we can assign no reason, the affirmation obviously expresses a simple intuition.

Not only do we pass from the special truth to the general truth by an intuition of the equality of two relations; but a like intuition constitutes each of the steps by which the special truth is reached. In the demonstration of such special truth, the propositions previously established are explicitly or implicitly referred to; and the relations that subsist in the case in hand are recognized as equal to relations which those previously-established propositions express. This will be seen on subjecting a demonstration to analysis. The one belonging to the foregoing theorem is inconveniently long. We shall find a fitter one in Proposition xxxii.

" If the side of any triangle be produced, the exterior angle is equal to the two interior and opposite angles; and the three interior angles of every triangle are together equal to two right angles.

" Let A B C be a triangle, and let one of its sides B C be produced to D; then the exterior angle A C D is equal to the two interior and opposite angles C A B, A B C; and the three interior angles of the triangle, namely A B C, B C A, C A B, are together equal to two right angles.

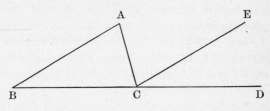

DEMONSTRATION.

" From the point C draw the straight line C E parallel to A B; and because A B is parallel to C E, and A C meets them, the alternate angles B A C, A C E are equal.

"Again, because A B is parallel to C E, and

ANALYSIS.

It was demonstrated in a previous case, that there is a relation of co-existence between the parallelism of two lines and the equality of the alternate angles made by a line meeting them. It is perceived that the parallelism of the lines must coexist with the equality of the angles in this case also. That is, the present relation is seen to be equal to a relation previously established.

In a foregoing proposition, it was shown that of the angles made by a

B D falls upon them, the exterior angle E C D is equal to the interior and opposite angle A B C;

but the angle A C E was shown to be equal to the angle B A C; therefore the whole exterior angle A C D, is equal to the two interior and opposite angles C A B, A B C.

"To these angles add the angle A C B; then the angles A C D, A C B are together equal to the three angles C B A, B A C, A C B.

"But the angles A C D, A C B, are together equal to two right angles;

line cutting two parallel lines, the exterior is equal to the interior and opposite. Here there are two parallel lines and a line cutting them; and the cognition which the demonstration expresses is, that the relation between lines and angles which held before, holds now—that this is a like relation, an equal relation.

Immediate intuitions: first, that the whole is equal to its parts; and second, that things which are equal to the same thing are equal to each other. Which last, as we shall see at a future stage, is an intuition of the equality of two relations.

An intuition that when to equal magnitudes the same magnitude is added, the sums are equal: an intuition which is itself a consciousness of the equality of two relations—the relation that subsists between the magnitudes before the addition is made, and the relation that subsists after it is made.

In a previous case it was ascertained that the angles which a straight line made with another straight line upon one side of it, were either two right angles, or equal to two right angles; and the thing now perceived is, that the relation between lines and angles in this case, is exactly like the relation in that case—in other words, the two relations are equal.

therefore also the angles C B A, B A C, A C B, are together equal to two right angles.

"Therefore if a side of any triangle be produced, the exterior angle is equal to the two interior and opposite angles; and the three interior angles of every triangle are equal to two right angles. Q.E.D."

An intuition that things which are equal to the same thing are equal to each other; which, as before hinted, is itself known through an intuition of the equality of two relations.

An intuition that the relation between lines and angles found to subsist in this triangle, subsists in any triangle, in all triangles—that the relation in every other case is equal to the relation in this case.

Thus in each step by which the special conclusion is reached, as well as in the step taken from that special conclusion to the general one, the essential operation gone through is the establishment in consciousness of the equality of two relations. And as, in each step, the mental act is undecomposable—as for the assertion that any two such relations are equal, no reason can be assigned save that they are perceived to be so; it is manifest that the whole process of thought is thus expressed.

§ 283. Perhaps it will be deemed needless to prove that each step in an algebraic argument is of the same nature; since it has been shown that the axiom—Relations which are equal to the same relation are equal to each other, twice involves an intuition of the above-described kind; and since the implication is, that reasoning which proceeds upon this axiom is built up of such intuitions. But it may be well definitely to point out that only in virtue of such intuitions do the successive transformations of an equation become allowable. Unless it is perceived that a certain modification made in the form of the equation, leaves the relation between its two sides the same as before—unless it is seen that each new relation established is *equal* to the foregoing one, the reasoning is vicious. A convenient mode of showing that the mental act continually repeated in one of these analytical processes is of the kind described, is suggested by an ordinary algebraic artifice. When a simplification may be thereby achieved, it is usual to throw any two forms of an equation into a proportion—a procedure in which the equality of the relations is specifically asserted. Here is an illustration: not such an one as would occur in practice, but one that is simplified to serve present purposes.

$$2xy = y^2$$
$$2x = y$$
$$2xy : y^2 :: 2x : y$$

or, as it is otherwise written

$$2xy : y^2 = 2x : y$$

and if proof be needed that this mode of presenting the facts is legitimate, we at once obtain it by multiplying extremes and means; whence results the truism—

$$2xy^2 = 2xy^2.$$

This clearly shows that the mental act determining each algebraic transformation, is one in which the relation expressed by the new form of the equation is recognized as equal to the relation which the previous form expresses.

CHAPTER IV.

IMPERFECT AND SIMPLE QUANTITATIVE REASONING.

§ 284. Ability to perceive equality implies a correlative ability to perceive inequality: neither can exist without the other. But though inseparable in origin, the cognitions of equality and inequality, whether between things or relations, differ in this; that while the one is definite the other is indefinite. There is but one equality; but there are numberless degrees of inequality. To assert an inequality involves the affirmation of no fact, but merely the denial of a fact; and therefore, as positing nothing specific, the cognition of inequality can never be a premiss to any specific conclusion.

Hence, reasoning which is *perfectly* quantitative in its results, proceeds *wholly* by the establishment of equality between relations, the members of which are either equal or one a known multiple of the other. Conversely, if any of the magnitudes standing in immediate relation are neither directly equal nor the one equal to so many times the other; or if any of the successive relations which the reasoning establishes are unequal; the results are *imperfectly* quantitative. The truth is illustrated in that class of geometrical theorems in which it is asserted of some thing that it is greater or less than some other; that it falls within or without some other; and the like. Let us take as an example the proposition—" Any two sides of a triangle are together greater than the third side."

"Let A B C be a triangle; any two sides of it are, together, greater than the third side; namely, B A, A C, greater than B C; and A B, B C, greater than A C; and B C, C A, greater than A B.

"Produce B A to D, and make A D equal to A C; and join D C.

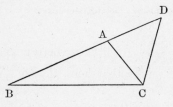

"Because D A is equal to A C, the angle A D C is equal to the angle A C D;	A relation equal to a previously-established relation.
but the angle B C D is greater than the angle A C D;	An immediate intuition of inequality.
therefore the angle B C D is greater than the angle A D C.	An immediate intuition of the equality of two relations of inequality, which have one term in common, and the other terms equal.
"And because the angle B C D is greater than the angle B D C, and that the greater side is opposite to the greater angle, the side D B is greater than the side B C;	A relation equal to a previously-established relation.
but D B is equal to B A, A C;	An immediate intuition that when to two magnitudes standing in the relation of equality, the same magnitude is added, the resulting relation equals the original relation.

therefore B A, A C are greater than B C.

An immediate intuition of the equality of two relations of inequality which have one term in common, and the other terms equal.

" In the same manner it may be demonstrated that the sides A B, B C are greater than C A, and B C, C A greater than A B."

The relations subsisting in other cases are equal to the relation subsisting in this case.

It will be observed that here, though the magnitudes dealt with are unequal, yet the demonstration proceeds by showing that certain relations among them are equal to certain other relations: though the primary relations (between quantities) are those of inequality, yet the secondary relations (between relations) are those of equality. And this holds in the majority of imperfectly-quantitative arguments. Though, as we shall see by and by, there are cases in which both the magnitudes and the relations are unequal, yet they are comparatively rare; and are incapable of any but the simplest forms.

§ 285. Another species of imperfectly-quantitative reasoning occupies a position in mathematical analysis, like that which the foregoing species does in mathematical synthesis. The ordinary algebraic inequation supplies us with a sample of it. Thus, if it is known that $a + \dfrac{x^2}{\sqrt{y}}$ is less than $a + v \sqrt{y}$, the argument instituted is as follows:—

$$a + \frac{x^2}{\sqrt{y}} \quad < \quad a + x\sqrt{y}$$
$$\frac{x^2}{\sqrt{y}} \quad < \quad x\sqrt{y}$$
$$x^2 \quad < \quad xy$$
$$x \quad < \quad y.$$

In this case, as in the case of equations, the reasoning proceeds by steps of which each tacitly asserts the equality of the new relation to the relation previously established, with this difference, that instead of the successive relations being relations of equality, they are relations of inferiority. The general process of thought, however, is the same in both.   This will be obvious on considering that as the inferiority of x to y can be known only by deduction from the inferiority of $a + \dfrac{z^2}{\sqrt{y}}$ to $a + x\sqrt{y}$; and as it can be so known only by the intermediation of other relations of inferiority; the possibility of the argument depends on the successive relations being recognized as severally equal.   It is true that these successive relations need not be specifically equal; but they must be equal in so far as they are defined. In the above case, for example, the original form of the inequation expresses a relation in which the second quantity bears a greater ratio to the first, than it does in the form which follows; seeing that when equals are taken from unequals, the remainders are more unequal than before. But though in the *degree* of inferiority which they severally express, the successive relations need not be equal, they must be equal in so far as being relations of inferiority goes; and this indefinite inferiority is all that is predicated either in premiss or conclusion.

Here, too, should be specifically remarked the fact hinted in a previous chapter; namely, that the reasoning by which an inequation is worked out, palpably proceeds on the intuition that relations which are equal to the same relation are equal to each other.   The relations being those of inequality, the filiation of the last upon the first can only thus be explained; and the parallelism subsisting between inequations and equations, in respect of the mental acts gone through in solving them, confirms the conclusion before reached that in equations this intuition is involved, though less manifestly.

Of imperfect quantitative reasoning, the lowest type is that in which the successive relations are known only as relations of inequality—are presented in a way which does not define them as either those of superiority or inferiority. For instance:—

$$\frac{x^2}{y} \text{ is unequal to } y$$
$$x^2 \text{ is unequal to } y^2$$
$$x \text{ is unequal to } y.$$

In this case the deductive process is the same as before. The successive relations are perceived to be alike in respect to their inequality, though it is not known whether the antecedents or the consequents are the greater. There is a definite co-ordination of the successive relations, though each relation is defined to the smallest possible extent.

§ 286. Incidentally, much has been implied respecting simple quantitative reasoning throughout the foregoing analyses. The steps into which every compound quantitative argument is resolvable, are simple quantitative arguments; and we have already found that each of them involves the establishment of equality or inequality between two relations. It will be convenient, however, to consider by themselves a class of simple quantitative arguments which are of habitual occurrence: some of them axioms; some of them nearly allied to axioms.

Let us commence with the familiar one—" Things which are equal to the same thing are equal to each other." By reasoning like that already used in an analogous but more complex case, it may be shown that this axiom expresses an intuition of the equality of two relations. Thus, putting A, B and C, as the three magnitudes, it is clear that if A and C are contemplated by themselves in immediate succession, their equality cannot be recognized; since it is only because equality to B is common to the two that they can be known as equal. If, on the other hand, B is interpolated in consciousness, and the three are contemplated serially—A, B, C, or C, B, A,—then A and C do not occur in the juxtaposition implied by consciousness of their equality. There remains no alternative but that of contemplating them in pairs, thus:—

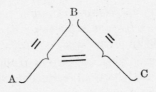

When A and B are united together in the single concept —a relation of equality; and when C and B are united into another such concept; it becomes impossible to recognize the equality of these two relations of equality which possess a common term, without the equality of the other terms being involved in the intuition.

That the mental act is of the kind described, will be made clear by taking a case in which some of the magnitudes dealt with have ceased to exist. Suppose A to represent a standard measure preserved by the State; and let a surveyor be in possession of a measure B, which is an exact copy of the original one A. Imagine that in the course of his survey the measure B is broken; and that in the meantime the building containing the standard measure A, has been burnt. Nevertheless, by purchasing another measure C, which had also been made to match the standard A, the surveyor is enabled to complete his work; and knows that his later measurements will agree with his earlier ones. By what process of thought does he perceive this? It cannot be by comparing B and C; for one of these was broken before he got the other. Nor can it be by comparing them serially—B, A, C, and C, A, B; for two of them have ceased to exist. Evidently, then, he thinks of B and C as both copies of A: he contemplates the *relations* in which they respectively stood to A; and in recognizing the sameness or equality of these relations, he unavoidably recognizes the equality of B and C.　　Here let us notice a fact having an important bearing, not only on this, but on endless other cases—the fact, namely, that the mind may retain an accurate remembrance of a *relation*, when it is unable to retain an accurate remembrance of the *things* between which the relation subsisted. To vary the above illustration—suppose a surveyor has had opportunities, at the respective times when he bought them, of comparing the measures B and C with the standard A. It becomes possible for him, at any time afterwards, to remember with precision the relation of equality in which B stood to A: he can see in thought that exact agreement which they displayed when placed side by side. But he cannot remember the magnitudes themselves with anything like this precision.　　And now observe the implication. When two objects that have not been seen in juxtaposition are remembered, an approximate idea of their relative magnitudes may be formed, if they are markedly different; but if they are nearly of a size, the judgment is as likely to be wrong as right in deciding which is the greater. If, then, two magnitudes separately observed, cannot afterwards be represented in consciousness so distinctly that their equality or inequality can be determined; and if, on the other hand, a relation of equality that was once ascertained by juxtaposing two magnitudes *can* be represented in consciousness with perfect distinctness, and recognized as equal to some other relation of equality; it becomes manifest that, in cases like the above, the truth perceived *cannot* be reached by remembering the magnitudes, but *can* be reached by remembering the relations.

Divergent from this original type are certain intuitions in which the thing known is the relation, not between two relations of equality having a common term, but between two relations of inequality having a common term. Thus, if A is greater than B, and B greater than C, then A is greater than C; and conversely if they are severally less instead of greater. The act of thought may be symbolized thus:—

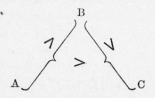

The relation A to B being given as a relation of superiority, while that of C to B is given as a relation of inferiority, it is known that the relation A to B is greater than the relation C to B; and as the term B is common to the two relations, the intuition that the relation A to B is greater than the relation C to B, cannot be formed without involving the intuition that A is greater than C.

Again, if A is greater than B, and B is equal to C; we know that A is greater than C. And if the first relation is one of equality and the second is one of inequality, there is a kindred intuition. In these cases, or rather in the first of them, we may express the mental act thus:—

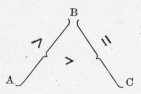

Here, as before, the magnitude B being common to both, the relation A to B cannot become known as greater than the relation C to B without the superiority of A to C being known. Two relations having a common term cannot be conceived unequal, unless the remaining terms are unequal. And just as two magnitudes placed side by side, cannot be perceived unequal without its being at the same time perceived which is the greater; so, of two conjoined relations, one cannot be perceived greater than the other without its being at the same time perceived which includes the greater magnitude.

§ 287. Of simple quantitative intuitions embodied in axioms, or capable of being so embodied, we have next to consider the class in which not three magnitudes but four are involved. On such axioms proceed the successive transformations of an equation.

Among them the most familiar are these:—The sums of equals are equal. If equals are taken from equals the differences are equal. If equals are multiplied by equals the products are equal. If equals are divided by equals the quotients are equal. These are of course accompanied by axioms expressing converse intuitions such as:—If to equals unequals are added the sums are unequal. If equals are divided by unequals the quotients are unequal, etc. Some of the intuitions of this order are more complex. I may name those by which it is known that if from unequals equals are taken, the remainders are more unequal; and, conversely, that if to unequals equals are added, the sums are less unequal. To such generic cases may be added the specific ones in which the first pair of unequals being known to stand in a relation of superiority, the second pair are known to stand in a still greater relation of superiority, or a less relation, according to the operation performed; and similarly when the relation is one of inferiority. Thus,

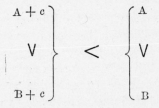

$$\left.\begin{array}{c} \text{A} + c \\ \vee \\ \text{B} + c \end{array}\right\} \; < \; \left\{\begin{array}{c} \text{A} \\ \vee \\ \text{B} \end{array}\right.$$

if $A + c$ is greater than $B + c$; then, in a still higher degree is A greater than B—an intuition which may be expressed by the foregoing symbol.

For present purposes it is needless to detail the varieties belonging to this class. It will suffice to remark, alike of these cases in which the thing perceived is the inequality of two relations, and of the antithetical cases in which the equality of two relations is perceived, that they differ from the previous class in this; that the relations are not conjoined ones but disjoined ones. Throughout the previous class, of which the simplest type is the axiom—" Things which are equal to the same thing are equal to each other," there is invariably one term common to the two relations; while throughout this class, of which as a typical sample we may take the axiom—" If equals be added to equals the sums are equal," the compared relations have no term in common. Hence in this second series, the relations being perfectly independent and distinct, the mental processes into which they enter are more readily analyzable. It is at once manifest that each of the axioms above given, involves an intuition of the equality or inequality of two relations; and, indeed, the fact is more or less specifically stated throughout. In each case there is a certain relation, the terms of which are modified after a specified manner; and there is then an assertion that the new relation is or is not equal to the old one—an assertion which, being based on no argument, expresses an intuition.

§ 288. One further fact respecting these two groups of intuitions remains to be noticed. They have a common root with those which proportions express. The one group is related in origin to that species of proportion in which the second of three magnitudes is a mean between the first and third; and the other group to that species in which the proportion subsists between four separate magnitudes. Thus the axiom—" Things which are equal to the same thing are equal to each other," may, if we call the things A, B and C, be written thus:—

$$A : B \; : : \; B : C.$$

And again, the axiom—" The sums of equals are equal," may, if we put A and B for the first pair of equals, with C and D for the second pair, be expressed thus:—

$$A : B \; : : \; A + C : B + D.$$

The intuitions by which proportions are established, differ from the majority of the foregoing intuitions simply in their greater definiteness—in their complete quantitativeness. The two compared relations are always exactly equal, whatever the magnitudes may be—are not joined by the indefinite signs meaning greater than or less than; and when the proportion is expressed numerically, it not only implies the intuition that the two relations are equal, but the figures indicate what multiple, or submultiple, each magnitude is of the others.

CHAPTER V.

§ 289. Quantitative Reasoning involves the three ideas—coextension, coexistence, and connature;·* or to speak less accurately but more comprehensibly—sameness in the quantity of space occupied, sameness in the time of presentation to consciousness, and sameness in kind. It involves these either positively by asserting them, or negatively by denying them. This proposition calls for an expanded statement.

The germ out of which Quantitative Reasoning grows —the simple intuition of the equality of two magnitudes, necessarily involves all these ideas. There can be no comparison between magnitudes unless they are of the same kind; and their coextension cannot be perceived unless they are coexistent. It is thus with positively-quantitative geometry in general. Each of its propositions predicates the coextension or non-coextension of two or more connatural things which coexist; or the coexistence of certain things asserted to be coextensive, or the reverse, with certain other things known to be coextensive, or the reverse. And its demonstrations proceed by asserting that certain coexistent, connatural things are invariably coextensive, or the reverse; or that certain connatural and

---

* I coin this word partly to avoid an awkward periphrasis; and partly to indicate the kinship of the idea signified, to the ideas of coexistence and coextension. As we have already in use the words *connate* and *connatural*, the innovation is but small; and will, I think, be sufficiently justified by the requirement.

coextensive things invariably coexist with certain other things.   When the propositions are numerical, and when, as frequently happens in Algebra and the Calculus generally, *duration* is one of the elements dealt with, it would appear that coexistence is not involved; and further, that when *force* and *value* are the other elements of the question, there is not even any implication of coextension.   These, however, are illusions resulting from the abstract character of numerical symbols. Representing equal units, and groups of equal units, of any order whatever; and being, as it were, created at any moment for the purposes of calculation; numerical symbols seem, at first sight, independent alike of Space and Time. The fact, however, is exactly the reverse. On tracing them back to their origins, we find that the units of Time, Force, Value, Velocity, &c., which figures may indiscriminately represent, were at first measured by equal units of Space. The equality of times becomes known either by means of the equal spaces traversed by an index, or the descent of equal quantities (space-fulls) of sand or water. Equal units of weight were obtained through the aid of a lever having equal arms (scales). The problems of Statics and Dynamics are primarily soluble, only by putting lengths of lines to represent amounts of forces. Mercantile values are expressed in units which were at first, and indeed are still, definite weights of metal; and are therefore, in common with units of weight, referable to units of linear extension. Temperature is measured by the equal lengths marked alongside a mercurial column. Thus, abstract as they have now become, the units of calculation, applied to whatever species of magnitudes, do really stand for equal units of linear extension; and the idea of coextension underlies every process of mathematical analysis. Similarly with coexistence. Numerical symbols are, it is true, purely representative; and hence may be regarded as having nothing but a fictitious existence. But one of two things must be admitted respecting the reasoning processes carried on by means of them. Either these processes imply a conscious reference to the things symbolized—in which case the equalities predicated are really those previously observed between coexistent things; or else the things symbolized cease to be thought of, and the relations among the symbols are alone considered—in which case these symbols require to be made coexistent to consciousness before their relations can be determined. In fact, the phenomena of motion and sequence can be treated quantitatively, only by putting coexistent magnitudes to represent magnitudes that do not coexist. The relative lengths of two times, not being ascertainable directly, has to be indirectly ascertained by comparing the spaces which a clock-finger traverses during the two times; that is, by comparing coexistent magnitudes. Hence, regarding it in the abstract, we may say that the Calculus in general is a means of dealing with magnitudes that do not coexist, or are not homogeneous, or both, by first substituting for them magnitudes that do coexist and are homogeneous, and afterwards re-translating these into their original forms.

That perfect quantitative reasoning deals exclusively with intuitions of the coextension of coexistent magnitudes which are connatural, will, however, be most clearly seen when it is remarked that the intuitions of coextension, of coexistence, and of connature, are the sole perfectly definite intuitions we can frame. On placing two equal lines side by side, we can perceive with precision that they are equal; but we cannot, if one is greater than the other, perceive with like precision how much greater it is. Our only mode of precisely determining this, is to divide both into small *equal* divisions, of which the greater contains so many and the less so many: we have to fall back on the intuition of coextension. Again, while we can know with exactness that two things coexist, we cannot, when one thing follows another, know with like exactness the interval of time be-

tween them. Definitely to ascertain this, we use a scale of
time made of coextensive units of space. Once more, we
recognize with perfect definiteness, equality of nature in
those things which admit of quantitative comparison. That
straight lines are homogeneous, and can stand to one
another in relations of greater and less, though they cannot
so stand to areas or cubic spaces; that areas are connatural with areas, and cubic spaces with cubic spaces;
that such and such are magnitudes of force, and such and
such are magnitudes of time—these are intuitions that have
as high a degree of accuracy as the foregoing ones. Beyond
these three orders of intuitions, however, we have none that
are perfectly definite. Our perceptions of degree and quality
in sound, colour, taste, smell; of amount in weight and
heat; of relative hardness; of relative duration; are in
themselves inexact. Hence, as we know that by quantitative reasoning of the higher orders, perfectly definite results
are reached; it follows that the intuitions out of which it is
built must be exclusively those of coexistence, connature,
and coextension.

Here, to show the various combinations into which these
intuitions enter, and also to bring into view sundry facts
not yet noticed, let me group in their ascending order the
successive forms which quantitative reasoning assumes.
Certain unavoidable repetitions will, I think, be justified by
the clearer comprehension to be given.

§ 290. The intuition underlying all quantitative reasoning is that of the equality of two magnitudes. Now the
immediate consciousness that—

$$A = B$$

implies three things:—First, that A and B are coexistent;
for otherwise, they cannot be so presented to consciousness
as to allow of a direct recognition of their equality. Second,
that they are magnitudes of like kind, that is, connatural or
homogeneous; for if one be a length and the other an area,

no quantitative relation can exist between them. Third, that they are not *any* homogeneous magnitudes, but are magnitudes of linear extension; seeing that these alone admit of that perfect juxtaposition by which exact equality must be determined—these alone permit their equality to be tested by seeing whether it will merge into identity, as two equal mathematical lines placed one upon the other do —these alone exhibit that species of coexistence which can lapse into single existence. Thus the primordial quantitative idea unites the intuitions of coextension, coexistence, and connature in their most perfect forms.

 To recognize the negation of this equality—to perceive that A is unequel to B—or, more explicitly, to perceive either that—

$$A > B, \quad \text{or} \quad A < B$$

involves no such stringent conditions. It is true that, as before, A and B must be connatural magnitudes. But it is no longer necessary that they should be coexistent; nor that they should be magnitudes of linear extension. Provided the superiority or inferiority of A to B is considerable, it can be known in the absence of one or both; and can be known when they are magnitudes of area, bulk, weight, time, velocity, &c.

The simplest act of quantitative reasoning, which neither of these intuitions exhibits when standing alone, arises when the two are co-ordinated in a compound intuition; or when either of them is so co-ordinated with another of its own kind. When, by uniting two of the first intuitions thus—

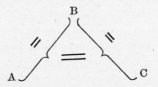

we recognize the equality of A and C, it is requisite, as before, that if the equalities of A to B, and B to C are to be

known immediately, the magnitudes shall be those of linear
extension, though, if the equalities have been mediately
determined, the magnitudes may be any other that are
homogeneous; but it is no longer necessary that all of
them shall coexist. At one time A must have coexisted
with B; and at one time B must have coexisted with C;
but the intuitions of their equalities having once been
achieved, either at the same time or separate times, it
results from the ability we have to remember a specific
relation with perfect exactness, that we can, at any subsequent time, recognize the equality of the relations A to B
and B to C, and the consequent equality of A and C;
though part, or even all, of the magnitudes have ceased to
exist.

By uniting the first and second intuitions, and by uniting
the second with another of its own kind, we obtain two
compound intuitions, formulated as follows:—

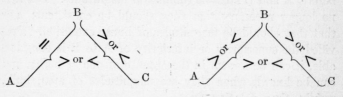

In the first of these cases it is requisite, when the relations are immediately established, that the magnitudes be
linear; but not so if the equality of A and B has been
mediately established; and while A and B must have co-
existed, it is not necessary that B and C should have done
so. In the second case the magnitudes need not be linear;
but, if the inequalities are considerable, may be of any
order. Further, it would at first sight appear that they
need none of them be coexistent. But this is not true. For
if the superiority or inferiority of A to B and of B to C is so
great that it can be perceived by comparing the remembrances of them, then the superiority or inferiority of A to
C can be similarly perceived without the intermediation of

B; and the reasoning is superfluous. The only cases to which this formula applies, are those in which the inequalities are so moderate that direct comparison is required for the discernment of them; whence it follows that each pair of magnitudes must have been at one time coexistent.

The next complication, characterizing all quantitative reasonings save these simplest and least important kinds just exemplified, arises when, in place of conjoined relations, we have to deal with disjoined relations—when the compared relations instead of having one term in common have no term in common. Wherever there are four magnitudes instead of three, sundry new laws come into force; the most important of which is, that the magnitudes need no longer be all of the same order. In every one of the foregoing cases, we have seen that while the intuition of coexistence is sometimes not immediately involved but only mediately so, even where the judgment reached is perfectly quantitative; and while, where the judgment is imperfectly quantitative, the intuition of coextension is not involved, save as the correlative of non-coextension; the intuition which *is* uniformly involved is that of the con-nature of the magnitudes—their homogeneity, their same-ness in kind. Without this no one of the judgments given is possible. But with disjoined relations it is otherwise. The four magnitudes may be all homogeneous; or they may be homogeneous only in pairs, either as taken in succession or alternately. Let us consider the resulting formulæ.

When all the magnitudes are homogeneous we have for the first group of cases the symbol—

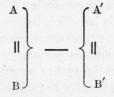

in which each of the disjoined relations is one of equality, and the second is some transformation of the first. This, as before shown, represents the mental act taken in every step of an equation; and stands for the several axioms—When equals are added to, subtracted from, multiplied by, or divided by, equals, the results are equal. For the second group of cases we have the symbol—

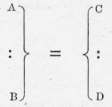

in which each of the relations is one of inequality. This comprehends all cases of proportion: whether they be the numerical ones in which the degrees of inequality are definitely expressed; or the geometrical ones (as those subsisting between the sides of similar triangles) in which the degrees of inequality, though known to be alike, are not definitely expressed. For the third group of cases, forming the antithesis to the two preceding groups, and being but imperfectly quantitative, we have the symbol—

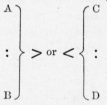

which represents such general truths as that if equals be taken from unequals the remainders are more unequal; that if to equals unequals be added, the sums are unequal; and so forth. Respecting these three groups of cases in which the magnitudes are all homogeneous, it needs only be added that the equality or inequality asserted between the two pairs, always refers directly or indirectly to the space-relations of their components, and not to their time-relations.

Passing to the class of disjunctive pairs of relations in which the several magnitudes are not all homogeneous, we find that the equality predicated between the relations may refer either to comparative extension or comparative existence.   The first group of them may be symbolized thus:—

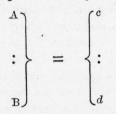

so as to indicate the fact that the magnitudes of the first relation are of one species, while those of the second relation are of another species.   It comprehends cases in which one line is to another line as one area to another area, or in which a bulk is to a bulk as a weight to a weight—cases like those in which it is seen that triangles of the same altitude are to each other as their bases, or that the amounts of two attractions are to each other as the masses of the attracting bodies.   Here it is manifest that though the first pair of magnitudes differs in kind from the second pair, yet the antecedent and consequent of the one bear to each other the same quantitative relation as those of the other; and hence the possibility of ratiocination.   The second group of cases belonging to this class may be thus formulated.

$$\left.\begin{matrix} A \\ : \\ b \end{matrix}\right\} = \left\{\begin{matrix} C \\ : \\ d \end{matrix}\right.$$

Here each relation consists of two heterogeneous magnitudes, as a line and an angle; but the two antecedents are of the same nature and the two consequents are of the same nature. Neither of the compared relations can be a quantitative one; since in neither have the components that connature implied by the assertion of relative magnitude. Hence the two relations can be equal only in respect of the *coexistence* of their elements; and, as it would seem, considerations of quantity are no longer involved. There are conditions, however, under which this form represents reasoning that is truly quantitative; namely, when the coexistence pre-supposes certain defined quantitative relations by which the heterogeneous magnitudes are indirectly bound together. Thus, when the theorem—" The greater side of every triangle has the greater angle opposite to it," is quoted in the proof of a subsequent theorem, the act of thought implied is of the kind above symbolized. The greater side (A) of a triangle, has been found to stand in a special relation of coexistence with the greater angle (b); and in some other triangle the greater side (C) and greater angle (d) are perceived to stand in the *same* or an *equal* relation. This relation is not simply that of coexistence: it is coexistence in certain respective positions. And though there can be no *direct* quantitative relation between a side and an angle, yet, by being contained between the two lesser sides, the greater angle is put in *indirect* quantitative relation with the greater side. It may be held, however, that in this, as in the innumerable like cases which occur in geometrical reasoning, A, b, C, and d should be severally regarded rather as relations between magnitudes, than as magnitudes themselves. To elucidate this question let us consider the theorem—" The angle in a semicircle is a right angle." Here the word " semicircle " denotes definitely quantitative relations—a curve all parts of which are *equi*distant from a given point, and which has its extremities joined by a straight line passing through that point. The words " angle in a semicircle," denote further quantitative relations: negatively quantitative if not positively quantitative. And the thing asserted is, that

along with this group of quantitative relations coexists
that other group of quantitative relations which the term
" right angle " denotes between two lines containing it.
Taking this view, the reasoning will stand thus:—

DEMONSTRATED CASE.	ANY OTHER CASE.

A ⎫
(The relations consti-
tuting the angle in
this semicircle) ⎪
(Coexist with) : ⎬ = ⎰ C (The relations constituting the angle in
that semicircle)
(The relations consti-
tuting a right angle.) b ⎭ ⎱ : (Coexist with)
d (The relations consti-
tuting a right angle.)

Such seems to be the more correct analysis of those
kinds of quantitative reasoning above described, in which
the antecedents are not homogeneous with the consequents.

The only further complication needing consideration here,
is the one arising when, instead of *two* equal relations, we
have to deal with *three*. As from that first simple intuition in which two magnitudes are recognized as equal, we
passed, by union of two such intuitions, into a compound
one involving three magnitudes; so from the foregoing
cases in which two relations are recognized as equal,
we now pass, by a similar duplication, to the still more
complex case in which three relations are involved. This
brings us to the axiom—" Relations that are equal to the
same relation, are equal to each other; " formulated, as we
before saw, after this fashion:—

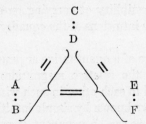

In which symbol it will be seen that each pair of relations

is united in thought, after the same general manner as any of the pairs lately treated of. The various modifications of this form which result when the relations are unequal, it is unnecessary to detail. And it is also unnecessary to dwell on those yet more complicated forms which result when this conjunctive arrangement is replaced by a disjunctive arrangement—when, in place of three relations, we have to deal with four; as in the case of the axiom given at the outset (§ 277)—" Relations which are severally equal to certain other relations that are unequal to each other, are themselves unequal." The process of evolution has been sufficiently exemplified to render this, and the allied intuitions, readily comprehensible.

All that needs further be done is to point out how, yet successive developments, we have advanced from a simple intuition of the equality or inequality of two magnitudes, to a highly complex intuition of the equality or inequality of relations between relations.

§ 291. Quantitative reasoning thus followed in its genesis, shows us that, either mediately or immediately, it always involves, in their positive or negative forms, some or all of the ideas—sameness in the nature of its magnitudes; sameness in their quantity; sameness in their time of presentation to consciousness; and sameness in degree between relations of the same nature subsisting among them. It will be well, finally, to remark that we may see, even à priori, the impossibility of carrying on any quantitative reasoning, save by intuitions of the equality or inequality of relations.

It is the purpose of a quantitative argument to determine with definiteness the relative magnitudes of things. If these things stand to each other in such wise that their relative magnitudes are known by simple intuition, argument is not involved. There can be argument, therefore, only when they are so circumstanced as not to be directly comparable.

Hence their relative magnitudes, if determined at all, must be determined by the intermediation of magnitudes to which they are comparable. The unknown quantitative relation between A and E, can be ascertained only by means of some known quantitative relations between each of them and B, C, D; and it is the aim of every mathematical process to find such intermediate known relations as will bring A and E into quantitative comparison. Now no contemplation of magnitudes alone can do this. We might go on for ever considering B, C, and D, in their individual capacities, without making a step towards the desired end. Only by observing their modes of dependence can any progress be made. If A and E are in an unknown quantitative *relation* which we desire to determine, we can determine it only as being equal or unequal to certain other *relations*, which we know mediately or immediately. There is no way even of specifically expressing the relation save by this means. The ascertaining what a thing *is* or *is not*, signifies the ascertaining what things it is like or not like—what class it belongs to. And when, of the previously unknown relation between A and E, we say we have discovered it, completely or partially, our meaning is that we find it to be the same, or not the same, as some relation which is known. Hence it results, *à priori*, that the process of quantitative reasoning must consist in the establishment of the equality or inequality of relations.

CHAPTER VI.

PERFECT QUALITATIVE REASONING.

§ 292. Thus far we have dealt with reasoning which has for its fundamental ideas, coextension, coexistence, and connature; and which proceeds by establishing cointension * in degree, between relations that are connatural. We have now to consider a kind of reasoning in which the idea of coextension forms no necessary element: that, namely, by which we determine the coexistence or non-coexistence of things, attributes, or relations, that are connatural with certain other things, attributes, or relations. It was pointed out that the intuitions of coextension, coexistence, and connature, are the only perfectly definite intuitions we are capable of; and the only intuitions, therefore, through which we can reach exact conclusions. One class of these

---

* The words *tense, tension, intense, intension*, are already in use. *Intension* being synonymous with *intensity, cointension* will be synonymous with *cointensity;* and is here used instead of it because the parallelism with *coextension* is thus indicated. The propriety of calling relations more or less *intense*, according to the degrees of difference between their terms, may not be at first sight apparent. All quantitative relations, however, save those of equality, involve the idea of *contrast*—the relation of 5 : 1 being called greater than the relation of 2 : 1, because the contrast between 5 and 1 is greater than the contrast between 2 and 1. And since contrast is habitually spoken of as *weak* or *strong*, as *feeble* or *intense*, the word *intension* seems a fit one to express the *degree* of any relation as distinguished from its *kind*. *Cointension* is consequently here chosen, to indicate the equality of relations in respect of the contrast between their terms.

conclusions, in which the *quantity* of certain existences of determinate quality is predicated, has been examined. It remains to examine a class in which the thing predicated is either the *quality* of certain determinate existences, or the existence of certain determinate *qualities*.

The last chapter incidentally exhibited the near connexion between these kinds of reasoning. It was shown that when of two compared relations, each consists of heterogeneous magnitudes which admit of no quantitative comparison, the two relations can be considered equal, only in respect to the coexistence of the components of each. We saw that many geometrical theorems simulate this form; expressed by the symbol—

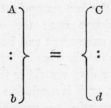

the fact predicated being the coexistence of C and *d*, standing in the same relation as A and *b*, which were proved coexistent; (say the equiangularity and equilateralness of a triangle.) As was pointed out, however, the terms of each relation are, in these cases, not really heterogeneous magnitudes, but heterogeneous relations among magnitudes that have definite though indirect quantitative connexions. When, contrariwise, the terms of each relation are simple heterogeneous magnitudes, or heterogeneous groups of relations having no implied quantitative connexions, we pass to the order of reasoning now to be treated of; in which equality is asserted of two relations that are alike in the natures of their terms, and in the coexistence of each antecedent with its own consequent.

Before proceeding I must meet an objection that may be raised to the use of the word *equality* in the sense here given to it. Commonly we apply it only to attributes. We speak of equal lengths, breadths, areas, capacities; equal times, weights, velocities, momenta; equal temperatures, sounds, colours, degrees of hardness; and we speak of equal ratios or relations, when the terms are magnitudes; but we do not speak of relations of coexistence as equal. Here, however, we are dealing, not with words in their conventional applications, but with the mental acts which words mark; and these, when they are of the same character, must have the same name.   The true interpretation of equality is *indistinguishableness*. Distances, and sizes, and weights, we call equal when no differences can be discerned between them. We assert the equality of two ratios—two relations of extension—when the contrast in amount between the first antecedent and its consequent, cannot be distinguished from the contrast in amount between the second antecedent and its consequent. And, similarly, we may assert the equality of two relations of existence, when the one does not differ from the other in respect of time—when each is a relation of *co*existence. As two relations of coextension are properly considered equal, though each of them consists of magnitudes that are unlike in everything but length; so two relations of coexistence may properly be considered equal, though the elements of each are unlike in everything but the period of their presentation to consciousness.   Or, to put the matter in an *à priori* form—Every phenomenon, when considered in connexion with any other, must be known either as occurring before it, as being simultaneous with it, or as occurring after it. But all objects of thought, and among others relations of time, may be compared, and their likenesses or unlikenesses recognized. The time-relation of events that occur simultaneously, is different from the time-relation of events that occur one after the other. Two sequences are alike in so far as they are sequences; and each of them is unlike a coexistence. Hence, if there are time-relations so completely alike as to be indistinguishable, they may properly be called *equal.* Such time-relations we have in all co-existences. Consequently when, having learnt that certain two attributes invariably coexist, we, in any new case, know that where we see the one we shall find the other; it may as truly be said that the mental act implied is a recognition of the equality of two relations, as when, in similar triangles of which two homologous sides are known, we infer the area of one triangle from that of the other.

§ 293. This being understood, we now pass to those reasonings in which the things asserted are not the co-extensions or non-coextensions of certain coexistences, but either, on the one hand, the coexistence or non-coexistence of certain attributes or groups of attributes, or, on the other hand, the simultaneity or non-simultaneity of certain changes or groups of changes. Reasonings of this order, which, instead of explicitly predicating *both* space-relations and time-relations, explicitly predicate time-relations only, exhibit, in a large group of cases, that same necessity often ascribed exclusively to quantitative reasonings. This group of cases is divisible into two sub-groups; the one including disjoined relations and the other conjoined relations—the one always involving four phenomena and the other only three.

The first of these sub-groups—represented by the formula last given, and, like geometrical reasoning, predicating necessary coexistence, but, unlike it, saying nothing of co-extension—includes the countless cases in which, from certain observed attributes of objects, we infer the presence of certain other attributes that are inseparable from them. When, on feeling pressure against an out-stretched limb, I conclude that there is something before me having extension—when, on seeing one side of an object, I know that there is an opposite side; this order of reasoning is exemplified. Were it not that perpetual repetition has consolidated these cognitions into what may be termed

organic inferences, it would be at once seen they stand on
a like footing with those in which the equilateralness of a
triangle is known from its equiangularity, when the coexistence of these has once been recognized. Under
another head we shall hereafter consider these cases more
closely. At present it concerns us only to notice that the
mental act implied, is an intuition of the equality of two
disjoined time-relations—the one, a generalized relation of
invariable coexistence, established by an infinity of experiences having no exception, and therefore conceived as a
necessary relation; the other, a particular relation of coexistence, in which one term is not perceived but is
implied by the presence of the accompanying term. To
formulate an example:—

(Tangible substance)	A	a	(This mass of rope)
(Universally, or neces- sarily, coexists with)	$:$ $\quad=$	$:$	(Coexists with)
(Limiting surfaces)	B	b	(Two ends, which un- coiling it will disclose.)

And similarly in all cases of necessary attributes as distinguished from contingent attributes.*

Of that subdivision of perfect qualitative reasoning which
proceeds by recognizing the equality or inequality of conjoined relations, the examples are not abundant. The fact
predicated in any one of them is either the coexistence or
non-coexistence of certain things, as determined by their
known relations to some third thing, or else the simul-

* The choice of letters in this formula needs explanation. By using
capitals in the first relation and small letters in the second, I intend to
signify, on the one hand, the general or class relation, and, on the other,
the particular relation contemplated. Letters of the same names are used
to match the fact that the antecedents are homogeneous with the antecedents, and the consequents with the consequents. While the use of
roman letters for the antecedents and italic letters for the consequents
implies that the antecedents differ in nature from the consequents—that
the two are heterogeneous.

taneity or non-simultaneity of certain events, as determined by their known relations to some third event. If, of two persons together passing the open door of a building, the one sees a barrel of gunpowder inside while the other sees a boy with a light in his hand, it is clear that, on immediately hearing an explosion, the adjacent coexistence of the light with the gunpowder is inferable: the data being that the one observed the adjacent coexistence of the light and the building, while the other observed the adjacent coexistence of the gunpowder and the building. If, again, certain two other persons heard the explosion, and, on comparing notes, found that each was setting out to meet the other at the moment of its occurrence; it is a necessary inference that they set out at the same time. These two classes of cases, dealing respectively with coexistent or non-coexistent things, and with co-occurring or non-co-occurring changes, are so nearly allied that it is needless to treat of them both. Confining our attention to the latter class, we may represent the sub-division of it above exemplified, thus:—

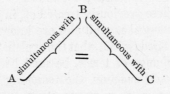

In this symbol the letters stand, not for objects but for events; and the simultaneity of A and C is recognized by an intuition analogous to that by which their equality would be recognized, were they magnitudes both equal to a third.

We need not treat in detail the antithetical group of cases in which, of three events, the first and second being known to have occurred simultaneously and the second and third being known to have occurred non-simultaneously, it is inferred that the first did not occur simultaneously with the third. But it will be well to notice the specific cases in which something more than non-simultaneity is known: those, namely, in which the inference is that one event preceded or succeeded a certain other event. Thus, if A and B go in company to a public meeting, and B on coming away early meets C entering the door; then A, on afterwards hearing of this, knows that he was there before C. Or if, supposing them all to go separately, C on arriving finds B already present, and B tells him that on his (B's) arrival he found A present; then, though he should not see him, C knows that A was there before himself. Using the letters to stand for the events (not the persons), these cases may be represented thus:—

It is needless to detail the possible modifications of these, or to argue at length that the intuitions must be essentially of the kind thus symbolized; for the cases are so obviously analogous to those previously treated of, in which the relations of two unequal magnitudes are known by the intermediation of a third (§ 286), that the explanation there given may, with a change of terms, be used here. Indeed, as this analogy itself suggests, the reasoning exemplified by these last cases is, in a vague sense, quantitative. So long as only coexistence or non-coexistence, simultaneity or non-simultaneity, is asserted, *quantity* of time does not enter into the question. But when the ideas *before* and *after* are involved, there would seem to be a mental comparison of periods, as measured from some common point. The times of particular occurrences are relatively fixed by means of their respective relations to the past—are regarded as farther, or not so far, down the current of time; and can only be thus regarded by comparing the respective intervals between them and occurrences gone by. Whether, as in the first of the following figures, we represent each of the events A, B, and C, as the terminus to its own particular line of causation; or whether, as in the second, we represent them simply as unconnected occurrences,—

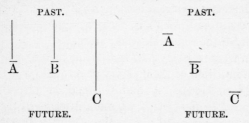

PAST.   PAST.

$\overline{A}$ $\overline{B}$ $\overline{A}$

                                              $\overline{B}$

              C $\overline{C}$

FUTURE.   FUTURE.

—it is equally manifest that in determining the unknown relation of A and C, by means of their known relations to B, we conceive all their times of occurrence as measured from some past datum. Our course is to compare the lengths of these times, and to recognize the inferiority of the length A to the length C, by means of the known relations they respectively bear to the length B. Where this datum is, matters not; for the respective periods measured from it will retain their several relations of equality, inferiority, or superiority, however far back, or however near, it is placed.   We get clear proof that the process of thought is as above described, when, from these vaguely-quantitative predications expressed by the words *before* and *after*, we pass to those definitely-quantitative predications reached by using space as a measure of time—when we pass to cases in which. by our clocks, we determine *how much* before or after. On hearing that one event occurred at four and another at five, we know that the first was an hour earlier than the last; and here the names of the hours show us that we recognize the relation of these events in time, by means of their respective relations to twelve o'clock—the datum from which their distances are measured. Similarly with the interval between any two historical events. This we ascertain by severally referring them to the commencement of the Christian era.

And if, to determine specifically the respective positions in time of two occurrences which cannot be brought into direct relation, we habitually compare their distances from some point in the past; it can scarcely be doubted that when we merely determine their positions generally, as before or after, the process gone through is, though vague and almost unconscious, of the same essential nature.

But in whatever way performed, this mental act is necessarily an intuition of the equality or inequality of two relations. If the events A and C stand in just the same time-relation to an event B, or, more strictly—if their time-relations to it are *equal ;* then the cognition that they are simultaneous is involved. They cannot be thought of as both occurring at the same time with C, or at equal intervals before it, or after it, without being thought of as simultaneous. Conversely, if the events A and C are known to stand in different time-relations to the event B—if their time-relations to it are *unequal ;* then the cognition of their non-simultaneity is involved. Whence it unavoidably follows, that when the difference of the time-relations is expressed more specifically —when the terms *before* and *after* are used—the intuition must be essentially of the same character: be the mode in which the comparison of relations is effected what it may.

§ 294. It seems to me, that in conclusions of this kind only, are involved the axioms which Mr. Mill considers are involved in the syllogism. If we include simultaneity (momentary coexistence) in our idea of coexistence at large, it may be said that all the foregoing cases of conjunctive intuitions, severally recognize one or other of the two general propositions—" Things which coexist with the same thing coexist with one another," and—" A thing which coexists with another thing, with which other a third thing does not coexist, is not coexistent with that third thing." But in no other ratiocinative acts, I think, than those above exemplified, are these self-evident truths tacitly asserted.

That they cannot be the most general forms of the mental process said to be represented by the syllogism, will become manifest on considering that they refer positively or negatively to one time only; whereas the syllogism, as involving in its major premiss an appeal to accumulated experiences, refers to *two* times—to time present and time past. The axiom—" Things which coexist with the same thing coexist with one another," cannot, however often repeated, help us to any knowledge beyond that of the coexistence of an indefinite number of things; any more than the axiom— " Things which are equal to the same thing are equal to one another," can, by multiplied application, do more than establish the equality of some series of magnitudes. But the act of thought which every syllogism professes to represent, besides involving a consciousness of the particular coexistence predicated in the conclusion, involves a consciousness of those before-known coexistences which form the data for that conclusion. Moreover, while such before-known coexistences are implied, it is not requisite that they shall be still knowable. The two terms of the inferred coexistence may alone continue in being. The entities presenting parallel coexistences may have been every one annihilated. How, then, can the mental act by which the predication is effected, be formulated in an axiom which involves *three coexistent terms?*

Has not Mr. Mill been here misled by a verbal ambiguity of a kind which he himself has pointed out, as one " against which scarcely any one is sufficiently on his guard " ? Towards the close of Chapter III. of his Logic, he says:— " Resemblance, when it exists in the highest degree of all, amounting to undistinguishableness, is often called identity, and the two similar things are said to be the same. * * * as when I say that the sight of any object gives me the *same* sensation or emotion to-day that it did yesterday, or the *same* which it gives to some other person. This is evidently an incorrect application of the word *same ;* for the feeling which I had yesterday is gone, never to return; what I have to-day is another feeling, exactly like the former perhaps, but distinct from it; * * * * By a similar ambiguity we say, that two persons are ill of the *same* disease; that two persons hold the *same* office." Now, that an *équivoque* of this nature is involved in the above formula, will, I think, be seen on examining the passage which introduces that formula. At page 200 (3rd edition) * Mr. Mill says:—

" The major premiss, which, as already remarked, is always universal, asserts, that all things which have a certain attribute (or attributes) have or have not along with it, a certain other attribute (or attributes). The minor premiss asserts that the thing or set of things which are the subject of that premiss, have *the first-mentioned attribute ;* and the conclusion is, that they have (or that they have not) the second. Thus in our former example,

All men are mortal,
Socrates is a man,
therefore
Socrates is mortal,

the subject and predicate of the major premiss are connotative terms, denoting objects and connoting attributes. The assertion in the major premiss is, that along with one of the two sets of attributes, we always find the other: that the attributes connoted by ' man ' never exist unless conjoined with the attribute called mortality. The assertion in the minor premiss is that the individual named Socrates possesses *the former attributes ;* and it is concluded that he possesses also the attribute mortality."

Both in the general statement and in the example, I have italicised the words in which the misleading ambiguity lies. Let us confine our attention to the example. When it is said that " Socrates possesses *the former attributes*," the

---

* In the seventh edition the passage will be found on p. 197. No change of substance or expression has been made in it.

literal meaning of the words, and the meaning Mr. Mill's axiom ascribes to them, is, that Socrates possesses attributes not *exactly like* those connoted by the word " man," but the *same* attributes. Only by this interpretation are the elements of the syllogism reducible to three—1st, the set of attributes possessed by all men and by Socrates; 2nd, the mortality of other men; 3rd, the mortality of Socrates. But in calling the attributes which constitute Socrates a man, the *same* as those by which other men are characterized, is there not a misuse of words parallel to that involved in saying that two persons are ill of the *same* disease? Persons said to have the *same* disease, are persons presenting similar groups of special phenomena not presented by other persons. Objects said to have the *same* attributes (as those of humanity), are objects presenting similar groups of special phenomena not presented by other objects. And if the word *same* is improperly used in the one case, it must be improperly used in the other. This being admitted, it follows that the elements of the syllogism cannot be reduced to less than four. (1). The set of attributes characterizing any or each of the before-known objects united into the class which the major premiss names: which set of attributes must be represented in consciousness either (plurally) as possessed by every sample of the class that can be remembered, or (singularly) as possessed by some one sample of it figured to the mind as a type of the class; and which, therefore, cannot be considered as *less* than one, though it may be considered as *more*. (2). The particular attribute predicated in the major premiss as always accompanying this set of attributes; and which, according as we are supposed to think of it as possessed by several remembered samples of the class, or by a typical sample, may be considered as many, or as one; but cannot be less than one. (3). The set of attributes presented by the individual (or sub-class) named in the minor premiss: which set of attributes being essentially like (not the same as) the first-named set of attributes, this individual is recognized as a member of the first-named class. (4). The particular attribute inferred as accompanying this essentially-like set of attributes. And if the elements of the syllogism cannot be reduced to less than *four* it is manifest that the axiom—" Things which coexist with the same thing coexist with one another," which comprehends only *three* things, cannot be the general proposition which each particular syllogism involves. Only to that limited class of conjunctive propositions lately exemplified, can such an axiom apply.*

§ 295. Returning from this parenthetical discussion,

* I regret being obliged still to differ from Mr. Mill on this point. In editions of his *System of Logic* later than that from which I have quoted, he replies to my criticism. Let me deal with a secondary issue before passing to that primary one respecting which, I fear, no reconciliation of view is possible.

Mr. Mill says:—" Mr. Spencer has misunderstood me in another particular. He supposes that the coexistence spoken of in the axiom, of two things with the same third thing, means simultaneousness in time. The coexistence meant is that of being jointly attributes of the same subject. The attribute of being born without teeth, and the attribute of having thirty-two teeth in mature age, are in this sense coexistent, both being attributes of man, though *ex vi termini* never of the same man at the same time." In answer, I would first remark that if in ordinary speech such a use of the word is proper, it may be doubted whether it is proper in Logic, where precision of meaning is essential; and that the literally-true statement of the relation is, that in the infant, toothlessness coexists with the *power of developing* thirty-two teeth at maturity. In the second place, I would point out that if coexistence is to be interpreted in this comprehensive sense, there needs some means of distinguishing between the very dissimilar relations expressed by it. Thus, the proposition that in man rudimentary teeth coexist with rudimentary hair, expresses a literal relation of coexistence. Similarly, when I assert that in man virility coexists with a deep voice, I assert of two attributes that they are simultaneously possessed by the same thing. But if the relation of coexistence may be asserted between all attributes possessed by a man throughout his life, it may be said that rudimentary teeth coexist with a deep voice. The circumstances that we must qualify this proposition by saying that the attribute of having rudimentary teeth in infancy, coexists with the attribute of having a deep voice at maturity, shows that coexistence is here to be understood in a sense qualified by the words infancy and maturity. In the absence of qualifying words (and the axiom we are considering contains none) coexistence must be understood there has still to be noticed that species of perfect qualitative reasoning in which the thing predicated is some necessary relation of phenomena in succession. We have already considered cases of unconditional coexistence; and here we have to glance at cases of unconditional sequence.

As, in the first group, we were concerned only with those relations of co-existence the negations of which are inconceivable; so, in this second group, we are concerned only with those relations of antecedence and sequence which it is impossible to think of as other than we know them. To take a case—If, on entering a room, I find in a distant corner the chair which I had previously placed near the

in the literal sense in which I have used it; or else, being taken in either sense, confusion must result.

On turning to the main issue, whether the syllogism contains four indispensable elements or only three, I find that Mr. Mill's explanation discloses a difference of view which is fundamental. He says:—" The question between Mr. Spencer and me is merely one of language; for neither of us (if I understand Mr. Spencer's opinions rightly) believes an attribute to be a real thing, possessed of objective existence; we believe it to be a particular mode of naming our sensations, or our expectations of sensation, when looked at in their relation to an external object which excites them." Further on, in developing the doctrine that the things dealt with in the syllogism are the feelings excited in us by external objects, and that the syllogism does not recognize the external objects themselves, he says that the axiom in question " might be thus worded: Two *types of sensation* each of which coexists with a third type, coexist with one another."

I am sorry to say that on this general question I diverge from Mr. Mill in a way which seems to render impossible any agreement on the special question. For the things named in the premisses and conclusion of a syllogism, I conceive to be those objective existences which are the correlatives of my subjective states. To take again Mr. Mill's instance:—The " men " spoken of in the major premiss, I hold to be so many separate objective entities, and not so many recurrences of an idea in me. The stoppage of breathing in each of these men (which is the sensible phenomenon implied by the abstract word " mortal ") I regard as a change that occurs separately in each man—there are many distinct cessations of breathing as there are distinct men. Socrates I understand to be another independent entity, like the entities classed as men. And the cessation of his breathing I consider as another change, distinct numerically, but like in nature, to the changes these other men have one by one exhibited. To make as clear as possible the interpretation I put on the terms used in syllogism, and at the same fire, it is a necessary conclusion that it has traversed the intervening space: I am unable to conceive that it has reached its present position, without having passed through positions intermediate between that and its past position. Further, it is a necessary conclusion that some agency (very probably, though not certainly, human) has produced this change of place: it is inconceivable that there should be this effect without a cause. Here we have nothing to do with the analyses of these inferences further than to observe that, like the previous ones, they are reached by intuitions of the equality of relations. The relation between this effect as a consequent and some force as an antecedent, is conceived as one with an infinity of such relations; differing in detail, but alike in presenting uniformity of succession. And similarly with the relation between changed position and transit through space.

time to show the double duality of its composition, let me take a case in which the matter is not complicated by plurality of the major premiss. Suppose that I am a naturalist to whom there is sent (say from the still unexplored interior of New Guinea) a mammal of a kind never before seen; and that, on dissecting it, I discover eight cervical vertebræ, instead of the seven by which *Mammalia* are almost universally characterized. Suppose that there is afterwards sent to me another mammal like the first in external size, form, structure, colours, etc.; and that I proceed to dissect this with the expectation of finding in it the anomalous eighth cervical vertebra. What are the terms with which I am dealing; and what is the course of my thought? I consider that my reasoning refers to two individually-distinct objects beyond my consciousness, having the two individually distinct attributes specially named. And considering this, I cannot reduce the elements of my reasoning to less than four—(1) the individual mammal I first examined; (2) the extra cervical vertebra in which it differed from nearly all other mammals; (3) the second individual mammal having special traits which make it *like* the first; (4) the *like* extra cervical vertebra which I expect to find. Now, though here the inferred relation is based on a single previous experience of a like relation (and the inference would be hazardous were it not for the wide induction that these structural correlations are usually constant in the same species), yet it is clear the course of the thought does not differ from its course when the major premiss is plural; and it is further clear that though plurality of the major premiss may be supposed to make the terms more than four, it cannot make them less than four.

CHAPTER VII.

IMPERFECT QUALITATIVE REASONING.

§ 296. While the conclusions of perfect qualitative reasoning are of such kinds that their negations cannot be conceived, those of imperfect qualitative reasoning can have their negations conceived with greater or less difficulty. The approximation of the two is, however, so close, that some members of the second class may readily be mistaken for members of the first. Thus the relation between visible and tangible attributes is such, that on receiving the ocular impressions representing an adjacent object, we cannot help concluding that there exists an adjacent object which, on putting our hands to it, will give them sensations of resistance; and by those whose experiences are very scanty, no other conclusion is conceivable. But our familiarity with looking-glasses and with optical illusions, renders it just possible for us to imagine that where there is an appearance there may be no answering solid substance. Judging from the unhesitating confidence with which, from moment to moment, cognitions of this order are accepted as guides, we might suppose them to be no less certain than those lately exemplified, in which from the invariable coexistence of tangibility with limiting surfaces we infer that an object of which we perceive one side must have another side; but we see that the two classes differ when rigorously analyzed. So, again, with cases like that incidentally cited at the close of the last chapter, in which the mortality of a par-

ticular individual is inferred from the mortality of mankind
in general. Next to impossible as it seems for any one to
believe of himself, or of another, that he will not die; yet
avoidance of death is not only conceivable, but history shows
us that in times past it was even believable.

§ 297. Imperfect qualitative reasoning is distinguished
from perfect qualitative reasoning by the relative indefiniteness of its intuitions. Beginning with those grades in
which the negation of the inference can be conceived only
by the greatest effort; descending through those in which it
can be conceived with less and less effort; and ending with
those in which it presents itself to the mind almost as
readily as the affirmation; it is throughout discriminated
from perfect qualitative reasoning, and from quantitative
reasoning, by the peculiarity that the compared relations are
no longer to be considered as *equal* or *unequal*, but as *like*
or *unlike*.

That complete indistinguishableness which characterizes
the compared relations of definite necessary reasoning, is
found only among the simple phenomena of number, space,
time, force—is not predicable of the relations subsisting
among those comparatively complex phenomena whose dependencies cannot be known, or are not yet known, as
necessary. The knowledge that the ratio A : B is equal to
the ratio $\dfrac{A}{2} : \dfrac{B}{2}$, is an exact intuition. The contrast in
magnitude between A and B is perceived to be indis-
tinguishable from that between half A and half B. The relations not being severally made up of many component relations, the comparison between them gives a result which is
simple and precise. But when, from the general truth that
motion is a constant antecedent of sound, we infer, on
hearing a sound, that something has moved; or when, from
human mortality at large, we infer the mortality of a par-

ticular individual; the compared relations cannot be called *equal*, but can only be called *like*. Let us observe the wherefore of this.   The known relation between sound and motion as its antecedent, is not thought of as one definite relation; but as an average of many definite relations varying in the amounts, qualities, and intervals, of their antecedents and consequents. Hence the particular relation between a sound heard and a motion inferred, cannot be held *equal* to the general one; because this lacks the definiteness implied by such a predication. Even when from the nature of the sound the character of the antecedent motion is known—when from a loud crash it is concluded that a heavy body has fallen; there is still only *likeness* in the compared relations, though it is a likeness that approaches nearer to equality. For though the repeatedly-experienced relation between a loud crash and the fall of a heavy body, is far more specific than is the general relation between sound and motion; yet it is not so specific that either the size or nature of the body can be known with any precision; as it could be were the compared relations *equal* in the true sense of the word.   Similarly in the second case. Though the relation between life and death is such that we can with certainty say of any individual that he will die; yet we cannot with certainty say either the time or the manner. He may die tomorrow by accident; or next year by disease; or fifty years hence of old age. While the generalization from which our conclusion is deduced, is specific in the respect that the phenomena of life are invariably followed by those of death; yet the infinity of cases included in the generalization differ more or less in every other respect. The particular relation which the conclusion recognizes, exactly parallels no particular relation before known, and has only one peculiarity in common with all the relations with which it is grouped; and therefore *likeness* only can be asserted of it and not equality. Did we regard the relation between life and death in the abstract as purely one of succession—could we exclude all consciousness of the interval, so as to recognize no difference between the death of an infant and that of a centenarian—we might with propriety consider all cases of the relation as equal; but our inability to do this necessitates the use of the more general word.

Indeed, it needs but to observe the contrasted applications we commonly make of these words, to see the validity of the distinction. The things we habitually call equal, are either simple sensations or simple relations. We talk of *equal* lengths, breadths, and thicknesses; *equal* weights and forces; *equal* temperatures and degrees of light; *equal* times and velocities. When speaking accurately we do not, in respect to any of these, use the word *like;* unless in the qualified form "*exactly alike,*" which is synonymous with *equal*. Nor, when the compared magnitudes of these kinds are almost *equal*, do we allow ourselves to call them *like*, in virtue of their near approximation. Wherever the terms of the comparison, being both elementary, have only one aspect under which they can be regarded, and can be specifically posited either as distinguishable or indistinguishable, we call them either *unequal* or *equal*. But when we pass to complex things, exhibiting at once the attributes, size, form, colour, weight, texture, hardness—things which, if equal in some particulars, are rarely equal in all, and therefore rarely indistinguishable; then we use the term *like* to express, partly the approximate equality of the several attributes separately considered, and partly the grouping of them after a parallel manner in time and space. Similarly with the relations involved in reasoning. If simple, they are recognized as *equal* or *unequal;* if complex, as *like* or *unlike*.

§ 298. This premised, it will at once be seen that those cases of imperfect qualitative reasoning commonly given in Treatises on Logic, as illustrating the process of thought

said to be expressed by the syllogism, severally exhibit
intuitions of the likeness or unlikeness of relations. When,
to quote a familiar case, it is said—" All horned animals are
ruminants; this is a horned animal; therefore this animal is a
ruminant; " the mental act indicated is a cognition of the
fact that the relation between particular attributes in this
animal, is like the relation between homologous attributes
in certain other animals. It may be symbolized thus:—

(The attributes constituting a horned animal)	A			a	(The attributes constituting this a horned animal)
(Coexist with)	:	is like	:	(Coexist with)
(The attributes constituting a ruminant animal.)	B			b	(The attributes constituting this a ruminant animal.)

That this formula—the relation between A and *B* is like
the relation between a and *b*—represents the intuition,
will, from our present stand-point, be obvious. Only in
virtue of the perceived *likeness* between A and a—
the group of attributes involved in the conception of a
horned animal, and the group of attributes presented by
this particular animal—can any such inference be valid, or
even be suggested. Further, the attributes implied by the
term "ruminant," can be known only as previously
observed or described; and the predication of these as
possessed by the animal under remark, is the predication of
attributes *like* certain before-known attributes. Once more,
there is no assignable reason why, in this particular case, a
relation of coexistence should be thought of between these
attributes and those signified by the words "horned
animal," unless as being *like* certain relations of coexistence
previously known; and whether the thinking of this
relation can be otherwise accounted for or not, it is clear
that the predication cannot otherwise have any probability,
much less certainty.   To state the case with
greater precision—Observe, first, that as the unseen
attribute predicated cannot, on the one hand, be supposed

to enter the mind save in some relation to its subject; and that as, on the other hand, the relation cannot be thought of without the subject and the predicated attribute being involved as its terms; it follows that the intuition which the inference expresses, must be one in which subject, predicate, and the relation between them, are jointly represented. Observe, next, that while subject and predicate are separately-conceivable things, the relation between them cannot be conceived without involving them both; whence it follows that only by thinking of the relation can the elements of the intuition be combined in the requisite manner. Observe, lastly, under what form this relation must be thought. Since the subject is recognized as *like* certain others previously known, with which it is classed; and since the attribute predicated is conceived as *like* an attribute possessed by these previously-known members of the class; and since the relation between the subject and the predicated attribute is proved, by the truth of the predication, to be *like* the relation subsisting in these previously-known members of the class; it must be by recognizing the relation as *like* certain previously-known relations, that the conclusion is reached.

On contemplating the parallelism between this species of reasoning and that species of mathematical reasoning which is confessedly carried on by comparison of relations, we shall find this interpretation confirmed. The unknown fact predicated in a syllogism, is perfectly analogous to the unknown fourth term in a proportion. Let us take cases.

SYLLOGISM.	A	:	B	is like	a	:	b
	the fermentation of wort	is simultaneous with	the evolution of carbonic acid		the fermentation in this vat of wort		

PROPORTION.	A	:	B	equals	a	:	b
	the walking a mile	is simultaneous with	the lapse of fifteen minutes		the walking this quarter of a mile		

In each of these acts of ratiocination (mark the word) the

fourth term *b*, represents the thing inferred; and seeing, not only that it is similarly related to its data in the two cases, but that the data stand in like relations to one another, the essential likeness of the mental processes is manifest. No doubt they have their differences; but an examination of these serves but to show the fundamental agreement.   Let us make a close comparison.   The fact that the predication in the first is qualitative while in the second it is quantitative, though true in the main, and important as a general distinction, is not true in an absolute sense.   When strictly analyzed, both prove to be qualitative and both in some degree quantitative.   A glance at the forms in which the two inferences present themselves to the mind, will render this obvious.   The first (that carbonic acid is being evolved) is, in the main, and as verbally expressed, merely qualitative—refers to the *nature* of a certain process and a certain product; and the second (that a specified portion of time will elapse), though distinguishable as quantitative, is by implication qualitative also; since not only is a magnitude predicated, but a magnitude of *time:* the thing inferred is defined alike in *nature* and *amount.* As thus regarded, then, the first inference is qualitative, and the second both qualitative and quantitative.   If we examine the two inferences still more closely, and, neglecting the words in which they are expressed, consider the mental states those words describe, we shall see a still nearer approach.   For though the first inference as verbally rendered (carbonic acid is being evolved) is in no respect quantitative; yet the idea so rendered is joined with an idea of quantity, more or less definite.   The experiences by which it is known that fermenting wort gives out carbonic acid, are accompanied by experiences of the quantity given out; and vague as these may be, they are yet such that when the brewer says a certain vat of fermenting wort contains carbonic acid, he thinks of the carbonic acid as more, certainly, than a cubic foot; less, certainly, than the total capacity of the vat: the quantity is thought of as in some

ratio to the quantity of wort.   Again, in the second case,
though the inference as verbally rendered (the lapse of three
minutes and three-quarters) is specifically quantitative; yet
the idea so rendered, *if examined in its primitive form*, is
not specifically quantitative.   A man who has walked a
mile in fifteen minutes, and, observing that he has a quarter
of a mile still to go, infers the time it will take to reach his
destination, does not primarily infer *three minutes and three-
quarters:* he primarily infers *a short time*—a time indefinitely conceived as certainly less than ten minutes, and certainly
more than one. By a process based on the perceived
equality of the relations between time and distance, he can
afterwards calculate the interval exactly. But, as it will
not be contended that he can know the exact interval without calculation; and as it must be admitted that before
making the calculation he has an approximate notion of the
interval; it must be confessed that though his ultimate
inference is definitely quantitative, his original one is but
indefinitely quantitative.   The two inferences,
then, as at first formed, are alike in being qualitative and
indefinitely quantitative; and they differ simply in this—
that while in the one, the quantitative element is neglected
as incapable of development, in the other, it is developed
into a specific form. Seeing, then, that the parallelism between them is so close, it cannot be questioned that as the
last is reached by an intuition of the equality of two relations, so the first is reached by an intuition of the likeness
of two relations.*

* The foregoing analysis, in which it is incidentally pointed out that
every act of specifically-quantitative reasoning is preceded by a provisional act of qualitative reasoning (which is only potentially quantitative), suggests an interesting analogy between these particular processes
of reasoning, and the general evolution of reasoning. For not only is it
true that, in the course of civilization, qualitative reasoning precedes
quantitative reasoning ; not only is it true that, in the growth of the individual mind, the progress must be through the qualitative to the quantitative ; but it is also true, as we now find, that every act of quantitative
reasoning is qualitative in its initial stage.

It is unnecessary here to illustrate or analyze that kind of so-called syllogistic reasoning by which negative inferences are reached. It differs from the foregoing kind simply in this; that the fact recognized is not the likeness, but the unlikeness, of two compared relations. Nor is it requisite to say anything about the different forms and modes of the syllogism; which obviously seek to express, partly the order in which the terms of the two relations are contemplated, and partly the extent to which the relations hold, as being either universal or partial. A psychological analysis like the present, properly includes nothing beyond an explanation of the general nature of the mental process involved.

Neither will it be needful to treat of that compound qualitative reasoning exemplified in all cases where an inference is reached, not by a single intuition of the likeness or unlikeness of relations, but by a connected series of such intuitions. Analogous as such cases are to those of compound quantitative reasoning examined in previous chapters, and consisting, like them, of successive inferences that are sometimes severally perfect and sometimes only part of them perfect; it will suffice to refer the reader to §§ 282, 284, for the general type, and to his own imagination for instances.

§ 299. But before leaving that division of imperfect qualitative reasoning which proceeds from generals to particulars, it is desirable to notice the fact that, by an easy transition, the so-called syllogistic reasoning passes into what is commonly known as reasoning by analogy. We shall find that this last differs from the first, simply in the much smaller degree of likeness which the terms of the inferred relation bear to those of the known relations it is supposed to parallel.

In the syllogism as ordinarily exemplified, the things classed together as the subject of the major premiss have usually a great number of attributes in common, besides the one particularly predicated of them. The individual or sub-class which the minor premiss names, has also a great number of attributes in common with this class named in the major premiss. And it is only because of this extensive community of attributes that the inferred attribute is asserted. Thus, when it is argued—" All men are mortal; this is a man; therefore this man is mortal; " it is clear that the individual indicated, and all members of the class to which he is referred, exhibit a high degree of similarity. Though they differ in colour, stature, bulk, in minor peculiarities of form, and in their mental manifestations; yet they are alike in so many leading characters that there is no hesitation in grouping them together. When, again, it is argued—" All horned animals are ruminants; therefore, this horned animal is a ruminant; " we see that though the sub-classes—such as oxen, deer, and goats—which are included in the class horned animals, differ considerably in certain respects; and though the particular horned animal in question, say an ibex, differs very obviously from all of them; yet they have various traits in common besides having horns. If, taking a wider case, we say that since all mammals are warm-blooded this mammal is warm-blooded; it will be remarked that the class—including whales, mice, tigers, men, rabbits, elephants—is far more heterogeneous. If, once more, we infer the cold-bloodedness of a fly from the general fact that all annulose animals are cold-blooded; the class, including worms, crabs, butterflies, spiders, mites, centipedes, beetles, is more heterogeneous still. And the heterogeneity approaches its extreme, when we draw an inference from the proposition that all animals contain nitrogen.   But now let it be noticed that in these latter cases, in which the objects grouped together have so many differences, the probability of the conclusion come to, depends on the previous establishment of the asserted relation throughout a great variety of the sub-classes included in the general class. Had only oxen and goats been found to ruminate, the presumption that any other species of horned animal ruminated would be but weak. The warm-bloodedness of a new kind of mammal would be but doubtfully inferable if only a dozen other kinds were known to be warm-blooded: no matter how many of each kind had been tested. In each of these cases the reasoning, while yet the general fact was unestablished, would be merely analogical; and would be so recognized. Take a parallel instance. The elephant differs from most mammals in having the teats placed before the fore limbs, and also in the structure of the hind limbs, which have their bones so proportioned that where there is usually a joint bending backwards, there is a joint bending forwards. In both these peculiarities, however, the elephant is like man and the primates generally; while at the same time it approaches them in sagacity more nearly than any other creature does. If, now, another species organized after the same fashion were discovered, and much intelligence were to be expected from it, the expectation would imply what we call an inference from analogy; and vague as this analogy would be, it would not be more vague than that which led to the expectation that other horned animals ruminated, while yet rumination had been observed only in oxen, goats, and deer. Moreover, just as when to oxen, goats, and deer, were added many other genera in which the like relation subsisted, the basis of deduction was so far enlarged as to give the inferred rumination of a new horned animal something more than analogical probability; so, were the relation between special intelligence and physical characteristics above described, found in a hundred kinds of mammalia, the inference that a mammal possessing these physical characteristics was intelligent, would be an ordinary deduction; and might serve logicians as an example of syllogizing, equally well with the preceding one.   Thus, premising that in the syllogism the word " all " means—all that are known (and it can never mean more), it is clear that ordinary syllogistic deductions differ from analogical ones, simply in degree. If the subjects of the so-called major and minor premisses are considerably unlike, the conclusion that the relation observed in the first will be found in the last, is based on analogy; which is weak in proportion as the unlikeness is great. But if, everything else remaining the same, the assemblage named in the major premiss has added to it species after species, each of which, though considerably unlike the rest, has a certain group of attributes in common with them, and with the subject of the minor premiss; then, in proportion as the number of different species becomes great, does the conclusion that a relation subsisting in every one of them subsists in the subject of the minor premiss, approach to a deduction.

In an order of more remote analogical reasoning, we find much unlikeness between the predicates, as well as between the subjects. To formulate an example:—

(The growth of an individual organism)	A			A	(The growth of a society)
(Is simultaneous with)	:	is like		:	(Is simultaneous with
(The subdivision of functions among its parts.)	b			b	(The division of labour among its members.)

In this case, the likeness in virtue of which a society is referred to the class, organisms, is very distant; and there is not much apparent similarity between the progress of organic economy and that of industrial economy. Hence the inference might be considered but little more than an idle fancy, were it not inductively confirmed by past and present history.

And now, let us not overlook the bearing of these cases on the general argument. Note, first, that analogical reasoning is the antipodes of demonstrative reasoning; both as being uncertain and as having widely dissimilar things for the terms of its relations. While in mathematical and other necessary inferences, the things dealt with have few attributes, and the relations among them are capable of accurate determination as *equal*, or exactly alike; and while in imperfect deductive reasoning the things dealt with have many attributes which, though somewhat different, have so much in common that most of their relations may properly be called *like;* in analogical reasoning the things dealt with are, in many respects, conspicuously *unlike;* and the presumption that they are like in respect of some particular relation becomes correspondingly small.   Secondly, let it be remarked that while ordinary class-reasoning is, under one aspect, parallel to that species of mathematical reasoning which recognizes the equality between one relation of 2 : 3, and all other relations of 2 : 3; reasoning by analogy is, under the same aspect, parallel to that species of mathematical reasoning which recognizes the equality between the relation 2 : 3 and the relation 6 : 9—an equality called a numerical analogy.   In the third place observe that as, in the case of analogical reasoning, the likeness of the relations is the thing contemplated (since it would never occur to any one to consider society as an organism, until he had perceived that certain relations between the functions of its parts are like the relations between the functions of the parts constituting an animal); and as perfect quantitative reasoning confessedly proceeds by intuitions of the equality or exact likeness of relations; we have yet further grounds for holding that all orders of reasoning which lie between these extremes, and which insensibly merge into both, are carried on by a similar mental process.

§ 300. From that kind of imperfect qualitative reasoning which proceeds from generals to particulars, we now pass to that kind which proceeds from particulars to generals: in other words—to inductive reasoning. From our present stand-point the fundamental differences of these, as well as their fundamental similarities, become clearly apparent. Both kinds are seen to be carried on by comparison of relations; and the contrast between them is seen to consist solely in the numerical preponderance of the premised relations in the one case, and of the inferred relations in the other.

If the known relations grouped together as of the same kind, outnumber the unknown relations conceived to be like them, the reasoning is deductive; if the reverse, it is inductive. In the accompanying formula, arranged to exhibit this contrast, the group of attributes in virtue of which the things are named, are symbolized by A, or A, or a, according as they are thought of as possessed by all, or some, or one; and for the particular attribute or set of attributes predicated as accompanying this group, the letter *B*, or *B*, or *b*, is used, according as the subject of it is all, some, or one.

DEDUCTION.   INDUCTION.

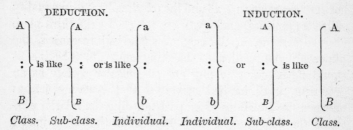

Class. Sub-class. Individual. Individual. Sub-class. Class.

The first form might be filled up thus:—Like the general observed relation between living bodies and fertilized germs, is the relation between these infusoria and fertilized germs, or is the relation between this entozoon and a fertilized germ. The second form might be filled up thus:—Like the observed relation between the development of this plant and its progress from homogeneity to heterogeneity of structure, or like the observed relation between the development of these animals and their progress from homogeneity to heterogeneity of structure, is the general relation in all organisms between development and progress from homogeneity to heterogeneity of structure.

Some possible criticisms on this exposition must be noticed. In the formula of the inductive process, as well as in the illustration, I have introduced the generalization of a whole class of cases from the observation of a single case—a generalization which seems illegitimate. To this objection there are two replies. The first is that our immediate subject is not logic, but the nature of the reasoning process, whether carried on conclusively or otherwise. If, as will not be denied, many people found general conclusions on solitary instances—if, as must be admitted, the mental process by which they advance from data to inference is the same in nature where the data are insufficient as where they are sufficient; then, an account of this mental process may properly include examples of this kind. The second reply is, that throughout a wide range of cases such inductions are legitimate. When it has been demonstrated of a particular equilateral triangle that it is equiangular, it is forthwith inferred that all equilateral triangles are equiangular; and countless general truths in mathematics are reached after this fashion. Hence, a formula for induction not only *may* but *must* include the inference from the singular to the universal. A further criticism which will perhaps be passed is, that in quoting as an instance of deduction, the argument that infusoria have fertilized germs because living bodies in general have them, a questionable instance has been given; as is proved by the fact that there are many by whom this conclusion is rejected. My answer is again twofold. Most of the deductions by which every-day life is guided are of this imperfect order; and hence, whether valid or invalid, they cannot be excluded from an account of the deductive process. Further, I have chosen a case in which the conclusion is open to possible doubt, for the purpose of implying that in all cases of contingent reasoning, the unknown relation predicated can

never possess anything more than a high degree of probability—a degree proportionate to the frequency and uniformity of the parallel experiences.

This doctrine is, I am aware, quite at variance with that
held by some logicians. Irrespective of the distinction
between necessary and contingent matter, Sir William
Hamilton contends not simply that there are both Deductions and Inductions in which the conclusion is absolutely
necessitated by the premisses, but that all other Deductions
and Inductions are extra-logical. To discuss this question
fully, would carry us too much away from our subject.
Such brief criticisms only can be set down, as seem requisite
for defence of the opposite doctrine.   Among
general objections to Sir William Hamilton's argument (see
Discussions, &c., pp. 156 to 166), may be noted the fact that
he uses the word *same* in place of the word *like*, after a
fashion equally ambiguous with that pointed out in the last
chapter. Moreover, he employs the words *whole* and *parts*
(to stand for a logical class and its constituent individuals)
in a mode implying that in thinking of a whole we definitely think of *all* the contained parts—an assumption
totally at variance with fact. No one in arguing that because all men are mortal, this man is mortal, conceives the
whole " all men," in anything like a complete circumscribed
form. His conception answers neither to the objective
whole (all the men who exist and have existed), which infinitely exceeds his power of knowing; nor to the subjective whole (all the men he has seen or heard of), which it
is impossible for him to remember. Yet unless logical
wholes are conceived in a specific manner, Sir William
Hamilton's doctrine cannot stand; for the perfect Induction and perfect Deduction which alone he allows to
be the subject-matter of Logic, imply wholes that are
known by " enumeration (actual or presumed) of *all* the
parts."   Again, let us consider the results following from this distinction which Sir William Hamilton

draws between the logical and the extra-logical. Other logicians, he says, have divided Induction " into *perfect* and *imperfect*, according as the *whole* concluded, was inferred from *all* or from *some* only of its constituent parts." This he considers to involve " a twofold absurdity; " and asserts that that only is logical induction which infers the *whole* from the enumerated *all*. If this be so, there arises the question—What is the nature of that so-called *imperfect* induction which infers wholes from *some* only of the constituent parts? Sir William Hamilton says it is extra-logical. Still it is a species of reasoning—a species by which the immense majority of our conclusions are drawn; and *rightly* drawn. Hence, then, there are two kinds of Induction (as well as of Deduction), one of which is recognized by the science of Logic while the other is ignored by it. This somewhat startling implication will lead us to a very astonishing conclusion if we ask the essential nature of the difference, which, according to this hypothesis, exists between the logical and the extra-logical. When, proceeding by the so-called imperfect induction, I infer from the many instances in which I have seen butterflies developed from caterpillars, that all butterflies are developed from caterpillars; it is clear that the inference contains multitudinous facts of which I have never been cognizant: from a few known phenomena, I conclude innumerable unknown phenomena. On the other hand, suppose I proceed by the so-called perfect induction, which does not allow me to predicate of the whole anything that I have not previously observed in every one of the parts, and which, therefore, does not permit, as logical, the conclusion that all butterflies are developed from cater-pillars; what will then be the course of my reasoning? It must be that as each of the butterflies (which I have observed) was thus developed, the whole of the butterflies (which I have observed) were thus developed; and here it is clear that the so-called conclusion contains nothing but what is previously asserted in the premiss—is simply a *colligation* under the word *whole*, of the separate facts indicated by the word *each*—predicates nothing before unknown. See then the contrast between these two kinds of mental procedure. In the one, from something known, something unknown is predicated; in the other, from something known, nothing unknown is predicated. Yet both are called reasoning—the last logical; the first extra-logical. This seems to me an impossible classification. The two things stand in irreconcilable opposition. Agreeing, as I do, with Sir William Hamilton in considering it absurd to include in logic both perfect and imperfect induction, I do so on exactly opposite grounds; for this which he calls perfect induction, I conceive to be not reasoning at all, but simply a roundabout mode of defining words. All reasoning, Inductive or Deductive, is a reaching of the unknown through the known; and where nothing unknown is reached there is no reasoning. The whole process of stating premises and drawing conclusion, is a wanton superfluity if the fact which the conclusion asserts is already given in experience. Suppose I have noticed that A, B, C, D, E, F, &c. severally possess a given attribute; do I then, by this so-called Induction, group them together as all possessing such attribute, that I may be afterwards able by the so-called Deduction to infer that E or F possesses it? Certainly not. By the hypothesis, I have already noticed that E and F possess it; and knowing this by a past perception, have no need to reach it by inference. Yet this ascent from the known constituent parts to the constituted whole, is all that Sir William Hamilton recognizes as logical Induction; while the descent from such constituted whole to any, some, or one, of such constituent parts, is all that he recognizes as logical Deduction. And thus, in the endeavour to establish necessary logical forms, he exhibits forms which the intellect never employs; nor ever can, with any propriety, employ.

Returning from this digression, which certain anticipated objections made needful, we have to observe that the inductive process above formulated, applies alike to the establishment of the simplest relations between single properties, and the most complex relations between groups of properties and between groups of objects. As is now usually admitted, the process by which a child reaches the generalization that all surfaces returning bright reflections are smooth to the touch, is fundamentally like that by which the physiologist reaches the generalization that, other things equal, the heat of an animal is proportionate to the activity of its respiration. Between those earliest organically-registered inductions on which are based the almost automatic deductions that guide our movements from moment to moment, and those latest ones which only the highly-cultured man of science can draw, may be placed a series connecting them by scarcely sensible gradations. The members of it differ in several ways—partly in the comparative infrequency with which the relations are experienced; partly in the increasing complexity of the terms between which the relations subsist; and partly in the increasing complexity of the relations themselves. Throughout the whole series, however, the essential act of thought is a cognition of the likeness between certain before-known relations and certain relations not yet known by perception, but represented by imagination. And the trustworthiness of this cognition varies sometimes according to the numerical ratio between the observed and unobserved relations, sometimes according to the simplicity of their nature, sometimes according to their analogy to established relations, sometimes according to all these.

Any detailed consideration of the conditions under which the inductive inference is valid, would here be out of place. We have now only to examine the mental act by which such inference is reached; and this is the same in *form* whether the data are adequate or not. The only further remark called for is that (excluding the mathematical inductions before named) when the observed relations are very few in number, or when the terms between which they subsist differ much from the terms of the relations classed with them, or both, we have what is known as an hypothesis. Thus, to quote an example from a recent controversy, if we argue that—

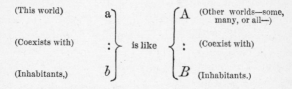

it is clear that, though inductive reasoning is simulated in form, the presumption that the relations are like is not strong; and nothing beyond probability (which some think but small) can be claimed for the inference. Were the likeness between the terms of the known and unknown relations greater—were all other worlds physically like this world in most particulars; the hypothesis would have increased probability. And then if, of worlds thus physically similar, we ascertained that hundreds, thousands, tens of thousands, were inhabited; the inference that all were inhabited would become an ordinary induction. Whence it becomes manifest not only that, as we all know, hypothesis must precede induction, but further, that an hypothesis *is* an induction in the incipient stage: capable of being developed into one if there are facts for it to assimilate; likely to dwindle away if there are none.

§ 301. To the foregoing two orders of imperfect qualitative reasoning—that which proceeds from generals to particulars, and that which proceeds from particulars to generals —has to be added a third order, which Mr. Mill names reasoning from particulars to particulars. This, as he points out, is the primitive kind of reasoning; habitually exemplified in children and in the higher animals. And, as he also conclusively shows, it is the kind of reasoning by which most of our daily acts are guided.

The simplest form of it is that in which, from a single instance of an experienced relation, another like relation is inferred. This is the form to which both Induction and Deduction may be degraded by continually diminishing the number of their observed or predicated facts; and it is thus the form which lies midway between them, as the common root whence they diverge. In all the examples of reasoning hitherto given, either the known relations serving for data were plural, or the unknown relations predicated were plural, or both were plural. But in this aboriginal reasoning, both the premised and the inferred relations are singular. The mental act is an intuition of the likeness (or unlikeness) of one relation to one other relation. The burnt child who, having once experienced the connexion between the visual impression of fire and the painful sensation which fire produces in the skin, shrinks on again having his hand put near the fire, is mentally possessed by a represented relation between fire and burning, similar to the before-presented relation. In this simplest and most imperfect ratiocination, we may clearly see that the thing remembered, which stands for premiss, is a relation; that the thing conceived, which stands for inference, is a relation; that the presentation of one term of this inferred relation (the fire) is followed by the representation of its other term (burning); that the relation thus conceived, is so conceived solely because there is a past experience of the relation between fire and burning; and that hence, by the very conditions of its origin, the new relation is conceived as *like* the previously-known one.

The verification thus furnished of the general view set forth is complete. For it is manifest that while, by the multiplication of experiences, the known and unknown relations, instead of being respectively one and one, become many and many, and so originate Deduction and Induction, the act of thought by which the inference is reached, remains throughout fundamentally similar.

CHAPTER VIII.

REASONING IN GENERAL.

§ 302. Before summing up the evidence, and presenting under its most general form the doctrine which the foregoing chapters present in detail, a question of much interest must be discussed. We have to consider the current doctrines respecting logical forms; to see whether the syllogism has any uses, and, if so, what they are. Further we have to inquire how there has arisen the absolute opposition between those who affirm that the syllogism presents analytically the mode in which all men reason, and those who affirm that the syllogism is valueless. In the words of Mr. Mill, one set of writers " represent the syllogism as the correct analysis of what the mind actually performs in discovering and proving the larger half of the truths, whether of science or of daily life, which we believe; while those who have avoided this inconsistency, and followed out the general theorem respecting the logical value of the syllogism to its legitimate corollary, have been led to impute uselessness and frivolity to the syllogistic theory itself, on the ground of the *petitio principii* which they allege to be inherent in every syllogism."

With the remark that what follows must not be taken as an admission that the doctrine of the syllogism is coextensive with logical doctrine in general, which is much the wider, I proceed to point out that there is a possible reconciliation between these antagonists. But it is a reconciliation which, strangely enough, is to be effected only by denying the tacit assumption of both, that the syllogism refers to the dependencies of our *thoughts*, and by affirming, contrariwise, that it refers to the dependencies of *things*. Those who do not avowedly recognize the antithesis of subject and object, must, I think, end by accepting one of these opposite estimates of the syllogism and rejecting the other; but for those who acknowledge that subject and object are separate realities, there is a way of bringing these views into harmony, by showing how each is right in one sense and wrong in another. A distinction exists which, in consequence of its highly abstract nature, is not easily perceived, between the science of Logic and on account of the process of Reasoning—a distinction which, once seized, disposes completely of the difficulty. The distinction is, in brief, this, that Logic formulates the most general laws of correlation among existences considered as objective; while an account of the process of Reasoning, formulates the most general laws of correlation among the ideas corresponding to these existences. The one contemplates in its propositions, certain connexions predicated, which are necessarily involved with certain other connexions given: regarding all these connexions as existing in the *non-ego*—not, it may be, under the form in which we know them, but in some form. The other contemplates the process in the *ego* by which these necessities of connexion come to be recognized.

Why this distinction has eluded observation, it is not difficult to see. Logic on the one hand, and the theory of Reasoning on the other, deal with relations from which all concrete terms are, as far as possible, expelled. They are severally obliged to use some terms (which, however, are by preference symbolic, so that they may express indifferently any kind of existence, attribute, action, or even relation); otherwise the relations dealt with cannot be expressed, or distinguished from one another.   But they intentionally ignore the natures of the terms, and occupy themselves with the most general dependencies of these most abstract relations.   The result is that, in the absence of terms definitely specified as belonging either to the outer world or to the inner world, the two sets of relations, belonging the one to the outer world and the other to the inner world, become indistinguishable.   Hence there arises this confusion between Logic, which is as much a division of the science of objective existence as Mathematics, and the theory of Reasoning, which is a division of subjective science.

To show that the affirmations of Logic refer to the connexions among things considered as existing apart from our consciousness, and not to the correlative connexions among our correlative states of consciousness, we need but to take the case of logical propositions as numerically quantified, in the system of Prof. de Morgan.   I quote Mr. Mill's condensed statement of the doctrine; for Prof. de Morgan's own statements are so encumbered with details and symbols, that I cannot find in his work one that is at once brief and adequate.

" From the premises Most B's are C's, most B's are A's, it may be concluded with certainty that some A's are C's, since two portions of the class B, each of them comprising more than a half, must necessarily in part consist of the same individuals.   Following out this line of thought, it is equally evident that if we knew exactly what proportion the ' most ' in each of the premises bear to the entire class B, we could increase in corresponding degree the definiteness of the conclusion.   Thus if 60 per cent. of B are included in C, and 70 per cent. in A, 30 per cent. at least must be common to both; in other words, the number of A's which are B's, and of C's which are A's, must be at least equal to 30 per cent. of the class B."

If we make the syllogism not only numerically definite, but, in place of symbolical terms, put terms that express realities, the objective character of the relations we are considering becomes still clearer. Suppose, in the case above-named, the class B stands for the total number of animals, partly oxen, partly sheep, on a farm. Suppose the class C comprehends all the sheep; while the class A comprehends all the diseased animals. Then if most of the animals are sheep, and if most of the animals are diseased, it is certain that some of the diseased are sheep: the oxen being the numerically-smaller cases, cannot by themselves, even if they are all diseased, fulfil the statement that most of the animals are diseased. But now, apart from words and symbols, what is the fact we mean to assert? We mean to assert that if we separated the diseased animals from the healthy, we could not form a group of the entities classed as diseased animals, which should be the larger half of the entire assemblage, without taking into it some of the entities classed as sheep: *we are unquestionably contemplating necessary objective relations.* With equal clearness is this truth implied by the performance of the syllogistic process mathematically, after the methods discovered by Prof. Boole. To quote the words of Prof. Jevons—" Boole showed incontestably that it was possible, by the aid of a system of mathematical signs, to deduce the conclusions of all these ancient modes of reasoning, and an indefinite number of other conclusions. Any conclusion, in short, that it was possible to deduce from any set of premises or conditions, however numerous and complicated, could be calculated by his method." Now, since it is admitted that mathematical analysis deals with relations which are considered as objectively existing, and, in the last resort, tests its conclusions respecting the necessary inter-dependencies of these objective relations by appeal to actual perception; it must be admitted that this form of mathematical analysis to which Logic is reducible, does the same thing. But the clearest proof that relations among objective existences form the subject-matter of

49

Logic, is yielded by the mechanical performance of logical inference. Prof. Jevons has devised a machine of such kind that, its keys being pressed down in proper order in conformity with the premises of the given logical proposition, the conclusion is presented by the combinations which the machine displays. Here it is undeniable that the relation disclosed is an objective one; and it is equally undeniable that the thing ascertained is, that this objective relation was necessarily involved in those other objective relations which constituted the premises. We have nothing to do with thought at all. We have to do with inter-dependencies among outer things or agencies. The machine having been set to represent objects and attributes in certain relations, evolves certain necessarily-accompanying relations, such as would otherwise be ascertained by actual examination of the objects and attributes.

A conclusion harmonizing with this may, indeed, be reached *à priori*. If there is a division of science, properly to be called Concrete, which treats of existences considered in all their fulness as objective entities—if there is another division of science, fitly distinguishable as Abstract-Concrete, which treats separately of the various modes of force which these existences exhibit, still considering these modes of force as objective—if, of the remaining division of science, which is truly Abstract, there is a part that treats of quantitative relations considered as separate from related things, still, however, considering these quantitative relations as objective; then there must remain a further most general part of this Abstract division, which, ignoring all distinctions of being, attribute, quantity, treats of the necessary correlations common to all cases, still considering these necessary correlations as objective. There must be such a science of universal objective correlations; and that science is Logic.

The propositions of Logic, then, primarily express necessary dependencies of things, and not necessary dependencies of thoughts; and in so far as they express necessary dependencies of thoughts, they do this secondarily—they do it in so far as the dependencies of thoughts have been moulded into correspondence with the dependencies of things. I say advisedly, "*in so far as*"; for there are certain absolute unlikenesses of nature between the outer dependencies and the inner dependencies, which for ever forbid anything more than a symbolic correspondence, as we shall hereafter see more clearly. The greater part of the necessary objective correlations are *statical*, while all the necessary subjective correlations are *dynamical;* and only in so far as dynamical correlations may be so arranged as to symbolize statical correlations, can the necessary dependencies of Reason be made to parallel the necessary dependencies of Logic.

I have reserved to the last, a mode of illustrating the relation of Logic to the other sciences, which will, I think, show unmistakably that it must be classed as objective. Suppose I am giving to a child a lesson in Mathematics, carried on after that concrete method which teachers, were they wise, would habitually adopt as an initiation. I take a number of its marbles—say, fifty. I show to it that four rows of four, placed side by side, will make a square containing sixteen; and I show it that out of its fifty marbles it can make three such squares, and have two marbles remaining. Again, I show it that by placing together five rows of five each, it may make a larger square, which, on counting, proves to contain twenty-five; and further, I lead it to observe that its fifty marbles will serve to make exactly two such squares. Once more, I suggest the experiment of making a line of seven marbles and placing seven such lines next to one another: the result being the discovery that out of its fifty marbles only one remains over when this square is made. Having thus introduced it by sensible experiences to the numerical truths that four fours make sixteen, and three sixteens forty-eight; that five fives make twenty-five, and that there are two twenty-fives in fifty, and so on; and having simultaneously introduced it to certain correlative geometrical truths respecting the natures of squares, and the relations between their areas and their sides; I go on to draw its attention to some truths of another class. By long use, many of the marbles have become chipped—more than half, according to the complaint made. I have myself observed in the course of these experimental lessons, that there are more streaked marbles than plain ones. And now I point out to the child that as, out of all its marbles, the number chipped is greater than the remaining number, and that as out of all its marbles there are more streaked than plain, some of the streaked marbles must be chipped. Examination proves this to be the fact. By way of showing that this fact is a necessary one, I take other marbles, and make up a group of fifty in which, to fulfil the conditions of the case, there are twenty-six streaked and twenty-four plain, and in which all the plain ones are chipped; and then I ask the child to make out of this fifty a group of chipped marbles that is larger than the remaining group of unchipped ones. It cannot do so. Though all the plain ones are chipped, they do not amount to one-half; and it finds that a group of chipped marbles amounting to more than one-half, cannot be formed unless some of the streaked marbles are chipped. And now what is the truth here disclosed to it? Nothing else than the truth expressed in the quantified syllogism, that if most B's are C's, and most B's are A's, some A's are C's.   See, then, the inevitable implication. No one questions the fact that while I was using these marbles to exemplify arithmetical truths and geometrical truths, I was contemplating, and was teaching, necessary objective correlations. Can it be that when I used these same marbles to exemplify necessities of correlation among groups and sub-groups, distinguished by certain marks, I passed from the region of objective necessities to the region of subjective necessities? No one will, I think, have the hardihood to assert as much. There is no choice but to leave these most general laws of correlation which Logic formulates, outside along with the laws of numerical correlation and geometrical correlation; or else, bringing them into the mind as laws of thought, to bring with them these mathematical laws as laws of thought in the same sense, and, by other steps equally unavoidable, to merge all objective facts in subjective facts: thus abolishing the distinction between subject and object.

And now having recognized the truth that Logic is a science pertaining to objective existence, and that so understood it has a definite function and value; and having recognized the correlative truth that Logic cannot be a science pertaining to subjective existence—cannot be a statement of laws of thought; we shall be prepared for appreciating the several independent proofs of the implied proposition that we do not reason by syllogism. To these we will now pass.

§ 303. There appears to be among logicians a general agreement that a certain abstract truth said to be involved in every syllogism, is recognized by the mind in going through every syllogism; and that the recognition of this abstract truth under any particular embodiment, is the real ratiocinative act. Nevertheless, neither the *dictum de omni et nullo*—" that whatever can be affirmed (or denied) of a class may be affirmed (or denied) of everything included in the class;" nor the axiom which Mr. Mill evolves—" that whatever possesses any mark possesses that which it is a mark of; " nor indeed any axiom which it is possible to frame, can, I think, be rightly held capable of expressing the ratiocinative act.

Saying nothing of special objections to be urged against these or kindred propositions, they are all open to the fundamental objection that they state substantive truths perceived by reason; not the mode of rational perception. Each of them expresses a piece of knowledge; not a method of knowing. Each of them generalizes a large class of cognitions; but does not by so doing approach any nearer to the nature of the cognitive act. Contemplate all the axioms —" Things that are equal to the same thing are equal to each other; " " Things that coexist with the same thing coexist with each other; " and so forth. Every one of them is a rational cognition; and if any logical axiom be added to the number, it also must be a rational cognition. These axioms, then, are all of one family—become known by similar intellectual acts. But if so, how can the addition of a new one to the list answer the question—What is the common nature of these intellectual acts?—what is the course of thought by which axioms become known? Axioms can belong only to the subject-matter about which we reason, and not to reason itself—imply cases in which an objective uniformity determines a subjective uniformity; and all these subjective uniformities can no more be reduced to one than the objective ones can.

The distinction drawn in the foregoing section between the science of Logic and the theory of Reasoning, at once opens a way out of this secondary perplexity. We can admit that these logical axioms express universal truths, without admitting that they are axioms tacitly asserted in drawing valid inferences. For, understanding Logic to be the most abstract of the objective sciences, made up, like other objective sciences, of truths some special and some general, we may expect to find among these certain *most* general truths. If it has for its subject-matter objective relations among terms the natures of which are ignored— if it occupies itself solely with the various necessities of correlation among these relations; it is clear that there will be some *universal* necessity of correlation—some axiom. Such an axiom is therefore to be accepted as expressing absolute dependencies in the *non-ego*, which imply answering absolute dependencies in the *ego*—not, however, absolute dependencies in the *ego* that are recognized as such in reasoning.

The utmost that any analysis of reason can effect is to disclose the *act of consciousness* through which these and all other mediately known truths are discerned; and this we have in the inward perception of likeness or unlikeness of relations. But a truth of this kind does not admit of axiomatic expression, because the universal *process* of rational intelligence cannot become solidified into any single *product* of rational intelligence.

§ 304. A true theory must be co-extensive with all the facts. Let us bring the theory of logicians to this test. We shall find that the simplest deliverances of reason as well as its most complex deliverances, have alike a form which the syllogism fails utterly to represent.

For how are we to express syllogistically the data for the conclusion that " things which are equal to the same thing are equal to one another," or for the conclusion that " if from unequals equals be taken, the remainders are more unequal " ? Neither of these truths is reached by direct external perception. Nor has either of them been reached through successive experiences of past cases, in which the alleged connexion of facts existed; which it must have been if the warrant for it is of a kind to be formulated in a syllogism. Each of these truths is reached by an intuition of reason; but it is an intuition of which the theory of reason, as logicians present it, gives no account whatever. All the various simple axioms,. quantitative and qualitative, treated of in the preceding chapters, are extra-syllogistic; and if so, one of two things is inevitably implied—either that there is a kind of reasoning formulated by syllogism and another kind of reasoning so entirely different that syllogism cannot formulate it, or else that syllogism does not formulate reasoning at all.

If it be urged that these axiomatic truths are truths recognized by the simplest order of reasoning, and that syllogizing represents reasoning of a developed order, the defence serves but to bring on a still more serious attack. For the syllogism can as little express the most involved deliverances of reason as it can express its simplest deliverances. There are ratiocinative acts much more complex than those which the syllogism professes to formulate, that cannot by any manœuvre be brought within it. Of these I have given an example at the outset (§ 277). The engineer who, from the fact that a tubular bridge built by him is only just strong enough, infers that a tubular bridge similar in all respects but of double the size will not support itself; goes through a process of thought which is in a much higher degree rational, than that through which the mortality of one man is inferred from the mortality of all men. Yet it is not expressible by syllogism. No single case has occurred before in his experience on which he bases this conclusion; nor have such cases occurred in the experiences of other men. Yet by a mental act which, though complicated, is not separable into steps, he rightly draws the inference: he recognizes in a particular case the general truth that ratios which are severally equal to certain other ratios that are unequal to each other, are themselves unequal. Not indeed that he overtly proceeds upon this complex axiom. He has never been taught it; he would seek for it in vain among acknowledged axioms; and he does not become aware of it even when tacitly asserting it. Hence besides the fact that neither his experiences nor those of others have furnished a major premiss for the conclusion he draws, we have the fact that he is unconscious of the class of inferences in which his particular inference is included. Nevertheless, having the data before him, he reaches through an intuition that is undeniably rational, and rational in an unusually high degree, the truth involved in those data.

The syllogism then, if taken to represent the form of the inferential act, has the fundamental fault that it fails to cover the whole of the ground it professes to cover. It falls short at both ends. There are simple deliverances of reason and complex deliverances of reason, both of them having the highest degree of certainty, which are entirely extra-syllogistic—cannot, however violently dislocated, be brought within the syllogistic form. Consequently, if it be admitted that a true expression of the ratiocinative act must be one applicable to all ratiocinative acts; it must be concluded that the ratiocinative act is not truly expressed by the syllogism.

§ 305. From indirect examinations of the syllogism, let us turn to a direct examination of it. This will quickly lead us to the same conclusion. We shall find that the syllogism is a psychological impossibility.

To get rid of all misleading implications, let us take an unhackneyed case. When I say,—

> All crystals have planes of cleavage;
> This is a crystal;
>   therefore,
> This has a plane of cleavage;

and when it is asserted that this describes the mental process by which I reached the conclusion; there arises the question —What induced me to think of " All crystals "? Did the concept " All crystals," come into my mind by a happy accident, the moment before I was about to draw an inference respecting a particular crystal? No one will assert such an absurdity. It must have been, then, that a consciousness of the particular crystal identified by me as such, was antecedent to my conception of " All crystals." This, however, it will be said, is merely a formal objection; which may be met by putting the minor premiss first. True; but this objection is introductory to a fatal one. For the mind being, as we see, occupied about the individual crystal before it is occupied about the class; there result the two inquiries—(1), Why, having been conscious of the individual crystal, should I, in this particular case, go on to think of the class, crystals; instead of thinking of some other thing? and (2), Why, when I think of the class crystals, should I think of them as having planes of cleavage; instead of thinking of them as angular, or as polished, or as brittle, or as having axes? Is it again by a happy accident that, after the individual, the class is overtly called to mind? and further, is it by a happy accident that the class is called to mind as having the special attribute I am about to predicate? No one will dare to say, yes. How happens it, then, that after the thought—" This is a crysal," there arises the thought—" All crystals have planes of cleavage; " instead of some other of the thousand thoughts which association might next bring up? There is one answer, and only one. *Before consciously asserting that all crystals have planes of cleavage, it has already occurred to me that this crystal has a plane of cleavage.*   Doubtless it is the registered experience I have had respecting the cleavage of crystals, which *determines* me to think of this crystal as having a plane of cleavage; but that registered experience is not present to my mind *before* the special predication is made, though I may become conscious of it subsequently. The process of thought which the syllogism seeks to describe, *is not that by which the inference is reached, but that by which it is justified ;* and in its totality is not gone through at all, unless the need for justification is suggested. Each may at once convince himself of this by watching how any of his most familiar inferences originate. It is stated that Mr. So-and-so, who is ninety years old, is about to build a new mansion; and you instantly laugh at the absurdity—a man so near death making such preparation for life. But how came you to think of Mr. So-and-so as dying? Did you first repeat to yourself the proposition—" All men must die? " Nothing of the kind. Certain antecedents led you to think of death as one of its attributes, without previously thinking of it as an attribute of mankind at large. To any one who considered Mr. So-and-so's folly not manifest, you would probably say—" He must die, and that very shortly: " not even then appealing to the general fact. Only on being asked *why* he must die, would you either in thought or word resort to the argument—" All men die, therefore Mr. So-and-so must die."

Obviously, then, the process of thought formulated by the syllogism, is in various ways irreconcilable with the process of reasoning as normally conducted—irreconcilable as presenting the class while yet there is nothing to account for its presentation; irreconcilable as predicating of that class a special attribute while yet there is nothing to account for its being thought of in connexion with that attribute; irreconcilable as embodying in the minor premiss an asser-tory judgment (this is a man) while the previous reference to the class men implies that that judgment had been tacitly formed beforehand; irreconcilable as separating the minor premiss and the conclusion, which ever present themselves to the mind in relation.

All that may rightly be claimed for the syllogism is, that by conveniently exhibiting the data, it enables us deliberately to verify an inference already drawn; pro-vided this inference belongs to a particular class. I add this qualification because its use, even for purposes of verification, is comparatively limited. One limitation is in-dicated in the foregoing section; where we saw that there are many inferences of a kind so certain as to be called axiomatic, which do not admit of having their terms arranged syllogistically. This is not all. To a large class of the cases commonly formulated in syllogisms, there applies the current criticism that a *petitio principii* is involved in the major premiss; since no test of the *objective* reality of the alleged correlation is yielded unless the *all* asserted can be asserted absolutely: the implication being that the syllogism here serves simply to aid us in re-inspecting our propositions; so that we may see whether we have asserted much more than we absolutely know, and whether the conclusion is really involved in the premises, as we supposed. Beyond those

syllogisms in which the major premiss expresses a truth
that can be known as strictly universal, the only syllogisms
which can be said to formulate objective correlations in such
way as helps us to test the alleged necessity of certain
inferred correlations, in the quantified syllogism; and even
this, though it covers a large class of necessary objective
correlations, does not cover them all.   Instance the one
contained in this old puzzle with a new face:—Suppose there
are more persons in a town than there are hairs on any one
person's head; then there must be at least two persons in
the town with the same number of hairs on their heads.   In
this implication we see very clearly the existence of those
necessary objective correlations which, as above contended,
form the matter of the most abstract objective science; and
we see also that Logic, considered as this science, comprehends much which cannot be included in the established
logical forms.

§ 306. Here ending this parenthetical discussion, which
in various ways brings us to the conclusion that Logic, instead of being a science of certain subjective correlations is a
science of certain objective correlations, and that syllogizing
is a mode of so representing some of these objective correlations as to facilitate the observation of their inter-
dependencies, we return to our immediate subject—the
theory of Reasoning. This we have now to consider under
its most general aspects; which we are all the better prepared to do after considering the general aspects of an
opposed theory.   Especially has a clear understanding of
the matter been furthered by the criticisms set down in the
last section; where I have drawn attention to a fact hitherto
passed over with the view of avoiding inconvenient complication, but which must now be deliberately recognized.

For, as some readers have perhaps already perceived, the
objection made to the syllogism because its terms stand in
an order unlike that followed by them in a normal act of
reasoning, is partially applicable to many of the formulæ

given in preceding chapters. It may be truly said that these represent, not the primary and direct reasoning, gone through almost spontaneously without distinct assertion of the data, but the secondary and indirect reasoning, consciously gone through. To express any deduction by saying of the compared relations that,

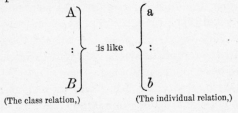

(The class relation,)   (The individual relation,)

is to raise the insuperable difficulty above suggested—that the class, with its appropriate predicate, cannot in order of thought precede the individual and that which we predicate of it; or, in other words—that we do not think of the class of before-known relations as *like* the single present relation; but we think of the single present relation as *like* the class. Just as, before writing down the proportion $3 \overset{\text{acres.}}{:} 162 \overset{\text{£.}}{::} 4\frac{1}{2} \overset{\text{acres.}}{:} \overset{\text{£.}}{—}$, I must have already recognized the unknown relation sought, as equal to the known relation premised: otherwise the writing down the premised relation would be unaccountable.

Hence, to symbolize the deductive process in a complete manner, the inferred relation must be placed before, as well as after, the class of relations to which it is assimilated; thus—

Primary or provisional inference.   Secondary or verified inference.

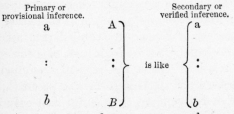

The first of these three represents that act of thought in

which, on the presentation of some object (a), there is suggested to the mind some unperceived attribute (b), as possessed by it. This act is simple and spontaneous; resulting,
not from a *remembrance* of the before-known like relations
(A : B), but merely from the *influence* which, as past experiences, they exercise over the association of ideas. Commonly, the inference thus determined suffices us, and we
pass to some other thought; but if a doubt is internally
or externally suggested, then the acts of thought represented by the rest of the symbol are gone through—we have
a process of conscious reasoning.

And here, respecting this series of mental acts, there
occurs a consideration of some interest and importance. It
is universally admitted that induction must precede deduction—that we cannot descend from the general to the particular, until we have ascended from the particular to the
general. The fact now to be remarked is, that not only of
reasoning in its *ensemble* does this hold, but also, in a qualified sense, of each particular inference. A few pages back
it was pointed out that as, in the development alike of the
general mind and the individual mind, qualitative reasoning
precedes quantitative reasoning; so, each particular act of
quantitative reasoning grows out of a preceding act of qualitative reasoning. We are now introduced to the analogous
law that as, in mental progress, both general and particular,
induction precedes deduction; so, every particular act of
deduction properly so called, implies a preparatory act of
induction.   For may we not properly say that
the mental transition from the spontaneously-inferred relation with which every deductive process must commence, to
the class of relations it belongs to, parallels the act by
which the mind originally passed from particular relations
to the general relation? True, the particular relation is
now not an observed one; and in so far the parallel does
not hold. Still, it is conceived as existing; and only because it is so conceived does the class of such relations come

into consciousness. The sequence of thought follows the channel through which the induction was before reached. As each separate deductive act involves an ascent from the particular to the general, before the descent from the general to the particular, the historic relation between induction and deduction is repeated. In all cases of deduction there is either an induction made on the spur of the moment (which is often the case), or there is an automatic re-thinking of the induction before made.

Resuming our immediate topic, it is to be remarked that the amended, or rather completed, form under which the deductive process is above represented, remains in perfect accordance with the doctrine developed in foregoing chapters, that reasoning is carried on by comparison of relations. For whether the singular relation is thought of before the plural, or the plural before the singular, or first one and then the other; it remains throughout manifest that they are thought of as like (or unlike) relations, and that the possibility of the inference depends on their being so thought of.

§ 307. And now, that the truth of the doctrines enunciated in foregoing chapters may be still more clearly seen, let us glance at the series of special results that have been reached, and observe how harmoniously they unite as parts of one whole.

We noticed that perfect quantitative reasoning, by which alone complete previsions are reached, involves intuitions of coextension, coexistence, and connature, in the things reasoned about; besides connature and cointension in the compared relations. In other words, we saw that in this highest reasoning there is equality among the terms in Space, Time, Quality, and among their relations in kind and degree; and that thus not only does the idea of likeness rise to its greatest perfection (equality), but it appears under the greatest variety of applications. While we saw that in imperfect quantitative reasoning where non-co-extension is predicated, either indefinitely (these magnitudes are unequal) or definitely (this magnitude is greater than that), the idea of exact likeness is no longer so variously involved.   We next found that in perfect qualitative reasoning, the intuition of coextension ceases to appear, though there is still coexistence and connature among the terms, along with connature and cointension among the relations subsisting between those terms; and that thus there is another diminution in the number of implied intuitions of equality. And further we found that in parti-perfect qualitative reasoning, where non-coexistence is predicated either indefinitely (these things do not exist at the same time) or definitely (this follows that), the number of such implied intuitions is again reduced; though there yet remains equality in the natures of the things dealt with, and in the natures of the compared relations.   We have now to notice, what was not noticed in passing, that in imperfect qualitative reasoning we descend still lower; for in it, we have no longer complete equality of nature among the terms of the compared relations. Unlike lines, angles, forces, areas, times, &c., the things with which ordinary class-reasoning deals are not altogether homogeneous. The objects grouped together in an induction are never exactly alike in every one of their attributes; nor is the individual thing respecting which a deduction is made, ever quite indistinguishable in character from the things with which it is classed. No two men, or trees, or stones, have the same absolute uniformity of nature that two circles have. Similarly with the relations between terms of such kinds: though they remain connatural, they do not remain cointense. And thus in our contingent every-day inferences, we have only likeness of nature in the entities and attributes involved; equality of nature in the relations between them; and more or less of likeness in the degrees of those relations. The subjects must be like;

the things predicated of them must be like; and the relations must be homogeneous, if nothing more. Even when we come to the most imperfect reasoning of all—reasoning by analogy—it is still to be observed that, though the subjects and predicates have severally become so different that not even likeness of nature can be safely asserted of them, there still remains likeness of nature between the compared relations. If the premised relation is a sequence, the inferred one must be a sequence; or they must be both coexistences. If one is a space-relation and the other a time-relation, reasoning becomes impossible. As a weight cannot be compared with a sound, so there can be no comparison between relations of different orders. This fact, that as we descend from the highest to the lowest kinds of reasoning, the intuitions of likeness among the elements involved become both less perfect and less numerous, but never wholly disappear, will hereafter be seen to have great significance.

Passing from the elements of rational intuitions to their forms, we find that these are divisible into two genera. In the one the compared relations, having a common term, are conjoined; and in the other the compared relations, having no common term, are disjoined. Let us glance at the several species comprehended under the first of these genera. Having but three terms, these have for their types the forms—

$$A : B \text{ is equal to } B : C ;$$
its indefinite negation,
$$A : B \text{ is unequal to } B : C ;$$
and its definite negation,
$$A : B \text{ is } \left\{ \begin{array}{c} \text{greater} \\ \text{or less} \end{array} \right\} \text{ than } B : C.$$

Suppose in the first of these forms, A, B, and C represent magnitudes of any order; then, if they are severally equal, we have the axiom—" Things that are equal to the same

thing are equal to each other;" and if they are severally
unequal, we have a case of mean proportionals. In the
second form, if A, B, and C are magnitudes, we have the
converse of the above axiom; while the thing determined
is the inequality of A and C. And in the third form, the
thing determined is the superiority or inferiority of A to C.
Again, suppose A, B, and C are times, either at which
certain things continuously exist or at which certain events
occur; then, the first form represents the axioms—"Things
that coexist with the same thing coexist with each other,"
and "Events which are simultaneous with the same event
are simultaneous with each other." The second form stands
for the converse axioms; and predicates the non-coexistence or non-simultaneity of A and C. While the third
symbolizes cases in which A is concluded to be before or
after C. To make these facts clear, let us formulate each
variety.

SPACE-RELATIONS.

A is equal to B; B is equal to C; therefore A is equal to C.

A is equal to B; B is unequal to C; therefore A is unequal to C.

A is equal to B; B is $\left\{ \begin{array}{c} \text{greater} \\ \text{or less} \end{array} \right\}$ than C; therefore A is $\left\{ \begin{array}{c} \text{greater} \\ \text{or less} \end{array} \right\}$ than C.

A is $\left\{ \begin{array}{c} \text{greater} \\ \text{or less} \end{array} \right\}$ than B; B is $\left\{ \begin{array}{c} \text{greater} \\ \text{or less} \end{array} \right\}$ than C; therefore A is $\left\{ \begin{array}{c} \text{greater} \\ \text{or less} \end{array} \right\}$ than C.

TIME-RELATIONS.

A $\left\{ \begin{array}{c} \text{is simultane-} \\ \text{ous with} \end{array} \right\}$ B; B $\left\{ \begin{array}{c} \text{is simultane-} \\ \text{ous with} \end{array} \right\}$ C; therefore A $\left\{ \begin{array}{c} \text{is simultane-} \\ \text{ous with} \end{array} \right\}$ C.

A $\left\{ \begin{array}{c} \text{is simultane-} \\ \text{ous with} \end{array} \right\}$ B; B $\left\{ \begin{array}{c} \text{is not simul-} \\ \text{taneous with} \end{array} \right\}$ C; therefore A $\left\{ \begin{array}{c} \text{is not simul-} \\ \text{taneous with} \end{array} \right\}$ C.

(and similarly if there is coexistence instead of simultaneity)

A $\left\{ \begin{array}{c} \text{is simultane-} \\ \text{ous with} \end{array} \right\}$ B; B is $\left\{ \begin{array}{c} \text{before or} \\ \text{after} \end{array} \right\}$ C; therefore A is $\left\{ \begin{array}{c} \text{before or} \\ \text{after} \end{array} \right\}$ C.

A is $\left\{ \begin{array}{c} \text{before or} \\ \text{after} \end{array} \right\}$ B; B is $\left\{ \begin{array}{c} \text{before or} \\ \text{after} \end{array} \right\}$ C; therefore A is $\left\{ \begin{array}{c} \text{before or} \\ \text{after} \end{array} \right\}$ C.

It must not be supposed, however, that Time-relations
and Space-relations are the only ones that can enter into

these forms. Relations of Force, under its various manifestations, may be similarly dealt with. To use the Kantian
nomenclature, there is Extensive quantity (in Space); Pro-
tensive quantity (in Time); and Intensive quantity (in the
degree of the Actions that occur in space and time). It is
true, as before shown, (§ 25) that intensive quantities, as
those of weight, temperature, &c., cannot be accurately
reasoned about without substituting for them quantities of
extension, as by the scales and the thermometer; but it is
none the less true that there is a simple order of inferences
respecting intensive quantities, exactly parallel to those
above given. If, for example, a ribbon matched in colour
some fabric left at home, and matches some other fabric at
the draper's, it is rightly inferred that these fabrics will
match each other; or if, on different occasions, a piece of
music had its key-note pitched by the same tuning-fork, it
is to be concluded that the pitch was alike on both occasions. Similarly in various other cases, which it is needless
to specify. In all of them, as well as in the cases above
given, the intuition, both in its positive and negative forms,
is represented by the symbol—

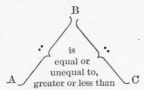

The only further fact of importance to be named respecting
this genus of rational intuitions is, that not only are the two
relations homogeneous in nature, but all the three terms are
so likewise. Whence, in part, arises the extremely-limited
range of conjunctive reasonings.*

* I ought here to mention that some year and a half since (this was
written in 1855), in the course of a conversation in which the axiom—
"Things that coexist with the same thing coexist with each other," was
referred to, it was remarked by a distinguished lady—the translator of

The other genus of rational intuitions, distinguished by having four terms, and therefore two separate or disjoined relations, is represented by the typical forms—

A : B is equal to C : D ;

its indefinite negation,

A : B is unequal to C : D ;

and its definite negation,

A : B is $\left\{ \begin{array}{c} \text{greater} \\ \text{or less} \end{array} \right\}$ than C : D.

To which must be added the two modified forms which result when the reasoning is imperfect—

A : B is like C : D ;

and its negation,

A : B is unlike C : D.

Supposing, in the first of these five, the letters represent homogeneous magnitudes; then, when A equals B, and C equals D, we have a representation of the several axioms— If equals are added to, subtracted from, multiplied by, &c.,

Strauss and Feuerbach (now universally known as George Eliot)—that perhaps a better axiom would be—"Things that have a constant relation to the same thing have a constant relation to each other." Not having at that time reached the conclusion that a formula having but three terms cannot express our ordinary ratiocinations, which involve four; I was greatly inclined to think this the most general truth to which the propositions known by reason are reducible: the more so as, being expressed in terms of relations, it assimilated with many results at which I had already arrived in the course of analyzing the lower intellectual processes. As will appear, however, from the preceding chapters, subsequent inquiry led me to other conclusions. Nevertheless, this suggestion was of much service in directing my thoughts into a track which they might not else have followed. Respecting this axiom itself, it may be remarked that as the word *constant* implies *time* and *uniformity*, the application of the axiom is limited to necessary time-relations of the conjunctive class. But if, changing the word constant for a more general one, we say— Things which have a definite relation to the same thing have a definite relation to each other ; we get an axiom which expresses the most general truth known by conjunctive reasoning—positive and negative, quantitative and qualitative.

equals, the results are equal; and when each of the two
ratios is not one of equality, we have an ordinary proportion. Supposing that the four terms are not homogeneous
throughout, but only in pairs, then the formula stands for
common geometrical reasoning; and when the things represented are not magnitudes, but simply entities and
attributes that are alternately homogeneous, we have the
reasoning by which necessary coexistences and sequences
are recognized. Again, in the second and third forms, if all
the terms are homogeneous magnitudes, inequations and
certain axioms antithetical to the above are symbolized; if
the magnitudes are but alternately homogeneous, there is
typified that imperfect geometrical reasoning by which
certain things are proved always greater or less than certain
others; and when the letters stand not for magnitudes
but simply for entities, properties, or changes, we have
that species of necessary qualitative reasoning which
gives negative predications. Lastly, by the fourth and
fifth forms are signified all orders of class-reasoning; from
that which is next to necessary to that which is in the
highest degree problematical: inclusive alike of Induction,
Deduction, Analogy, and Hypothesis. All these sub-genera
and species of Disjunctive Reasoning are representable by
the one symbol—

$$A \atop B \Biggr\} \quad \begin{matrix} \text{is equal or} \\ \text{unequal to,} \\ \\ \text{greater or} \\ \text{less than,} \\ \\ \text{like or} \\ \text{unlike,} \end{matrix} \quad \Biggl\{ {C \atop D}$$

And the several varieties may be classified in three distinct
modes, according as the basis of classification is—(1) the
degree of resemblance between the two relations; (2) the
nature of the compared relations; and (3) the comparative
number of the premised and inferred relations. Under the
first of these classifications, we have the divisions—Positive

and Negative; Perfect, Parti-perfect, and Imperfect; Necessary and Contingent; Analogical.   Under the second, we
have the two great divisions—Quantitative and Qualitative;
of which the one may be Proportional, Algebraic, or Geometrical, according as the terms of each relation are or are
not homogeneous, and are or are not equal; and of which
the other may refer to either coexistences or sequences,
whether between attributes, things, or events.   Under the
third, we have reasoning divided into Inductive, Deductive,
Hypothetical; which are classifiable according to the
numerical ratio between the premised and inferred relations, as follows:—

> Premised   Inferred
> Relations.   Relations.

If from *one* to *one*, the reasoning is from particulars to
particulars; and is valid or doubtful
according to the natures of the
terms.

If from *one* to *all*, we have a species of induction that is
valid or doubtful according to the
natures of the terms.

If from *few* to *all*, it amounts to ordinary Hypothesis.

If from *many* to *all*, it is Induction proper.

If from *some* to *one*, it is what we may call Hypothetical deduction.

If from *all* to *one*, ⎫
If from *all* to *some*, ⎬ it is Deduction proper.

Respecting the disjunctive form of reasoning one further
remark should be made; namely, that it includes certain
inferences which can be classed neither with the inductive, the deductive, the process from particulars
to particulars, nor any of their modifications.   These are
the inferences at once drawn, and correctly drawn, without an established truth for a premiss, and in cases that
have not been before paralleled in experience.   Thus, if A be
but a fiftieth part less than B, it is at once inferable that a

half of A is greater than a third of B. Neither a general principle nor a particular experience, can be quoted as the ground for this conclusion. It is reached directly and independently by a comparison of the two relations named; and is satisfactorily explicable neither on the hypothesis of forms of thought, nor on the experience-hypothesis as ordinarily interpreted. We may aptly term it a *latent* inference; and its genesis, like that of many others, is to be properly understood only from that point of view whence these antagonist hypotheses are seen to express opposite sides of the same truth. Of this more in the sequel. Here it is to be observed that while the species of reasoning thus exemplified is obviously effected by comparison of relations, and so conforms to the theory above set forth, it does not conform to any of the current theories.

Respecting those most involved forms of reasoning analyzed in the first chapter, which deal not with the quantitative or qualitative relations of things, but with the quantitative relations of quantitative relations, it is needless now to do more than remind the reader that they arise by duplication of the forms above given; and that in their highest complications they follow the same law. Perceiving as he thus will that the doctrine set forth applies to all orders of reasoning—from the simplest to the most complex; from the necessary to the remotely contingent; from the axiomatic to the analogical; from the most premature induction to the most rigorous deduction—he will see that it fulfils the character of a true generalization: that, namely, of explaining all the phenomena.

§ 308. One other group of confirmatory evidences deserves notice—the group supplied by our ordinary forms of speech. Already some of these evidences have been incidentally pointed out. They are so numerous and so significant, that even standing alone they would go far to justify the doctrine which has been developed.

Thus we have the Latin *ratio*, meaning reason; and *ratiocinor*, to reason. This word *ratio* we apply to each of the two quantitative relations forming a proportion; and the word *ratiocination*, which is defined as " the act of deducing consequences from premisses," is applicable alike to numerical and to other inferences. Conversely, the French use *raison* in the same sense that *ratio* is used by us. Throughout, therefore, the implication is that *reason*-ing and *ratio*-ing are fundamentally identical.   Further, be it remarked that *ratiocination*, or reasoning, is defined as "the *comparison* of propositions or facts, and the deduction of inferences from the comparison." Now every proposition, or asserted fact, involving as it does a subject and a some-thing predicated of it, necessarily expresses a relation. Hence the definition may properly be transformed into, " the comparison of relations, and the deduction of inferences from the comparison." But the only thing effected by compa-rison is a recognition of the likeness or unlikeness of the compared things; and therefore inferences said to be de-duced from the comparison, must result from the recognition of the likeness or unlikeness of relations.   Again, we have the word *analogy*, applied alike to proportional reasoning in mathematics and to the presumptive reasoning of daily life. The meaning of analogy is, " an *agreement* or *likeness* between things in some circumstances or effects, when the things are otherwise entirely different; " and in mathematics, an analogy is " an agreement or likeness be-tween " two ratios in respect of the quantitative contrast be-tween each antecedent and its consequent. So that in either case, to " deny the analogy," is to deny the assumed like-ness of relations.   Then we have the common ex-pressions—" by *parity* of reasoning," and " the cases are not upon a *par*." Parity means *equality ;* and being upon a par means being upon a *level ;* so that here, too, the essential idea is that of likeness or unlikeness. Note, also, the familiar qualifications,—" *cæteris paribus*," "other things equal; " which are used with the implication that when all the remaining elements of the compared cases stand in like relations, the particular elements in question will stand in like relations. There is the notion of parallelism, too. It is an habitual practice in argument to draw a *parallel*, with the view of assuming in the one case what is shown in the other. But parallel lines are those that are always *equi*-distant—that are *like* in direction; and thus the fundamental idea is still the same. Yet another group of words has significance. Men reason by *similes* of all orders, from the parable down to the illustration; and *similarity* is constantly the alleged ground of inference, alike in necessary and in contingent reasoning. When geometrical figures are known to be similar, and the ratio of any two homologous sides is given, the values of all the remaining sides in the one, may be inferred from their known values in the other; and when the lawyer has established his precedent, he goes on to argue that *similarly*, &c. Now as, in geometry, the definition of similarity is, equality of ratios among the answering parts of the compared figures; it is clear that the similarity on the strength of which ordinary inferences are drawn, means—likeness of relations. Once more there is the language used to express *proportion*. Not only is the process of thought by which both our simplest and our most complex conclusions are reached, fundamentally one with that employed in proportional reasoning; but its verbal expression often simulates the same form. As in mathematics we say—*As* A is to B, *so* is C to D; so in non-quantitative reasoning we say—*As* a muscle is strengthened by exercise, *so* is the rational faculty strengthened by thinking. Indeed, this sentence supplies a double illustration; for not only does each of the two inferences it compares exhibit the proportional form, but the comparison of them itself exhibits that form.

Thus words and phrases afford us consistent testimony. It is manifest, that our habitual modes of expression bear witness to the truth of the foregoing analysis.

§ 309. And now, as an appropriate finish to this lengthened exposition, let me point out how the conclusion we have come to may be reached even *à priori.* When, towards the close of this Special Analysis, we look at the ultimate elements of consciousness, it will be abundantly manifest that the phenomena of reasoning cannot be truly generalized in any other way. But without waiting for this most conclusive proof eventually to be arrived at, it may be demonstrated in two ways that every inference involves an intuition of the likeness or unlikeness of relations. Already, incidental reference has been made to these *à priori* arguments; but they claim a more definite statement than they have hitherto received.

Both of them are based on the very definition of reason, considered under its universal aspect. What is the content of every rational proposition? Invariably a predication—an assertion that something is, was, or will be, conditioned (or not) in a specified manner—that certain objects, forces, attributes, stand to each other thus or thus, in Time or Space. That is, every rational proposition expresses *some relation.* But how only is a relation thinkable? It is thinkable only as of a certain *order*—as belonging to some *class* of before-known relations. It must be with relations as with their terms; which can be thought of as such, or such, only by being thought of as members of this or that class. To say—" This is an animal," or " This is a circle," or " This is the colour red; " necessarily implies that animals, circles, and colours have been previously presented to consciousness. And the assertion that this is an animal, a circle, or a colour, is a grouping of the new object perceived with the similar objects remembered. In like manner the inferences—" That berry is poisonous," " This solution will crystallize; " are impossible even as conceptions, unless a knowledge of the relations between poison and death, between solution and crystallization, have been previously put into the mind; either immediately by experience or mediately by description. And if a knowledge of such relations pre-exists in the mind, then the predications —" That berry is poisonous," " This solution will crystal-lize; " imply that certain new relations are thought of as belonging to certain classes of relations. It follows that, contemplated from this point of view, *reasoning is a classi-fication of relations.* But what does classification mean? It means the grouping together those which are *like*—the separation of the *like* from the *unlike.* Briefly, then, when inferring any relation, we are obliged to think of it as one (or not one) of some class of relations; and to think of it thus, is to think of it as like or unlike certain other rela-tions.

Passing to the second *à priori* argument, let us consider what is the more specific definition of Reasoning. Not only does the kind of proposition called an inference, assert a re-lation; but every proposition, whether expressing mediate or immediate knowledge, asserts a relation. How, then, does knowing a relation by Reason differ from knowing it by Perception? It differs by its *indirectness.* A cognition is distinguishable as of one or the other kind, accord-ing as the relation it embodies is disclosed to the mind *directly* or *indirectly.* If its terms are so presented that the relation between them is immediately cognized—if their coexistence, or succession, or juxtaposition, is knowable through the senses; we have a perception. If their co-existence, or sequence, or juxtaposition, is not knowable through the senses—if the relation between them is mediately cognized; we have a ratiocinative act. Reason-ing, then, is *the indirect establishment of a definite relation between two things.*   But now the question arises —By what process can the indirect establishment of a definite relation be effected? There is one process, and only one. If a relation between two things is not directly knowable; it can be disclosed only through the intermedia-tion of relations that are directly knowable, or are already

known.   Two mountains not admitting of a side by side
comparison, can have their relative heights determined only
by reference to some common datum line; as the level of
the sea.   The connexion between a certain sound and the
blowing of a distant horn, can arise in the mind only by
the help of a before-perceived connexion between such a
sound and such an action.   Observe, however, that in
neither case can any progress be made so long as the
relations are separately contemplated.   Knowledge of the
altitude of each mountain above the sea, gives no knowledge of their relative altitudes, until the two relations of
their tops to the sea are thought of together, as having a
certain relation.   The remembrance that a special kind of
sound is simultaneous with the blowing of a horn, leads to
nothing unless this general relation is thought of in connexion with the particular relation to be inferred.   Hence,
every ratiocinative act is *the indirect establishment of a
definite relation between two things, by the process of establishing a definite relation between two definite relations.*

These truths—That Reasoning, whether exhibited in
a simple inference or in a chain of such inferences, is
the indirect establishment of a definite relation between
two things; and that the achievement of this is by one or
many steps, each of which consists in the establishment of
a definite relation between two definite relations; embody,
under the most general form, the various results arrived at
in previous chapters.*

* A brief statement of the theory of Reasoning here elaborated in detail, will be found in an essay on "The Genesis of Science," published in
the *British Quarterly Review*, for July, 1854 (since republished, with other
essays in a permanent form).   In that essay I have sought to show that
scientific progress conforms to the laws of thought here set forth.   It
contains accumulated illustrations of the fact that the discoveries of exact science, from the earliest to the latest, severally consists in the establishment of the equalities of relations.   That the progress of human
reason, as viewed in its concrete results, should throughout exemplify
this generalization, as it does in the clearest manner, affords further confirmation of the foregoing analysis.

CHAPTER IX.

§ 310. I need scarcely recall the closing section of the last chapter for the purpose of showing that there is a close alliance between Reasoning and Classification; for every student of Reasoning had this truth thrust upon him at the outset of his studies. The alliance is much closer than is supposed, however. Their dependence is reciprocal—Reasoning presupposes Classification, and Classification presupposes Reasoning. This statement seems to involve a contradiction; and would do so, were Reasoning and Classification wholly distinct things. But the solution of the apparent paradox lies in the fact that they are different sides of the same thing—are the necessary complements of each other. Already in describing reasoning as the classification of relations, its near approach to the classification of entities has been implied. And if we remember that on the one hand, classification of relations involves classification of the things or attributes between which they subsist, while, on the other hand, classification of entities involves classification of the relations among their constituent attributes; the kinship of the two will appear still closer. Let us compare them in detail.

The idea underlying all classification is that of *similarity*. When we group an object with certain others, we do so because in some or all of its characters it resembles them.

Whether it be in putting together as of one kind, the extremely-like individuals constituting a species; whether it be in uniting under the general division, *Vertebrata,* such diverse creatures as a fish and a man, a snake and a bird; or whether it be in regarding both animate and inanimate objects as members of the great class, solid bodies; there is always *some* community of attributes—always *some* similarity in virtue of which they are colligated. But, as was lately pointed out, similarity in its strictest sense means equality of relations, and in its less strict sense means likeness of relations. When it is said that the two triangles ABC, DEF, are similar, the specific assertion involved is, that AB is to BC, as DE to EF; or, generally, that the quantitative relation between any two sides of the one, is equal to that between the homologous sides of the other.

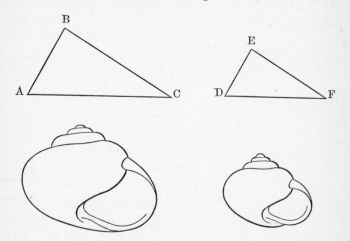

And when the two annexed shells are classed as of the same species, the implied perception of similarity is a perception that the relations among the several parts of the one are equal to, or like, those among the homologous parts of the other: not only the space-relations, but to a great extent the relations among colours, textures, and so on. What, then, is the difference between these acts of thought? From the perception of similarity in the triangles, there is evolved an inference respecting the value of some side; and from the perception of similarity in the shells, there is evolved the idea of identity of class. How is this? An answer is easily found.　　　　Similarity has several implications. After the perception of similarity any one of these may present itself to consciousness; and according as one or other of the two leading kinds of implication is thought of, we have reasoning or we have classification. It is impossible to perceive anything to be similar to another, or others, without, to some extent, thinking of that other, or those others. At the same time it is impossible to perceive similarity between things, without being more or less conscious of that likeness of relations among their elements which constitutes their similarity. Either of these two latent implications may become the subject of distinct contemplation. If we consciously recall the things to which this particular one is similar, we classify; if, consciously dwelling on the likeness of relations, we think of certain implied attributes, we reason.

" But how," it may be asked, " does this prove that classification presupposes reasoning; as well as that reasoning presupposes classification? It may be true that the intuition of similarity is their common root. It may be true that our conscious inferences involve acts of classing. But it does not, therefore, follow that our conscious acts of classing involve inferences." The reply is, that in all ordinary cases the majority of the like relations in virtue of which any object is classed with certain before-known objects, are not presented in perception but represented in an act of reason. The structural, tangible, gustable, ponderable, and other sensible characters ascribed to an orange, are not included in the visual impression received from the orange; but, as all admit, are inferred from that impression. Yet these various inferred characters are included in the concept—an orange. When I reach out my hand towards this reddish-yellow something, under the belief that it is juicy, and will slake thirst, I have already, in judging it to be an orange, conceived it as having various attributes besides the observed attributes; every one of which I know to exist, only by the same process that I know the juiciness to exist. The act of classing, then, involves a whole group of inferences; of which the particular inference avowedly drawn is only one. And had some other been drawn, as that the taste was sweet, what is now distinguished as the inference would have been one of the data; that is, one of the attributes involved in the judgment—this is an orange.   Should it be said that these various unspecified attributes are not inferred in the act of classing, but that the entire thought implied is—All reddish-yellow, spherical, polished, pitted bodies of a certain size are juicy; the untruth of the position will be seen on re-membering what takes place if a mock-orange made of painted stone is laid hold of. The *unexpected* weight and hardness, instantly lead to a change of classification: it is at once perceived that the body is not an orange. And this fact proves that something else than juiciness had been inferred; had been wrongly inferred; and had involved a wrong classification.

And here we see another vice of the theory which identifies syllogizing with reasoning. That theory proceeds upon the supposition that the act of referring any individual object to a class, is not an act of inference. The constant assumption is that the minor premiss, " This is a —," is immediately known; whereas it is always known mediately. Reasoning is already involved in the cognition of the very data out of which reasoning is said to be evolved. On the hypothesis that the syllogism represents the entire ratiocinative process, it is contended that its conclusion is necessary. Meanwhile, the all-essential fact which it posits as the foundation of that conclusion, is itself known by an unexpressed ratiocination. The concluded fact, and the fact from which it is concluded, stand on the same footing. The proposition—That which I see is an orange, has no greater certainty than the proposition —That which I see is juicy. The visual impressions of shape, size, colour, and surface, received from it, form the sole ground for both propositions. The wider inference— It is an orange, can give no extra validity to the narrower inference—It is juicy; seeing that for the first there is no more evidence than for the last. Yet the doctrine of the syllogism implies that the one is the warrant for the other— implies that I can *directly* know that this something belongs to the class oranges, and, by so doing, can *indirectly* know that it is juicy!

No such insuperable difficulty stands in the way of the theory that has been enunciated. A consciousness of similarity, underlying at once the act of classification or general inference, and the act of ratiocination which gives any special inference, is the basis of either or both. Along with the visible attributes of an orange, there are mentally represented in various degrees of distinctness, some, many, or all of the attributes before found in relation with such visible attributes; and, according to the mode in which they are represented, the thing predicated is the class, or some one or more of the attributes. Let the unperceived attributes be thought of in their totality, without any of them becoming specially prominent to consciousness; then, the object in being mentally endowed with all the characteristics of its class, is conceived as one of that class, or is classified. Let a single unperceived attribute, or a single group of such attributes, arrest consciousness, and occupy it to the partial exclusion of the other unperceived attributes; then, we have a special inference, or what is verbally embodied as such.   Of course the two processes being thus related, run into each other so readily and rapidly that probably neither ever occurs without the other. It is

scarcely possible that the aggregate of unperceived attributes should be thought of, without some of them being
represented more vividly than the rest; and it is scarcely
possible that any one of them should so engross the mind
as to banish all others entirely.   Always the attribute
inferred has for its indistinct back-ground, those many
accompanying attributes which constitute the conception of
the object as one of a class; and always among the many
attributes united in this classing conception, some stand out
as incipient inferences.   A latent classing accompanies the
inferential act; latent inferences accompany the act of
classing; and each continually arousing the other, alternates
with it in consciousness.

Our conclusion, then, is perfectly consistent with all that
has gone before; and, indeed, serves as a complement to it.
Likeness of relations is the intuition common to reasoning
and classification; and it results in one or the other, according as the relations thought of are partial or total.

§ 311. If we regard the name of a thing as a kind of conventional attribute, it will be manifest that when the thing
is presented, this conventional attribute becomes known as
any unseen real attribute becomes known—by an act of inference.   The immediately-perceived properties are thought
of as standing towards various unperceived properties in relations like those previously experienced; and among these
unperceived properties, is that of calling forth from human
beings a certain articulate sound—the name.   It is true that
this property is not inherent, but depends on an almost
fortuitous relation established between the thing and a
limited class of minds.   But the like is true of various other
properties which we commonly ascribe to the thing itself.
As all admit, the so-called secondary qualities of body are
not intrinsic, but are the affections produced in our organs
by unknown agents; and they so vary that the same thing
may seem heavy or light, warm or cold, pleasant or disagree-

able, according to the age, state, or character of the individual. If, then, these subjective and partially-incidental affections are called attributes of the objects affecting us, and are often ascribed to them inferentially; we may say that the purely subjective and mainly-incidental affection which an object produces in us when it suggests its name, is also in a strained sense an attribute, and becomes known by a similar mental process.

But it is by no means necessary to the argument that names should be thus considered as factitious attributes. The fact that the articulate sound by which an observed object is known, arises in consciousness after the same manner that an unperceived attribute does, may be rendered manifest without seeking any kinship between the things themselves. Observe what happens with a child. The word *orange*, which it probably first hears on a sample of that fruit being given to it, and which is often repeated in connexion with similar sensible characters, is established in its mind as a phenomenon having a more or less constant relation to the various phenomena which the orange presents. Not having as yet any notions of necessary and accidental relations, the particular sound accompanying the particular appearances, is as much grouped with them as the particular taste is. When the particular appearances recur, a relation (like the previously-experienced relation) between them and this sound, is as likely to be formed in consciousness as a relation between them and the taste. The mental act is essentially the same; and though subsequent experiences modify it in so far as the resulting conception is concerned, they cannot alter its fundamental nature. The genesis of the thought by which a thing is named remains identical in form; and to the last, as at the first, likeness of relations is the intuition implied in it.

Still more manifest becomes the kinship between naming and reasoning, when we call to mind that originally a name is a copy of some real attribute of the thing named. It is

inferable alike from the prattling of children and from the
speech of savages, that all language is in the beginning
mimetic. Wherever we can trace to their origin the symbols
used to convey thoughts—whether it be in the infantile
habit of naming animals by imitating their cries; whether it
be in the signs spontaneously hit upon by deaf-mutes, or in
those by which travellers in strange lands express their
wants; whether it be in the dramatic gestures used by the
uncivilized man to eke out his imperfect vocabulary, or in
the simulative words of which that vocabulary so largely
consists—we see that the notion of likeness underlies all
language, and also that the symbols of thought, both vocal
and mechanical (and even literal also), are at first *reproduc-
tions* of the things signified. And if names, in their earliest
forms, are either directly or metaphorically descriptive of
one or more distinctive attributes; then, primarily, an act of
naming is an inference becoming vocal. If a Bosjesman,
catching sight of some wild animal, conveys the fact to his
fellows by pointing towards it and mimicking the sound it is
known to make; beyond doubt this sound came into his
mind as an inferred attribute. And it differs from any other
inferred attribute solely in this, that instead of being simply
represented in his consciousness it is re-represented by his
voice. Thus beyond the fact that to ourselves the name of
a thing occurs in thought just as any inferred attribute
occurs, we have the fact that, originally, a name was *literally*
an inferred attribute transformed—was an inference which,
arising in the mind of one man by a representative act, was
forthwith presentatively conveyed by him to other men.*

Developing as language does by insensible modifications

---

* When this passage was written (1854), I had the advantage only of
such scattered illustrations as general reading had furnished. I did not
know how abundant and various was the evidence that might be brought
in support of the proposition it embodies. In the recent work of Mr.
Tyler on *The Early History of Mankind*, large accumulations of such
evidence will be found.

and complications out of this primitive process of naming, it follows throughout the same general law. Almost losing, though it ultimately does, the marks of its inferential genesis, it needs but to watch the use of new metaphors and the coining of new words, to see under a disguised form, the same fundamental intuition of likeness of relations.

§ 312. From the acts of Classification and Naming, let us pass to the act of Recognition. When the relations subsisting among any group of attributes are not simply *like* the relations subsisting among some before-known group, but are in most, if not in all respects, *equal* to them; and when the attributes themselves (as those of height, breadth, colour, &c.) are also *equal;* then we conclude the object presenting them to be the *same* object which we before knew.

Recognition differs from classification partly in the fact that the two compared groups of relations usually present a much higher degree of likeness, but mainly in the fact that not only are the relations alike but the constituent attributes are alike. There are two kinds of differences which objects display: differences between their sensible properties, as considered separately; and differences between the modes in which these sensible properties are co-ordinated, or related to one another. And if there are no discernible differences between the corresponding properties or the corresponding relations, we know the object as one previously perceived—we identify it—we recognize it.   To speak more specifically—If, passing over all those wider classes, such as minerals, plants, &c., whose members present very few relations in common; and those narrower but still very comprehensive classes, such as houses, crystals, quadrupeds, which have more decided similarities; and again, those yet narrower ones called genera—if, passing over all these, we confine our attention to those narrowest classes which severally contain individuals of the same kind, as asses, fir-trees, balloons; we see that while in respect of each attribute there need not be equality, there must be equality, or at least extreme likeness, in respect of the mode in which the attributes are combined. Whether the ass be six feet long or four feet long—whether dark brown or light brown, does not affect the classification; providing the *proportions* of its body and limbs in their ensemble and details, are nearly the same as those of other asses. It matters not whether the height of the fir-tree be five feet or a hundred feet; it is still classed as a fir-tree, if the *relations* of the branches to each other and to the stem, in position, direction, and length, together with the proportions and groupings of the pin-shaped leaves, are like those of fir-trees in general. But that a particular thing or place should be identified as a thing or place before seen, implies (in most cases) not only that the elements which compose the perception stand to one another in relations that are indistinguishable from the remembered relations; but that each element individually is indistinguishable from the remembered element answering to it.

I say in most cases, because our experience of the changeableness of things often leads us to assert identity where, besides some failure of likeness between the perceived and the remembered attributes, there is even some failure of likeness between the relations in which they stand to one another. Though, if the body be inanimate, we look for sameness in the dimensions and their several ratios, we are not prevented from knowing it again by the absence of a corner, or by some change of colour, or by the loss of polish. And an animate body may be recognized as a particular individual, even though it has greatly altered in bulk, in colour, and even in proportions—even though a limb has disappeared, the face become thin, and the voice weak. But when, as here, the identity is perceived in virtue of some very distinctive attributes and relations which remain unaltered, it is manifest that the impressions are interpreted by the help of sundry generalizations respecting the changes to which certain classes of bodies are liable; and that thus the act of simple recognition, properly so called, is greatly disguised. It should be remarked, too, that in cases of this kind the distinction between Recognition and Classification is very liable to disappear. It frequently becomes a question whether the observed object is the one before seen, or another of the same class.

But we shall best see what are the requisites to Recognition, by taking a case in which an individual cannot be recognized because of its extreme likeness to the other individuals constituting the class. Suppose that, while taking a needle from among sundry others of the same size, the whole paper-full is dropped on the floor. To fix upon the one which was about to be taken, is known to be hopeless. Why? Because the needles are so exactly alike in all respects, that no one of them is distinguishable from the others. Classification and Recognition here merge into one; or rather, there is no recognition of the individual, but only of the species. Suppose, now, that the selected needle is a larger one than the rest. What follows? That it can be readily identified. Though it may be perfectly *similar* to the others—though the ratios of the several dimensions to one another may be exactly *like* the homologous ratios in the rest—though there may be complete *equality of relations* among the attributes; yet these attributes, separately considered, differ from the corresponding attributes in the others. Hence the possibility of recognition. In this case we see both the positive conditions under which only recognition can take place, and the negative conditions. We see not only that the object identified must re-present a group of phenomena just like a group before presented; but also that there must be no other object presenting a group which is just like.

Of course it follows that Recognition, in common with Classification, is a modified form of reasoning. I do not mean that reasoning is involved in cases where great change has taken place, as where a tree that has wholly outgrown recollection is identified by its relative position; but I mean that where the recognition is of the simplest kind—where the recognized object is unaltered, there is still a ratiocinative act implied in the predication of its identity. For what do we mean by saying of such a thing that it is the *same* which we before saw? And what suffices us as proof of the sameness? The conception indicated by the word *same*, is that of a definite assemblage of correlated phenomena, not *similar* to a before-known assemblage, but *indistinguishable from* a before-known assemblage. On perceiving a group of attributes answering in all respects to a group perceived on a previous occasion, and differing in some respects from all allied groups, we *infer* that there coexists with it a group of unperceived attributes that likewise answer, in all respects, to those previously found to coexist with the perceived group. Should any doubt arise as to the identity of the object, then, by more closely inspecting it, by feeling it, by examining its remote side, by looking for a mark before observed, we proceed to compare the inferred attributes with the actual ones; and if they agree, we say the object is the same. While from minute to minute throughout our lives we are presented with groups of phenomena differing more or less from all preceding groups, we are also continually presented with groups of phenomena that are indistinguishable from preceding groups. Experience teaches us that when the perceived portion of one of these groups is indistinguishable from the corresponding portion of one before perceived; then, the remaining portions of the two are also indistinguishable. And the act of recognition is simply an inference determined by this general experience, joined to that particular experience which the recognition presupposes.

So that, regarding them both as forms of reasoning, Recognition differs from Classification simply in the greater speciality and definiteness of the inferred facts. In classing an observed object as a book, the implied inference is that along with certain visible attributes there coexist such others as the possession of white leaves covered with print. In the recognition of that book as So-and-so's Travels, the implied inference is, that these white leaves are covered with print of a particular size, divided into chapters with particular titles, containing paragraphs that express particular ideas. Thus the likeness of relations involved in the intuition, is both more exact and more detailed.

§ 313. The general community of nature thus shown in mental acts called by different names, may be cited as so much confirmation of the several analyses.

In preceding chapters, we saw that all orders of Reasoning —Deductive and Inductive, Necessary and Contingent, Quantitative and Qualitative, Axiomatic and Analogical— come under one general form. Here, we see both that Classification, Naming, and Recognition are nearly allied to one another, and that they, too, are severally modifications of that same fundamental intuition out of which all orders of reasoning arise. Nor are Classification and Naming allied only as being both of inferential nature; for they are otherwise allied as different sides of the same thing. Naming presupposes Classification; and Classification cannot be carried to any extent without Naming. Similarly with Recognition and Classification, which are also otherwise allied than through their common kinship to ratiocination. They often merge into each other, either from the extreme likeness of different objects, or the changed aspect of the same object; and while Recognition is a classing of a present impression with past impressions, Classification is a recognition of a particular object as one of a special group of objects.

This weakening of conventional distinctions—this reduction of these several operations of the mind, in common with all those hitherto considered, to variations of one operation, is to be expected as the result of analysis. For it is a characteristic of advancing science to subordinate the distinctions which a cursory examination establishes; and to show that these pertain, not to Nature, but to our language and our system.

CHAPTER X.

THE PERCEPTION OF SPECIAL OBJECTS.

§ 314. The several mental processes treated of in the last chapter, must be glanced at under their obverse aspect. We found Classification and Recognition to be allied forms of the act by which surrounding things become known. It remains to be pointed out that surrounding things can become known only by acts of Classification or Recognition.

Every perception of an external object involves a consciousness of it as such or such—as a something more or less specific; and this implies, either the identification of it as a particular thing or the ranging of it with certain kindred things. Every complete act of perception implies an expressed or unexpressed " assertory judgment "—a predication respecting the nature of that which is perceived; and the saying what a thing *is* is the saying what it is *like* —what class it belongs to. The same object may, according as the distance or the degree of light permits, be identified as a particular negro; or more generally as a negro; or more generally still as a man; or yet more generally as some living creature; or most generally as a solid body. In each of which cases the implication is, that the present compound impression is like certain past compound impressions. When, as sometimes happens from mental distraction, we go on searching for something actually in our hands, or overlook something directly under our eyes, we get clear proof that the mere passive reception of the group of sensations produced by an object, does not constitute a perception of it. A perception of it can arise only when the group of sensations is consciously co-ordinated and their meaning understood. And as their meaning can be understood only by help of those past experiences in which similar groups have been found to imply such and such facts, the understanding of them involves their assimilation to those groups—involves the thinking of them as like those groups, and as having like accompaniments. The perception of any object, therefore, is impossible save under the form either of Recognition or of Classification. .

The only qualification . of this statement that seems needed, concerns cases in which some kind of thing is seen for the first time—cases, therefore, in which a thing is known not as *like*, but as *unlike*, the things previously known. Under such conditions it appears that as there exists no previously-formed class, there is no Classification. But further consideration will show that there is a general classification, in default of a special one. Suppose the object to be an animal just discovered. Though, in the act of perception, it may not be thought of under the class mammals or the class birds, it is still thought of under the class living beings. Suppose there is doubt whether the object is animate or inanimate. It is nevertheless perceived as a solid body, and classed as such. The primary act, then, is still a cognition of likeness of a more or less general kind; though there may subsequently arise a cognition of a subordinate unlikeness to all before-known things.

Whether this law holds when we descend to the simplest kinds of cognition, it would be premature here to inquire; for at present we have to do only with those involved cognitions by which surrounding objects are severally distinguished as complex wholes. To meet all possible criticisms, however, the statement may be qualified by saying that a special perception is possible, only as an intuition of the likeness or unlikeness of certain present attributes and relations, to certain past attributes and relations.

§ 315. As implied above, the perception by which any object is known as such or such, is always an acquired perception. All psychologists concur in the doctrine that most of the elements contained in the cognition of an observed object, are not known immediately through the senses, but are mediately known by instantaneous ratiocination. Before a visual impression can become a perception of the thing causing it, there must be added in thought those attributes of trinal extension, size, solidity, quality of surface, &c. &c., which, when united, constitute the nature of the thing as it is known to us. Though these seem to be given in the visual impression, it is demonstrable that they are not so, but have to be reached by inference. And the act of knowing them is termed acquired perception, to signify the fact that while really mediate, it appears to be immediate.

The like holds of those various actions which objects exhibit: the perceptions of them are similarly acquired, and similarly imply classification. If an adjacent person at whose back we are looking turns half round, the only thing immediately known is the sudden change in the visual impression. Standing alone this change has no meaning. It comes to have a meaning only when by accumulated experiences it is found that all such changes are accompanied by alterations in the relative positions of the parts, as ascertained by touch. We do not *see* the turning: we *infer* the turning. We conceive a certain relation between the changes we see and the motions we might feel, which is *like* numberless previously-experienced relations; we *classify* the present relation with a series of past relations; and we signify it by a word *like* the words used to signify those past relations. The visible transformation which a piece of melting lead undergoes, can convey no knowledge unless it is already known that certain appearances always coexist with liquidity. And what seems to be a perception of the melting is, in reality, a rational interpretation of the appearances—a classing of them with the like appearances before known, and an assumption that they stand towards certain other phenomena in relations parallel to the before-known relations.

Thus the cognitions by which we guide ourselves from moment to moment, in the house and in the street, are all of them acquired perceptions; all of them involve the classification or recognition of attributes, groups of related attributes, and the relations between such groups; all of them embody inferences; all of them imply intuitions of likeness or unlikeness of relations.

§ 316. And here we see again that the divisions made among the various mental processes have merely a superficial truth. At the conclusion of Chapter VIII., Reasoning was defined as the *indirect* establishment of a definite relation between two things; in contrast to Perception, in which the relation is established *directly*. But now we find that all those perceptions by which complex objects become specifically known, also involve the indirect establishment of relations. Though on contemplating the lights and shades and perspective outlines of a building, the fact that it is a solid body seems to be immediately known, yet analysis proves that its solidity is known mediately. And this analysis is confirmed by the stereoscope, which, by simulating the evidence of solidity, induces us to conceive as solid that which is not solid. Obviously, therefore, the indirect passes into the direct by long-continued habit. Just as the meaning of a word in a new language, though at first remembered only by the intermediation of the equivalent word in a known language, by and by comes to be remembered without this intermediation; so, by constant repetition, the process of interpreting our sensations becomes so rapid that we appear to pass directly to the facts which they imply.　　Still more manifest will appear the purely relative truth of this division, when it is observed that what seem unquestionably direct cognitions are united by insensible gradations with indirect ones. If I stand a hundred yards from the front of a house, the shape of that front seems to be known immediately: the relations of the parts are all directly presented to consciousness. But if I stand within a yard of the front and look up at it, the outlines, as then apparent, are not in the least like those seen from a distance; and the conception I now form of its shape must be *inferred* from the greatly distorted outlines I see. Yet between a hundred yards and one yard, there are ten thousand points from which may be had as many views, each differing inappreciably from its neighbours. Evidently, then, the transition from a *directly*-perceived shape to an *indirectly*-perceived shape is insensible.　　When to facts of this kind is added the fact that we often skip the intermediate steps of an habitual argument, and pass at once from the premises to a remotely-involved conclusion—when we thus see that in conscious reasoning also, the tendency is for indirect processes to become more and more direct; we are forced to admit that it is only relatively, and not absolutely, that Reasoning is distinguished from Perception by its indirectness.

CHAPTER XI.

§ 317. The relation established between object and subject in the act of perception, is threefold. It assumes three distinct aspects, according as there is some kind of activity on the part of the object, on the part of the subject, or on the part of both. If, while the subject is passive, the object is working an effect upon it—as by radiating heat, giving off odour, or propagating sound; there results in the subject a perception of what is usually termed a secondary property of body, but what may be better termed a dynamical property. If the subject is directly acting upon the object by grasping, thrusting, pulling, or any other mechanical process, while the object is reacting, as it must, to an equivalent extent; the subject perceives those variously-

---

* The divisions thus designated, answer to those which Sir William Hamilton classes as Secondary, Secundo-primary, and Primary. While coinciding in the general distinctions drawn in his dissertation, I do so on other grounds than those assigned; and adopt another nomenclature for several reasons. One is that the names Primary, Secundo-primary, and Secondary, implying, as they in some degree do, a serial genesis in time, do not, as it seems to me, correspond with the true order of that genesis, subjectively considered; while, objectively considered, we cannot assign priority to any. Another is that these terms, as used by Sir William Hamilton, have direct reference to the Kantian doctrine of Space and Time, from which I dissent. And a third is that the terms above proposed are descriptive of the real distinctions among these three orders of attributes.

modified kinds of resistance which have been classed as the secundo-primary properties, but which I prefer to class as statico-dynamical. And if the subject alone is active—if that which occupies consciousness is not any action or re-action of the object, but something discerned *through* its actions or reactions—as size, form, or position; then the property perceived is of the kind commonly known as primary, but here named statical.

The three classes of attributes thus briefly defined, which will hereafter be successively considered at length, are usu-ally presented to consciousness together. The space-attri-butes are knowable only through the medium of resistance and the other force-attributes. Tangible properties are generally perceived in connexion with form, size, and posi-tion. And of the non-tangible ones, colour is mostly asso-ciated with the surfaces of solids, and cannot be conceived apart from extension of two dimensions. An object held in the hands and regarded by the eyes, presents to conscious-ness all three orders of attributes at once. It is known as something resisting, rough or smooth, elastic or unelastic; as something having both visible and tangible extension, form, and size; as something whose parts reflect certain amounts and qualities of light; and, on further examination, as something specifically scented and flavoured.

In conformity with the method hitherto pursued, of setting out with the most involved combinations, resolving these into simpler ones, and these again into still simpler ones; our analysis of the perception of body will be best initiated by taking an exhaustive perception as above described, and considering what are the relations among its various ele-ments. And to simplify the problem, it will be well to treat first of those *contingent* attributes known as secondary, and here called dynamical; so that after having analyzed these in themselves, and in their relations to the *necessary* attributes, we may deal with the perception of necessary attributes as divested of everything that is extraneous.

§ 318. Beginning with these contingent attributes as contemplated in themselves, let us first consider the propriety of classing them as dynamical.

The most familiar ones are obviously manifestations of certain forms of force. Of sound, we know that it becomes sensible to us through vibrations of the *membrana tympani*, and that these vibrations are caused by waves in the air. We know, too, that the body whence these proceed must be thrown into a vibratory state by some mechanical force; that it thereupon propagates undulations through surrounding matter; and that in this purely dynamical action consists the production of sound. Respecting heat we know that it may be generated mechanically, as by compression or friction, and that, conversely, it is itself capable of generating mechanical force. We find that in its reflections and refractions, it conforms to the law of composition of forces; and that, by the now-established undulatory theory, its multiplied phenomena are resolved into dynamical ones. Further, there is the fact that on holding a thermometer near the fire, the same agent which causes in the hand the sensation of warmth causes motion in the mercury. The phenomena of colour, again, are reducible to the same category. The reflections and refractions of light are inexplicable, save mechanically; and only on the theory of undulations can polarization, diffraction, &c., be accounted for. Light is now recognized as one form of the primordial force, which may otherwise manifest itself as sensible motion, as electricity, as heat, as chemical affinity. In the fact that great heat is accompanied by luminosity, joined to the fact that great heat may be generated mechanically, we clearly trace the transformation; while, conversely, we find light producing a dynamic effect, alike in all photographic processes and in those molecular re-arrangements which it works in certain crystals. Nor must we forget that while, under ordinary circumstances, matter only reflects and modifies the light falling upon it;

yet under fit chemical conditions, it becomes an independent source of light. Though not the immediate effects of radiant forces, odours are demonstrably dynamic in their origin. The established doctrine of evaporation implies that the giving-off of particles which produces odoriferousness, must be ascribed to molecular repulsion. Those diffused molecules constituting the scent of a body, must have been propelled from the surfaces of that body before they acted upon the nostrils; and hence it follows that a certain form of activity in the object, is the efficient cause of a sensation of smell in the subject. The only secondary attribute not obviously dynamic is that of taste. But the close alliance existing between taste and smell is almost of itself sufficient to prove that if one is dynamic so is the other. When we bear in mind that for a body to have any gustable property implies some degree of solubility in the saliva, without which its particles cannot be carried by endosmose through the mucous membrane of the tongue, and cannot therefore be tasted; and when we further bear in mind that the diffusion of particles through liquid is analogous to their diffusion through air, and that the molecular repulsion causing the last has its share in the first; we shall see further reason to consider the sensation of taste as due to an objective activity.

But the dynamic nature of the secondary attributes is most clearly seen when, instead of contemplating the object as acting, we contemplate the subject as acted upon. All can testify that the flavours of certain drugs are so persistent as to continue to give feelings of disgust, long after the drugs themselves have been swallowed. A pungent odour causes a sneeze; and the smell from a slaughterhouse or boneyard creates a nausea which so tyrannizes over consciousness, as to exclude every thought but that of escape. A flash of lightning, or any sudden change in the amount or quality of the light surrounding us, instantly changes the currents of our thoughts. And still more significant is the fact that a strong glare abruptly thrown on his face, will often awaken a sleepy person. Similarly with changes of temperature. Any one standing with his hands behind him cannot have a red-hot iron put close to them without his ideas being at once directed into a new channel; and if the degree of heat passes a certain point, he will draw away his hands automatically. So, too, is it with sounds. They may create either pleasurable or painful states of consciousness. They often distract the attention against the will. When loud, they cause involuntary starts in those who are awake; and either waken those who sleep, or modify their dreams.   If, then, in these extreme cases, the so-called secondary attributes of body are unquestionably dynamic, they must be so throughout. If we find the eyes made to water by mustard taken in excess; vomiting excited when squeamish by the smell of a steamer's cabin; a blinking of the eyes, and a painful sense of dazzling, caused by looking at the sun; a scream called forth by a scald or burn; an involuntary bound produced by an adjacent explosion; it becomes an unavoidable conclusion that those properties of things which we know as tastes, scents, colours, heats, sounds, are effects wrought on us by forces in the environment. The subject undergoes a change of state determined by some external agency, directly or indirectly proceeding from an object. Though there may arise in him, during the interpretation of its outward cause, various internally-determined states; yet, in so far as the change itself is concerned, he is simply recipient of an objective influence. In respect to all these so-called secondary attributes, the object is *active* and the subject is *passive*.

Let us next observe that, with the exception of taste which is in some respects transitional, these dynamical attributes are those by which objects act upon us through space. By means of the light it radiates or reflects, an outward thing renders itself visible when afar off. At various degrees of remoteness, objects in states of sonorous vibration arrest our attention. We are made aware of the presence of odoriferous substances while only in their neighbourhood. Masses of hot matter affect us when near to them. Unlike hardness, softness, flexibility, brittleness, and all the statico-dynamical attributes, which are cognizable by us only through actual contact, either immediate or mediate; unlike the statical attributes, shape, size, and position, which do not in themselves affect us at all, but become known only by acts of constructive intelligence; these dynamical attributes modify consciousness at all distances, from that of a star downwards. Eyes, ears, nose, and the diffused nervous agency through which temperature is appreciated, are inlets to the influences of objects more or less distant; and the ability that distant objects have thus to work changes in us, again exhibits their inherent activity.

These attributes are further distinguished by the peculiarity that they are, in a sense, separable from what we commonly call body. Light in varying intensities is known as pervading surrounding space. The many tints assumed by the sky are not, in so far as our senses are concerned, the attributes of matter. And by casting the prismatic spectrum on a succession of surfaces, or by observing how the iris in the spray of a cascade moves with every change in the position of the eye, proof is gained that colour, in its various qualities, is not an inherent property. The like holds with respect to the relation between sounds and vibrating objects; which we learn only by a generalization of experiences. To the incipient intelligence of an infant, noise does not involve any conception of body. In an oft-recurring echo, the sound has come to have an existence separate from the original concussion—continues after the vibrating body which caused it has become still. We frequently hear sounds produced by things that are neither visible nor tangible to us, but are simply inferred. And by the phrase,—" What's that? " commonly uttered on hearing an unusual noise, it is clearly implied that the noise has been identified as such before any object has been thought of as causing it.   Odours, again, are often perceived when wafted far from the substances diffusing them.   A room scented by something placed in it, may retain the scent long after the thing has been removed. We may be strongly affected by an entirely new smell while ignorant what produces it, or from which side it comes.   Similarly with heat.   In a cloudy summer we often feel marked changes of temperature that are not traceable to any special object.   The warmth of a room heated by hot-water pipes may be felt for some time before it is discovered whence the warmth proceeds.   So even is it with gustable properties.   Though ordinarily the things which we taste are simultaneously known to us as fluid or solid matters, yet it needs but to remember the persistence of disagreeable flavours, even after the mouth has been rinsed, to perceive that sapidity can be dissociated from body: understanding by the word body, something perceivable as extended and resisting.   Here again, then, the dynamical attributes stand apart from the statico-dynamical and statical ones; for none of those modifications of resistance constituting the one class, nor those tangibly-perceived modes of extension constituting the other (visible extension being but symbolical of tangible extension), can be recognized apart from the objects to which they belong.

Note, again, that these dynamical or secondary attributes are incidental.   Different bodies exhibit them in countless degrees and combinations; and each body exhibits them more or less, or not at all, according as surrounding conditions determine.   In the dark, things are all of them colourless.   In the light, their appearances vary as the light varies in kind and degree.   The colour of a dove's neck changes with the position of the observer's eye;

while that of some crystals and fluids is reversed when the light is transmitted instead of being reflected. Under ordinary circumstances most objects are silent. Those that emit sound do so only under special influences; and the sound that any one of them emits is in great measure determined by the nature or intensity of the influences. A great number of substances are inodorous; and of the rest, the majority cannot be perceived to have any smell unless held close to the nostrils. Things that are almost scentless at low temperatures may become strongly scented at high ones. Very many bodies have no taste whatever; and the sapid qualities of others vary according as they are hot or cold. The temperature of the same mass may be such as to give a sensation of greater or less heat; or such as to give no appreciable sensation at all; or such as to give a sensation of greater or less cold. Thus the incidental character of these attributes is manifest. To a person specially circumstanced, an object may be at once colourless, soundless, scentless, tasteless, and of such temperature as to produce no thermal effect upon him; or the object and the circumstances may be such that he shall be variously affected by one, or two, or three, of these dynamical attributes. But it is otherwise with the statico-dynamical and statical attributes. For while different bodies present different amounts of resistance and extension; and while in the same body the resistance and extension admit of more or less variation; there is no body *without* resistance and extension.

Lastly, let it be noticed that these so-called secondary attributes of body, which we find distinguishable from the rest as being dynamical, as acting through space, as cognizable apart from body, and as manifested by body only incidentally, are not, in any strict sense, attributes of body at all. I do not mean simply that, being dissociable from body, body can readily enough be conceived without them; nor do I mean that what we call colour, sound, and the rest, are subjective effects produced by unknown powers in the objects; but I mean that these unknown powers are literally not in the objects at all. Rightly understood, the so-called secondary attributes are manifestations of certain forces which pervade the Universe; and which, when they act upon bodies, call forth from them certain reactions. On being struck, a gong vibrates; and by communicating its vibrations to the air, or any intermediate substance, affects an auditor with a sensation of sound. What is the active cause of that sensation? It is not the gong: it is the force which, being impressed on the gong, is changed by its re-action into another shape. When the Sun shines on any mass of matter, some of his rays are absorbed while some are reflected. In most cases the light being decomposed, its reflected portion affects us as colour; and by special masses of matter it is refracted and dispersed in chromatic bands. That is, a certain force emanating from the Sun impresses itself on matter, and is, by the counter-action of matter, more or less metamorphosed. The heat given off by burning coal, and by a briskly-hammered piece of iron, are reactions called forth, in the first case by the chemical action of the surrounding oxygen, in the second by mechanical pressure. The molecular repulsion whence odorife-rousness results, is one of the reactions consequent on the reception of heat—is known to vary as the heat varies; and could heat be entirely withheld, odours would cease. Throughout, therefore, these attributes are, if considered in their origin, activities pervading space; and can be ascribed to body only in the sense that body when exposed to them, reacts upon them, modifies them, and is known to us through the modifications. Strictly speaking, one of these simple sensations of colour, sound, scent, &c., involves a series of actions and re-actions of which the object proximately yielding it mani-fests but the last. The light, or mechanical force, or heat, serving as its conspicuous cause, itself resulted from pre-

vious actions and reactions, which lead us back into an indefinite past filled with changes. But confining our attention to the elements with which we have immediately to
deal, we see that rightly to understand one of these dynamic attributes, implies the contemplation of three things:
—First, a force, either diffused as light and heat or concen-
trated as momentum; second, an object on which some of
that force is impressed, and which in so far as it is a recipient of force is passive, but in so far as it reacts and determines that force into new forms and directions is active;
and third, a subject on whom some of the transformed force
expends itself in producing what we term a sensation, and
who as the recipient of this transformed force is passive,
but who may be rendered active by it.

Literally, then, the so-called secondary attributes are
neither objective nor subjective; but are the triple products
of the subject, the object, and the environing activities.
Sound, colour, heat, odour, and taste, can be called attributes of body only in the sense that they imply in body certain powers of reaction, which appropriate external actions
call forth. These powers of reaction, however, are neither
the attributes made known to us as sensations, nor those
vibrations or undulations or molecular repulsions in which,
as objectively considered, these attributes are commonly
said to consist; but they are the occult properties in virtue
of which body modifies the forces brought to bear upon it.
Nevertheless, it remains true that these attributes, as manifested to us, are dynamical. And in so far as the immediate
relation is concerned, it remains true that in respect of these
attributes the object is active and the subject is passive.

§ 319. Let us now proceed to define the perception which
we have of a body presenting these non-necessary attributes,
in conjunction with the necessary attributes; that is—a
body as ordinarily perceived.

On taking up and contemplating an apple, there arises in

consciousness, partly by presentation through the senses and partly by representation through the memory, what seems to be one state, but what analysis proves to be a very complex combination of many states. The greater number of these remain to be considered analytically in subsequent chapters, and can here be simply enumerated. Among them we have, first, the coexistence in time of the contemplating subject and the contemplated object. Further we have that relative position of the two in space which we call proximity. We have also that group of impressions on the finger-ends, which leads us to conceive the object as not only having a position in space but as occupying space, and a certain limited amount of space. Yet again we have that more involved series of tactual and motor impressions gained by moving the fingers about it, and constituting our notion of its tangible shape. To these must be added that supplementary set of impressions by which we recognize its surface as smooth; and that other set by which we form an idea of its hardness. Passing from these fundamental data acquired through the tactual and muscular senses, we have to note the impressions through which the apple's coexistence in time and adjacency in space are visually as well as tactually known. With these we must join the impressions which make up our conception of its visible bulk and figure. And we must not omit those which indicate to us a correspondence between the data received through the eyes and those received through the fingers. ·But now, along with the statical and statico-dynamical attributes primarily known through combined sensations of resistance and motion, and some of them re-known through combined ocular sensations of light, shade, and focal adjustment, we find certain other attributes standing in various orders of relation. Joined with the attributes of position, size, and form, as visually perceived, is the attribute of colour (including in the word all possible modifications of light), recognized as coexistent in time and coincident in space with these statical attributes. This relation admits of some variation, however. For though, when our consciousness of colour entirely ceases, our consciousness of visible form, size, and place, ceases with it; yet by alterations in the amount and quality of the light, our impression of colour may be variously changed without any change being produced in our consciousness of form, size, and place. While it is generically absolute this connexion is specifically conditional. Note this, however, that the relation of coincidence in time and space between the several impressions we have of the visible attributes and those we have of the tangible ones, is entirely conditional. It depends on the presence of light; on the opening of the eyes; and on the object being within the field of view. Unless each of these three conditions is fulfilled, no relation of coincidence in time and space between these two sets of attributes can be established. Similarly with the odour. This, being but weak, can be perceived to accompany the other attributes only when the apple is placed near the nostrils and air drawn in. The presence of a certain taste is in like manner unknowable, save through actions similarly special. Thus, the common characteristic of the dynamical attributes, is the extreme conditionality of their coexistence with the statico-dynamical and statical ones, in so far as our consciousness is concerned. Though our perceptions of the softness, roughness, flexibility, &c., of any body examined by the fingers, are conditional on our performance of certain manipulations as well as on the nature of the body; yet the general perception of resistance is wholly unconditional. Though our perceptions of the specific extension of the body —its size and shape—are similarly conditional on its character and on our acts; yet the general perception of extension is wholly unconditional. *Some* resistance and *some* extension are the invariable and necessary elements of the cognition. Be the body what it may, and be the part of the skin touched by the body what it may, if it is perceived

at all, it is perceived as something resisting and extended.
But the perception of the dynamical attributes as coexistent
with the rest, depends not only on the nature of the object
and on our acts, but also on the exposure of the object to
certain agencies pervading the environment.

Here, then, is the general result. Any total perception,
uniting the three orders of attributes in one cognition, is a
state of consciousness formed thus:—Along with certain
general impressions of resistance and extension, *unconditionally* standing to each other and the subject in relations
of co-existence in time and adjacency in space; and along
with certain specialized impressions of resistance and specialized impressions of extension, *conditionally* standing to
each other and the subject in similar space-relations and
slightly-modified time-relations; there are certain impressions of a different order standing in a *doubly conditional*
manner to the previous ones, to the subject, and to one another, in space and time relations still further modified.
This definition must not, however, be taken as exhaustive;
for nothing is said of all the inferred facts bound up with
the perceived facts—nothing of those many minor conditions and accompaniments, only to be described at the cost
of pages. It is intended simply to exhibit, in as precise a
way as the present stage of the analysis admits, the general
mode in which our cognitions of the several orders of attributes are united in ordinary perception—simply to display
the relationship in which, as known to us, the dynamical
attributes of body stand to its other attributes; so that having duly contemplated this relationship, we may go on to
analyze the perception of the statico-dynamical and statical
attributes by themselves.

§ 320. The mental act effecting one of these perceptions
next claims our attention. So far, we have considered only
the several elements which compose the perception; and
there has yet to be considered the process by which they

are co-ordinated. This is what may be termed a process of *organic classification*.

As explained in preceding chapters, the " assertory judg-ment " involved in every perception of an object, is an act of either classification or recognition. According as it is more or less specific, a perception involves the thought— " This is a dog; " or, " This is something alive; " or, " This is a solid body." It is not requisite that the assertory judg-ment should be verbally expressed, either outwardly or inwardly; but that the perceived object must be more or less consciously referred to its class, is manifest from the fact that when, after some ordinary thing has been put under his eyes a person cannot tell what the thing was, we say that he did not perceive it. Though the need-ful impressions were made on his senses, he did not so attend to them as to become conscious of their im-port. Had he done so, his subsequent ability to name the thing would imply that he had recognized its nature; that is, its class. Now this semi-conscious classification which every complete perception of an object involves, is *necessarily preceded by a still less conscious classification of its constituent attributes, of the relations in which they stand to one another, and of the conditions under which such attri-butes and relations become known*. At first sight, this seems an incredible proposition—incredible both as asserting what self-analysis gives no evidence of, and as implying a mental activity inconceivably great. Nevertheless, inquiry will show that, *à priori*, the perception of an object is not otherwise possible, and also that direct experience, not less than analogy, implies the performance of some such spon-taneous assimilation.

Observe first the necessities of the case. If, instead of that which I perceive to be an apple, there had been pre-sented something having like form and colours but measur-ing a yard in diameter, I should not have concluded it to be an apple. Or if, while the bulk and colours were as usual,

the form had been cubical or pyramidal, I should have regarded it as something else than an apple. And similarly if,
though like in other respects, it had been sky-blue, or covered
with spines, or as heavy as lead. What now is implied?
Clearly this, that before the object is recognized as an apple,
each of the chief constituent attributes is recognized as *like*
the homologous attribute in other apples. The bulk is perceived to be like the bulk of apples in general; the form
like their forms; the colour like their colours; the surface
like their surfaces; and so on. The elements constituting
the total perception, are severally classed with the before-
known like elements; just as the entire group is afterwards
classed with the before-known like groups.   Moreover, there is a classing not only of the constituent attributes but of their relations. If the apple be one marked
with streaks of red, then these must run in certain directions. Were they to run equatorially, it would be at once
decided that the object was not an apple; as also, if the
stem and the remnant of the calyx did not stand towards
each other in specific positions. That is, the relations of
coexistence and proximity and arrangement subsisting
among the constituent attributes, must also be recognized
as like certain before-known relations—must be classed with
them.   Further, there must be classed the conditions
under which the attributes and relations become known.
The colours and visible form of an apple being perceivable
only during the presence of light, it results that a consciousness of light, regarded as a condition like the before-
known conditions, becomes an indirect component of the
perception: to prove which, it needs but remember that the
form and colours of an apple if seen in the dark, would be
regarded not as implying an apple but as implying an
optical illusion. Its weight, again, is perceived as coexistent with its tangible properties; but only when it is lifted.
No sensation of weight, save one obtained under this condition like certain remembered conditions, could be ascribed

to the apple, or become an element in the perception of it. Thus, then, there is a classing of the several attributes with the like before-known attributes, of the relations subsisting among them with like before-known relations, and of the conditions under which they are perceived with like before-known conditions. And the classification of the object as an apple is the cumulative result of these constituent classifications.

" Can such a complicated set of mental acts be performed so rapidly as to leave no trace in consciousness? " The question is pertinent. I have already, by the phrase " *organic* classification," indicated what I conceive to be the solution of this difficulty; and it needs but to note the stages through which our acts of classing pass from the conscious to the unconscious, to see that the facts point to this solution. Let any one walking through the Zoological Gardens, meet with an animal he has read about but has not before seen. How does he endeavour to determine its kind? He considers its separate characteristics—observes successively its size, its general shape, its head, its feet, its tail, its hair, its colour—classes these respectively as large, as broad, as pointed, and so forth—does in a less definite way what a zoologist in a parallel case does systematically; and if he succeeds in classing the creature, he succeeds by thus thinking of the likenesses of its constituent attributes and their relations to those of creatures he has heard of, read of, or seen drawings of. Let him pass on to some beast before seen but not familiar, as the sea-bear. His first sight of it is accompanied by a distinct act of classing, and by a repetition of the name, either aloud or to himself. Let him walk by cages having inmates he has often watched, as the lions, and the act of classing will obtrude upon his consciousness much less distinctly. Now let him leave the gardens. On passing the horses standing at the gates, he will be conscious that they are horses; but he will not specifically identify them as such in deliberate acts of thought.

And when he reaches the streets, though each of the hundred individuals passing him every minute is distinguished as man, woman, boy, or girl—is classed, that is—the mental act is performed so rapidly as scarcely to interrupt the current of his thoughts. Now this ever-increasing facility and quickness in classing complex groups of attributes, implies an ever-increasing facility and quickness in that classing of the attributes themselves, their relations, and the conditions under which they are perceived, that begins with infancy. Forms, sizes, distances, colours, weights, smells, and the rest, though once consciously classed, gradually during childhood come to be classed less and less consciously; and this classification being simpler than any other, beginning earlier and being almost infinitely repeated, grows more rapid than any other: eventually becoming practically automatic.

To verify this interpretation it needs but to remind the reader that he has, within his own experience, a case in which the entire progress from conscious to unconscious classification is traceable. When learning to read, the child has to class each letter by a distinct mental act. This symbol A, has to be thought of as like certain others before seen, and as standing for a sound like certain sounds before heard. By practice these processes become more and more abbreviated, or less and less conscious. Presently the power is reached of classing by one act a whole group of such symbols—a word; and eventually an entire cluster of words is recognized instantaneously. Now, were it not that these steps can be recalled, it would seem absurd to say that when the reader takes in at a glance the sentence —" This is true," he not only classifies each word with the before-known like words, but each letter with the before-known like letters. Yet, as it is, he will see this to be an unavoidable inference. He knows that such acts of classing were performed at first; and as no time can be named at which they were given up, it follows that the entire change has arisen from a progressive increase of rapidity, which has finally made them almost automatic. And if this has taken place with acts of classing commenced so late as five or six years old, still more must it have taken place with those simpler acts commenced at birth.

The foregoing definition of the perception of body as presenting the three orders of attributes, therefore requires to be supplemented by this explanation; that the several attributes, the relations in which they stand to one another and to the subject, as well as the conditions under which only such attributes and relations are perceived, have to be thought of as like before-known attributes, before-known relations, and before-known conditions.

CHAPTER XII.

§ 321. If we imagine a human being without sight, hearing, taste, smell, or the sense of temperature; then the only attributes of body cognizable by him, will be the statico-dynamical and the statical. All the knowledge he can gain by touching, pressing, pulling, and rubbing things, as well as by moving his limbs, or body, or both, in contact with them, comes under these heads: the one comprehending knowledge which implies an activity on his part, and a re-activity on the part of the things; the other comprehending knowledge which implies his independent internal activity in putting together certain of the impressions he has received.

These statico-dynamical and statical attributes are usually presented to consciousness closely united. When in the dark any object is examined by the hands, more or less definite perceptions of its softness, smoothness, elasticity, &c., are joined with more or less definite perceptions of its position, size, and form. These two classes of perceptions may accompany each other with various degrees of incompleteness; but *some* connexion between them is invariable. As will hereafter be shown, it is questionable whether primordially they exist in this relation; but without doubt by the adult human consciousness, all tactile resistances are unconditionally known as coexistent with *some* extension, and all tactile extensions are unconditionally known as coexistent with *some* resistance.

In pursuance of the method hitherto followed, we have now to analyze one of these complex tactual perceptions in its totality. As in the last chapter we attended mainly to the contingent attributes and their relations to these essential ones, with a view of afterwards leaving the contingent out of consideration; so here, it will be best to treat more especially of the resistance-attributes, so that having observed how we perceive them and their relations to the extension-attributes, we may proceed to deal with the extension-attributes by themselves.

§ 322. Note first why these resistance-attributes which have been termed secundo-primary, may be more appropriately termed statico-dynamical.

They are all of them known as manifestations of mechanical force. They are all results of attraction, of repulsion, and of that property in virtue of which a body's reaction upon a disturbing agent varies as the quantity of motion which that disturbing agent impresses upon it.* They are the attributes of body involved alike in its standing and in its acting. That capacity which matter has of passively retaining, while undisturbed, its size, figure, and position, may rightly be regarded as statical; while that

* I use this awkward circumlocution to avoid an inaccuracy. Among the sources, physically considered, of the secundo-primary attributes, Sir William Hamilton enumerates *inertia.* But inertia is not a force : it is simply the negation of activity. It is not a positive attribute : it is a purely negative one. There is a very general belief that matter offers some absolute opposition to anything tending to displace it. This is not the fact. Take away all extrinsic hindrance—all friction, all resisting medium— and an infinitesimal force will produce motion ; only the motion will be infinitesimal, in consequence of the law that the velocity varies as the momentum (or force impressed) divided by the mass. Were inertia a force, all the calculations of astronomers respecting planetary perturbations and the like, would be erroneous. The term *vis inertiæ* is a misnomer.

capacity which it has of meeting by a proportionate counter-acting force, any force brought to bear upon it, must be considered as dynamical; and the fact that these capacities cannot be dissociated, but are two sides of the same capacity, is expressed by uniting the descriptive terms. Add to this, that if we class those attributes in respect of which the object is active while the subject is passive, as dynamical; and if we class as statical those in respect of which the subject is active while the object is passive; then we must class as statico-dynamical those in respect of which subject and object are both active.

Attributes of this class are more numerous than would be supposed. The resistances offered by objects to forces tending to raise them—their weights—originate only the attributes of *Heavy* and *Light;* which indicate amounts of gravitative force in relation to bulk. But the opposition which objects offer to compression or tension, is distinguishable not only in its relative amounts but in its kinds. Of bodies that resist in different modes as well as in different degrees, we have the *Hard* and *Soft;* the *Firm* and *Fluid;* the *Viscid* and *Friable;* the *Tough* and *Brittle;* the *Rigid* and *Flexible;* the *Fissile* and *Infissile;* the *Ductile* and *Inductile;* the *Retractile* and *Irretractile;* the *Compressible* and *Incompressible;* the *Resilient* and *Irresilient;* and (combined with figure) the *Rough* and *Smooth.** Of these

---

* With some exceptions this is Sir William Hamilton's classification. I do not, however, separate, as he attempts to do, the attributes which (physically considered) imply molecular attraction (as the Retractile) from those which imply molecular repulsion (as the Resilient); because, in reality, all of them imply both. As there is a balance of the molecular attractions and repulsions in an undisturbed body, a body cannot have any of its molecules disturbed by an external force without both the attractive and repulsive forces coming into active opposition. On examining the fracture of a piece of wood broken transversely, part of the area will be seen to exhibit marks of tension and part of compression; and the line dividing these parts is called the "neutral axis." A body cannot exhibit ductility or retractility without being partially thrown into a state of compression; seeing that the extending force cannot be applied to the body without compressing it somewhere.

pairs of attributed qualities, several are purely relative—are simply degrees of the same. This is manifestly the case with *Hard* and *Soft*, *Firm* and *Fluid*, *Compressible* and *Incompressible*. But there are some, as *Ductile* and *Inductile*, which are not united by insensible gradations.

§ 323. Before defining our perceptions of these attributes, it is requisite that we should consider the several distinct sensations resulting from the direct actions of body upon us; together with those which accompany our direct actions upon body. There are two in respect of which body is active while we are passive, and two in respect of which we are active while body is passive. Those which we may class as of objective origin, are the sensations of *touch* and *pressure*. Those which originate subjectively are the sensations of *muscular tension* and *muscular motion*. Let us consider them seriatim.

When one of the fingers is brought gently in contact with anything, when a fly settles on the forehead, or when a hair gets into the mouth, there arises the sensation of *touch proper*. This sensation is undecomposable—is not accompanied by any sensation of pressure; and though we always ascribe it to some resisting object, we cannot say that the resistance is given in the sensation. That the sensation is caused by mechanical force, we know; but we know this mediately. Mechanical force is immediately knowable by us only as that which opposes muscular action; and as, in this case, muscular action is not called forth, mechanical force can only be inferred.

If the hand be opened out on the table and a weight be placed on one of the fingers, there results the sensation of *pressure*, which is clearly distinguishable from the last. In most of our tactual impressions the two are so mixed as to be not easily discriminated. But if we compare the feeling caused by a fly on the forehead, with that caused by a weight on the finger, we shall perceive that no increase in

the intensity of either will produce the other. That the
two differ not in degree but in kind, will be yet more
clearly seen on remembering that the sensation of tickling,
which a continuity of touch proper produces, is the strongest when the touch is extremely light; and that when
the touch becomes heavy the sensation of tickling ceases.
Contrasting them physiologically, we may presume that
the sensation of touch proper results from a stimulation
of nerves in the skin, while that of pressure results from a
stimulation of nerves in the subjacent tissues; that hence,
by very gentle contact the nerves in the skin alone are
affected, while by rougher contact the nerves in both are
affected; that consequently, in passing from gentle to
rough contact by degrees, the single feeling at first experienced becomes masked by another feeling that arises
gradually; and that thus is produced the habitual confusion
of the two. It remains to be noticed that the sensation of
pressure, though often associated with that of muscular
tension, often exists apart from it; as in the example above
given, and as in the ever-present experience of the reactive
pressure of whatever surface supports the body.

The sensation of *muscular tension* also, is capable of existing separately. On holding out the arm horizontally,
and still more on dealing similarly with the leg, a sensation
is felt which, tolerably strong as it is at the outset, presently
becomes unbearable. If the limb be uncovered and kept
from contact with anything, this sensation is associated
with no other.

Allied to the sensation accompanying tension of the
muscles, is that accompanying the act of contracting them
—the sensation of *muscular motion*. Concerning the state
of consciousness induced by muscular motion, and concerning the ideas of Space and Time which are connected with
it in adult minds, something will be said hereafter. For present purposes it will suffice to notice the peculiarity of this
sensation. While from a muscle at rest no sensation arises;

while from a muscle in a state of continuous strain there arises a continuous sensation which remains uniform for some time; from a muscle that is contracting or relaxing there arises a sensation which is undergoing increase or decrease.

The several sensations thus distinguished, and more particularly the last three, are those which, by their combinations in various degrees and relations, constitute our perceptions of the statico-dynamical attributes of body. Let us consider some of the perceptions thus constituted.

§ 324. When we express our immediate experiences of a body by saying that it is *hard*, what are the experiences implied? First, a sensation of pressure of considerable intensity is implied; and if, as in most cases, this sensation of pressure is given to a finger voluntarily thrust against the object, then there is simultaneously felt a correspondingly-strong sensation of muscular tension. But this is not all. Feelings of pressure and muscular tension may be given by bodies which we call soft, provided the compressing finger follows the surface as fast as it gives way. In what then consists the difference between the perceptions? In this; that whereas when a soft body is pressed with increasing force, the sensations of pressure and muscular tension, while they increase synchronously, are necessarily accompanied by certain sensations of muscular movement; when a hard body is pressed with increasing force, these sensations of increasing pressure and tension are *not* necessarily accompanied by sensations of muscular movement—not, at least, by any that are appreciable. Considered by itself, then, the perception of softness may be defined as the establishment in consciousness of a relation of simultaneity between three series of sensations—a series of increasing sensations of pressure; a series of increasing sensations of tension; and a series of sensations of motion. And the perception of hardness is the same, with omission of the last series. As,

however, hardness and softness are names for different degrees of the same attribute, these definitions must be understood in a relative sense.

Take again the attribute of *resilience*, as displayed in
such a body as caoutchouc. The perception of it manifestly
includes as one component, the perception of softness; but
it includes something more. When the finger is thrust
against some soft but irresilient body, as wet clay, the three
concurrent series of sensations of pressure, tension, and
motion, are followed (on the withdrawal of the finger) by
sensations of motion only; but when it is thrust against a
piece of caoutchouc, these three concurrent series of sensations are followed by three other series in the reverse
order. Following the finger, the withdrawal of which implies serial sensations of muscular motion, the caoutchouc
gives a decreasing series of sensations of pressure, and a
decreasing series of sensations of that muscular tension implied by the pressure. Thus the perception of resilience is
definable as the establishment in consciousness, of a relation of sequence between the group of co-ordinated sensations constituting the perception of softness, and a certain
other group of co-ordinated sensations similar in kind but
opposite in serial order.

The perceptions of *roughness* and *smoothness* refer not to
the degree or kind of cohesion subsisting among the particles of a body, but to the quality of its surface; and hence
have little in common with the foregoing. The motion by
which either of them is gained, is not in the line of pressure
but at right angles to it. The accompanying sensations,
partly of pressure, partly of touch proper, do not form an
increasing or a decreasing series; but are either uniform (as
when smoothness is perceived) or irregularly varied (as when
roughness is perceived). The perception of smoothness,
then, consists in the establishment in consciousness of a relation of simultaneity between a special series of sensations of
motion, and a uniform sensation of touch proper, or pres-

sure, or both. While in the perception of roughness, the like sensations of motion are known as simultaneous with a broken series of sensations of touch, or pressure, or both.

It is unnecessary thus to analyze our perceptions of all the statico-dynamical attributes above enumerated. What has been said renders it sufficiently manifest, that they severally consist in the establishment of relations of simultaneity and sequence among our sensations of touch, pressure, tension and motion; experienced as increasing, decreasing, or uniform; and combined in various modes and degrees. This is all which it here concerns us to know.

§ 325. Passing from these preliminary analyses to the general subject of the chapter—the perception of body as presenting statico-dynamical and statical attributes, we find that it is made up of the following elements. The relations of coexistence in time and adjacency in space between subject and object; the combined impressions which make up our ideas of a more or less specific size and a more or less specific shape; the further impressions included in our notions of surface; those included in our notions of texture; and those many others signified by the terms ductility, elasticity, flexibility, &c.: all of them referred to a place in space that is approximately the same, and to a time that is common to them all.

Merely re-stating these several constituents of the perception, which were to some extent incidentally described in the last chapter, it remains to specify more definitely than before, the kind of union subsisting among them. When in the dark the presence of some object is revealed by accidental collision, we have, along with certain unexpected sensations of pressure and muscular tension, a vague conception of a something extended; and, as previously explained, this relation of coexistence between resistance and extension is unconditional—is independent alike of the will of the subject and the quality of the object. The special elements of the perception are conditional. If the nature of the object is to be ascertained, its reactions must be called forth by certain appropriate actions of the subject. The sensations it gives us must become known as sequent to certain sensations we give ourselves. There must be particular kinds of volition and the particular changes of internal state that follow them, before the changes resulting from external impressions can be received. It is true that some of the resistance-attributes, as hardness and softness, usually become involuntarily known in the act of collision; though this is not necessary, since, when moving with out-stretched hands, the gentlest touch suffices to prove the existence of *something*, before yet we can know aught of its nature. But to determine whether the body is rough or smooth, flexible or rigid, ductile or inductile, implies correlative subjective activities of a complicated kind; and the modifications of consciousness accompanying these, must become essential elements of the perceptions. Hence a statico-dynamical attribute is perceived through a union of internally-determined impressions with externally-determined impressions; which combined group of impressions is known as the consequent of those internally-determined changes constituting volition.

Defined in its totality, then, the perception of body as presenting statico-dynamical and statical attributes, is a state of consciousness having for its primary elements the impressions of resistance and extension *unconditionally* united with each other and the subject in relations of coincidence in time and adjacency in space; having for its secondary elements the impressions of touch, pressure, tension, and motion, variously united with one another in relations of simultaneity and sequence, that are severally *conditional* on the nature of the object and the acts of the subject, and all of them *conditionally* united with the primary elements by relations of sequence; and having for its further secondary elements certain yet undefined relations (constituting the cognitions of size and form, hereafter to be analyzed), which are also *conditionally* united alike with the primary elements and the other secondary elements.

Such being the *constituents* of the perception, the *act* of perception consists in the classing these constituents, each with others of its own order. As shown in the last chapter, no one of them can be known for what it is, without being assimilated to the before-known ones which it resembles. And from the classing of each impression with like remembered impressions, each relation with like remembered relations, and each condition with like remembered conditions, results that classing of the object in its totality which is synonymous with a perception of it.

CHAPTER XIII.

THE PERCEPTION OF BODY AS PRESENTING STATICAL ATTRIBUTES.

§ 326. From that class of attributes known to us solely through one or other kind of objective activity; and from that further class known to us through some objective re-activity called forth by a subjective activity; we now pass to that remaining class known to us through a subjective activity only.

In respect of its space-attributes—Bulk, Figure, and Position—body is altogether passive; and the perception of them is wholly due to certain mental operations. Unlike heat, sound, odour, &c., which are presented to consciousness by no acts of our own, but often in spite of our acts— unlike roughness, softness, pliability, &c., of which we become conscious by the union of our own acts with the acts of things; extension under its several modes is cognizable through a wholly-internal co-ordination of impressions: a process in which the extended object has no share. Though the data through which its extension is known, are supplied by the object; yet, as those data are not the extension, and as until they are combined in thought the extension is unknown, it follows that extension is an attribute with which body does not impress us, but which we discover through certain of its other attributes. To an uncritical observer, the visible form of an object seems as much thrust upon his

164

consciousness by the object itself, as its colour is. But on remembering that the visible form is revealed to him only through certain modifications of light; that these modifications are produced not by the form, but by certain occult properties of the substance having the form; and that if the body had no power of reacting on light, the form would be invisible; it will be seen that the form is known not immediately but mediately. When it is further remembered that in the dark the shape and size of anything are knowable only through tactual and muscular sensations gained by acts of exploration; and that consciousness of the shape and size depends on the thinking of these in certain relations; it will no longer be questioned that in the perception of the space-attributes, the object is wholly passive while the subject is active.

The propriety of distinguishing Bulk, Figure, and Position as statical attributes, may perhaps be questioned. In mechanics, statics and dynamics are allied to one another as closely as the circle is allied to the ellipse, into which it passes by insensible steps; whereas the attributes that are here classed as statical, differ wholly and irreconcilably from those classed as dynamical. The reply is that the terms as now used are to be understood, not in the mechanical sense, but in a more general sense. Statical attributes are those which pertain to body as standing or existing. Dynamical ones are those which pertain to it as acting. If it be admitted that the so-called secondary attributes of body, which, as we find, imply its activity, are rightly termed dynamical; it must be admitted that the so-called primary ones, which, as implying passivity, are their antitheses, may be properly distinguished as statical.

§ 327. Whether the space-attributes of body are any of them knowable through the eyes alone, has been a disputed question. That our perceptions of distance are not originally visual, but result from muscular experiences, which visual experiences serve to symbolize, is admitted. And that at least one out of the three dimensions of body, involving as it does the idea of greater or less remoteness from us, can be known only through muscular experiences, must also be admitted. But our inability to conceive of colour save as having extension of two dimensions, seems to imply that superficial magnitude is, to a certain extent, knowable by sight. Though it is manifest that superficial magnitude as known by sight is purely relative—that the same surface, according as it is placed close to the eye or a mile off, may occupy the whole field of view, or but an inappreciable portion of it; yet as, while an object is visible at all, it must present *some* length and breadth, it may be argued that superficial extension *in the abstract*, is originally perceivable through the eyes, as much as colour is. This conclusion is in one sense true and in another sense untrue. The relation between its untruth and its truth will be best seen by considering first a criticism upon it and then the reply.

Along with the conception of visible superficial extension there goes a conception of distance. Imagine a surface a foot square to be placed a yard from the eye, at right angles to the axis of vision; and imagine that four straight lines are drawn from its angles to the centre of the eye. Suppose now that a surface of six inches square be interposed at half the distance, so as to subtend to the eye the same apparent area; and that another of three inches square be interposed between this and the eye in the same manner; and so on continuously. It is manifest that were it possible to repeat this process *ad infinitum*, the area subtended by the four converging lines would disappear at the same moment that the distance from the point of convergence disappeared; and that hence, all our experiences conforming as they must to the laws of convergent rays, we can have no conception of a visible superficies without an accompanying conception of a distance between that superficies and the sentient

surface. Consequently, if distance is not conceived *à priori*
area is not conceived *à priori*.   To this the reply
is, that there can be no such series of diminishing areas
subtending the same angular space. The argument ignores the structure of the eye; and supposes vision to continue under conditions that must absolutely prevent it. I
do not mean only that the supposed diminishing areas will,
as their including lines converge, presently come in contact with the eye itself; but I mean that long before they
do this, the assumed diminution of the area becomes op-
tically impossible. Though successively diminishing areas
subtending the same angular space may be arranged as
described so long as the eye is not approached too closely,
yet as soon as the limit of its shortest focal adjustment
is passed, this no longer holds: the retinal area occupied
by the image, while it becomes gradually indefinite, enlarges rather than diminishes. And when we thus see that
both the size of the eye and its optical adjustments necessarily enter as factors into the perceptions of visual areas
and distances, it becomes manifest that there is a sense in
which the consciousness of visual area is pre-determined
by the inherited structure; not, indeed, to the same extent
as the accompanying sense of colour is so pre-determined,
but to some extent—to the extent that the visual organ, by
its own size and constitution, furnishes certain limits within
which the space-interpretations given to an impression of
colour must eventually fall.

But a clearer understanding of the matter will be obtained,
if we consider more at length a visual impression as it is
received at the periphery of the nervous system. The retina,
examined microscopically, presents a tesselated pavement
made up of minute rods and cones packed side by side, so
that their ends form a surface on which the optical images
are received. As far as can be made out, each of these
rods and cones is supplied by a separate nerve-fibril; and
is, as must be supposed, capable of independent stimulation.

That the joint action of these retinal elements may be the more easily comprehended, let us suppose an analogous structure on a large scale. Imagine that an immense number of fingers could be packed side by side, so that their ends made a flat surface; and that each of them had a separate nervous connexion with the same sensorium. If anything were laid on the flat surface formed by these finger-ends, an impression of touch would be given to a certain number of them—a number great in proportion to the size of the thing. And if two things successively laid on them differed in shape as well as in size, there would be a difference not only in the *number* of finger-ends affected, but also in the kind of *combination*. What would be the interpretation of any impression thus produced, while as yet no experiences had been accumulated? Would there be any idea of extension? Certainly not a developed idea, though there would be the crude material of an idea.   To simplify the question, let the first object laid upon these finger-ends be a straight stick; and let us name the two finger-ends on which its extremes lie, A and Z. If now it be said that the length of the stick will be perceived, it is implied that the distance between A and Z is already known, or in other words, that there is a pre-existent idea of a special extension: which is absurd. If it be said that the extension is implied by the simultaneous excitation of B, C, D, E, F, and all the fingers between A and Z, the difficulty is not escaped; for no idea of extension can arise from the simultaneous excitation of these, unless there is a knowledge of their relative positions; which is itself a knowledge of extension. By what process then can the length of the stick become known? It can become known only after the accumulation of certain experiences, by which the series of fingers between A and Z becomes known. If the mass of fingers admits of being moved bodily, as the retina does; and if, in virtue of its movements, something now touched by finger A is next touched by finger B, next by C, and so on; and if these experiences are so multiplied by motion in all directions, that between the touching by finger A and by any other finger, the number of intermediate touches that will be felt is known; then the distance between A and Z can be known—known, that is, as a series of states of consciousness produced by the successive touchings of the intermediate fingers—a series of states comparable with any other such series, and capable of being estimated as greater or less. And when, by numberless repetitions, the relation between any one finger and each of the others is established, and can be represented to the mind as a series of a certain length, we may understand how a stick laid on the surface so as at the same moment to touch all the fingers from A to Z inclusive, will be taken as equivalent to the series A to Z—how the *simultaneous* excitation of the entire row of fingers, will come to stand for its *serial* excitation—how thus, objects laid on the surface will come to be distinguished from one another by the relative lengths of the series they cover, or when broad as well as long, by the groups of series which they cover—and how by habit these simultaneous excitations, from being at first known indirectly by translation into the serial ones, will come to be known directly, and the serial ones will be forgotten: just as in childhood the words of a new language, at first understood by means of their equivalents in the mother tongue, are presently understood by themselves; and if used to the exclusion of the mother tongue, lead to the ultimate loss of it. The greatly-magnified apparatus here described, being reduced to its original shape—the surface of finger-ends being diminished to the size of the retina, the things laid on that surface being understood as images cast on the retina, and its movements in contact with these things being understood as movements of the retina relatively to the images —some conception will be formed of one part of the process by which our ideas of visual extension are de-

54

veloped.　　　　　But now a very well-grounded criticism demands our attention. When the retina is thus described as made up of closely-packed units, separately excitable because connected with a nervous centre by separate fibres; and when it is argued that the excitation of any series of these comes to be known by experience as indicative of a certain linear extension; the interpretation is in great measure contained in the facts assumed. It is forgotten that in these clustered retinal elements, with their multitudinous separate fibres running to a place where they are put in relation with other nervous structures which receive the special impressions from special motions of the retina, there pre-exist the appliances through which such equivalences are to be established. The nervous structures concerned, no less than the optical and muscular structures, are already in great measure developed: certainly all the efferent and afferent fibres, and certainly to some considerable extent the central plexuses by which the visual impressions, serial and simultaneous, are co-ordinated. So that in fact the correlations and equivalences said to be established by experience between special retinal excitations received serially, and the answering retinal excitations which, when received simultaneously, indicate certain extensions, are lying latent in the structures with which the explanation sets out. All that can be reasonably inferred is, that these correlations and equivalences, mainly pre-determined by the structure of the organism, are changed from their potential to their actual forms by the experiences of the organism; and further that while the experiences disclose these latent connexions between certain nervous actions and between certain correlative states of consciousness, they further the development of the structures and determine their details—serving at the same time to give definiteness to their actions and to the accompanying perceptions.　　　　　To this important qualification there must, however, be added an equally-important counter-qualification. Though the explanation above given is inadequate if taken as applying only to the individual, it is not inadequate if taken as applying to the immeasurable series of antecedent individuals supposed by the hypothesis of Evolution. On referring back to the expositions contained in Part V., it will become manifest that the correlations between visual impressions and extensions, established little by little and inherited with continual accumulations, generation after generation, admit of being interpreted in the way described.

This analysis, however, involved as it is even in its simplest form, and much more involved as it is when taken with the qualifications just indicated, carries us only part way towards a solution of our problem—the perception of body as presenting statical attributes. Those motions of the eye required to bring the sentient elements of the retina successively in contact with different parts of the image, being themselves known to consciousness, become components of the perception. So too do those motions required to produce due convergence of the visual axes; and those further motions required to adjust each eye to the proper focus. Even when the several series of states of consciousness thus resulting, have been combined with those which proceed from the retina itself, they cannot give that developed notion of extension possessed by adults, until motions of the limbs and body have yielded those experiences through which distances are measured; and these are impossible without those accompanying tactual experiences that give the limits to distances. To examine in detail these various groups of elements which go to make up our perception of visible extension, would take up more pages than can here be spared. Nor is it needful for the establishment of general principles that they should be thus examined. The foregoing analysis shows that, leaving out of view other requirements (all of which involve motion and the accompanying states of conscious-

ness), no image cast on the retina can be understood, or
even distinguished from another image widely different in
form, until relations have been established between the
separate sensitive agents of which the retina is constructed;
that no relation between any two such agents can be known
otherwise than through the series of sensations given by the
intervening agents; that such series of sensations can be
obtained only by motion of the retina; and that thus the
primitive element out of which our ideas of visible extension
are evolved, is a cognition of the relative positions of two
states of consciousness in some series of such states consequent upon a subjective motion.   Not that such
relation between successive states of consciousness gives in
itself any idea of extension. We have seen that a set of
retinal elements may be excited simultaneously, as well as
serially; that so, a quasi-single state of consciousness becomes the equivalent of a series of states; that a relation
between what we call *coexistent positions* thus represents a
relation of *successive positions ;* that this symbolic relation
being far briefer, is habitually thought of in place of that
which it symbolizes; and that, by the continued use of such
symbols and the union of them into more complex ones, are
generated our ideas of visible extension—ideas which, like
those of the algebraist working out an equation, are wholly
unlike the ideas symbolized, and which yet, like his, occupy
the mind to the entire exclusion of the ideas symbolized.

The fact, however, which it now more particularly behoves us to remember, is, that underlying all cognitions of
visible extension, is the cognition of relative position among
the states of consciousness accompanying motion.

§ 328. From the visual perception of body as presenting
statical attributes, we pass to the tactual perception of it—
to such perception of Form, Size, and Position, as a blind
man has. And before dealing with this perception in its
totality, let us look at its components: considering these

first as known to us, and then in our mode of knowing them.

It is an anciently-established doctrine that Form or Figure, which we may call the most complex mode of extension, is resolvable into relative magnitude of parts. An equilateral triangle is one of which the three sides are alike in their lengths. An ellipse is a symmetrical closed curve, of which the transverse and conjugate diameters are the one greater than the other. A cube is a solid having all its surfaces of the same magnitude, and all its angles of the same magnitude. A cone is a solid, successive sections of which, made at right angles to the axis, are circles regularly decreasing in magnitude as we progress from base to apex. Any object described as narrow, has a breadth of small magnitude compared with its length. A symmetrical figure is one in which the homologous parts on opposite sides are equal in magnitude. Moreover, an alteration in the form of anything, is an alteration in the comparative sizes of some of its parts—a change in the relations of magnitude subsisting between them and the other parts. Hence, form being resolvable into relations of magnitude, we may go on to analyze that out of which these relations arise—magnitude itself.

On passing from a mode of extension which consists in relations of magnitude, to consider magnitude itself, it would seem that relativity is no longer involved; but this is not really the case. Of absolute magnitude we can frame no conception. All magnitudes as known to us are thought of as equal to, greater than, or less than, certain other magnitudes. In speaking of a house as large, we mean large in comparison with other houses; in calling a man short, we mean short in comparison with most men; in describing Mercury as small and a certain pin's head as big, we mean in comparison with planets and pins' heads respectively. And further we can have no general notion of magnitude save one constructed out of the magnitudes

given to us in experience, and therefore, thought of in relation to them. In what, then, consists the difference between
figure and size as known to us? Simply in this:—When
thinking of a thing's figure, we think of the relations of
magnitude which its constituent parts bear to one another;
but when thinking of its size, we think of the relation of magnitude which it, as a whole, bears to other
wholes. Still there remains the question—What
is a magnitude considered analytically? The reply is—It
consists of relations of position. When we conceive anything as having a certain bulk, we conceive its opposite
limiting surfaces as more or less removed from each other;
that is—as related in position. When we think of a particular area, we think of a surface having boundary lines
standing to one another in specific degrees of remoteness;
that is—as related in position. When we imagine a line of
definite length, we imagine its termini as occupying places
in space having some positive distance from each other;
that is—as related in position. A solid is decomposable
into planes; a plane into lines; lines into points; and as
adjacent points cannot be conceived as distinct from each
other, without being conceived as having relative positions,
it follows that every cognition of magnitude is a cognition
of relations of position, which are presented to consciousness
as like or unlike other relations of position.

This analysis brings us to the remaining space-attribute
of body—Position. Like Magnitude, Position cannot be
known absolutely; it can be known only relatively. The
position of a thing is inconceivable, save by thinking of that
thing as at some distance from one or more other things.
Imagine a solitary point A, in space which has no assignable
bounds; and suppose it possible for that point to be known
by a being having no locality. What can be predicated respecting its place? Absolutely nothing. Imagine another
point B, to be added. What can now be predicated respecting the two? Still nothing. Neither point having any

attribute save position, the two are not comparable in themselves; and nothing can be said of their relative position from lack of anything with which to compare it. The distance between them may be either infinite or infinitesimal, according to the measure used; and as, by the hypothesis, there exists no measure—as space contains nothing save these two points, the distance between them is unthinkable. But suppose that a third point C, is added. Immediately it becomes possible to frame a proposition respecting the positions of the three. The two distances A to B, and A to C, serve as measures to each other. The space between A and B may be compared with the space between A and C; and the relation of position in which A stands to B, is thinkable as like or unlike the relation in which A stands to C. Position, then, is not an attribute of body in itself, but only in its connexion with the other contents of the universe.

Relations of position are of two kinds: those which subsist between subject and object; and those which subsist between either different objects, or different parts of the same object. Of these the last are resolvable into the first. On remembering that in the dark a man can discover the relative positions of two objects only by touching first one and then the other, and so inferring their relative positions from his own position towards each; and on remembering that by vision no knowledge of their relative positions can be reached save through a perception of the distance of each from the eye; it becomes clear that ultimately, all relative positions may be decomposed into relative positions of subject and object.

These conclusions—that Figure is resolvable into relative magnitudes; that Magnitude is resolvable into relative positions; and that all relative positions may finally be reduced to positions of subject and object—will be fully confirmed on considering the process by which the space-attributes of body become known to a blind man. He puts out his hand, and touching something, thereby learns its position with respect to himself. He puts out his other hand, and meeting no resistance above, or on one side of, the position already found, gains some negative knowledge of the thing's magnitude—a knowledge which three or four touches on different sides of it serve to render positive. And then, by moving his hands over its surface, he acquires a notion of its figure. What, then, are the elements out of which, by synthesis, his perceptions of magnitude and figure are framed? He has received nothing but simultaneous and successive touches. Each touch established a relation of position between himself and the point touched. And all he can know respecting magnitude and figure—that is, respecting the relative positions of these points to one another—is necessarily known through the relative positions in which they severally stand to himself.

Our perceptions of all the space-attributes of body, being thus decomposable into perceptions of positions like that gained by a single act of touch, we have next to inquire what is contained in a perception of this kind. Obviously to perceive the position of anything touched, is to perceive the position of that part of the body in which the sensation of touch arises. Whence it follows that our knowledge of the positions of objects, is built upon our knowledge of the positions of our members towards one another—knowledge both of their fixed relations, and of those temporary relations they are placed in by every change of muscular adjustment. That this knowledge is gained by bringing each part in contact with the others and moving the parts over one another in all possible ways; and that the motions as well as the touches involved in these mutual explorations, are known by their reactions upon consciousness; are propositions that scarcely need stating. But it is manifestly impossible to carry the analysis further without analyzing our perception of motion. Relative position and motion are two sides of the same experience. We can neither conceive motion without conceiving relative position, nor discover relative position without motion. For the present, therefore, we must be content with the conclusion that, whether visual or tactual, the perception of every statical attribute of body is resolvable into perceptions of relative position which are gained through motion.

§ 329. Before defining in its totality the perception of body as presenting statical attributes, it is needful to remark that the resisting positions which, as co-ordinated in thought, constitute the consciousness of Magnitude or of Figure, must be aggregated—must be continuous with an assemblage of intermediate resisting positions. If they are discontinuous—if they are separated by positions that do not resist, we have a perception not of the space-attributes of one body, but of the space-attributes of two or more.

Premising this, and omitting as doubly mediate our visual perceptions, we may say that the perception of body as presenting statical attributes, is a composite state of consciousness, having for its primary elements the indefinite impressions of resistance and extension, *unconditionally* united with each other and with the subject in relations of coincidence in time and adjacency in space; and having for its secondary elements sundry definite impressions of resistances, variously united with each other in relations of simultaneity and sequence that are severally *conditional* on the nature of the object and the acts of the subject, and all of them *conditionally* united with the primary elements by relations of sequence.

To which there is only to add, as before, that these being the *materials* of the perception, the *process* of perception consists in the unconscious classing of these impressions, relations, and conditions, with the like before-known ones.

CHAPTER XIV.

THE PERCEPTION OF SPACE.

§ 330. In the last chapter, much has been tacitly asserted respecting our perception of Space. The consideration of occupied space cannot be dissociated from the consideration of unoccupied space. The two being distinguished as resistant extension and non-resistant extension, it is impossible to treat of either without virtually treating of both. Substantially, therefore, the inquiry on which we are now to enter must be a continuation of the one just concluded. Before commencing it, something must be said in answer to those who, holding with Kant that Space is a form which belongs to the subject and not to the object, consider all attempts to analyze our consciousness of it as absurd.

Among these, is Sir William Hamilton; who says that "it is truly an idle problem to attempt imagining the steps by which we may be supposed to have acquired the notion of extension; when in fact we are unable to imagine to ourselves the possibility of that notion not being always in our possession."

On this proposition the first comment to be made is that a philosopher, dealing with questions of so subtle a kind, becomes a doubtful guide when he hampers the statement of his doctrine by a phrase which seems to mean something but really means nothing; as in the last clause of the passage I have quoted. The entire fact to which Sir W.

Hamilton refers is this:—I am conscious of space. I seek to expel the consciousness of space and fail. I try to recall a time when I had not the consciousness of space and cannot do so. And I express the result of these attempts by saying that I cannot imagine myself as not having the consciousness of space. But now, (supposing even that this statement is admissible without reservation, which it is not) to say that I cannot imagine the "possibility" of ever having been without this consciousness, is to use words which have no answering thoughts. If I cannot now get rid of the consciousness of space, and (which is tacitly implied) cannot think of any past experiences free from that consciousness; I am thereby debarred from predicating to myself anything about the "possibility" or impossibility of ever having been without the consciousness. For to imagine the possibility of the absence is really to imagine the absence itself. If I use words not idly as mere symbols, but for their proper purpose of indicating certain states of my mind, then, when I say that I can think of a thing as possible, I mean that it lies within the power of my representative faculty to put together in thought the terms of the proposition. And therefore if I ask whether it is possible or impossible to think of myself as having ever been without the notion of space, I imply that it lies within the power of my representative faculty to associate or dissociate the two terms of the proposition, self and space. But if I have already recognized the fact that I cannot expel this consciousness, I have recognized the fact that it is beyond the power of my representative faculty to associate or dissociate the terms of the proposition; and that therefore all question about the possibility or impossibility of imagining any other state is excluded.

But now, granting for argument's sake all which Sir William Hamilton has the power to allege, that we cannot conceive ourselves as ever having been without the notion of extension, it does not follow either that extension is a form of intuition, or that we are disabled from analyzing the notion we have of it. Those who have followed the line of argument running through Parts III., IV., and V., and more especially those who remember the contents of §§ 208, 237—247, will see that our inability to banish from our minds the idea of space is readily to be accounted for on the experience-hypothesis. If space be an universal form of the *non-ego*, it must produce some corresponding universal form in the *ego*—a form which, as being the constant element of *all* impressions presented in experience, and therefore of *all* impressions represented in thought, is independent of every *particular* impression; and consequently remains when every particular impression is, as far as possible, banished. And then, to the argument that whether extension is a form of intuition or not, our inability to conceive ourselves as ever having been without it, disables us from analyzing it, I reply, that while we may be disabled from analyzing it directly we may remain able to analyze it indirectly. Though examination of mental processes subjectively may not disclose any anterior elements out of which to construct the consciousness of space; yet, by examining mental processes objectively, we may gain the means of conceiving how our own consciousness of space was constructed. As we learn vicariously that our eyes make visible movements when we glance from one thing to another, though we can never see our own eyes move; so we may learn vicariously how space has become a form of thought, even admitting that we cannot conceive our consciousness as remaining in the absence of this form.

But what is here granted for argument's sake may be rightly denied. This alleged inability to conceive of consciousness as existing without the notion of extension, I, for one, do not admit. I find it quite possible to think of myself as having possessed states of consciousness not involving any notion of extension—quite possible to imagine trains of thought in which space is not implied. It is a vice of the older psychology, and of the Kantian psychology included, that it habitually deals only with the consciousness of the adult: ignoring the obvious fact that the developed apparatus of thought possessed by the adult is not possessed by the infant, but is slowly evolved; and ignoring the further fact that associations unquestionably established and consolidated by experience, are so carried by us into all our thinkings that we are constantly in danger of attributing to the undeveloped mind ideas which only the developed mind possesses. It is a further vice of the Kantian psychology in its exposition of this hypothesis respecting forms of intuition, that, instead of citing in proof intuitions of all orders, it cites intuitions of those orders only with which the consciousness of space is most directly connected in experience. If we refuse thus to limit the inquiry—if passing over the sensations gained through touch and vision, we contemplate certain others; and if we figure ourselves as devoid of certain perceptions that are *known* to be acquired; it at once becomes easy to conceive ourselves as having thoughts that do not imply space.

Remembering that, as Sir William Hamilton himself expresses it, " we are never aware even of the existence of our organism, except as it is somehow affected; " let us suppose a human being absolutely without experience, and therefore, as yet unacquainted with his own body. It is admitted by Kant that space being but a *form* of intuition cannot exist before intuition—cannot be known in itself antecedently to experience, but that it is disclosed in the act of receiving experiences. His doctrine is that the matter of perception being given by the *non-ego*, and the form by the *ego*, the form and the matter come into consciousness simultaneously. In the supposed case, therefore, there is yet no notion of space.   Let the first impressions received be those of sound. No one will allege that sound, as an affection of consciousness, has any space-attributes. And even those who have little considered such questions will admit that our knowledge of sound as coming from this or that point in space, is a knowledge gained by experience—is a knowledge not *given* along with the sound but *inferred* from certain modifications of the sound. When being deluded by a ventriloquist and led to draw wrong inferences, or when, respecting the whereabouts of a humming gnat at night we can draw no inference, we get clear proof that primarily sound is known only as pure sensation.   Further, let it be observed that the sensation of sound is of a kind which does not in itself make us " aware of the existence of our organism, as somehow affected." Only by experience do we learn that we hear through the ears. Auditory impressions are so indistinctly localized that, in spite of their associations, most adults even will perceive that in the absence of acquired knowledge they would not know whereabouts in the body they were sentient. Hence, in the supposed state of nascent intelligence, sensations of sound, not having in themselves any space-implications, and not in themselves disclosing any part of the organism as affected, would be nothing more than simple affections of consciousness, which would admit of being remembered and compared without any notion of extension being involved.   Having duly contemplated the case thus objectively presented, any one ordinarily endowed with imagination, will, I think, by closing his eyes, arranging his body so as to give as few disturbing sensations as possible, and banishing to the greatest extent practicable all remembrance of surrounding things, be able to conceive a state in which a varied series of sounds known as severally like and unlike, and thought of solely in respect to their mutual relations, would be the entire contents of consciousness.

With such further reasons for holding that Space, considered as subjective, is derived by accumulated and consolidated experiences from Space considered as objective, we may be encouraged to continue that analysis of our perception of it collaterally entered upon in the last chapter.

§ 331. Let us start afresh from the conclusions there reached. They were that, whether visual or tactual, every perception of the space-attributes of body is decomposable into perceptions of relative position; that all perceptions of relative position are decomposable into perceptions of the relative position of subject and object; and that these relations of position are knowable only through motion. Such being now our data, the first question that arises is—How, through experiences of occupied extension, or body, can we ever gain the notion of unoccupied extension, or space? How, from the perception of a relation between resistant positions, do we progress to the perception of a relation between non-resistant positions? If all the space-attributes of body are resolvable into relations of position between subject and object, disclosed in the act of touch—if, originally, relative position is only thus knowable—if, therefore, position is, to the nascent intelligence, incognizable except as the position of something that produces an impression on the organism; how is it possible for the idea of position ever to be dissociated from that of body?

This problem, difficult of solution as it appears, is really a very easy one. If, after some particular motion of a limb there invariably came a sensation of softness; after some other, one of roughness; after some other, one of hardness— or if, after those movements of the eye needed for some special act of vision, there always came a sensation of redness; after some others, a sensation of blueness; and so on —it is manifest that, in conformity with the laws of association, there would be established constant relations between such motions and such sensations. If positions were conceived at all, they would be conceived as invariably occupied by things producing special impressions; and it would be impossible to dissociate the positions from the

things. But as we find that a certain movement of the
hand which once brought it in contact with something hot,
now brings it in contact with something sharp, and now
with nothing at all; and as we find that a certain movement
of the eye which once was followed by the sight of a black
object, is now followed by the sight of a white object, and
now by the sight of no object; it results that the idea of the
particular position accompanying each one of these movements, is, by accumulated experiences, *dissociated* from
objects and impressions. It results, too, that as there are
endless such movements, there come to be endless such
positions conceived as existing apart from body. And it
results, further, that as in the first and in every subsequent
act of perception, each position is known as coexistent with
the subject, there arises a consciousness of countless such
coexistent positions; that is—of Space. This is not offered
as an ultimate interpretation; for, as before admitted, the
difficulty is to account for our notion of relative position.
All that is here attempted is, partially to explain how, from
that primitive notion, our consciousness of Space in its
totality is built up.

Carrying with us this idea, calling to mind the structure
of the retina as described in the last chapter, and remembering the mode in which the relations among its elements are
established, it will, I think, become possible to conceive how
that wonderful perception we have of visible space is generated. It is a peculiarity of sight that it makes us partially
conscious of many things at once. On now raising my
head, I take in at a glance, desk, papers, table, books,
chairs, walls, carpet, window, and sundry objects outside;
all of them simultaneously impressing me with various
details of colour, suggesting surface and structure. True, I
am not *equally* conscious of all these things at the same
time. I find that some one object at which I am looking
is more distinctly present to my mind than any other, and
that the one point in this object on which the visual axes

converge is more vividly perceived than the rest. In fact, I have a perfect perception of scarcely more than an infinitesimal portion of the whole visual area. Nevertheless, even while concentrating my attention on this infinitesimal portion, I am in some degree aware of the whole. My complete consciousness of a particular letter on the back of a book, does not exclude a consciousness that there are accompanying letters—does not exclude a consciousness of the book—does not exclude a consciousness of the table on which the book lies—nay, does not even exclude a consciousness of the wall against which the table stands. All these things are present to me in different degrees of intensity—degrees that become less, partly in proportion as the things are unobtrusive in colour and size, and partly in proportion as they recede from the centre of the visual field. Not that these many surrounding things are definitely known as such or such; for, while keeping my eyes fixed on one object, I cannot make that assertory judgment respecting any adjacent object which a real cognition of it implies, without becoming, for the moment, imperfectly conscious of the object on which my eyes are fixed. But notwithstanding all this, it remains true that these various objects are in some sense present to my mind—are incipiently perceived—are severally tending to fill the consciousness—are each of them partially exciting the mental states that would arise were it to be distinctly perceived.

This peculiarity in the faculty of sight (to which there is nothing analogous in the faculties of taste and smell; which, in the faculty of hearing, is vaguely represented by our appreciation of harmony; and which is but very imperfectly paralleled in the tactual faculty by the ability we have to discern irregularities in a surface on which the hand is laid) is clearly due to the structure of the retina. Consisting of multitudinous sensitive elements each capable of independent stimulation, it results that when an image is received by the retina, each of those sensitive elements on which the variously-modified rays of light fall, is thrown into a state of greater or less excitement. Each of them, as it were, *touches* some particular part of the image; and sends inwards to the central nervous system the impression produced by the touch. But now observe that, as before explained, each retinal element has come to have a known relation to every one of those around it—a relation such that their synchronous excitation serves to represent their serial excitation. Lest this symbolism should not have been fully understood, I will endeavour further to elucidate it. Suppose a minute dot to be looked at—a dot so small that its image, cast on the retina, covers only one of these sensitive elements, A. Now suppose the eye to be so slightly moved that the image of this dot falls on the adjacent element B. What results? Two slight changes of consciousness: the one proceeding from the new retinal element affected; the other from the muscles producing the motion. Let there be another motion, such as will transfer the image of the dot to the next element C. Two other changes of consciousness result. And so on continuously: the consequence being that the relative positions in consciousness of A and B, A and C, A and D, A and E, &c., are known by the number of intervening states. Imagine now that instead of these small motions separately made, the eye is moved with ordinary rapidity; so that the image of the dot sweeps over the whole series A to Z in an extremely short time. What results? It is a familiar fact that all impressions on the senses, and visual ones among the number, continue for a certain brief period after they are made. Hence, when the retinal elements forming the series A to Z are excited in rapid succession, the excitation of Z commences before that of A has ceased; and for a moment the whole series A to Z remains in a state of excitement together. This being understood, suppose the eye is turned upon a line of such length that its image covers the whole series A to Z. What results? There is a simultaneous excitation of the series A to Z, differing from the last in this; that it is persistent, and that it is unaccompanied by sensations of motion. But does it not follow from the known laws of association, that as the simultaneous excitation is common to both cases, it will, in the last case, tend to arouse in consciousness that series of states which accompanied it in the first? Will it not tend to *consolidate* the entire series of such states into one state? and will it not thus come to be taken as the equivalent of such series? There cannot, I think, be a doubt of it. And if not, then we may see how an excitement of consciousness by the coexistent positions constituting a line, serves as the representative of that serial excitement of it which accompanies motion along that line. Let us return now to the above-described state of the retina as occupied by an image or by a cluster of images. Relations of coexistent position like those we have here considered in respect to a particular linear series, are established throughout countless such series in all directions over the retina: so putting each element in relation with every other. Further, by a process analogous to that described, the state of consciousness produced by the focal adjustment and convergence of the eyes to each particular point, has been made a symbol of the series of coexistent positions between the eyes and that point. After dwelling awhile on these facts, the genesis of our visual perception of space will begin to be comprehensible. Every one of the retinal elements simultaneously thrown into a state of partial excitement, arousing as it does not only a partial consciousness of the sensation answering to its own excitement, but also a partial consciousness of the many relations of coexistent position established between it and the rest, which are all of them similarly excited and similarly suggestive; there results a consciousness of a whole *area* of coexistent positions. Meanwhile the particular consciousness that accompanies adjustment of the eyes, calling up as it does the line of coexistent positions lying between the subject and the object specially contemplated; and each of the things, and parts of things, not in the centre of the field, exciting by its more or less definite image an incipient consciousness of its distance, that is, of the coexistent positions lying between the eye and it; there is awakened a consciousness of a whole *volume* of coexistent positions—of Space in three dimensions. Along with a *complete* consciousness of the one position to which the visual axes converge, arises a *nascent* consciousness of an infinity of other positions—a consciousness that is nascent in the same sense that our consciousness of the various objects out of the centre of the visual field is nascent. One addition must be made. As the innumerable relations subsisting among these coexistent positions were originally established by motion; as each of these relations came by habit to stand for the series of mental states accompanying the motion which measured it; as every one of such relations must, when presented to consciousness, still tend to call up in an indistinct way that train of feelings accompanying motion, which it represents; and as the simultaneous presentation of an infinity of such relations will tend to suggest an infinity of such experiences of motion, which, as being in all directions, must so neutralize one another as to prevent any particular motion from being thought of; there will arise, as their common resultant, that sense of *ability to move*, that sense of *freedom for motion*, which forms the remaining constituent in our notion of Space.

Any one who finds it difficult to conceive how, by so elaborate a process as this, there should be reached a notion apparently so simple, so homogeneous, as that which we have of Space, will feel the difficulty diminished on recalling these several facts:—First, that the experiences out of which the notion is framed and consolidated are in their essentials the same for ourselves and for the ancestral races of creatures from which we inherit our organizations, and that these uniform ancestral experiences, potentially present in the nervous structures bequeathed to us, constitute a partially-innate preparedness for the notion; second, that the individual experiences which repeat these ancestral experiences commence at birth, and serve to aid the development of the correlative structures while they give them their ultimate definiteness; third, that every day throughout our lives, and throughout the whole of each day, we are repeating our experiences of these innumerable coexistences of position and their several equivalences to the serial states of feeling accompanying motions; and fourth, that after development is complete these experiences invariably agree —that these relations of coexistent positions are unchangeable—are ever the same towards each other and the subject —are ever equivalent to the same motions. On bearing in mind this inheritance of latent experiences, this early commencement of the experiences that verify and complete them, this infinite repetition of them, and their absolute uniformity; and on further remembering the power which, in virtue of its structure, the eye possesses of partially suggesting to the mind countless such experiences at the same moment; it will become possible to conceive how we acquire that consolidated idea of space in its totality, which at first seems so inexplicable. On developing somewhat further a late illustration, we shall be enabled to conceive this still more clearly. By habit each of the groups of letters now before the reader has acquired a seemingly-inherent meaning—has ceased to be a mere series of straight and bent strokes, and has actually, as it were, *absorbed* some of the thought for which it stands. Moreover in our intellectual operations, these clusters of symbols have come to be the elements with which we think, and are so habitually used to the exclusion of the things they signify, as to cause frequent mistakes. This being so, it is easy to see how, with symbols learnt much earlier, symbols incomparably more simple, uniform, and exact, symbols

used every instant of our waking lives, a like transformation
and substitution has been carried much further. And when
this is understood, it may also be understood how the state
of consciousness answering to any group of coexistent
positions made known by the senses, has supplanted in our
minds the series of states of consciousness to which it was
equivalent; and how, consequently, our space-perceptions
have become a language in which we think of surrounding
things, without at all thinking of those experiences of motion which this language expresses.

§ 332. Its most finished form will be given to this interpretation by going on to consider how it enables us to understand the origin of the space-intuitions which we
recognize as necessary. The general theory of these the
reader will at once see is that they are the fixed functions
of fixed structures that have become moulded into correspondence with fixed outer relations. In elaborating this
general theory into a more special form, such repetitions as
may be needed will, I think, be justified by the result.

I take a pin's head, place it on a table, retreat towards
the far side of the room, and presently reach a distance at
which I can no longer see the pin's head. The structure
I have inherited determines a fixed limit to the distance at
which a fixed area can produce on me a visual impression.   The pin's head becomes visible again as I
approach the table; its apparent area (or quantity of consciousness of coexistent positions it produces in me) goes
on increasing; until at length, when my eye is within a few
inches, this area becomes the largest possible consistent with
that definiteness implied by a perception of the object and
its place as such and such. For if my eye continues to be
brought nearer, the apparent area, while enlarging, becomes
gradually more confused in character and indefinite in outline; so that in the absence of previous knowledge I should
be unable to say from what it proceeded.   Thus

there are both near and remote limits to the distance at which a given extension can so affect me as to cause a visual consciousness of it. That is to say, the organization bequeathed to me partially pre-determines the relations between certain outer magnitudes and distances and certain inner perceptions to be produced by them.

More than these limitations are thus potentially present. Between each consciousness of an area subtended by any object and the consciousness of the distance at which it subtends this area, there is a relation lying latent in the optical, muscular, and nervous structures—not a relation such that at the outset its terms are completely adjusted; but a relation such that the one consciousness arouses a vague form of the other, which individual development and experience make a definite form. The image of a square foot placed ten yards off, covers a precisely-limited area of the retina; and at the same time the muscular contractions by which the two eyes are converged on the square foot, and focally adjusted to it, form a combination which alone can produce clear vision of an object ten yards off. Thus the inherited structure is such that the square foot placed at the distance of ten yards cannot be distinctly perceived without there arising a relation between a specific number of the retinal elements covered by the image and a specific adjustment of the ocular muscles: both implying specific states of consciousness. And similarly with every other distance. This is not all. While the retinal area covered by the image of the square foot at each distance, has a definite relation to the muscular adjustment required to bring it into focus at that distance; there is also a definite relation between every different position of the square foot to the right or to the left, above or below, and the particular group of retinal elements which its image will cover; and there is also a definite relation between every such position and the particular set of muscular movements required to direct the eyes upon it so as to bring its image into the centre of the retina. All these correlations are in great measure pre-established—are pre-established so far as the inherited organization is developed at the time it comes into activity; and this activity can do no other than complete the structure, and change the innate vague connexions among the accompanying states of consciousness into definite connexions.

To a like extent pre-determined by the inherited organization, and similarly made precise by the individual experiences which accompany the development of this inherited organization, are the correlations between these visual impressions and the tactual and muscular impressions derived by the limbs from the same objects. The square foot a yard off requires a certain muscular motion to reach it, and other muscular motions to move the hands round it; and the quantities and combinations of these are related to the quantities and combinations of the visual impressions yielded by the square foot at that distance. The square foot cannot be brought nearer, or moved towards either side, without there occurring simultaneous changes, definitely related to one another, between the feelings which tactual exploration gives and the feelings which vision gives. And the like holds between the visual feelings and the feelings that attend locomotion, when the object is beyond reach. Clearly, correlations of these kinds are dependent on the sizes and structures of the body and limbs, as standing in connexion with the sizes and structures and positions of the eyes. Not forgetting the fact that the same sensations of touch may be gained by muscular adjustments that differ somewhat, we may say that the conceptions of space-relations to be disclosed in experience by muscular motions, are mainly fixed beforehand by the inherited structures.*

---

* A qualification must be appended. It may properly be objected to this doctrine, when offered for full acceptance, that it takes no note of the changes of proportions among visual and motor appliances that go on during development. The length of a man's arm is some three times the

Little more need be said to make it clear how certain primary space-relations are presented to consciousness under the form of necessary relations. If a segment of a circle be looked at, the image of it cast on the retina is necessarily such that the arc covers a greater number of retinal elements than the chord; and since each of these retinal elements yields its separate impression to consciousness, the series of impressions produced by the arc is felt as larger than the series produced by the chord. This continues to hold however much the arc is flattened: so long as it has any perceptible curvature at all, it is felt to be longer than the chord uniting its extremes. Parallel experiences are derived from the ocular muscles. Carrying the eye along the line of the curve, yields to consciousness a greater quantity of sensation than carrying the eye along the chord does. As the curve is flattened this difference

length of an infant's arm; but neither the diameter of a man's retina nor the space between his eyes is anything like three times that of the corresponding dimension in the infant. Consequently the ocular adjustments and answering sensations which vision of a near object produces in an infant, bear ratios to the muscular adjustments and feelings which tactual exploration of it gives, different from the ratios which they bear to one another in a man. Hence that these nervo-muscular acts and accompanying mental states which answer to certain positions in space, are pre-adjusted in the race under a special form like that which they have in the adult, seems untenable. Two considerations serve to dispose of this difficulty; while they qualify in a needful way the original statement. The one is, that the correlation of structures and of potential mental states accompanying their actions, being inherited by the infant in a proximate form, is progressively modified by the daily activities that accompany development, until it reaches the complete form : individual experiences thus serving to finish what is but rudely sketched out at birth. The other is, that apart from activities and concomitant experiences, there go on spontaneously, during development, structural modifications which complete the adjustment of the organism to the environment, as that adjustment existed in adult ancestors. Among many undeniable proofs of this, the most conspicuous is furnished by the establishment of the reproductive capacity. Various correlated developments in different parts of the organism, including the nervous centres, commence at puberty, and complete themselves quite independently of functional actions. Evidently, diminishes; but some of it continues as long as the curve continues appreciable. Thus the truth that a straight line is the shortest line between two points, lies latent in the structures of the eyes and the nervous centres which receive and co-ordinate visual impressions. We cannot think otherwise because, during that adjustment between the organism and the environment which evolution has established, the inner relations have been so moulded upon the outer relations that they cannot by any effort be made not to fit them. Just in the same way that an infant's hand, constructed so as to grasp by bending the fingers inwards, implies ancestral hands which have thus grasped, and implies objects in the environment to be thus grasped by this infantine hand when it is developed; so the various structures fitting the infant for apprehensions of space-relations, imply such apprehensions in the past by its ancestors and in the

then, we have good ground for the belief that the correlations here in question, different in the child from the answering correlations in the adult, undergo a continuous re-adjustment during the growth of the child, in virtue of processes equally spontaneous with those which determine its growth: the experiences it receives from moment to moment during the development, serving but to facilitate the re-adjustment pre-determined by its constitution. Nevertheless, while we ascribe the general forms of these correlations to inherited structures, and ascribe to inherited tendencies the modifications that go on in these structures during growth, we must not overlook the fact that individual experiences are capable of doing much. Not only in the sensations they yield do they furnish the concrete terms for these relations out of which our space-consciousness is built; and not only by their repetitions do they serve to give precision to the consciousness of each particular relation; but they work such effects upon the associations of ideas and answering nervous connexions as suffice, in some cases, to invert the inherited relations. The testimony of the microscopist demonstrates this. As before pointed out (§ 204), he becomes in course of time so accustomed to see in the microscopic image a reversal of those motions which his fingers produce in the object he is examining, that he ceases to be conscious of the contradiction—nay more, when he comes to use an "erecting glass," which re-reverses the apparent motion and makes it in the same direction as it would appear without the microscope, he becomes completely puzzled, and bungles just as he did when he originally had to learn to reverse the motions.

future by itself. And just as it has become impossible for the hand to grasp by bending the fingers outwards instead of inwards; so has it become impossible for those nervous actions by which we apprehend primary space-relations to be reversed so as to enable us to think of these relations otherwise than we do.

It will probably be remarked that this view approaches to the view of Liebnitz; and some perhaps will think that it does not differ very widely from that of Kant. Already I have pointed out (§ 208) that the hypothesis of Evolution " supplies a reconciliation between the experience-hypothesis as commonly interpreted and the hypothesis which the transcendentalists oppose to it; " and here we see how complete the reconciliation is. For while we are enabled to recognize the truth which lies in the doctrine of a " pre-established harmony," and the truth which lies in the doctrine of " forms of intuition; " we are enabled to interpret these truths as corollaries from the doctrine that all intelligence is acquired through experience: we have but to expand this doctrine so as to make it include, with the experience of each individual, the experiences of all ancestral individuals. By regarding these data of intelligence as *à priori* for the individual, but *à posteriori* for that entire series of individuals of which he forms the last term, we escape the difficulties of both hypothesis as currently understood.

The argument may be fitly concluded by glancing at sundry peculiarities in our conception of space, quite irreconcilable with the Kantian hypothesis, but harmonizing completely with the hypothesis that has been set forth.

§ 333. Our various epi-peripheral feelings carry with them the consciousness of space in degrees that range from no consciousness up to extremely vivid consciousness. As already pointed out, sensations of sound do not of themselves yield the consciousness of space: it is only through

experience that we associate them with outer objects. Much
the same may be said of odours. No thought of position
originally accompanies a sensation of smell: it is by experiment that we learn the connexions between smells and
things yielding them, and so come to think of them as in
space. Some space-consciousness accompanies the sensation of taste: not only through the tactual feelings it gives
to the tongue and palate do we know the position of a sapid
morsel, but we can vaguely perceive its whereabouts by
a localized intensity of the sensation of taste. Relatively
clear and extensive and varied is the space-consciousness
that goes along with tactual feelings. Though the man
born blind has but a very imperfect notion of space, and a
notion composed in a different way from that of persons
who can see, yet it is a notion much greater than that
given along with taste. But so immensely more vivid
and comprehensive is the consciousness of space accompanying visual sensations, that we habitually think of it
as accompanying these only. 　　　　　Now let us ask,
with what other series of contrasts do these contrasts go?
They go along with the contrasts between the mobilities
of the sense-organs, relatively to the stimuli they receive.
The sensitive surface within either ear cannot be so moved
about in relation to the incoming vibrations as to expose
now one part and now another to them: all that can be done
is to shift the head in such way as to vary the intensity of
the sound-waves that fall on either ear and on the two ears.
Similarly with smell. The olfactory tract is fixed in relation to the body of inhaled odour: it can simply be brought
as a whole nearer to or further from the source of the sensation. Along with tastes we have seen that a certain amount
of space-consciousness is directly given; and here we see
that the sense-organ is movable with respect to the source
of its stimulation. Far more marked is the mobility of the
sentient surface in relation to the object affecting it, when
we pass to the case of touch; and it is observable, also,

that the space-consciousness accompanying tactual sensations is clear in proportion as the parts whence the sensations come are mobile. We cannot form any such distinct conceptions of the sizes and shapes of things explored by our backs or legs, as we can of the sizes and shapes of things explored by our hands. But it is when we come to the eyes that we reach the greatest mobility of the parts relatively to their stimuli: not, indeed, relatively to the actual outer objects, but relatively to the images of those objects cast on the retinæ. For the retinæ, made up of multitudinous independent sensitive agents, can be moved with immense facility all about the images falling upon them. With a quickness almost too great to note, the contractions that converge the eyes and adjust their foci are effected; and by other contractions the clustered feelers which make up the retinæ are swept from side to side, and up and down, over the image; touching all its parts in countless combinations and successions. Here, then, we have the highly-significant fact that the space-consciousness accompanying each kind of sensation derived from the outer world, is great in proportion to the variety and rapidity of the sensations of motion which go along with the receipt of it —a fact obviously to be expected if the foregoing interpretation is true.

Another peculiarity in our perception of space is worth noting. If the reader, while looking at his hand or any equally-close object, will consider what consciousness he has of the space lying between it and his eyes, he will perceive that his consciousness of it is, as it were, exhaustive. He has an extremely complete or detailed perception of it. If he now directs his eyes to the farther side of the room, and contemplates an equal portion of space there, he finds that he has much less knowledge of it. He has nothing like so intimate an acquaintance with its constituent parts. If, again, looking through the window, he observes what consciousness he has of a space a hundred yards away, he discovers it to be in still less specific consciousness. And on gazing at the distant horizon he becomes aware that he has scarcely any perception of that far-off space—has rather an indistinct *con*ception than a distinct *per*ception. But this is exactly the kind of knowledge that would result from experiences organized as above described. Of the space within range of our hands we have the most complete perception, because we have had myriads of experiences of relative positions within that space. And of space as it recedes from us we have a less and less complete perception, because our experiences of relative positions contained in it have been fewer and fewer.

A kindred peculiarity in our space-perceptions, which was indicated in § 119, has a like implication. We saw that when the eyes are adjusted to see any object, or part of an object, " we become conscious of the space it occupies, and of the closely-environing space, with much more distinctness than we are conscious of any other space." Now if our consciousness of space results from organized and inherited experiences, verified and completed during the activity and development of the individual, this peculiarity must inevitably result from the ordinary process of association. For those feelings, visual, tactual, and muscular, which accompany the disclosure of any position occupied by an object, or part of an object, have been, in the experiences of ourselves and our ancestors, oftener associated with the feelings accompanying disclosure of adjacent occupied positions than they have with the feelings accompanying the disclosure of remote positions. Obviously the frequency and directness of the associations have always been proportionate to the proximity. Hence, from the law of association it is an immediate corollary that when the eyes are converged on any point, we become clearly conscious of the space around it, and that when we turn the eyes to a second point this consciousness fades, and gives place to a similar distinct consciousness of the space around this second point.　　　No less significant is the concomitant peculiarity that while we are conscious of the space between our eyes and anything at which we look, we are not simultaneously conscious of the space beyond: unless it contains objects which are impressing their images upon us. This fact will be most clearly recognized on observing how at night, when the shutters are closed and no sound reminds us of the outer world, we have no distinctly-presented consciousness of outer space. We are spontaneously conscious of the space within the walls, but we are not spontaneously conscious of the space beyond the walls. And when imagination makes us conscious of this space beyond the walls, we become conscious of it by thinking of ourselves as looking at the objects it contains, and so remembering the spaces between us and them. Now this is manifestly just what the hypothesis implies. For the explorations which reveal the position of any object to us, are always explorations which acquaint us with the space between us and it, but not with the space beyond it.

The feelings accompanying certain abnormal states of the nervous system, furnish confirmatory evidence. De Quincey, describing some of his opium-dreams, says that " buildings and landscapes were exhibited in proportions so vast as the bodily eye is not fitted to receive. *Space swelled*, and was amplified to an extent of unutterable infinity." It is not at all an uncommon thing with nervous subjects to have illusive perceptions in which the body seems enormously extended: even to the covering an acre of ground. Now the state in which these phenomena occur, is one of exalted nervous activity—a state in which De Quincey depicts himself as seeing in their minutest details the long-forgotten events of his childhood. And if we consider what effect must be produced on the consciousness of space, by an excitement during which forgotten experiences are revived in extreme abundance and vividness, we shall see that it

will cause the illusion he names. Of the surrounding positions, in part potentially registered in the inherited organization and in part disclosed by the individual's actions, only
some are present to consciousness at any instant. Memory,
inherited and acquired, fails to bring back more than a
small portion of the impressions received. Now imagine
multitudes of the fading experiences suddenly to revive, and
to become definitely present to consciousness. What must
result? It must result that space will be known in comparatively microscopic detail. Within any portion of it,
ordinarily thought of as containing a certain quantity of
positions, a much greater quantity of positions will be
thought of. Between the eye and each point looked at,
whose distance is commonly conceived as equivalent to a
certain series of positions, a far more extensive series will
be conceived; and as the length of each such series is the
mind's measure of the distance, all distances will appear increased, all points will appear more remote, and it will seem
that space has " swelled," as De Quincey expresses it.

And now mark that while these several peculiarities in
our space-perceptions harmonize with, and receive their interpretations from, the experience-hypothesis, taken in that
expanded form implied by the doctrine of Evolution, they
are not interpretable by, and are quite incongruous with, the
Kantian hypothesis. Without insisting on the fact that
our sensations of sound and odour do not originally carry
with them the consciousness of space at all, there is the fact
that along with those sensations of taste, touch, and sight
which do carry this consciousness with them, it is carried
in extremely different degrees—a fact quite unaccountable
if space is given before all experience as a form of intuition.
That our consciousness of adjacent space is far more complete than our consciousness of remote space, is also at
variance with the hypothesis; which, for aught that
appears to the contrary, implies homogeneity. Similarly
with that variation in the distinctness of surrounding parts

of space which occurs as we turn our eyes now to one point and now to another: were space a subjective form not derived from experience, there should be no such variation. Again, the contrast between the spontaneous consciousness of space within a room, and the consciousness of the space beyond its walls, which does not come spontaneously, is a contrast for which there seems no reason if space is a fixed form. And so, too, that in morbid states space should appear " swelled," is, on the Kantian theory, unaccountable; seeing that the *form* of intuition should remain constant, whether the intuition itself be normal or abnormal.

§ 334. Leaving here the inquiry concerning our perception of Space in its totality, a few further words are called for respecting that relation of two coexistent positions, in our consciousness of which the problem ultimately centres. From time to time in the progress of the argument, something has been done towards showing that it is an aggregate of simultaneous states of consciousness, symbolizing a series of states to which it is found equivalent. But, as before said, it is desirable to postpone the more definite analysis of this perception until the perception of motion is dealt with. At present the only reason for recurring to it, is to point out the indissoluble union between the cognition of space and the cognition of coexistence; and afterwards to point out what is implied by this.

The idea of space involves the idea of coexistence, and the idea of coexistence involves the idea of space. On the one hand, space cannot be thought of without coexistent positions being thought of. On the other hand, coexistence cannot be thought of without at least two points in space being thought of. A relation of coexistence implies two somethings that coexist. Two somethings cannot occupy absolutely the same position in space. And hence coexistence implies space. If it be said that one body can have coexistent attributes, and that therefore two attributes can coexist

56

in the same place; the reply is, that body itself is unthinkable except as presenting coexistent positions—a top and a
bottom, a right and a left. Body cannot be so diminished,
even in imagination, as to present only one position. When
it ceases to present in thought more than one position,
it ceases to be body. And as attributes imply body—as a
mere position in space can have no other attribute than that
of position, it follows that a relation of coexistence, even
between attributes, is inconceivable without an accompanying conception of space.

If now it should turn out that in the first stage of mental
development a relation of coexistence is not directly cognizable, but is cognizable only by a duplex act of thought—
only by a comparison of experiences, the theory of the
transcendentalists will be finally disposed of. When it
comes to be shown that the ultimate element into which the
consciousness of space is decomposable—the relation of coexistence—can itself be gained only by experience; the utter
untenableness of the Kantian doctrine will become manifest.
That this will be so shown, the reader must at present take
for granted. I am obliged thus to forestall the argument,
because it would be inconvenient, during an analysis of the
several orders of relations, to recur at any length to the
controversy respecting space.

§ 335. To complete the chapter it needs but to say that
the process of organic classification, shown in previous cases
to constitute the act of perception, is very clearly exhibited
in the perception of space.

The materials of the perception having been gained in the
way described, the co-ordination of them into any particular
perception consists in the assimilation of each relation of
position to the like before-known relations. In every glance
we cast around, the distinct consciousness of the distance of
each thing looked at, and the nascent consciousnesses of the
distances of various neighbouring things, alike imply class-

ings of present distances with remembered distances. These distances being one and all unknowable under any other condition, there is no alternative but to admit this. And the fact that numberless such classings should be simultaneously made by us without attracting our attention, simply shows to what perfection the process of automatic classification is brought by infinite repetition throughout the lives of all ancestral organisms, as throughout our own lives.

Since the two foregoing chapters have been stereotyped and in part printed, it has occurred to me that due attention has not been paid in them to those early stages in the development of the visual perception of space, which were indicated in the "Physical Synthesis." The cause of this inadequate attention has been that while revising these chapters (which were originally written before the synthetical divisions were fully thought out) the conceptions set forth in them have so far possessed me that I have overlooked some qualifications which should be made, in addition to those which have been made. These I now append.

In §§ 233–5 will be found a sketch of the process by which, in a creature having the general type and movements of a rudimentary fish, there may in course of time be established a structure of the kind required to co-ordinate its muscular motions with its visual impressions. On considering the implications of the argument running through those sections, it will be seen that we must infer the gradual rise of nervous connexions such that impressions received through the eyes from small objects before the creature, will produce, automatically, muscular movements such as will bring its head up to the objects. That is to say, within a certain region of space around and in front of the creature's head, the positions are in a sense known— known so far that the visual impression received from something occupying any one of them is correlated with the muscular tensions gone through in turning the body and moving the head up to this something. That correlations of this direct kind between visual impressions and muscular motions do exist, is proved by the actions of every fish from moment to moment. And that such correlations are inherited in the form of automatically-acting sets of nervous plexuses, is proved by the fact that they effectually guide the young fish while so undeveloped that it still carries the remains of a yelk-bag attached to its abdomen. Indeed, it is obvious, á priori, that if these correlations were not pre-established in its organization, the young fish

could not survive; since, in the absence of food supplied by a
parent, it would starve before such correlations could be established
by its own experiences—even supposing that its own experiences
commencing *de novo* would suffice, which is a strong supposition.
Thus, it is undeniable that quite early in the course of nervous
evolution, there arises something which seems like a visual space-
consciousness; that this arises without tactual explorations; and
that it is mainly fixed in the inherited nervous structure.

But now let us not assume too much—let us not err by inferring the possession of a visual space-consciousness like our own.
That inverse anthropomorphism by which we are continually led
to interpret the actions of inferior animals in terms of human
ideas and feelings, will mislead us here if we do not take care.
It is natural to suppose that a rudimentary creature which, being
impressed by an adjacent object, moves itself in the way required
to lay hold of this object, must have a consciousness of position
such as we have. Yet I believe it may be shown that between
the two modes of consciousness there is an enormous difference.
Let us look closely into the matter.

We are not warranted in crediting an animal with a higher type
of consciousness than its actions imply. And supposing its actions
are interpretable without further assumptions, we are not warranted
in crediting it with a consciousness containing elements that have
nothing corresponding to them in its own experiences or the experiences of its ancestry : this is a necessary implication of the Evolution-hypothesis. Hence in considering the nature of the space-
consciousness described, we have to ask what are the elements given
in the experiences which, as organized, constitute it. We shall
find that they are limited almost entirely to experiences of successions.   When a fish-like creature of the kind supposed,
impressed by a small object before it on the right, so moves its tail
as to bring the axis of its body into a line with the object; and
when by lateral undulations of its body it brings its head up to the
object : what are the changes undergone by its nervous centres ? A
series of re-actions accompanying the actions of the muscles, and
a series of visual impressions; first limited to one eye, then joined in
an imperfect way by the two eyes (for a fish's visual axes do not
converge), and then forming a series the members of which, partially joined, become larger and stronger as the object is neared.
The only approach to experiences of coexistence are the experiences
of concurrence between the two series—the series of muscular tensions and the series of increasing visual impressions. But two
concurrent series in Time, contain no such element as that of continuous coexistence, which forms the unit of consciousness of Space.
To perceive, in the human sense, the locality of an object, is to be
simultaneously conscious of the whole series of coexistent positions

lying between the subject and the object : and, as concluded in the foregoing chapter, this implies that these positions, first known in succession, have been simultaneously known through their occupancy by things simultaneously impressing us. How the primitive fish is guided by serial experiences only, will become conceivable on observing that the consciousness it has is analogous to the consciousness we should have if we were moved through dark space containing sounding bodies without being aware of our motion; for we should then know of an impending contact with a sounding body by the increasing loudness of the sound.   Any difficulty that may be found in conceiving such a type of consciousness, will disappear on cross-examining a man born blind; and on finding that beyond the small portions of adjacent space which, when occupied by things, yield to his limbs simultaneous impressions, and so reveal coexistent positions, he has no consciousness of space, save in the successively-presented terms that accompany his movements through it. He finds his way partly by the sounds which, on previously going to a place, he heard in a certain order; partly by the successive touches which accompanied this series of sounds; and partly by the series of steps and accompanying estimate of time : the whereabouts of the place in remote space as we conceive it, is inconceivable by him. Even a square table he knows only in terms of the touches and tensions, partly simultaneous but mainly successive, accompanying exploration of it; and gets a crude idea of its squareness only when *told* that it is like a small square thing which he can grasp all at once. When we bear in mind that the congenitally-blind man inherits that complex nervous structure in which the human space-consciousness is latent, we shall see that even such dim notions as he can form of positions a little beyond the reach of his hands, are to be ascribed to the aid which this inherited structure gives him in eking out his tactual experiences; and that in the absence of this inherited structure, with all its reflex suggestions, he would know nothing of things in space save as occurring at certain places in the series of his conscious states. Now though it seems strange to illustrate the consciousness of a creature which can see but has no limbs with which to explore, by comparing it to the consciousness of one who can tactually explore but cannot see ; yet the two are parallel thus far, that in both there are states of consciousness presented only in series, and that in the absence of any means by which such series can be presented simultaneously, there can arise no consciousness of the coexistent positions to which the serial positions are equivalent. We are helped to understand that a complete consciousness of occupied space can arise only when, by the motion of a limb over a surface, a series of muscular tensions joined with a series of tactual impressions yielded by the successive points touched, goes along with a continuous visual impression received from all these points; and that a complete consciouness of unoccupied space can arise only when it is found that the serial tensions received from the moving limb, and the serial visual impressions received from it, can occur without any successive tactual impressions and without any simultaneous visual impressions from all the positions which previously yielded such tactual impressions.

There is good reason to think, therefore, that the consciousness of space is reached through a process of evolution, which begins with it in so rudimentary a state that it cannot properly be called a consciousness of space, in the sense we ordinarily give to the word; and that in the course of the evolution new elements are added, combinations between these and the primitive elements are formed, and the consciousness becomes more complex at the same time that it integrates and widens.

[The interpretation of the genesis of our Space-consciousness contained in the foregoing chapter, with its appended note, originally set forth in the first edition of this work, published in 1855, has since then gained some acceptance among psychologists of the naturalistic school, and has become current in Germany. At the same time it has aroused the antagonism of the transcendental school, and has, in various places, been attacked by the neo-Kantists. Preoccupations long prevented me from taking any notice of their criticisms, but I at length found it needful to deal with them ; and, in the number of *Mind* for June 1890, singled out for reply the work of Prof. Watson, entitled *Kant and his English Critics*. To this reply I have thought it desirable to give a permanent place. It will be found in the Appendix.

CHAPTER XV.

§ 336. The near relationship between our notion of Time and our notion of Space, is implied in current forms of speech. In the phrase " a great space of time," a magnitude of one serves to denote a magnitude of the other. Conversely, the tourist in Switzerland whose inquiries respecting distances are answered in *stunden*, or hours; and the savage who, in common with the ancient Hebrew, has a place described to him as so many days' journey off; find times used to express spaces. The like reciprocity of symbolism occurs in science. Beyond the facts that a second of time is a function of the length of the pendulum, and that our hours are measured by spaces on the dial, there is the fact that a degree, which was originally a day's journey of the Sun along the ecliptic, has become the name of an angular space.

Joined to the arguments contained in the last chapter, these facts possess much significance. *That in early ages, and in uncivilized countries, men should have expressed Space in terms of Time, and that afterwards, as a result of progress, they should have come to express Time in terms of Space;* is a circumstance giving strong support to the views recently developed. While it shows conclusively that the phenomena of coexistence and those of sequence, *are* made to stand for each other in the mind; it also shows,

207

repeated on a higher platform, that gradual supplanting of mental sequences by their equivalent coexistences, lately described as the process by which our cognition of Space is acquired. Just as we saw that the series of states of consciousness accompanying any motion, becomes consolidated into a quasi-single consciousness of the coexistent positions (or space) traversed during that motion, which single consciousness afterwards expresses to the mind the series it was equivalent to; so we see that the series of states of consciousness implied by " a day's journey," becomes consolidated into a consciousness of the coexistent positions traversed (measured by miles or leagues), which practically-single state of consciousness has supplanted in thought and word the series of states represented by it. Any one wishing yet further examples of this mental substitution, will find one on observing how habitually he thinks of the spaces on the clock-face instead of the periods they stand for—how, on discovering it to be half an hour later than he supposed, he does not represent the half-hour in its duration, but scarcely passes beyond the sign of it marked by the finger. Such illustrations make it easy to conceive that the use of coexistences to symbolize sequences, which in these complex cases has become so habitual, has in the simplest cases become organic.

This reciprocity between our cognitions of Space and Time, alike in their primitive and most developed forms, being understood; and the consequent impossibility of considering either of them entirely alone, being inferred; let us go on to deal more particularly with Time.

§ 337. As the notions of Space and Coexistence are inseparable, so are the notions of Time and Sequence. It is impossible to think of Time without thinking of some succession; and it is equally impossible to think of any succession without thinking of Time. Time, like Space, cannot be conceived except by the establishment of a relation between at least two elements of consciousness: the difference being that while, in the case of Space, these two elements are, or seem to be, present together, in the case of Time they are not present together.

The doctrine that Time is knowable only by the succession of our mental states calls for little exposition: it is so well established a doctrine. All that seems here necessary, is to re-state it in a way which will bring out its harmony with the foregoing doctrines. To this end, it will be well first to recall the fact that the cognition is entirely relative. When treating of the "Relativity of Relations" (§ 91), it was pointed out that the apparent lengths of sequences vary with "the structure of the organism, with its size, with its age, with its constitutional state, with the number and vividness of the impressions it receives, and with their relative positions in consciousness."

Omitting, as not relevant to the present inquiry, those causes of variation that go along with difference of species, we may say that our notion of any period of time, is determined by the length of the series of remembered states of consciousness experienced during that time. I say advisedly *remembered* states of consciousness. For as any series of states of consciousness can be known only by memory; and as any of the states that have occurred but are not represented in memory cannot be components of the series; it results that the series of remembered states can alone serve as the measure between a past and a present state. And hence the explanation of all such facts as that an interval looked back upon by a child, appears longer than the same interval looked back upon by an adult; since, out of the same series of experiences, many which being novel to the child make deep impressions on it, are so familiar to the adult as to make scarcely any impressions. And the length of the series of remembered states of consciousness being thus our measure of time, we have no longer any difficulty in understanding cases in which vivid ideas, following each other with extreme rapidity, cause a night to seem like a hundred years, or, as in some drowning persons, a few minutes to represent a whole life.

When, however, we say that the time between two events is recognized by the series of remembered states of consciousness intervening, what do we more specifically mean? These two events were known to us by the states of consciousness they produced. Before the first of these there were countless other states of consciousness. Since the last of them there have been others. Between them there were others. We know them, therefore, as having certain *places* in the whole series of states of consciousness experienced during our lives. The time at which each occurred is known to us as its *position* in the series. And by the time between them, we mean their *relative positions* in the series. As any relation of coexistent positions—any portion of space, is conceived by us as such or such, according to the number of other positions that intervene; so, any relation of sequent positions—any portion of time, is conceived by us as such or such, according to the number of other positions that intervene. Thus, a particular time is a relation of position between some two states in the series of states of consciousness. And Time in general, as known to us, is *the abstract of all relations of position among successive states of consciousness.* Or, using other words, we may say that it is *the blank form in which these successive states are presented and represented ; and which, serving alike for each, is not dependent on any.*

For here we have to note the fact, parallel to a fact noted when treating of Space, that since in the series of our states of consciousness the same positions, as estimated by their distances from the state that is passing, have been occupied by states of all kinds, these positions become known apart from states of each particular kind. If at a certain distance back in the train of my thoughts, there was always a feeling of colour, there would be an established association between that place and that feeling. But as this same place is now filled by a tactual sensation, now by an auditory sensation, and now by a sensation coming from the palate, or the nostrils, or the viscera; it results that the place is dissociated from special sensations and from special kinds of sensations. And the same thing having happened with every other place, known as nearer or more remote, the whole series of these places, considered as separate from the feelings that may be in them, or as unoccupied by feelings, comes to be aggregated into a consciousness of Time, considered as the blank form of all relations of sequence; just as we saw that there similarly arises the consciousness of Space, as the blank form of all relations of coexistence.

§ 338. By defenders of the Kantian hypothesis, it will probably be contended that the consciousness of Time is given along with the first sequence experienced, which cannot otherwise be known as a sequence. I reply that it is not at first known as a sequence; and that the full consciousness of it as a sequence, and of Time as its form, arise through the same accumulated experiences.

It is, doubtless, to be concluded that even in a nascent consciousness the successive states must be severally recognized as standing to one another in certain relations of position—either as occurring next to one another, or as separated by intervening states. Though, at first, probably no considerable portion of the series of states can be contemplated at once, and no *distant* members of it brought into relation, yet the simplest cognition implies that sundry of the *proximate* members of it are co-ordinated and their respective places known in some vague way. But neither the contemplation of any two states of consciousness that stand in certain relative positions, nor the thinking of their relation of position as like some other relation of position, gives, in itself, the notion of Time; although it is the raw material

out of which that notion is constructed. Time, as conceived
by us, is not any one relation of position in the series; nor
any relation between two such relations; but is the abstract
of all such relations, and cannot possibly be conceived until
many of them have been known and compared. To elucidate this let us consider a parallel case.   Suppose
an incipient intelligence to receive two equal impressions of
the colour red. No other experiences having been received,
the *relation* between these two impressions cannot be thought
of in any way; because there exists no other relation with
which it can be classed, or from which it can be distinguished. Suppose two other equal impressions of red are
received. There can still exist no idea of the relation
between them. For though there is a repetition of the
previously-experienced relation, yet since no thing can be
cognized save as of some kind; and since, by its very
nature, kind implies the establishment of difference; there
cannot, while only one order of relation has been experienced, be any knowledge of it—any thought about it.
Now suppose that two unequal impressions of red are received. There is experienced a second species of relation.
And if there are afterwards presented many such pairs of
impressions, the members of which are severally equal and
unequal, it becomes possible for the constituents of each
new pair to be vaguely thought of as like or unlike, and as
standing in relations like or unlike previous ones. I say
vaguely thought of, because, while various impressions of
the colour red are the sole things known, the cognitions of
their likenesses and unlikenesses will not be distinctly
separable from the impressions themselves. When, however,
pairs of impressions belonging to some other species come
to be received—as of the colour green in different intensities—the occurrence among these also of some that are
like and of others that are unlike, will tend to dissociate
these relations from the colours green and red. And gradually as, by accumulation of experiences, there are found

to be like and unlike sounds, tastes, smells, resistances, temperatures, &c., the relationships which we signify by these words like and unlike, will become partially separable in thought from particular impressions: the ideas of *likeness* and *unlikeness* will begin to arise, and will become more distinct and more abstract in proportion to the multiplicity of kinds of impressions presenting them. Manifestly, then, the ideas of likeness and unlikeness are impossible until after multitudes of things have been thought of as like and unlike. Similarly in the case before us. After various relations of position among states of consciousness have been contemplated, have been compared, have become familiar; and after experiences of different relations of position have been so accumulated as to dissociate the idea of the relation from all particular positions; then, but not till then, can there arise that abstract notion of *relativity of position* among successive states of consciousness which constitutes the notion of their several places in time, and that abstract notion of *aggregated relative positions* which constitutes the notion of Time in general.

§ 339. How far the consciousness of Time is, in its general character, fixed by the inherited structure in a way like that in which the consciousness of Space is fixed, is an interesting question. That there is some kind of pre-determination we may feel tolerably certain; while we may suspect the pre-determination to be less specific than that to which we here compare it.

When treating of the " Relativity of Relations," (§ 91), it was pointed out that the consciousness of Time must vary with size, with structure, and with functional activity; since the scale of time proper to each creature is composed primarily of the marks made in its consciousness by the rhythms of its vital functions, and secondarily of the marks made in its consciousness by the rhythms of its locomotive functions: both which sets of rhythms are immensely

different in different species. Consequently, the constitution
derived from ancestry settles the general character of the
consciousness within approximate limits. In our own case,
for example, it is clear that there are certain extremes
within which our units of measure for time must fall. The
heart-beats and respiratory actions serving as primitive
measures, can have their rates varied within moderate
ranges only. The alternating movements of the legs have
a certain degree of slowness below which we cannot be
conscious of them, and a certain degree of rapidity beyond
which we cannot push them. Similarly with measures of
time furnished by sensible motions outside of us. There are
motions too rapid for our perceptions, as well as motions too
slow for our perceptions; and such consciousness of time as
we get from watching objective motions must fall between
these extremes.

To what extent the larger consciousness of Time is pre-
determined, and to what extent it is determined by individual
experiences, are also points about which nothing very definite can be said. Still, we may see grounds for concluding
that the lengths of the periods over which consciousness
can range in such way as to grasp them, are approximately
limited by inherited nervous structures. For the power to
estimate an interval of hours or days depends on the power
to represent the events that have occurred during its lapse.
The inability of an old person to remember what he was
doing two days ago, shows us that as fast as the series of
impressions lately received becomes less easily representable, the estimation of recent long intervals becomes im-
practicable. This case, which illustrates the result of
defective function, I cite merely to indicate the connexion
between consciousness of time and faculty of representation.
And having done this, it remains only to point out that since
structure is the primary condition to representation (in so
far that with a given degree of structure there cannot be
more than a given amount of representation), it follows that

the consciousness of time in its wider reach must be potentially fixed in its general character by the organization.

§ 340. Such being the genesis and nature of our consciousness of Time, considered generally, we have but further to ask in what consists the process of perceiving a time.

Strictly speaking, perception here passes very nearly into conception. For while in perception as commonly exemplified many or most of the components of the consciousness are presented while some are represented, in the perception of a portion of time, nearly all the components are represented: only the passing feelings are given in vivid forms, and all the rest are given in their faint forms. But making this qualification, it only needs to say respecting the perception of a portion of time, that it consists in the classing of the relation of serial positions contemplated as forming it, with certain before-known relations—the cognition of it as like such before-known relations.

CHAPTER XVI.

THE PERCEPTION OF MOTION.

§ 341. As shown by the foregoing discusssions, our ideas of Motion, Time, and Space, are so intimately connected that it is extremely difficult to disentangle them. On the one hand it has, I think, been made clear that Space and Time are knowable only through Motion. On the other hand it is by some contended, with great apparent truth, that Motion is unknowable except as in Space and Time; and that, therefore, notions of Space and Time must pre-exist. Taking which two positions together, there seems no course left but to adopt the Kantian hypothesis; and conclude that Time and Space are forms of sensibility which are disclosed in the act by which Motion is perceived. A closer consideration, however, will show that there is an alternative.

For though the consciousness of Motion cannot be formed by the developed mind, without an accompanying consciousness of Space and Time; it does not follow that the consciousness of Motion in the *un*developed mind is similarly accompanied. It does not follow that because the connexion between the notions is now indissoluble, it was always so. The confusion has arisen from the unwarrantable assumption, that certain impressions received through the senses were originally understood in a way just like that in which they are understood after the accumulation of multitudinous experiences—an assumption at variance with the established facts of Psychology. Do we not know that the form of a house is comprehended by the child, after a manner in which the infant cannot comprehend it? Do we not know that the daily rising and setting of the sun, are thought of in completely different ways by a savage and by an astronomer? Do we not know that the physicist thinks of sound, or of light, or of heat, in a manner utterly unlike that in which the clown thinks of them? Moreover, is it not admitted that much of our acquired knowledge becomes so consolidated as to disable us from dissociating its elements—that on grasping an apple we cannot, without great difficulty, so confine our consciousness to the sensations of touch as to avoid thinking of the apple as spherical—that we find it impossible, when looking at a neighbouring object, to shut out all thought of the distance and attend only to the visual sensations? And when we unite these two general facts, that by combining its experiences the mind acquires conceptions quite different from those it originally had, and that such of these as are invariably combined, and perpetually combined, become fused into conceptions that are undecomposable by introspection; does it not become manifest, both that the idea of Motion which accompanies developed intelligence is distinct in nature from the idea of Motion which undeveloped intelligence frames, and that it has become impossible for the one to think of Motion as the other thought of it? It is a vicious assumption that what are necessities of thought to us, are necessities of thought in the abstract.

"But how," it may be asked, "is it possible for us to deal with Motion as known in some form different from that in which we know it? How are we to treat of a conception which we cannot ourselves have?" Very readily. For though in our adult consciousness of Motion the ideas of Space and Time are inextricably involved, there is another element in that consciousness which we may see

57

would remain were the ideas of Space and Time absent.
Though on moving my arm, even in the dark, I cannot
become conscious of the motion without being simultaneously conscious of a space traversed and a time occupied in traversing it; yet it is obvious to me that the
muscular sensations accompanying the motion, are quite distinct in nature from the notions of Space and Time associated with them. I find no difficulty in so far isolating
these sensations, as to perceive that the consciousness of
them would remain were my notions of Space and Time
abolished. And I find no difficulty in conceiving that
Motion is thinkable by a nascent intelligence as consisting
of these sensations, while yet the notions of Space and Time
are undeveloped.

Seeing, then, that the primitive consciousness of Motion
may readily be conceived to have contained but one of the
elements ultimately included in it, we may properly inquire
whether, out of such a primitive consciousness of Motion,
the consciousness we have of it may be evolved.

§ 342. To open this inquiry systematically, let us first
look at the data furnished by preceding chapters.

We saw that our consciousness of Space is an abstract of
all relations among coexistent positions; that the germinal
element of the consciousness is the relation between two coexistent positions; that every relation between two coexistent positions is resolvable into a relation of coexistent
positions between the subject and an object touched; that
this relation of coexistent positions between subject and
object, is equivalent to the relation of coexistent positions
between two parts of the body when adjusted by the muscles
to a particular attitude; and that thus the question—How
do we come by our cognition of Space? is reducible to the
question—How do we discover the relation of coexistent
positions between two sentient points on our surface?

Our consciousness of Time we saw to be the abstract of

all relations among successive positions in the series of our states of consciousness. We saw that the germinal element out of which this conception is developed, is a relation of position between two states of consciousness; and that every relation of position between two states of consciousness is known by the number of remembered intervening states.

Respecting Motion, we know that as through it only are changes in consciousness originally produced, through it only can relations of position among successive states of consciousness be disclosed; and that, for the same reason, through it only can be disclosed the relations of position among coexistences. At the same time we know that whether Motion is or is not originally cognizable in any other way, it is from the beginning cognizable through the changes of consciousness it produces. If it be a subjective motion, as that of a limb, it is present to the mind as a continuous but varying series of sensations of muscular tension. If it be an objective motion, as that of something traversing the surface of the body, or as that of something passing before the eyes, it is still present to the mind as a continuous series of sensations: in the one case the sensations that result from touching a succession of points on the skin; in the other case the sensations that result from exciting a succession of points on the retina. And if the motion be both subjective and objective, as when one part of the body is drawn over another part, or as when a limb is extended within view of the eyes, then it is present to the mind as a double series of sensations: in the one case, as a series of muscular sensations joined with a simultaneous series of tactual sensations; in the other case, as a series of muscular sensations joined with a simultaneous series of visual sensations. Finally, when the hand is moved over the body within view of the eyes, motion is present to the mind as a triple series of sensations—muscular, tactual, visual—occurring simultaneously.

Passing over for the present the visual phenomena, let us deal with the question in which centres the whole controversy respecting the genesis of our ideas of Motion, Space, and Time: the question, namely—How do we become cognizant of the relative positions of two points on the surface of the body? Such two points considered as coexistent, involve the germinal idea of Space. Such two points disclosed to consciousness by two successive tactual sensations, involve the germinal idea of Time. And the muscular sensations by which, when self-produced, these two tactual sensations are separated, involve the germinal idea of Motion. The questions to be considered then, are—In what order do these germinal ideas arise? and—How are they developed?

§ 343. Already, in treating of visible extension (§ 327), and the visual perception of space (§ 331), and in showing how serial states of consciousness are consolidated into simultaneous states which become their equivalents, the way has been prepared for answering these questions. The process of analysis partially applied to retinal impressions, has now to be applied, after a more complete manner, to impressions on the body at large.

To this end, taking for our subject a partially-developed creature, having a nervous structure that is able to receive the data for the cognition, but in which the data are not yet co-ordinated, let us call the two points on its body between which a relation is to be established, A and Z.* Let us

* In the first edition I had here set out with a newly-born infant: thus implying that the organization of experiences to be explained, occurs in the course of an individual life. The "Special Analysis" having been originally written before the "Special Synthesis," (as their order in the first edition shows), its conclusions were not worked out into full harmony with those which the Evolution-hypothesis led me to in the "Special Synthesis." As the revised argument of the foregoing chapters has made manifest, however, we must recognize these relations now to be dealt with, as potentially established in the nervous structure inherited by the infant. The intra-

assume these two points to be anywhere within reach of the limbs. By the hypothesis, nothing is at present known of these points; either as coexisting in Space, as giving successive sensations in Time, or as being brought into relation by Motion. If now the creature moves a limb in such a way as to touch nothing, there is a certain vague reaction upon its consciousness—a sensation of muscular tension. This sensation has the peculiarity of being indefinite in its commencement, indefinite in its termination, and indefinite in all its intermediate changes. Its strength being proportionate to the degree of contraction, it follows that as the limb starts from a state in which there is no contraction, and as it can reach a position requiring extreme contraction only by passing through positions requiring intermediate degrees of contraction, and as the degree of contraction must therefore form a series ascending by small increments from zero, the sensations of tension must also form such a series. And the sensations accompanying all subsequent movement must similarly form series that either increase or decrease; since a muscle cannot pass from any one state to any other without going through all the intermediate states. Thus, then, the creature, on moving its limb backwards and forwards without touching anything, has a consciousness not definitely divisible into states; but a consciousness the variations of which pass insensibly into one another, like undulations of greater or less magnitude. Manifestly, such a consciousness is but a nascent

uterine modifications it has gone through, have already repeated in a short time, those modifications slowly produced by the experiences of ancestral races during an immeasurable time. But the argument remains in essence the same, whether we conceive the progressive changes to be wrought in a long series of individuals which successively bequeath the modifications produced by experience, or whether we conceive them to be wrought in a continuously-existing individual. The partially-developed creature assumed above, must therefore be understood as a continuously-existing individual, or else as receiving in the course of its life such modifications as are ordinarily received only during the lives of species and genera and orders.

consciousness. While its states are thus indistinctly separated, there can be no clear comparison of them; no classing
of them; no thought, properly so called; and consequently, no ideas of Motion, Time, or Space, as we understand them.   Suppose that the limb touches
something. A sudden change in consciousness is produced
—a change that is incisive in its commencement, and, when
the limb is removed, equally incisive in its termination. In
the midst of the continuous feeling of muscular tension,
vaguely rising and falling in intensity, there all at once
occurs a distinct feeling of another kind. This feeling,
beginning and ending abruptly, constitutes a definite state
of consciousness; and becomes, as it were, a *mark* in consciousness. Other such marks are produced by other such
acts; and in proportion as they are multiplied there arises
a possibility of comparing them, both in respect to their
strengths and in respect to their relative positions. At the
same time the feelings of muscular tension being, as it
were, divided into lengths by these super-posed marks,
become similarly comparable; and so there are acquired
materials for a simple order of thought. Observe, also, that
while these tactual sensations may, when several things are
touched in succession, produce successive marks in consciousness, separated by intervening muscular sensations,
they may also become concurrent with these muscular sensations; as when the end of the limb is drawn along a
surface. And observe further, that when the surface over
which the end of the limb is drawn is not a foreign body,
but some part of the creature's own body, these muscular
sensations, and the continuous tactual sensation joined with
them, are accompanied by a series of tactual sensations proceeding from that part of the skin over which the limb is
drawn.

See then what happens and what is implied. When the
creature moves the end of a limb along the surface of its
body from A to Z, there are simultaneously impressed on

its consciousness three sets of sensations—the varying series of sensations proceeding from the muscles in action; the series of tactual sensations proceeding from the points of the skin successively touched between A and Z; and the continuous sensation of touch from the end of the limb. Now it might be argued that some progress is made towards the notion of space, in the simultaneous reception of these sensations—in the contemplation of them as coexistent; seeing that the notion of coexistence and the notion of space have a common root, or, in other words—seeing that to be conscious of a duality or multiplicity of sensations, is the first step towards being conscious of that duality or multiplicity of points in space which they imply. It might also be argued that as, when the limb is moved back from Z to A, the serial sensations occur in a reverse order, there is thus achieved a further step in the genesis of the notion; since coexistent things are alone capable of impressing consciousness in any order with equal vividness. But merely indicating these considerations, let us pass to the essential consideration. Every subsequent motion of the limb over the surface from A to Z results in the like simultaneous sets of sensations; and hence these, in course of time, become indissolubly associated. Though the series of tactual sensations, A to Z, being producible by a foreign body moving over the same surface, can be dissociated from the others; and though, if this surface (which we will suppose to be on the head) be withdrawn by a movement of the head, the same motion of the limb with its accompanying muscular sensations, may occur without any sensation of touch; yet when these two series are linked by the tactual sensation proceeding from the end of the limb, they necessarily proceed together, and become inseparably connected in thought. Consequently, the series of tactual sensations A to Z, and the series of muscular sensations which invariably accompanies it when self-produced, serve as equivalents; and being two sides of the same experience, suggest each other in consciousness. *The successive feelings on the skin being excited, association brings up ideas of the habitually-correlated feelings in the limb; and the feelings in the limb being excited, association brings up ideas of the habitually-correlated feelings on the skin.* Due attention having been paid to this fact, let us go on to consider what must happen when something touches, at the same moment, the entire surface between A and Z. This surface is supplied by a series of independent nerve-fibres, each of which separately is affected by an impression falling within a specific area of the skin, and each of which produces a separate state of consciousness. When the finger is drawn along this surface, these nerve-fibres A, B, C, D, . . . Z, are excited in succession; that is—produce successive states of consciousness. But when something covers the whole surface between A and Z, they are excited simultaneously; and produce what tends to become a single state of consciousness. Already in a parallel case (§ 331) I have explained how, when impressions originally known as coming one after another come all at once, their sequent positions are transformed into coexistent positions, which, when consolidated by frequent presentation, are used in thought as equivalent to the sequent positions; and it is needless here to repeat the explanation. What it now concerns us to notice is this:—*that as the series of tactual feelings A to Z, known as having sequent positions in consciousness, is found to be equivalent to the accompanying series of muscular feelings; and as it is also found to be equivalent to the simultaneous tactual feelings A to Z, which are presented in coexistent positions; it follows that these two last are found to be equivalents to each other.* A series of muscular sensations becomes known as corresponding to a series of coexistent positions; and being habitually joined with it, becomes at last unthinkable without it. Thus, the relation of coexistent positions between the points A and Z (and by implication all intermediate points), is necessarily disclosed by a comparison of experiences: the ideas of Space, Time, and Motion, are evolved together. When the successive states of consciousness A to Z, are thought of as having relative positions, the notion of Time becomes nascent. When these states of consciousness occur simultaneously, their relative positions, which were before sequent, become coexistent; and there arises a nascent consciousness of Space. And when these two relations of coexistent and sequent positions are both presented to consciousness along with a series of sensations of muscular tension, a nascent idea of Motion results.

The development of these nascent ideas by further accumulation and comparison of experiences, will be readily understood. What has been described as taking place with respect to one relation of coexistent positions, or rather, one linear series of such positions, is, during the same period, taking place with respect to countless other such linear series in all directions over the body. The like equivalence between a series of coexistent impressions of touch, a series of successive impressions of touch, and series of successive muscular impressions, is being established between every pair of points that can readily be brought into relation by movements of the limbs.

§ 344. But now a criticism has to be met and a qualification to be made. Exposition of the involved process we are dealing with, cannot be so carried on as to keep all parts of the process simultaneously in view; and, for simplicity's sake, I have described the development of this triple consciousness of Motion, Time, and Space, as though some elements of it were fully organized before the rest, and independently of them. The truth is, however, that the three notions are evolved concurrently—the development of certain components preceding by a little the development of other components.

For, careful study of the matter makes it manifest that if

we set out with a surface of skin supplied with the nerve-fibres required for yielding to consciousness all the separate tactual feelings A to Z, we assume much that has to be explained. The pre-existence of these several independent nerve-fibres and of the several independent central elements connected with them, which on being excited through them yield to consciousness states that are distinguishable from one another, is, in fact, the pre-existence of a potential consciousness of the positions A to Z—a consciousness so far potential that anything touching simultaneously the whole surface A to Z, produces the consciousness of these positions as coexistent. Hence the questions immediately arise— How came there to be this series of nerve-fibres having separate peripheral and central terminations? And is not the whole explanation begged when the pre-existence of such structures is taken for granted?

To these questions I answer that the process of genesis is carried on after a manner like that by which processes of organic genesis in general are carried on; namely, by reciprocal aid—by an action and reaction such that each increment of development in one agency makes possible increments of development in other agencies. Were we to describe the evolution of the digestive system, the vascular system, and the respiratory system, in a way which made it appear that the stomach having arisen there then arose a heart for the distribution of the absorbed nutriment, and that there then arose lungs serving to purify this nutriment; we should, by placing the facts in this simple serial order, greatly misrepresent the course of evolution. There is, throughout, an inter-dependence such that superior digestive organs cannot be formed in the absence of superior organs for circulating and aërating the blood; and such that a development of the circulatory organs is not possible in the absence of respiratory organs which are considerably developed. Nevertheless, while this mutual assistance is indispensable, it remains true that these functions make one

another possible in the order named. Until there is a
supply of absorbed nutriment, organs for distributing it
can have no function; and until there are organs for distributing it, organs for aërating it can have no function. In
the course of their evolution absorption must go before
circulation, and circulation before respiration; but this
order being maintained, their evolution advances *pari
passu*. Similarly with the processes we are considering. We have to recognize them as instrumental to
one another in so far that no one can advance independently;
and yet we have to recognize them as preserving a relation
such that the first must make a step before there can be a
step of the second, and the second must make a step before
there can be a step of the third. Or, to speak definitely,
the structures through which are given to consciousness
separate impressions from adjacent parts of the skin, must
develop a stage before there can be a further stage of
development in the structures through which is gained the
consciousness of these positions as tactually and muscu-
larly disclosed in succession by the motion of a limb over
them; and both must develop a stage before there can be
a further development in structures through which is
gained the consciousness of these positions as coexistent,
and as having their distance known in terms of the successive tactual and muscular feelings that accompany transit
from one to other.

Thus, then, we have so far to modify the foregoing explanations as to conceive the triple consciousness of
Motion, Time, and Space, to be undergoing evolution along
with evolution of the body in general—the evolution of
bulk whereby it acquires an extended surface, having more
numerous separate portions capable of having separate
nerve-fibres; the evolution of structure whereby limbs are
developed and acquire greater and more varied capacities
for motion and locomotion; and the evolution of nerves and
nerve-centres which is the concomitant of these evolutions.

We have to regard the perpetual converse of the organism
with its environment, and of its parts with one another by
mutual explorations, as building up this triple consciousness,
element by element; as the nervous system itself is built up,
fibre by fibre and cell by cell. And we have to regard each
new structural unit of any order, with the accompanying
functional unit of consciousness which it yields, as no sooner
established than it begins to co-operate in producing new
units of the other orders.

Certain physiological experiments yield strong support to
the belief that this mutual exploration by surfaces of the
body, itself aids the multiplication of separate sentient areas,
at the same time that it develops the consciousness of their
relations. The facts ascertained by Weber imply that the
degree of tactual discrimination in any part, is not so much
proportionate to the multiplied contacts of the part with surrounding objects, as it is proportionate to the exposure of the
part itself to habitual exploration by other parts. Thus, the
surface of the face, which is not at all used for tactually
examining things, has nevertheless much capacity for distinguishing relative positions. The cheek has as great a
perceptive power as the palm of the hand, and the lower
part of the forehead has a greater perceptive power than
the back of the hand: the interpretation being that there is
a continual converse between the hands and the face. To
see that this is the reason, we have but to observe that the
middle of the fore-arm, the middle of the thigh, the middle
of the back of the neck, and the middle of the back, which
are surfaces least explored by the hands, have only one-
sixth of the tactual discrimination possessed by the cheek—
a fact quite inexplicable teleologically. Hence, then, we
have an inductive basis for the belief that as in the fingers
of a blind man accustomed to read raised characters, there
goes on that multiplication of nerve-fibres implied by the
increased perceptiveness; so, in the course of general evolution, there goes on in any surface a multiplication of nerve-

fibres proportionate to the multiplicity of separate touches, whether produced by the exploration of other things or by self-exploration; and that where it results from self-exploration, there also go on the above-described concomitant developments.

We have now only to glance at one or two general corollaries from these interpretations.

§ 345. Besides the establishment of a connexion in thought between each *particular* muscular series and the *particular* tactual series, both successive and simultaneous, with which it is associated in act; and besides the implied establishment of a knowledge of the special muscular adjustments required to touch each special part; there must be a still more decided establishment of a connexion between muscular series in general and series of sequent and coexistent positions in general; since this connexion is repeated in every one of the particular experiences. And when we consider the infinite repetition of these experiences, we shall have no difficulty in understanding how their components become so consolidated, that even when the hand is moved in the dark without touching anything, it is impossible to be conscious of the muscular sensations without being conscious of the sequent and coexistent positions—the Time and Space—in which it has moved.

Observe again, that as, by this continuous exploration each point on the skin is put in relation with multitudinous points that lie not in one direction only but in all directions, it follows that when an object of some size is placed on the skin, the impressions from all parts of the area covered being simultaneously presented to consciousness, occupy coexistent positions before consciousness: whence results an idea of the superficial extension of that part of the body. The idea of this extension is really nothing more than a simultaneous presentation of all the impressions proceeding from the various points it includes, which

have previously had their several relative positions measured
by means of the series of impressions separating them. Any
one who hesitates respecting this conclusion, will, I think,
adopt it, on critically considering the perception he has
when placing a book against his cheek—on observing that
the perception is made up of many elements which he
cannot think of all together—on observing that there is
always one part of the whole surface touched, of which he
is more distinctly conscious than of any other part—and on
observing that to become fully conscious of any other part,
he has to traverse in thought the intervening parts; that is,
he has to think of the relative positions of these parts by
vaguely recalling the series of states of consciousness which
a motion over the skin from one to the other would involve.

It is needless now to dwell on that development of these
fundamental ideas which results when the visual experiences
are united with the tactual and muscular experiences. Being
merely a further complication of the same process, it may
readily be traced out by joining with the above explanations,
those given when treating of visible extension and space.
Here I need only add that, by serving clearly to establish
in our minds the identity of subjective and objective motion, sight enables us to dissociate Motion almost entirely
from those muscular sensations through which it is primarily
known to us; and that by doing this, and by so reducing our
idea of Motion to that of coexistent positions in Space occupied in successive positions in Time, it produces the apparently necessary connexion between these three ideas.

§ 346. We conclude, then, that the consciousness of
Motion, originally present under the form of a series of
muscular sensations, serves by its union with tactual experiences to disclose Time and Space to us; and that, in the
act of disclosing them, it becomes clothed with the ideas of
them, and ultimately becomes inconceivable without these
ideas.

It remains to say that the perception of Motion, as we know it, consists in the establishment in consciousness of a relation of simultaneity between two relations—a relation of coexistent positions in Space, and a relation of sequent positions in Time (with which, however, there necessarily goes the consciousness of a something that occupies these positions successively). And in the act of perception, these jointly-presented relations are severally assimilated to the like relations before known. Thus the perception of great velocity is possible only by simultaneously thinking of two coexistent positions as *remote*, and two sequent positions as *near:* which words remote and near, imply the classing of the two relations with previously-experienced ones. And similarly with perceptions of the kind of motion, and the direction of motion.

CHAPTER XVII.

THE PERCEPTION OF RESISTANCE.

§ 347. We may conclude, *à priori*, that of the various impressions received by consciousness, there must be some most general impression. The building up of our experiences into a complex structure, implies a fundamental experience on which the structure may rest. By successive decompositions of our knowledge into simpler and simpler components, we must come at last to the simplest—to the ultimate material—to the substratum. What is this substratum? It is the impression of resistance. This is the primordial, the universal, the ever-present constituent of consciousness.

It is primordial in the sense that it is an impression of which the lowest orders of creatures show themselves susceptible, and in the sense that it is the first species of impression received by the highest creatures: it is appreciated by the nerveless tissue of the zoophyte, and is presented in a vague manner even to the nascent consciousness of the unborn child.

It is universal, both as being cognizable (using that word not in the human but in a wider sense) by every creature possessing any sensitiveness, and usually as being cognizable by all parts of the body of each—both as being common to all sensitive organisms, and mostly as being common in greater or less degrees to their entire surfaces.

It is ever present, inasmuch as every creature, or at any rate every terrestrial creature, is subject to it during the whole of its existence. Excluding those lowest animals which make no visible response to external stimuli, and those which float passively suspended in the water, there are none but what have, at every moment of their lives, some impressions of resistance; proceeding either from the surfaces on which they rest, or from the reactions of their members during locomotion, or from both.

Thus, impressions of resistance as being the earliest that are appreciated by the sensitive creation regarded as a progressive whole, as well as by every higher animal in the course of its evolution; and as being more or less appreciated by all parts of the body in the great majority of animals; are necessarily the first materials put together in the genesis of intelligence. And as being the impressions continuously present in one form or other throughout life, they necessarily constitute that thread of consciousness on which all other impressions are strung—form, as it were, the weft of that tissue of thought which we are ever weaving.

But leaving general statements, let us go on to consider these truths somewhat in detail.

§ 348. That our perception of Body has for its ultimate elements impressions of resistance, is a conclusion to which all the foregoing analyses point. In the order of thought (and of any other order we can know nothing) resistance is the primary attribute of body; and extension is a secondary attribute. Here is the evidence.

We know extension only through a combination of resistances. We know resistance immediately by itself; for though to a developed intelligence the consciousness of position is given along with the consciousness of resistance, it is clear that were the consciousness of position absent this would not involve the absence of the consciousness of resistance. Again, a thing

58

cannot be thought of as occupying space, except as offering resistance. Even though but a point, if it be conceived to offer absolutely *no* resistance, it ceases to be anything—becomes *no*-thing. Resistance is that by which occupied extension (body) and empty extension (space) are differentiated. And the primary property of body, considered as a different thing from not-body, must be that by which it is universally distinguished from not-body: namely, resistance.   Moreover, it is by resistance we determine whether any appearance is body or not. Resistance without appearance we decide to be body; as when striking against any object in the dark. Appearance without resistance we decide not to be body; as in the case of optical illusions.   Once more there is a thing which we know to be body *only* by its resistance; namely, air. We should be ignorant that there is such a thing as air, were it not for its resistance; and we endow it with extension by an act of inference. So that, not only is body primarily known as resistant, and subsequently, through a combination of resistances, is known as occupying space; but the kind of body we call gaseous presents to our senses no other attribute than that of resistance.

That our cognition of Space can arise only through an interpretation of resistances, is a corollary from preceding chapters. The ultimate element into which our notion of Space is resolvable, was shown to be the relation between two coexistent positions. And that such two coexistent positions may be presented to consciousness, it is necessary that they should be occupied by things capable of impressing us; that is—by resistant things. Space in itself, having no sensible properties, would be for ever unknowable to us did it not contain objects. Even Kantists do not contend that it is knowable by itself; but say that our experiences of things are the *occasions* of its disclosure to us. And as all our experiences of things are ultimately resolvable into either resistances or the signs of resistances, it follows that on any hypothesis, Space is cognizable only through experience of resistances.

Similarly with Motion. As was shown in the last chapter, subjective motion is primarily known as a varying series of states of muscular tension, that is—sensations of resistance. The series of tactual sensations through which it is also known when one part of the body is drawn over another, are sensations produced by something that resists. And the objective motion recognized by sight, is fully understood only when it is recognized as equivalent to the subjective motion known through the muscular and visual sensations conjoined; as when we move our own limbs within view of the eyes. So that the developed consciousness of motion grows out of a consciousness of a certain order of resistances.

Our notion of Force, also, has a parallel genesis. Resistance, as known subjectively in our sensations of muscular tension, forms the substance of our consciousness of force. That we have such a consciousness, is a fact which no metaphysical quibbling can set aside. That we must think of force in terms of our experience—must construct our conception of it out of the sensations we have received, is also beyond question. That we have never had, and never can have, any experience of the force by which objects produce changes in other objects, is equally indisputable. And that, therefore, our notion of force is a generalization of those muscular sensations which we have when we are ourselves the producers of changes in outward things, is an unavoidable corollary.   How force as so conceived is afterwards inevitably ascribed to all external workers of change, is easy to see. Every one experiences the same sensible effects when body strikes against him, as when he strikes against body. Hence he is obliged to represent to himself the actions of body upon him as like his action upon it. And the sensible antecedent of his action upon body being the feeling of muscular tension, he cannot conceive its action upon himself as of like nature, without vaguely thinking of this muscular tension, that is, of force, as the antecedent of its action.

Thus, Matter, Space, Motion, Force—all our fundamental ideas, arise by generalization and abstraction from our experiences of resistance. Nor shall we see in this anything strange if we contemplate, under its simplest aspect, the relation between the organism and its environment. Here is a subject placed in the midst of objects. It can learn nothing of them without being affected by them. Being affected by them implies their action upon its surface. Their action must be either action by direct contact, or action through some intermediate agency. In virtue of the law of gravitation, their primary and continuous action is by direct contact. In the nature of things, also, their all-important actions, both destructive and preservative— through enemies and through food—are by direct contact. Hence, action by direct contact being the primary action, the unceasing action, the all-important action, as well as the simplest and most definite action, becomes the kind of action which all other kinds of action represent. And the sensation of resistance through which this fundamental action is known, becomes the mother-tongue of thought; in which all the first cognitions are registered, and into which all symbols afterwards learnt are interpretable.

§ 349. The matter will be further elucidated, and this last position especially confirmed, on observing that all the sensations through which the external world becomes known are explicable by us only as resulting from certain forms of force as thus conceived.

As already shown (§ 318), the so-called secondary attributes of body are dynamical. Science determines them to be the manifestations of certain energies possessed by matter; and even before scientific analysis they are seen to imply the actions of things upon us. But we cannot think of the actions of things upon us, except by ascribing to them powers or forces. These powers or forces must be presented to our minds in terms of our experiences. And, as above shown, our only experience of force is the feeling of muscular tension which we have when overcoming force: this constitutes our consciousness of force, and our measure of force. Hence, besides the fact that our experiences of resistance form the original materials of thought; and besides the fact that our other experiences are employed by us as the representatives of these original experiences; there is the fact that we cannot understand these other experiences except by translating them into terms derived from our original experiences.

A concomitant truth of much significance is that resistance, as disclosed by opposition to our own energies, is the only species of external activity which we are obliged to think of as subjectively and objectively the same. *We are disabled from conceiving mechanical force in itself under a form different from mechanical force as ordinarily presented to consciousness* The axiom—" Action and reaction are equal, and opposite," applied as it is not only to the actions of objects on one another, but to our actions on them and their actions on us, implies a conception of the two forces as equivalent, both in quantity and nature; seeing that we cannot conceive a relation of equality between magnitudes that are not connatural. How happens it that in this case alone we are compelled to think of the force outside of us as like the force we feel? Sound we can very well conceive as consisting in itself of vibrations, having no likeness whatever to the sensation they produce. The impressions we have of colour can, without much difficulty, be understood as purely subjective effects resulting from an objective activity to which they have not even a distant analogy. And similarly with heat, smell, and taste. Why, then, can we not represent to ourselves the force with which a body resists an effort to move it, as a something quite unlike the feeling of muscular tension which constitutes the effort? There are all-sufficient reasons, of which we will first look at the accessory ones.   Whether we strike or are struck, the sound, the indentation, the sensations of touch, pressure, and pain, are of the same kinds; and this furthers the conception of identity in their causes. We can make the force which is known to our consciousness as muscular tension, produce an effect like that produced by an external body—as when, taking one of the weights out of a pair of scales in equilibrium, we raise the antagonist weight by pressing down the empty scale with the hand: an experience which suggests equivalence between our effort and the pull of gravity. We can store up our own force in objects, and make them afterwards expend it in producing results such as it would have directly produced— as when we strain a bow and let its recoil propel the arrow: an experiment having a suggestiveness greater even than that of the last.   These, however, as above implied, are but secondary causes. Let us pass to the primary cause.   This is *that there exists no alternative mode of representing this force to consciousness*—no other experience, or combination of experiences, by which we can figure it to our minds. The liberty we have to think of light, heat, sound, &c., as in themselves different from our sensations of them, is due to our possession of other sensations by which to symbolize them—namely, those of mechanical force; and it needs but to glance at any theory of light, heat, sound, &c., to see that we *do* think of them in terms of mechanical force, that is, in terms of our muscular sensations. But if we attempt to think of mechanical force itself as different from our impression of it, there arises the insurmountable difficulty that there is no remaining species of impression to represent it. All other experiences having been expressed to the mind in terms of this experience, this experience cannot be expressed to the mind in any terms but its own. To be conceived, mechanical force must

be represented in some state of consciousness. This state
of consciousness must be one directly or indirectly resulting
from the actions of things on us or our actions on them.
The states of consciousness produced by all other actions
than mechanical action, we already represent to our minds
in states such as those produced by mechanical action.
There remains, therefore, no available state of consciousness
save that produced by mechanical action. Hence it is impossible for us to represent mechanical action to ourselves
in any other state of consciousness than that which it produces in us. Though the proposition that objective force
differs in nature from force as we know it subjectively, is
verbally intelligible; and though the supposition that the
two are alike commits us to absurdities that cannot be entertained; yet to frame a conception of force in the *non-ego*
different from the conception we have of force in the *ego*
is utterly beyond our power.

§ 350. Having thus seen that the perception of resistance
is fundamental, alike in respect of genesis, in respect of
universality, and in respect of continuity; and that consequently it is also fundamental as being the perception into
which all other perceptions are interpretable, while itself
interpretable into none; we may proceed to consider it
analytically.

As shown when treating of the statico-dynamical attributes of body, the sensations concerned in our various
perceptions of resistance are those of touch proper, pressure, and muscular tension. The sensation of touch proper
does not in itself give an immediate knowledge of resistance; but is simply the sign of something capable of resisting. When the contact is so gentle as to produce no
feeling of pressure, it cannot be said whether the object is
soft or hard, large or small. It is *inferred* that there is
something: just as it would have been had a sensation of
sound or colour been received. Hence the sensation of
touch proper may be left out of the inquiry.

Knowledge of resistance, then, is gained through the sensations of pressure and muscular tension. These may occur separately. When I am wholly inactive, I have the sensation of pressure only—either from the reaction of the surface on which I rest, or from the action of a weight placed on some part of my body, or from both. When I bring my forces to bear on outward objects—when my body is active and objects are reactive—I have coexistent sensations of pressure and muscular tension. And when, as on raising my arm into a horizontal position, the bodily action is such as to call forth no direct reaction from objects, I experience the sensation of muscular tension alone. Here the fact to be more particularly noticed, is, that whenever the sensations of pressure and muscular tension coexist, they vary together. Now that I am holding my pen gently between the fore-finger and thumb, I have a slight sensation of pressure and a slight sensation of muscular tension. If I grasp the pen hard, both increase in intensity; and I find that I cannot change one without changing the other. The like relation is observable on raising light and heavy weights; or on thrusting against small and large objects. Hence these sensations become known as equivalents. A given feeling of pressure is thinkable as tantamount to a certain feeling of muscular tension; and *vice versâ*. And now there arises the inquiry—Which of these two is habitually used in thought as the sign and which as the thing signified?

In point of time the two are co-ordinate. From the very first, a developing creature experiences the reaction upon consciousness accompanying the action of its muscles. From the very first it has sensations of pressure from the surfaces on which it rests, and from the things laid hold of. But equally early though they are, it may be readily proved that in the order of constructive thought the sensation of muscular tension is primary and that of pressure secondary.   This will be made tolerably manifest by the simple consideration, that sensations of pressure caused by the weight of the body and by incident agencies, can at first give no notions of what we understand as resistance or force; seeing that before they can give such notions there must exist ideas of weight and of objective action. Originally the sensations of pressure which a developing creature passively receives, being unconnected in experience with definite antecedents and consequents, are as isolated and meaningless as sensations of sound or odour. Not to dwell upon this fact, however, further than to point out that the *involuntarily-produced* sensations of pressure may be left out of the question, let us, in the first place, observe that the *voluntarily-produced* sensations of pressure are second in order of time to the sensations of muscular tension. Before the creature can experience the feelings which neighbouring objects give to its moving limbs, it must experience the feelings which accompany motions of its limbs. In the second place we have to note that the muscular sensations are more general than the voluntarily-produced sensations of pressure; for the voluntarily-produced sensations of pressure occur only when the energies are employed upon external bodies, while the muscular sensations occur *both* when the energies are thus employed, and when they are employed in moving and holding up the limbs themselves. Further we have to remember that while only *some* of the sensations of pressure are voluntarily produced, *all* the sensations of muscular tension are voluntarily produced. And yet again there is the fact that when both are voluntarily produced—as when some object is grasped, or lifted, or thrust against—the muscular sensation is always present to consciousness as the antecedent while the sensation of pressure is the consequent; and that any variation in the last is known as following a variation in the first. Among the intelligible experiences of a developing creature, therefore, the sensation of muscular tension, being alike the earliest, the most general, and that which immediately precedes the sensation of pressure when-ever the origin of that sensation is known, becomes the sensation in which all experiences of resistance are registered. Hence the reason why, when anything pushes against us, we do not think of its force in terms of the pressure experienced, but in terms of the effort which that pressure signifies. Hence the fact that when calling to mind the weight of an object, we do not call to mind the intensity of the tactual impression which results on lifting it, but the intensity of the accompanying muscular strain.

That the consciousness of muscular tension forms the raw material of primitive thought, will be most clearly seen on considering that at first it is the only available measure of external phenomena. The acquisition of knowledge is from the beginning experimental. Were a creature to remain passive in the midst of surrounding objects, it could never arrive at a comprehension of them. It can arrive at a com-prehension of them, only by active exploration. But what is the condition under which alone such an exploration will answer its end? How can the properties of things be com-pared, and estimated, and classified? By means of some *common measure* already possessed. The creature's only mode of determining the amounts of external activities, is by ascertaining how much of its own activity they are severally equivalent to. As inanimate objects cannot act on it in such way as to disclose their properties, it must call out their reactions by acting on them; and to become cog-nizant of their reactions implies some scale of action in itself. Thus, then, the sense of muscular tension, of which this scale is constituted, necessarily becomes the primitive element in our intelligence.

§ 351. Respecting the perception of resistance, that is of muscular tension, it has still to be pointed out that it con-sists in the establishment of a relation between the muscular sensation itself and that state of consciousness which we call *will*—a relation such that the unbalanced surplus of feeling of whatever kind, which for the moment constitutes the will, is the antecedent of the muscular sensation, and coexists with it while it lasts. That the muscular sensation alone does not constitute a perception of resistance, will be seen on remembering that we receive from a tired muscle, a feeling nearly allied to, if not identical with, that which we receive from a muscle in action; and that yet this feeling, being unconnected with any act of volition, does not give any notion of resistance.

To which there is only to add that in the act of perception this relation is classed with the like before-known relations; and that in so classing it consists the knowledge of the special muscular combination, adjustment, and degree of force exercised.

CHAPTER XVIII.

§ 352. As foregoing chapters have made sufficiently manifest, the term Perception is applied to mental states infinitely varied, and even widely different in their natures. Between the consciousness of a vast landscape and the consciousness of a minute dot on the surface of this paper, there exist countless gradations which pass insensibly one into another; and which yet unite extremes almost too strongly contrasted to be classed together. A perception may vary indefinitely in complexity, in degree of directness, and in degree of continuity. We will glance at its variations under these heads.

In one of the primitive cognitions of resistance lately treated of, perception may rise but a step above simple sensation. Conversely, when watching the evolutions of a ballet, there is a consciousness not only of the multiplied relations of coexistent positions which constitute our notions of the distance, size, figure, and attitude of each dancer—not only of the various space-relations between the figure of each dancer and the several colours of her dress—not only of the relations of distribution among the dancers; but also of the many relations of sequence which the body and limbs of every dancer exhibit in their movements with respect to one another, and of those yet more involved relations of sequence exhibited in the movements of every dancer

244

with respect to the rest.   In degree of directness, again, there is a similarly-marked contrast between the perception that some surface touched by the finger is hard, and the perception that a building at which we are looking is a particular cathedral. The one piece of knowledge is almost immediate. The other is mediate in a double, a triple, a quadruple, and even in a still higher degree. It is mediate inasmuch as the solidity of that which causes the visual impression is inferential; mediate inasmuch as its position, its size, its shape, are inferential; mediate inasmuch as its material, its hollowness, are inferential; mediate inasmuch as its ecclesiastical purpose is an inference from these inferences; and mediate inasmuch as the identification of it as a particular cathedral, is a still more remote inference resulting from the union of these inferences with those many others through which the locality is recognized.   In like antithesis stand the degrees of continuity in our respective perceptions, now of an electric spark, now of a waterfall we are watching. And when we add the fact that our perceptions, or at any rate our visual perceptions, are continuous in Space as well as in Time— that when looking at a landscape and turning our eyes to different parts of it, we cannot say how many perceptions take in the panorama or where each perception ends; it will be abundantly-manifest that the state of consciousness which we call a perception is scarcely ever discontinuous with its like.

Thus a perception merges insensibly into others of its own kind, both synchronous and successive; and into others which we class as of different kinds, both superior and inferior. It passes at the one extreme into reasoning and at the other borders upon sensation. It may include innumerable relations simultaneously co-ordinated, or but a single relation. It cannot be demarcated from the nascent perceptions that coexist with it, nor (where the thing perceived is in motion) from the perceptions which follow it.

So that, however convenient a term Perception may be for common purposes, it must not be understood as signifying any truly scientific division.

§ 353. The only valid distinction to be drawn is that between Perception and Sensation. Though from time to time referred to with more or less distinctness by early philosophers, it is only in later times that this distinction has been currently acknowledged; and it is but recently that the relation between the two has been specifically formulated in the doctrine of Sir William Hamilton, " that, above a certain point, the stronger the Sensation, the weaker the Perception; and the distincter the perception the less obtrusive the sensation; in other words—though Perception proper and Sensation proper exist only as they coexist, in the degree or intensity of their existence they are always found in an inverse ratio to each other." Before criticizing this doctrine, which seems to me rather an adumbration of the truth than the truth itself, it will be needful to state the exact meanings of Sensation proper and Perception proper.

Manifestly every sensation, to be known as such, must be perceived; and hence, as thus considered, all sensations are perceptions. A mere physical affection of the organism does not constitute a sensation proper. While absorbed in thought I may be subject to undue heat from the fire, uncomfortable pressure from a hard seat, or a continual noise from the street; and though my sentient organs are very decidedly affected, I may yet remain unconscious of the affections—may become conscious of them only when they pass a certain degree of intensity; and only then can I be said to experience them as sensations.   Nor is this all. In Sensation proper, at least if it is a sensation of touch or heat or pain, I not only contemplate the affection as an affection of myself—as a state through which my consciousness is passing or has passed; but I also contemplate it as existing in a certain part of my body—as stand-

ing in certain relations of position. I perceive *where* it
is.   But though under both these aspects Sensation must be regarded as one species of Perception, it will
readily be seen to differ widely from Perception proper—
from the cognition of an external object. In the one case,
that which occupies consciousness is something contemplated as belonging to the *ego;* while in the other, it is
something contemplated as belonging to the *non-ego.* And
these it is which, as Sensation proper and Perception proper,
are asserted to coexist in degrees of intensity that vary inversely.

That this is not altogether a correct assertion, will, I
think, become apparent on carefully examining the facts as
determined by experiment. Let the finger be brought
against some hard rough body—say the jagged surface of
a broken stone, the back of a ribbed sea-shell, or anything
capable of giving a tactual impression of some complexity.
Between the pressure used in ordinary touch and the pressure which is painful from its intensity, there are many
gradations; and Sir William Hamilton's doctrine implies
that, beginning with the pressure needful for distinct perception, and increasing it until the pain becomes unbearable, the perception gradually decreases in vividness while
the sensation gradually increases in vividness; but that
neither at the beginning nor the end does the one exclude
the other. Do the facts correspond with this statement?
We shall find that they do not.   During the
ordinary gentle pressure, consciousness is occupied entirely
about the surface and its irregularities. No thought is
taken of the sensations through which the surface and its
irregularities are known. To attend to these sensations
rather than to the objective phenomenon implied by them,
requires a decided effort; and when they are thought of, it
is in a state of consciousness quite distinct from the previous
one. If the pressure be slowly increased, there is not a
slow decrease in the vividness of the perception and a slow

increase in the vividness of the sensation; but the consciousness remains, as before, occupied about the surface:
the hardness and roughness of which become the peculiarities most contemplated as the pressure becomes greater.
Though the sensation may now be more easily thought of
than before, and rises into greater distinctness when it is
thought of, it can still be thought of only in a second state of
consciousness not included in the original one. But observe
what happens on pushing the experiment further. If the
pressure be increased so far as to produce decided pain,
there results quite a different state of consciousness, in
which the thing contemplated is the subjective affection
and not its objective cause. When the pain reaches any
considerable intensity, it will be found that the perception
has not only altogether ceased, but that it can be recalled
into consciousness only by an effort. And it will also become manifest that were the nature of the object producing
the painful pressure not already known, it would be unknowable.   Generalizing the facts, then, it would
seem, not that Sensation and Perception vary inversely,
but that they exclude each other with degrees of stringency
which vary inversely. When the sensations (considered
simply as physical changes in the organism) are weak, the
objective phenomenon signified by them is alone contemplated. The sensations, if not absolutely excluded from
consciousness, pass through it so rapidly as not to form
appreciable elements in it; and cannot be detained in it, or
arrested for inspection, without a decided effort. When the
sensations are rendered somewhat more intense, the perception continues equally-vivid—still remains the sole occupant
of consciousness; but it requires less effort than before to
make them the subjects of thought. If the intensity of the
sensations is gradually increased, a point is presently
reached at which consciousness is as likely to be occupied
by them as by the external thing they imply—a point at
which either can be thought of with equal facility, while

each tends in the greatest degree to draw attention from the other. When further intensified, the sensations begin to occupy consciousness to the exclusion of the perception; which, however, can still be brought into consciousness by a slight effort. But finally, if the sensations rise to extreme intensity, consciousness becomes so absorbed in them, that only by great effort, if at all, can the thing causing them be thought about.*

* Those who test this statement experimentally, should remember that the mere act of observing the *current* phenomena of consciousness, introduces a new element into consciousness, which tends to disturb the processes going on. The observations should be oblique rather than direct —should be made, not *during*, but *immediately after*, the appropriate experiences.

Since the foregoing passages were written in 1855, some interesting verifications have presented themselves—two of them quite recently. In *Nature* for August 18, 1870, Mr. R. B. Hayward, giving an account of a defective appreciation of colour under which he labours, remarks that his eyes differ in respect to their degrees of defectiveness, and that the eye which is the least appreciative of colours is the most appreciative of forms. In a subsequent number of the same periodical (Sept. 1, 1870), Mr. L. Marshall gives like testimony. Until I met with these facts, I had supposed that the increased vividness of colouring which becomes apparent in a landscape when it is looked at with the eyes inverted, results from a change in the distribution of the colours falling upon the retina—a change such that each part receives a kind of light to which it is unaccustomed, and is therefore more sensitive. That this cannot be the chief cause, however, becomes manifest on observing that this brightening of the colours occurs in parts of the landscape which, casting their images upon the middle portion of the retina, affect the same elements of it in both positions of the eye, and also on observing that nearly if not quite as great an effect results when instead of inverting the eyes the head is so placed as to bring them into a vertical line. The true interpretation, to which the testimonies I have just cited pointed, lies in this antagonism between Sensation and Perception. When objects are looked at in the ordinary way, consciousness is chiefly occupied in interpreting the impressions made on the retina—is filled with the associated ideas which constitute knowledge of the objects seen as such or such; and so long as they are thus looked at it is impossible to prevent acts of recognition from taking place and absorbing a share of the attention. But when the eyes are inverted, or otherwise so placed as to throw out of gear all those relations of forms and distributions of parts through which the objects are identified, the

What now is the real nature of this mutual exclusion?
Is it not an instance of the general fact that consciousness cannot be in two equally distinct states at the same
time; and that in proportion as the predominance of one
state becomes more marked the suppression of other states
becomes more decided? I cannot know that I have a
associated ideas implied by the identifications do not readily arise, and
consciousness remains so much the more occupied by the sensations of
colour which compose the images received.

And here, indeed, we are naturally led to the physical interpretation of
this antagonism. If from the subjective effects we pass to the objective
counterparts of them, we see clearly the necessity of this inverse relation.
For when from such an object as the ribbed sea-shell above instanced,
there come to a nerve-centre moderate waves of molecular disturbance
initiated by the pressures of its projections on the finger-end, there is an
instant escape of these waves through plexuses of fibres to other centres;
where there are awakened the correlative feelings which make up the consciousness of relative position, visible form of surface, degree of hardness,
&c. These associated nervous actions are so nearly automatic that it is
impossible to arrest them. Along the well-established channels there is so
instantaneous an escape of the nerve-waves, which, if arrested, would be
the equivalents of tactual feelings, that there are no consciously-recog-
nized tactual feelings; but instead, consciousness becomes filled with all
the associated ideas of form and appearance and inferred nature—there
is perception. But now suppose that by a stronger pressure the amounts
of the afferent nerve-waves are much increased. The various channels
which draft off from the first nerve-centre reached, these larger waves of
molecular motion, plus the molecular motion disengaged by them in this
centre, becoming filled to the extent of their capacities, do not carry off
the entire discharge so swiftly; and that disturbance in the tactual centre
itself which answers to the feeling of touch, becomes a more considerable
element—it becomes easier for the feeling of touch to be kept in consciousness. And then when the pressure has been made so hard as to
cause pain, these plexuses through which ordinarily the escaping waves
awaken the appropriate associated ideas, are no longer anything like adequate to draft off all the force brought to, and disengaged in, the tactual
centre. The surplus that cannot be drafted off becomes so great, and the
correlative feeling so intense, that the associated elements of consciousness become obscured—sensation now predominates and perception disappears. On referring to the "Special Synthesis," and more especially to
§ 211, the reader will find that this explanation harmonizes with the one
there given of the relation between conscious and unconscious nervous
action, and is verified by it.

sensation, without, for the moment, having my attention specially occupied with that sensation. I cannot know the external thing causing it, without, for the moment, having my attention specially occupied with that external thing. As either cognition rises, the other ceases. If, as Sir William Hamilton asserts, the two cognitions always co-exist, though in inverse intensities, then if, beginning at either extreme, the conditions be slowly changed, so that while the cognition most distinctly present to the mind becomes gradually less distinct, the other becomes gradually more distinct; there must arrive a time when they will be equally distinct—when the subjective and objective phenomena will be thought of together with equal clearness; which is impossible. It is true that under such change of conditions there comes a time when the subjective and objective phenomena attract attention in equal degrees, and are thought of *alternately* with equal facility. And it may even be admitted that while either is being thought of, the other is nascent in thought. But saying this is not saying that they occupy consciousness together.

§ 354. Perception proper and Sensation proper, will however be best understood, and the purpose of the present chapter most furthered, by considering their antagonism under the light of preceding analyses.

In all cases we have found that Perception is an establishment of specific relations among states of consciousness; and is thus distinguished from the establishment of these states of consciousness themselves. When apprehending a sensation the mind is occupied with a single subjective affection, which it classes as such or such; but when apprehending the external something producing it, the mind is occupied with the relations between that affection and others, either past or present, which it classes with like relations. The sensation is known as an undecomposable state of consciousness.

The outward object is known through a decomposable state of consciousness; and is identified in virtue of the manner in which the component states are united. Now the contemplation of a special state of consciousness, and the contemplation of the special relations among states of consciousness, are quite different mental acts—acts which may be performed in immediate succession, but not together. To know a relation is not simply to know the terms between which it subsists. Though when the relation is perceived the terms are nascently perceived, and conversely, yet introspection will show that there is a distinct transition in thought from the terms to the relation, and from the relation to the terms. While my consciousness is occupied with either term of a relation, I am distinguishing it as such or such—assimilating it to its like in past experience; but while my consciousness is occupied with a relation, that which I discriminate and class is the effect produced in me by transition from the one term to the other. That the whole matter centres in the question—How do we think of a relation as distinguished from the terms between which it subsists? will be plain from the fact that Sir William Hamilton, while implying that it is something more, himself says that in one respect, "perception proper is an apprehension of the relations of sensations to each other." Joining which doctrine with the one here contended against, we see that, according to his hypothesis, the sensations and the relations between them can be simultaneously thought of with equal degrees of distinctness, or with any other relative degrees of distinctness—a manifestly-untenable proposition.

The only further remark called for is, that Perception cannot be correctly defined as "an apprehension of the relations of *sensations* to each other"; since in nearly all perceptions many of the elements are not presented but represented. When passing the finger over a rough surface, the perception contains very much more than the co-ordinated sensations immediately experienced. Along with these there go the remembered visual impressions produced by such a surface, which cannot be kept out of the mind, and in the suggestion of which the perception largely consists; and there are automatic inferences respecting the texture and density of the substance. Again, when gazing at some one object, it will be found that objects on the outskirts of the field of view are recognized more by representation than by presentation. If, without moving his eyes, the observer will consider what is contained in his direct consciousness of these outlying objects, he will find that they impress him simply as ill-defined patches of colour; that were it not for his previous experiences he would not know the meanings of these patches; and that in perceiving what the objects are, he ekes out the vaguely-presented impressions with some comparatively-distinct represented ones. What thus manifestly happens with perceptions of this order, happens in one form or other with all perceptions. In fact, when analyzed to the bottom, all perceptions prove to be acquired perceptions. From its simplest to its most complex forms, Perception is essentially a diagnosis.

§ 355. To express most generally the truth that has been variously illustrated in detail—Perception is a discerning of the relation or relations between states of consciousness, partly presentative and partly representative; which states of consciousness must be themselves known to the extent involved in the knowledge of their relations.

Under its simplest form (a form, however, of which the adult mind has few, if any, examples) Perception is the consciousness of a single relation. More commonly, a number of relations are simultaneously presented and represented; and the relations among these relations are cognized. Most frequently, the relations of relations of relations are the objects of perception; as when any neighbouring solid body is regarded.　And very often—as when observing the motions of an animal, which are known to us as the relations between certain highly-complex relations of position now present and certain others just past—a still more involved relativity is contemplated.

Further, it is to be noticed that in the ascending grades of Perception there is an increase not only in the number and complexity of the relations grasped together, but also in the variety of their kinds.　Numerous relations of position, of extension, of coexistence, of sequence, of degrees in all sensible qualities, are co-ordinated in one thought; or what appears to us such.

Add to which that, as heretofore pointed out in each special case, the act of perception is the establishment of a relation of likeness between the particular relation or group of relations contemplated, and some past relations or groups of relations—the assimilation of it to such past relations or groups of relations—the classing of it with them.

§ 356.　It now remains only to apply the analysis thus far pursued to the relations themselves.　By successive decompositions we have found that our intellectual operations are severally performed by establishing relations, and groups of relations, among those undecomposable states of consciousness directly produced in us by our own actions and the actions of surrounding things.　But what are these relations?　They can be nothing more than certain secondary states of consciousness, arising through connexions of the primary states.　Unable as we are to transcend consciousness, we can know a relation only as some modification of consciousness.　The original modifications of consciousness are the feelings aroused in us by subjective and objective activities; and any further modifications of consciousness must be such as result from combinations of these original ones.　In all their various kinds and compounds, what we call relations can be to us nothing more than the modes in which we are affected by bringing together sensations, or remembered sensations, or both. Hence what we have next to do is, first to resolve the special kinds of relations into more general kinds, ending with the primordial kinds; and then to ascertain what are the ultimate phenomena of consciousness which these primordial kinds express.

CHAPTER XIX.

§ 357. Of all relations the most complex is that of Similarity—that in virtue of which we range together objects of the same species, notwithstanding their differences of magnitude, and in virtue of which we group under the same head, phenomena of causation that are widely contrasted in degree. Already, in treating of Reasoning and of Classification, much has been said of this relation which forms their common basis. Here it needs only to state what it is when considered under its most general aspect.

The similarity which we predicate of natural objects belonging to the same species, is made up of many component similarities. Two horses unlike in size, are similar not only as wholes, but are also similar in their parts. The head of one is similar to the head of the other; the leg to the leg; the hoof to the hoof; the eye to the eye. Even the parts of the parts will be found more or less similar; as, on comparing two corresponding teeth, the crown to the crown, and the fangs to the fangs. Nay, such minute components as the hairs show in their structures this same parallelism. One of these ordinary similarities, therefore, consisting of an intricate plexus of similarities held together in similar ways, and resolvable as it consequently is into simple similarities, will, by implication, be analyzed in analyzing one of these simple similarities.

Though similarities of sequences do not admit of a complication parallel to that which similarities of coexistences admit of, yet they admit of another species of complication; namely, that arising from composition of causes and composition of effects. There are similarities of simple sequences and similarities of complex sequences. By the gravitation of a weight, the string to which the weight hangs may be elongated, and there may be no other appreciable results; while by the joint action of a certain temperature, a certain amount of moisture, and a certain miasm, upon an individual of a particular diathesis, who happens to be in a particular state, there may be produced the immense complication of effects constituting a disease. Each of these sequences is classed with others which we call similar; and in conjunction with them may form a premiss for future conclusions. And though, in the first case, we have a single antecedent and a single consequent, while, in the second case, we have a group of antecedents and a group of consequents—though in this second case the antecedent is not a force but a variety of forces united in a special plexus of relations, and the consequent is not an effect but a variety of effects united in a special plexus of relations; yet, we so obviously think of a composite cause and a composite effect, as related in the same way that a simple cause and a simple effect are related, that in treating of similar sequences we may confine our attention to the simple ones, as those out of which the others arise by complication of the terms.

Thus, then, choosing some primitive type of each, we have to consider what there is in common between similar coexistences and similar sequences.

§ 358. Of the one class, similar triangles furnish the most convenient example; and as an example of the other, we may take the uniform sequence of heat upon compression.

It is needless to do more than remind the reader, that in both of these cases the similarity resolves itself into either equality of relations or likeness of relations—that triangles are similar when any two sides of the one bear to each other a relation equal to that which the homologous sides of the other bear to each other; and that when classing as similar the various cases in which compression produces heat, the likeness of the relations between compression and heat in those various cases, is the sole thing meant. Here it concerns us, not to dwell upon the fact that Similarity is likeness of relations, but to consider what this likeness of relations implies.

In the first place, we have to note that while it implies likeness in nature between the two antecedents and between the two consequents, it does not imply likeness in their amounts; but that, in nearly all cases, though not necessarily, the two antecedents are quantitatively unlike and the two consequents are quantitatively unlike. Two triangles may be similar, though any side of the one is a score times as great as the homologous side of the other; and though to-day a small disengagement of heat results from the pressure of a hundred pounds, while to-morrow a great disengagement results from the pressure of a hundred tons, the cases are classed as similar. So that thus regarded, similarity may be described as the likeness of relations whose antecedents are like in kind but mostly unlike in degree, and whose consequents are like in kind but mostly unlike in degree.

This likeness of relations has itself two phases. It may be both qualitative and quantitative; or it may be only qualitative. It may be a likeness of the relations both in kind and in degree; or it may be a likeness in kind only. Hence arise the two orders of Similarity—perfect and imperfect: the similarity on which mathematical reasoning proceeds and the similarity on which the reasoning of daily life proceeds. Thus, in the case of the triangles, the intuition of similarity implies, first, that the relations between extensions presented in the one, are compared in thought with the like kinds of relations presented in the other. There can be no idea of similarity if a relation of coexistence between two sides of one triangle, is brought before consciousness along with some relation of extension between two sides of the other. Evidently, therefore, the primary element in the intuition of perfect similarity is—likeness of nature between relations. And then, joined to this, is the secondary element—likeness of degree between these connatural relations. The relations must be of the same order; and each antecedent must bear to its consequent a contrast of the same strength. In imperfect similarity, however, the only specific implication is—likeness of nature in the relations. When, in any new case, we think of heat as caused by compression, the implied similarity between such new case and previous cases, is simply a consciousness of connatural relations, of which the two antecedents are connatural and the two consequents are connatural. Nothing is said of degree. The new relation between compression and heat is simply thought of as a sequence like in kind to certain before-known sequences; and though there may be a vague idea of the quantity of heat as varying with the quantity of compression, this is not included in the predication.

Hence, while imperfect similarity involves the connature of relations whose antecedents are connatural and whose consequents are connatural; perfect similarity involves also the cointension of such connatural relations.

§ 359. Speaking most generally, then, the consciousness of Similarity arises when two successive states of consciousness are severally composed of like states of consciousness arranged in like ways. And when complete it is a consciousness of the cointension of two connatural relations between states of consciousness, which are respectively like in kind but commonly unlike in degree. This being the consciousness of a single similarity, it results that when, as in ordinary cases, the similarity consists of many component similarities, each of the compared states of consciousness contains many relations which are severally connatural and cointense with the corresponding relations in the other.

Concerning Dissimilarity it needs only to be said that (neglecting all those ordinary misapplications of the word in which it is used to describe any kind of unlikeness, and confining our attention to dissimilarity proper) it is a consciousness of the non-cointension of two connatural relations between states of consciousness which are respectively like in kind, but commonly unlike in degree.

The relations of Similarity and Dissimilarity being thus proximately decomposed into certain more general relations, the further analysis of them is involved in the analysis of these more general relations; to which let us now proceed.

CHAPTER XX.

§ 360. Keeping to the subjective point of view, and regarding every relation as some state of consciousness holding together other states of consciousness, it is first to be remarked that relations of cointension are of two kinds. The states of consciousness between which they subsist may be primary or secondary—may be simple states or the relations among simple states. Of these, the kind exemplified in the last chapter, and the kind we must here first deal with, is that subsisting between states of consciousness which are themselves relations.

§ 361. To know two states of consciousness as related implies a change in consciousness. That there may be a relation, there must be two states between which it subsists; and before there can be two states, definitely contemplated as such, there must be some change of state. On the one hand, no change in the state of consciousness can arise without involving two states standing in some relation; and on the other hand, no relation can arise until consciousness undergoes some change of state. These are two sides of the same necessary truth.

Now changes in consciousness differ widely in their kinds. The mental transition from a flash to an explosion is totally unlike that from a touch to a burn. Between an impression

produced by the colour of a rose and one produced by its
odour, there is a contrast quite different from the contrast
between the impressions of hardness and transparency which
a crystal gives. Differences of kind among the changes in
consciousness from one simple state to another, have, indeed,
two orders: each of them extensive. There are the changes
experienced when from a sensation of one class, we pass to
a sensation of a wholly-unrelated class—changes that are of
various kinds; and there are the changes experienced when
from a sensation of one class, we pass to a sensation of the
same class but of another species—changes that are also
various in their kinds; though less widely unlike than the
others.   To speak more specifically:—We have, on
the one hand, those most extreme changes which occur on
passing from a colour to touch, from a taste to a sound, from
a burn to a smell, from a sense of pressure to one of cold,
from a feeling of roughness to one of dazzling, &c. On the
other hand, we have the less extreme changes which occur
on passing from one colour to another—as red to green,
yellow to blue, pink to grey; or on passing from one taste
to another—as bitter to sour, sour to sweet, sweet to bitter;
or on passing from one sound to another, or from one smell
to another. This is not all. When the transitions, instead
of being from sensation to sensation are from percept to
percept, or from concept to concept, there arise other orders
of changes still more varied in their kinds.

Not only, however, do changes in consciousness differ
widely in their *kinds* but they differ widely in their *degrees*.
The differences in their degrees are divisible into two classes
—those which arise when the successive states of consciousness are unlike in nature; and those which arise
when the successive states of consciousness are like in
nature.   Observe first these differences of degree
if the states are of unlike natures. If some loose gunpowder
is exploded, the transition from the impression of light to
that of a faint sound, is not the same as the transition from

the impression of light to that of a loud sound, which results if the powder is fired out of a pistol. Nor is the transition from the sensation of touch to that of temperature the same when grasping wood as when grasping iron. And evidently throughout all the various orders of changes above indicated, the like contrasts subsist.　　Equally multiplied and familiar are those other contrasts, subsisting between changes in consciousness that do not alter the nature of its state but only the intensity. Thus when, of two doors intervening between his ear and some continuous sound, one is suddenly opened, the change in a listener's consciousness is not so great as when both doors are suddenly opened. Nor, when contemplating in succession two allied shades of bright purple placed side by side, is the change in consciousness so great as on transferring the gaze from either of them to an adjacent shade of lilac.　　And here we have to note that those changes in consciousness which do not affect the nature of its state, are much more measurable than the others. Two alterations of intensity in the same kind of feeling, may be known as like or unlike in degree, far more completely than two transitions from one kind of feeling to another. And, indeed, it is doubtful whether these last can be considered measurable at all—whether the change from a light to a sound, being, as it were, total, must not be held as the same in degree with all other changes from light to sound : however much the relative amounts of light or sound may vary. But be this as it may, it is clear that in such cases all minor differences are dwarfed by the greatness of the contrast; and that, consequently, no accurate discriminations among the degrees of the changes can be made.

Now changes in consciousness, which we thus find to be various not only in kind but in degree, are themselves cognizable as states of consciousness: not, indeed, as simple states, but as states in which the transitions from state to state are the things contemplated. However it may seem that the change itself can be nothing additional to the states themselves, it is unquestionable that we have the power of thinking of the change itself as something more than the two states individually considered. Possibly there is a physiological reason for this. Sundry facts point to the conclusion that the change itself constitutes a fleeting state of feeling, distinguishable from the less fleeting states which it links together. Every one knows that a violent change in the sensations is accompanied by a species of shock. Even though it be expected, a bright flash of light will cause the eyes to wink; and yet light of the same brilliancy, if continuous, can be steadily looked at without difficulty. The sudden application of cold water to the skin produces a start, notwithstanding a previous determination to bear it unmoved; and yet an equally intense sensation of cold, when once established, can be borne with equanimity. Nay, extremely marked transitions among the ideas will occasionally produce analogous effects. Many will readily call to mind cases in which the sudden remembrance of something important that had been forgotten, or the reception of unexpected news, produced a sensible shock. Whence it may be inferred that as the violence of changes in the state of consciousness is a thing of degree, all such changes are accompanied by some feeling however slight.*

But whether a change in consciousness be or be not knowable as something more than the juxtaposition of a preceding and a succeeding state, it is undeniable that we can so think of changes in consciousness as to distinguish their various kinds and degrees. In whatever way I cognize the transition from a sensation of touch to one of sound, it is beyond question that I can think of it as unlike in nature to the transition from a sensation of touch to one of cold. Whether in thinking of a change I think only of the two

---

* On referring to Part II., the reader will find, in § 65, a more satisfactory exposition of this doctrine. I have preferred to let the above paragraph stand as it did in the edition of 1855: making only some omissions and verbal amendments.

successive states, or whether I think of the effect wrought in me by the contrast between them, it remains alike true that in passing from an impression of the brightest green to one of bright green, and from one of bright green to one of pale green, I am conscious of two changes which are the same in kind but different in degree. And to say that I am conscious of these changes as such or such, *is to say that they are states of my consciousness.*

And now observe the implication. Being able to think of differences in kind and degree, not only between successive sensations but also between successive changes among sensations, it results that these changes are classifiable as the original sensations are. As two sensations can be known as like or unlike in kind; so can two changes among them be known as like or unlike in kind. And as two sensations that are like in kind can be known as like or unlike in intensity; so can two changes among them that are like in kind be known as like or unlike in intensity. We can recognize changes as connatural, or the reverse; and connatural changes we can recognize as cointense, or the reverse.

As above pointed out, however, changes in consciousness are nothing else than what we call relations. There can be no phenomena of consciousness beyond its successive states and the modes of succession of its states—the states themselves and the changes from one state to another. And since what we distinguish as relations are not the primitive states themselves, they can be nothing else than the changes from state to state. The two answer in all respects. We can think neither of a change nor of a relation without thinking of the two terms forming its antecedent and consequent. As we cannot think a relation without a change in consciousness from one of its terms to the other; so we cannot think a change without establishing a relation between a preceding phenomenon and a succeeding one.

The bearing of this conclusion on the inquiry before us is

this. Relations, subjectively considered, being nothing but changes in the state of consciousness, it follows that the cointension of relations is the cointension of such changes; or, in other words—likeness in degree between changes like in kind.

§ 362. Not much need be added respecting the simpler relation of cointension: that, namely, of which the terms are not relations among states of consciousness but the primary states of consciousness themselves. This is of course definable as—likeness in degree between feelings like in kind.

Nor, respecting the relation of non-cointension is it requisite to say more than that it is unlikeness in degree between either changes like in kind or feelings like in kind.

The only further remark to be made, is one concerning the use of the words cointension and non-cointension to denote these orders of relations. All our ideas of intensity, when traced to their origin, refer to the degrees of our feelings. We speak of intense heat and cold, intense pressure, intense pleasure and pain, intense passion, intense bitterness and sourness, intense irritation: in all of which cases we speak of feelings in respect to their degrees. Hence, in comparing simple states of consciousness that are alike in kind, we observe their relative intensities. If their intensities are equal, they must be called cointense; and the equality of their intensities is cointension. As the changes in consciousness are also different in respect of their violence, and are accompanied by some species of momentary feeling, they also are comparable in respect to their intensity; whence it follows that cointension is predicable of such changes, that is of relations, when they are alike in kind and degree.

CHAPTER XXI.

THE RELATIONS OF COEXTENSION AND NON-COEXTENSION.

§ 363. As was shown when treating of Space and of the statical attributes of Body, all modes of extension are resolvable into relations of coexistent positions. Space is known to us as an infinitude of coexistent positions that do not resist; Body as a congeries of coexistent positions that do resist. The simplest extension therefore, as that of a line, must be regarded as a series of coexistent positions; equal lines, as equal series of coexistent positions; and coextension, as the equality of separate series of coexistent positions.

It was explained at considerable length, that a series of coexistent positions is known to the developed mind through the simultaneous excitation of some series of independent sensitive agents distributed over the surface of the body; and that this simultaneous excitation being the equivalent and symbol of the successive excitations, the successive excitations are those in which all phenomena of extension, subjectively considered, must ultimately be expressed.

Hence, extension, as originally known, must be some succession of connatural states of consciousness of a special order; and as before shown, it must, in its primary form, be that order of states produced by the united sensations of motion and touch. Two equal extensions, then, are originally known to us as two equal series of united sensations of motion and touch. And coextension, when reduced to its lowest terms, means—equality in the lengths of such series; that is—equality in the numbers of the states they severally include.

Two objections to this definition should be noticed. It may be considered a misuse of language to call that which we feel when drawing a finger over the skin, a *series* of states of consciousness; since the sensations of motion and touch are continuous. But saying nothing of the fact that the nerves which are one after another excited by the moving finger are independent, and must be supposed to convey separate impressions to the nervous centres, it will suffice to reply that though, in cases of this kind, the consciousness seems unbroken and homogeneous, it is in fact, *marked out* into many separate portions. A little introspection will show that during one of these seemingly-persistent feelings, the attention is transitorily occupied with various other things—with surrounding objects, with sounds, with the idea of self, &c. &c. What we are liable to take for a continuous state of consciousness, is really a state traversed by numerous incidental states which, by dividing it into portions, reduce it to a series of states. The second objection is that coextension, as ordinarily determined by the juxtaposition of the coextensive objects, involves no comparison between two series of states of consciousness, but merely an observation that the ends of the objects coincide. This mode of ascertaining coextension, however, is clearly an artifice, based on the experience that extensions separately known to us through the equal series of states they produce, always manifest this coincidence of their ends when placed side by side. As we are here dealing, not with the artificial test of coextension, but with the notion of coextension as it naturally arises, the objection is invalid: more especially as we have thus far considered, not the developed consciousness of coextension but that primary consciousness out of which it is developed.

§ 364. The nature of our developed consciousness of co-extension will now readily be understood. The successive impressions through which extension is originally presented, having been transformed into synchronous impressions—the whole chain of connatural states, at first known in their serial positions, having become known in their coexistent positions; their consolidated states of consciousness resulting, become comparable, and their likeness or unlikeness re-cognizable, just as the chains of states to which they are equivalent. Each of these consolidated states is produced by the simultaneous stimulation of a certain number of in-dependent nerves; and, physiologically considered, that likeness in the two states which constitutes the intuition in question, results from a likeness in the number and combi-nation of the independent nerves simultaneously stimulated: supposing always that these nerves are distributed with like abundance on the two surfaces affected by the compared ex-tensions.*

As implied by much that has gone before, it is this simul-taneity in the excitation of independent nerves which gives the notion of coexistence, underlying that of extension, and therefore that of coextension. Only when coexistence has come to be thus disclosed, can extension and coextension, as we comprehend them, be conceived; seeing that exten-sion implies coexistence in the parts of the thing extended.

* I add this qualifying clause for the purpose of recognizing the signifi-cant fact, that the estimation of a given extension is experimentally proved to vary according to the number of independent nerve-fibres supplied to the surface affected by this extension. One of the results established by Weber is that "two points, at a fixed distance apart, feel as if more widely sepa-rated when placed on a very sensitive part, than when touching a surface of blunter sensibility. This may be easily shown by drawing them over regions differently endowed; they will seem to open as they approach the parts acutely sensible, and *vice versâ*." (See Bain, *The Senses and the In-tellect*, p. 173, Third Ed.) This result harmonizes very satisfactorily with all the conclusions reached in preceding chapters; and it is especially in-structive as verifying, in an unexpected way, the explanation given in § 333 of the exaggerated estimates of space accompanying certain abnormal states.

Extension, therefore, as known by the developed mind, being made up of many elementary consciousnesses of co-existence; the relation of coextension cannot be exhaustively analyzed without analyzing the relation of coexistence. But in so far as the nature of our consciousness of coexistence has been incidentally explained, the relation of coextension, as subjectively considered, may be understood—may be de-fined as the likeness of two compound states of conscious-ness, visual or tactual, in respect of the number and order of the elementary relations of coexistence which they severally include: such compound states of consciousness being severally produced by the consolidation of what were originally known as serial states.

To which, for form's sake, it may be added that the rela-tion of non-coextension is definable as the unlikeness of such two compound states of consciousness.

CHAPTER XXII.

THE RELATIONS OF COEXISTENCE AND NON-COEXISTENCE.

§ 365. Though to the developed mind apparently unde-composable, the relation of coexistence must be originally compound. Coexistence implies at least two things. These two things cannot occupy consciousness at the same instant in the same degree. And as they cannot pass through con-sciousness in simple succession, since they would then be known as sequent and not as coexistent, it follows that coexistence can be disclosed only by some duplex act of thought. True, the terms of a relation of coexistence of the simplest kind appear to be known, not in two states of consciousness but in one. The opposite ends of a short line looked at, or the opposite sides of a stick which is grasped, seem presented in a single intuition. But it needs only to recall the extremely complex process by which our percep-tions of objects are built up, and to remember that what in the infant is an elaborate synthesis afterwards becomes an instantaneous cognition regarded as quite direct, to see that no apparent simultaneity in the consciousness of the two things between which there is a relation of coexistence, can be taken as disproving their original seriality. Leaving general considerations, however, let us look at the matter more nearly.

§ 366. If the eyes be directed to two small dots placed

close together on a sheet of paper, the facts that there are two, that they coexist, and that there is a certain space between them, certainly appear to be given in the same immediate intuition; and it seems a scarcely credible proposition that by a nascent intelligence they can neither be known as two, nor as coexistent, nor as having relative positions. But on reconsidering the conclusion reached in the chapters on Space, Time, and Motion, it will, I think, be manifest that at first, any two such dots can produce nothing but an indefinite visual sensation, as simple as one of sound or smell.   For as was shown, the possibility of distinguishing the impression made on the retina as consisting not of one element but of two, implies, in the first place, that the retina has been so far developed that it consists of parts capable of being separately excited. It implies, in the second place, an accompanying development of the nervous centre such that the separate stimulations of these separate parts are distinguishable from one another in consciousness. But before these independent peripheral agents and independent central agents connected with them have been thus evolved, there must have been experiences accumulated and registered in these structures: the experiences by which the structures are produced, are themselves the experiences out of which grows a knowledge of the separateness.   Or to state the case more conclusively:—Coexistence being unthinkable without a space in which the things may coexist, it follows that the two dots described cannot be known as coexistent without being also known as out of each other—as at some distance from each other. But, to suppose that when two sentient points on the surface of the organism are first simultaneously stimulated, some particular distance is thereby suggested, is to fall into the absurdity of supposing that an idea of some particular distance already exists in the mind. Evidently by a nascent intelligence the space between the two coexistent points is incognizable; and as their coexistence cannot be otherwise conceived, it follows that at first they cannot be known as coexistent.

From all which it is an obvious corollary, that the relation of coexistence is disclosed by the same experiences which disclose extension. But now we have to observe an additional trait in these experiences. The repeatedly-described consolidation of serial states of consciousness into quasi-single states, is not the whole of the process by which the ideas of coexistence and extension are evolved. It is the peculiarity alike of every tactual and visual series which enters into the genesis of these ideas, that not only does it admit of being transformed into a composite state in which the successive positions become simultaneous positions, *but it admits of being reversed*. The chain of states of consciousness A to Z, produced by the motion of the hand over an object, or of the eye along one of its edges, may with equal facility be gone through from Z to A. Unlike those states of consciousness constituting our perceptions of environing sequences, which do not admit of unresisted changes in the order of their components, those which constitute our perceptions of coexistences may have the order of their components inverted without effort—occur as readily in one direction as the other. And this is the especial experience by which the relation of coexistence is disclosed. Let us glance at the chief phases of this experience.

Recurring to the adjacent dots, it will be observed that though very close and very small, they can never be both *perfectly* present to consciousness at the same time. The one on which the visual axes converge, is alone recognized with complete distinctness. The other, clearly before the mind as it seems, cannot be perceived with the highest degree of definiteness until the visual axes converge upon it; and when the gaze is thus transferred, the dot first contemplated ceases to be so definitely perceived. Moreover, if, while the eyes are fixed on one of the dots, the thoughts are directed to the other, it will be found that in proportion as the other is distinctly thought of, the one to which the eyes are fixed tends to lapse out of consciousness. Either of which facts makes it clear, both that the serial experiences never wholly cease to be used, and that, even under the most favourable circumstances, the two terms of a relation of coexistence are not *absolutely* coexistent to the mind. Let us now observe what happens with dots further apart. If they are extremely minute, it will be found that even when there is only an inch between them, the one becomes invisible if the eyes are directed to the other, and cannot be known as coexistent with it except by a definite transfer of the attention. If they are dots of moderate sizes, the consciousness of one will be accompanied by some consciousness of the other until they are separated by a space of six or eight inches: beyond which, this nascent consciousness disappears. With larger objects there must be a larger interval—or, more strictly speaking, a greater subtended angle—to produce the same result. But however large the objects, there is a distance at which either ceases to be in any degree presented to the mind when the eyes are directed to the other. The unregarded object, when moved towards the outskirts of the field of view, does not disappear suddenly; but fades into nothingness gradually. And as, between those relative positions of two things in which their coexistence can be known only by a slight turn of the head, and those in which it can be known only by turning the head half round, there is also a series of imperceptible transitions; it follows that the coexistence of two dots lying close together, and that of two objects lying respectively behind and before the observer, are known in modes which are joined by insensible gradations, and must be primordially the same. In both cases, the terms of the relation of coexistence cannot be perfectly present to consciousness at the same moment. In both cases, motion is required to bring that term of the relation of which there is either no consciousness or but imperfect consciousness, distinctly before the mind. And the differences are partly between the amounts of motion, and partly between the degrees of consciousness of this second term, which vary from no consciousness up to almost perfect consciousness.

This being understood, let us ask how the coexistence of two things not visible together is known. When a man, having just seen some object A, sees another object B, he usually asserts their coexistence on the strength of this single observation. He is enabled to do this by an accumulation of experiences which warrant the induction that certain groups of phenomena are persistent. But what does he mean by persistent? He means that the groups of phenomena are of a kind which he can again become conscious of with the same vividness as before. He means that on turning his head, the object A will impress him as it did at first. His assertion that A and B coexist means that the vivid states of consciousness which they severally produce in him, can be alternated as often as he pleases. Leaving, however, the coexistence that is known inferentially, we must here concern ourselves with those primordial experiences which yield the notion of co-existence. By an incipient intelligence, two things A and B, seen in succession, cannot be known to differ in their persistence from two sounds heard one after the other. In either case there is nothing but a sequence of impressions. How, then, do the two relations come to be distinguished? Simply by finding that whereas the terms of the first can be known in the reverse order with equal vividness, those of the second cannot. It is perpetually found that while certain states of consciousness follow each other with as much facility and clearness in one direction as in the opposite (A, B—B, A) others do not; and hence results a differentiation of the relation of coexistence from that of sequence.

More manifest still will this become, on remembering that

there are coexistences which even the adult never knows otherwise than through this test. While writing, I feel in my foot the warmth of the fire; I am aware of the pressure of my arm on the desk; I see the paper on which I write; and I hear a cart in the street. I find it impossible, however, to think of all these things at the same instant. I cannot join the heat, the sound, the pressure, and the whiteness, in the same state of consciousness; and still less can I be simultaneously conscious of their respective causes. How, then, do I know that I am receiving these various impressions at one time? How do I know that the external objects producing them are coexistent? I know it from the fact that I can be successively conscious of these various feelings in any order with equal facility.

§ 367. The equal facility with which the terms of a relation of coexistence can be thought of in either order, is knowable by us only through an internal feeling. That we habitually notice the feelings accompanying changes in consciousness, cannot be questioned, since we distinguish them by words. When we speak of a thing as *hard* to think, or *easy* to believe, we express by these adverbs the presence or absence of mental tension. In the one case, the consequent can be made to follow the antecedent only by a great effort; in the other, by little or no effort. When attempting to remember a forgotten name, or when continuing to puzzle over some calculation, or when trying to form an unusually-complex conception, there is a distinct consciousness of inward strain. Whence it is clear that the states of consciousness constituting a thought, may follow one another without difficulty or with any degree of difficulty; and that the difficulty is known to us by the feeling accompanying the transition.

Consequently, to distinguish the relation of coexistence as one of which the terms will follow one another through consciousness in either order with equal facility, is to say that there is a likeness or equality of the two feelings of facility which accompany respectively, the change from antecedent to consequent, and the change from consequent to antecedent. There may not be a likeness or equality of the two feelings produced by the contrasts of the terms, for these nearly always differ according to the order in which the terms are contemplated; but there is a likeness or equality of the two feelings of resistance—or rather in this case, non-resistance—which occur at the moments of transition.

So that the relation of coexistence under its primary simple form, is to be defined as a union of two relations of sequence, which are such that while the terms of the one are exactly like those of the other in kind and degree, and exactly contrary to them in their order of succession, the two relations are exactly like each other in the feeling which accompanies the succession. Or otherwise, it may be defined as consisting of two changes in consciousness, which, though absolutely opposite in other respects, are perfectly alike in the absence of strain. And of course the relation of non-coexistence differs in this, that though one of the two changes occurs without any feeling of tension, the other does not.

§ 368. It may be worth while to point out, that these conclusions are indicated even by *à priori* considerations. For if, on the one hand, the great mass of external phenomena are statical, or not actively changing; and if, on the other hand, perpetual change is the law of internal phenomena—the condition under which only consciousness can continue; there arises the question—How can outer statical phenomena be represented by inner dynamical phenomena? How can the no-changes outside be symbolized by the changes inside? That changes in the *non-ego* may be expressed by changes in the *ego*, is comprehensible enough; but how is it possible for objective rest to be signified by subjective motion? Evidently there is only one possibility. A consciousness ever in a state of change, can represent to itself a no-change, only by an inversion of one of its changes —by a duplication of consciousness equivalent to an arrest —by a regress which undergoes a previous progress—by two changes which exactly neutralize each other.

Finally, the reader should be reminded that this analysis of the relation of coexistence, showing that it is a relation disclosed by experience, supplies an ultimate disproof of the hypothesis that Space is a form of intuition; since the consciousness of coexistence is the primitive element out of which the consciousness of space is built—is the element without which even the germ of that consciousness is impossible.

CHAPTER XXIII.

§ 369. After what has been said concerning it in § 360, but little need here be added respecting the relation of con-nature. It is of two kinds. In the one, the terms between which it subsists are themselves relations, or changes in consciousness. In the other, they are the primitive states of consciousness between which such changes occur. Let us first glance at the more complex of these.

When treating of the relation of cointension, it was pointed out that simple changes from one primitive state of consciousness to another are of several classes. There are those in which the antecedent and consequent states are of different orders—as when the transition is from a tone to emotion; those in which they are of different genera—as when the transition is from a flash of light to a bang; those in which they are of the same genera but of different species —as when the transition is from the colour green to the colour red; and those in which they are of the same species, but of different degrees—as when the transition is from a faint sound to a loud one. And these being the different kinds of change between states of consciousness dis-tinguished as simple feelings, it is manifest that when the states of consciousness become composite, a great multi-plicity of kinds of changes arise—changes from greater to less in magnitude, from slow to quick in velocity, from ascent to descent, &c. Hence those various orders of changes implied by the negations of the relations already treated of—the changes indicated by the terms dissimilarity,

non-cointension, non-coextension, non-coexistence.　And
hence also those processes of consciousness through which
we class lines with lines, areas with areas, bulks with bulks
—all of them distinguished by us as different orders of relations; that is, different orders of changes among the states
of consciousness.

Nothing is to be said respecting the connature of relations
in its various modes, beyond describing it; for the relation
of connature is not decomposable into other relations.　That
two changes in consciousness are of like kind, is a fact of
which we can give no account further than that we perceive
it to be so.　When two transitions in consciousness produce
in us two like feelings, we know nothing more than that we
have the like feelings.　It is true, as will be shown in a
subsequent chapter, that it is possible to say specifically
what we mean by asserting the likeness of these feelings.
But beyond this it is impossible to go.

As subsisting between relations, therefore, the relation of
connature must be defined as—likeness of kind between two
changes in consciousness.

§ 370. Respecting the relation of connature as subsisting, not between relations, but between primary states of
consciousness—feelings or the representations of them—
still less is to be said.　What is the nature of the feelings
which we have of warmth, of blueness, of pressure, of sweetness, no one can say.　They are undecomposable elements
of thought with which analysis can do nothing.　And when
we assert the connature of any two such feelings—their likeness in kind—we express an intuition of which we can say
nothing further than that we have it.　Though, as will by
and by be seen, the intuition may be otherwise expressed,
it cannot be decomposed.

To justify the title of the chapter, it must be added that
the relation of non-connature is—unlikeness in kind between either changes in consciousness or the states which
they connect.

CHAPTER XXIV.

THE RELATIONS OF LIKENESS AND UNLIKENESS.

§ 371. At length continued analysis has brought us down to the relations underlying not only all preceding relations, but all processes of thought whatever. From the most complex and most abstract inferences down to the most rudimentary intuitions, all intelligence proceeds by the establishment of relations of *likeness* and *unlikeness*. Duly to appreciate this truth, we must glance at the successive conclusions arrived at in preceding chapters.

In the highest kinds of compound quantitative reasoning, we found that each of the several intuitions which make up a demonstration, not only involves the relation of *likeness* under its highest form—that of *equality*—but involves it in the most various ways. We found that in descending step by step to the lower kinds of reasoning, the intuitions of *likeness* included in each ratiocinative act become less numerous and less perfect; but that to the last, *likeness* of relations is necessarily involved. The classification of objects, we found to imply a perception of the *likeness* of a new group of relations to a before-known group, joined with more or less *unlikeness* of the individual attributes; while recognition implies *exact likeness* both of the individual attributes and their relations, to those of groups before known. And we further saw that the perception of a special object is impossible save by thinking of it as *like* some

before-known class or individual.   The perception
of Body, as presenting its three orders of attributes, we
found to imply a classing of the several attributes, their
relations to each other, and the conditions under which they
are disclosed, with *like* attributes, relations, and conditions.
It was shown that our perceptions of Space, Time, and Motion, arise by a discovery of the *equivalence* of certain states
of consciousness, serial and simultaneous; and further, that
no particular space, time, or motion, can be thought of without the relation of *likeness* being involved.   More
recently we have seen that the higher orders of relations are
severally resolvable into relations of *likeness* and *unlikeness*
whose terms have certain specialities and complexities.
Similarity, was defined as the cointension of two connatural
relations between states of consciousness which are themselves *like* in kind but commonly *unlike* in degree.   Cointension, we found to be, *likeness* in degree either between
changes in consciousness that are like in kind, or between
states of consciousness that are *like* in kind.   It was shown
that coextension is the *likeness* of two composite states of
consciousness, in respect of the number and order of the
elementary relations of coexistence which they severally include.   Coexistence, was resolved into two sequences whose
terms are exactly *alike* in kind and degree, exactly *unlike*,
or opposite, in their order of succession, and exactly *alike* in
the feeling which accompanies that succession.   Connature
was defined as *likéness* in kind either between two changes
in consciousness or between two states of consciousness.
And each of these relations we found to have its negative, in
which *unlikeness* is the thing predicated.

Seeing, thus, that the knowing of successive states and
changes of consciousness as like or unlike, is that in
which thinking consists, we have next to inquire what
is the essential nature of those phenomena in consciousness which we signify by the words likeness and unlikeness.

§ 372. Things can be truly defined only in terms more general than themselves; and hence unless there is some relation underlying the relations of likeness and unlikeness, they must be indefinable. Strictly speaking, no such more general relation exists. The only relation remaining to be dealt with is one that is co-ordinate with them—one that is in fact another side of the same mental phenomena. All we can do is to describe likeness and unlikeness in terms of this remaining relation, and to describe this remaining relation, when we come to it, in terms of likeness and unlikeness —to exhibit them as the necessary complements of each other.

This premised, the question above asked will be most readily answered by comparing the relations of likeness and unlikeness together. The essential nature of each will best be shown by contrasting it with the other. In what, then, consists the difference between the two mental processes by which these relations are disclosed?

If I cut in two a sheet of blue paper, and place the pieces at some distance apart; and if I also place at some distance apart, two pieces of paper of different colours—say red and green; I have in the first pair a relation of likeness and in the second pair a relation of unlikeness. What constitutes my knowledge of each of these relations? On glancing from one of the blue pieces to the other, I am conscious of passing from one state to another state, which is new in so far as it is separate from, and subsequent to, the first, but which is not otherwise new. On glancing from the red to the green, I am conscious of passing from one state to another state, which is new not only as being subsequent, but which is otherwise new. Suppose now that I place the blue pieces close together, joining the edges which were made by the cut; and that I also place the red and green pieces close together. What happens? The two blue pieces are not now known in two distinct states of consciousness: the two states of consciousness practically merge into one. The red and green pieces, however, placed no matter how close, still produce two states when contemplated.   Similarly with sounds. A sustained note made by the voice or by an instrument, may be unbroken and homogeneous, or it may be interrupted by some slight flaw, serving nominally to divide it into two notes that are exactly alike. But while, when we listen to such a note, consciousness may with almost-equal propriety be considered in one state or two states, when we listen to any musical interval we very decidedly experience two states.

It is sufficiently manifest, then, that by the words unlike and like, we signify the occurrence or non-occurrence of *change* in consciousness. Leaving out of sight for a moment that fleeting consciousness which marks a transfer of the attention, and which strictly considered is a change, we may say that by unlikeness and likeness we mean respectively, *change* and *no change* in consciousness. The two terms of a relation of unlikeness are two states of consciousness forming the antecedent and consequent of a *change* in consciousness. The two terms of a relation of likeness are the antecedent and consequent of what, in one sense, is *no change ;* seeing that it leaves consciousness in the same condition as before.

§ 373. As implied, however, this is but an approximate statement which, if interpreted literally, describes an impossibility. For as the relation of likeness implies two states of consciousness; and as two states of consciousness, if not themselves different, cannot exist as separate states unless they are divided from each other by some state that is different; it follows that a relation of likeness implies a change, or rather changes, in consciousness.   Accurately speaking, therefore, a relation of likeness consists of two relations of unlikeness which neutralize each other. It is a change from some relatively-enduring state A to another state x (which represents the feeling we have while passing from one of the like things to the other), and a change from this transitory state x to a second relatively-enduring state A: which second state A would be indistinguishable from the first state were it not divided from it by the state x, and which merges into such first state when the state x disappears from the approximation of the two like stimuli in space or time.

Very many relations of unlikeness similarly consist of two relations of unlikeness, which, however, fail to neutralize each other. In all cases where the two terms of the relation do not follow through consciousness in juxtaposition—as when the unlike things looked at are some distance apart, or when between unlike sounds a brief interval of time elapses—there are three states of consciousness involved; the original state A, the transition state x, and that state of which we predicate unlikeness, B. But the primordial relation of unlikeness consists of two states only. When two notes differing in pitch strike the ear in quick succession, so as to leave no time for any intervening thought or sensation—when a flash of lightning for a moment dispels the darkness—when any one state of consciousness is directly supplanted by another state, there is established a relation of unlikeness.

Thus, then, the relation of unlikeness is the primordial one—is the relation involved in every other relation; and can itself be described in no other way than as a *change* in consciousness.

CHAPTER XXV.

THE RELATION OF SEQUENCE.

§ 374. As was said in the last chapter, this remaining relation is but another side of the one there treated of. Sequence is change; and change, as known by us, is the unlikeness of a present state of consciousness to a past state. While on the one hand, the two terms of the relation of unlikeness cannot be known without a change in consciousness, on the other hand, there cannot be a change in consciousness without there being two states standing in a relation of unlikeness. The fundamental or undecomposable relation must have two terms—two juxtaposed states of consciousness. These must be unlike, otherwise they will constitute not two states but one. To be known as unlike they must be known in succession, since consciousness cannot be in two states at the same time. The ultimate relation, therefore, is nothing more than a *change* in the state of consciousness; and we call it either a relation of unlikeness or a relation of sequence, according as we think of the *contrast* between the antecedent and consequent states, or of their *order*.

Beyond thus describing each aspect of this relation in terms of the other aspect, no account can be given of it. Like every primordial experience—like the sensation of redness or that of warmth, it transcends analysis. All that is left to be done is to classify the relations of sequence, and

to inquire how the classes are distinguished from one another.   To do this completely is by no means easy, and
would occupy more space than can here be afforded.   It
must suffice to describe the leading distinctions.

§ 375. It is tolerably manifest that these distinctions cannot be originally given in the consciousness of the sequences
themselves. By a nascent intelligence, the relation between
two sensations that severally answer to some external cause
and effect, can not be known as essentially unlike that between two sensations that follow one another fortuitously.
The two relations are two changes in consciousness, and
nothing more. If, then, some changes, some sequences, are
afterwards found to differ in nature from others, the difference must be in some collateral property disclosed by
further experience.   What is that property?

Comparison of a few cases will show us the answer to
this question. After hearing in immediate succession two
notes of different pitch, no difficulty is found in making
those notes—or rather, the ideas of them—pass through
consciousness in the reverse order.   After an ascending
fifth has been struck on the piano, it is easy to represent
the sounds so as to make a descending fifth: the two states
of consciousness produced may readily be re-thought in
inverted sequence.   Not that the two states thus voluntarily
changed in their order, are entirely like the original states.
Though they are like in their natures they are widely unlike
in their intensities.   While the original states, which we
know as two sensations of sound, are vivid, the two ideas
which we find may be transposed are faint repetitions
of them.   And this it is which distinguishes one of these
reversible sequences from a coexistence. If the successive
states of consciousness **A, B,** can be made to occur in the
opposite order, **B, A,** without any diminution of vividness,
the relation between them is what we know as coexistence.
But if the states **A, B,** when they occur in opposite order,

can be made to do so only as the weak states B, A, the relation between them is that of reversible sequence. Thus
much to prevent misapprehension. What it now concerns
us to observe is, that there are sequences whose terms
having been presented in one order, admit of being represented in the opposite order with great facility. Not that
they occur in this opposite order with as much facility as in
the original order. Two feelings that were experienced in
a certain succession, tend, when recalled, to pass through
consciousness in a like succession; and it is in virtue of
their tendency to do this that we know them to have
occurred in that succession; or rather, it is their recurrence in this succession which *constitutes* our knowledge of
their original succession. But though, when uninterfered
with, the represented feelings follow one another in an order
like that in which the presented ones followed; yet, in cases
such as the one instanced, the slightest effort of volition
reverses the order—an effort so slight as to be unaccompanied by any sense of tension. That *some* effort is required, may be inferred; since, while the represented
impressions *involuntarily* follow one another in the original
order, they do not follow in the opposite one, unless
voluntarily. This, however, is the sole appreciable distinction. And these are the sequences which, objectively
considered, we class as *accidental*.

If now, instead of two phenomena that have occurred in a
fortuitous succession, or in a succession which to our
ignorance seems fortuitous, we take two phenomena that
have occurred in a certain order with considerable regularity, we shall find that the relation subsisting between the
states of consciousness answering to them has a somewhat
different quality. Instance the shouting to any one and the
turning of his head. These two phenomena, frequently
experienced in this order, have produced a mental connexion such that the occurrence of the one almost inevitably
suggests an idea of the other. Moreover, the states of con-

sciousness thus associated in experience have no tendency to occur in the opposite order. The turning of another person's head does not make us think of a shout. Nevertheless, there is little or no difficulty in reversing the order of these states. The thought of a person turning his head may be instantly followed by the thought of a shout, if we so will it. Sequences of this kind then, are distinguished by the peculiarity that though, when the antecedent is presented or represented, a representation of the consequent cannot without difficulty be prevented from rising in consciousness, yet these two states can readily have their order of succession changed. And this is the character of the sequences which, objectively considered, we class as *probable*.

When, however, we pass from *non-necessary* sequences to *necessary* sequences, we find not only that the states of consciousness are so connected that when the antecedent is presented it is impossible to prevent the consequent from following it, but also that the antecedent and consequent do not admit of transposition. As an illustration of the first peculiarity, may be taken our inability to think of a heavy weight as breaking the string by which it is suspended, without thinking of the weight as falling. And the last peculiarity is illustrated in the fact that the relation between a blow and an antecedent motion, cannot be represented to the mind in the reverse order.

§ 376. Thus the relation of sequence, considered subjectively as a change in consciousness, is of three general kinds. The fortuitous, in which the two terms are as nearly as may be *alike* in their tendency, or want of tendency, subsequently to suggest each other; and in which the change may be reversed in thought with a feeling of non-resistance *like* that with which it originally occurred. The probable, in which the terms are *unlike* in their tendency to suggest each other; but in which the usual

order of the terms may be inverted with but little effort.
And the necessary, in which the antecedent being presented or represented to consciousness, the consequent cannot be prevented from following; and in which the direction of the change cannot be changed.

Leaving though it does much to be explained, this statement will serve to show that the classification of sequences
is itself effected through other sequences. This classification, depending on the different modes in which the
sequences comport themselves when tested, involves, at the
outset, the ideas of *like* and *unlike;* while the process of
testing them is itself an observing of the degrees of *likeness*
or *unlikeness* between certain feelings they severally yield
under experiment. And since the relations of likeness and
unlikeness are the one a double sequence and the other a
single sequence, it results that the classing of sequences
implies the making them the terms of secondary sequences.
As all relations are finally reducible to one, which is
nothing else than a *change* in consciousness, it follows, even
à priori, that all relations among the changes in consciousness must themselves be other changes.

CHAPTER XXVI.

CONSCIOUSNESS IN GENERAL.

§ 377. Successive decompositions of the more complex phenomena of intelligence into simpler ones, and of these into still simpler ones, have at length brought us down to the simplest; which we find to be nothing else than a change in the state of consciousness. This is the element out of which are composed the most involved cognitions. Analysis leaves us no alternative but to hold that the perception of a vast landscape consists in a multitude of co-ordinate changes; and that of co-ordinated changes, also, consists the most abstract conception of the philosopher.

This result, reached by taking to pieces our cognitions, is, indeed, the one indicated by *à priori* considerations. To be conscious is to think; to think is to put together impressions and ideas; and to do this, is to be the subject of internal changes. It is admitted on all hands that without change, consciousness is impossible: consciousness ceases when the changes in consciousness cease. If, then, incessant change is the condition on which only consciousness can continue, it would seem to follow that all the various phenomena of consciousness are resolvable into changes. Even from a general view of the facts, therefore, may be prophesied the issue to which a detailed analysis has led us.

Still more clearly may this same issue be foreseen, when it is remembered that we can become conscious only through the changes caused in us by surrounding things. Here is an organism placed in the midst of objects. If it is uninfluenced by them, it can know nothing of them—think nothing of them. Their existence cannot be revealed to it unless by the effects they produce on it—the changes they work in it. Only through changes can it be made conscious of an external world; and only out of changes can be constructed that knowledge of an external world which is possible to it.

But a full comprehension of this truth that the primordial element of all intelligence is simply a change, and that every complex mental phenomenon is a co-ordinated group of changes, will best be gained by arranging synthetically the results lately reached by analysis. After contemplating in their order of genesis, a few of the primitive cognitions treated of in recent chapters, both the particular conclusions there reached, and the general conclusion based upon them, will be clearly understood.

§ 378. As already sufficiently explained, absolute quiescence in consciousness is cessation of consciousness. To constitute a consciousness, however, incessant change is not the sole thing needed. If the changes are altogether at random, no consciousness, properly so called, exists. Consciousness is not simply a succession of changes, but an *orderly* succession of changes—a succession of changes *combined and arranged* in special ways. The changes form the raw material of consciousness; and the development of consciousness is the *organization* of them. This premised, let us consider under what conditions consciousness becomes nascent.

The lowest form of consciousness that can be conceived, is that resulting from the alternation of two states. When there is a change from state A to state B, and from state B to state A—that is when states A and B come into existence as the antecedents and consequents of changes, each change constitutes a phenomenon in consciousness; and the recurrence of such changes becomes a consciousness. Not that such a consciousness is one which we can realize to ourselves, or one which would ordinarily be termed consciousness. We must regard it as the first step towards the evolution of consciousness proper—a step such as we may imagine to have been taken in the lowest animals that manifest sensibility. But now let us inquire what is given in this first step. By the hypothesis, the second state B differs from the first state A—constitutes a second state only in virtue of being different; that is to say, A and B are *unlike*. That there can exist any cognition of them as unlike is not to be supposed. Such a cognition implies a complicated mental act that becomes possible only after considerable development. All we have now to note is, that this first phenomenon is one of the experiences out of which are ultimately elaborated the ideas of *change*, of *sequence*, of *unlikeness*. Suppose that there occurs the change B to A. Here are the materials for a second relation of sequence—a second relation of unlikeness. But this is not all. There has now arisen a second state A, *like* the first state A. Data have been presented which, in an advanced consciousness, would constitute a relation of *likeness*. At present, however, even supposing a latent capacity for thinking such a relation, it cannot be thought from lack of experiences to class it with. Let there occur another change, A to B. This constitutes a second relation of unlikeness, of the same nature as the one first established—a change or relation *like* the before-experienced relation. There are now given the materials which, did there exist a power of co-ordinating them, might compose a thought. There have arisen two relations of likeness between primitive states of consciousness—between A and A, and B and B; and also a relation of likeness between two changes—between two relations of unlikeness. By a practised consciousness, this second change or relation would be thinkable as like the first—might be classed with it, or assimilated to it. Let another change B to A arise. A further relation of unlikeness is presented, like a foregoing one. And by a perpetual repetition of these changes A—B, B—A, the two states and their two relations tend to become more and more cognizable. Thus, even in a consciousness of the lowest imaginable type, there are foreshadowed the relation of sequence, the relation of unlikeness among the sensations, the relation of likeness among the sensations, the relation of unlikeness among the changes, and the relation of likeness among the changes. The earliest possible experiences are those supplying the raw material from which these cognitions are developed.

Suppose that a third estate, C—a third kind of sensation, is now joined to the others. Further relations of likeness and unlikeness between states and between changes result. But not simply can there occur a greater variety of phenomena of the same kind: new kinds of phenomena become possible. The two states A, B, we have assumed to alternate with equal facility in each direction A—B, B—A. If, however, the new state C frequently follows B but never precedes it, there results an experience of two orders of change which become known by contrast: the duplex change A—B, B—A, answering to the relation of co-existence, and the single change B—C, answering to the relation of sequence proper. Moreover, after this introduction of a third state, it becomes possible for some particular combination to be established as one of more frequent recurrence than the others; and the recurrence of such particular combination, B—A—C for example, supplies the material for a relation of likeness, not between one single change in consciousness and previous changes, but between a group of changes and previous groups. Nor is this all. The more varied experiences that now arise of the relations of likeness and unlikeness, which subsist between several kinds of primitive states, several kinds of single changes, and several kinds of compound changes, afford data for the consciousness of likeness and unlikeness in general, apart from the particular terms between which they were first established.

Supposing this introduction of new sensations, new changes, and new combinations among them, to be carried on step by step, let us mark what must result from that universal law, that the more frequently mental states have occurred in a certain order the more easily and rapidly do they follow one another in that order. In proportion as the specially-combined states D—B—A—C, have been repeated, the time occupied in the transition from the first to the last becomes abbreviated; and ultimately this series of states and changes takes no more time than one of its constituents originally did. The consequence is, that these compound changes tend to become more and more clearly thinkable as single phenomena in consciousness—more and more readily classable with the like previous phenomena and distinguishable from others. But now observe the important fact that in proportion as a chain of such changes is consolidated into a single change, *in the same proportion do the several sensations which form the antecedents and consequents of the changes, become present together.* When the compound change D—B—A—C, takes place, as it ultimately does, almost instantaneously, it results that before the first sensation or idea D, has ceased, the others B, A, C, have severally arisen. Hence there is produced a consolidated consciousness in which many sensations appear to be simultaneously presented—a consolidated consciousness answering to some outward object that habitually gives this group of sensations. And we have but to conceive an endless progress in this consolidation of changes, to comprehend how there can arise the consciousness of complex things—how the objects with which human intelligence deals become thinkable as like and unlike—how the highest acts of perception and reason become possible.

§ 379. Of course the actual genesis of intelligence is incomparably more complex than it is here represented to be. This description simply shadows forth the nature of the process—exhibits the fundamental principles of it. The successive complications above suggested in rapid succession, can in reality arise only by insensible degrees. Each order of experiences must be registered in the nervous structures by long-continued habit, before any higher order can be dealt with. Each constantly-united group of states of consciousness must be more or less completely fused into one state, before any further complexity can be reached by the combination of such groups. In respect of its progress, this organization of experiences must conform to the laws of organization in general; and must therefore be extremely slow.

Taking the above description, however, as exhibiting the *method* of the process in its most general outlines, it will serve to show that at the very outset there are involved the materials of those fundamental relations to which analysis has, from the very beginning, pointed. It will serve to make more comprehensible how, out of change, kind of change, degree of change, facility of change, arrangement of change, &c., the infinitely-varied states of consciousness may be elaborated. And it will serve to suggest how, by the ever-progressing consolidation of changes—the running together of larger and larger groups and series of them—there can arise, out of internal phenomena originally successive, the means of representing those extremely-complicated phenomena of coexistence which constitute the external world.

CHAPTER XXVII.

RESULTS.

§ 380. Among the truths to be gathered from the fore-going chapters, one of the most significant is that there exists a *unity of composition* throughout all the phenomena of intelligence. At the outset we saw that the most complex processes of reasoning are resolvable into intuitions of likeness and unlikeness between terms more or less involved. Under various modes, complications, and degrees of perfection, these intuitions were found to be traceable not only throughout all kinds of reasoning, but throughout all kinds of perception: constituting in every case the general structure of the cognition, whatever its particular substance. And we have recently seen, both analytically and synthetically, that these intuitions are foreshadowed in the very first stages of an incipient consciousness.

Standing together, this consistency in its particular results and their subordination to one general result, supply strong confirmation of the analysis; both as a whole and in its several parts. But they will be seen to supply yet stronger confirmation if we reflect that it is inferable, even *à priori*, that analysis must disclose some such universal law. For whatever may be the conditions under which alone consciousness can exist, they must be common to all kinds and degrees of consciousness. They must be disclosed along with the initial phenomena of consciousness; and must underlie each of the more complex phenomena built out of these initial phenomena. In other words—there must be some *form of thought,* exhibited alike in the very lowest and the very highest manifestations of intelligence. Hence, when we find that in the first changes of the simplest conceivable consciousness, data for the relations of likeness and unlikeness are given—that these relations form but another side of the very changes which constitute the nascent consciousness; we may conclude that these relations must be the foundation of all intelligence. And this being the conclusion reached at every successive stage of an analysis pursued quite independently of any such *à priori* consideration, there can, I think, scarcely be a doubt of its correctness.

The various divisions, therefore, which we ordinarily make among our mental operations, and which psychologists have mostly regarded as marking out distinct faculties, have merely a superficial truth. They are to be understood as indicating modifications of detail which distinguish phenomena that are essentially similar—modifications which do but mask that fundamental unity of composition possessed by all cognitions whatever.

§ 381. Contemplating the facts from another point of view, we may see that not only the *form* of thought, but the *process* of thought, is the same throughout. The mode in which the elements of a compound quantitative argument are dealt with by the mind, is essentially similar to the mode in which the elements of every other human thought are dealt with; and the impressions received by inferior intelligences, even down to the very lowest, are dealt with after a like mode.

We saw that all reasoning is definable as the classification of relations. We saw that the perception of an object is possible only by the classing of a present group of attributes and relations with a past group. We saw that the constituents of any complex perception must be severally classed with previously-known constituents of the same order. And we saw that not even the simplest attribute or relation can be known until there exist others with which it can be ranged; since the knowing it is the thinking of it as one with certain others—the classing it with those others. Nay, the relation of unlikeness itself is cognizable only as like previously-experienced relations of unlikeness—is incognizable unless there exist other relations with which it may be classed.　　　　　As above hinted, this law applies not to human thought alone. The life of the lowest sentient being is made possible only by an organic classification of impressions. The condition on which every creature exists is, that it shall behave in special ways under special stimuli —that contact with nutritive matter shall modify its motions in a manner different from that in which contact with innutritive matter modifies them—that one impression shall lead it to attack, another to hide, and so on. Manifestly, if there is no adaptation between its acts and surrounding circumstances, it must quickly cease to live. And if it exhibits any adaptation, it can do so only because certain impressions made upon it call forth one kind of action, while others call forth another kind. There must exist in it some means whereby these impressions are distinguished as such or such, or are classified—some organic registry of external differences and similarities. Not that there need be anything like what we know as a consciousness of external differences and similarities: there needs only an innate capability of acting thus or thus, according to the nature of the stimulus. But so far as this implies it, the organism must have a power of appreciating differences and similarities—a power of automatic classification.

Clearly, then, the law is the same throughout. When regarded under its fundamental aspect, the highest reasoning is seen to be one with all the lower forms of human thought, and one with instinct and reflex action, even in their simplest manifestations. The universal process of intelligence is the *assimilation* of impressions. And the differences displayed in the ascending grades of intelligence are consequent upon the increasing complexity of the impressions assimilated.

§ 382. A further change in our stand-point introduces us to a still wider view of mental phenomena—discloses an exhaustive definition of them, whether considered separately or in their totality.

We have seen that the condition on which alone consciousness can begin to exist, is the occurrence of a change of state; and that this change of state necessarily generates the terms of a relation of unlikeness. We have seen that not simply does consciousness become nascent by virtue of a change, but that consciousness can continue only while changes continue—only while relations of unlikeness are being established. Hence, consciousness can neither arise nor be maintained without the occurrence of differences in its state. It must be ever passing from some one state into a different state. In other words—there must be *a continuous differentiation* of its states.

But we have also seen that the states of consciousness successively arising, can become elements of thought only by being known as like certain before-experienced states. If no note be taken of the different states as they occur—if they pass through consciousness simply as images pass over a mirror; there can be no intelligence, however long the process be continued. Intelligence can arise only by the classification of these states. If they are severally taken note of, it must be as more or less like certain previous ones. They are thinkable only as such or such; that is, as like certain others before-experienced. The act of knowing them is impossible except by classing them with those of the same nature—assimilating them to those of the same nature. In being known, then, each state must become one with certain previous states—must be integrated with those previous states. Each successive act of knowing must be an act of integrating. That is to say, there must be *a continuous integration* of states of consciousness.

These are the two antagonist processes by which consciousness subsists—the centrifugal and centripetal actions by which its balance is maintained. That there may be the material for thought, consciousness must every moment have its state differentiated. And for the new state hence resulting to become a thought, it must be integrated with before-experienced states. This perpetual alternation is the characteristic of all consciousness from the very lowest to the very highest. It is distinctly typified in that oscillation between two states, constituting the simplest conceivable form of consciousness; and it is illustrated in the most complex thinkings of the most cultivated man.

This law is displayed also in the general progress of thought. These small differentiations and integrations that go on from moment to moment, result in those great differentiations and integrations which constitute mental development. Every case in which an advancing intelligence distinguishes between objects, or phenomena, or laws, that were previously confounded together, implies a differentiation of states of consciousness. And every case in which such advancing intelligence recognizes as of the same essential nature, objects, or phenomena, or laws, that were previously thought distinct, implies an integration of states of consciousness.

Under its most general aspect, therefore, all mental action whatever is definable as *the continuous differentiation and integration of states of consciousness.*

§ 383. The only fact of importance remaining to be pointed out, is the harmony which subsists between this final result and that reached by a kindred science. The widest truth disclosed by the inquiries of biologists is parallel to the one at which we have just arrived.

As there are two antagonist processes by which consciousness is maintained, so there are two antagonist processes by which bodily life is maintained. By the actions it is exposed to every tissue is being differentiated; and every tissue is integrating the materials supplied by the blood. No function can be performed without the differentiation of the tissue performing it; and no tissue is enabled to perform its function save by the integration of nutriment. In the balance of these two actions the organic life is maintained. By each new integration an organ is fitted for being again differentiated; while each new differentiation enables the organ again to integrate. And as with the psychical life, so with the physical—the stopping of either process is the stopping of both.

Moreover the parallel equally holds under the second aspect. Commencing as a uniform mass of matter, every organism is evolved by the differentiation and integration of parts. So, too, on contemplating the phenomena of organization at large as exhibited throughout creation, we find that the integration of elements which perform the same function, goes on *pari passu* with the differentiation of elements which perform diverse functions. That advance from homogeneity to heterogeneity, in which all organization consists, is wholly effected by this duplex action.

Thus, in two senses, there is a continuous differentiation and integration throughout the body; as, in two senses, there is a continuous differentiation and integration throughout the mind.

When we remember that the laws of structure and function must necessarily harmonize; and that the structure and function of the nervous system must conform to the laws of structure and function in general; we shall see that the parallelism here roughly indicated is such as might be expected. We shall see that the ultimate generalizations of Psychology and Physiology must be, as they here appear, different sides of the same primordial truth: both are expressions of the same fundamental process of Life.

PART VII.

GENERAL ANALYSIS.

CHAPTER I.

§ 384. When at the outset " The scope of Psychology " was considered, it was pointed out (§ 53) that " that which distinguishes Psychology from the sciences on which it rests, is, that each of its propositions takes account both of the connected internal phenomena and of the connected external phenomena to which they refer. * * * Suppose that A and B are two related manifestations in the environment —say, the colour and taste of a fruit; then, so long as we contemplate their relation by itself, or as associated with other external phenomena, we are occupied with a portion of physical science. Now suppose that a and b are the sensations produced in the organism by this peculiar light which the fruit reflects, and by the chemical action of its juice on the palate; then * * * we pass into the domain of Psychology the moment we inquire how there comes to exist within the organism a relation between a and b that in some way or other corresponds to the relation between A and B."

The problem of Psychology as thus posited, presents different aspects according as one or other of the inter-dependencies among these relations is made the dominant topic. Bearing in mind that the law of the relation A B, is the problem of Objective Science, which takes for granted that $a\,b$ answers to it, we have to observe that the problem of Subjective Science is divisible into two problems,

according as it inquires into the nature of the connexion a b (the rest being taken for granted) or according
as it inquires into the nature of the connexion between A B
and a b. For, representing these inter-dependent relations

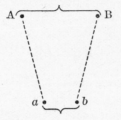

diagrammatically as above, we may, setting out with A B as
known, and assuming as known the connexions of A with
a, and of B with b, go on to ask in what way the relation
a b is established in correspondence with A B. Or, on the
other hand, setting out with a b as known, we may ask
how the other inter-dependencies become known—whether
we have any warrant for asserting the connexions of
a with A and of b with B? and if so, what that warrant is?

In the foregoing divisions of this work the first of these
problems has been dealt with under its several aspects.
Taking for granted the objective A B, and its connexion
with the subjective a b, we have examined how the correspondence of the subjective a b is established—tracing out
the process first of all synthetically and then analytically.
We have now to enter upon the other problem—the theory
of the connexion between A B and a b. In other words, we
now pass from our inquiry concerning the nature of the
human mind to an inquiry concerning the nature of human
knowledge.

This, which is the last problem, has not uncommonly been
dealt with as the first. The unlikelihood of success when it
is so dealt with, will be manifest on glancing at the conditions of the case.

§ 385. Knowledge implies something known and something which knows; whence it follows that a theory of knowledge is a theory of the relation between the two. Observe how distinct are the three things.

Here, on the one hand, is an aggregate of propositions respecting objects; and each group of these propositions, as for instance those constituting the science of Astronomy, we regard as expressing certain connexions which continue to hold whether we continue conscious or not. Here, on the other hand, is an aggregate of propositions concerning states of consciousness; and we regard these propositions as expressing certain connexions which continue to hold irrespective of the continuance of any other connexions. And now here are certain propositions which do not assert connexions among Things, and which do not assert connexions among Thoughts, but which assert connexions between Things and Thoughts. Or, to speak strictly, though they tacitly assert certain connexions among Things and certain connexions among Thoughts, which are indispensable elements of them, yet the connexions with which they are immediately concerned are those between Things and Thoughts. 			If, then, we distinguish Objective Science as the theory of the known and Subjective Science as the theory of that which knows; it becomes manifest that a theory of knowledge, which answers to what is commonly called Metaphysics, is a co-ordination of the two. And if so, a true theory of knowledge involves a true theory of that which knows and a true theory of that which is known; since error in either factor must involve error in the product. Doubtless, in a sense, all three questions must be rightly answered in rightly answering any one. But while a true theory of knowledge is impossible without a true theory of the thing knowing and a theory of the thing known which is true as far as it goes; and while it follows that advance towards a true theory of any one depends on advances towards true theories of the others; it is, I think manifest that, since a true theory of knowledge implies a true co-ordination of that which knows with that which is known, the ultimate form of such a theory can be reached only after the theories of that which knows and of that which is known have reached their ultimate forms.

The only hopeful course is the course which has been pursued, not by metaphysicians, but by mankind at large. It is this:—first, to accumulate and classify crude observations and inferences, such as constitute the mental pos-sessions of the savage and the rustic. Next, as the accumulation increases, becomes organized, and is freed from its grosser errors, to observe how the errors are separated from it; and so to get a rude conception of the knowing process and the process of discriminating truth from falsehood. The rudimentary theory of knowing, accepted provisionally, has then to be used as a means of further purifying and system-atizing that which is known. Along with the growth of that which is known—the gradual expulsion of falsities from the mass of truths—the frequent detection of that which is as-sumed in the midst of that which is proved; there goes a continuous activity of the process of knowing and a con-tinuous opportunity of examining it—an opportunity that becomes ever better as the antithesis between fact and fancy becomes clearer. Thus, the theory of the Known and the theory of the Knowing advance step by step, yielding mu-tual aid—each further progress of the one making possible a further progress of the other. Meanwhile the theory of Knowledge, growing into definiteness as its factors become definite, advances towards the condition of a true theory a stage behind its advancing factors; and has to assume its finished shape after these have assumed their finished shapes.

That the theories of the Known and of the Knowing have assumed their finished shapes, and that a finished theory of Knowledge is now possible, would, of course, be an absurd assumption. But if it be granted that the theory of the Known has been reduced to a more systematic form, and that the theory of the Knowing has also been better systematized, it is to be inferred that we are in a position for reconsidering the theory of Knowledge. Let us observe where we stand.   The Abstract Sciences long ago reached a sufficient degree of development. The Abstract-Concrete Sciences have now made such great advances that we may fairly consider ourselves as understanding the laws of the more important physical actions. The Concrete Sciences, dealing with the continuous transformations of sensible existences taken altogether, or in groups, or singly, have been severally progressing in definiteness and coherence—a definiteness and coherence now made greater by the recognition of certain laws which hold of the transformation in general and in detail.   Meanwhile, examination of the actions of the Knowing has been lately carried on with the aid of this fuller and more precise account of the Known. In the preceding volume Objective Science has helped us to explain the genesis and nature of the process of knowing; and in the Part just closed we have examined analytically the knowing process under all its forms, from the most complex down to the most simple, reaching at last a conclusion respecting that which is essential to it throughout.

Such being our preparations, we have now to examine afresh the theory of Knowledge; and see what revision of it may be made by the help of these revised theories of the Known and the Knowing.

§ 386. To do this will be to redeem the promise made by implication in *First Principles*, when dealing with " The Data of Philosophy." It was there argued (§ 39) that " developed intelligence is framed upon certain organized and consolidated conceptions of which it cannot divest itself; and which it can no more stir without using than the body can stir without help of its limbs. In what way,

then, is it possible for intelligence, striving after Philosophy,
to give any account of these conceptions, and to show either
their validity or their invalidity? There is but one way.
Those of them which are vital, or cannot be severed from
the rest without mental dissolution, must be assumed as
true *provisionally*. The fundamental intuitions that are
essential to the process of thinking, must be temporarily
accepted as unquestionable: leaving the assumption of their
unquestionableness to be justified by the results." And it
was further argued (§ 40) that "setting out with these
fundamental intuitions provisionally assumed to be true—
that is, provisionally assumed to be congruous with all other
dicta of consciousness—the process of proving or disproving the congruity becomes the business of Philosophy; and
the complete establishment of the congruity becomes the
same thing as the complete unification of knowledge in
which Philosophy reaches its goal."

This much having been premised, we asked what data
Philosophy needs; and after glancing at the genesis of
them, we accepted as its data certain primary conceptions
taken for granted in every act of daily life, and assumed as
beyond question in scientific investigations of all orders.
Since then we have been occupied in carrying on the unification indicated; and thus far have found everywhere
the required congruity. We are now called upon to
reconsider these provisional assumptions. The process of
unification, as carried on throughout the great classes of
phenomena distinguished as Biology and Psychology, has
brought us at length to these assumptions themselves; and
the question here to be met is, whether they admit of being
unified with the coherent body of conclusions to which acceptance of them has led us. For some critics hold that
under a final analysis there evolve irreconcilable incongruities between these postulated dicta of consciousness and
the conclusions which consciousness otherwise interrogated
leads us to. Hence it becomes needful to look closely at

these postulates and to test the arguments of those who deny their validity.

§ 387. In other words, we have to take up the vexed question of Subject and Object. The relation between these, as antithetically-opposed divisions of the entire assemblage of manifestations of the Unknowable, was our datum. The fabric of conclusions built upon it must be unstable if this datum can be proved either untrue or doubtful. Should the idealist be right, the doctrine of Evolution is a dream.

Some definite issue, then, must here be reached. Either by critical examination we must be forced to relinquish all the inferences we have thus far drawn; or we must be driven into that position, apparently satisfactory to some, in which are entertained two mutually-destructive beliefs ; or we must discover that the reasonings of idealists and sceptics are fallacious. I need scarcely say that the last result is the one to be expected.

CHAPTER II.

THE ASSUMPTION OF METAPHYSICIANS.

§ 388. When a schoolboy takes up to his teacher a sum in long division, he is not uncommonly told to " prove it." Returning to his desk, he multiplies the divisor by the quotient, and adds to the product the remainder, if there happens to be one. Supposing the amount which results is found to agree with the dividend, the inference is that the division has been rightly performed; but if the two disagree, error, either in the division or in the process by which it was checked, is inferred. Imagine, however, that the boy, while recognizing the disagreement, asserts that he has performed both processes rightly. His teacher will conclude that he is either impertinent or stupid. But should his comprehension of arithmetical principles be unquestionable, and should there be no reason to doubt his sincerity, the teacher will probably begin to suspect incipient insanity. And if he presently finds that his pupil, in dealings with his school-fellows, habitually buys and sells on the assumption that his multiplications are correct, though they are habitually contradicted by the long divisions which he affirms to be correct, he will conclude that if there is not incipient insanity there is some inexplicable mental twist.

Substitute for the intellectual processes here supposed, intellectual processes of a partially-different kind, and we have something like the attitudes assumed by idealists and sceptics. The parallel holds so far as this, that by them, too, intelligence is brought to bear on a given problem; that through a certain complex mode of action of this intelligence they reach a particular conclusion; that through another mode of action of this intelligence an utterly incongruous conclusion is reached; and that while they continue to affirm the first conclusion they continue to believe the second: some of them, indeed, (as Hume) admitting that " Nature, by an absolute and uncontrollable necessity, has determined us to judge " that to be true which we have yet no rational ground for concluding to be true.

I put the case thus strongly with the view of distinctly raising the question—How happens it that metaphysicians have so unfaltering a faith in one mode of intellectual action, and are so ready to treat with comparative disregard the results reached through another mode of intellectual action? How is it that they have unbounded confidence in their long division, and so little confidence in the multiplication by which it is checked? Why do they tacitly assume the error to be in the short process rather than in the long one?

§ 389. The answer to this question is, that metaphysicians greatly over-value a particular mode of mental action. They tacitly assume the supreme authority of certain highest and most recently-developed powers which have been the leaders to immense conquests; and they act as though this supremacy were unconditional. Through Reasoning multitudes of marvellous results have been reached, and Reasoning has come to excite an amount of faith greatly in excess of that which is its due.

The proximate causes of imposing effects always draw to themselves exaggerated respect. An example is furnished by the prevalent feeling shown towards the press as a teaching agency. " I read it in a book," is a phrase often to be heard among the half-educated as equivalent to " it must be true." Even the better-educated habitually manifest the same feeling in a smaller degree. A statement made by some sottish penny-a-liner, or the conclusion drawn in the leading article of some shilling-a-liner who writes opinions to order, is received with a degree of confidence far greater than that which would be given to the man himself. Nay, we may detect the illusion in the now current belief that the nation is about to be moralized by lessons learnt out of school-books. Print upon paper having been so widely instrumental in diffusing information, and the knowledge of all the highly cultivated having been mainly acquired through print upon paper, there has been established such an intimate association between truth and print upon paper, that much of the reverence given to the one gathers round the other.

Similarly with reasoning. By it we have been led up from the few, simple, vague notions of the savage to the multitudinous, complex, and definite truths which now so largely serve to guide us. By it we have been helped to explore a Universe compared with which our Earth is a grain of sand, and to detect the structure of a monad compared with which a grain of sand is an Earth. By it we have complicated and perfected those arts of life which require cyclopædias to describe them. Hence there has naturally arisen an awe of Reason which betrays many into the error of supposing its range to be unlimited; and which betrays others, who recognize the limitations of its range, into the error of supposing that within these its dicta are above question.

§ 390. Another influence has favored the establishment of this autocracy among the faculties. Reason has been instrumental in putting down the inferior forms of mental government—the government by prejudice, the government by tradition, &c.; and wherever it has replaced them tends to play the despot in their stead. For of the developing mind, as of a developing society, it seems to be a law that progress towards the highest form of government, is through forms each of which establishes a new ruling power that behaves only a little less tyrannically than the ruling power it displaced. Or, to change the figure, we may say that by extinguishing other superstitions Reason makes itself the final object of superstition. In minds freed by its help from unwarranted beliefs, it becomes that to which an unwarranted amount of belief is given. It absorbs, as it were, the strengths of all the errors it has subdued; and the unquestioning respect once felt for all these errors, swells by accumulation into a servility which never dreams of asking for the credentials of this power that has expelled them.

In thus describing the worship of that which puts down superstitions as in itself the final superstition, we come, indeed, much nearer to literal truth than at first appears. For this worship implies the assumption that by shaping consciousness into a particular form, there is given to it some power independent of the power which belongs intrinsically to its substance. Reasoning, however, is nothing more than re-coördinating states of consciousness already co-ordinated in certain simpler ways; and re-coördination can no more give to the results reached a validity independent of that possessed by the previously-coördinated states, than cutting a piece of wood into a certain shape can give it a power independent of that which the substance of the wood already has.

§ 391. The remarkable fact is that this excessive confidence in Reason, as compared with simpler modes of intellectual action, is not seen in those by whom Reason has been employed with such astonishing results. Men of science, now as in all past times, subordinate the deliverances of consciousness reached through mediate processes to the deliverances of consciousness reached through im-

mediate processes; or, to speak strictly, they subordinate
those deliverances reached through prolonged and conscious
reasoning, to those deliverances reached through reasoning
that has become so nearly automatic as no longer to be
called reasoning.   The astronomer who has, through the
elaborate quantitative reasonings which we call calculations,
concluded that a transit of Venus will commence on a
certain day, hour, and minute, and who on turning a telescope to the Sun at that time sees no black spot entering on its disc, infers an untruth in his calculations—
not an untruth in those relatively-brief and primitive acts
of thought which make up his observation.   The chemist
whose reasoned-out formula for a new compound implies
that the separated precipitate put into his scales should
weigh a grain, and who finds that it weighs two grains, at
once abandons the verdict of his reasoning; and never
dreams of calling in question the verdict of his direct perception.   So is it with all classes of the men whose joint
efforts have brought our knowledge of the Universe to its
present coherent comprehensive state.   It is rather among
the spectators of these vast achievements of Reason that
we find this exaggerated estimate of its power; and in the
minds of these spectators its usurpation is often marked in
proportion as the converse with Nature has been remote.

Of course, I shall not be suspected of taking sides with
those who would subordinate Reason to Faith.   The question raised is that of the comparative validities of beliefs
reached through complex intellectual processes and beliefs
reached through simple intellectual processes.   I put in a
demurrer to the tacit assumption that the complex processes are the relatively-authoritative ones; and ask the
warrant for this assumption.   I draw attention to the fact
that metaphysicians, setting out with this as their postulate,
seem unconscious that they have postulated anything; and
may be brought to a stand by demanding proof that their
postulate has a greater certainty than the counter-postu-

late. Deliverances of consciousness are of two kinds—the one given through a process comparatively direct, the other given through a process comparatively indirect. The mass of men take for granted that when the results of the two processes are at variance, those reached by the direct process must be accepted; and men of science, who use both processes to most purpose, agree with the mass of men in unhesitatingly assuming this supremacy of the direct process. The few metaphysicians, however, assume that the indirect process is supreme. Here, as a first step in the criticism of their conclusions, comes the question—Why is the indirect process supreme? If they can give a satisfactory answer, they establish a claim to proceed with their case. If not, the illusion is as likely to be with them as with their opponents.

As likely, I have said—I should have said more likely. For here we have only to ask how their assumption is to be justified, to find that there is no possible way of justifying it. In the trial of Reason *versus* Perception, Reason claims superior trustworthiness. If this claim is challenged, Reason can do no more than employ some process of Reason to justify the claim. But such process of Reason itself needs to be proved valid if Reason in general needs to be proved valid. The validity of Reason is already taken for granted in any argument by which the superior trustworthiness of Reason is to be shown. There can be nothing but a disguised *petitio principii*. If, of two witnesses brought into court to testify each on his own behalf, A asserts one thing and B the opposite thing, B does not increase his credibility by any number of assertions which severally take for granted his credibility. Reason, then, is absolutely incapable of justifying its assumption. An assumption it is at the outset. An assumption it must remain to the last.

CHAPTER III.

§ 392. The meaning acquired by each word during its development has been determined partly by its genealogy and partly by its environment. To the one are traceable the natures and powers of its component parts, which severally once had distinct meanings that are still implied though inconspicuous. To the other are traceable the successive differentiations which have given it the particular form and adaptations it now possesses. That each word has derived from a long ancestry its present constitution, and that a complete understanding of it is in many cases to be obtained only by studying ancestral words, is a familiar truth; though a truth not duly remembered in philosophical discussions. But that the constitution of each word has, in the course of its descent, been ever undergoing modifications fitting it to co-operate with environing words, is a correlative truth which is not familiar. Yet the second factor is no less important than the first. Words have become specialized and defined only in the course of those actions which they have joined one another in performing. The meaning of every one has been gradually restricted by the growth of others, which have trenched upon the sphere it once occupied alone. Every one has come to have special classes of words, and often special groups of those classes, with which it habitually acts. And in many cases, adjustable appendages are formed by which it articulates with the other words that give to it its power, direction, and effectiveness.

Otherwise expressing these truths, we may say that each word has both an intrinsic connotation and an extrinsic connotation. It does not simply imply, with various degrees of distinctness, the meanings of ancestral words; but it implies also the meanings of coexisting words, which limit and extend and individualize its meaning, and in the absence of which it is meaningless. Let us consider in the concrete these two kinds of connotation.*

Suppose we take for our example the adjective brown. Philologists, of whom Grimm is one, trace this back to a word common to the Aryan languages, meaning " to burn." Some derivatives of this refer to a brightness like that of flame; and the derivatives *braun, bruun, bruen, bruin, brun, bruno, brunus,* which in sundry languages mean *brown,* refer to the colour produced in a thing exposed to flame. That is to say, as originally used the word described a certain kind of appearance metaphorically, by reference to one of the concomitants of a certain process wrought in an object. There were contained in the consciousness summoned up by the word, combined ideas of temperature, touch, pressure, form, motion, given by the thing and the action connoted; and without all these the meaning acquired could never have been acquired. It matters not to the argument whether the derivation above given be the true one or not. Some derivation of this kind, implying experiences of special objects or actions or both, there certainly was. We have but to call to mind recent names for colours, as *orange* and *lilac,* to be fully assured that all names of colours were originally special, and became general only by dropping

---

* I believe I am giving here, and throughout this chapter, meanings that are wider than usual to the words *connote* and *connotation ;* but the license appears to be justified by the derivation, and is needful for my purpose.

their intrinsic connotations. And if so, the verbal sign *brown* cannot now be used to convey the idea *brown*, without tacitly implying some such intrinsic connotations.

We will now look at the extrinsic connotations of the word. To think of *brown*, is simultaneously to think of colour. I cannot have that consciousness of it which constitutes cognition, without referring it to its class. This involves a further extrinsic connotation. Colour is an abstract word which has no meaning in the absence of experience of colours; so that there are indirectly connoted other distinct colours, forming along with *brown* the class to which *brown* is referred in being thought of. This is not all. Colour is thinkable as a kind of feeling, only by contrast with other kinds of feelings—to identify a state of consciousness as colour, is simultaneously to distinguish it from touch, taste, smell, sound, &c. Great classes of feelings are thus connoted by the class colour, which is connoted by the colour *brown.*   Take another group of extrinsic connotations. The consciousness of colour involves the consciousness of space of two dimensions; and be it true or not that in the undeveloped consciousness an area of colour cannot be conceived without conception of distance going with it, there can be no question that by the time the word *brown* is used, distance is connoted, and that there is also connoted the consciousness of position. Hence the word *brown* is meaningless unless space of three dimensions, more or less specialized by limitations of place, and size, and form, is simultaneously conceived. Time, too, is extrinsically connoted. I do not mean merely that the relation of coexistence, under which an area of *brown* has to be represented, can be known only by contrast with non-coexistence, that is, with succession; but I mean that the consciousness of *brown* tacitly implies past experiences of *browns*, with which it is classed as like; and to think of *brown* in terms of a before-known feeling is to be conscious of time.   Merely just indicating remoter connotations, such as the general relations of likeness and difference involved in all the foregoing connotations, it will be sufficiently manifest that there can be no consciousness answering to the word *brown,* unless there go along with it numerous consciousnesses denoted by other words not mentioned. Only by co-operation with the many thoughts answering to these many words, does the thought *brown* become possible.*

This being understood, we are prepared to examine the language used by metaphysicians, and to mark all its direct and indirect implications.

§ 393. At the outset of his *Principles of Human Knowledge,* Berkeley discusses the use of abstract words; observing, very truly, that in no case can an abstract word be rendered into thought without some one or more of the concrete meanings embraced by it being thought of. He says:—" I can consider the hand, the eye, the nose, each by itself abstracted or separated from the rest of the body. But then whatever hand or eye I imagine, it must have some particular shape or colour. * * * And it is equally impossible for me to form the abstract idea of motion distinct from the body moving, and which is neither swift nor slow, curvilinear nor rectilinear; and the like may be said of all other abstract general ideas whatsoever." Having professedly cleared the ground from the ambiguities due to the careless use of abstract words, Berkeley commences his argument. We will interpret its words after his own principle of interpretation, and as defined by their connotations, intrinsic and extrinsic.

In the first paragraph of the succeeding chapter, we come upon these words—*"By sight I have the ideas of light and of colours."* Let us take *seriatim* each member of this statement and consider all that is meant by it.   The word *by is*

---

* For another exposition of this general doctrine see Second Edition of *First Principles,* § 39.

a highly abstract word—so abstract that we are very apt to overlook the relation, having at least two terms, invariably implied by it. Its intrinsic connotations are lost in the remote past; but its extrinsic connotations, abundantly obvious, will suffice us. Originally the word means " near " or " close; " as " to sit *by*," " to pass *by*." Proximity being the root-notion, there come the secondary notions of proximity with agency, either subjective or objective; as in " hit *by* a stone," " broken *by* me." And then a further complication gives us proximity through an agent; as in " I voted *by* proxy," " I learnt it *by* telegraph." Always, therefore, the word *by* connotes two or more things, in relation of position, or action, or both. To put it in Berkeley's way, " I cannot by any effort of thought conceive " what *by* means, unless I think of two somethings that are adjacent, or are brought into relation by something adjacent to both. So that the expression *by sight* implies in its first member something else than sight. The word *sight* itself, yields us the like implications with still greater distinctness. It is applied both to the faculty of vision and to a thing seen—*a sight;* and in the Anglo-Saxon *gesight* this latter meaning seems to have been the dominant one. Be this as it may, the word *sight* intrinsically connotes something seen and something seeing. Along with its original signification there was posited the relation of subject and object; and if this relation be supposed absent its meaning is gone. More than this is true. No thought answering to the word *sight* can be framed without thinking of a visual organ. *Sight* is an abstract word having no signification if there does not exist in the mind the idea of an eye and of the function of an eye. If, as Berkeley says, it is " impossible for me to form the abstract idea of motion distinct from the body moving; " then with no less certainty may I say that it is impossible for me to form the abstract idea of *sight* distinct from an eye seeing and an object on which it is turned. Thus the word *sight* expanded into its full meaning, immediate and remote, tells us specifically what the word *by* told us generally—that there is some unspecified existence in some relation of proximity.   Next comes the third word of the sentence, *I.*   We need not go into the vexed question of the notion of personal identity. Nor need we dwell on the fact that, as originally used, and as used by the mass of mankind now, *I* means the individuality as a whole; of which the extended organism forms in thought the dominant element. It will not be needful, either, to commit ourselves to any speculative conclusions respecting the original meanings of the personal pronouns, of which it is said that the first means " the here " and the second " the near to the here "—derivations which seem to me extremely doubtful. It will suffice to point out the unquestionable fact that the personal pronouns exist, and acquire meanings, only by their relations to one another.   Nowhere can there be found a language which has a pronoun in the first person without one in the second person—an " I " without a " thou." Leaving out all question of the intrinsic connotation of the word *I,* its extrinsic connotation has all along been, and still continues to be, the existence of that which is *not I:* primarily under the form of another like individual; secondarily under forms implying other such individuals; and tertiarily under forms implying entities of alien kinds.   We come now to the word *have,* Such light as is thrown by philologists on the intrinsic connotations of this word, implies that its deepest known root signified " to touch " or " to grasp "— signified, therefore, the action of a hand upon something seized. How truly this is the original meaning of the word, we have evidence in its still-extant legal use. To seize means, in Law, " to take possession; " and " seizin " means both " possession " and " the thing possessed." So that " to have," originally connoted a connexion between the organism and an external object. It acquired wider meanings gradually, as this connexion became more indirect and various; and only by a comparatively-late metaphor was applied to mental modifications. Even now it would be meaningless in the absence of the multitudinous ideas of outer things which go along with it. *I have*, is a combination of words that can give rise to a thought, only by connoting a distinction between something which I have and something which I have not. If all things stand in that relation to me implied by the notion of possession, then possession ceases to be thinkable from the absence of a correlative. So that both by its intrinsic and its extrinsic connotations, the word *have* necessarily involves the thought of existence other than self-existence.   The next inquiry is, what do we mean directly and indirectly by *idea?* Both its derivation and its current use imply a something that is connected with something else. The primitive rendering of the Greek word *ιδέα*, is form. Thence came the secondary notion of a semblance as distinguished from a reality. And then, in the Platonic philosophy, we have the meanings so inverted that *ιδέαι* are the eternal archetypes of which sensible things are the temporary antitypes. Throughout all these meanings, however, there is one element constant—the connexion of the *idea* with something of which it is the *idea :* be it the connexion of form with substance, of semblance with reality, or of divine matrix with objects moulded from it. This intrinsic connotation of an existence which is not the *idea*, has survived alike in philosophy and in common life; and whatever he may profess, no one can use the word without carrying this connotation into his thoughts.   Whoever doubts this, needs but to ask the implications of the succeeding word, *of*. It is a highly-abstract word expressing a relation—a relation, it may be, between one thing and another, or between a thing and an attribute, or between an object and an act, or between a cause and an effect; but a relation universally and necessarily implying two terms, as " a son *of* John," " the smell *of* a rose," "the kick *of* a horse." So that the word *of* extrinsically connotes two existences, just as much as the word *idea* does; and the two words together, *idea of*, jointly connoting this second existence, are meaningless in its absence—can no more be rendered into thought than the words " motion of " can be rendered into thought without a consciousness of something that moves. We come lastly to the word *colour* (for we may omit *light* as being dealt with in dealing with *colour*). Already we have seen that colour is unthinkable without the extrinsic connotations of time, extension of two dimensions, position, class, likeness, difference, &c.; and that if conceived as some particular colour, which Berkeley says it must be, it intrinsically connotes a something conspicuous for that colour. Now we have further to observe that this particular colour, characterizing some object it originally connoted, is the missing term of the relation expressed in blank by the words *idea of*. Here is the second existence implied by the first existence *idea*, as well as by the connecting link *of*, expressing relation. Not only do we find on examining critically the thoughts that are indispensable for giving meanings to these words, that *colour* and *idea* refer to two different existences; but we also find that the existence to which the word *colour* refers, is indissolubly bound up with other existences conditioned in a particular way.* And so it turns out that

---

* It may be well to shut the door upon the idealist who seeks an escape from this interpretation. He will perhaps say that by *the ideas of colours*, is to be understood—the ideas belonging to the class of ideas distinguished as colours; and that Berkeley means to state that he has various classes of ideas which he distinguishes as those of touch, of taste, of smell, of sound, &c., each one of which when it occurs he distinguishes as of, or belonging to, its class. That this is not what the words mean will be obvious on taking a parallel case. Suppose, referring to oysters, I call them the animals of mollusca; will it be admitted that I have correctly expressed myself as meaning animals of the class mollusca? Suppose, further, that the interpretation of the word animal is itself in dispute. Can we accept an unusual rendering which requires us to suppose the sentence incomplete, when the usual rendering makes sense of the sentence as it stands?

every word of the sentence tells the same story. Alike by
its inherited constitution, and by those specializations which
enable it to co-operate with other words, it proves itself to
be organized in conformity with the fundamental relation
of subject and object. The same story is told by each clause
of the sentence. *By sight I have*, if we reduce it from
the abstract to the concrete, as Berkeley insists that we
ought, inevitably means that *I*, through the *agency of my
eye*. receive *something;* and it is impossible to think of receiving something through an agent without being conscious of a third thing from which my agent receives
that something. The other clause, *idea of red* (to reduce
the abstract *colour* to a concrete) just as certainly involves
the same consciousness—involves the two separate existences *idea* and *red*, as much as " son of John " involves the
two separate existences, John and his son. When we put
together these clauses, the indefinite meaning of the first,
which is that through an agent I receive something from
something, is made definite; and I learn that through this
agent I receive from something *red* an *idea*, which I call
an *idea of red*. The whole sentence, then, its divisions, and
its ultimate parts, separately and jointly yield this meaning; and no one, metaphysician or other, can so suppress
the established associations of the words as to keep this
meaning out of his mind.

But now suppose we give the metaphysician full license.
Let us accept his words as he wishes them to be accepted;
and assume, for the nonce, that it is possible to exclude all
consciousness of their intrinsic and extrinsic connotations.
Let us grant Berkeley his entire position: saying with him
that the only existences are in the mind, and that the
being of everything is the being perceived. And let
us imagine that his words imply nothing whatever beyond
these states of mind or ideas. Let us suppose all this, I
say; and then, rigorously adhering to his interpretation, let
us observe what becomes of his proposition—*by sight I have*

the ideas of light and of colours. Following Berkeley's precepts, and putting for the abstract word *sight* its concrete meaning, we have, as indispensable elements of the thought, an eye directed upon something, and also a possessor of the eye. Leave out any one of these, and *sight* cannot be rendered into consciousness. If there is a possessor without an eye, there is no sight; if there is an eye without a possessor, there is no sight; if there are the eye and its possessor but nothing to be seen, there is no sight. Recognizing these three indispensable components of the conception *sight*, we have now, according to the Berkeleian hypothesis, to consider these components as so many ideas, or clusters of ideas. An eye can be to us nothing more than a combination of the ideas known as colours, arranged in a way to produce the ideas of certain forms, connected in thought with certain ideas of touch and of pressure that are combined into ideas of tangible size, shape, softness, elasticity, &c., and which are also connected with certain ideas of motions disclosing these other ideas. And now the proposition is that through these clustered and connected ideas, adjusted in a certain ideal way to something else which must be an idea, I have an idea of colour. If the reader finds himself enlightened by this statement, he must have a mental structure of a very unusual kind. When, however, he has conceived what it means, there rises before him a far greater difficulty of conception. For this complex cluster of ideas called an eye, through which he has ideas of colour, is itself composed partly of ideas of colour, and partly of other ideas, which, when defined, prove severally to involve ideas of colour. Thus if we put x to stand for colour (of which the several kinds involved may be signified by x_1, x_2, x_3, &c.), y to stand for visible form (which is also multiple), z to stand for tangible form (similarly multiple), v and w for softness, elasticity, &c.; and if we put θ and π to stand respectively for motion and muscular tension, and ϕ for the visible thing; then we may, in a rude way, but far too simply, represent the idea of colour according to Berkeley's hypothesis by the following equation:—

$$x = \frac{(x\,y + x_1\,y + x_2\,y_1 + x_3\,y_2) \times \dfrac{z + 2\,z_1 + 2\,z_2}{v\,w + v_1\,w_1}}{20\,\theta\,x_4\,y_5 \times 20\,\pi} \times \delta$$

The absurdity of assuming in the explanation, that the thing to be explained is already known, thus made manifest by symbolizing the explanation, becomes an absurdity raised to the nth power when we carry the inquiry a little further. For on seeking the value of z, standing for the idea of tangible form, we find that since the idea of touch implies the idea of a tactual organ, which is known through ideas of colour (by all at least who, having sight, can understand the terms of the definition), z itself has to be defined by a formula that involves x. Similarly with others of the symbols. Each of them in the foregoing equation must have substituted for it an expression containing both itself and $x;$ and the like substitutions may be made for each of the terms of the substituted expressions *ad infinitum*, without arriving any nearer to a result.

Among mathematicians, rendering the value of an unknown quantity in terms of itself and of other unknown quantities involving it, is regarded as unsatisfactory; but among metaphysicians values so rendered seem very acceptable.

§ 394. The language of Hume furnishes matter for such further criticism as is needful. The following extract will serve as a text:—

"Here, therefore, we may divide all the perceptions of the mind into two classes or species, which are distinguished by their different degrees of force and vivacity. The less forcible and lively are commonly denominated THOUGHTS or IDEAS. The other species want a name in our language, and in most others; I suppose, because it was not requisite for any, but philosophical purposes, to rank them under a general term or appellation. Let us, therefore, use a little freedom, and call them IMPRESSIONS; employing that word in a sense somewhat

different from the usual. By the term *impression*, then, I mean all
our more lively perceptions, when we hear, or see, or feel, or love, or
hate, or desire, or will. And impressions are distinguished from ideas,
which are the less lively perceptions, of which we are conscious, when
we reflect on any of those sensations or movements above mentioned."

Obviously these words might be dealt with as the words
of Berkeley have been dealt with. No more when used by
Hume than when used by Berkeley, can the word *idea* be
freed from those intrinsic and extrinsic connotations of
which there is no overt recognition; and the like intrinsic
and extrinsic connotations inevitably accompany the word
impression and determine its meaning. For though we are
told by Hume that the word is employed by him " in a
sense somewhat different from the usual; " and though he
perhaps means to say that an impression is not to be taken as
connoting a thing impressing and a thing impressed; yet it
may be contended that these connotations are surreptitiously
carried into the argument, and that no word can be substituted which does not carry such connotations. But passing over this, as having been already said by implication,
let us here pursue another line of criticism.

And first as to the force of the words accompanying
those which we have more especially to consider. Hume
begins by classifying " the perceptions of the mind "—using
the word perceptions, however, not in the modern sense,
but in a sense which covers all states of consciousness;
since he includes under it sensations, emotions, desires,
volitions, and the recollections of these. By classifying
these perceptions, or states of consciousness, he tacitly
asserts that they exist. As he does not avowedly posit the
existence of anything else, and as it is the purpose of his
reasoning to show that the existence of anything else is
doubtful, we must conclude that the existence of " perceptions of the mind," or what we now call states of consciousness, is at any rate beyond doubt. What, then, are we to
understand by *being* or *existing?* When, by dividing them,

65

Hume alleges the *existence* of impressions and ideas, does he give the ordinary meaning to the word? It is to be supposed so, since he does not warn us that he is about to give it any other meaning. Yet the notions which the · words *being* and *existing* convey do not seem appropriate for his purpose. To *be* is " to remain," " to be fixed." *Existence* is defined as " continued being," " duration," " continuation." Persistence is the root-notion running through all the meanings. So long as a pain persists we say it *is* still there; so long as breathings, pulsations, and other vital movements persist, we say there *is* life. The flash of lightning not having persisted is regarded as having ceased to be; while we assert the existence of sunlight so long as sunlight remains. Above all, it is this continuity, or endurance, or fixity, or persistence, which we especially mean when we assert the existence of what we call objects; among which, too, we draw the distinction between existing or ceasing to exist according as we do or do not find persistence.   Considerable difficulty arises in thus interpreting the words *being* and *existing* when we use them in connexion with impressions and ideas. For there are some of these, as the crack of a whip, which do not persist for any appreciable time; and there are others, as the feeling received from a seat, which persist for a long time. If we are to speak of the existence of such *impressions* in the way that is most consistent with the ordinary use of the word, I suppose we must say that they respectively exist as long as they persist. And now, thus interpreting the word as best we can in its application to Hume's *impressions* and *ideas*, let us observe the result.

I have what, for consistency's sake, I will call the impressions of mountains; and in the midst of them I have the impression of a black dot. I am walking, and after an immense number of the muscular and tactual impressions I call steps, the impression of the black dot becomes a little larger and clearer. I go on, and in the course of another half-hour's walking I perceive a change of shape, as well as of size—the impression is now larger vertically than horizontally. Approaching nearer, the shape insensibly becomes more definite while the subtended area becomes greater; and at length my suspicion that the impression I am receiving is what I call a man is confirmed: I can distinguish his head and his arms. As I come still closer all the details grow distinct, and the impression, sensibly changing at every step, rapidly enlarges until it occupies a considerable part of the visual area. If I continue my approach, the impression begins to exclude other visual impressions—nay more, after it has excluded all others, if I persist in advancing my eye, the lateral parts of the impression disappear from the field of view, the central part goes on enlarging, and when my eye is quite close to a button, I have an impression only of the button with a small portion of the surrounding cloth. All these changes have been perfectly continuous; so that from the original black dot to the fully-expanded impression of a man, and from this to the impression of a bit of his dress finally filling the whole visual consciousness, there is nowhere a place at which any sensible break occurs. The matter becomes considerably complicated on observing that as I move round, carrying my eye hither and thither close to this so-called man, I have continuously-changing impressions which have no separate individualities, and which yet become from moment to moment totally distinct from one another. Now the pattern of his waistcoat comes into view, disappearing laterally as I move; now the cloth covering his arm; now the collar of his coat, his shirt-collar, his hair. I cannot, by any mark, cut off one of these panoramically-changing states from another; and yet the motion of my eye is perpetually followed by a state which has nothing in common with that which existed a moment before. Again, if being now on one side of the man or behind him, I begin to retreat, a continuously-changing consciousness of another order begins: the impression, unlike the first in the distribution of its parts, dwindles as I retire; and may, if I go back far enough, vanish into a point. Without further detail it will be obvious that for every direction in space there is a different serially-changing consciousness producible by approach or recession; and that motion round the man at every distance, and in every plane, will also produce a changing consciousness contrasted more or less with all the others. Moreover, if we suppose that the man, instead of being stationary, is himself walking or otherwise moving, every one of these changing conscious-nesses becomes itself the possible root of innumerable other series, differing from one another as the man's motions differ. So that without counting the variations producible by variations in the quantities and qualities of light, we may say that the visual impressions thus gene-rated admit of millions of metamorphoses; all of them so related that it is possible to pass from any one to any other by infinitesimal gradations, and which yet are such that multitudes of them contrast with one another as strongly as can be imagined.

And now what is my visual impression of a man? Leav-ing out all the rest, let us take the changing consciousness originally described, which, beginning as a dot, expands without breach of continuity until it occupies the whole vis-ual field; which, at first without sensible distinction of parts, develops by infinitesimal gradations into a multitude of variously-shaped and variously-coloured components; and which, during the last stage of the approach, enlarges so as to pass more and more beyond the limits of the visual field, until at length the visual field is wholly occupied by a small portion of it, that may be gradually exchanged for another small portion, and this for another. What, I ask again, is my visual impression of a man? Three imagin-able answers only can be given. It is the state of con-sciousness existing at any moment during the time in which consciousness is undergoing these changes; or it is a certain set of such states that occur during a certain part of the time; or it is the sum of the series of states occurring during the whole time. Let us observe what each of these possible answers commits us to. If by the impression of a man, as one of those " perceptions of the mind " that are alone said to exist, I am to understand the sum of all these consciousnesses, then I am obliged to say that the individual thing which I know as the impression of a man, is at the same time all those many things which I have distinguished as different—the small dot, the appreciable figure, the thing that shuts out everything else from view; and I have not only to do this, but also to include those multitudinous different states producible in me by close inspection of his different parts, since these are continuous with one another and with the impression that commenced as a dot. If, again, the existing something which I call the impression of a man, is to be understood as including only a part of the series, there arise the unanswerable questions—what part of the series? on what principle am I to cut out of the series some portion that is continuous with the rest at both of its extremes? and by what names shall I call the excluded parts of the series? And if, to avoid these insuperable difficulties, I take the third course, and say that by the impression of a man is to be understood any one phase of this continuously-changing consciousness, then I find myself in difficulties no less insuperable. In the first place, to consider any one transverse section of this continuously-changing consciousness, as that impression the existence of which I am entitled to assert, besides implying an arbitrary separation of what was not in the least separate in my consciousness, implies the assertion of as many such existences as this continuous consciousness can be divided into. In the second place, it raises the unanswerable question—at what stage does that expanding impression which I receive as my eye comes near, cease to be the impression of a man and become the impression of this or that part of his dress? And in the third place, I find myself obliged to admit that this impression of a man, of which alone I may assert the existence, is something which, having come into existence, instantly ceases to exist —something which has a persistence that is inappreciable.　　　　See then the alternatives. To say that the existence which I call the impression of a man, is the totality of all these changing phases of my consciousness, is to say that by unity I mean multiplicity; and is also to say that by a thing which exists, I mean an almost-infinite series, the remoter members of which are absolutely different and no two which are present together. And if, to avoid the absurdity of calling that an existing thing which is a heterogeneous multitude of things, successively appearing and disappearing, I say that the impression of which I assert existence is the impression I have at any one stage of my approach, then the thing which I say exists is a thing which has no persistence at all: existence no longer means persistence, but the reverse.

Thus it turns out that if the words *impressions* and *ideas* are supposed not to have the connotations which they actually have, the words along with which they are used cease to have their ordinary meanings and get opposite ones. So long as I interpret to myself an *impression* as connoting something that impresses and something that is impressed— so long as I recognize these two somethings as independent existences of which the one affects the other, the meaning of the word *impression* remains intelligible; and all these peculiarities of an *impression* above detailed, become comprehensible as caused by the changing relations between the two existences. But if I suppose myself capable of thinking of an *impression* as existing without these two connoted existences; then it results that in giving to it a meaning which it has not, I take away from the co-operating words all the meanings they had.

§ 395. I had intended here to examine other words and expressions used in metaphysical controversy; and to trace out the process by which metaphysicians, rising to abstractions and thence to abstractions of abstractions, take their stand upon these and proceed to abolish the realities from which the abstractions are derived—apparently supposing that the abstractions continue to exist. But it is, I think, needless to continue.

What has been said above discloses the significant fact that *language absolutely refuses to express the idealistic and sceptical hypothesis.* No manœuvring enables it to bring up by themselves the states of consciousness overtly referred to, while excluding the states of consciousness referred to by implication. If the words are used, as they must in fact be used by every one, metaphysician or other, with all the intrinsic and extrinsic connotations they have acquired; then we find that separately and jointly they imply existence beyond consciousness. If, while unable really to free the words from these connotations, we suppose them to be freed, the result is that in seeking to define their meanings we can do nothing more than express each in terms of itself. And we also find that when absolute existence is claimed for what, by the connotations of the words, is shown to have only relative existence, the result is either to make *unity* mean *multiplicity*, or to make *existence* mean *absence of persistence.* The choice is in every case between self-contradiction, or entire absence of meaning, or complete inversion of meaning.

Language has, in fact, been throughout its development moulded to express all things under the fundamental relation of subject and object, just as much as the hand has been moulded into fitness for manipulating things presented under this same fundamental relation; and if detached from this fundamental relation, language becomes as absolutely impotent as an amputated limb in empty space.

CHAPTER IV.

THE REASONINGS OF METAPHYSICIANS.

§ 396. Let us grant the metaphysicians all which the two foregoing chapters have denied. Let us not stop them by asking the warrant for their tacit assumption that the mode of intellectual action distinguished as reasoning is more trustworthy than any other mode of intellectual action. Let us allow their language to pass without comment: assuming that the words they use can be used without implying all that is to be disproved. And now supposing this, let us examine their reasonings and see whether they can make out their case.

Of course it will be impossible to do more than deal with typical examples. We will begin, as before, with Berkeley.

§ 397. Imaginary conversation affords great facilities for gaining a victory. When you can put into an adversary's mouth just such replies as fit your purpose, there is little difficulty in reaching the desired conclusion. Berkeley's *Dialogues of Hylas and Philonous* furnish abundant illustrations of this. *Hylas* repeatedly assents to propositions which, on his opponent's own principles, he should not have assented to. Soon after setting out, *Philonous*, with the view of proving the subjectivity of heat, obtains from *Hylas* the admission that an " intense degree of heat is a very great pain." He then asks—" Is your material substance a senseless being, or a being endowed with sense and perception?" To which *Hylas* replies—"It is senseless, without doubt." "It cannot, therefore, be the subject of pain," continues *Philonous*. "By no means," rejoins *Hylas*. And *Philonous* then argues that as an intense heat is a pain, and as a pain cannot exist in a senseless material substance, it follows that an intense heat can exist only in a perceiving mind. But what right has *Hylas* to make the answers he does? The argument sets out with the position that sensible things are the only things we certainly know; these sensible things are defined as "the things we immediately perceive by the senses;" and *Philonous*, resolutely ignoring everything else, says:—"Whatever other qualities, therefore, you speak of, as distinct from these, I know nothing of them." Had *Hylas* as he should have done, taken the same ground, the dialogue would have run thus:—

Phil. Is your material substance a senseless being, or a being endowed with sense and perception?

Hyl. I cannot say.

Phil. How do you mean you cannot say?

Hyl. I mean that like you, "I know nothing" of any qualities of bodies save those I immediately perceive through the senses; and I cannot immediately perceive through the senses whether material substance is senseless or not.

Phil. But you do not doubt that it *is* senseless?

Hyl. Yes; in the same way that you doubt my external reality—doubt whether I am anything more than one of your ideas. Did we not, at the beginning, Philonous, distinguish between things known immediately and things known mediately?

Phil. Yes.

Hyl. Did you not make me admit that sensations are the only sensible things—the only things immediately perceived; and that I cannot know the causes of these sensations immediately, but can only know them mediately by reasoning?

Phil. I did.

Hyl. And your whole argument is an attempt to show that these things which I know mediately—these things which I infer as the causes of my sensations, do not exist at all.

Phil. True.

Hyl. How, then, can you put any trust in my reply, if I say that matter is not sensitive? The only sensitiveness I can immediately perceive is my own.

Phil. You know that I am sensitive.

Hyl. Yes, but how? I see you turn when spoken to and shrink when burned. From such facts, joined with my personal experiences, I *infer* that you are sensitive as I am; and if you must have an answer to your question, I *infer* that matter is not sensitive, because it shows no such signs.

Phil. Well.

Hyl. Well! do you not see that if you adopt this answer your whole reasoning is vitiated? You set out to disprove a certain portion of my mediate knowledge. To do this, you now ask from me another portion of my mediate knowledge, as you have already asked several, and will, I suppose, ask more. You are combining these many portions of mediate knowledge, and will draw from them a conclusion; and this conclusion—this piece of *doubly* mediate knowledge, you will, I suppose, offer to me in place of the mediate knowledge you would disprove. Certainly I shall reject it. I demand that every link in your argument shall consist of *immediate* knowledge. If but one of them is an inference, and not a thing " immediately perceived by sense," I shall say that your conclusion has the same uncertainty with this that you combat, *plus* the uncertainty attendant on all argument.

This, though sufficient to bring *Philonous* to a stand, is not the line of cross-examination best fitted to show his self-contradiction. *Hylas*, if he saw still more clearly the nature of the fallacy, might proceed to pull off its disguises somewhat in this manner:—

Phil. Is your material substance a senseless being, or a being endowed with sense and perception?

Hyl. What if I reply that it is endowed with sense and perception?

Phil. You are trifling with me.

Hyl. But suppose I affirm, in all sincerity, that material substance has feeling.

Phil. Then your reply is extremely absurd.

Hyl. What do you mean by " absurd "?

Phil. By absurd, I mean " that which is opposed to manifest truth "—" that which is inconsistent with reason, or the plain dictates of common sense."

Hyl. Very good; but to make sure that we understand one another respecting the meaning of absurdity, let us take a case. Suppose I ask you to draw a revengeful straight line.

Phil. That is a sufficiently-absurd proposal. I cannot even think of a revengeful straight line, much less draw one.

Hyl. Tell me now, *Philonous,* how you perceive the implied proposition that a straight line can be revengeful, to be a manifestly-untrue proposition, or, as we here call it, an absurd proposition? You know it to be absurd through some process of thinking, do you not?

Phil. Certainly.

Hyl. I suppose that before you can recognize the absurdity of the assertion that there can be a revengeful straight line, you must think more or less clearly of the two things between which the incongruity exists. So long as you are conscious of a straight line only, you are not conscious of any absurdity. So long as you are conscious of revenge only, you are not conscious of any absurdity. You are conscious of absurdity only when you try to think of revenge as a property of a straight line, and find that it is absolutely impossible to unite the two ideas.

Phil. That is manifest.

Hyl. One further question—When you consider that I am absurd if I tacitly assert that there can be a revengeful straight line, you do so because the absurdity is clear to your own consciousness?

Phil. Yes. I must perceive the absurdity myself before I can attribute it to you.

Hyl. We are agreed thus far, then; that to be conscious of an absurdity it is needful to be conscious of two things avowedly or tacitly alleged to be congruous, but between which there exists some great incongruity; and that when you call a proposition of mine absurd, you do so because it seems absurd to you.

Phil. That is what I have said.

Hyl. Now let us return to our question. You ask me whether material substance is a being endowed with sense and perception. I reply that it *is* endowed with sense and perception; and you call my reply absurd.

Phil. I do.

Hyl. That is to say, the proposition that material substance can feel, appears to your mind an absurd proposition.

Phil. Unquestionably.

Hyl. Have we not agreed, *Philonous*, that before you can be conscious of an absurdity you must be conscious of the two things between which there exists the perceived incongruity?

Phil. We have.

Hyl. In this case one of the two terms is material substance. The other of the two terms is feeling or sense. And in being conscious of the absurdity of the proposition that material substance possesses sense, you have to be conscious of the two incongruous things, sense and material substance.

Phil. Well, I—

Hyl. Yes; no wonder you stammer. I have detected you in recognizing that very existence which you pretend not to recognize. All the while that you were questioning

me about what you are pleased to call *my* material substance, you were thinking about *your* material substance—
about a material substance which was just as much present
to your consciousness as to mine.

Thus Berkeley's argument is brought to a dead-lock at
the outset, whatever answer is given. If to his question
respecting the sensibility of matter there be given the reply
which is alone consistent with his hypothesis, that it is impossible to say, his argument cannot proceed. And the acceptance of the reply that it is *not* sensitive, is equally fatal
with the rejection of the reply that it *is* sensitive. Since
neither the truth of the one, nor the untruth of the other,
can be discerned without a recognition of the subject
(material substance) as well as the predicate (sense and perception).

§ 398. In the last chapter I have quoted a paragraph
from Section II. of Hume's *Inquiry concerning Human Understanding*—the paragraph in which he divides " all the
perceptions of the mind into two classes or species," which
he calls, respectively, *Impressions* and *Ideas*. The distinction he draws between these is that the first are original and
the second are derivative; or, to use his own words—" all
our ideas or more feeble perceptions are copies of our impressions or more lively ones." Having alleged that we
have no real ideas but what are thus derived, he proceeds
to make this derivation the test of real ideas, and winds up
the Section by saying:—

" When we entertain, therefore, any suspicion that a philosophical
term is employed without any meaning or idea, (as is but too frequent),
we need but inquire, *from what impression is that supposed idea derived?*
And if it be impossible to assign any, this will serve to confirm our
suspicion."

Passing over some two pages treating " Of the Association of Ideas," we come to Section IV. entitled " Sceptical

Doubts concerning the Operations of the Understanding,"
which begins thus:—

"All the objects of human reason or inquiry may naturally be
divided into two kinds, to wit, *Relations of Ideas*, and *Matters of Fact*.
Of the first kind are the sciences of Geometry, Algebra, and Arith-
metic, and, in short, every affirmation which is either intuitively or
demonstratively certain. *That the square of the hypothenuse is equal to
the squares of the two sides*, is a proposition which expresses a relation
between these figures. *That three times five is equal to the half of thirty*,
expresses a relation between these numbers. Propositions of this kind
are discoverable by the mere operation of thought, without dependence
on what is anywhere existent in the universe. Though there never
were a circle or triangle in nature, the truths demonstrated by Euclid
would for ever retain their certainty and evidence.

"Matters of fact, which are the second objects of human reason,
are not ascertained in the same manner; nor is our evidence of their
truth, however great, of a like nature with the foregoing. The contrary of every matter of fact is still possible, because it can never
imply a contradiction, and is conceived by the mind with the same
facility and distinctness, as if ever so conformable to reality. *That
the sun will not rise to-morrow*, is no less intelligible a proposition, and
implies no more contradiction, than the affirmation, *that it will rise*.
We should in vain, therefore, attempt to demonstrate its falsehood.
Were it demonstratively false, it would imply a contradiction, and
could never be distinctly conceived by the mind."

Here, then, in Sections II. and IV. are two classifications;
in the one of which " all the perceptions of the mind " are
divided into *impressions* and *ideas*, and in the other of
which " all the objects of human reason or inquiry " are
divided into *relations of ideas* and *matters of fact*. The
first question to be asked is—What connexion exists between the two assemblages of things thus respectively divided? Is the assemblage called " perceptions of the mind "
coextensive with the assemblage called " objects of human
reason or inquiry " ? As Hume has not told us, we must try
and ascertain for ourselves.

If the two assemblages are not coextensive, there are
three possibilities. The first assemblage may include the

second and something more; or the second may include the first and something more; or while the two have a part in common, each may contain something which the other does not. Let us test these respective assumptions. If there are " objects of human reason or inquiry " that are not " perceptions of the mind," then it is possible for human reason to perceive things which do not become " perceptions of the mind " in being perceived; and this is a contradiction in terms. If, conversely, the assemblage, called " perceptions of the mind," includes, but exceeds in extent, the assemblage called " objects of human reason or inquiry," then there are some " perceptions of the mind " that are not " objects of human reason or inquiry " —a curious proposition which at once calls for a definition of those which are, as distinguished from those which are not. And if the third possibility is the one intended—if while the two assemblages overlap, each contains something which the other does not, then there are both some " objects of human reason or inquiry " that are not " perceptions of the mind," and there are some " perceptions of the mind " that are not " objects of human reason or inquiry: " there arise two insurmountable difficulties.

Hume, therefore, must intend us to understand the two assemblages to be coextensive; or rather, there is but one assemblage called by different names. The aggregate which in the one Section is divided into *impressions* and *ideas*, is, in the other Section, divided into *relations of ideas* and *matters of fact*. Hence there suggests itself as a preliminary question—How do these different classifications of the same assemblage stand to one another? This question subdivides into several questions, which we will consider *seriatim*. What are *relations?* Nothing was said about relations when the " perceptions of the mind " were divided into *impressions* and *ideas*. Is it meant that relations are not " perceptions of the mind "? If so, then though ideas are " perceptions of the mind " the relations between them are not; and if the relations between them are not " perceptions of the mind," what are they? where are they? and how do we become conscious of them? When, failing to answer these questions, we infer that relations are included among the " perceptions of the mind; " there comes the inquiry—under which of its subdivisions, impressions or ideas? Suppose we say they are to be classed with impressions. Then a *relation of ideas* consists of two ideas and an impression—a conception irreconcilable with the definition given of impressions and ideas, since it requires us to conceive of two copies of past impressions joined together by a present impression. If, contrariwise, a relation is to be classed among ideas; then, as we are told that whatever is known as an idea was previously known as an impression, we have to ask—Where is that impression to which the idea called a relation corresponds?   Here we are introduced to a still more serious question—What about the *relations of impressions?* If, as we are told, " all our ideas are copies of our impressions; " it follows that if there are relations of ideas there must be relations of impressions. For suppose there are not. Then we must say (1) that impressions exist out of relation to one another—exist in such wise that we can perceive them individually, and yet cannot at the same time perceive them to be one before another, or one like another, or one different from another. We must also say (2) that impressions having generated ideas, which are copies of them, these can exist in relation—can be known as like or unlike, before or after, though their originals cannot. And we must further say (3) that since such relations between ideas are not copies of relations previously known between impressions, they are either existences of a new order, or else they are ideas that have not pre-existed as impressions: a conclusion which contradicts the fundamental proposition.   Let us try to amend Hume's classification, so far as seems needful to avoid these fatal criticisms. Let us qualify his statement that " all the objects of human reason or inquiry " are divisible into *relations of ideas* and *matters of fact*, by recognizing *relations of impressions* as included in the assemblage to be divided. Shall we make of this a third class? or is it to be identified with the class, *matters of fact?* Clearly it cannot be identified with the class, *matters of fact*. For Hume distinguishes between *relations of ideas* and *matters of fact* by this, that the " contrary of every matter of fact is still possible," whereas the contrary of what he calls a relation of ideas is not possible. Now since we find ourselves obliged to conclude that relations of ideas are derived from relations of impressions, it follows that as relations of ideas are necessary, the relations of impressions they are derived from must be necessary. If not, whence comes the necessity? Are we to suppose that the necessity arises in the relations between the copies, and did not exist in the relations between the originals? We cannot say this; and unless we do say it, we must say that the *relations of impressions* are not what Hume calls *matters of fact;* since he distinguishes these as being not necessary.   Thus it becomes manifest, on comparing these two classifications, that they cannot by any manœuvring be reconciled. All possible suppositions made with the view of reconciling them, lead us into contradictions and absurdities.

Suppose we pass over these incongruities between the two classifications, and study the second classification by itself. The moment we begin to look carefully into it we find ourselves in perplexities. Here are some of them.   When an aggregate assemblage is divided into two classes, we do not expect each class to contain members of the other—we do not, when separating objects into animate and inanimate, make each division such that it contains both living things and not-living things. Hence we must suppose that Hume's two classes, *relations of ideas* and *matters of fact*, are mutually exclusive: no matter of fact is a relation of ideas; and no relation of ideas is a matter

66

of fact. If his two classes are to be thus conceived, however, we must give to the titles of them very unusual meanings. According to Hume's definition, it is *not* a matter of fact that 2 and 2 make 4: this is a relation of ideas. According to Hume's definition, the conclusion that the sun will rise to-morrow is *not* a relation of ideas: this he instances as a matter of fact. Obviously, language is here greatly strained from its ordinary acceptation; for that 4 results from adding 2 to 2, is commonly cited as a matter of fact which there is no gainsaying. With some reason, therefore, we might hesitate to follow an argument in which words are employed in senses so arbitrary, until some guarantee is offered that we shall not be betrayed into error by giving them their ordinary senses. But waiving this, let us ask what is meant by saying that the proposition— "the sun will rise to-morrow," does not express a relation of ideas. Does it express a relation of impressions? This cannot be; for impressions exist only in time present, and the word "to-morrow" implies time future. If, then, the conclusion—"the sun will rise to-morrow," is "a perception of the mind," it must be admitted that, as it does not consist of impressions, it must consist of ideas. Do these ideas exist out of relation? If so, what is the purpose of the proposition—"the sun will rise to-morrow"? Is it not the purpose of every proposition to assert a relation? See, then, the predicament. This which Hume instances as a *matter of fact*, must either be at the same time a *relation of ideas*, or else his definitions of *impressions* and *ideas* must be abandoned. But now let us overlook these further incongruities. Let us accept in all faith, this division of the "objects of human reason or inquiry" into *relations of ideas* and *matters of fact ;* and let us see whether we can put under one or other of these two heads, all the "objects of human reason and inquiry" that arise. Suppose I say that a rope, of which I see one end, has got another end. Shall I call this a matter of fact or a relation of ideas? On trial it refuses to come under either. If it is a matter of fact, then since, as Hume tells us, " the contrary of every matter of fact is still possible," it must be possible for the rope of which I see one end to have no other end—the absence of another end can " be distinctly conceived by the mind," to use his own words. Shall we say this? If not, we choose the second alternative, and class it as a relation of ideas. Let us see how it agrees with this class. Hume says that propositions respecting relations of ideas " are discoverable by the mere operation of thought, without dependence on what is anywhere existent in the universe." But if so, this proposition that a rope of which I see one end has got another end, cannot be a relation of ideas; for I cannot think it without thinking of something existent. To speak of an end of a thing is nonsense if there is no thing to have the end. Hence this is neither a relation of ideas nor a matter of fact; and Hume's division of " all objects of human reason or inquiry " into these classes fails.

Turning from these multitudinous fallacies of classification and definition, let us now observe Hume's mode of arguing; and see how far it conforms to the principles he lays down. If, in a philosophical work, we came upon a chapter entitled " Unhesitating Faith in the Operations of the Understanding," we should of course expect to find in it large claims. An attempt to show that the ultimate nature of matter may be ascertained, would not surprise us; or we might read without astonishment the assertion that the ultimate nature of the existence out of which consciousness is evolved, may be discerned. Even in a chapter thus entitled, however, we should be taken aback by the assumption that we can know not only the ultimate truths presented by the Universe as it exists, but also that we can know what would remain true if the Universe did not exist. How, then, shall we express our amazement on finding such an assumption in a chapter entitled " Sceptical Doubts con-

cerning the Operations of the Understanding "? Yet Hume
makes this assumption. The test by which he professes to
distinguish *relations of ideas*, is that their truth does not
depend " on what is anywhere existent in the universe "—
they would remain true were there nothing in the Universe.
So that the Understanding is supposed to be capable of
perceiving what would hold under conditions which *do not*
exist; while " sceptical doubts " are entertained respecting
its ability to perceive what holds under the conditions which
do exist! And the marvellous fact is that this exalted
faith in the Understanding, furnishes a *datum* for the argument which is to justify " sceptical doubts " concerning it!
On the belief in its transcendent power is based the proof
of its utter impotence! To show, in a direct way,
the illegitimacy of this proceeding, we have but to apply
Hume's own test, above quoted. He tells us that when we
suspect a philosophical term is used without any meaning
or idea, " we need but inquire, *from what impression is that
supposed idea derived?* and if it be impossible to assign
any, this will serve to confirm our suspicion " that the
term is meaningless. Let us ask, then—Where is the *impression* corresponding to the *idea* of a Universe in which
mathematical truths hold " without dependence on what is
anywhere existent in it "? There is no such impression;
consequently there is no such idea; consequently the proposition is empty sound.

Were it requisite to carry the criticism further, and to
examine the validity of the conclusions which Hume draws
from his premises, several lines of inquiry might be pursued,
of which I will briefly indicate the directions. He
asserts that " the foundation of all our reasonings and conclusions concerning the relation of cause and effect is *experience*." Suppose we put the question—experience of *what?*
Hume began by dividing " all perceptions of the mind "
into impressions and ideas, and tacitly professed to postulate nothing else. Must we then say that this *experience*,

through which we discover relations of cause and effect, is experience of impressions and ideas?—are these particular connexions among our states of mind, determined by the recurrences of particular connexions among our states of mind? This is to make their connexions self-determining. For if not, how come some connexions to recur so as to produce in thought the relation of cause and effect, while others do not so recur? The very conception of *experience* implies something of which there is experience—implies something which determines particular connexions of thought rather than other connexions; and so implies this very notion of cause which is said to be derived from experience. We are further told that when a man has found certain things habitually joined together in experience, there is " a principle which determines him to form " the conclusion that there is a secret power or cause connecting them; and that this principle is *custom* or *habit*. Now what is *habit?* Humes tells us to test the reality of a professed idea by asking for the impression from which it is derived. Where, then, is the impression corresponding to the idea, *habit?* I know of none. If Hume cites cases of often-recurring actions and often-recurring thoughts (say, of words and their meanings) as showing us the establishment of connexions by habit, I answer that according to his own interpretation, nothing is presented in experience except the recurrent impressions and ideas; and that no one can point out an impression answering to the idea *habit*, any more than he can point out an impression answering to the idea *cause*. And here we are introduced to the further question that might be asked—How can *experience* and *habit* be assigned as giving origin to the notion of *cause*, without involving the notion of cause in the explanation? How is it possible to convey the thought that experience *produces* in us this notion, without taking as the very basis of the thought the notion of causation? How is it possible to speak of habit as a " principle which *deter-*

mines" (i.e., *causes*) us to think of things as causally related, without including this conception of cause in the explanation? The conception of cause is surreptitiously re-
introduced in the very act of explaining it away. As usual
with metaphysicians, proof of the non-existence of a thing
is based on the assumption of its existence.

Such, as I have said, might be the lines of criticism
pursued were it requisite to carry the inquiry further.
But further inquiry is, I think, manifestly unnecessary.
Either the sceptical conclusions Hume draws are legitimately deducible from the premises he lays down, or they
are not. If they are not so deducible, then his reasoning,
being inconsequent, need not be examined. If they are
legitimately deducible, then they are invalidated by the
badness of the premises. A logical apparatus that is to
overturn the deepest of human beliefs, must have an extremely firm base; must have parts rigid enough to bear
any strain; and must have these parts so firmly articulated
that there is no dislocating them. Far from finding that
the co-ordinated groups of propositions with which Hume
sets out, fulfil this requirement, we find them incapable of
bearing any strain at all—we find them altogether incoherent. Nay, worse than incoherent. On trying to fit them
together, to see how they will work as an argument, we discover that the different parts absolutely refuse to join one
another; and tumble apart as fast as they are placed in
apposition.

§ 399. It is curious to see a doctrine which positively
contradicts our primary cognitions, chosen as a refuge from
another doctrine which simply doubts them. In the
philosophy of Kant, however, this is done. Scepticism,
questioning all things, professes to decisively affirm nothing.
Kantism, in anxiety to escape it, decisively affirms things
contrary to universal belief.

I propose here to examine somewhat fully the Kantian

doctrine that Time and Space are subjective forms which have nothing objective corresponding to them: being prompted to do this not only with the view of further illustrating metaphysical reasonings, but because the doctrine itself still keeps its hold on many minds.*

If all B is made possible by A—cannot exist in the absence of A, we must call A original and B derivative. If C's and E's, and F's, &c., cannot exist in the absence of B, it is obviously a mistake to make their existence primarily de-

---

* Throughout this discussion I use the expression "forms of intuition," and avoid the expression "forms of thought," which I used in the first edition of this work; and for using which I have, along with other writers, been blamed. In the course of a controversy carried on in *Nature*, from January 3 to February 10th, 1870, it was pointed out by Mr. Lewes, who was one of those charged with this misrepresentation, that among others who have used the phrase "forms of thought" to express this doctrine of Kant, are sundry professed Kantists, as Dr. Whewell and Sir W. Hamilton (a great stickler for precision); and he might have added to these, Dr. Mansel, who is also an exact writer, not likely to have misapprehended or misstated his master's meaning. The fact is that, relatively to the question at issue, whether Time and Space belong to the *ego* or to the *non-ego*, the distinction is wholly unimportant, and indeed irrelevant. If some one were to quote the statement of a certain chemist, to the effect that broadcloth is a nitrogenous substance; and if another were to contradict him, saying— no, his statement is that wool is a nitrogenous substance; the objection would, I think, be held frivolous, when the question in dispute was whether the matter of wool contains nitrogen or not. And I do not see much more pertinence in the objection that Kant called Time and Space "forms of intuition" (raw material of thought), and not "forms of thought" itself (in which the raw material is woven together); when the thing contended is, that Time and Space belong neither to woven thought nor to its unwoven materials.

Here, beyond this general reply to the charge of misrepresentation, I may give the special reply which lies patent in the foregoing division of this work. This reply is, that no such divisions as those which Kant makes of human intelligence into Intuition, Understanding, and Reason, are tenable. Whoever has followed with attention the successive steps of the Special Analysis, through which we were led down without break from the highest Compound Quantitative Reasoning to that lowest consciousness in which two simple states are known as like or unlike, will see that this classification of Kant is not fundamental; and that a criticism based upon it cannot stand.

pendent upon B to the ignoring of A; and still more so if
their existence is dependent directly upon A as well as indirectly through B. I use this symbolic illustration to prepare the way for the statement that the so-called mental
forms, Time and Space, are the B of our alphabet; that the
A of our alphabet, by which the B becomes possible, is the
consciousness of likeness and unlikeness; and that the C,
D, F, &c.—the intuitions and conceptions presented and
represented in Time and Space—are directly dependent on
this consciousness of likeness and unlikeness, as well as indirectly dependent on it, through the derivative forms Time
and Space. The only true " form," whether of Intuition,
or of Understanding, or of Reason, is the consciousness of
likeness and unlikeness; which is common to all acts of intelligence whatever.

The assertion that subjective Time and Space are forms
derived from this primordial form, will take metaphysical
readers by surprise. Nevertheless, analysis will show it to be
undeniable. Whatever is separable into parts contains that
which is contained in the parts. If the consciousness of space
includes consciousnesses of parts of space, then whatever is
necessary to the consciousness of a part of space is necessary
to the consciousness of space. Now no consciousness of
any space, linear, superficial, or solid, is possible save under
the universal form of all consciousness—the dual relation of
like and unlike. A space of three dimensions can, in
respect of its size, be conceived only as less than the
space including it and greater than the space it includes; or
as like some magnitudes of space before presented, and
unlike others. No shape can be given to it in thought but
what implies limiting surfaces that are unlike in their positions, unlike (some of them necessarily) in their directions,
like or unlike in their areas. Each limiting surface must be
imagined as either having or not having all its parts in the
same plane—like in their directions, or unlike in their
directions; and the limiting lines of each limiting surface

are inconceivable except as some of them unlike in direction and the others as either unlike or like in direction (parallel). Nay, each one of these limiting lines can be represented only under the same form: all its parts must be thought of as like in direction (constituting it a straight line) or they must be thought of as some or all of them unlike in direction (constituting a crooked line or a curved line). Even when we reduce the space-consciousness to its ultimate components, this necessary form of it is equally manifest, if not, indeed, more manifest. That two positions may be conceived as related, they must be conceived as like or unlike in distance, or direction, or both. And if the ultimate component of the space-consciousness can be known only through the consciousness of like and unlike, then, *à fortiori*, the space-consciousness as a whole can be known only through this same consciousness of like and unlike.* Still more obvious, if it be possible, is the fact that the consciousness of Time can exist only through the consciousness of like and unlike. It needs but to listen to the tickings of a clock, or to feel one's pulse, to be aware that the essence of the time-consciousness is the consciousness of unlikenesses among the positions of the successive impressions, in relation to the impression now passing. Had we no consciousness of differences in their distances, as measured by differences in the numbers of intervening states, we should be conscious of them as existing all together—time-consciousness would be impossible.

* Kant does, indeed, appear to assert that there is a transcendent intuition of Space which goes before all consciousness of its parts. He says:— "These parts cannot antecede this one all-embracing space, as the component parts from which the aggregate can be made up, but can be cogitated only as existing in it. Space is essentially one, and multiplicity in it." Now if by this it is meant that there is an intuition of Space which involves no consciousness of near and remote; or that there is a consciousness of near and remote which involves no consciousness of parts; then I can only say that this intuition of Space is one I cannot discuss, for I do not possess it.

Having thus observed in what position these derived
mental forms, Time and Space, stand towards the ultimate
mental form, we are in a better position for weighing the
reasons given by Kant for regarding Time and Space as
ultimate mental forms. We will begin with Space.   As
pointed out in § 330, the proposition on which the Kantian
doctrine proceeds, that every sensation caused by an object
is given in an intuition which has Space for its form, is not
true: it is true only when the surfaces that receive the impressions can have their parts moved relatively to the agents
producing the impressions.* It will be manifest, also, to
any one who studies Kant's statement, that he refers only to
the visual space-consciousness: saying nothing about the

---

* Should any one need more evidence than was before given that the
sensation of sound is not presented under this so-called universal form,
will find it if he compares his musical ideas with his ideas of things he
has seen and touched. Let him first call to mind any object or place,
and observe that he is obliged to represent it in space ; let him similarly
call to mind the tactual impressions which any object gave him, and observe that these, too, are unrepresentable except as in space; and let him
note that here, where the sensation had space for the form under which
it was presented, it has also space for the form under which it is represented. Now let him observe what happens when some melody takes
possession of his imagination. Its tones and cadences go on repeating
themselves apart from any space-consciousness—they are not localized.
He may or may not be reminded of the place where he heard them—
this association is incidental only. Having observed this, he will see that
such space-implications as sounds have, are learnt in the course of individual experience, and are not given with the sounds themselves. Indeed,
if we refer to the Kantian definition of form, we get a simple and conclusive proof of this. Kant says form is "that which effects that the content of the phænomenon can be arranged under certain relations." How
then can the content of the phenomenon we call sound be arranged ? Its
parts can be arranged in order of sequence—that is, in Time. But there
is no possibility of arranging its parts in order of coexistence—that is, in
Space. And it is just the same with odour. Whoever thinks that sound
and odour have Space for their form of intuition, may convince himself
to the contrary by trying to find the right and left sides of a sound, or to
imagine an odour turned the other way upwards. So that there are two
orders of external phenomena not presented under the so-called universal
form of external intuition.

totally-different space-consciousness slowly developed in those who are born blind. But passing over all this, let us critically test his assertions respecting the behaviour of the visual space-consciousness. He says:—"We never can imagine or make a representation to ourselves of the non-existence of space, though we may easily enough think that no objects are found in it." Now this proposition may be disputed;—first, on the ground that when every trace of ideal existence has been expelled, relative distances become unthinkable from want of something to yield the thought of mark or measure, and that without the consciousness of relative distances there can be no consciousness of Space; second, on the ground that the shape and extension of a body do not, as Kant alleges, survive in thought when the body's properties are absolutely suppressed in thought, since limits are thinkable only in terms of idealized properties originally known through sensations; and third, on the ground that whoever supposes the space-consciousness remains after he has expelled all ideas of objects, has forgotten to expel the idea of his own body, which furnishes him with units of measure if he has no others, and that could he suppress his own body in thought (which he cannot), the consciousness of Space would disappear, because there would be nothing left to yield relativity of position. But merely indicating these minor criticisms, I pass to the major criticism; namely, that the fact which Kant here supposes he has proved is not the fact he set out to prove. The Space which, as he above says, remains after we have conceived all things to disappear, is the Space in which they were *imagined*—the ideal Space in which they were *represented*, and not the real Space in which they were *presented*. The Space said to survive its contents, is the form in which *re-intuition* takes place; not the form in which *intuition* takes place. Kant says that the *sensation* (mark the word) produced by an object, is the matter of intuition, and that the Space in which we perceive this matter is the form of intuition. To prove this he turns from the Space known through our open eyes, and in which the said intuition occurs, to the Space known when our eyes are closed, and in which the re-intuition or imagination of things occurs; and having alleged that this ideal Space survives its contents, and therefore must be a form, leaves it to be inferred that the real Space has been shown to be a form which survives its contents. But the real Space cannot be thus shown to survive its contents. The Space we are conscious of in actual perception, stands on just the same footing with the objects perceived: neither of them can be suppressed from consciousness. So that if survival of its contents is the test by which " a form " is distinguished, the Space in which intuitions are given is not a form.   Still more obvious is a parallel criticism on the parallel reason given for asserting that Time is an *à priori* form of intuition. Kant says:—" With regard to phænomena in general, we cannot think away time from them, and represent them to ourselves as out of and unconnected with time, but we can quite well represent to ourselves time void of phænomena." Now since he has already told us that " all which relates to the inward determinations of the mind is represented in relation of time; " and that " of time we cannot have any external intuition, any more than we can have an internal intuition of space "; it is manifest that the phenomena of which we can conceive Time to be void, are internal phenomena. For, if otherwise, the statement must be that while Time is an internal form, the phenomena of which we are able to conceive it void are external—are already out of it; which is nonsense. His proposition is, then, that we can represent to ourselves this form of our internal intuitions as persisting when all the matter of those intuitions has vanished. So far from recognizing this as a self-evident truth, it seems to me a self-evident untruth. In the first place, it is impossible to suppress these internal intuitions of which

Time is said to be the form: to suppose it possible, is to suppose that we may get rid of all thoughts and yet continue to think. And, in the second place, though quite unable to rid ourselves of the ideas filling this internal form of intuition, we may readily perceive that the successive positions of these ideas in the ever-passing series, yield us the consciousness of those intervals which make up the consciousness of Time; and that in the absence of all ideas marking these positions, consciousness of Time would disappear. So that of these assertions respecting the behaviour of these two forms of intuition, both are deniable. Instead of forming a trustworthy basis for a system of beliefs at variance with the universal dictum of consciousness, these two propositions would tend to discredit a system of beliefs that was in harmony with that dictum.

Accepting, however, these propositions for argument's sake; and accepting as necessarily involved the conclusion that Time and Space are forms of intuition; let us consider how the several statements made respecting them are to be reconciled with one another. Kant tells us that Space is a form of intuition in which all the sensations caused by external objects occur; and he also tells us that " the original representation of space is an intuition *à priori*, and not a conception." Elsewhere he unites these statements, saying —" but space and time are not merely forms of sensuous intuition, but *intuitions* themselves." Suppose we try to render this proposition into thought. Let us, if we can, conceive a thing as being both the *matter* of intuition and the *form* of intuition. We look at an object; and the doctrine is that we can perceive it only in Space as its form. Now let us remove the object—Space, considered as its form, remaining. This Space we are said to know as an intuition: Space is here the *matter* of the intuition—that which occupies consciousness. What, then, is the *form* under which this *matter* is presented? No form having been named, we must conclude either that the same thing is at once form and matter of intuition, or that there may be matter of intuition without any form; in which case why need any matter of intuition have form?   If we inquire more closely, this irreconcilability becomes still clearer. Kant says:—" That which in the phænomenon corresponds to the sensation, I term its *matter ;* but that which effects that the content of the phænomenon can be arranged under certain relations, I call its *form.*" Carrying with us this definition of form, as " that which effects that the content * * * can be arranged under certain relations," let us return to the case in which the intuition of Space is the intuition which occupies consciousness. Can the content of this intuition " be arranged under certain relations," or not? It can be so arranged, or rather, it *is* so arranged. Space cannot be thought of save as having parts, near and remote, in this direction or the other. Hence if that is the form of a thing " which effects that the content * * can be arranged under certain relations," it follows that when the content of consciousness is the intuition of Space, which has parts " that can be arranged under certain relations," there must be a form of that intuition. What is it? Kant does not tell us—does not appear to perceive that there must be such a form; and could not have perceived this without abandoning his hypothesis that the space-intuition is primordial.   For on pushing the inquiry—What is the form of intuition under which this alleged form of intuition is presented or represented to consciousness? we are brought back to the conclusion above drawn: it is presented or represented under the universal form of likeness and unlikeness. It is this form which " effects that the content " (when consciousness is occupied by the intuition of Space) " can be arranged under certain relations "—relations of like or unlike distance, and like or unlike direction. We see, as before, that the dual relation of like and unlike is the form of this so-called form, as well as the form of all the concrete experiences presented under it.*

A further step may now be taken. We will assume that Kant's premises are incontestable, and his conclusion irresistible. We will assume that the space-consciousness and the time-consciousness behave as he alleges, and that therefore we must agree with him in saying that they are forms of intuition. We will also imagine ourselves to have got over the difficulty of conceiving a thing to be both the matter of intuition and its form—both that which is conditioned in consciousness and that which conditions it. And having supposed all this, we will observe the position

---

* In an appendix to his Essay on the "Laws of Verse," Prof. Sylvester has republished from *Nature* the controversy to which I have referred above. In an additional note he says:—" It is clear that if Mr. Spencer had been made aware of the broad lines of demarcation in Kant's system between Intuition, the action or the product of the Sensibility, and Thought, the action or product of the Understanding (the two belonging, according to Kant, to entirely different provinces of the mind), he would have seen that his supposed refutation proceeded on a mere misapprehension of Kant's actual utterance and doctrine on the subject. If Mr. Spencer will restore to Kant the words really used by him, the sentence will run thus:—' If space and time are forms of intuition, they can never be thought of; since it is impossible for anything to be at once the *form* of thought and the *matter* of thought;' and his epigram (for Mr. Spencer must have meant it rather as an epigram than as a serious argument) loses all its point. Was it likely *à priori* that Kant (*the* Kant) should have laid himself open to such a *scholar's-mate* at the very outset of his system?"

I have only to remark that Prof. Sylvester's mode of rendering my criticism pointless, is a very curious, but not, I think, a very conclusive one. He has substituted Kant's words for my words in one part of the sentence quoted (from *First Principles*, p. 49), while he has made no corresponding substitutions in the correlative parts of the sentence. Had he put "intuition" for "thought" everywhere, instead of only in one place, my sentence would have run thus:—"If space and time are forms of intuition they can never be intuited; since it is impossible for anything to be at once the *form* of intuition and the *matter* of intuition." I fail to see that in the sentence as thus altered the point is lost: if it was there before, it is there now. Indeed, as I think the text shows, the change of expression which Prof. Sylvester's objection has led me to make, renders the disproof much clearer than it was before. Whether that disproof is rightly described by his metaphor, is a question that does not concern me—he is responsible for its use, not I.

in which we stand.　　　　　　Consider, first, the thing affirmed—that Time and Space are subjective forms, or properties of the *ego*. Is it possible to realize the meaning of these words? or are they simply groups of signs which seem to contain a notion but really contain none? An attempt to construct the notion will quickly show that the latter is the fact. Think of Space—of the thing, that is; not of the word. Now think of self—of that which is conscious. Having clearly represented them, put the two together, and conceive the one as a property of the other. What results? Nothing but a conflict of two thoughts that cannot be united. It would be as practicable to imagine a round triangle. What, then, is the worth of the proposition? As Mr. Mansel, himself a Kantist, says in his subtle work, *Prolegomena Logica:*—" A form of words uniting attributes not presentable in an intuition, is not the sign of a thought, but of the negation of all thinking. Conception must thus be carefully distinguished, as well from mere imagination, as from a mere understanding of the meaning of words. Combinations of attributes logically impossible may be expressed in language perfectly intelligible. There is no difficulty in understanding the meaning of the phrase *bilinear figure*, or *iron-gold*. The language is intelligible, though the object is inconceivable." If this be true, Kant's statement is empty sound. If, as Sir William Hamilton puts it, those propositions only are conceivable of which subject and predicate are capable of *unity of representation*, then is the subjectivity of Space inconceivable; for it is impossible to bring the two notions, *Space* and *property of the ego*, into unity of representation.　　　　Consider next that which is, by implication, denied. To affirm that Time and Space belong to the *ego*, is simultaneously to affirm that they do not belong to the *non-ego*. Beyond the above positive proposition, which it is impossible to think, there is thus a correlative negative proposition, which it is equally impossible to think. While, in the one case,

the assertion is that two things are united in fact which
we are wholly unable to unite in thought; in the other
case, the assertion is that two things are disunited in
fact which we are wholly unable to disunite in thought.
By no effort can any one separate, or think away, Space
and Time from the objective world, and leave the objective
world behind. The proposal to imagine a square divested
of its equiangularity is a kindred proposal. And if the
implied statement that a square has an existence apart
from its equiangularity, though a verbally-intelligible
statement, is unthinkable and meaningless, then no less
unthinkable and meaningless is the implied statement
that objects have an existence apart from Space and Time.

Nor are we committed to these two impossibilities of
thought only—there are sequent impossibilities. The
Kantian doctrine not only compels us to dissociate from
the *non-ego* these forms as we know them, but practically
forbids us to recognize, or suppose, *any* forms for the
non-ego. Kant says that " Space is *nothing else* than the
form of all phænomena of the external sense, that is, the
subjective condition of the sensibility, under which alone
external intuition is possible." This is a tacit affirmation
that there is no form of objective existence to which it
corresponds; since, if there were, it would be *something
else* than the subjective condition of the sensibility. He
says, too, that " Time is *nothing but* the form of our internal intuition. * * * it inheres not in the objects themselves, but *solely* in the subject (or mind) which intuites
them." And he distinctly shuts out the supposition that
there are forms of the *non-ego* to which these forms of the
ego correspond, by saying that " Space is not a conception which has been derived from outward experiences, * * * the representation of space cannot be bor-
rowed from the relations of external phænomena through
experience." Let us observe, then, the two alternative conclusions respecting the *non-ego*, between which we have to

67

choose.   The first is that the *non-ego* is formless.
Though, as existing internally, the matter of every intuition has its form, yet, as existing externally, the object to
which this intuition relates has no form.   As we have seen,
Kant defines *form* as " that which effects that the content   *   *   *   can be arranged under certain relations."
Understanding form in this sense, then, we must say that
the *non-ego* cannot have its content arranged under certain
relations.   But to say this is to say that the *non-ego*
has no parts, since to have parts is to have content arranged
in relations; and it is equally to say that it is not a whole,
for a whole necessarily implies parts of which it is the sum.
Whence the proposition amounts to this, that the *non-ego,*
having neither whole nor parts, cannot be thought of as
existing; and we are landed in Absolute Idealism, which is
contrary to the hypothesis.*   The alternative proposition is that the *non-ego* has a form, but that this
produces no effect on the *ego* in the act of experience.

---

* Let me here append the passage from which I have just quoted, for
the purpose of indicating what is either a confusion of statement or a change
in the meanings of the words used.   Kant says:—" The effect of an object
upon the faculty of representation, so far as we are affected by the said
object, is sensation.   That sort of intuition which relates to an object by
means of sensation, is called an empirical intuition.   The undetermined
object of an empirical intuition, is called *phænomenon.*   That which in the
phænomenon corresponds to the sensation, I term its *matter ;* " (here, remembering the definition just given of phenomenon, objective existence
is manifestly referred to) " but that which effects that the content of the
phænomenon can be arranged under certain relations, I call its *form.*"
(So that *form,* as here applied, refers to objective existence.)   " But that
in which our sensations are merely arranged, and by which they are susceptible of assuming a certain form, cannot be itself sensation."   (In
which sentence the word *form* obviously refers to subjective existence.)   At
the outset, the "phenomenon" and the "sensation" are distinguished as
objective and subjective respectively; and then in the closing sentences
the *form* is spoken of in connexion first with the one and then with the
other, as though they were the same.   This passage occurs on the first
page of the *Critique of Pure Reason* (p. 21 of *Meiklejohn's translation*).
Mr. Lewes has obliged me by comparing the words with the original,
and finds the translation to be accurate.

Though the objective existence contained under some objective form is capable of impressing the subject, and producing sensation, yet this sensation is conditioned wholly by the subjective form: the objective form is completely inoperative. So that whatever arrangement there may be in the content of the *non-ego*, the effect wrought on the *ego* has its content arranged purely according to the form of the *ego*. One arrangement of the *non-ego* is just as good as another, in so far as the *ego* is concerned. As it follows from this that no differences among our sensations are determined by any differences in the *non-ego* (for to say that they are so determined is to say that the form under which the *non-ego* exists produces an effect upon the *ego*); and as it similarly follows that the order of coexistence and sequence among these sensations is not determined by any order in the *non-ego*; we are compelled to conclude that all these differences and changes in the *ego* are self-determined. We are, as before, driven into Absolute Idealism, and the premises are contradicated.

To complete the criticism it remains but to remind the reader that the facts of consciousness supposed to be interpretable only on the Kantian hypothesis, are interpretable on the Experience-hypothesis, when it is adequately expanded. In the preceding Parts of this work, and more especially in the last of them, we have seen that if, in pursuance of the Doctrine of Evolution, we suppose the modifications produced by experience to be inheritable, it must happen that if there are any universal forms of the *non-ego*, these must establish corresponding universal forms in the *ego*. These forms, being embodied in the organization, will impress themselves on the first intuitions of the individual; and will thus appear to antecede all experience. But they will nevertheless be forms which, when analyzed, prove to be derived from that same ultimate consciousness of likeness and unlikeness into which all experience is resolvable: just as we have found.

And now let us sum up the Kantian argument—limiting ourselves to the case of Space. Kant tells us that Space is the form of all external intuition; which is not true. He tells us that the consciousness of Space continues when the consciousness of all things contained in it is suppressed; which is also not true. From these alleged facts he *infers* that Space is an *à priori* form of intuition. I say *infers*, because this conclusion is not presented in necessary union with the premises, in the same way that the consciousness of duality is necessarily presented along with the consciousness of inequality; but it is a conclusion voluntarily drawn for the purpose of explaining the alleged facts. And then that we may accept this conclusion, which is not necessarily presented along with these alleged facts which are not true, we are obliged to affirm several propositions which cannot be rendered into thought. When Space is itself contemplated, we have to conceive it as at once the form of intuition and the matter of intuition; which is impossible. We have to unite that which we are conscious of as Space with that which we are conscious of as the *ego*, and contemplate the one as a property of the other; which is impossible. We have at the same time to disunite that which we are conscious of as Space, from that which we are conscious of as the *non-ego*, and contemplate the one as separate from the other; which is also impossible. Further, this hypothesis that Space is " nothing else " than a form of intuition belonging wholly to the *ego*, commits us to one of the two alternatives, that the *non-ego* is formless or that its form produces absolutely no effect upon the *ego ;* both of which alternatives involve us in impossibilities of thought. And all these impossibilities of thought, offered to us along with a supposed necessary inference from supposed facts, we are to accept that we may escape a difficulty of interpretation assumed to be insurmountable, but which is readily surmounted!

§ 400. One other example of metaphysical reasoning may be fitly added—an example lineally descending from the last. It will show us how that rejection of the direct testimony of consciousness which Kantism involves, leads to contradiction when joined with that acceptance of the direct testimony of consciousness implied by "Natural Realism."

Sir William Hamilton, who, from some passages in his writings (see, for instance, p. 882 of the *Dissertations*), might be supposed to hold that Space is *both* a law of thought and a law of things; but who proves himself to be a disciple of Kant by saying—" It is one merit of the philosophy of the conditioned, that it proves Space to be only a law of thought, and not a law of things; " has been led by his Kantism into a suicidal argument. In his trenchant criticism on Dr. Brown, he brings into strong relief the inconsistency of that writer by putting side by side two positions respectively received and repudiated by him. The passage, which will be found at page 90 of the *Dissertations*, is as follows:—

" *I cannot but believe that material things exist :—I cannot but believe that the material reality is the object immediately known in perception.* The former of these beliefs, explicitly argues Dr. Brown, in defending his system against the sceptic, *because irresistible, is true.* The latter of these beliefs, implicitly argues Dr. Brown, in establishing his system itself, *though irresistible, is false.*"

Now when Sir William Hamilton asserts that Space is " only a law of thought, and not a law of things," he falls into an inconsistency of the same kind as that which he here exposes. To show this it needs but to make a small addition to the foregoing passage, and to change the names, thus:—

I cannot but believe that material things exist :—I cannot but believe that the material reality is the object immediately known in perception :—I cannot but believe that the space in which material realities are perceived is objectively real.

The two former of these beliefs, explicitly argues Sir William Hamilton, in defending his system against the sceptic, *because irresistible, are true.* The latter of these beliefs, implicitly argues Sir William Hamilton, in establishing his system itself, *though irresistible, is false.*

We are not now concerned with the tenability of Dr. Brown's position, or with the tenability of Sir W. Hamilton's criticism. We have to note only that if Sir W. Hamilton's argument is conclusive against Dr. Brown, a parallel argument is conclusive against himself; and that either the criterion he erects is no criterion, or that his belief respecting the subjectivity of Space is disproved by his criterion.

§ 401. Such, then, are metaphysical reasonings; not selected from the works of one writer or one school, but from the works of a series of writers of different schools —Berkeley, Hume, Kant, Hamilton. While disagreeing in other respects, these writers agree in the professed rejection of some or many of the fundamental *dicta* of consciousness. The passages quoted and criticized have been typical passages directly referring to these fundamental *dicta;* and the reasonings have been reasonings considered sufficient to disprove them. Have they the requisite cogency? So far from having it, they are full of defects which would invalidate quite ordinary inferences.

In one case we find that what is to be denied in the conclusion is tacitly affirmed in the premises. Now transcendent mental capacity is made the basis for proof of mental incapacity; and disproof of our consciousness of a thing is made to proceed upon our consciousness of another thing which the same argument disproves. To escape from a difficulty of thought, half-a-dozen impossibilities of thought are offered by way of refuge. And once more, the test of true cognitions, which is alleged to be final, is, without any assigned reason, assumed to be worthless in respect of particular cognitions.

CHAPTER V.

NEGATIVE JUSTIFICATION OF REALISM.

§ 402. The foregoing three chapters contain a general survey of the metaphysical position. We have seen that metaphysicians proceed on a tacit assumption which they make no attempt to justify; and which cannot possibly be justified. We have seen that the words they use, one and all, turn traitors; and along with every proposition they are set to express, persist in expressing some fatal counter-proposition. We have also seen that the reasonings framed out of these propositions cannot be coerced into establishing that which they are intended to establish; but have to take for their fulcrum that which is to be dis-established, and are powerless when that fulcrum is removed.

For ordinary purposes such an examination, leading to such results, might be held sufficient. Here, however, it is not intended as more than an introduction. It foreshadows the analytical argument on which we are now to enter, and still more vaguely the synthetical argument that is to supplement it—the one a negative justification of Realism and the other a positive justification of Realism.

By a negative justification of Realism, I mean a proof that Realism rests on evidence having a greater validity than the evidence on which any counter-hypothesis rests. By such proof the realistic belief is negatively justified; inasmuch as no belief having a better justification exists.

Before proceeding to an ultimate analysis, we will advance the examination a stage by making a proximate analysis.

CHAPTER VI.

THE ARGUMENT FROM PRIORITY.

§ 403. Twice in the course of this work (§§ 204 and 332, *note*) I have named, as illustrating in a remarkable way the effect of habit, the power acquired by microscopists of so moving objects under a microscope as to neutralize the apparent inversions of their motions. This adjustment, which is such that, to move the object to the right the fingers must be moved to the left, and to move it up they must be moved down, is, after long practice, made automatically, and comes to seem quite natural—so natural that when, for certain purposes, there is used an " erecting glass," which brings the visible motions into their ordinary relations with the tactual motions, these relations seem to be unnatural; and the microscopist is as much perplexed by this normal connexion of impressions as he originally was by the abnormal one.

Habit, thus shown to produce so striking a result in the sphere of simple external perception, is capable of producing a no less striking result in the sphere of that complex internal perception which we call reasoning. Here, too, by frequently presenting sequences of thought under an inverted relation, there is gradually superinduced the belief that this is their direct relation. From persistently contemplating them in a certain hypothetical order, exactly opposite to their real order, the hypothetical order eventually comes to appear as the real order and the real order as the hypothetical.

368

This is the attitude of mind generated by habit in the metaphysician. So accustomed is he to look through the introspective instrument which reverses the succession of his experiences, that the reversed succession is taken by him for the direct succession; and when he is made to look through an " erecting glass " which rectifies the succession, everything seems to him turned the wrong side up.

From this introductory parallel let us pass to the argument which it pre-figures.

§ 404. The postulate with which metaphysical reasoning sets out, is that we are primarily conscious only of our sensations—that we certainly know we have these, and that if there be anything beyond these serving as cause for them, it can be known only by inference from them.

I shall give much surprise to the metaphysical reader if I call in question this postulate; and the surprise will rise into astonishment if I distinctly deny it. Yet I must do this. Limiting the proposition to those epi-peripheral feelings produced in us by external objects (for these are alone in question) I see no alternative but to affirm that the thing primarily known, is not that a sensation has been experienced, but that there exists an outer object. Instead of admitting that the primordial and unquestionable knowledge is the existence of a sensation, I assert, contrariwise, that the existence of a sensation is an hypothesis that cannot be framed until external existence is known. This entire inversion of his conception, which to the metaphysician will seem so absurd, is one that inevitably takes place when we inspect the phenomena of consciousness in their order of genesis: using, for our " erecting glass," the mental biography of a child, or the developed conception of things held in common by the savage and the rustic.

During his early days a boy eats, plays, pulls to pieces his toys, quarrels with his brothers, and carries on a life in which things, and persons, and places, and acts, become familiar, and are dealt with in a way implying an apprehension of them essentially similar to that which adults have. During the same period there is acquired a knowledge of language sufficient for understanding and expressing simple propositions respecting objects, properties, and relations. But now let us ask, at what age does the boy first use any word ending in " ation "; and how many years is it before the meaning of " sensation " can be explained to him? Its first component " sense," understood as the general name for hearing, sight, touch, taste, and smell, is for a long time incomprehensible. The force of the ending, " ation," cannot by any possibility be known until the power of forming abstractions has been considerably developed. And the doubly-abstract term " sensation," remains for a still longer period without meaning. Equally obvious, or even more obvious, is the child's inability to know that he has sensations, when we remember his inability to form a definite conception of his own individuality. No urchin from the nursery speaks of himself as " I." He regards himself as an object. Hearing himself called " Georgy," he will say " Give Georgy," when he wants something; or will plaintively indicate " Georgy " as the cause of the evil when he has hurt himself. Such a form of speech as " I hurt myself," is never heard among young children. That synthesis of all the experiences and powers, past and present, constituting the conception of self, is far beyond the ability of an undeveloped intelligence. So that neither the subject nor the predicate of the proposition—" I have a sensation," can be even separately framed by a child, much less put together.

The notion of personal identity, though more developed in the savage, is still so imperfectly developed that he cannot form the consciousness which the metaphysician posits as primordial. In the languages of the lowest races there are no words answering to " mind " and " ideas." The uncivilized man has, indeed, got the belief in another self that goes away in dreams, and leaves the body for a longer time at death; but this other self, as conceived by him, is simply a duplicate, visible and tangible as the body is. He has no name for that which is conscious, or for that aggregate of thoughts and feelings called by us " consciousness; " and if he wants to convey the fact that he perceives something not present to the senses, he can do it only by likening his perception to external vision, and his internal power to an eye.* So that he is devoid of that conception of self as a sentient principle, which the metaphysical proposition implies; just as much as he is, in common with the child, devoid of any such notion as " sensation." We need but remember that his language has not even a general word for tree, as considered apart from particular kinds of trees, to see at once the absurdity of crediting him with these highly abstract ideas.

It is superfluous, however, to go so far for proof. Any labourer or farmer will furnish it. Tell him that the sound he hears from the bell of the village church exists in himself; and that in the absence of all creatures having ears, there would be no sound. When his look of blank amazement has waned, try and make him understand this truth which is so clear to you. Explain that the vibrations of the bell are communicated to the air; that the air conveys them as waves or pulses; that these pulses successively strike the membrane of his ear, causing it to vibrate; and that what exist in the air as mechanical movements become in him the sensation of sound, which varies in pitch as these movements vary in their rapidity of succession. And now ask yourself, what are these things you are telling him about? When you speak to him of the bell, of the air, of the mechanical motions, do you mean so many of his ideas?

---

* I do not assert this only as an inference from primitive languages. Some time since I had the opportunity of putting direct questions on the point to Dr. Theophilus Hahn, who was brought up among the Hottentots, has a full command of their language, and complete familiarity with their modes of thought; and he entirely verified the à priori implications.

If you do, you fall into the astounding absurdity of supposing that he already has the conception which you are trying to give him. By the bell, the air, the vibrations, then, you mean just what he means—so many objective existences and actions; and by no possibility can you present to him this hypothesis that what he knows as sound exists in him, and not outside of him, without postulating, in common with him, these objective realities. By no possibility can you show him that he knows only his sensations, without supposing him to be already conscious of all these things and changes causing his sensations.

Up to a considerably-advanced stage of his mental development, every one thinks of properties not simply as implying objects, but as being objectively what they seem to him subjectively. Aided by the " erecting glass " used above, even the metaphysician, perplexed by involved reasonings, will not fail to remember that originally he regarded colours as inherent in the substances distinguished by them; that sweetness was conceived as an intrinsic property of sugar; that hardness and softness were supposed actually to dwell in stones and in flesh. And perhaps he will recollect that only after a considerable amount of practice in throwing intellectual somersets, did he succeed in inverting his original conception; so as to think of the impression produced on him as that which is immediately known, and the outer object causing it as known mediately, so far as it is known. Remembering all which, he will see that the Idealistic hypothesis not only came long after the Realistic belief, but that when he succeeded in framing the Idealistic hypothesis he did so only by the help of the Realistic belief.

§ 405. Let us digress a moment to observe the source of these metaphysical confusions. The error has been in confounding two quite distinct things—having a sensation, and being conscious of having a sensation.

To be impressed by a colour, a sound, or an odour, and thereupon to perform some motion conducive to self-preservation, is a simple act perpetually performed by creatures of low grade—an act closely allied to reflex acts, and passing insensibly into these. We may figure its nature by imagining to ourselves, so far as we can, the process of sneezing, as occurring without a contemplating self to watch it and think about . it. A sensation thus existing before there exists an introspective consciousness, is a sensation of the kind spoken of by metaphysicians as being immediately given in consciousness, in contradistinction to the outer agent producing it, which can be but mediately given. And did they simply argue that the conception of the outer agent eventually framed, is framed out of such sensations, and stands in relation to them as secondary and derived, their position would be tenable enough. But it is one thing to say that in such a creature the sensations are the things originally given, while their objective cause comes in course of time to be inferred; and it is quite another thing to say these sensations can be known *as sensations,* by such a creature. So long as a creature is simply recipient of sensations, and so long as it has got only far enough to make the synthesis of these implied in the conception of an object—nay, so long as it has not reached the still more complex synthesis required to conceive the object and itself as independent existences, it cannot reach that consciousness of sensation which the metaphysician assumes to be primordial.

For, as we have seen above, this consciousness of having a sensation, which the metaphysical argument postulates, is the consciousness framed by a distinctly-individualized self, which long antecedent experience has clearly distinguished from a not-self. The metaphysical argument identifies two things which are at the very opposite extremes of the process of mental evolution. The simple consciousness of sensation, uncomplicated by any consciousness of subject or object, is doubtless primordial. Through immeasurably long and complex differentiations and integrations of such primordial sensations and derived ideas, there develops a consciousness of self and a correlative not-self. And far later than this is reached a final stage, at which it becomes possible for the developed self to contemplate its own states as affections produced in it by the not-self. And this final stage is spoken of as though it were the initial stage!

§ 406. Returning from this digression, that which we are concerned here to note, is that the Realistic conception is everywhere and always, in child, in savage, in rustic, in the metaphysician himself, prior to the Idealistic conception; and that in no mind whatever can the Idealistic conception be reached except through the Realistic one. Realism must be posited before a step can be taken towards propounding Idealism.

Now if any one, in proof that his friend died last week, produced a letter from his friend dated yesterday, announcing his own death, we should think that even Irish extraction would scarcely suffice to account for the illogicality. To say that a man is dead, and then to give, as evidence of his death, that which supposes him to be alive, implies a scarcely-imaginable blindness to the contradiction between premises and conclusion. And yet in what does this contradiction differ essentially from that which, having implicitly postulated external objects, evolves the conclusion that sensations only can be known, and that objects causing them are hypothetical, or even non-existent?

In brief, then, the argument from priority is this;—that in the history of the race, as well as in the history of every mind, Realism is the primary conception; that only after it has been reached, and long held without question, does it become possible even to frame the Idealistic conception, while resting upon the Realistic one; and that then, as ever after, the Idealistic conception, depending on the Realistic one, must vanish the instant the Realistic one is taken away.

CHAPTER VII.

THE ARGUMENT FROM SIMPLICITY.

§ 407. A bullet fired at a target a hundred yards off, may miss it; but if fired at the same target placed a thousand yards off, the probability of missing is much less. In walking over a frozen lake a quarter of a mile wide, you are not unlikely to slip down; but if the frozen lake is a mile wide, there is but little probability that you will slip down in walking over it. During an hour's ramble in April, there is a moderate chance that you may be caught in a shower; but if your ramble occupies the whole day, your chance of being caught in a shower is relatively small. These propositions, which look so eminently insane, will serve to exemplify, in a startling way, one kind of absurdity which pervades metaphysical conclusions.

For if we compare the mental process which yields Realism, with the mental process said to yield Idealism or Scepticism, we see that, apart from other differences, the two differ immensely in their lengths. The one is so simple and direct as to appear, at first sight, undecomposable; while the other, long, involved, and indirect, is not simply decomposable but requires much ingenuity to compose it. Ought we then to hold that in the short and simple process there is less danger of going wrong than in the long and elaborate process; or ought we to hold, with the metaphysician, that in the long and elaborate process we shall not go wrong, though we go wrong in the short one?

This comparison will be objected to on the ground that the two processes differ not in their lengths only but in their natures. Doubtless they do this. As we shall see in the next chapter, the process carrying us to the Realistic conception, is qualitatively so immensely superior that, lengths being supposed equal, its outcome is far more trustworthy than that of the process carrying us to the Idealistic conception. But claiming nothing here for this superiority, the two processes are, otherwise, so far alike that they may be properly compared in respect to their lengths. This will need a little explanation.

§ 408. The metaphysical argument, whatever be its particular species, habitually begins by offering proof that the Realistic belief is inferential. Now in one case and now in another, the listener is made to admit that the thing present to his consciousness is some feeling; that along with, say, a particular sensation of colour, there have habitually been joined, through certain motions made, sensations of hardness or softness, of smell, of taste, of temperature; that when he again has this particular sensation of colour, he *infers* that these other sensations will follow if he makes the appropriate motions; that this is the whole content of his consciousness; and that if he thinks there is any objective substratum serving as cause for this cluster of sensations, its existence is *an inference*—the inferred substratum can never be itself presented in consciousness. Thus the metaphysician shows that the Realistic belief is reached through a process of drawing conclusions—a process of reasoning. Consequently, as his own belief is also reached through a process of reasoning, the two processes are comparable in respect to their lengths. Let us see how they stand when thus compared.

In the first place, this alleged demonstration that the Realistic belief is inferential, itself consists of many inferences. Whatever risk there may be in drawing

the Realistic inference, is a risk over and over again en-
countered in drawing the successive inferences proving the
inferential nature of Realism. And hence to suppose the
inference of Realism disproved by this series of inferences,
is to suppose, as above, that while there is much danger in
one step there is little danger in many steps. Nay, the case
is even stronger; for whatever difference there is between
the natures of these inferential steps, is in favour of that
taken by Realism, which is far simpler than any one of those
taken in showing the inferential character of Realism. Let
it be granted that knowledge of the external object is
reached by synthesis. Is it not obvious that the alleged
demonstration of its synthetic origin, consists of syntheses,
each of which is more complex than the one called in question?

This, however, is by no means all. After the supposed
disproof of Realism comes the supposed proof of Idealism
or Scepticism. This has throughout the same character,
and involves throughout the same multiplication of possibilities of error. The conception to be justified cannot even
be framed without uniting several highly-synthetic acts;
and every step of the argument used to justify it, is synthetic
in a still higher degree. Take, for example, the proposition of Berkeley—" Ideas exist in Mind." Here are three
syntheses. *Idea* is a general word applicable to each of
our multitudinous states of consciousness of all orders; and,
as we see in the child, can be understood only after the
putting together of many experiences. *Mind* is a synthesis of states of consciousness—is a thing we can form no
notion of without re-*membering*, re-*collecting*, some of our
mental acts. Every conception of relation is a synthesis—
that of inclusion being one. The child is enabled to recognize one thing as *in* another, by observations similar to,
and simultaneous with, those which teach it the externality
of things; and until these observations have been generalized, the proposition that ideas are *in* mind is un-

thinkable. Thus, each of the words *idea, in, mind,* presupposes a synthesis; and the proposition—" Ideas exist in mind," is a synthesis of syntheses. Passing from the proposition of Idealism to its reasoning, it might be shown that each of its syllogisms is a synthesis of syntheses; and that its conclusion, reached by putting together many syllogisms, is a synthesis of syntheses of syntheses.

§ 409. Here, then, in its briefest form, is the issue raised:—That deliverance of consciousness which yields Realism, is either immediate or mediate. If it is immediate, everything is surrendered, and the controversy ends. If it is mediate, then it is comparable in its intrinsic nature with that deliverance of consciousness which is said to yield Idealism: this also is mediate. Being both mediate, the question arises—In what respect do they differ? and their most conspicuous difference we find to be that while the first involves but a single mediate act, the second involves a succession of mediate acts, each of which is itself made up of several mediate acts. Hence, if the one mediate act of Realism is to be invalidated by the multitudinous mediate acts of Idealism, it must be on the supposition exemplified at the outset; namely, that if there is doubtfulness in a single step of a given kind, there is less doubtfulness in many steps of this kind.

CHAPTER VIII.

§ 410. A man passing an acquaintance when it is dusk, may feel some doubt about his identity—a doubt he would not feel in broad daylight. A witness testifying to words whispered at the other end of a room, scarcely dares to assert their import as positively as if they were spoken in loud tones close to him. The truthworthiness of any outer perception is universally held to be great, in proportion as the elements of it are distinctly presented.

In like manner among ideas, we always put greater faith in those of which the components can be clearly recalled, than in those of which the components can be dimly recalled. If I repeat a sentence I heard a moment since, while the impressions made on me are quite fresh, I feel, and my hearers feel, far greater confidence in the exactness of my repetition than if the sentence was one I heard last week. The description of a person or a place seen yesterday, is regarded as much less liable to be erroneous than the description of a person or a place seen a year ago or ten years ago.

Immensely more marked is a further contrast of kindred nature. Deliverances of consciousness given in the vivid terms we call sensations, excite a confidence immeasurably exceeding the confidence excited by deliverances given in the faint terms we distinguish as ideas. If I think I left

379

a book on the table in the next room, and on going to fetch
it find it is not there, I do not suppose that the presence of
the book on the table as mentally represented, is comparable in certainty to its absence as actually observed. If, when
humming an air I heard yesterday on a musical box, I
imagine its cadences as taking this or that particular turn;
and if to-day on hearing again this same air on the musical
box, I find the cadences are not as I thought; it never
occurs to me to accept my recollection and reject my perception.

By all persons, then, and in all cases, where the characters
of the acts of consciousness are in other respects the same,
the deliverances given in vivid terms are accepted in preference to those given in faint terms. Obscure perceptions
are rejected rather than clear ones; remembrances which
are definite are trusted rather than those which are indefinite; and, above all, the deliverances of consciousness composed of sensations, are unhesitatingly preferred to those
composed of the ideas of sensations.

§ 411. The one proposition of Realism is presented in
vivid terms; and each of the many propositions of Idealism
or Scepticism is represented in faint terms. Let us grant
that in both cases the process of thought is inferential.
The two are nevertheless contrasted in this, that the single
inference of the one is made up of elements most, if not all,
of which have the highest degree of distinctness; while the
many inferences of the other are severally made up of extremely indistinct elements. Suppose we consider a moment the composition of a link in the Idealistic argument.

Each link is a consciousness that some one thing or
group of things, which comes within a larger group of
things distinguished by a certain character, has also that
character. In the process of thought yielding the conclusion, there is thus a mental representation of a sub-class
(the representation being usually but partial); there is a

representation of the including class (usually extremely partial); there is a representation of the predicated character as common to all members of the including class (also extremely partial); and there is a representation of the one class as included in the other (a representation also symbolized by a few cases taken to stand for all). Hence, besides the fact that the elements out of which this complex consciousness is formed are of the indistinct order, we have the fact that the groups of these indistinct elements are but indistinctly represented as groups; and that the inclusion of the one by the other is but indistinctly represented.

But the indistinctness of the terms composing each inference of the Idealist, is far greater than thus appears. For the classes of things dealt with are not simple representations: they are mostly representations of representations. If I allege anything about sensations, I do not allege it simply of some one assemblage, as sounds (which I can but very inadequately think of in their varieties), or of some other assemblage, as colours (which I can still less adequately think of in their varieties), or of odours only, or tastes only, or touches only: I allege it of all these heterogeneous and multitudinous classes together. So that when I make, or when I accept, any general statement respecting sensations, I can but hurriedly think over the indistinct ideas of a few of them, and join with this fragmentary representation an extremely vague notion of all the rest as supposed to be represented; and then, in a way equally vague, I have to observe that some represented character, said to belong to these things supposed to be represented, therefore belongs to some group, the inclusion of which is represented in an equally feeble manner.

Nay, not even now is the haziness of the consciousness fully described. For each of these successive propositions making up the Idealist's argument, is expressed in the symbols we call words. These symbols may or may not

be translated into the equivalent thoughts.   In many instances they are not translated—the equivalent thoughts are
not called into consciousness.   The words are just recognized as commonly standing for certain values, without its
being ascertained whether their values are forthcoming:
just as cheques and bills are accepted and passed on, without inquiring whether there are assets to meet them.   So
that very frequently there is not even the indistinct representation, or re-representation, described; but only a symbolic representation of this!

§ 412. See, then, the contrast.   Supposing that the deliverances of consciousness which yield Realism and Idealism respectively, were otherwise alike in their degrees of
validity; it would still happen that since the Realistic deliverance is given in terms of the highest possible distinctness,
while the Idealistic deliverance is given in terms of the ex-
tremest indistinctness, the Idealistic deliverance could not
be accepted without asserting that things are most certainly
known in proportion as they are most faintly perceived.

CHAPTER IX.

A CRITERION WANTED.

§ 413. The three short chapters just concluded, have advanced our analysis a stage by disentangling, and presenting separately, the three essential contrasts between the Realistic conception and the conceptions opposed to it. Let us glance at them separately and jointly.

The Realistic conception is prior in order of time; and the Idealistic conception cannot be framed in its absence. The one is independent, the other dependent upon it; and the Idealist, affirming that which is dependent, denies that on which it depends. The consciousness in which Realism rests is reached by a single inferential act; while the consciousness professed to be reached by Idealism, is reached by a series of inferential acts. The Idealist proposes that, distrusting the single inferential act, we shall have faith in a series of them. The elements of the act of thought which yields Realism as its result, are extremely vivid and absolutely definite; while the elements of each one of the acts of thought said to yield Idealism, are extremely faint and very indefinite. We are asked to accept all these successive results given in faint, indefinite terms; and, on the strength of them, to reject the result given in vivid, definite terms.

Stated thus nakedly, each of these tacit proposals is seen to involve the negation of a principle of rational thinking; and, even taken by itself, any one of them is obviously fatal to a doctrine which makes it. What, then, shall we think of the doctrine which requires us to negative all these three principles of rational thinking simultaneously? Yet this is what the metaphysical doctrine in general does. The primary independent belief, the belief reached most directly, the belief given in terms of the highest distinctness, is to be abandoned as baseless; and we are to take as well based the belief which is secondary and dependent, which rests on complex indirect evidence, and on evidence that is extremely indistinct. All three criteria of certainty guarantee the first, while the direct negations of these criteria are united to form the postulate of the last; and yet the last proposes to overthrow the first!

Need we wonder, then, at the strangeness of these metaphysical systems, as contemplated by those who have not cultivated " the art of puzzling one's-self methodically "? Need we wonder if the uninitiated pass them by with unconcern, mingled, it may be, with more or less of contempt? Speculations which set out by inverting all those tests men commonly use in the pursuit of truth, are not unnaturally thus met.

§ 414. But now we have to enter upon a further stage of our inquiry. It is not enough to be clear that a doctrine is erroneous; it is not enough even to disentangle the error from its disguises; it is further requisite—and in this case above all others requisite—that we should trace down the error to its simplest form and find its root.

We have abundant reason for suspecting that there is a root of error common to all these systems which seem to establish beliefs that are absolutely incongruous with our primary belief. I do not mean simply that the difficulty of thinking them, much more of accepting them, furnishes ground for this suspicion; but I mean that, apart from the particular results reached, their general aspects are eminently suggestive of an all-pervading fallacy. Each of them requires us to choose between these alternatives:—that there is some fundamental flaw in its method, or that reason necessarily leads to unreasonable conclusions. And while it is possible to think the first of these, it is impossible to think the second. For clearly all metaphysics can be nothing but an analysis of our knowledge by means of our knowledge— an inquiry by our intelligence into the decisions of our intelligence. We cannot carry on such an inquiry without taking for granted the trustworthiness of our intelligence. How then can we legitimately end in proving something at variance with our primary beliefs, and so proving our intelligence fundamentally untrustworthy? Intelligence cannot prove its own invalidity, because it must postulate its own validity in doing this.

Manifestly, then, there must be some unrecognized datum, the overlooking of which makes possible this suicidal conflict. Each side of the argument involves the tacit assumption that intelligence proceeding after some manner or other can reach a valid conclusion; for on each side intelligence is used. If one of these deliverances of intelligence is wrong—if of two contradictory propositions uttered by it, both cannot be accepted; then does not any choice which is made imply some ultimate principle of thought that is conformed to more in the one case than in the other? And is it not clear that before there can be agreement on the general issue there must be agreement on the particular issue —what is this ultimate principle.

§ 415. The need for some such preliminary agreement is best seen on contemplating the general conduct of the controversy; which, in the absence of a common ground, amounts to little more than beating the air. The argument of the Realist habitually fails from not having as a fulcrum some universally-admitted truth which the Idealist also has to admit. Right as Reid may have been in his conviction, he cannot be said to have demonstrated that he was so. His *Inquiry into the Human Mind* contains no disproof of Scepticism, but is little more than an elaborate protest against it. In his later work, the *Essays on the Intellectual Powers of Man*, he continues to adopt as premises what the sceptic rejects as conclusions. Having thrown down his gage, he remains outside the lists, and merely hurls at his opponent an occasional sarcasm.

In the Dissertation appended to his edition of Reid's works, Sir William Hamilton places the Common-sense Philosophy on a more satisfactory footing. But though he gives systematic form to its doctrines, he does not render it criticism-proof. Among the self-evident propositions with which he sets out, are these:—

"Consciousness is to be presumed trustworthy until proved mendacious."

"The mendacity of consciousness is proved, if its data, immediately in themselves, or mediately in their necessary consequences, be shown to stand in mutual contradiction."

Now a sceptic might very properly argue that this test is worthless. For as the steps by which consciousness is to be proved mendacious are themselves acts of consciousness; and as they must be assumed trustworthy in proving that consciousness is not so; the process results in assuming the trustworthiness of particular acts of consciousness, to prove the mendacity of consciousness in general.

Perhaps it will be replied that, could it be shown, a contradiction between the data of consciousness would still be the justification of Scepticism—that though it would not prove the certainty of falsehood, which implies somewhere a test of truth, it would yet prove the impossibility of determining any judgment to be either true or false. The rejoinder is, that the cognition of a contradiction between two primary data of consciousness, implying as it does the union of those two data in a certain relation, is a more complex operation of consciousness than the cognition of either datum by itself; that any untrustworthiness of consciousness, did it exist, must render the compound cognition more uncertain than the simple cognitions; that hence the consciousness of a contradiction can never have so great a validity as either of the primary data of consciousness between which it is supposed to exist; that thus the only logical scepticism must be directed against the seeming contradiction; and that, consequently, Scepticism must destroy itself at the first step.

Doubtless all this, merely serving to show that the mendacity of consciousness cannot be proved, and that the effort to establish either the validity or invalidity of consciousness is analogous to the mechanical absurdity of trying to lift the chair one sits on, does not diminish the credibility of consciousness—merely shows that its credibility must be assumed. Sir William Hamilton's test simply fails to help us: the only harm being that the offer of a valueless guarantee, lays open to cavil that which it is put forward to insure.

One further thing, however, which much concerns us here, is shown. Proving, as the foregoing criticism does, that an assumption of the trustworthiness of consciousness *in general*, fails to help us; and seeing, as we have done, that there must exist somewhere in consciousness a way of determining trustworthiness; we are left with the implication that there has to be found some *particular mode* of consciousness which is trustworthy in comparison with all other modes.

§ 416. Otherwise stating the case, we must, in place of a vague, unmethodic deliverance of consciousness, substitute some precise, methodic deliverance. In the language of Evolution, we have to rise from a less definite to a more definite form of mental action. And this, indeed, is an aspect of the matter which we may advantageously pause a moment to consider.

It is with mental progress as with all other progress, that along with increasing integration and increasing heterogeneity there goes increasing definiteness; and in the region of the intellect, as everywhere else, exactness can be reached only through stages of decreasing inexactness. It is impossible to get accuracy from undeveloped minds; and undeveloped minds dislike prescribed ways of obtaining accuracy. Cooks hate weights and scales—prefer handfuls and pinches; and consider it an imputation on their skill if you suggest that definite measures would be better. There are uneducated men who trust their own sensations rather than the scale of a thermometer—will even sometimes say the thermometer is wrong, because it does not agree with their sensations.　　　 The like holds with language. You cannot get uncultivated people, or indeed the great mass of people called cultivated, to tell you neither more nor less than the fact. Always they either over-state or under-state; and regard criticism or qualification of their strong words as rude or perverse.　　　 So, too, is it with the processes of thinking carried on by those who are wanting in power or discipline of thought. They guess at results. They will not deliberately examine premises and conclusion. They are impatient if you hint a doubt whether the case in question belongs to the class they have referred it to; or whether that class invariably possesses the character they predicate of it. In short, just in proportion as their ability to reason is small, they resent any attempt to bring their conclusion, or any part of their argument, to the test.

Now though among men who philosophize, there has commonly been a prolonged exercise of the reflective powers; though they recognize the need for method and precision; and though by studying Logic many have deliberately prepared for carrying on the higher mental processes correctly; yet even among them there is a remnant of indefiniteness and an apparent reluctance to use the final precaution required to reach definiteness. Not only is there an ignoring of the question—What is it which makes one deliverance of consciousness preferable to another? but there is no readiness to join issue on the question, and to let conclusions stand or fall by the result.

Yet to them, if to no others, it should be obvious that there must be somewhere, in some shape, some fundamental act of thought by which the validities of other acts of thought are to be determined. Unaided internal perception can no more suffice to build up subjective science than unaided external perception can suffice to build up objective science. As we cannot by simple outward inspection determine with exactness the relation between two objects; so we cannot by simple inward inspection determine with exactness the relation between two states of consciousness. In the one case, as in the other, some method of verifying our empirical cognitions must be found, before any sure results can be reached. We have to proceed in the ascertainment of internal truths, as we proceed in the ascertainment of external truths—we have to make a particular mode of perception the guarantee of all other modes.

§ 417. Press them home, and the antagonist schools of philosophy are both compelled to recognize some ultimate law of intelligence which from the beginning dominates over all conclusions; and which must be tacitly, if not avowedly, recognized before any conclusion can be accepted rather than some other.

Whoever says there are mental forms or innate powers, thereby asserts the pre-existence of something which imposes itself on all that is given in experience. If, before experience begins, there is possessed an inherited framework of thought; then the structure of that framework must fix, in great part if not entirely, the manner in which the experiences are dealt with. Hence before any conclusions, metaphysical or other, can be established, there has to be answered the previous question—In what way do the inherited forms of mental action determine our thoughts in respect to such conclusions?

Those who deny the existence of anything innate, and refer the whole of every mental phenomenon to experience, are in the like position. Suppose that at birth there exists nothing to determine the way in which impressions received from without shall be dealt with. Still there is not escaped the conclusion that all rational thinking is governed by some principle which is established before rational thinking begins. For what has been going on during the long period between birth and the time when there is a possibility of philosophizing? what has been taking place in this which we call *self*, before there is reached the power of *self*-interpretation—if it ever is reached? The very hypothesis alleges that the experiences have been during all this time in course of classification and organization. There have been developing multitudinous strong associations—various habits of mind and conceptions that have grown rigid—sundry fundamental forms into which the experiences have been put together. Evidently, then, the natures of these, fixed long before the higher mental activities become possible, must govern these higher mental activities. Self-interpretation is a process of thought; the nature of that process is already determined before self-interpretation can begin; the validity of this pre-determined process must be taken for granted in accepting the results of self-interpretation—even if self-interpretation leads to the conclusion that there is nothing in mind but experiences. That is to say, the necessities of thought which experience has produced, must be postulated as unquestionably true before they can be resolved into experiences.

In every case, then, by every school, something has to be assumed. A certainty greater than that which any reasoning can yield, has to be recognized at the outset of all reasoning—be it the reasoning which proposes to show that necessary truths are *à priori*, or be it the reasoning which proposes to show that necessary truths are products of experience.

§ 418. How imperative is the recognition of an ultimate test of truth may, however, be best shown by asking what happens if none is recognized. Let us see the result of analyzing pure Empiricism, or, as Prof. Masson has called it, Experientialism.

Throughout its argument there runs the tacit assumption that there may be a Philosophy in which nothing is asserted but what is proved. It proposes to admit into the coherent fabric of its conclusions, no conclusion that is incapable of being established by evidence; and thus it takes for granted that not only may all derivative truths be proved, but also that proof may be given of the truths from which they are derived, down to the very deepest. The consequence of this refusal to recognize some fundamental unproved truth, is that its fabric of conclusions is left without a base. Giving proof of any special proposition, is assimilating it to some class of propositions known to be true. If any doubt arises respecting the general proposition cited in justification of this special proposition, the course is to show that this general proposition is deducible from a proposition of still greater generality; and if pressed for proof of such still more general proposition, the only resource is to repeat the process. Is this process endless? If so, nothing can be proved—the whole series of propositions depends on some unassignable proposition. Has the process an end? If so, there must eventually be reached a widest proposition—one which cannot be justified by showing that it is included by any wider—one which cannot be proved. Or to put the argument otherwise:—Every inference depends on premises; every premise, if it admits of proof, depends on other premises; and if the proof of the proof be continually demanded, it must either end in an unproved premise, or in the acknowledgment that there cannot be reached any premise on which the entire series of proofs depends.

Hence Philosophy, if it does not avowedly stand on some datum underlying reason, must acknowledge that it has nothing on which to stand—must confess itself to be baseless.

§ 419. From all points of view, then, we discern the same implication. Before there can be a settlement of these prolonged controversies, there must be found something which all sides admit as a transcendent certainty. Obviously this must be the test of certainty itself; for no truth can be so certain as that test by which its certainty is recognized.

In the next chapter and the two succeeding it, we will consider where this test is to be found, what it is, and how to apply it.

CHAPTER X.

§ 420. If I wish to ascertain whether $\frac{7}{9}$ is greater or not greater than $\frac{13}{16}$, I cannot do it by direct contemplation. To reach any trustworthy conclusion I must reduce the two fractions to fractions of a common denomination; and then, by comparing their numerators, I can perceive which is the greater. Before an investment in England can be contrasted with an investment in America, pounds must be changed into dollars or dollars into pounds: only then can the difference in interest be known. It is so, too, in a more involved way with every scientific investigation and every application of science to the arts. Say that in a given case it has to be found whether wood or coal is the more economical fuel for burning in a steam-engine furnace. Quantities of the two fuels must be reduced to some common denomination either of weight or bulk; and such calculations made as will show in equal units of money, how much a unit of the one kind of fuel costs more than a unit of the other. Further, the effect produced by the engine with a unit of each kind of fuel, has to be found in terms of horse-power: a unit of work in which the respective amounts of work done may be expressed and compared. And, eventually, by means of such reductions and comparisons, it is ascertained that a unit of work costs so many units of money with the one fuel and so many with the other.

69   393

Everywhere, then, exact results are reached only by comparing things of the same denomination; and where the things to be compared are of different denominations, one of them must be reduced to the same with the other, or else the equivalent of each in a denomination different from either must be found. This method we have now to apply. By this means only can exact results be reached in that field we are exploring.

§ 421. The units with which we have here to deal are propositions. These are the ultimate components of knowledge. The simplest intuition equally with the most complex rational judgment, has the same fundamental structure: it is the tacit or overt assertion that something is or is not of a certain nature—belongs or does not belong to a certain class—has or has not a certain attribute.

No state of consciousness can become an element of what we call intelligence, without becoming one term of a proposition which is implied if not expressed. Not only when I *say* "I am cold," must I use this universal verbal form for stating a relation; but it is impossible for me clearly to *think* I am cold, without going through some consciousness having this form. The mere recognition of a sensation as being a sensation of cold, cannot occur without the sensation being thought of as like certain before-known sensations; and it cannot be so thought of without making a tacit assertion respecting it. Everywhere throughout the Special Analysis, we saw that the intellectual process is, from beginning to end, essentially the same in method. From the first stages in which simple feelings are identified and discriminated, to the last stages in which the most intricate clusters of things and acts and relations are grouped with their similars and separated from their dissimilars, the difference is not in the ultimate nature of the mental act, but in the extent to which it is complicated. Alleged distinctions into Intuition, Understanding, and Reason are surface-distinctions. A consciousness propositional in its form, is involved in recognizing an odour to be of this or that kind, just as much as in recognizing State-education to be a kind of Socialism.

Propositions, then, constitute the common denomination to which all systems of belief, simple or complex, have to be reduced, before we can scientifically test them. Propositions are the units of composition out of which Realism and Idealism are alike framed; and if we are rigorously to compare Realism and Idealism in respect of their validities, we must first compare their respective units of composition. The problem before us is to ascertain what qualitative differences, if any, exist between the propositions out of which these conflicting systems are composed.

§ 422. Various groupings of propositions result, according as these or those differences among propositions are considered. Of the many possible classifications, only two essentially concern us here; and of these we may first take the one dividing them into the simple and the complex. There are some propositions which tacitly assert little more than they avowedly assert; while there are other propositions, in which what is tacitly asserted immensely exceeds in amount what is avowedly asserted.

The proposition—" I have a pain," may be called, in contrast with most propositions, a simple one; though even it involves the unexpressed propositions that I have a body, that this body has a part in which this pain is localized, and that I have before had pains with which I class this as like in general nature. Strictly speaking, no such thing exists as an absolutely-simple proposition, implying nothing beyond one subject and one predicate known in relation. Nevertheless, though the simplest proposition connotes sundry other propositions, there is a broad line to be drawn between it and the great mass of propositions, which severally make multitudes of predications beyond that which they appear to make. Let us consider one of these ordinary propositions—seemingly very simple but really very complex.

On a bench before me is a seated figure, and I think, or perhaps say—There is an old man. Not to dwell upon the most general propositions, that this is a solid body, and that it exists at a certain distance in a certain direction, let us enumerate the chief special propositions involved. These are that specially-shaped areas of colour in special relations of position imply a dress; that within a dress there exists a living body; that the particular combination of forms and colours shows the living body within to be a man and not a woman; that the bent back turned towards me, with the head bowed forwards, indicates that the man is old—all which special propositions severally involve general propositions respecting these relations as observed in past experience. To prove that my overt predication includes these many tacit predications, we have only to remember that the living body within the dress *may* be female instead of male; or, further, that instead of being a living body it *may* be a dummy, such as tailors put in their windows. I see the figure move, however—the head turns. Here I find verification if any be needed: the proposition tacitly asserted being, that all objects which have certain aspects and which move are living. It may happen, however, that this, along with the other tacit propositions included in my overt proposition, is false—the seat *may* be a seat at Madame Tussaud's, and the figure *may* be the wax figure of Cobbett, with head moved now and then automatically. This instance I do not give to show the untrustworthiness of ordinary propositions; for in the immense majority of cases, these, with all their implied propositions, are true. I do it to show distinctly the number of propositions included in an ordinary proposition which appears simple; and the many possibilities there are that this proposition may be falsified by the falsification of one or other of the included propositions.

How much is often asserted by implication that does not seem to be asserted, and what erroneous conclusions hence result, will be better shown by an illustration of another kind. On a cold winter's night, a gas-light seen through the window of a cab, or a light in a shop looked at through a pane that has been much rubbed, is surrounded by a halo. Whoever examines will see that this halo is caused by scratches on the glass; the curves of which are arcs of circles having the light for their centre. The proposition which expresses the result of his observation, and seems to assert no more than the result of his observation, is that on the part of the glass through which he looks, the scratches produced by rubbing are arranged concentrically with the light. If, however, he should be startled by the strangeness of this proposition, and should so be led to inquire, he will find, on moving his head about, that through whatever part of the glass he looks, there is round the light a similar halo of illuminated concentric scratches. This discovery makes it clear that the proposition he originally affirmed to himself (that the glass was scratched in curves concentric with the light) was entirely misleading. He perceives how, along with the proposition that there existed these concentric scratches, he had inadvertently included another proposition; namely, that there did not exist on the same spot scratches otherwise arranged, immeasurably exceeding in number the concentric scratches. He learns that in fact the scratches on any part of the glass have no concentric arrangement at all; but run in countless directions with multitudinous curvatures. And at length he discovers the truth to be that under the conditions of the case, only the few scratches which happened to run concentrically, reflected the light and came into view; while the immensely-more numerous scratches having other directions, remained invisible. This example is typical of a wide range of complex propositions, in which, along with certain conspicuous facts affirmed, there is a tacit denial of facts of an

opposite kind, which are by the necessities of the case inconspicuous. The popular generalization that "murder will
out," is one in point. Along with the open affirmation that
many murders, at first concealed, have been afterwards discovered (the cases of discovery being thus rendered conspicuous) there goes the implied affirmation that there are
not as many or more murders, at first concealed, which
always continue concealed (the cases of non-discovery thus
necessarily remaining inconspicuous). Current conclusions
drawn from statistical evidence, by political reasoners even of
high culture and scientific discipline, furnish many kindred
examples.

From this somewhat discursive discussion we are brought
round to our immediate topic, on observing that the last-
named cause of error in complex propositions, is a cause
which pervades all class-reasoning: including that which
metaphysicians employ. I do not mean merely that every
general proposition predicating something of a class, is a
highly-complex proposition, because it colligates the many
propositions severally made respecting the individuals of the
class; but I mean, further, that there is in all cases a marked
tendency for the very act of predication to bring into pro-
minence those members of the class which fulfil the predication, and to leave in the background those members of the
class, if there are any, which do not fulfil it. An example
in point may be recalled from the chapter on the "Reasonings of Metaphysicians." Kant alleges that all sensations
given to us by objects have Space as their form. Beyond
the fact that this general proposition affirms many particular
propositions, and may be invalidated by whatever in-
validates any one of them; there is the fact that the sensations of sight and touch, which fulfil the predication, are
those which, when Space is spoken of, come into the fore-
ground of consciousness: leaving in the background those
which have not Space as their form. And hence the
result that Kant has affirmed of all sensations what does

not hold of sound or odour; and that this complex proposition of his has passed current, though some of the particular propositions included in it would not have passed.

Clearly, then, that we can compare conclusions with scientific rigour, we must not only resolve arguments into their constituent propositions, but must resolve each complex proposition into the simple propositions composing it. And only when each of these simple propositions has been separately tested, can the complex proposition made up of them be regarded as having approximately a validity equal with that of a simple proposition which has been tested.

§ 423. Before we can clearly discern that fundamental character distinguishing the propositions we accept from those we reject, there needs a further classification—one in which propositions are grouped according as their terms are real or ideal, or partly one and partly the other. As every proposition expresses some relation between some two terms, we must use the same word in all cases to express the mental act by which the relation is known. The only appropriate word is *cognition;* and we have here, therefore, to distinguish among the various orders of cognitions which propositions express, according as the elements of them occur in perception, or in thought, or in the two combined.

When the content of a proposition is the relation between two terms both of which are directly presented, as when I pinch my finger and am simultaneously conscious of the pain and of the place where it is, we have a simple *presentative cognition*. If next day I remember that my finger was pinched, the consciousness of the relation between the pain and the finger, differing from the original consciousness in having faint terms instead of vivid terms, but otherwise the same in nature, is a simple *representative cognition*. If when pinched I see that the thing pinching me is a vice, the content of the proposition is that along with certain presented appearances there go the tangible form, substance, and structural characters which make up my conception of a vice, all which are represented; and hence the cognition is a *presentative-representative* one. If I afterwards, when not seeing it, say that that which pinched me was a vice, the content of the proposition is in part *representative* and in part *re-representative :* the visual impression, which is the first term of the relation I assert, I represent, and the accompanying attributes which I think of as going along with the visual impression, I re-represent. And here we observe that cognitions, as they thus pass into the representative and re-representative, become *constructively compound*—each term becomes one in which are included many propositions that are tacitly asserted in the way shown above. From this stage we pass to another in which the cognitions also become *cumulatively compound*. Thus, to carry out the same illustration, if to this case of pinching by a vice, I add the various other cases in which I have been pinched by a closing door, or by a drawer, or by a heavy weight, and make the general assertion that masses of dense matter made to approach one another with much force, will pinch the flesh that comes between them; it is manifest that the content of the proposition is a relation between two terms, each of which is *constructively re-representative* and also *cumulatively re-representative*.

And now, bearing in mind these distinctions among the cognitions which are expressed by propositions, suppose we go on to observe how they severally behave under examination.

§ 424. Let us say that a friend with whom I am staying in the country shows me a favourite cow. I see it to be brown and white—brown patches on a white ground. While I look at the animal, the cognition which I have that here is a smaller area of brown within a larger area of white is such that the subject and its predicate continue to exist together: I cannot find any interval during which the white as the containing, and the brown as the contained, cease to have this relation. Months afterwards I inquire about the favourite cow, and describe it as the cow with the white spots on the brown ground. My cognition respecting the relations of the colours, no longer presentative but now representative, is such that the two terms do not maintain the same persistent relation. When I am told that instead of white patches on a brown ground, the cow has brown patches on a white ground, the elements of the representation cease to exist in the relation under which I had thought them: in interpreting the statement which negatives my own, I think of the patches as brown and the ground as white. But now mark that while these terms of my overt proposition do not coexist in the unchanging relation which they had when I saw the cow, certain implied propositions have the same character in the representation as they had in the presentation. That these colours subtended certain areas, that they were at some distance from my eyes, that there were two of them, are implied propositions the terms of which coexist in the representation just as invariably as they did in the presentation. In this simple case, then, we see that an ordinary proposition is composed of several propositions which differ essentially in their character; since in some the predicate never ceases to exist while its subject is before consciousness, but in others it may cease to exist.

On turning to more complex propositions, we find a much larger proportion of the component propositions have the character that the subject and predicate do not invariably exist in the relation alleged. When, as in the case given above, I see before me the back of a seated figure, and say—" There is an old man; " various of the included propositions are such as admit of the predicate ceasing to coexist with its subject. If any one suggests that the person within the dress is not an old man but a young man putting on the appearances of age, the proposition that along with the appearances there exists an old man, changes: the rendering of the counter-proposition into thought, involves the representation of a young man as existing along with them. Or if it is alleged that the occupant of the dress is a woman, or that it is some inanimate matter with which the dress is stuffed, these predicates are represented and the original predicate ceases for the time to exist. So, too, is it when instead of the conception of life as the cause of movement, it is suggested that the movement is automatic. But here, as before, it is observable that though in the entire proposition—" This is an old man," there are many included propositions of which the subjects and predicates do not invariably exist in the relations alleged; there are other propositions the elements of which have this unchanging coexistence. While looking at the figure, its colours never exist out of their space-relations. Along with the cognition of its near side there invariably coexists the cognition of a remote side; and similarly, with the consciousness of it as a visible object, there invariably coexists the consciousness of some position in front, more or less special in direction.

§ 425. Here, then, we have a broad distinction among propositions. There are some the predicates of which always exist along with their subjects; and there are others of which the predicates do not always exist along with their subjects. Those of the first class express cognitions such that the thing alleged continues before consciousness as long as the thing of which it is alleged continues before consciousness; and those of the second class express cognitions such that the thing alleged may disappear from consciousness while the thing of which it is alleged remains. These are respectively the cognitions we necessarily accept and the cognitions we do not necessarily accept. Passing over the second class, as not here concerning us, we find in the first class two distinct orders, at which we must glance.

There are cognitions in which the coexistence of the two

terms is but *temporarily* absolute. These are the simple
cognitions of the presentative order. Suppose I gaze at
the Sun. The proposition—" I perceive light," then becomes one in which, along with the subject (self), there
invariably exists the predicate (sensation of light). Not
for an instant is this predicated sensation of light interrupted by a consciousness of darkness. As long as I gaze
at the Sun, so long does this absolute coexistence of the two
terms of the cognition continue; and so long I can do no
other than accept the cognition. It is thus, too, with certain immediately-presented relations. If, turning my eyes
to the left, I see an object, the consciousness that it exists
in this relation of position towards self, continues invariably
to exist while I continue to look at it. I can, indeed,
superpose on this vivid consciousness of the object as existing on my left hand, a faint consciousness of its hypothetical
transfer to the right hand, and of myself as seeing on the
right hand; but this faint consciousness does not replace
the vivid consciousness: the relation as I perceive it persists as long as my eyes are directed to the object. And
the like holds with simple relations of objects to one
another. If, of two straight lines placed side by side, A is
much longer than B, I cannot, while contemplating the two,
find any moment at which this consciousness of their difference ceases to exist, or is reversed. There are
certain presentative-representative cognitions having this
same character. When I feel the resistance of a body, the
proposition that it has extension, is one of which the predicate coexists absolutely with its subject. The extension
presented in consciousness along with the resistance, may
be great or may be small; but the consciousness of *some*
extension exists as long as the consciousness of the resistance exists. And the like holds when this cognition becomes
wholly representative: the imagination of resistance has invariably coexisting with it the imagination of extension.

In the other order belonging to this first class, the union
of subject and predicate is *permanently* absolute. Such

cognitions are those which contain general abstract relations, quantitative or qualitative. The axioms of Mathematics express cognitions which are such that along with
the consciousness of the subject the consciousness of the
thing predicated invariably exists; and many of the more
special mathematical propositions have the same character.
One of these is the proposition that any two sides of a
triangle are greater than the third side.   We have
the same trait in those most abstract cognitions which
Logic formulates. If there exist more A's than B's; and
if in some mixed group of the two, the B's exceed the A's
in number; then, outside of this group, there must exist
more A's than B's. Here we have a cognition such that,
given in consciousness the relations specified, and the relation predicated will always be found with them.

One important distinction among these sub-classes,
making up this general class of propositions, remains to
be noticed; and it is one of great significance. In the
simplest of them, whether the terms be real or ideal,
or whether they be feelings or relations, the connexion of
the predicate with its subject is so close that its coexistence
cannot be kept out of consciousness; whereas in the more
complex of them the invariably-coexistent thing predicated
has to be sought for in consciousness. When I say that I
am dazzled by the Sun, or when, touching a body in the dark,
I say that it must have some extension, the predicates of
the propositions not only invariably coexist with their subjects (the one as long as I look at the Sun, and the other
whenever I perceive or imagine any object), but they invariably coexist with them in such ways that they cannot be
overlooked. Whereas in those cumulatively-representative
cognitions which Logic formulates, the invariable coexistence predicated is often inconspicuous, and may be overlooked. Thus, in the case above given, the conclusion that
outside the group described there must exist more A's than
B's, does not conspicuously coexist with the premisses: the
premisses may be represented without the conclusion being

thought of. Though here, as before, the relation inferred does invariably exist in consciousness along with the relations given, it exists implicitly and not explicitly. It may not be sought for, and in some cases search may fail to disentangle it. *So that the simplest step in reasoning, necessarily made relatively complex by including several propositions, can never yield a consciousness of invariable coexistence of the same unmistakable kind.*

And here we are naturally introduced to the ultimate question. When we divide cognitions into those of which the predicates invariably exist along with their subjects, and those in which they do not, there arises the question—How do we ascertain their invariable existence? To this question let us now address ourselves.*

* In this chapter, and in the two chapters which follow, I have used terms different from those which I originally used. Throughout the corresponding part of the argument, as it was set forth in the first edition of this work, I described as "beliefs which invariably exist," what I have here described as "cognitions of which the predicates invariably exist along with their subjects." My reason for making this change of expression, is that the word *belief*, having two radically-opposed meanings, admits of being misinterpreted. It is habitually applied to dicta of consciousness for which no proof can be assigned: both those which are unprovable because they underlie all proof, and those which are unprovable because of the absence of evidence—both those which are most certain and those which are most uncertain. And this ambiguity necessarily brings some confusion into the thoughts, even where it does not lead to positive error. A further reason for not employing the word *belief*, is that men are liable to confound the things they truly believe with the things they believe they believe. Very commonly in Philosophy, as in Theology, there is a formal acceptance of a proposition without any real acceptance of it—without any proper representation of that which it asserts. The proposition having had its two *terms* identified in thought as known terms; and having had the *relation* it names identified as a known relation; it is often supposed that the specified terms have been brought together before consciousness in the specified relation, and believed; when in fact they do not admit of being brought together before consciousness in this relation at all, and cannot therefore be believed in the proper sense of the word. This confusion is a fruitful source of error which it is very desirable to avoid. It must be admitted, however, that the word *cognition*, as above used, is also objectionable; since its implications are too positive. But there is no available word that is unobjectionable, and the objections to this are the least weighty.

CHAPTER XI.

THE UNIVERSAL POSTULATE.*

§ 426. To ascertain whether along with a certain subject a certain predicate invariably exists, we have no other way than to seek for a case in which the subject exists without it; and we conduct the search by trying to replace this invariably-existing predicate by some other, or by trying to suppress it altogether without replacing it.

This is what, in other words, we describe as trying to conceive the negation of a proposition. If, having touched a body in the dark, and having become instantly conscious of some extension as accompanying the resistance, I wish to decide whether the proposition—" Whatever resists has extension," expresses a cognition of the highest certainty, how do I do it? I endeavour to think away the extension from

---

* The above title is identical with that of an article which I published in the *Westminster Review* for October, 1853; setting forth in outline the doctrine now set forth more fully, in this chapter and the one succeeding it. The article named was in part a criticism on the controversy between Mr. Mill and Dr. Whewell, respecting the nature of necessary truths—a criticism in which, agreeing with Mr. Mill in rejecting Dr. Whewell's conception of necessary truths, I ventured to differ from him respecting the value of a certain test by which Dr. Whewell said they were discriminated, but by which they are not discriminated. Mr. Mill replied in the next edition of his *Logic;* and a rejoinder from me has since been published in the *Fortnightly Review,* followed by a re-rejoinder from him in later editions of his *Logic.* The amicable controversy that has thus been long pending between us, I am now obliged to resume. Both on personal and on general grounds, I am very sorry to be still at issue with Mr. Mill on this fundamental question. For two reasons, especially, I regret having to contend against the doc-

the resistance. I think of resistance, and endeavour to keep extension out of thought. I fail absolutely in the attempt. I cannot conceive the negation of the proposition that whatever resists is extended; and *my failure to conceive the negation*, is the discovery that along with the subject (something resisting) *there invariably exists* the predicate (extension).

Hence the inconceivableness of its negation is that which shows a cognition to possess the highest rank—is the criterion by which its unsurpassable validity is known. If the negation of a cognition is conceivable, the discovery of this amounts to the discovery that we may or may not accept it. If its negation is inconceivable, the discovery of this is the discovery that we are obliged to accept it. And a cognition which we are thus obliged to accept, is one which we class as having the highest possible certainty. To assert the inconceivableness of its negation, is at the same time to assert the psychological necessity we are under of thinking it, and to give our logical justification for holding it to be unquestionable.

That a cognition which has withstood this test, is therefore to be accepted as unquestionable, is, however, not universally admitted. We have now to consider the reasons given for not admitting it.

trine of one whose agreement I should value more than that of any other thinker. In the first place, the difference is, I believe, superficial rather than substantial; for it is in the interests of the Experience-Hypothesis that Mr. Mill opposes the alleged criterion of truth; while it is as harmonizing with the Experience-Hypothesis, and reconciling it with all the facts, that I defend this criterion. In the second place, this lengthened exposition of a single point of difference, unaccompanied by an exposition of the numerous points of concurrence, unavoidably produces an appearance of dissent very far greater than that which exists. Mr. Mill, however, whose unswerving allegiance to truth is on all occasion so conspicuously displayed, will recognize the justification for this utterance of disagreement on a matter of such profound importance, philosophically considered; and will not require any apology for the freedom with which I have criticized his views while seeking to substantiate my own.

§ 427. And first let me exclude all possible misinterpretations of terms. One of the mischiefs wrought by the pestilent habit of exaggeration, is that some of the words used for scientific and philosophical purposes have their force and precision destroyed: instance *infinite* and *infinitely*, which even from the mouths of scientific men who should know better, may now be heard applied to quite ordinary quantities and differences. The meaning of *inconceivable* has been made uncertain by habitual misuse of this kind. People wishing to express strongly their disbelief in something alleged, have used this word for the purpose; and thus *inconceivable* has come in many minds to be the equivalent of *incredible*. This vitiated meaning of the word has been assumed to be that which I intended to give it throughout the argument here presented in a revised form—a misapprehension which had not occurred to me as one that might arise. Lest this misapprehension should again arise, let me here define and illustrate what I mean by inconceivable, as distinguished from incredible or unbelievable.

An inconceivable proposition is one of which the terms cannot, by any effort, be brought before consciousness in that relation which the proposition asserts between them—a proposition of which the subject and the predicate offer an insurmountable resistance to union in thought. An unbelievable proposition is one which admits of being framed in thought, but is so much at variance with experience, in which its terms have habitually been otherwise united, that its terms cannot be put in the alleged relation without effort. Thus, it is unbelievable that a cannon-ball fired from England should reach America; but it is not inconceivable. Conversely, it is inconceivable that one side of a triangle is equal to the sum of the other two sides—not simply unbelievable. The two sides cannot be represented in consciousness as becoming equal in their joint length to the third side, without the representation of a triangle being destroyed; and the concept of a triangle cannot be framed without the simultaneous destruction of a concept in which these magnitudes are represented as equal. That is to say, the subject and predicate cannot be united in the same intuition—the proposition is unthinkable. It is in this sense only that I have used the word inconceivable; and only when rigorously restricted to this sense, do I regard the test of inconceivableness as having any value.

§ 428. A leading objection made by Mr. Mill to the test of the inconceivableness of its negation, as a test whereby an unquestionably-true proposition may be discriminated, is that propositions once accepted as true because they withstood this test, have since been proved false. He says:—
" There was a time when men of the most cultivated intellects, and the most emancipated from the dominion of early prejudice, could not credit the existence of antipodes; were unable to conceive, in opposition to old association, the force of gravity acting upwards instead of downwards." *

Already in the last chapter, where we distinguished

---

* Some of the further instances which Mr. Mill gives of beliefs, the negations of which were once thought inconceivable but are now conceived, are not open to the objection about to be made in the text. I do not quote them, however, because they cannot, I think, be rightly said to have undergone the change he alleges. Mr. Mill says that Newton held an etherial medium to be a necessary implication of observed facts; but that it is not now held to be a necessary implication. I do not think, however, that scientific men "have at last learnt to conceive the sun *attracting* the earth without any intervening fluid;" any more than they have learnt to "conceive the sun *illuminating* the earth without some such medium." The most that can be said is that they have given up attempting to conceive how gravitation results. If, however, an astronomer avowed that he could conceive gravitative force as exercised through space absolutely void, my private opinion would be that he mistook the nature of conception. Conception implies representation. Here the elements of the representation are the two bodies and an agency by which either affects the other. To conceive this agency is to represent it in some terms derived from our experiences—*that is, from our sensations*. As this agency gives us no sensations, we are obliged (if we try to conceive it) to use symbols idealized from our sensations—imponderable units forming a medium.

between simple propositions and complex propositions, it was pointed out that no scientific comparisons can be made except between propositions of the same denomination. It was shown by implication that a test legitimately applicable to a simple proposition, the subject and predicate of which are in direct relation, cannot be legitimately applied to a complex proposition, the subject and predicate of which are indirectly related through the many simple propositions implied. To this criticism of Mr. Mill, therefore, my reply is that the propositions erroneously accepted because they seemed to withstand the test, were complex propositions to which the test is inapplicable; and that no errors arising from its illegitimate application can be held to tell against its legitimate application.

If the question be asked—How are we to decide what is a legitimate application of the test? I answer that already, in restricting its application to propositions which are not further decomposable, I have pointed to the needful distinction. This question is so all-important a one, however, that I must be excused for endeavouring to give such further answer to it as will leave no possibility of misapprehension. Perfectly concrete examples of the applicability of the test and of its inapplicability will best serve the purpose.

A and B are two lines. How is it decided that they are equal or not equal? No way is open but that of comparing the two impressions they make on consciousness. I know them to be unequal by an immediate act if the difference is great, or if, though only moderately different, they are close together; and supposing the difference is but slight, I decide the question by putting the lines in apposition when they are movable, or by carrying a movable line from one to the other when they are fixed. In any case, I obtain in consciousness the testimony that the impression produced by the one line differs from that produced by the other. Of this difference I can give no further evidence than that I am conscious of it, and find it impossible, while contemplating the lines, to get rid of the consciousness. The pro-

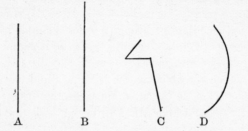

A   B   C   D

position that the lines are unequal is a proposition of which the negation is inconceivable. But now suppose it is asked whether B and C are equal; or whether C and D are equal. No positive answer is possible. Instead of its being inconceivable that B is longer than C, or equal to it, or shorter, it is conceivable that it is any one of the three. Here an appeal to the direct verdict of consciousness is illegitimate; because on transferring the attention from B to C, or C to D, the changes in the other elements of the impressions so entangle the elements to be compared, as to prevent them from being put in apposition. If the question of relative length is to be determined, it must be by rectification of the bent line; and this is done through a series of steps, each one of which involves an immediate judgment akin to that by which A and B are compared. Now as here, so in other cases, it is only simple percepts or concepts respecting the relations of which immediate consciousness can satisfactorily testify; and as here, so in other cases, it is by resolution into such simple percepts and concepts, that true judgments respecting complex percepts and concepts are reached. That things which are equal to the same thing are equal to one another, is a fact which can be known by direct comparison of actual or ideal relations, and can be known in no other way: the proposition is one of which the negation is inconceivable, and is rightly asserted on that

warrant.   But that the square of the hypothenuse of a
right-angled triangle equals the sum of the squares of the
other two sides, cannot be known immediately by comparison of two states of consciousness.   Here the truth can be
reached only mediately, through a series of simple judgments
respecting the likenesses or unlikenesses of certain relations:
each of which judgments is essentially of the same kind as
that by which the above axiom is known, and has the same
warrant. · Thus it becomes apparent that the fallacious
result of the test which Mr. Mill instances, is due to a mis-
application of the test.

And now mark that in respect of those questions legitimately brought to judgment by this test, there is *no* dispute about the answer.   From the earliest times on record
down to our own, men have not changed their beliefs
concerning the truth of number.   The axiom that if equals
be added to unequals the sums are unequal, was held by the
Greeks no less than by ourselves, as a direct verdict of consciousness from which there is no appeal.   Each step in
each demonstration of Euclid we accept, as they accepted
it, because we immediately see that the alleged relation is
as alleged; and that it is impossible to conceive it otherwise.

§ 429. Even were there no such distinction as that above
drawn, Mr. Mill's inference might still, I think, be properly
contested.   Beyond the reply that the errors instanced are
errors which arise from applying to complex propositions a
test applicable only to simple propositions, there is a further
reply.   The failure of any method has two possible causes—
badness of the method itself being one, and the other being
inability to use it: even for its legitimate purposes.

In alleging that if a belief is said by some to be necessary,
but by others to be not necessary, the test of necessity is
thereby shown to be no test, Mr. Mill tacitly assumes that
all men have adequate powers of introspection; whereas
many are incapable of correctly interpreting consciousness

in any but its simplest modes, and even the remainder are liable to mistake for dicta of consciousness what prove on closer examination not to be its dicta. Take the case of an arithmetical blunder. A boy adds up a column of figures, and brings out a wrong total. Again he does it, and again errs. His master asks him to go through the process aloud, and then hears him say " 35 and 9 are 46 "—an error which he had repeated on each occasion. Now, without discussing the mental act through which we know that 35 and 9 are 44, it is clear that the boy's misinterpretation of consciousness, leading him tacitly to deny this necessity by asserting that " 35 and 9 are 46," cannot be held to prove that the relation is not necessary. Misjudgments of this kind, often made even by disciplined accountants, merely show that there is a liability to overlook the necessary connexions in our thoughts, and to assume as necessary others which are not. And what occasionally happens in calculation, frequently happens in more complex thinking: men do not distinctly translate into their equivalent states of consciousness the words they use. This negligence is with many so habitual, that they are unaware that they have not clearly represented to themselves the propositions they assert; and are then apt, quite sincerely though erroneously, to say that they can think things which it is really impossible to think.

Even supposing it were true that the test is proved to be fallacious in every case where men have differed respecting the conceivability or inconceivability of a proposition; would it therefore follow that the test is untrustworthy in those multitudinous cases in which there is, and always has been, universal agreement? I think not. I think it would no more follow than it would follow that the process of reasoning is invalid because in certain cases men starting from the same data reach opposite conclusions. We consider an inference logically drawn from established premisses to be true. Yet, very often, men have been wrong in the

inferences they have thought logically drawn.   Do we,
therefore, argue that it is absurd to consider an inference
true " on no other ground " than that it is logically drawn
from established premisses?   No; we say that though men
may have taken for logical inferences, inferences which were
not logical, there nevertheless *are* logical inferences; and
that we are justified in assuming the truth of what seem to
us such, until better instructed.   Similarly, though men
may have supposed some things inconceivable which were
not so, there may still be inconceivable things; and the
inability to conceive the negation of a thing, may still be
our best warrant for believing it.

§ 430.   Another aspect of the question may now be considered.   Against the hypothesis that axiomatic truths are
necessities of thought, independent of, and antecedent to, all
experience, Mr. Mill opposes the hypothesis that axiomatic
truths are inductions from experience.   He says that " when
we have often seen and thought of two things together, and
have never in any one instance either seen or thought of
them separately, there is by the primary law of association
an increasing difficulty, which may in the end become insuperable, of conceiving the two things apart."   From which
passage, as from various others, it is obvious that " these
inseparable associations " which constitute necessities of
thought, and are regarded as axioms, Mr. Mill supposes to
be formed in each individual by the experiences he acquires
during his life.   That the point of view from which my
criticisms are made may be the better understood, I must
remind the reader that I coincide with neither of these
opposing hypotheses entirely, but with both of them in part.
As said in § 332, I regard " these data of intelligence as
á priori for the individual, but *à posteriori* for that entire
series of individuals of which he forms the last term."   And
now, making this remark to prevent misapprehension, let
me point out that, even accepting Mr. Mill's version of the

Experience-Hypothesis, a good plea may still be put in for the test of inconceivableness.

For let us suppose it to be true that at any stage of civilization, a man's ability or inability to form a given conception depends wholly on the experiences acquired, either through his own converse with things or through the accumulated knowledge derived from other men's converse with things—knowledge which his education unites with his own knowledge. And suppose it to be also true that by a widening and multiplying of these experiences, first-hand and second-hand, men are enabled to conceive things before inconceivable by them. Still, supposing all this, it may be fairly argued that as the best warrant men can have for a belief is the perfect agreement of all preceding experience in support of it; and as, at any given time, a cognition of which the negation remains inconceivable, is, by the hypothesis, one that has been verified by all experiences up to that time; it follows that at any time the inconceivableness of its negation is the strongest justification a cognition can have.

What is the purpose of critically examining our thoughts, or analyzing the dicta of consciousness? To insure a correspondence between subjective beliefs and objective facts. Well, objective facts are ever impressing themselves upon us; our experience is a register of these objective facts; and the inconceivableness of a thing implies that it is wholly at variance with the register. Even were this all, it is not clear how, if every truth is primarily inductive, any better test of truth could exist. But it must be remembered that while many of the facts impressed upon us, are occasional; and while others are very general; some are universal and unchanging. These universal and unchanging facts are, by the hypothesis, certain to establish beliefs of which the negations are inconceivable; while the others are not certain to do this; and if they do it, facts subsequently met with will reverse their action. Hence when, after an immense accumulation of experiences, there remain beliefs of which the negations are inconceivable, most, if not all of them, must correspond to universal objective facts. If there be, as Mr. Mill holds, absolute uniformities in Nature; if these uniformities produce, as they must, absolute uniformities in our experience; and if, as he shows, these absolute uniformities in our experience disable us from conceiving the negations of them; then, answering to each absolute uniformity in Nature habitually repeated in our experience, there must exist in us a belief of which the negation is inconceivable, and which is absolutely true. In this wide range of cases, subjective inconceivableness corresponds to objective impossibility. Throughout the great body of our consciousness, consisting as it does of things presented from moment to moment under definite relations of space, time, and number, the test of inconceivableness is valid. Perpetually-repeated experiences have generated in us cognitions of logical relations, mathematical relations, and some simple physical relations, for the necessity of which the inconceivableness of their negations is a guarantee unhesitatingly accepted. And if among those undecomposable propositions alone admitting of justification by this test, there are still some which, having its warrant, are nevertheless untrue (though I see no reason to think this); it must still be admitted that such simple propositions, verified by this test, express the net result of our experiences up to the present time, which is the best warrant possible for them.

The argument I have here repeated with slight modifications, has been replied to by Mr. Mill. He says:— "Even if it were true that inconceivableness represents the 'net result' of all past experience, why should we stop at the representative when we can get at the thing represented? If our incapacity to conceive the negation of a given supposition is proof of its truth, because proving that our experience has hitherto been uniform in its favour, the real evidence for the supposition is not the inconceivableness, but the uniformity of experience. Now, this, which is the substantial and only proof, is directly accessible. We are not obliged to presume it from an incidental consequence. If all past experience is in favour of a belief, let this be stated, and the belief openly rested on that ground: after which the question arises, what that fact may be worth as evidence of its truth?"

Of the instances which Mr. Mill goes on to give of uniformities in experience that were inadequate proofs of truth, I have to remark, that, like instances previously given, they are not of the class to which alone the test of inconceivableness is applicable; since they have not the required simplicity, nor has their recurrence made the least approach to the almost-infinite frequency of those uniformities we are considering. Remarking this, I pass to the essential question— Why in place of the derivative test of inconceivableness should there not be used the experiences from which it is derived? I reply that for the great mass of our cognitions we cannot employ such a method of verification for several reasons:— First, the implied enumeration of experiences, if possible, would postpone indefinitely the establishment of any conclusion as valid; second, no such enumeration of experiences is possible; and third, if possible, the warrant gained for the conclusion could never be as great as that of the test objected to. Let us consider each of these reasons.   Suppose, before accepting as certain the proposition that any rectilinear figure must have as many angles as it has sides, I had to think of every triangle, square, pentagon, hexagon, &c., which I have ever seen, and to verify the asserted relation in each case; the time required for the rehearsal of all these memories would be so great that the proposition affirmed to-day could not be verified before to-morrow. Were such a verification needed before asserting it to be a necessary truth that a body of which the near side is felt has got a remote side, a month would be spent before the certainty could be affirmed and the argument proceeded with.   But no such enumeration of the experiences on the strength of which a cognition is to be affirmed as certain, is ever possible: only a few of them can be recalled. The great mass of those which, according to this hypothesis, should form the inductive basis for the truth alleged, have gone for ever; and further, it is to be observed that they have disappeared most in the cases of those truths that are most certain. How many separate occasions can I name on which I have consciously observed that where I perceived a near side of a thing I found also a remote side? Probably not one-millionth of the occasions on which this truth has been presented in my experience.   Beyond this quantitative defect in the proposed inductive basis for affirmation, there is an equally grave qualitative defect. The imperfection of memory is such that the register itself, by which certainty is to be established, is itself uncertain. Whether in boyhood I did or did not notice that when from two unequal masses I cut off equal slices the remainders were more unequal than before, or that two unequal groups of marbles were made more unequal by taking the same number from each, I cannot now say with any positiveness, even if at all. How then can the validity of such an axiom ever be known if it has for warrant nothing beyond memories that are not only so few but also so doubtful?   Yet again, it is to be noted that since the testimony of conscious experiences is given only through memory; and since the worth of this testimony depends wholly on the trustworthiness of memory; the proposal to test the validity of a truth alleged to be necessary by recalling the experiences it generalizes, implies the tacit assertion that the trustworthiness of memory is more certain than is the alleged truth. This can surely not be said. Our experiences themselves so frequently prove memory to be treacherous, that we can more readily think any one of its testimonies untrue than we can think it untrue that if equals be added to equals the sums are equal. Lastly, even granting the assumed trustworthiness of memory, the same conclusion would still evolve. For the most that can be said for the experiences to which memory testifies, is that we are obliged to think we have had them—cannot conceive the negation of the proposition that we have had them; and to say this is to assign the warrant which is repudiated.

But now, to the question put by Mr. Mill in the above-quoted passage, there comes that deeper reply hinted at the beginning of the section. I hold that the inconceivableness of its negation affords a far higher warrant for a cognition than does any enumeration of experiences, even though exact and exhaustive, for the reason that it represents experiences almost infinitely numerous in comparison. If nervous modifications produced by often-repeated nervous acts are inheritable, accumulate from generation to generation, and result in nervous structures that are fixed in proportion as the outer relations to which they answer are fixed, then the test has a worth immeasurably transcending the worth of any test furnished by individual experiences. Instead of relatively-feeble nervous associations caused by repetition in one generation, we have organized nervous connexions caused by habit in thousands of generations—nay, probably millions of generations. Space-relations have been the same not only for all ancestral men, all ancestral primates, all ancestral orders of mammalia, but for all simpler orders of creatures. These constant space-relations are expressed in definite nervous structures, congenitally framed to act in definite ways, and incapable of acting in any other ways. Hence the inconceivableness of the negation of a mathematical axiom, resulting as it does from the impossibility of inverting the actions of the correlative nervous structures, really stands for the infinity of experiences that have developed these structures. As certainly as the eyes before birth imply by their lenses light to be hereafter re-

fracted, imply by their *retinæ* images of objects presently to
be received, imply by the muscles that move them, variations
of position in these objects; so certainly do the nervous structures which co-ordinate ocular impressions with one another
and with impressions received from the limbs, imply all
those essential space-relations hereafter to be simultaneously
disclosed and verified by personal experience. Hence it
obviously follows that objective necessities of relation in
space, are represented by established nervous structures implying latent subjective necessities of nervous action; that
these last constitute pre-determined forms of thought produced by the moulding of Thought upon Things; and that
the impossibility of inverting them, implied by the inconceivableness of their negations, is a reason for accepting
them as true, which immeasurably transcends in value any
other reason that can be given.

§ 431. How is this view held by Mr. Mill respecting the
test of inconceivableness, reconcilable with his view respecting the nature of valid proof? In the second of his two
chapters on " Demonstration and Necessary Truths," where
he calls in question the necessity commonly ascribed to the
deductive sciences, he says:—

" The results of those sciences are indeed necessary, in the
sense of necessarily following from certain first principles,
commonly called axioms and definitions; that is, of being
certainly true, if those axioms and definitions are so; for the
word necessity, even in this acceptation of it, means no more
than certainty. But their claim to the character of necessity
in any sense beyond this . . . . . must depend on the previous establishment of such a claim in favour of the definitions and axioms themselves."—Chapter vi.

Here, and throughout the argument, Mr. Mill assumes
that there is something more certain in a demonstration
than in anything else—some unquestionableness in the steps
of our reasoning, which is not possessed by the axioms

they start from. Can this assumption be justified? In each successive step the dependence of the conclusion upon its premisses, is a truth of which we have no other proof than that the reverse is inconceivable. And if this be an insufficient warrant for asserting the necessity of the axiomatic premiss, it is an insufficient warrant for asserting the necessity of any link in the argument.

That logical necessity and mathematical necessity must stand or fall together, is, I think, inevitably implied by an analogy which Mr. Mill himself draws. In an earlier chapter he contends that by analysis of the syllogism we arrive at " a fundamental principle, or rather two principles, *strikingly resembling the axioms of mathematics.* The first, which is the principle of affirmative syllogisms, is, that things which coexist with the same thing, coexist with one another. The second is the principle of negative syllogisms, and is to this effect: that a thing which coexists with another thing, with which other a third thing does not coexist, is not coexistent with that third thing." But though Mr. Mill here indicates that the truth, " things which coexist with the same thing coexist with one another," strikingly resembles the truth, " things which are equal to the same thing are equal to one another "; he claims for the former a necessity which he denies to the latter. When, as above, he asserts that the deductive sciences are not necessary, save " in the sense of *necessarily following* from certain first principles, commonly called axioms and definitions; that is, of being *certainly* true, *if* those axioms and definitions are so "—he assumes that while the mathematical axioms possess only hypothetical truth, this logical axiom involved in every step of the demonstration possesses absolute truth. I do not see how this position is to be defended. Unless it can be shown that the truth, " things which coexist with the same thing coexist with one another," has some higher warrant than the impossibility of thinking the reverse, I see no escape from the admission that axioms and demonstrations stand on the same footing. If necessity be denied to the one it must be denied to the other; and while we are debarred from knowing any first principle as certain, we are also debarred from knowing as certain each step in the argument by which the uncertainty of a first principle is shown: there remains for us nothing but universal scepticism.

It seems to me, however, that Mr. Mill really does admit the test of the inconceivableness of the negation to be valid, when he admits the test of the *reductio ad absurdum* to be valid. His recognition of this as a criterion of mathematical necessity, will be found on p. 289; and his recognition of it as a criterion of logical necessity will be found on p. 292 (*Logic*, 7th ed.). On the latter of these pages he says:—" If any one denies the conclusion notwithstanding his admission of the premises, he is not involved in any direct and express contradiction until he is compelled to deny some premise; and he can only be forced to do this by a *reductio ad absurdum*, that is, by another ratiocination: now, if he denies the validity of the reasoning process itself, he can no more be forced to assent to the second syllogism than to the first." That is to say, unless he " denies the validity of the reasoning process itself," any one who " denies the conclusion notwithstanding his admission of the premises " can be forced into a " direct and express contradiction " by the *reductio ad absurdum*. But reduction to an absurdity is reduction to an inconceivable proposition. So that the choice lies between accepting a proposition of which the negation is inconceivable, or abandoning reasoning altogether.

§ 432. Of objections to the test of inconceivability, it remains but to notice the one pointed out by Sir W. Hamilton in his edition of Reid (p. 377). In proof that inconceivability is not a criterion of impossibility, he cites the fact, that " we can neither conceive, on the one hand, an ultimate minimum of space or time; nor can we, on the other, conceive their infinite divisibility. In like manner, we cannot conceive the absolute commencement of time, nor the utmost limit of space, and are yet equally unable to conceive them without any commencement or limit." The implication being, that as there must be either minimum or no minimum, limit or no limit, one of the two inconceivable things must in each case be true.

This conclusion Sir W. Hamilton considers to be necessitated by the law of the Excluded Middle, or, as it might be more intelligibly called, the law of the Alternative Necessity. A thing must either exist or not exist: there is no third possibility. Now so long as this is alleged to be a law of thought in its relations to phenomenal existence, no one can call it in question. But Sir W. Hamilton extends the law beyond the limits of thought, and draws a positive conclusion respecting noumenal existence. As inevitably happens in every such case, his conclusion is merely verbal. If, in place of the words of his propositions respecting Space and Time, we endeavour to put ideas, we shall see that the terms of the propositions are not thoughts but the negations of thoughts; and that no real inference is evolved at all. Clearly to understand this, we must pause a moment to observe how the law of the Excluded Middle results. When remembering a certain thing as in a certain place, the place and the thing are mentally represented together; while to think of the non-existence of the thing in that place, implies a consciousness in which the place is represented but not the thing. Similarly, if, instead of thinking of an object as colourless, we think of it as having colour, the change consists in the addition to the concept of an element that was before absent from it: the object cannot be thought of first as red and then as not red, without one component of the thought being totally expelled from the mind by another. The doctrine of the Excluded Middle, then, is simply a generalization' of the universal experience that some mental states are directly destructive of other states. It formulates a certain absolutely-constant law, that no positive mode of consciousness can occur without excluding a correlative negative mode; and that the negative mode cannot occur without excluding the correlative positive mode: the antithesis of positive and negative, being, indeed, merely an expression of this experience. Hence it follows that if consciousness is not in one of the two modes, it must be in the other. But under what conditions only can this law of consciousness hold? It can hold only so long as there are positive states of consciousness that can exclude and can be excluded. If we are not concerned with positive states of consciousness at all, no mutual exclusion takes place, and the law of the Alternative Necessity does not apply.   Here, then, is the flaw in Sir W. Hamilton's proposition. That Space must be infinite or finite, are alternatives of which we are not obliged to regard one as necessary; seeing that we have no state of consciousness answering to either of these words as applied to the totality of Space, and therefore no exclusion of two antagonist states of consciousness by one another. Both alternatives being unthinkable, the proposition should be put thus:—Space is either   or is   ; neither of which can be conceived, but one of which must be true. In this, as in other cases, Sir W. Hamilton continues to work out the forms of thought when they no longer contain any substance; and, of course, reaches nothing more than semblances of conclusions.

But even were there no such reply as this, Sir W. Hamilton's argument might still be met. He says that inconceivability is no criterion of impossibility. Why? Because, of two propositions, one of which must be true, it proves both impossible—proves that Space cannot have a limit, because a limit is inconceivable, and yet that it must have a limit, because unlimited Space is inconceivable—proves, therefore, that Space has a limit and has no limit, which is absurd. How absurd? Absurd, because " it is impossible for the same thing to be and not to be." But how do we *know* that it is impossible for the same thing to be and not to be? What is our criterion of *this* impossibility? Can Sir W. Hamilton assign any other than this same inconceivability? If not, his reasoning is self-contradictory; seeing that he assumes the validity of the test in proving its invalidity.

§ 433. And now let us sum up this argument which has been made so elaborate by the necessity of meeting criticisms. Its leading propositions may be succinctly expressed as follows:—

An abortive effort to conceive the negation of a proposition, shows that the cognition expressed is one of which the predicate invariably exists along with its subject; and the discovery that the predicate invariably exists along with its subject, is the discovery that this cognition is one we are compelled to accept. It is a necessary relation in consciousness; and to suppose there can be any higher warrant, is to suppose that there are relations which are more than necessary.

That some propositions have been wrongly accepted as true, because their negations were supposed inconceivable when they were not, does not disprove the validity of the test, for these reasons:—(1) that they were complex propositions, not to be established by a test applicable only to propositions no further decomposable; (2) that this test, in common with any test, is liable to yield untrue results, either from incapacity or from carelessness in those who use it; (3) that if it were needful to abandon the test because an absolute guarantee against the misuse of it cannot be found, still more needful would it be to abandon logical principles, the misapplications of which are immeasurably more numerous; but that (4) as applied only to the undecomposable propositions which embody the ultimate relations of number,

71

space and time, the test when used with due care has ever yielded, and continues to yield, uniform results.

That experiences of the relations among phenomena in the past, form the only basis for our present knowledge of such relations, is fully admitted. But if it be a fundamental law that connexions of ideas become strong in proportion as they are repeated, then the adjustment between Thought and Things, produced even by the experiences of individual life, must be such that perpetually-repeated absolute relations in things, will generate relations in thought that are also absolute. But the test of the inconceivableness of their negations, used by us to discover which relations among our thoughts are absolute, represents a justification transcendently greater; for the absolute relations in our thoughts are the results not of individual experiences only, but of experiences received by ancestral individuals through all past time.

Reasoning itself can be trusted only on the assumption that absolute uniformities of Thought correspond to absolute uniformities of Things. For logical intuitions there is no warrant assignable other than that assignable for all intuitions accepted as certain; namely, the impossibility of thinking the opposite. Unless it be alleged that the consciousness of logical necessity has a different origin, and a higher origin, it must be admitted that the consciousness of logical necessity is just as much a product of past experiences as is every other consciousness of necessity. Consequently, it must either be said that the experiences which yield the consciousness of logical necessity, are simpler, more distinct, more direct, and more frequently-repeated, than are the experiences which yield any other consciousness of necessity (and this is just the reverse of the fact); or else it must be conceded that the consciousness of logical necessity can have no higher warrant (though it may have a lower) than the consciousnesses of other necessities. It is therefore a corollary from the Experience-Hypothesis itself, in whatever way interpreted, than an argument which questions the authority of such truths as mathematical axioms, can do so only by claiming for the less-deeply-rooted necessities of thought a validity which it denies to the more-deeply-rooted necessities of thought.

Finally, let me point out that any one declining to recognize the Universal Postulate, can consistently do this only so long as he maintains the attitude of pure and simple negation. The moment he asserts anything—the moment he even gives a reason for his denial, he may be stopped by demanding his warrant. Against every " because " and every " therefore " may be entered a demurrer, until he has said why this proposition he affirms is to be accepted rather than the counter-proposition. So that he cannot even take a step towards justifying his scepticism respecting the Universal Postulate without, in the very act, confessing his acceptance of it.

CHAPTER XII.

§ 434. We are now prepared to formulate a method of deciding between conflicting conclusions. In every way we have been forced to admit that for those ultimate cognitions on which all others depend, the Universal Postulate is our only warrant—that for each of them the sole justification is the invariable existence of the predicate along with its sub-ject, tested by an abortive effort to cause non-existence. This is our guarantee for the reality of consciousness, of sensations, of personal existence: no mental effort enables us to suppress, even for a moment, either element of a proposition expressing one of these ultimate truths. This is our guarantee for each axiom: the only reason we can give for accepting it, is that on trying we find no alter-native cognition can be framed. And this is our guarantee for every step in a demonstration. To gain the strongest conviction possible respecting any complex fact, we either analytically descend from it by successive steps, each of which we test by the inconceivableness of its negation, until we reach some truth which we have similarly tested; or we synthetically ascend from such truth by such steps.

Still, there rises the question—How are we to choose be-tween opposing conclusions, each of which claims to be legi-timately drawn from premisses alleged to be beyond doubt? Arguments of all kinds, including those of metaphysicians, which we have here to value, proceed upon the tacit assump-tion that each datum, and each successive step, has that indubitable warrant the nature of which we have been examining. On behalf of each counter-argument the same tacit assumption is made. So that in deciding which of two irreconcilable inferences is true, we do not at first sight seem to be helped by this analysis so laboriously made.

A satisfactory way of appraising conflicting arguments nevertheless exists. Already an escape from the difficulty has been opened by distinguishing between simple propositions and complex propositions. As was said in the last chapter but one, definite results are to be reached only by comparing things of the same denomination. The relative validities of involved propositions cannot be directly known; but the simple propositions they severally contain must be separated before, by putting these side by side with antagonist ones of equal simplicity, any judgment can be formed. This holds alike where the cognition is simultaneously complex (as tacitly including many cognitions along with that which is avowed); where the cognition is serially complex (as being reached through the chain of cognitions constituting an argument); and still more where it is both simultaneously and serially complex.

Two reasons may be distinguished for insisting on this testing process. One is that, in proportion as propositions are compound, direct comparisons of them must be hazardous; because their component propositions, each of which is an inlet to possible error, cannot be severally tested and verified. The other is, that only when compound propositions are resolved into their constituents, can it be seen what are the relative numbers of assumptions in the two, and what are the relative possibilities of error hence resulting.

And here we come within clear view of the desired method —a method which must hold good whether the Universal Postulate be absolutely trustworthy or not.

§ 435. For suppose it could be shown that a cognition of which the predicate invariably exists along with its subject, though the most certain possible to us, is not necessarily true. Let it be admitted for argument's sake that, either from insufficient experience, or from non-agreement between subject and object, the inconceivable and the impossible may not correspond even within our mental range. Let us go to the extreme of assuming that for the validity of no one single act of thought is the Universal Postulate a perfect warrant. Let all this, I say, be granted. Still, be the test fallible or not, the probability of error in any inference will increase in proportion to the number of times the truth of the test has been assumed in arriving at the inference. If the postulate be uniformly valid, it must yet happen that, as we are liable to mental *lapsus* we shall occasionally think we have its warrant when we have not; and in each case the chances of our having done this will vary directly as the number of times we have claimed its warrant. If the postulate be not uniformly valid, then a further source of error is introduced, the effects of which will vary in the same ratio. Hence, on either supposition, that must be the most certain conclusion at which, starting from the postulate itself, we arrive by the fewest assumptions of the postulate.

We recognize this fact in our ordinary modes of proof. We hold it more certain that 2 and 2 make 4, than that $5 + 7 + 6 + 9 + 8$ make 35. We find that every fresh assumption of the postulate involves some risk of error; and, indeed, where the calculation is intricate, and the assumptions therefore numerous, experience teaches us that the likelihood of there having been a wrong assumption made, is greater than the reverse likelihood. So, too, in argument. We lose faith in a long series of steps, however logical they seem; and habitually test the inference by appeal to fact— that is, *we confidently accept the inference only when it has been verified by a single use of the postulate.**

---

* It never occurred to me that this statement was wanting in clearness; but it appears to have been misunderstood in more quarters than one. For example, at page 28 of his *Physical Ethics*, Mr. Alfred Barratt adverting to it

§ 436. Two possible sources of error involved by the multiplied use of the postulate, are indicated in the foregoing section. Of these Mr. Mill in his reply recognizes, I think, only one; and that the one which I have merely granted for argument's sake—not the one on which I have dwelt as of actual and admitted importance. A somewhat lengthy quotation from his chapter on " Theories concerning Axioms," will be here requisite:—

" In every reasoning, according to Mr. Spencer, the assumption of the postulate is renewed at every step. At each inference we judge that the conclusion follows from the premises, our sole warrant for that judgment being that

says:—"The weakness of a long argument lies, not as he supposes, on the frequent use of the Postulate, (for if it is the standard of certainty, it can never introduce uncertainty, any more than equals added to equals a hundred times would remain less certainly equal than at first); but only in the multiplied danger of its misuse." As in the above paragraph I have said that "every fresh assumption of the postulate involves some risk of error," I think I have sufficiently indicated that " the multiplied danger of its misuse " is the source of " the weakness of a long argument."

Having here to correct one of Mr. Barratt's misapprehensions, I may fitly seize the occasion for correcting several others. On page 37 (note), proposing to amend the accounts I have given of Memory, Reason, &c., Mr. Barratt tells me that " Reason too involves something more than the mere sequence of ideas—it involves the recognition and conscious classification both of the ideas themselves and of the relation between them." Considering that I have occupied several chapters of the " Special Analysis " in elaborately demonstrating this truth, is it not a little remarkable that it should be thus pointed out to me. Again, on page 40 (note) he says:— " It may be answered that Mr. Spencer only differs from us in his use of the word consciousness, which he confines to the meaning of Perception or Knowledge." Now, in saying this, Mr. Barratt does not simply misrepresent me, but he contradicts the representation of me which he has given on page 300; where he has commented on the distinction I draw between definite consciousness and indefinite consciousness—this last being placed in contrast with that which is distinguished as Perception or Knowledge. Similarly, on page 46, Mr. Barratt, after giving an account of the antagonism between Sensation and Perception, which is a brief re-statement of the one I have given in the chapter on " Perception in General," proceeds, in the appended note, to comment on my remark that "no act of cognition can be *absolutely* free from emotion," by saying:—" The rea-

we cannot conceive it not to follow. Consequently if the
postulate is fallible, the conclusions of reasoning are more
vitiated by that uncertainty than direct intuitions; and the
disproportion is greater, the more numerous the steps of the
argument.

" To test this doctrine, let us first suppose an argument
consisting only of a single step, which would be represented
by one syllogism. This argument does not rest on an assumption, and we have seen in the preceding chapters what the
assumption is. It is, that whatever has a mark, has what it
is a mark of. The evidence of this axiom I shall not consider at present; let us suppose it (with Mr. Spencer) to be
the inconceivableness of its reverse.

son of this Mr. Spencer cannot see, because of his mistake about consciousness, which leads him to the theory that emotion and cognition have
no real difference." This Mr. Barratt says, though the very section from
which he quotes (see chapter on "The Feelings") is a delineation of the
contrast between the two; in which I have said that, " though differing
from Sir William Hamilton respecting the interpretation of the antagonism
between Perception and Sensation, I quite agree with him in the doctrine,
that the same antagonism holds between cognition and emotion in general."
Equally at variance with fact is the representation on page 52 of the
" grave error " into which I have fallen; as is also the representation of the
doctrine of mine referred to on page 89. Kindred mis-statements of other
men's conceptions occur; as, for instance, where Mr. Barratt says—" But
Mr. Spencer is not justified in adopting Von Baer's expression of the law
of evolution, which identifies it with the integration of matter and the
dissipation of motion. For the least observation shows that such an expression of it applies at most to the inorganic world." I am not aware
that Von Baer used any such expression, or had any such conception.
Certainly I did not adopt it from him. All I adopted from him was his
generalization that each organism, in the course of its development, pro-
gresses from homogeneity to heterogeneity. I may add that as Mr. Barratt's remarkable facility of misapprehension characterizes his criticisms
on the "Theory of the Absolute," discussion of them would be profitless,
even were this a fit place.

I regret having thus to speak of one whose work has much merit, and
who, in several places, refers to me in sympathetic language. But the
amount of mischief done to an author by repeatedly debiting him with
serious mistakes which he has not made, and then proceeding to rectify
them, is greater than can be compensated by occasional laudation.

" Let us now add a second step to the argument: we require, what? Another assumption? No: the same assumption a second time; and so on to a third, and a fourth. I confess I do not see how, on Mr. Spencer's own principles, the repetition of the assumption at all weakens the force of the argument. If it were necessary the second time to assume some other axiom, the argument would no doubt be weakened, since it would be necessary to its validity that both axioms should be true, and it might happen that one was true and not the other: making two chances of error instead of one. But since it is the *same* axiom, if it is true once it is true every time; and if the argument, being of a hundred links, assumed the axiom a hundred times, these hundred assumptions would make but one chance of error among them all."

Even were the source of error here dealt with, that on which I have above insisted, it might still be held that multiplied use of the postulate involves increased possibility of error. Were an argument formed by repeating the same proposition over and over again, it would be true that any *intrinsic* fallibility of the postulate would not make the conclusion more untrustworthy than the first step. But an argument consists of unlike propositions. Now since Mr. Mill's criticism on the Universal Postulate is that in some cases, which he names, it has proved to be an untrustworthy test; it follows that in any argument consisting of heterogeneous propositions, there is a risk, increasing as the number of propositions increases, that some one of them belongs to this class of cases, and is wrongly accepted because of the inconceivableness of its negation.

But the danger of error alleged in the foregoing section, is not the *intrinsic* one ; which I have admitted hypothetically, but not in fact. The danger of error I refer to is the *extrinsic* one ; arising from the treachery of thought, as it is ordinarily carried on. It is not from the constitution of the warrant itself that mistake is to be apprehended; but from that inattentiveness which leads us to suppose that we have the warrant when we have it not. If, by some remote chance, a Bank of England note I take in payment, is not cashed when presented, because there are no assets to meet it, I am betrayed into a loss because of the imperfect trustworthiness of the document itself; but if I inadvertently accept in payment, a note of the Bank of Elegance, supposing it to be a note of the Bank of England, my loss is due, not to any untrustworthiness of the Bank of England note, but to my inaccuracy of observation. Errors of this kind, occurring occasionally in intellectual acts of all kinds, and endangering more especially the complex intellectual acts, are those I have in view. Take some instances. I look at my watch, and seeing it to be 11 o'clock, think I shall be quite in time for an appointment; find on arriving that I am an hour too late; and then discover that when I thought it was 11 o'clock, my watch marked five minutes to 12. Again, hearing some one described as short-sighted, I state, as conclusive proof to the contrary, the fact that I saw him reading with spectacles on; and spectacles used for reading imply aged or long sight. It turns out that I am wrong, however, not from any flaw in my conscious inference, but from a flaw in my automatic inference; for the person named, taking up a newspaper but for a minute, and keeping his spectacles on, was not reading through them but below them. When we pass to conscious reasoning, the possibilities of mistake become greatly multiplied. Each one of the data is liable to be wrong from direct error of observation, from inadequate number of observations, and from absence of counter-observations; and the introspection by which it is decided that the premises involve the conclusion, is liable to fail both from inadequate capacity and from undue rapidity. Indeed, it needs but to recall the treatises written on fallacies, to be impressed with the fact that, apart from any possible error in logical principles themselves, error is frequently made, even by the most careful, in the application of them; and that the probability of error consequently increases as the length of an argument increases.

§ 437. Do we not here then discern a rigorous test of the relative validities of conflicting conclusions? Not only as judged instinctively, but as judged by a fundamental logic, *that must be the most certain conclusion which involves the postulate the fewest times.*

We find that under any circumstances—whether the postulate be uniformly true or not, this must hold good. Here, therefore, we have a method of ascertaining the comparative values of all cognitions.

CHAPTER XIII.

ITS COROLLARIES.

§ 438. From this critical examination of the processes by which conflicting judgments are to be appraised, we return now to the judgments especially concerning us—those of metaphysicians. By the test arrived at, we have to estimate the worths of the Idealistic and the Sceptical conclusions, in contrast with the worth of the Realistic conclusion. Let us suppose all other things equal. Let us suppose that the anti-Realistic conclusion is perfectly independent, and can be reached without the Realistic conclusion being previously posited (which it cannot); let us suppose, too, that the anti-Realistic conclusion is given in terms as distinct as those in which the Realistic conclusion is given (which it is not); and thus supposing the two conclusions to be otherwise equally good, let us observe the numbers of assumptions made in reaching them respectively.

That the comparison may be fairly made, let the reader sweep his mind clear of all hypotheses, and bring it to bear afresh upon the facts. As far as he can, let him keep out these verbal symbols, so often mistaken for the things symbolized—this paper-currency of thought, which continually leads to intellectual insolvency. Let him expel from his consciousness everything that can be expelled: so reducing his consciousness to its pre-speculative state.

Now let him contemplate an object—this book, for instance. Resolutely refraining from theorizing, let him say what he finds. He finds that he is conscious of the book as existing apart from himself. Does there enter into his consciousness any notion about sensations? No: so far from such notion being contained in his consciousness, it has to be fetched from elsewhere, to the manifest disturbance of his consciousness. Does he perceive that the thing he is conscious of is an image of the book? Not at all: it is only by remembering his metaphysical readings that he can suppose such image to exist. So long as he refuses to translate the facts into any hypothesis, he feels simply conscious of the book, and not of an impression of the book—of an objective thing, and not of a subjective thing. He feels that the sole content of his consciousness is the book considered as an external reality. He feels that this recognition of the book as an external reality is a single indivisible act. Whether originally separable into premisses and inference or not (a question which he manifestly cannot here entertain), he feels that this act is undecomposable. And, lastly, he feels that, do what he will, he cannot reverse this act—he cannot conceive that where he sees and feels the book there is nothing. Hence, while he continues looking at the book, his belief in it as an external reality possesses the highest validity possible. It has the direct guarantee of the Universal Postulate; and it assumes the Universal Postulate *only once*.

§ 439. Here, by asserting that in Perception proper, knowledge of the object as existing externally is acquired by a mental act which, however composite it originally was, has become simple to the developed intelligence, I am tacitly denying the assertions made by Prof. Ferrier and Sir W. Hamilton. These writers, otherwise differing so much, agree in affirming that the knowledge of *self* and the knowledge of *not-self* are inseparable. The doctrine of Prof. Ferrier is that " The object of knowledge .* * * always is, and must be, the object with the addition of oneself,—object *plus* subject, * * * Self is an integral and essential part of every object of cognition." Similarly, Sir W. Hamilton says:—" In the act of sensible perception I am conscious of two things;—of *myself* as the *perceiving subject*, and of an external reality in relation to my sense as the *object perceived*. * * * Each of these is apprehended equally and at once *in the same indivisible energy* ;" or, as he elsewhere phrases it—" *in the same indivisible moment of intuition.*

It seems to me, on the contrary, that the consciousness of self and the consciousness of not-self, are the elements of an unceasing rhythm in consciousness—a perpetual alternation, ordinarily so rapid as to evade observation, though occasionally so much retarded as to be observable. Like the divergence already set forth (§ 353) from Sir W. Hamilton's interpretation of the antagonism between Sensation and Perception, is the divergence that arises here: this second divergence being, in truth, a corollary from the first. Just as before we saw that Sensation and Perception respectively dominate in consciousness with degrees of strength that vary inversely, thus excluding one another with varying degrees of stringency; so here we shall see that the consciousness of self and the consciousness of not-self, are ever tending each to exclude the other, but each failing to do this for more than an instant, save in those exceptional cases where it is raised to extreme vividness. Thus, on the one hand, when the external object or act is an astounding one, the observer partially loses consciousness of himself. He is, as we say, *lost* in wonder, or has *forgotten* himself; and we describe him as afterwards *returning* to himself, *recollecting* himself. In this state, the related impressions received from the external object, joined with representations of the objective changes about to follow, monopolize consciousness, and keep out all those feelings and ideas which constitute self-consciousness. Hence what is called " fascination;" and

hence the stupefaction on witnessing a tremendous catas-
trophe. Persons so " possessed " are sometimes killed from
the inability to recover self-consciousness in time to avoid
danger. Even those who are not thus paralyzed are apt
to show a kindred " absence of mind; " for such are
sometimes wounded without knowing it, and are surprised
to hear afterwards what they did while in peril—a fact
proving that their actions were automatic rather than conscious. Conversely, self-consciousness occasionally
rises to a degree in which the individual is, as we say,
absorbed in thought and oblivious of the things around.
Even intellectual pre-occupation may become so complete
that, passing in the street persons perfectly well-known
to us, we may look them in the face and be afterwards absolutely unaware that we have met them. And when consciousness is filled with intense pain, sensational or emotional, the thoughts of external things are almost excluded
—returning at relatively-long intervals in but an imperfect way.

Sir W. Hamilton's view is, I think, disproved by one of
his own axiomatic principles. At page 49 of his " Discussions, &c.," he says:—" Relatives are known only together:
the science of opposites is one. Subject and object, mind
and matter, are known only in correlation and contrast—and
by the same common act." Now, were all antitheses those
between self and not-self, nothing would remain to be said.
But there are numberless antitheses, *both* members of which
pertain to the not-self; and numberless others, *both* members
of which pertain to self—of the one class, full and empty,
near and remote; of the other, pleasure and pain, belief and
disbelief. According to the foregoing general law, each of
these pairs of relatives can be known only by the contrast of
its terms—near only as the correlative of remote, and so on.
But if the *ego* is always present to consciousness as the correlative of the *non-ego*, how can two elements of the *non-ego*
ever be conceived as the correlatives of each other? If I can

know *a part* only by contrast with *a whole*, then the two things present to consciousness together must be *whole* and *part*. If that which I contemplate as the correlative to *a part* is the *self* which recognizes it, then I cannot contemplate *whole* as its correlative. As, however, we know that *whole* and *part are* known as correlatives, it follows inevitably from the general principle above quoted, that while recognizing the relation between them, I am not recognizing the relation between myself as subject and either of them as object.

Even apart from these verifications of it, the general principle that consciousness cannot be in two distinct states at the same time, negatives the assertion that the consciousnesses of subject and object are absolutely simultaneous—occupy "*the same indivisible moment of intuition.*" When engaged in interpreting the related impressions which an objects yields, and identifying the object as such or such, it is not possible for consciousness to be also engaged in contemplating those impressions as affections of self, still less in contemplating the various other affections which make up self-consciousness. The presented impressions, bound up in a plexus of relations with one another and with represented impressions; and also bound up with those space-relations which constitute the knowledges of externality and position; form a consolidated consciousness the components of which are for the time inseparable. The proposition—" The book exists," is one of which subject and predicate are indissolubly united—one of which the negation is inconceivable; and it assumes the Universal Postulate but once. Complex as the cognition thus expressed originally was, it became fused into a simple cognition long before conscious reasoning commenced; and it remains simpler than any one of the cognitions out of which conscious reasoning is framed.

§ 440. And now, in respect of the numbers of their assumptions of the Universal Postulate, let us contrast with

Realism the anti-Realistic doctrines—or rather one of them; for it will be needless to go farther. We will take Hypothetical Realism, which is the comparatively-unassuming parent of the rest. No one can define this, or frame for himself any conception of it, without abandoning that state of consciousness in which he is simply percipient, and taking up a mental position from which he may perceive the act of percipience. Instead of this book which he holds and recognizes as existing, being the sole content of his consciousness, he has also to bring definitely into consciousness that highly-complex conception which he knows as self; and then he has to conceive the one as affecting the other. He postulates the book, he postulates himself, he postulates the power by which the first works a change in the last. The original cognition of the book as existing, cannot be even conceived to be a compound cognition without a roundabout process. Whereas this which is proposed in place of it, cannot be even conceived without assuming at least three things: each of three distinct propositions must be posited as true because the negation of it is inconceivable.

But the contrast is far more marked than this. No such doctrine as that of Hypothetical Realism can be framed without language. Shut out all words and all the speculations conveyed through words, and though the Realistic conception of the object remains as vivid as ever, the conception of Hypothetical Realism vanishes utterly. To bring it back again, you have not only to use the paper-currency of thought, and instead of your experiences themselves use symbols of your experiences (many of them doubly and triply symbolic); but you have to bring in those generalized ideas of forces, and actions, and causes, and effects, which severally postulate the validities of countless by-gone mental acts. Nor is this all. Beyond the numerous assumptions of the Universal Postulate implied in the words and in the generalized ideas without which Hypothetical Realism cannot even be conceived, there are those

72

numerous assumptions implied in the argument by which it is sought to be justified.

Even supposing, then, that each of these multitudinous assumptions of the Universal Postulate was equally unquestionable with that which Realism makes—even supposing each act by which I know the meaning of a word, or frame the abstract idea of a cause, was as irreversible as that which makes me join to the consciousness of a body's resistance the consciousness of its externality; it would still hold that, since each of these many assumptions has but at best the same warrant as the single assumption, the conclusion reached through the many must at best be far less certain than the conclusion reached through the one, because of the multiplied possibilities of error.

Of course, the reasoning which thus shows that Hypothetical Realism can never have a logical validity equal to that of Positive Realism, applies with still greater force to the derivative hypotheses of Idealism, Absolute Idealism, and Scepticism.

§ 441. We must, therefore, confess that Reason is utterly incapable of showing the unreasonableness of those primary deliverances of consciousness which yield Subject and Object as independent existences. While, as we before saw, it is impossible for Reason to prove its own superior trustworthiness, it is quite possible for it to prove its own inferior trustworthiness. Self-analysis shows that all its dicta being derivative, are necessarily less certain than those from which they are derived. To carry out the simile before used, if, as witnesses, Reason and Perception give opposite testimonies, and Reason claims to be believed in preference, cross-examination brings out the fact that Reason's testimony is nothing more than hearsay gained from Perception. By its own account, it cannot possibly have done anything more than compare and interpret the evidences which Perception has given. So long as it limits itself to detecting incongruities among these, and finding out where they have arisen, Reason performs an all-important function; but it exceeds its function, and commits suicide, when it concludes the evidence to be false in substance.

In this sphere, as in other spheres, Reason can do nothing more than reconcile the testimonies of Perception with one another. When it proved that the Sun does not move round the Earth, but that the Earth turns on its axis, Reason substituted for an old interpretation which was irreconcilable with various facts, a new interpretation which was reconcilable with them, while it equally well accounted for the more obvious facts. Reason did not question the existence of the Sun, the Earth, and their relative motion; but simply furnished an alternative conception of their relative motion. And, similarly, Reason in being brought to bear on those deliverances of consciousness which we distinguish as perceptions of the external world, has to rectify many of these by expelling the crude interpretations ordinarily bound up with them; but it has to do this in such subordination to the perceptions as to leave their essential testimonies unquestioned.

Finding that while Reason can do this it can never do more than this—finding that any hypothetical doubtfulness of the Realistic conception must be immeasurably exceeded by the resulting doubtfulness of every anti-Realistic argument, we find that Realism is negatively justified.

CHAPTER XIV.

POSITIVE JUSTIFICATION OF REALISM.

§ 442. Among the many contradictions which anti-Realistic hypotheses involve, is the contradiction between the assertion that consciousness cannot be transcended and the assertion that there exists nothing beyond consciousness. For if we can in no way be aware of anything beyond consciousness, what can suggest either the affirmation or the denial of it? and how can even denial of it be framed in thought? The very proposition that consciousness cannot be transcended, admits of being put together only by representing a limit, and consequently implies some kind of consciousness of something beyond the limit.

And then after this contradiction, there comes a further contradiction. The assertion that consciousness cannot be transcended, is accompanied by a tacit demand for some other proof of an external world than that which is given in states of consciousness. While that complex deliverance of consciousness which asserts its own limits is regarded as above question; and while its simple deliverance that something exists outside its limits is held to be invalid; there seems to be required of it some proof of this outer existence other than that given in terms of inner existence.

Clearly, one of two things—either objective existence can be known otherwise than in states of consciousness, which is granting everything; or else neither proof nor disproof of objective existence can be given otherwise than in states of consciousness. And in this case, if states of consciousness are held adequate to frame a disproof, they must be held adequate to frame a proof. Otherwise the whole question is prejudged by affirming the power to give a negative answer and denying the power to give an affirmative answer.

§ 443. Realism, then, is positively justified, if it is shown to be a dictum of consciousness working after its proper laws. When normal acts of thought, like those which establish the truths we hold most certain, are proved to be the acts of thought which yield the antithesis of Subject and Object, no further demonstration can be asked.

Hence we have to trace the processes by which the Realistic conception is built up. Its relative validity we have already seen to be immeasurably greater than that of any counter-conception; and now we have to test its absolute validity. Its absolute validity will be shown if we find it to be a necessary product of thought proceeding according to laws of thought that are universal.

Our analysis and our subsequent synthesis will be psychological rather than logical. We must here examine the fabric of consciousness itself, to ascertain in what way its components are united. The ultimate answer to the question—Why do we think certain things true rather than others? involves the question—Why do our states of consciousness hang together in this way rather than in that?

§ 444. In carrying on this inquiry, we shall have to shut out, so far as may be, the ordinary implications of thought. We cannot shut them out actually; we can shut them out only hypothetically. The Realistic interpretation of our states of consciousness, deep as the very structure of the nervous system, cannot for an instant be actually expelled. All we can do by way of maintaining the needful attitude is persistently to ignore these Realistic interpretations—to suppose ourselves without them, and limit our attention to states of consciousness considered simply as such.

Our first step will be to present under its psychological aspect that ultimate truth which we lately dealt with at great length under its logical aspect.

CHAPTER XV.

THE DYNAMICS OF CONSCIOUSNESS.

§ 445. When thought is carried on with precision—when the mental states we call words, are translated into the mental states they symbolize (which they often are not)—thinking a proposition consists in the occurrence together in consciousness of the subject and predicate. "The bird was brown," is a statement implying the union in thought of a particular attribute with a group of other attributes.

If the inquirer compares various propositions thus rendered into states of consciousness, he finds them unlike in respect of the facility with which the states of consciousness are connected and disconnected. The mental state known as *brown* may be united with those mental states which make up the figure known as *bird*, without appreciable effort, or may be separated from them without appreciable effort: the bird may easily be thought of as black, or green, or yellow. Contrariwise, such an assertion as "The ice was hot," is one to which he finds much difficulty in making his mind respond. The elements of the proposition cannot be put together in thought without great resistance. Between those other states of consciousness which the word *ice* connotes, and the state of consciousness named *cold*, there is a strong cohesion—a cohesion measured by the resistance to be overcome in thinking of the ice as *hot*. Further, he finds that in many cases the states of consciousness grouped together cannot be

447

separated at all. The idea of pressure cannot be disconnected from the idea of something occupying space. Motion
cannot be thought of without an object that moves being at
the same time thought of. These connexions in consciousness remain absolute under all circumstances.

Shutting himself up within the prescribed limits, let the
inquirer ask what he thinks about these various degrees of
cohesion among his states of consciousness—how he names
them, and how he behaves toward them. If there comes, no
matter whence, the proposition—" The bird was brown,"
subject and predicate answering to these words spring up
together in thought; and if there is no opposing proposition,
he unites the specified and implied attributes without effort,
and accepts it. If, however, the proposition is—" The bird
was necessarily brown," he makes an experiment like those
above described, and finding that he can separate the attribute of brownness, and can think of the bird as green or
yellow, he does not admit that the bird was necessarily
brown.   When such a proposition as " The ice was
cold " arises in him, the elements of the thought behave as
before; and so long as no test is applied, the union of the
consciousness of cold with the accompanying states of consciousness, seems to be of the same nature as the union between those answering to the words *brown* and *bird*. But
should the proposition be changed into—" The ice was
necessarily cold," a result happens different from that which
happened in the previous case. The ideas answering to subject and predicate are here so coherent, that they might
almost pass as inseparable, and the proposition be accepted.
But suppose the proposition is deliberately tested by trying
whether ice can be thought of as not cold. Great resistance
is offered in consciousness to this. Still, by an effort, he can
imagine water to have its temperature of congelation higher
than blood heat; and can so think of congealed water as hot
instead of cold.   Once more, in response to the
words—" Along with motion there is something that moves"

he represents to himself a moving body; and, until he tries an experiment upon it, he may suppose the elements of the representation to be united in the same way as those of the representations instanced above. But supposing the proposition is modified into—" Along with motion there is necessarily something that moves," the response made in thought to these words shows that the states of consciousness called up in this case are indissolubly connected in the way alleged. He tries to think of motion as *not* having along with it something that moves; and his inability to do this is the obverse of his inability to tear asunder the states of consciousness which constitute the thought to be tested.

Those propositions which withstand this strain, are the propositions he distinguishes as necessary. Whether or not he means any thing else by this word, he evidently means that in his consciousness the connexions predicated are, so far as he can ascertain, unalterable. The bare fact is that he submits to them because he has no choice. They rule his thoughts whether he will or not. Leaving out all questions concerning the origin of these connexions—all theories concerning their significations, the inquirer discovers that certain of his states of consciousness are so welded together that all other links in the chain of consciousness yield before these give way.

§ 446. Continuing to ignore implied existences beyond consciousness, let him now ask himself what he means by reasoning? Analysis shows him that reasoning is the formation of a coherent series of states of consciousness. He has found that the thoughts expressed, by propositions, vary in the cohesions of their subjects and predicates; and he finds that at every step in an argument, carefully carried on, he tests the strengths of all the connexions asserted and implied. He considers whether the object named really does belong to the class in which it is included—tries whether he can think of it as *not* like the things it is said to be like.

He considers whether the attribute alleged is really possessed by all members of the class—tries to think of some member of the class as *not* having the attribute. And he admits the proposition only on finding that there is a greater cohesion in thought between its elements, than between the elements of the counter-proposition. Thus testing each link in the argument, he at length reaches the conclusion, which he tests in the same way. If he accepts it, he does so because the argument has established in him an indirect cohesion between states of consciousness that were not directly coherent, or not so coherent directly as the argument makes them indirectly. But he accepts it only supposing that the connexion between the two states of consciousness composing it, is not resisted by some stronger counter-connexion. If there happens to be an opposing argument, of which the component thoughts are felt, when tested, to be more coherent; or if, in the absence of an opposing argument, there exists an opposing conclusion, of which the elements have some direct cohesion greater than that which the proffered argument indirectly gives; then the conclusion reached by this argument is not admitted.

Thus, a discussion in consciousness proves to be simply a trial of strength between different connexions in consciousness—a systematized struggle serving to determine which are the least coherent states of consciousness. And the result of the struggle is, that the least coherent states of consciousness separate, while the most coherent remain together: forming a proposition of which the predicate persists in the mind along with its subject.

§ 447. What corollary may the inquirer draw, or rather what corollary must he draw, on pushing the analysis to its limit? If there are any indissoluble connexions, he is compelled to accept them. If certain states of consciousness absolutely cohere in certain ways, he is obliged to think them in those ways. The proposition is an identical one.

To say that they are necessities of thought is merely another way of saying that their elements cannot be torn asunder. No reasoning can give to these absolute cohesions in thought any better warrant; since all reasoning, being a process of testing cohesions, is itself carrried on by accepting the absolute cohesions; and can, in the last resort, do nothing more than present some absolute cohesions in justification of others —an act which unwarrantably assumes in the absolute cohesions it offers, a greater value than is allowed to the absolute cohesions it would justify. Here, then, the inquirer comes down to an ultimate mental uniformity—a universal law of his thinking. How completely his thought is subordinated to this law, is shown by the fact that he cannot even represent to himself the possibility of any other law. To suppose the connexions among his states of consciousness to be otherwise determined, is to suppose a smaller force overcoming a greater—a proposition which may be expressed in words but cannot be rendered into ideas.

These results the inquirer arrives at without assuming any other existence than that of what he calls states of consciousness. They postulate nothing about Mind or Matter, Subject or Object. They leave wholly untouched the questions—what does consciousness imply? and how is thought generated? There is not involved in the analysis any hypothesis respecting the origin of these relations between thoughts—how there come to be feeble cohesions, strong cohesions, and absolute cohesions. Whatever some of the terms used may have seemed to connote, it will be found, on examining each step, that nothing is essentially involved beyond mental states and the connexions among them.

Should the inquirer enter upon the explanation of these facts, he must consider how any further investigation is to be conducted, and what is the possible degree of validity of its conclusions. Every hypothesis he entertains in trying to explain himself to himself, being an hypothesis expressible only in terms of his mental states, it follows that any process of explanation must itself be carried on by testing the cohesions among mental states, and accepting the absolute cohesions. His conclusion, therefore, reached through repeated recognitions of this test of absolute cohesion, can never have any higher validity than this test. It matters not what name he gives to his conclusion—whether he calls it a belief, a theory, a fact, or a truth. These words can be themselves only names for certain relations among his states of consciousness. Any secondary meanings which he ascribes to them must also be meanings expressed in terms of consciousness, and therefore subordinate to the laws of consciousness. Hence he has no appeal from this ultimate dictum.

§ 448. Here, then, is an all-sufficient warrant for the assertion of objective existence. Mysterious as seems the consciousness of something which is yet out of consciousness, the inquirer finds that he alleges the reality of this something in virtue of the ultimate law—he is obliged to think it. There is an indissoluble cohesion between each of those vivid and definite states of consciousness known as a sensation, and an indefinable consciousness which stands for a mode of being beyond sensation, and separate from himself. When grasping his fork and putting food into his mouth, he is wholly unable to expel from his mind the notion of something which resists the force he is using; and he cannot suppress the nascent thought of an independent existence keeping apart his tongue and palate, and giving him that sensation of taste which he is unable to generate in consciousness by his own activity. Though self-criticism shows him that he cannot know what this is which lies outside of him; and though he may infer that not being able to say what it is, it is a fiction; he discovers that such self-criticism utterly fails to extinguish the consciousness of it as a reality. So that even could no account of its genesis be given, this consciousness would still remain imperative. It cannot even be imagined to be untrue without imagining the absence of that principle of cohesion whereby consciousness is held together.

§ 449. But while it is impossible by reasoning either to verify or to falsify this deliverance of consciousness, it is possible to account for it. Manifestly, if our conclusions are simply expressive of the ways in which our states of consciousness hang together, this imperative consciousness which we have of objective existence, must itself result from the way in which our states of consciousness hang together.

Here, then, rises before us a definite course of inquiry. Let us examine the cohesions among the elements of consciousness, taken as a whole; and let us observe whether there are any absolute cohesions by which its elements are aggregated into two antithetical halves, standing respectively for Subject and Object.

Though in the course of this inquiry we shall have to use words which connote both Subject and Object—though in every illustration taken we shall have tacitly to posit an external existence, and in every reference to states of consciousness we shall have to posit an internal existence which has these states; yet, as before, we must ignore these implications.

CHAPTER XVI.

PARTIAL DIFFERENTIATION OF SUBJECT AND OBJECT.*

§ 450. States of consciousness which I name touches and pressures, come to me as I sit on this bench with the sea-breeze blowing in my face. Sounds from the breakers, motions of the waves that stretch away to the horizon, are at the same time present; and I am also aware of the Sun's warmth and the odour of sea-weed. These states I call, according to their respective classes, loud, or bright, or strong. They seem to fill the whole area of consciousness; but a closer inspection proves that they do not.

After that whiff of sea-weed smell which the breeze just brought me, there come colours and forms such as another

---

* In the chapter of *First Principles* entitled " The Data of Philosophy," we found a needful preliminary to be the division of all manifestations of existence into two great aggregates, implying the two existences distinguished as *ego* and *non-ego*. As an indispensable link in the argument more fully set forth in this work, I am obliged here to enumerate afresh the several contrasts between these two great aggregates of manifestations. I re-state them, however, with new illustrations and in a form more or less different. Further, in pursuance of a better method, I exclude from this chapter certain classes of phenomena which accompany, or are due to, emotion and volition, and the muscular movements produced by them. The delineation of these phenomena, transferred to the next chapter, will there be joined with the delineation of certain allied classes not before dealt with—classes that are all-important as establishing the independence of objective existence. In this chapter the antitheses described, will be such only as are observable during *absolute physical passivity*.

454

beach gave many years ago; as well as thoughts of all that happened when I first saw the sea. Along with this series there goes a secondary series, constituting what I know as language, helping me to distinguish and identify and connect the members of the first. Presently this particular double series passes into some other. A book in the hand of a lady passing by, introduces afresh certain connected states which reading lately aroused in me. And so, on watching narrowly, I find that in presence of all these aggregated colours, sounds, pressures, &c., which I am receiving, there keep appearing and disappearing certain others which belong to the same classes, but differ in intensity and are differently arranged and combined.

Excluding all theory as to their origins, the first cardinal fact to be set down is, that these two classes of states are respectively vivid and faint.

§ 451. While I sit, the light and the warmth diminish, the horizon becomes obscure, and presently a sea-fog drifting in hides everything but the shingle stretching out before me. The distant headland with its white cliff and sweep of green down above, is blotted out; as is also the pier to my right and the cluster of boats anchored on my left. What is implied in saying this? There is implied that the specially-shaped vivid patches of green and white which I distinguished as a distant headland, now remain with me as faint patches, having shapes and relative positions approximately the same; and the like holds with those produced in me by the pier and the boats. If I ask what would have happened if, never having been in the place before the previous night, the sea-fog then existing had continued up to the time I took my seat, I perceive that these faint states which I now call the distant headland and the pier would not have existed: they exist now as specially-combined faint states, only because they previously existed as similarly-combined vivid states. This I find to be the law of

all the combinations. After the bursting of each breaker,
I hear a rattle and a hiss which I know to be caused by the
shingle as it is drawn back by the under-tow. But if I had
not previously heard these sounds along with the sight of
pebbles as they were rolled over and knocked together, the
sounds I now hear would not have been followed by the
faint states representing this process. And on observing
the uncombined states themselves, I find the like holds.
Never having eaten a mangosteen, the name calls up in me
no faint state like that which the juice of the fruit would give
me. But a weak state which I distinguish as the taste of
a pine-apple arises after the name, because the answering
strong state has occurred in my experience.

Comparison shows me, then, that the vivid states are
original and the faint states derived. It is true that these
derivative states admit of being combined in ways not
wholly like the ways in which the original states were
combined. Having had the states yielded by trees, mountains, rocks, cascades, &c., thoughts of these may be
put together in shapes partially new. But if none of the
various forms, colours, and distributions have been vividly
presented, no faint re-combinations of them are possible.

§ 452. The wind changes, the sea-fog rises, and I see
again the waves, the horizon, the headland, the pier, the
boats. These are arranged just as they were, and exhibit
similar contrasts. True, the Sun is lower; and the colours
of the headland, the sea, the sky, have changed somewhat.
Still, this cluster of vivid visual states corresponds, substantially in its colours and absolutely in their relative
positions, with the cluster I saw before. Further, I observe
that neither the tints, nor the shapes, nor the distributions,
are in the slightest degree changeable by anything in my
consciousness. Sitting motionless, as I do, they severally
persist in their respective kinds and intensities; and are
held together in a rigid plexus. I am equally power-

less over the states I know as motions and sounds. The patch of white I call a sail, continues to pass across other patches of colour regardless of any thought I have; and after the changing cluster of appearances which I name a curling breaker, there inevitably comes, whether I wish it or not, a thud on the beach. These vivid and original states, then, have the further character that both their natures and their order have a temporary absoluteness.

Far otherwise is it with the faint derivative states. Though the order among these has certain general characters not admitting of change (as that which with every consciousness of colour unites some consciousness of superficial space, or that which along with every idea of touch joins some idea of position), yet all their special relations, as well as the states themselves, are readily changeable. While the sea-fog shut out the view, the faint states answering to the previously-seen headland and pier and boats, admitted of being transposed, or varied in their forms and colours, or excluded entirely, to be replaced by others in endless combinations. And the like holds among all other derivative states.

So that the vivid originals and the faint copies are contrasted as being, the one absolutely unalterable while I remain physically passive, and the other readily alterable while I remain physically passive.

§ 453. Each set of states has among its members both a simultaneous cohesion and a serial cohesion. I find no moment at which I am aware of any break of succession in either aggregate, or of its reduction to singleness.

While I remain at rest, there is a continuity of the sights, the sounds, the pressures, the odours, &c. If I sit till night has shut out the vivid visual states, still the sounds of the breakers and the rolling shingle persist, as do the pressure I feel from the seat, the odour of the sea-weed, and the feelings of touch and coolness which the wind gives me.

These maintain the integrity of the aggregate of vivid
states; and however many elements of this aggregate are
absent, I can never discover any moment when they are
diminished to single file, still less any moment when they
are all absent and the aggregate broken in two. For even
when from weariness I doze, I cannot become aware of any
discontinuity of the vivid states; since they continue so long
as the power of observing them continues and their presence
is known the instant consciousness is recovered.

The like is true of the faint states. These also have both
a simultaneous and a serial cohesion among themselves,
which is absolute in the sense that no state can be so separated
from accompanying states as to exist alone, or can be detached from preceding or succeeeding states. Plastic and
changeable as is the series of faint states, yet no break in
it, or end of it, can be found or even imagined; since any
state of consciousness in which an ending of these faint
states is represented, is itself a new state of the same kind.

Each set of states thus proves itself a persistent whole.
The first is present to me as made up of states rigidly bound
in simultaneous order; bound also beyond my control in
successive order. And the second is made up of states
bound together in a pliable rather than a rigid way: the
pliability being such, however, that while minor displace-
ments are easy, no total displacement constituting a break
is possible.

§ 454. The two aggregates thus contrasted as being the
one composed of the vivid originals and the other of the
faint copies, and each of which is coherent within itself,
longitudinally and transverscly, are not coherent in like
manner with one another. The one is absolutely independent and the other relatively independent.

In broad procession the vivid states—sounds from the
breakers, the wind, the vehicles behind me; changing
patches of colour from the waves; pressures, odours, and the

rest—move on abreast, unceasing and unbroken, wholly without regard to anything else in my consciousness. Their independence of the faint states is such that the procession of these, in whatever way it moves, produces no effect whatever on them. Massed together by ties of their own, the vivid states slide by resistlessly.

The procession of the faint states, however, while it has a considerable degree of independence, cannot maintain complete independence. The vivid states sweeping past always affect it in a greater or less degree—drag part of it with them by lateral cohesion. To the moving patches of colour yielded by the waves, there cling certain faint states which make up the conception of a cold, transparent liquid. The sounds from the pebbles rolled about by the waves, inevitably draw along ideas of shape and colour and hardness. And after each whiff of sea-weed smell, there rise up, vaguely or distinctly, thoughts of the black, wet, tangled masses yielding it. In this manner the vivid series may carry with it much or little of the faint series; but so long as the waking state continues, it always carries some. There is, nevertheless, a portion of the faint series, sometimes broad sometimes narrow, which moves on with a substantial independence. While gazing at the sea, the train of faint states set up by the sight of the lady with the book, may rise into a predominance and gain a momentum so great that the stream of vivid states scarcely affects it. Though entire unconsciousness of things around is rarely if ever reached, yet the consciousness of them may become very imperfect; and this imperfect consciousness, observe, results from the independence of the faint series becoming for the time so marked that very little of it clings to the vivid series.

We have, therefore, the further cardinal fact, that these two aggregates move on side by side with an independence that is absolute in the case of the one, while in the case of the other it is partial and sometimes nearly complete.

§ 455. The separateness of these two aggregates becomes yet more conspicuous when we examine the states composing each in reference to their order of succession. We find the significant fact to be that when for any consequent in the vivid series we can perceive the antecedent, that antecedent exists in the vivid series; and, conversely, in the independent part of the faint series, we find that for each of the faint consequents there is a faint antecedent. In other words, beyond the general cohesion which binds each aggregate into a whole, there are, in each aggregate, special cohesions between its particular members.

Thus, in the vivid series, after the changing forms and colours which, as united, I call a curling breaker, there comes a sound made by its fall on the beach. No combination of faint feelings serves to initiate this vivid feeling of sound; nor when I receive the vivid visual feelings from the curling breaker, can I prevent the vivid feeling of sound from following. Similarly with the motions of the boat that is being rowed in front of me; and similarly with the setting of the Sun and the changes of colour which follow. In all these cases, antecedents and consequents alike exist in the vivid series; as do also whatever links unite them, since nothing in the faint series affects their unions.

In like manner when we trace back our thoughts and the components of our thoughts, we discover that each coheres with a special preceding thought; and we discover that all these cohesions, some absolute, some strong, some feeble, have an order or method proper to themselves, which admits of being identified and expressed in terms of the faint series. And that the proximate cause of the order in the faint series lies within the faint series, is manifest from the fact that the faint series has a power of changing its own order.

So that the two aggregates present the additional trait of separateness that each has its own laws of coexistence and succession. These laws, too, present a significant contrast. Among the vivid states, there are not only certain general absolute uniformities of relation, but each particular relation when it occurs is absolute. Among the faint series, however, while certain of the laws are derived (as the states themselves are derived) from the vivid series; and while some of these uniformities in the faint series are absolute, like the corresponding uniformities in the vivid series; the particular relations in the faint series are, when they occur, not absolute, but may be changed with facility.

§ 456. A further distinction between the two aggregates is, that whereas in the one the antecedent to any consequent may or may not be within the limits of consciousness, in the other it is always within the limits of consciousness.

That white cumulus which has just come over the blue sky on the left, constitutes a change in the vivid series that was not preceded by anything I could perceive. Sudden as it was, the sensation of cold I lately had on the back of my hand took me by surprise; since, not having seen the cloud behind, I did not anticipate the rain-drop which caused the sensation. Now that I am startled from my reverie by the discordant brayings of a three-boy band, I perceive that though, after hearing the sound, there rises in me a cluster of faint states representing the antecedent, yet the antecedent not having been in sight, the sound broke across my train of thought without there being within either the vivid or the faint series anything to prepare me for it.

If, on the other hand, I consider what made me just now think of death from fever, I find the thought was preceded by the thought of abnormal molecular changes in the blood; and this was preceded by the thought of unstable molecules that had been taken into the blood by respiration; and this by the thought that such molecules are generated by decomposition in closed cavities, but not by open decomposition; and this by the thought that decomposition in closed cavities has been insisted on by those who undertake to look

after our health; and this by the visual impression from a
large iron drain-pipe, which runs over the beach down to
the sea.   Similarly throughout.   Every state in the faint
series has an identifiable antecedent, either in the faint
series or in the vivid series.

This difference is significant as implying a circumscription of the faint aggregate which the vivid aggregate has
not. The possibility of finding the antecedent to each consequent in the perpetually-passing series of faint states,
shows that it can be explored up to its boundary in all
directions: the boundary being either the vivid aggregate,
or the vacuity into which memory cannot pass.   But the
vivid aggregate admits of no such complete exploration.
Into that part of it immediately present there are ever entering new components, which make their appearance out of
some region lying beyond consciousness.

§ 457. This contrast becomes more conspicuous and
significant still when, to my experiences of the vivid aggregate as now presented, I add recollections of the ways in
which it comported itself when before presented. These
show to me in two ways that outside that part of it immediately present, there is always a region of potential antecedents, and potential vivid states, without known limits.

Thus if I consider simply the pebble which just shot
across my area of vision and fell into the sea, I can only say
that it was a change in the vivid aggregate, the antecedent of which was somewhere outside the vivid aggregate.
But such motions of pebbles have in past cases had for
their visible antecedents certain motions of boys; and
with the vivid states now produced by the falling pebble,
there cohere in consciousness the faint states representing some similar antecedent outside the aggregate of vivid
states.

This conception of the aggregate of vivid states, as having
beyond its present limits an unlimited region in which there

exist powers of producing such states, both in known combinations and in unknown combinations, gains further distinctness when I remember how small a portion of it is now present; what countless such portions have been before present; how continuously these have passed one into another; how wholly unexpected have often been the combinations they presented; and how incapable my explorations have been of exhausting their varieties.

So comparing the aggregate of the vivid states with the aggregate of the faint states, it results that this last is a whole mostly very familiar, the limits of which have at one time or other been everywhere visited; while the other is part of a whole which has no discoverable limits.

§458. If now I enumerate these several contrasts, I find the two aggregates marked off from one another by traits which, severally striking as they are, constitute when taken together a difference transcending all other differences; for no one member of either aggregate is distinguished from other members of the same aggregate, by traits so many and so strong. Here, placed in series, are the several contrasts.

STATES OF THE FIRST CLASS.	STATES OF THE SECOND CLASS.
1. Relatively vivid.	1. Relatively faint.
2. Predecessors in time (or originals).	2. Successors in time (or copies).
3. Unchangeable by volition in their qualities.	3. Changeable by volition in their qualities.
4. Unchangeable by volition in their simultaneous order.	4. Changeable by volition in their simultaneous order.
5. Unchangeable by volition in their successive order.	5. Changeable by volition in their successive order.
6. Form parts of a vivid aggregate never known to be broken;	6. Form parts of a faint aggregate never known to be broken;

7. Which is completely independent of the faint;

7. Which is partially independent of the vivid;

8. And has laws that originate within it.

8. And has laws partly derived from the other, partly peculiar to itself.

9. Have antecedents that may or may not be traceable.

9. Have antecedents that are always traceable.

10. Belong to a whole of unknown extent.

10. Belong to a whole restricted to what we call memory.

These several antitheses, uniting to form an antithesis which predominates over every other, are partly such as establish themselves in my consciousness not only without effort but without the possibility of prevention; and partly such as get established in my consciousness by processes that are in some degree voluntary. To understand completely how each aggregate hangs together and separates from the other, it is needful to observe what contrasts are known before any deliberation and what contrasts are deliberately known.

§ 459. On criticizing the investigation I have been making, I find that though I have remained physically passive, I have not kept out of my thoughts the remembrances of past activities and the various feelings they caused and disclosed. All those united faint states making up my ideas of liquidity, tangible form, coldness, &c., which are now attached to the patches of colour I call waves, I find have been attached by the help of experimental motions long ago repeatedly performed. Though I cannot now detach them, I can see that had I never gone through such motions the patches of colour would not have dragged with them the faint states representing such past experiences. In other words, I can see that if in addition to being passive now I had always been passive, the

separateness of the two aggregates would in some respects
have been even sharper than it is. Note the differences as
they would then have existed.

The procession of the vivid states, rigidly bound in order
of coexistence and succession, would, as now, have been
absolutely unaffected by anything in the procession of the
faint states; and the procession of the faint states, no longer
to the same degree dragged along by the procession of the
vivid, would have been still more manifestly independent.
In that case, the two aggregates would have demonstrated
their separateness by sliding by one another still more
readily than at present. Each would also, as now, show
itself to be without break. Evidently then the primary
differentiation of each from the other, and integration of
each with itself, precede all those experiences given by my
motion, and all the deliberate comparisons which my motion
makes possible.

The secondary antitheses (such as that the vivid are the
originals and the faint the copies; that the vivid are unchangeable in quality and order by volition, while the faint
are changeable by it in quality and order; that the laws of
each aggregate lie within itself; that antecedents are always
ascertainable in the one case and not always in the other;
and that there are limits to the one aggregate and no known
limits to the other) are antitheses which I perceive can be
established only by conscious comparisons—some of them,
however, being so obvious as to be recognized almost
automatically. But be the deliberation much or little, the
secondary antitheses it establishes serve to strengthen the
primary antithesis that is self-established.

Finally, I observe that the differentiation thus anteceding
thought, and afterwards verified and increased by thought,
is imperative in the sense that there is no possibility of
arresting the process by which it is from instant to instant
reproduced. When dealing with the "Associability of
Feelings" and the "Associability of Relations between

Feelings," it became manifest that in the act of cognition each feeling aggregates primarily with the great class it belongs to—falling more or less promptly into its particular order, genus, species, variety; that the like happens with relations between feelings; and that Intelligence is made possible only by such classings. Here we see that at the same time each feeling, and each relation, in being known, joins itself to one or other of these two great aggregates. There is no intermediate position possible for it—it gravitates instantly to the vivid or the faint. In cases where a momentary doubt occurs whether a certain slight sound is, as we say, real or ideal, or whether in the dusk a thing is actually seen or only fancied, an unpleasant tension accompanies the state of uncertainty. Even during the doubt it cannot be kept balanced between the two, but oscillates from the one to the other. And when, under optical or other illusions, this automatic segregation is to any considerable extent prevented, there arises a painful state of confusion—a feeling of impending chaos caused by shaking this foundation of our intelligence.

CHAPTER XVII.

COMPLETED DIFFERENTIATION OF SUBJECT AND OBJECT.

§ 460. On continuing, as I sit, the analysis which has disclosed the broad contrast set forth in the last chapter, I observe certain states not included in either of the aggregates there defined. When the sea-fog drifted away and the Sun reappeared, there arose in me a state additional to those states directly produced by the more vivid light and the restored view—a state which I distinguish as agreeable. The sea-weed smell when it brought back memories of places and persons, brought back also a phase of what I call emotion. Such components of consciousness, pleasurable and painful, divisible into classes and subclasses, differ greatly from the components thus far described: being extremely vague, being unlocalizable in space, and being but indefinitely localizable in time. That is to say, considered as members of the entire assemblage, they differ from other members in this, that I cannot perceive whereabouts they are in that assemblage, or how they are limited by its other members, coexistent and successive.

Do these peculiar states belong to either of the two aggregates already distinguished? and if so, to which? If I try to class them with the vivid or the faint, I am met by the difficulty that while each kind of them furnishes examples of both the vivid and the faint; and while, as before,

the vivid are the originals and the faint the copies; there
are numerous gradations uniting the vivid with the faint.
Certain ideas of occurrences may excite a slight feeling of
what I call vexation, which reflection may increase to an
anger like that which the occurrences themselves would
produce. And the occurrences themselves will at one time
arouse a less vivid feeling of anger than the representation
of them will at another time. So that the classification
by intensity here fails.

There are, however, other tests which suffice. Take first
that of cohesion. In a few cases, an emotion seems immediately coherent to a member of the vivid aggregate, as to a
beautiful colour or a sweet sound. But in the great mass
of cases the cohesion of an emotion is not to any vivid states,
but to certain faint states combined in particular ways.
Fear is not directly joined to the visual impressions produced by the mouth of a pistol turned towards me; but it
is joined to certain intermediate faint states, or ideas, called
up by these vivid states.   Again, an emotion has,
in common with the faint states, the trait that its antecedent is always traceable. Instead of being liable to occur,
as a number of the vivid series is, without previous presentation of some state with which it is habitually connected,
it never occurs without my being able to perceive something
to which it is attached, that is like something to which it
had been before attached.   Further, I find that
the laws to which these states conform, exist in the faint
series and not in the vivid series. Among the faint
states I can trace the particular groups which cause particular emotions; and can perceive relations between the
varying characters of these and the varying quantities of
the emotions caused.   As a corollary, I note the
further fact, that while the vivid aggregate may slide by
and produce little or no effect on the emotions, the faint
aggregate irresistibly carries with it the special emotions
belonging to its passing combinations. A feeling of grief

or of joy cannot persist if the sets of ideas to which it is related pass away, and are replaced by sets of other kinds.   And once more, these elements of consciousness have, in common with the aggregate of faint states, the character that there are limits which they do not exceed. I am familiar with all these feelings up to their bounds; and continued exploration does not disclose endless new regions and new combinations.

Thus the classification of them is clear. Though there are both vivid and faint emotions—actual emotions and the ideas of them—these all belong to the faint aggregate.

§ 461. These peculiar members of the faint aggregate have a general character of great significance—they tend to set up changes in a certain combination belonging to the vivid aggregate. I refer to the fact that the emotions initiate what are known as bodily movements. Not, indeed, that they alone possess this power; for the vivid aggregate has components of sundry kinds which, reaching great intensities, also do this, though in a different way. Passing over the effects of these, as here of no concern, it is to be noted that each emotion excites muscular contraction, great in proportion as it is strong.

Thus on hearing at my back a voice which I recognize as the voice of a friend, the particular sounds, unlike the many other vivid states of all kinds present to me, excite a wave of pleasurable feeling which puts an end to my quiescence. What is this which happens, considered from our present stand-point?   While I sat still, the sets of vivid states known to me as hand and knee were not manifestly distinguished from the rest of the vivid aggregate: they apparently belonged to it in just the same way as the seat and the shingle before me. But now the transformation caused by this emotion, makes me aware that the set of vivid states I call my hand has some connexion with the faint aggregate; for, after a feeling of muscular tension which the emotion excites, the hand suddenly changes its place. The knee, too, on which my hand was lying, similarly proves to have this peculiar relation to the emotions and the aggregate of faint states including them; for it also moves.　　　Of certain vivid states belonging to other classes, the like is true. The emotion felt goes on presently to initiate other muscular tensions, and after them special sounds—I speak. Over the vivid sounds of the waves and the shingle the aggregate of the faint states, including the emotions, has not the slightest power; but here is a peculiar group of vivid sounds which the faint series can set up—its antecedents and the law of its combinations are in the faint series.　　　How the like holds of sundry vivid feelings of touch, as those I have in rising, in speaking, and in stepping forwards to meet my friend, need not be particularized.

On further investigating this portion of the vivid aggregate which I find thus peculiarly related to the faint aggregate, it proves to be in sundry other ways distinguished from the rest. Here are the traits which mark it off.

Though as a whole the rest of the vivid aggregate is ever present, yet no one of its components, or combination of its components, is ever present. But this particular portion of the vivid aggregate is ever present, more or less distinctly. There is no time at which all components of it, both visual and tactual, are absent from consciousness.　　　A special cohesion is observable in this combination of vivid states. The members of the rest of the vivid aggregate, while they cohere in such wise that no severance can be made of the whole they form, do not permanently cohere under particular relations: though many groups of them do within themselves. But this peculiar group is especially coherent within itself; and such variability as is possible in the relations of its parts, never approaches to discontinuity.　　　It is quite sharply limited.   Instead of an aggregate which we may explore perpetually without finding any bounds, exploration renders the bounds of this portion of the vivid aggregate perfectly familiar.   The order of its components, both in coexistence and succession, is knowable in a relatively-high degree.   The rest of the vivid aggregate has an inexhaustible series of new combinations in space; but the combinations in space of this portion of the vivid aggregate are obviously limited.   Such of them as constitute the visible and tangible forms of the limbs are almost fixed; and those others which arise by changed attitudes of the limbs come within definite limits of variation.   So, too, is it with the laws of relation among its changes: these are comparatively specific.   Between certain muscular tensions, certain changes in the states I know as tangible forms, and certain changes in the states I know as visible forms, there are particular dependencies—dependencies much more fully knowable than those exhibited by changes throughout the rest of the vivid aggregate.

In some way or other, then, there is attached to the faint aggregate a particular portion of the vivid aggregate; and this is unlike all the rest as being a portion always present, as having a special coherence among its components, as having known limits, as having comparatively-restricted and well-known combinations subject to familiar laws, and especially as having in the faint aggregate the antecedents of its most conspicuous changes.

§ 462.   On pursuing the examination I come upon another series of significant facts.   The changes which states in the faint aggregate set up in this particular part of the vivid aggregate, prove to be the means of setting up special classes of changes in the rest of the vivid aggregate.

After a certain thought come the vivid changes which I call shutting my eyes; and forthwith the visual part of the vivid aggregate is absent.   I open them again—it re-appears.

I move my head, and while one part of the vivid aggregate goes out of consciousness, there comes into consciousness a part of corresponding extent which was not before present. I turn round, and all that part of the vivid aggregate which I know as visual is replaced by a part equally large but different, and which may have never been present before.   The like holds to some extent with sounds. By similarly setting up a much more complex set of vivid changes, I close my ears, and comparative stillness results; I take away my fingers, and there return into the vivid aggregate the members I had excluded.   Once more, multiplied tactual changes are caused by previous changes which my ideas set up in this peculiar limited portion of the vivid aggregate. Through bodily motions I get endless varieties and combinations of touches and pressures. Stretching out an arm I grasp, and there arises a particular group of these vivid states; I desist, and they cease.

Beyond thus shutting out, or admitting, parts of the vivid aggregate, and so changing it relatively, I am able, within limits, to change it absolutely. Ideas and emotions, exciting muscular tensions, give my limbs power to transpose certain clusters of vivid states. As I rise I lay hold of my umbrella, and make the set of visual states which I know by that name, move across the sets of visual states I know as the shingle and the sea. Unlike most changes in the vivid series, which, as I sat motionless, proved to be quite independent of the faint series, and to have antecedents among themselves, these changes in the vivid series have their antecedents in the faint series. Their proximate antecedents are, indeed, the touches, pressures and muscular tensions previously set up in this peculiar portion of the vivid aggregate; but these are set up by members of the faint aggregate.

Thus the totality of my consciousness is divisible into a faint aggregate which I call my mind; a special part of the vivid aggregate cohering with this in various ways, which I call my body; and the rest of the vivid aggregate, which has no such coherence with the faint aggregate. This special part of the vivid aggregate which I call my body, proves to be a part through which the rest of the vivid aggregate works changes in the faint, and through which the faint works certain changes in the vivid. And in consequence of its intermediate position, I find myself now regarding this body as belonging to the vivid aggregate, and now as belonging to the same whole with the faint aggregate, to which it is so intimately related.

§ 463. We have at length reached a point of view whence the experiences that give concreteness to these distinctions, and comparative solidity to the conceptions of self and notself, will be properly appreciated.

Thus far we have considered the body only as a combination of vivid states through which the rest of the vivid aggregate affects the faint aggregate, and through which the faint aggregate affects the rest of the vivid. We have now to consider the body as a combination of vivid states, some parts of which can initiate changes in its other parts, and can also have changes initiated by its other parts in them.

While my hand rested on my knee, neither of the two was distinguishable by any immediately-present character from the rest of the vivid aggregate; but when emotion led to transposition of them, they became distinguishable from it. This transposition not only changed their relations to the rest of the vivid aggregate, but also their relations to one another; and when transpositions of this kind are made in particular ways, they introduce elements which the experiences thus far considered do not contain. Observe now the simplest of these elements. I draw my hand over my knee. There is a vivid feeling I call touch, cohering in my consciousness with the cluster of vivid visual feelings I call my hand, which is being transposed by muscular tension. Meanwhile, that other part of the vivid aggregate I know as my knee, also has joined with it a feeling of touch; which, however, changes its place as the hand moves. Ignoring details, the noteworthy fact is that in one part of this peculiar vivid aggregate controlled by it, the faint aggregate actively causes a vivid change, and thereby sets up in another part of this peculiar vivid aggregate another vivid change, which differs from the first in this, that its immediate antecedent is not in the faint aggregate. That is to say, causes in the faint aggregate can, through one part of this vivid aggregate belonging to it, work in another part of this vivid aggregate belonging to it, effects like those producible by causes existing in the rest of the vivid aggregate.   Now I close my fingers in such way as to grasp my knee. After that antecedent in the faint aggregate which I call the resolve to do this, there come the feelings of muscular tension and pressure in my fingers, and the feeling of pressure in my knee. But vivid states of consciousness such as this pressure in my knee, have aforetimes followed changes in that part of the vivid aggregate which I have found to be absolutely independent of the faint. Here, then, is another case in which an antecedent existing among these faint states I group as my mind, by changing a particular group of the vivid states I know as my body, can set up in another group of these vivid states I know as my body, a change like the change set up in it by antecedents not discoverable either in my mind or in my body.   Once more, I seize between my fingers the flesh of my knee, and along with strong effort in the one place I feel sharp pain in the other. This pain differs in no respect from pains that have followed antecedents in that vivid aggregate which is wholly independent of the faint; though now the pain is traceable, through the intermediation of a special part of the vivid, to an antecedent in the faint.   Three kinds of experiences thus

unite to show me that like effects are producible by antecedents existing respectively in these two great antithetical
aggregates; and therefore unite to suggest that there must
be something in common between these antecedents. Or, to
express the fact simply as a fact of cohesion, I find that as
to these feelings of touch, pressure, and pain, when self-
produced, there cohere those states in my consciousness
which were their antecedents; it happens that when they
are not self-produced, there cohere with them in my consciousness the faint forms of such antecedents—nascent
thoughts of some energy akin to that which I used
myself.

One further verification is reached by one further set
of experiences. Sundry parts of the peculiar combination
of vivid states I call my body, are capable of being both
simultaneously and alternately active and passive—gene-
rators of vivid states and recipients of vivid states. I put
my right and left hands together, so that each grasps the
other. When, in response to my wish, the right contracts,
there come, along with feelings of tension in it, feelings
of pressure in the left hand; and *vice versâ* when I contract the left hand. Thus I get complete equivalence
between the modes of existence of vivid states directly
initiated by the faint, and those not directly initiated by
the faint. That which I am conscious of as effort in the
one hand, I am conscious of as pressure in the other: the
two varying together in degree. And on squeezing with
the other hand, this relation is inverted. Each hand, then,
is a seat of what I class among my states of consciousness as active power, and is a seat of that pressure which,
cohering with it, I call the effect of this power. If I
contract the hands alternately, each in succession yields
evidence of the equivalence; and if I contract them both
at once they yield simultaneous evidence of it. At the
same time, each hand opposes to the other what I distinguish as resistance. So that the sense of effort in

the grasping hand, the concomitant sense of resistance offered by the hand grasped, and the sense of pressure passively experienced in the hand grasped, become coherent states of consciousness—so coherent that no one of them can come into consciousness without dragging portions of the others with it.

§ 464. Consider how, in consequence of this, the experiences yielded by the rest of the vivid aggregate necessarily formulate themselves.

If I grasp the hand of my friend instead of my own, the hand with which I grasp is the seat of feelings like those I had before. The essential difference is, that along with these feelings I have not in my other hand the feeling of pressure. But to the effort of grasping and the resistance simultaneously perceived, there coheres the consciousness of a pressure existing in the hand grasped. Though this does not arise in a vivid form, as when the hand was my own, it irresistibly arises in a faint form. Similarly, when my friend's hand grasps mine, though I have not now in my consciousness the vivid sense of effort I had when I grasped it with my other, there irresistibly coheres with the received pressure a faint form of the effort equivalent to it—I have an idea of such effort as existing in my friend's hand; while, cohering with this, there also goes an idea of the feeling in him causing such effort.

When that which resists my grasp, instead of being shaped, coloured, or otherwise characterized, like some part of myself or another moving creature, groups itself in my consciousness with things I call inanimate, I am nevertheless unable to suppress from my consciousness the representation of the pressure occurring in it as the correlative of the resistance offered by it to my muscular effort. There arises in me an idea of strain, caused in that which yields me these vivid feelings. I cannot by any possibility exclude this consciousness of a force in the vivid aggregate somehow allied to that which I distinguish as force in the faint aggregate—cannot break the link which association has produced between these states of consciousness.

§ 465. To the experiences of passive resistance in the vivid aggregate which generate these connexions in consciousness, have to be added the experiences of its actual energies. These make the connexions still stronger.

A weight which I lift with difficulty, which I see lifted by another with what I know as marks of effort, and which afterwards I see raised by a steam-crane, inevitably excites in the other cases a consciousness of some force existing in it like that which antagonized my own force when I lifted it. A pain now produced in my knee by my own fist brought down upon it, and now produced in it by the blow of some foreign body which hit me unawares, has to be thought of in the second case as the equivalent of a force akin to that known as its antecedent in the first case. When, by muscular effort, I give a body motion through space, and know that its energy, as measured by the effects, is proportionate to the muscular energy I use; and when I see a body projected by some other agency work like effects; both its motion and its effects have cohering with them the consciousness of some cause of change equivalent to the cause I felt in my own limbs. So that to every motion in the vivid aggregate which has not for its antecedent a muscular tension excited by an emotion in me, there inevitably coheres a nascent consciousness of an antecedent which takes the vague form of some such tension—is symbolized by the sense of effort.

The general result is that the vivid aggregate, both as manifesting passive resistance and as manifesting active energy, inevitably comes to have associated with it in consciousness, the idea of power, separate from, but in some way akin to, the power which the faint aggregate perpetually evolves within itself.*

* To the analyses set forth in this chapter and its predecessor, it will perhaps be objected to that, referring as they constantly do to simultaneous and successive order among the vivid and the faint states, they postulate antecedent consciousness of Space and Time; one of which, at any rate, involves the notion of objective existence. On this criticism I may remark, in the first place, that in its initial form this distinction of order does not involve the developed consciousness of Space, as we have it (§§ 366, 7). And in the second place, I may remark that the exploration of the limbs by one another, which we found to be the process through which the conceptions of Space and Time become developed, turns out here to be also the process by which the conceptions of Subject and Object become sharply distinguished and severally integrated, The relation of Subject and Object is organized as a form of thought by the same experiences which organize Space and Time as forms of thought; and the organizations of them, going on *pari passu*, further one another.

CHAPTER XVIII.

DEVELOPED CONCEPTION OF THE OBJECT.

§ 466. It was pointed out in §§ 347-8 that the impression we call resistance, " is the primordial, the universal, the ever-present constituent of consciousness." " It is primordial in the sense that it is an impression of which the lowest orders of creatures show themselves susceptible." * * * " It is universal, both as being cognizable by every creature possessing any sensitiveness, and usually as being cognizable by all parts of the body of each." * * * " It is ever-present, inasmuch as every creature, or at any rate every terrestrial creature, is subject to it during the whole of its existence." And it was shown that this consequently " becomes the mother-tongue of thought; in which all the first cognitions are registered, and into which all symbols afterwards learnt are interpretable."

Hence along with the segregation of our states of consciousness into vivid and faint, the consciousness of something which resists comes to be the general symbol for that independent existence implied by the vivid aggregate. We have just seen that mutual exploration of our limbs, excited by ideas and emotions, establishes an indissoluble cohesion in thought between active energy as it wells up from the depths of our consciousness, and the equivalent resistance opposed to it; as well as between this resistance opposed to it and an equivalent pressure in the part of the

body which resists. Hence the root-conception of existence beyond consciousness, becomes that of resistance *plus*
some force which the resistance measures.

This essential element in our consciousness of the vivid
aggregate, is also the essential element in our consciousness
of each part distinguished as an individual object. The
unknown correlative of the resistance offered by it, ever
nascent in thought under the form of muscular strain—the
unknown correlative which we think of as defying our
efforts to crush or rend the body, and therefore as that
which holds the body together, is necessarily thought of
as constituting body. On remembering how difficult we
find it to conceive aëriform matter as body at all; how
liquid matter, so incoherent that it cannot preserve its
shape, is recognized as body in a qualified sense; and how,
where the matter is solid, the notion of body is so intimately
united with the notion of that which maintains continuity
that destruction of continuity is destruction of the body;
we shall see clearly that this unknown correlative of the
vivid state we call pressure, symbolized in the known terms
of our own efforts, constitutes what we call material substance.

§ 467. One other component of co-ordinate importance
enters into the conception. That which, to our thought,
constitutes a body, is that which permanently binds together
those infinitely-varied vivid states the body gives us, as
we change our relations to it and as it changes its relations
to us.

When, in examining Hume's argument, we inquired what
was meant by asserting the existence of *impressions*, and
implying that impressions with their faint copies, *ideas*, are
the only things known to exist; we found that impressions
have existence only in a sense utterly at variance with the
ordinary sense. After noting how the countless different
impressions yielded by an object we approach, or move

round, change from instant to instant, we saw that if any one of these vivid states of consciousness, or any cluster of them, is to be regarded as that which exists, then existence means absence of persistence.

Here, conversely, we have to note that that which persists, and therefore that which we must say exists, is the *nexus* to these ever-varying appearances. I walk round an object, or, if it is small, turn it about in my hands; and of the variously-formed patches of colour and other vivid states of consciousness it yields me, no one remains the same for more than an instant: each impression may pass through a score different phases in a second. Yet each is continuous through all its metamorphoses; and each preserves a continuity of its changing relations with its neighbours: all of them similarly changing and similarly coherent. Moreover, their cohesion is such that after I have made an entire circuit of the object, or, if small, turned it quite round, each patch of colour comes once more into view, and resumes the form it had at first, as well as the same relations to the rest. Further, if I make such movements of retreat that this cluster of vivid states disappears completely; and if for years I do not make the counter-movements needful to bring it again into consciousness; I nevertheless find that when I do make these counter-movements, it presents itself with its members substantially as they were before, and cohering under substantially the same relations.

So that among all the changes there is something permanent. These multitudinous vivid states of my consciousness had none of them any permanence; and the one thing which had permanence was that which never became a vivid state of my consciousness—the something which kept together these vivid states, or bound them into a group. By an ultimate law of my intelligence I class together the states of consciousness which are like, and class apart those which are unlike. The most conspicuous contrast presented

in the vivid aggregate as a whole, as well as in each of
its parts, is the contrast between that which perpetually
changes and that which does not change—between each
ever-varying cluster of vivid states and their unvarying
nexus. This transcendent distinction needs a name. I must
use some mark to imply this duration as distinguished from
this transitoriness—this permanence in the midst of that
which has no permanence. And the word existence, as
applied to the unknown *nexus,* has no other meaning. It
expresses nothing beyond this primordial fact in my experience.

§ 468. See, then, how completely, by observation of our
states of consciousness, and of the ways in which they
segregate, there is evolved a conclusion not in conflict with
our primitive beliefs but in harmony with them.

While we are physically passive, our states of consciousness
irresistibly separate themselves from instant to instant into
the two great aggregates, vivid and faint; each coherent
within itself, having its own antecedents, its own laws, and
being in various ways distinguished from the other. And
this partial differentiation between the two antithetical
existences we call Subject and Object, establishing itself
before deliberate comparison is possible, is made clearer by
deliberate comparison.

On changing from passivity to activity—on evolving the
feeling which excites muscular motion, and using the limbs
for mutual exploration, this partial differentiation is completed. For such exploration shows that muscular tension,
resistance, and pressure, are correlatives and equivalents;
that the vivid aggregate can initiate two out of these
three correlatives—the pressure and the resistance; and
that these imply a something equivalent to the third.
Hence the vivid aggregate necessarily comes to be thought
of as not simply independent of the faint, but as being,
like it, a fountain of power. And this conception of it as

a fountain of power, is made distinct by experiences of changes directly caused in us by it, like those directly caused in us by our own energies.

The general conception thus formed of an independent source of activity beyond consciousness, develops into a more special conception when we examine the particular clusters of vivid states aroused in us.   For we find that each cluster, distinguished by us as an object, is a separate seat of the power with which the objective world as a whole impresses us.   We find that while it is this power which gives unity to the cluster, it is also this power which opposes our energies.   And we also find that this power, holding together the elements of the cluster notwithstanding the endlessly-varied changes they undergo in consciousness, is therefore thought of by us as persisting, or continuing to exist, in the midst of all these manifestations which do not continue to exist.

So that these several sets of experiences, unite to form a conception of something beyond consciousness which is absolutely independent of consciousness; which possesses power, if not like that in consciousness yet equivalent to it; and which remains fixed in the midst of changing appearances.   And this conception, uniting independence, permanence, and force, is the conception we have of Matter.*

* It is not too late to name here an experience which should have been named in the last chapter—an experience which, perhaps more than any other, aids in developing the consciousness of objective power. If with one hand I grasp a finger of the other hand and pull, there occurs along with the central initiating motive a sense of strain in the arm which pulls. At the same time in the other arm which resists, there is an equivalent sense of strain with its equivalent central motive.   All these elements vary together.   If I pull the finger hard, there is a greater expenditure of internal power and a greater feeling of tension in the pulling arm; but there is more : I cannot put forth this harder pull if the other arm gives way—it must offer a resistance measured by an equivalent muscular tension and an equivalent central impulse.   Now the finger pulled is objective to the hand and arm pulling, just as much as though it were the finger of another person ; but as being a finger connected with my own conscious-

§ 469. And now before closing the chapter, let me parenthetically remark on a striking parallelism between the conception of the Object thus built up, and that which we shall find to be the proper conception of the Subject. For just in the same way that the Object is the unknown permanent *nexus* which is never itself a phenomenon but is that which holds phenomena together; so is the Subject the unknown permanent *nexus* which is never itself a state of consciousness but which holds states of consciousness together. Limiting himself to self-analysis, the Subject can never learn anything about this *nexus*, further than that it forms part of the *nexus* to that peculiar vivid aggregate he distinguishes as his body. If, however, he makes a vicarious examination, the facts of nervous structure and function as exhibited in other bodies like his own, enable him to see how, for each changing cluster of ideas, there exists a permanent *nexus* which, in a sense, corresponds to the permanent *nexus* holding together the changing cluster of appearances referable to the external body.

For, as shown in earlier parts of this work, an idea is the psychical side of what on its physical side is an involved set of molecular changes propagated through an involved set of nervous plexuses. That which makes possible this idea is the pre-existence of these plexuses, so organized that a wave of molecular motion diffused through them will produce, as its psychical correlative, the components of the conception, in due order and degree. This idea lasts while the waves of molecular motion last, ceasing

---

ness, I have in it, and the arm bearing it, a measure of the reaction that is equivalent to the action of my other arm. When instead of my own finger I pull the finger of another person, there arises a nascent consciousness, or idea, of a strain in the arm of that person. And when the object pulled is what I distinguish as inanimate, the reaction against the action of my arm is represented in my consciousness by the same symbol—a symbol which becomes very dominant when I grasp the opposite ends of an object with my two hands, and on pulling it, find that its cohesion is measured by its ability to transfer the sense of strain from the one arm to the other.

when they cease; but that which remains is the set of plexuses. These constitute the potentiality of the idea, and make possible future ideas like it. Each such set of plexuses, perpetually modified in detail by perpetual new actions; capable of entering into countless combinations with others, just as the objects thought of entered into countless combinations; and capable of having its several parts variously excited just as the external object presents its combined attributes in various ways; is thus the permanent internal *nexus* for ideas, answering to the permanent external *nexus* for phenomena. And just as the external *nexus* is that which continues to exist amid transitory appearances, so the internal *nexus* is that which continues to exist amid transitory ideas. The ideas have no more a continued existence than we have found the impressions to have. They are like the successive chords and cadences brought out from a piano, which successively die away as other ones are sounded. And it would be as proper to say that these passing chords and cadences thereafter exist in the piano, as it is proper to say that passing ideas thereafter exist in the brain. In the one case, as in the other, the actual existence is the structure which, under like conditions, again evolves like combinations.

It is true that we seem to have somewhere within us these sets of faint states answering to sets of vivid states which once occurred. It is true that in common life ideas are spoken of as being treasured up, forming a store of knowledge: the implied notion being that they are duly arranged and, as it were, pigeon-holed for future use. It is true that in psychological explanations, ideas are often referred to as thus having a continued existence. It is true that our forms of expression are such as to make this implication unavoidable; and that in many places throughout this work, the phrases used apparently countenance it: though, I believe, they are always transformable into their scientific equivalents, as above expressed. But here, as in

metaphysical discussions at large, where our express object
is to make a final analysis, and to disentangle facts from
hypotheses, it behoves us to recognize the truth that this
popular conception, habitually adopted into psychological
and metaphysical discussions, is not simply gratuitous but
absolutely at variance with experience. All which introspection shows us is, that under certain conditions there
occurs a state of consciousness more or less like that which
previously occurred under more or less like conditions.
Not only are we without proof that during the interval this
state of consciousness existed under some form; but so far
as observation reaches, it gives positive evidence to the
contrary. For the new state is never the same—is never
more than an approximate likeness of that which went before. It has not that identity of structure which it would
have were it a pre-existing thing presenting itself afresh.
Nay more; even during its presence its identity of structure
is not preserved—it is not literally the same for two seconds
together. No idea, even of the most familiar object, preserves its stability while in consciousness. To carry further
the foregoing simile, its temporary existence is like that of
a continuously-sounded chord, of which the components
severally vary from instant to instant in pitch and loudness.
Quite apart, however, from any interpretation of ideas as
not substantive things but psychical changes, corresponding
to physical changes wrought in a physical structure, it suffices to insist upon the obvious truth that the existence in
the Subject of any other ideas than those which are passing,
is pure hypothesis absolutely without any evidence whatever.

And here we come upon yet another face of that contradiction which the anti-Realistic conception everywhere
presents. For setting out from the data embodied in the
popular speech, which asserts both the continued existence
of ideas and the continued existence of objects, it accepts
the fiction as a fact, and on the strength of it tries to show

that the fact is a fiction. Continued existence being claimed for that which has it not, is thereupon denied to that which has it.

§ 470. Returning from this digression, it remains only to point out how, in the three chapters here ended, we have found that which we set out to find. The chapter on the "Dynamics of Consciousness" brought us to the conclusion that every mental process carried on to ascertain truth, is at bottom a process of testing the cohesions among our states of consciousness and accepting the absolute cohesions: which, in fact, we have no alternative but to accept. From this conclusion we saw it to follow that since, besides the cohesions within consciousness itself, its more vivid states have an indissoluble cohesion to something beyond consciousness, ever present as a limit to consciousness though never within it, we must accept this absolute cohesion with its implied something, in the same way that we must accept any other absolute cohesion. Having seen this, however, there still pressed for answer the question—How can there be formed within consciousness this notion of an existence that is not within consciousness? and we set ourselves to examine the cohesions among our states of consciousness, to see whether there does naturally evolve this notion. Simply by a process of observation we find that our states of consciousness segregate into two independent aggregates, each held together by some principle of continuity within it. The principle of continuity, forming into a whole the faint states of consciousness, moulding and modifying them by some unknown energy, is distinguished as the *ego ;* while the *non-ego* is the principle of continuity holding together the independent aggregate of vivid states. And we find that while our states of consciousness cohere into these antithetical aggregates, the experiences gained by mutual exploration of the limbs, establish such cohesions that to the principle of continuity manifested in the *non-ego* there inevitably clings a nascent consciousness of force, akin to the force evolved by the principle of continuity in the *ego*.

Thus the normal processes of thought inevitably originate this inexpressible but indestructible consciousness of existence beyond the limits of consciousness; which is perpetually symbolized by something within its limits.

CHAPTER XIX.

§ 471. The foregoing eighteen chapters have set forth the divisions and sub-divisions of an argument too extended and elaborate to be fully understood without a *résumé* of the various special conclusions which unite in supporting its general conclusion. They may be thus briefly stated and grouped.

The assumption of metaphysicians that Reason has an authority to which simpler modes of consciousness must yield, we saw to be not only gratuitous but absolutely incapable of justification. We found that the words of metaphysicians, when rendered into their full meanings, invariably connote, both intrinsically and extrinsically, that relation of Subject and Object which is questioned: so stultifying at every step those who use them to establish either belief or disbelief in this relation. And when analyzed, the reasonings of metaphysicians were shown either tacitly to assume that which they set out to disprove or to involve some equally-great absurdity.

On considering in the abstract the natures of the Realistic and Anti-Realistic positions respectively, we saw that Anti-Realism has nothing but three impossible postulates for its basis. It takes for granted that a conception which is primary and independent, can be abolished by means of conceptions which are secondary and dependent upon it. It takes for granted that if one mental act is single and simple, while another is composed of many acts each at best but similarly simple, there is a doubtfulness in the single act greater than in the series of such acts. And it takes for granted that when between deliverances of consciousness, given respectively in vivid states and in faint states, there is a contradiction, the deliverance given in faint states must be accepted in preference. Thus the derived is to set aside that from which it is derived; a series of links is to be regarded as stronger than any one of its single links; and consciousness is more to be trusted when its terms are indistinct than when they are distinct.

After inferring that some fundamental error must pervade the thinking which involves these impossible assumptions, we saw that a criterion of certainty was the first thing to be settled; since until both sides agree how a true proposition is to be distinguished from an untrue proposition, no step towards a conclusion can be made good. This committed us to such an analysis of propositions as distinguishes them into those which are decomposable and those which are no further decomposable—these last alone admitting of rigorous testing. And then, among the propositions which admit of rigorous testing, we discovered the fundamental difference to be, that in some the predicate invariably exists along with its subject, while in others it does not. Noting that a proposition of which the predicate invariably exists along with its subject, is one we therefore accept and cannot but accept, we went on to ask how propositions of this kind are to be discriminated from others. Discrimination we saw could be effected only by trying to find a case in which the subject exists without the predicate; and this is trying to conceive the negation of the proposition. Hence it became clear that a proposition of which the negation is inconceivable, must inevitably be accepted; and that such a proposition is true, is the Universal Postulate. After meeting the criticisms on this criterion, we finally discovered that not even a reason

for doubting its validity can be given without tacitly asserting its validity. This being our test of truth, it was next
pointed out that whether it be absolutely valid or not, the
probability of error in any conclusion reached, will be great
in proportion to the number of times the test has been used.

Having thus decided on a definite method of valuation,
we proceeded to value by it the Realistic and Anti-Realistic
conclusions. On examining their respective propositions,
and still more on examining the respective justifications
offered for them, we found that Anti-Realism, even were it
not open to other fatal criticisms, is open to the fatal criticism
that its possibilities of error are relatively multitudinous. It
cannot even frame its conception, still less construct its argument, without making many times over that assumption
which Realism makes but once. And thus is Realism negatively justified: any hypothetical uncertainty it may have
is incomparably less than that of Anti-Realism.

From negative justification we passed to positive justification. This we sought in the ultimate structure of consciousness: the implication being that Realism " is positively
justified, if it is shown to be a dictum of consciousness
working after its proper laws." On examining consciousness to ascertain what makes us think this or that, we saw
that our thoughts are inevitably determined by the relative
cohesions among our component states of consciousness.
Every instant ideas form trains that result from these cohesions; if there are opposing tendencies among them, the
strongest cohesions necessitate the course taken; and where
we have to examine them, we can do nothing more than
test the relative cohesions of their components and accept
the absolute cohesions. It is impossible even to imagine
any law of consciousness other than the law that the indissoluble cohesions remain with us instead of the dissoluble ones. All consciousness, rational, perceptive, or
whatever else we may name it, being framed in conformity
with this law, it results that if there is an indissoluble co-

hesion between the rest of consciousness and some consciousness symbolizing existence beyond its limits, we have
to accept this indissoluble cohesion in the same way as any
other—or rather in a way transcending every other; since
all other cohesions in consciousness will break sooner than
this. Realism, then, would be positively justified even were
the genesis of this consciousness of existence beyond consciousness inexplicable. But further examination of these
cohesions explains its genesis.

On watching how all its states behave, we find that consciousness separates into two aggregates, each so coherent
within itself that it can never be broken, but each having
an independence that is complete in the one case and partial
in the other. That is to say, before reasoning begins, and
quite regardless of any conclusions afterwards established
by reason, consciousness differentiates into the vivid and
faint aggregates in virtue of cohesions which, as we see,
determine all thought—each aggregate being relatively coherent within itself and relatively incoherent with the other.
These aggregates, clearly distinguished from one another
even during quiesence, become further distinguished when
there arise the states of consciousness which initiate and
accompany motion. By disclosing a constant cohesion between the consciousness of what I call energy in myself,
and certain changes in that special part of the vivid aggregate I call my body; and by disclosing the identity
between these changes and changes otherwise set up in
the rest of the vivid aggregate; these additional experiences produce in me an indissoluble cohesion between the consciousness of such other changes and the
consciousness of some other energy—a nascent sense of
effort in my consciousness symbolizing a cause of change
not in my consciousness. This hanging together of
the states of consciousness into the two aggregates of Subject and Object; and this cohesion of the *sense of power*
with the changes in the one, and consequent cohesion of the

idea of power with the changes in the other; result in conceptions of the two aggregates as independent existences. The conception of the independent objective existence, is rendered definite as experience makes coherent with it the consciousness of *permanence*, the consciousness of *antagonism* to our energies, and the consciousness of ability to *initiate changes* in us.

So that all results agree. Anti-Realism is betrayed by its assumption, by its language, by its reasonings; it is based on the negations of three cardinal principles of credibility; it tacitly denies an ultimate test of truth, the very questioning of which implies admission of it; and hence Realism is negatively justified. Further, Realism is positively justified by the discovery that the dynamics of consciousness necessitate the Realistic conception—the Realistic conception does not, as Hume puts it, result from a " natural propensity " at variance with the laws of thought; nor is it, as Sir W. Hamilton supposes, a miraculously-inspired belief; but it is an inevitable outcome of the mental process gone through in every valid argument.

§472. But now what is this Realism which is established as a datum long before reasoning begins, which immeasurably transcends reasoning in certainty, and which reasoning cannot justify, further than by finding that its own deliverances are wrong when at variance with it? Is it the Realism of common life—the Realism of the child or the rustic? By no means.

Near the beginning of this work, in a chapter on the " Relativity of Feelings," it was shown that " what we are conscious of as properties of matter, even down to its wieght and resistance, are but subjective affections produced by objective agencies which are unknown and unknowable." But while we saw that comparisons of our sensations with one another inevitably bring us to this conclusion, we also saw that every argument by which the relativity of feelings is proved " sets out by assuming objective existence," and cannot do otherwise. In the next chapter, on the " Relativity of Relations between Feelings," it was similarly shown that no relation in consciousness can " resemble, or be in any way akin to, its source beyond consciousness." Similarly, however, it was there pointed out that the assumption " inevitably made in all reasoning used to prove the relativity of relations," is " that there exist beyond consciousness, conditions of objective manifestation which are symbolized by relations as we conceive them."

The conclusion to which our General Analysis has brought us, is in perfect harmony with these conclusions, yielded by inductive inquiry at the outset. While *some* objective existence, manifested under *some* conditions, remains as the final necessity of thought, there does not remain the implication that this existence and these conditions are more to us than the unknown correlatives of our feelings and the relations among our feelings. The Realism we are committed to is one which simply asserts objective existence as separate from, and independent of, subjective existence. But it affirms neither that any one mode of this objective existence is in reality that which it seems, nor that the connexions among its modes are objectively what they seem. Thus it stands widely distinguished from Crude Realism; and to mark the distinction it may properly be called Transfigured Realism.

§ 473. A diagram will give the highest definiteness to the general and special results arrived at. It is possible to represent geometrically the relations which exist among the several hypotheses we have discussed—between Crude Realism, the idealistic and sceptical forms of Anti-Realism, and the Transfigured Realism which reconciles them.

To prepare himself for understanding the analogy about to be drawn, let the reader, if the theory of perspective has ever been rationally explained to him, call to mind the explanation. He remembers that, looking through the window at some object, say a trunk lying on the ground outside, he may, keeping his eye fixed, make dots with pen and ink on the glass so that each dot hides an angle of the trunk; and may then join these dots by lines, each of which hides one of the edges of the trunk. This done, he has on the surface of the glass an outline-representation such as we call a perspective view of the trunk—a representation of its form not as conceived but as actually seen. If now he considers the relation between this figure and the trunk itself, he finds the two variously contrasted. The one occupies space of three dimensions and the other space of two dimensions; the lines of the one are far longer than those of the other; the ratios among the lines of the one are unlike the ratios among the lines of the other; the directions in space of the representative lines are wholly different from those of the actual lines; the angles they make with one another are dissimilar; and so on. Nevertheless, representation and reality are so connected that the positions of his eye, the glass, and the trunk, being given, no other figure is possible; and if the trunk is changed in attitude or distance, the changes in the figure are such that from them the changes in the trunk may be known. Here, then, he has a case of a symbolization such that, along with extreme unlikeness between the symbol and the actuality, there is an exact though indirect correspondence between the varying relations among the components of the one and the varying relations among the components of the other.

A more involved case of the same general nature may now be taken. Suppose A B C D is the surface of a cylinder; suppose E is a cube, in front of it; and suppose that from some point beyond F there radiate the lines shown, severally passing through the angles of the cube, as well as other lines not shown, passing through all the points which form the edges of the cube. Then these lines, when inter-

cepted by the curved surface, will form a projected image
of the cube, as shown at G. Here it is observable, as before,

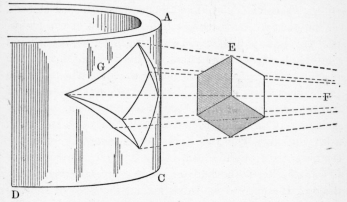

that the lengths, ratios, directions, &c., of the lines in the
image are wholly different from those in the solid; that the
angles also, both absolutely and in their relations to one
another, are different; and that so, too, are the surfaces,
both in their shapes and in their relative directions. But
beyond this it is observable that lines which are straight in
the cube are curved in its image; and that the flat surfaces
of the one are represented by curved surfaces in the other.
Yet further, it is to be noted that the laws of variation
among the lines in the image have become greatly involved:
if the cube be so moved laterally that the projected image
falls very much on the retreating surface of the cylinder,
some of the representative lines begin to elongate at much
greater rates than the others; and even the remoter parts
of each line elongate at greater rates than the nearer
parts. Nevertheless, in this case, as in the simpler one first
described, there is an absolutely-definite system of correspondences. Given as fixed, the cylinder, the dimensions of
the cube, and the point whence the lines radiate, and for
every position, distance, or attitude of the cube, there is a
corresponding figure on the cylinder; and no change in the

place of the cube, or in its attitude, can be made but what has an exactly answering change in the figure—a change so exactly answering that from the new figure the new place or attitude of the cube could be determined.

Thus we have a symbolization in which neither the components of the symbol, nor their relations, nor the laws of variation among these relations, are in the least like the components, their relations, and the laws of variation among these relations, in the thing symbolized. And yet reality and symbol are so connected that for every possible re-arrangement in the *plexus* constituting the one, there is an exactly-equivalent re-arrangement in the *plexus* constituting the other.

The analogy to be drawn is so obvious that it is scarcely needful to point it out in detail. The cube stands for the object of perception; the cylindrical surface stands for the receptive area of consciousness; the projected figure of the cube stands for that state of consciousness we call a perception of the object. Thus carrying out the parallel, we may understand very clearly how it becomes possible that a *plexus* of objective phenomena may be so represented by the *plexus* of subjective effects produced, that though the effects are totally unlike their causes, and though the relations among the effects are totally unlike the relations among their causes, and though the laws of variation in the one set of relations differ entirely from those in the other; yet the two may correspond in such way that each change in the objective reality causes in the subjective state a change exactly answering to it—so answering as to constitute a cognition of it.

But that which we are here chiefly concerned to note is that by thus representing the matter diagrammatically, a distinct idea is given of the relations among the several hypotheses we have been discussing. Crude Realism assumes that the lines and angles and areas on the curved surface are actually like the lines and angles and areas of

the cube. Idealism, observing how all these various elements in the projected figure change in themselves and in
their relations to one another when only change of place
or attitude has occurred in the cube, concludes that as
there is nothing in the figure which is like anything in the
cube, no such thing as a cube is implied; and that the only
existences are the figure and the containing surface. Hypothetical Realism, accepting these statements as to the non-
agreement between the figure and the cube, argues that
nevertheless the existence of the cube must be assumed:
cannot be alleged as a fact but must be admitted as a
needful hypothesis. Scepticism, carrying further the Idealistic criticism, contends that in the figure there is not only
nothing to afford proof of anything producing the figure,
but there is nothing to afford proof of any surface containing the figure; and that though there is a natural tendency
to believe in the existence of this surface, as well as in the
existence of the cube, we may reasonably doubt whether
these really exist. While Absolute Idealism, pushing to its
extreme the sceptical argument, asserts that the figure alone
exists, and that there are no such things as either the cube
or the surface. And now, rejecting all these conflicting
hypotheses considered as wholes, Transfigured Realism
takes an element from each. It affirms a connexion between
the cube and its projected image which reconciles whatever
is true in Realism with whatever is true in Anti-Realism.
With Crude Realism it agrees in asserting the existence of
the cube as being the primary certainty; but differs entirely
by asserting that there is no kinship of nature whatever
between the cube and the projected image. It joins
Idealism, Scepticism, and Hypothetical Realism, in affirming that the projected figure contains no element, relation,
or law, that is like any element, relation, or law, in the cube;
but it affirms against Idealism that the argument on which
this conclusion rests is impossible in the absence of the
cube; it affirms against Scepticism that besides the correla-

tive cube necessitated by the argument, there is also necessitated by the argument a receptive area for the figure;
while it blames Hypothetical Realism for admitting to be
hypotheses, what the arguments themselves assume to be
facts transcending in certainty all other facts.   Finally,
though it has a point of community with Absolute Idealism
in recognizing the truth that the projected figure can never
have within it any trait whatever either of the actual cube
from which it is projected or the actual surface on which it
is projected; yet it differs utterly by declaring that the
existence of these is implied as in a sense more certain than
that of the figure, since the existence of the figure is made
possible only by their existence.

The geometrical analogy thus helps us to see how Transfigured Realism reconciles what appear to be irreconcilable
views.   It was lately shown that existence, in the accepted
sense of the word, can be affirmed only of that variously-
conditioned substratum called the Object and that other substratum variously acted on by it, called the Subject; while
the effects of the one on the other, known as perceptions,
are changes having but transitory existences.   In the diagram we similarly see that the permanent existences are the
cube and the surface; while the projected image, varying
with every change in the relation between the cube and the
surface, has no permanent existence.   And just as we saw
that Subject and Object, as actually existing, can never be
contained in the consciousness produced by the co-operation
of the two, though they are necessarily implied by it; so
we see that neither the cube nor the surface can ever be
contained in the projected image of the one upon the other,
though this projected image can exist only on condition
that they pre-exist.

§ 474. And now the impossibility of all Anti-Realistic
beliefs having been shown by direct analysis in the preceding chapters, and having been again shown still more clearly

by this geometrical analogy, the final remark to be made is
that Anti-Realistic beliefs have never been held at all. They
are but ghosts of beliefs, haunting those mazes of verbal
propositions in which metaphysicians habitually lose themselves. Berkeley was not an Idealist: he never succeeded in expelling the consciousness of an external reality,
as we saw when analyzing his language and his reasonings.
Hume did not in the least doubt the existence of Matter or
of Mind: he simply persuaded himself that certain arguments ought to make him doubt. Nor was Kant a Kantist:
that Space and Time are nothing more than subjective
forms was with him, as it has been and will be with every
other, a verbally-intelligible proposition, but a proposition
which can never be rendered into thought, and can never
therefore be believed.

For here let me re-insist on the all-important distinction, ignored in metaphysical controversies, between thinking separately the components of a proposition, and thinking the proposition itself; which consists in combining the
two terms in the alleged relation. If any one tells me that
a sphere is equiangular, I can think separately of a sphere,
I can think separately of equiangularity as a character possessed by certain figures, and I can think separately of the
relation of coexistence. But though each of the two terms is
thinkable by itself as something that has been presented in
experience; and though the relation of coexistence is thinkable as one that is extremely familiar in experience; and
though the proposition is therefore verbally intelligible in
the sense that each of its words has a known meaning; yet
the proposition itself, considered as a whole, is utterly unintelligible. The conception of a sphere and the conception
of equiangularity cannot be made to coexist as object and
attribute in consciousness; and if they cannot be made
thus to coexist, the proposition that they do thus coexist
cannot be conceived, and therefore cannot be believed. Now
this confounding of propositions the components of which

can be thought only separately, with propositions of which the two terms can be thought in the relation alleged, characterizes all Anti-Realistic arguments and conclusions. When the Idealist says that what he knows as an object is a cluster of sensations contained in his consciousness, the proposition has intrinsically the same character as that which asserts the equiangularity of a sphere. The two terms, object and consciousness, are severally intelligible; and the relation of inclusion, considered apart, is intelligible; But the proposition itself, asserting that the object stands to consciousness in the relation of inclusion, is unintelligible; since the two terms cannot be combined in thought under this relation: no effort whatever can present, or represent, the one as within the limits of the other. And if it is not possible to conceive it within the limits, still less is it possible to believe it within the limits; since belief, properly so-called, pre-supposes conception.

Here, indeed, even more clearly than before, we may note what contradictory meanings are given to the word belief; and how fatal are the confusions hence arising. In § 425 we observed the origin of a remarkable ambiguity in the use of this word. Because they have in common the character that no reason can be assigned for them, those most certain propositions which underlie all proof, and those most doubtful propositions which are accepted without proof, are both classed as beliefs. Though otherwise radically unlike, propositions of these two kinds are, however, alike in this, that their terms cohere in consciousness —in the one case indissolubly and in the other case feebly. But now, marvellous to relate, Anti-Realism applies the word belief to a proposition of which the terms not only have no cohesion in consciousness, but cannot even be brought together in consciousness. The name is given to a proposition having a peculiarity absolutely opposite to that of the propositions ordinarily distinguished by the name.

So that, in fact, every Anti-Realistic system is not a fabric of ideas but a fabric of pseud-ideas. It is composed not of thoughts properly so-called, but of the forms of thoughts without any contents. Whether it be or be not a true saying that Mythology is a disease of language, it may be said with truth that Metaphysics, in all its Anti-Realistic developments, is a disease of language. For its Anti-Realistic developments are results of those abnormal combinations of linguistic symbols in which they no longer perform their functions as expressing ideas.

Nevertheless, we must not forget that these complicated aberrations of reason have been the concomitants of a legitimate, and indeed necessary, criticism. Crude Realism claimed as part of knowledge an unlimited territory which transcends knowledge. In showing how unwarranted is this claim, Anti-Realism went to the extreme of denying to Realism all territory whatever. Metaphysical controversy has been the settlement of the limit; and the history of it has been a history of those rhythms which antagonistic forces always produce—now causing excess on this side of the limit and now on the other. But as fast as the differentiation of Subject and Object approaches completion, the oscillations become less and less: and along with the purification of Realism from all that does not belong to it, the controversy ends: Realism contenting itself with affirming that the object of cognition is an independent existence, and Anti-Realism having shown that the cognition of it is entirely relative.

§ 475. Thus ends our examination of the Ultimate Question. We saw, when considering its nature, that Philosophy reaches its goal when it establishes universal congruity (*First Principles*, Part II., Chap. I.). Before stirring a step towards this goal, however, Philosophy has to assume the validity of certain primary dicta of consciousness; since before there can be thought there must be some data of thought. A general survey brought us to the conclusion

that the relation of Subject and Object was a dictum of consciousness which must be thus provisionally accepted.
Accepting it, the process of establishing congruities was
pursued, until at length it brought us round to the original
dictum; and we had then to consider whether this could be
absolutely justified. The foregoing chapters have led us
not only to the result that it harmonizes with all other dicta
of consciousness, but also to the result that every adverse
proposition is absolutely and in every way incongruous with
them.

Finally, then, we resume this originally-provisional assumption but now verified truth. Once more we are brought
round to the conclusion repeatedly reached by other
routes, that behind all manifestations, inner and outer, there
is a Power manifested. Here, as before, it has become clear
that while the nature of this Power cannot be known—while
we lack the faculty of framing even the dimmest conception
of it, yet its universal presence is the absolute fact without
which there can be no relative facts. Every feeling and
thought being but transitory—an entire life made up of
such feelings and thoughts being also but transitory—nay
the objects amid which life is passed, though less transitory, being severally in course of losing their individualities,
quickly or slowly; we learn that the one thing permanent
is the Unknowable Reality hidden under all these changing
shapes.

PART VIII.

CONGRUITIES.

CHAPTER I.

§ 475*a*. The foregoing divisions of this work have dealt with different aspects of psychological phenomena, and it remains now to co-ordinate these different aspects. Standing apart as they do, they may to some appear unconnected, and to others they may appear incongruous. It will be the aim of this division to show their congruity.

At the close of the first division it was pointed out that the Science of Psychology is distinguished by its duality of nature. Dealing with psychical phenomena as exhibited in the actions of animals and men which are visibly adjusted to surrounding actions, Objective Psychology carries on its inquiries concerning the *how* and the *why* of this correspondence, by external observation, as the sciences at large do. Contrariwise, Subjective Psychology, occupying itself with states of consciousness, their characters and relations, carries on its inquiries by internal observation, and is in so far unlike all other sciences.

Objective Psychology, as the reader will remember, falls into several parts. The first treats in the most general way of the adjustments between inner and outer actions by which living creatures maintain their lives. The second, dealing more specially with these adjustments, expresses them in terms of reflex action, instinct, reason, memory, feelings, will. The third interprets them as effected by a nervous system; and seeks to show how this nervous system is evolved by converse with the environment.   Subjective Psychology, again, has two great divisions. The one is concerned primarily with the order of states of consciousness as observed in self, and secondarily with the connexion between this order and the order of objective agencies to which it corresponds. The other is concerned with the general relation between consciousness and existence beyond consciousness.

The disclosure of congruities may best be carried on by successive stages. Limiting ourselves first to the conclusions constituting Objective Psychology, as set forth in the divisions entitled "General Synthesis," "Special Synthesis," " Physical Synthesis," we will observe their harmonies with one another. Passing then to the " Special Analysis," we will similarly observe how the several conclusions reached in it agree among themselves. The congruity between the set of conclusions contained in the synthetical division and the set of conclusions contained in the analytical division, will then occupy us. And the final part of the comparison will exhibit the agreement between that Transfigured Realism which the " General Analysis " leads to, and the conclusions drawn in the preceding divisions.

But before pointing out these more important verifications, it will be well to point out some less important ones. In Part I., "The Data of Psychology," certain truths yielded by Biology, and corollaries from them, were set down. Sundry empirical generalizations were reached in Part II., " The Inductions of Psychology." Our first step may fitly be to observe the congruities among these. And then the congruous results arrived at in the introductory parts we may carry with us, and from time to time observe how they agree with the results reached in the subsequent parts, analytical and synthetical.

CHAPTER II.

§ 475b. In a chapter on the " Structure of the Nervous System " it was shown that the simplest nervous apparatus consists of an internally-placed portion of unstable nerve-matter, to which there comes a nerve-fibre from a place where a stimulus is received, and from which there goes another nerve-fibre to a portion of substance which contracts when excited—an afferent fibre, an efferent fibre, and a minute ganglion through which the two are centrally connected. This being an ultimate nervous arc, we saw that for the formation of a nervous system out of such nervous arcs, there requires a third fibre, communicating between the primitive nerve-centre and other centres, either of like grade or of higher grade. So that taken together, an afferent fibre, an efferent fibre, and a centripetal fibre, with the intermediate ganglion-cell or cells, constitute what may be called the unit of composition of the nervous system. The general character of the structures resulting from combination and re-combination of units, we found to be such that all parts of the body, subject to various stimuli from the outer world, are placed in communication with one another, and with those contracting organs by which motions of all kinds are produced. And we observed how, during that evolution of the nervous system shown in the rise of great nervous centres, these simple relations among parts become united in complex groups of relations.

In considering "The Functions of the Nervous System," we saw that forces acting on the extremities of afferent nerves, set up molecular changes which are propagated in waves to the connected ganglia, where they set up other molecular changes greater in amount; and that through centripetal and efferent nerves, the changes thus set up are brought into relation with other changes simultaneously or subsequently set up by forces acting on other external organs, and also into relation with induced changes in the muscles. Impressions of all kinds and quantities from all parts of the periphery, are conveyed to a central receiver, and from this there go impulses which end in external actions: the receiver being thus a place where it becomes possible for the changes to be brought into such juxtaposition as permits identifications, discriminations, combinations.

And then in the chapter on "Æstho-physiology," several sets of evidences were united to show that "impossible as it is to get immediate proof that feeling and nervous action are the inner and outer faces of the same change, yet the hypothesis that they are so harmonizes with all the observed facts:" the implication being that the nervous structures which connect and combine what, under their objective aspects, are nervous changes, connect and combine what, under their subjective aspects, are states of consciousness.

§ 475*c*. From the general truths yielded by Biology as data to Psychology, we turn to the general truths which, in the next division, were grouped as "Inductions of Psychology." Those of chief moment may be summarized as follows.

The substance of Mind is in its ultimate nature inscrutable; but respecting its proximate nature we know something, and may, perhaps, eventually know more. Setting out with the sensation of sound, which is demonstrably composed of successive nervous shocks, it was argued that possibly, if not probably, all other feelings are compounded out of such primordial units of feeling; and that the heterogeneity of them results from different modes of compounding and re-compounding.

Passing from this hypothetical composition of what seem simple feelings, to the composition of mind as actually observable, we saw that it consists of feelings and relations between feelings. We recognized feelings as divisible into several classes and sub-classes; and we also recognized the relations between feelings as similarly divisible. Classes and sub-classes of feelings, besides being contrasted in their qualities, we found to be contrasted in other ways: some kinds being mutually limited in consciousness with great definiteness, others with less definiteness, others not at all; and being at the same time severally distinguished by strong cohesion with one another, by less cohesion, and by feeble cohesion. We also observed that in proportion to their definiteness of mutual limitation and strength of cohesion, is the capacity which feelings of each class have for uniting into clusters; and we saw that while feelings of the same class forcibly exclude one another from consciousness, feelings of one class have less power of keeping out those of another class, and the resistance of feelings to one another's entrance becomes small as their unlikeness of nature becomes great.

In a chapter on the "Relativity of Feelings," the familiar truth that both qualitatively and quantitatively the sensations excited by incident forces are unlike the forces, was exemplified under its various aspects. It was shown that feeling is relative to the nature and state of the organism: the feeling produced by a given agent being not only unlike in members of different species, but in members of the same species, and in different conditions of the same individual. And it was also shown that feeling is relative to the part of the organism on which the agent acts. As of feelings so of the relations between them: proof was given that they are relative to the character of the individual in species, size, and state.

Both feelings and the relations between them were shown to be revivable. The degree of revivability of a feeling we found to be greatest among feelings which are most relational; and we saw that it varies both according to the original strength of the feeling and according to the number of repetitions of it. Parallel truths were set down as holding of the revivability of relations.

Finally, we saw that both feelings and the relations between feelings are associable; and that their associabilities vary in their degrees after the same manner as do the traits already named.

§ 475*d*. Let us now put side by side the leading conclusions contained in the biological data and the leading conclusions established by psychological induction.

The hypothesis experimentally justified in one case, and extended as probable to other cases, that feeling of whatever order consists of variously-compounded units of feeling similar in kind, is congruous with the established fact that every nervous discharge is a series of pulses of molecular change. All nerve-fibres being substantially alike, all portions of nerve matter in which they end being substantially alike, and all discharges along them being formed of waves that rapidly succeed one another in like ways, the production of entirely unlike feelings, otherwise incomprehensible, is made comprehensible if the variously-compounded units of feeling are the subjective aspects of what objectively are variously-compounded series of nerve-waves.

Mind, as introspectively analyzed, we saw consists of feelings and relations between feelings, and this general composition of it is one answering to the general structure

of the nervous system. From all parts of the body to inferior centres, and again from these to higher centres, and
eventually to the highest, there pass lines of communication, which thus indirectly connect each part with all parts;
whence it results that the feeling aroused by a stimulus
in any part, can be put in relation with a feeling simultaneously or subsequently aroused in any other part. Answering as do the discharges along nerve-fibres to what we
know in consciousness as relations, and answering as do the
changes set up in nerve-centres to feelings, we see that
the composition of mind is congruous with the structure and
functions of the nervous system.

The conclusion that while the changes produced in
nerve-centres correspond to feelings, the discharges through
nerve-fibres correspond to the relations among feelings,
harmonizes with the fact that these lines of communication
through which relations are established, are most numerous in those parts where the greatest numbers of separate
feelings are initiated and combined: the extreme instance
being furnished by the organs of vision, which are distinguished alike by the multitudinousness of the fibres they
contain and by the multitudinousness of the related feelings which are excited in them to form a visual image.

It is a trait of nervous structure that the numerous fibres
proceeding from any specialized part, such as a sense-organ,
to a nervous centre, are more closely connected with one
another, centrally as well as peripherally, than they are with
the fibres proceeding from other such parts to their centres;
and a corresponding trait of consciousness is that feelings
of the same order are more associable with one another
than feelings of different orders: colours being more readily
connected in thought with colours than they are with
sounds, sounds more readily with sounds than with colours,
smells with smells more readily than with touches. This
holds with genera and species of feelings—the most nearly
alike being the most associable; and, conversely, there is

least associability between those great classes of feelings which are most widely contrasted in their origins and in the nervous structures appropriated to them—the feelings derived from the external world and those derived from the viscera. So that closeness of connexion between parts of the nervous system, and resulting closeness of connexion between nervous actions, go along with readiness in the corresponding mental states to form connexions. Whence also the truth that the clustering of feelings follows the same law: visual sensations aggregate into those large clusters which we identify as the appearances of objects; sounds combine simultaneously and successively into what we know as harmonies, melodies, sentences, &c.; and feelings of touch unite into those groups which form our concepts of tangible form.

If the rapid pulses of molecular change propagated along a nerve-fibre, producing disturbance in a connected nerve-centre, generate a special feeling—if every other special feeling is generated in like manner by a series of pulses, conveyed along some other fibre to some other portion of grey matter; the implication is that no likeness exists between the outer stimulus and the inner feeling. If, various as are the stimuli producing them (mechanical impacts, ærial waves, ethereal vibrations, chemical actions), the nervous discharges, all composed of recurrent pulses, are essentially similar; it is inconceivable that in the nerve-centres affected by them, they should be severally re-translated into the several special forces producing them. Thus the relativity of feelings as otherwise inferred, is verified by the disclosures of Biology concerning nervous structures and functions: these all imply it. And the results which Biology establishes respecting the effects of temperature, pressure, quantity and quality of blood, &c., on nervous action, correspond with the observed variations of feelings caused by variations of conditions; and thus further support the doctrine of their relativity.

Grant that the series of nerve-waves excited by an external force and propagated inwards, is that which, disturbing the connected nerve-centre, arouses in it the vivid feeling we know as sensation; then, the implication is that if this nerve-centre is feebly disturbed by nerve-waves otherwise reaching it, there will be aroused a faint form of this same feeling—an idea. Now as all parts of the nervous system are connected; as the connexions among the sensorial centres are intimate; and as, especially within each centre devoted to one order of sensations, the communicating fibres are close and multitudinous; it results that each nervous agent is continually liable to be slightly disturbed by these reverberating waves coming from adjacent disturbed nervous agents. So that to certain phenomena of nervous action, there correspond the phenomena of vivid and faint feelings, and the connexions among them. Manifestly this holds not of simple feelings only, but of clusters of feelings, and the connexions among such clusters.

Yet another parallelism may be added. We saw that feelings exclude one another from consciousness in different ways and degrees. Feelings of the same order stand in one another's way more than feelings of different orders. Attention to the sounds uttered by one person hinders perception of simultaneous sounds uttered by another; tactual examination of an object keeps out of thought, feelings of touch coming from other parts of the body; and so on. But the tactual sensations which an object yields do not obscure the sensations which the eyes at the same time derive from it; appreciation of a symphony conflicts but little with visual consciousness of the orchestra and the audience; and perceptions of tastes and smells do not interfere much with other perceptions received at the same time. Obviously this corresponds with the facts of nervous structure. Though a nervous centre appropriated to feelings of a certain kind, cannot be simultaneously occupied by two sets of such feelings without confusion; yet other nervous

centres can without confusion be simultaneously occupied
by their appropriate feelings.   This truth is even
more clearly shown us in the exclusion of faint feelings
by vivid feelings in different degrees. While looking
at one landscape, another landscape can be but faintly
imagined; while listening to one melody, it is next to impossible mentally to repeat another melody; while tasting
something bitter, it is difficult to call up in consciousness the
idea of sweetness. But contemplation of a landscape does
not prevent any musical air from being thought of; bodily
exertion impedes but in a small degree the remembrance of
words that have lately been uttered; and the idea of some
odour is almost, if not quite, as easy to recall while looking
at a bright colour as with the eyes closed: all of them facts
explained by that specialization of the nervous centres which
Biology discloses.

Between the Data and the Inductions, then, the congruities are many and complete. The structure and functions
of the nervous system harmonize with the laws of mental
phenomena in their leading traits.

CHAPTER III.

CO-ORDINATION OF SYNTHESES.

§ 475*e*. Though throughout the first two divisions, just summarized and compared, some tacit references were made to the Theory of Evolution.in connexion with the truths disclosed; yet, essentially, those truths were reached by external observation of existing creatures, or by internal observation of mental states and changes personally experienced. Throughout the three succeeding divisions, however, Evolution being avowedly assumed, the aim was not simply to set forth the leading truths of Objective Psychology as they now are, but also to explain how they have come to be what they now are.

The " General Synthesis " dealt with the phenomena of Mind under their broadest aspects, as part of the phenomena of Life. Life having been conceived as " the definite combination of heterogeneous changes, both simultaneous and successive, in correspondence with external co-existences and sequences," or more generally as " the continuous adjustments of internal relations to external relations," it was shown that, objectively considered, the evolution of mind is the evolution of these adjustments. Proof was given that the increasing power of self-conservation displayed by creatures of higher and higher grades, implies advance of these adjustments in extent, variety, complexity, definiteness. Being originally few, they augment in number; beginning as homogeneous, they become more heterogeneous; having at first narrow ranges in space and time, their ranges gradually widen; while at first simple, they grow in complexity; and from primitive vagueness they advance towards precision. Throughout this division, then, the conception of mental evolution was that of inner related actions that progress in correspondence to outer related actions throughout an ever-widening environment.

The succeeding division, " Special Synthesis," had for its purpose to interpret this progressing correspondence between inner and outer actions, in the terms commonly used when speaking of mental phenomena. It was pointed out that with advance in what we call intelligence, the connected changes known as psychical become more and more distinguished from the physical changes constituting bodily life, by their increasing seriality; and that in the highest intellectual processes, as chains of reasoning, the seriality of the mental changes becomes quite distinct. On inquiring after what general law mental states succeed one another, we found that " the strength of the tendency which the antecedent of any psychical change has to be followed by its consequent, is proportionate to the persistence of the union between the external things they symbolize; " and that hence results the general truth " that relations which are absolute in the environment are absolute in us, that relations which are probable in the environment are probable in us, that relations which are fortuitous in the environment are fortuitous in us." Passing then to the " Growth of Intelligence," it was shown that as mental development goes on, " the inner tendencies are proportioned to the outer persistences " with greater accuracy, in more numerous cases, and in cases of increasing complexity. And a corollary drawn was that " there must exist all grades of strength in the connexions between states of consciousness " answering to all degrees of persistence in the relations between things in the outer world. To the question "How are their various cohesions adjusted?" it was replied that "the inner cohesions are adjusted to the outer persistences by accumulated experiences of those outer persistences." This reply was shown to be in harmony with established beliefs respecting the influence of habit, as well as with the accepted doctrine of the association of ideas; and it was pointed out that if, in addition to the effects of individual experiences, we recognize the effects of ancestral experiences, organized and inherited, we get an adequate idea of the way in which the correspondence between inner and outer relations is evolved. In succeeding chapters these general conceptions were developed in detail. Reflex Action, Instinct, Memory, Reason, the Feelings, the Will, were interpreted as so many aspects, more or less special, of the correspondence between inner and outer actions, which is made ever wider and better by more multiplied and extended experiences of such outer actions.

Then in the "Physical Synthesis" was raised the final question presented by Objective Psychology—"How is Mental Evolution to be affiliated on Evolution at large, regarded as a process of physical transformation?—By what process is the organization of experiences achieved?" Distinguishing between Mind under its subjective aspect as consisting of states of consciousness, and Mind under its objective aspect as consisting of nervous changes; and admitting that these last had to be interpreted in terms of the re-distribution of matter and motion; we proceeded to inquire after what physical principle the nervous system has had its structure and functions adapted to the requirements. Quoting from *First Principles* the laws that "motion follows the line of greatest traction, or the line of least resistance, or the resultant of the two," and " that motion once set up along any line becomes itself a cause of subsequent motion along that line," we proceeded to trace, in pursuance of these laws, the genesis of nerves and of nervous systems, simple, compound, and doubly-compound. Setting out with the diffusion of molecular changes through undifferentiated tissue, we saw how, from repeated disturbances arising at the same place, there tend to arise special tracks of diffusion, which, becoming more definite with repetition, end in being lines of communication; and further, that the same physical actions which initiate such lines, tend to make them more permeable the more frequently discharges pass along them. Applied throughout, this principle enabled us to conceive how nervous systems of increasing degrees of complexity are evolved; and also how nervous discharges and the correlative connexions in consciousness, become so adjusted that the cohesions of mental states symbolize the persistences of the corresponding outer relations. The truth inductively established, that experience of the outer persistences produces the inner cohesions, was deductively interpreted as consequent on this general physical law; and we so reached an explanation of psychical phenomena, which extends from reflex actions up to discursive imaginations—from forms of thought up to casual associations of ideas.

The harmony among these synthetical divisions is thus conspicuous: the conclusions reached in the second and third, being successively more developed forms of the conclusions reached in the first.

§ 475*f*. That these conclusions, congruous with one another, are congruous with those contained in Parts I. and II., summarized in the last chapter, will also I think be manifest on comparing them.

Being an apparatus by which all parts of the body are put in communication with one another, the nervous system is a fit apparatus for carrying on psychical changes, considered as inner relations continuously adjusted to outer relations. That from the periphery of the organism at large, and from particular parts of it having special sense-organs, there proceed fibres to centres, where they are all connected with one another; and that from these centres there proceed fibres to contractile organs which initiate movements in the limbs; are facts harmonizing with the need for bringing internal actions into correspondence with external actions.

The simplest nervous apparatus, consisting of an afferent fibre, a ganglionic corpuscle, and an efferent fibre, of which the first conveys a stimulus and the last a discharge causing contraction, shows us, in its rudimentary form, an instrumentality for effecting a correspondence between impression and motion in an organism and related phenomena in the environment—two coherent inner changes answering to two persistently-related outer agencies. And the truth that this simple nervous arc, with its centripetal fibre communicating with other nervous arcs, is the unit of composition of the nervous system, answers to the truth that the unit of composition of nervous function is a discharge from one excited place to another place where excitement is produced, and to the truth that the unit of composition of psychical actions is a connected pair of psychical states brought into relation with other such pairs: the compounding of such units of structure and function in the course of nervous evolution, being accompanied by the compounding of such units of thought.

An obvious agreement exists between the developing structure of the nervous system set forth when dealing with the " Data of Psychology," and that increase of the correspondence in heterogeneity, in space, in time, in specialty, in complexity, set forth in the " General Synthesis." With production of more numerous sense-organs and connected centres, there goes capacity for receiving a greater variety of impressions from the external world, and the possibility of making a greater variety of adjustments; and as each sense develops, the possible discriminations made through it multiply and conduce to a like result. As the nerve-fibres proceeding inwards from the periphery, increase in numbers and kinds, and the nervous centres to which they carry stimuli become larger, the amount of nervous discharge centrally elicited, and of concomitant feeling, increases; so that there results an augmenting genesis of muscular motion, and a joining of greater activities with greater receptivities: the power of initiating those motions which effect adjustments, increasing with susceptibility to those stimuli which direct them. Moreover, with that complicating of the nervous centres which multiplies the relations established among parts of the nervous system, sensory and motor, there arises the possibility of more complex combinations of received impressions, and of resulting motions; giving ability to identify more complex groups of external phenomena, and to make more complex adjustments of the actions to them. Thus in various ways the evolving nervous system answers in its characters to the requirements of the evolving correspondence.

An agreement of a more special kind may be noted between certain traits in the order of nervous phenomena, and certain traits in the order of phenomena existing externally. We saw that " the relational element of Mind, as shown in mutual limitation, in strength of cohesion, and in degree of clustering, is greater between feelings of the same order than between feelings of one order and those of another; " and we saw that " this answers to the fact that the bundles of nerve-fibres and clusters of nerve-vesicles belonging to feelings of one order, are combined together more directly and intimately than they are with the fibres and vesicles belonging to feelings of other orders." Here we have to observe the fact that the corresponding orders of phenomena, as revealed to us in perception, present corresponding traits. Large assemblages of objects from which there come rays to a visual organ, produce from moment to moment, large assemblages of impressions: the outer distribution in relation to the sense-organ, is such as

to make possible very extensive clusters of responsive sensations. The fact that when, from the boundaries of the objects assembled, lines are drawn to a centre, the angles which
the objects subtend at that centre rigorously exclude one
another, answers to the fact that visual states of consciousness are mutually limited with great definiteness. And the
fact that these many sensations simultaneously received
through the eyes, limiting one another thus precisely, are
being perpetually received during our waking lives, answers to the fact that the degrees of cohesion among them
are extremely great. Though the attribute of objects
whereby they give us visual impressions, habitually coexists with the attribute whereby they give us impressions
of touch; yet, in our experience, the co-existence is not
presented with a frequency anything like as great as the
frequency with which the co-existence of visual impressions with one another is presented. Hence the fact that
mutual limitation, clustering, and cohesion, characterize
visual feelings in their relations with one another, and tactual
feelings in their relations with one another, more than they
characterize the relations between visual feelings and tactual
feelings, corresponds to a trait in the order of environing
phenomena as they are habitually impressed upon us. And
that the like holds among sounds and tastes will at once
be perceived. Thus the harmony before found between certain leading traits of nervous structures and certain leading
traits of feelings accompanying nervous actions, we now find
re-inforced by the harmony of both with certain leading
traits in the distribution of outer activities.

It is needless to dwell on the agreement between the
truths which the Data and Inductions set forth, and the
conclusions drawn in the " Physical Synthesis; " since, as
was implied at the time, the Physical Synthesis is a deductive interpretation of the truths previously established by
induction.

CHAPTER IV.

CO-ORDINATION OF SPECIAL ANALYSES.

§ 475*g*. Premising that analyses carried on methodically, must begin with the most complex things to be analyzed, and, resolving these into the less complex, proceed after the same manner until the simplest have been reached, we commenced with compound quantitative reasoning.

One of the intuitions composing reasoning of this highest kind, we found to be a consciousness of the equality or inequality of two relations between relations—a consciousness in which each term of the relation recognized, is itself a cluster consisting of two pair of related things, the relations of which are contemplated as equal or unequal. We next saw that in simple quantitative reasoning, the act of thought is an intuition of equality between two relations—is one of those component intuitions which, as united, form the more complex act of thought previously defined. Further, " we saw that in this highest reasoning there is equality among the terms in Space, Time, Quality, and among their relations in kind and degree; and that thus not only does the idea of likeness rise to its greatest perfection (equality), but it appears under the greatest variety of applications." So that considering it generally, a step in quantitative reasoning is one in which the relation established in consciousness is between two clusters of states of consciousness that are severally quite definite in their natures and in their relations to one another.　　　Decompositions of rational intuitions of successively lower kinds, brought us down to these final results:—first, that in all cases reasoning consists of a comparison of relations, resulting in the recognition of them as like or unlike, with a consequent determination of one related term before unknown, or but partially known; and, second, that in all cases it is a means of indirectly establishing a definite relation between two things where such definite relation cannot be directly established.

From Reasoning, which we thus found to be effected by a classification of relations—the like relations being assimilated in thought and the unlike distinguished—we passed to certain intellectual acts not usually included in Reasoning—" Classification, Naming, and Recognition." It was shown that the classification of relations and the classification of things, are but two aspects of one process; since conscious reasoning involves not only classification of relations, but classification of the things between which they exist; while classification of things involves that unconscious reasoning by which, from certain perceived attributes, we infer those unperceived attributes included in our conceptions of them as such or such. And our conclusion was that " likeness of relations is the intuition common to reasoning and classification: " naming and recognition being also shown to imply modifications of this same intuition.

After dealing with " Perceptions of Special Objects," in a chapter pointing out that they embody inferences and imply intuitions of likeness or unlikeness of relations, we went on to consider perceptions of body as presenting its various orders of attributes, and then to perceptions of Space, of Time, of Motion, of Resistance; and we reached the general result that " perception is a discerning of the relation or relations between states of consciousness, partly presentative and partly representative; which states of consciousness must be themselves known to the extent involved in

the knowledge of their relations." And we saw that the
process in every case implies that certain relations are classed
with their likes in past experience, while the terms among
which they exist are similarly classed with their likes in
past experience.

Then turning to relations themselves, and beginning with
Similarity and Dissimilarity as the most complex, these were
resolved into successively more simple ones; ending in the
relations of Likeness and Unlikeness, with the correlative relation of Sequence. The decomposition of relations thus
completed, disclosed the fact that in recognition of these
simplest, out of which all others are compounded, there
goes on the same process of consciousness: there is assimilation of its states with previously-experienced like states, and
of the transitions between them with previously-experienced
like transitions. This proved to be equivalent to the truth
that consciousness, perpetually undergoing changes, is constituted by the organization of these changes—the combination and arrangement of them in special ways: implying a grouping of the like and a separation of the unlike.

In a chapter summing up the results, it was pointed out
that these successive analyses disclosed "*a unity of composition* throughout all the phenomena of intelligence,"
and proved that the intuitions which compose the most complex processes of reasoning, " are foreshadowed in the very
first stages of an incipient consciousness." We inferred
that such a unity of composition is to be anticipated *à
priori*—that the fundamental " conditions under which
alone consciousness can exist, must be common to all kinds
and degrees of consciousness "—that " there must be some
form of thought exhibited alike in the very lowest and the
very highest manifestations of intelligence." And seeing,
as we did, that in " the simplest conceivable consciousness,
data for the relations of likeness and unlikeness are given,"
we concluded that there does exist from the beginning that

form of thought which characterizes it throughout its ascending stages of complexity. Passing from the *form* of thought to the *process* of thought, it was shown that this also is the same throughout: " the universal process of intelligence is the *assimilation* of impressions." Finally came the generalization that since consciousness can exist only by ceaseless change from each state to a different state; and since its states and changes can be arranged in order only by the classing of like with like, or union of each with its kind; it follows that " all mental action whatever is definable as *the continuous differentiation and integration of states of consciousness:* " in which ultimate character of psychical life we recognized a parallelism to an ultimate character of physical life.

§ 475*h*. That the conclusions to which these special analyses thus brought us, congruous as we have seen with one another, are also congruous with the conclusions reached in the synthetical divisions, will be manifest to every reader who remembers what those conclusions were. The conception of Life itself, as the continuous adjustment of inner relations to outer relations—a conception which we found to include at once the phenomena of bodily life and the phenomena of mental life—introduces us to an entire agreement between the general aspect of mental phenomena as objectively considered, and the general aspect of mental phenomena as subjectively considered. For if in all cases an intellectual act is the establishment in consciousness of a relation between two states; then, clearly, it has the nature which this continuous adjustment of inner relations to outer relations implies. Further, if inner relations are to be *adjusted* to outer relations, then, if in the outer relations there are likenesses and differences of nature, there must be answering likenesses and differences of nature in the corresponding inner relations: a requirement fulfilled if experience of the outer persistences produces the inner cohesions;

and a requirement harmonizing with the conclusion that there goes on a continuous assimilation in consciousness of its states and their relations to like states and relations in past experience.

In the objective division of our inquiry it was shown that the simplest nervous act consists of two habitually-related changes; of which one results from some external stimulus and the other accompanies an induced muscular contraction. Congruously, our subjective inquiry disclosed the truth that the simplest act of consciousness consists of two states occurring in relation, which severally repeat like states that have before occurred in like relation. In tracing up the evolution of intelligence objectively considered, we saw that there is a composition and consolidation of nervous acts into clusters larger and more varied, answering to the larger and more varied combinations of external phenomena which come within cognizance; but that to the last the essential act of advancing intelligence is that of establishing an inner connexion answering to the outer connexion: the form of the act remains the same however complex its components become. And so when considering intelligence subjectively, we found that while the terms between which relations are established in thought, become extremely involved in the highest mental processes, such as compound quantitative reasoning; yet the general form of the relation which thinking establishes between them is constant. It may be added that as our preliminary study of the nervous system disclosed a unit of composition of nervous structures and functions; and as we saw when studying the phenomena synthetically, that there was thus furnished a fit unit of composition for the inner relations which are progressively adjusted to outer relations; so we now see that there answers to this, the unit of composition into which consciousness was resolved in the course of our analysis.

When, at the outset, we dealt with mental phenomena

inductively, and among others the association of ideas, we concluded that this association is in all cases effected by the connecting of like with like: the so-called Law of Contiguity proving to be resolvable into the Law of Similarity. And our special analysis disclosed the truth that acts of consciousness, from the most complex to the most simple, are universally carried on by the classing of its states and relations with like states and relations in past experience. To which add that these results, congruous with one another, are congruous with the phenomena of nervous structure and function; since what we know as like feelings and like relations, correspond to like stimulations and discharges occurring in the same plexus.

When setting forth the " Data of Psychology," it was pointed out that the branching processes of nerve-cells, ramifying and intermingling in various ways and degrees with one another and with fibres, afford fit structures for making nervous channels of all degrees of definiteness, through which may pass discharges with all degrees of facility: there being, at the one extreme, direct unions of nerve-fibres with cells, and direct unions of cells with one another; while at the other extreme there are connexions no closer than those implied by the adjacency of extremely delicate cell-processes imbedded in the same matrix. In the " Physical Synthesis " was developed at large the hypothesis, that nervous communications, originally formed by the passage of molecular disturbances along lines of least resistance, are continually made more definite and more permeable by the recurrence of such disturbances. Recognizing the congruity between this hypothesis and the facts of minute nervous structure as just indicated, the congruity of both with sundry general truths otherwise reached is to be noted. We are furnished with an adequate explanation of nervous acts in all their degrees of promptness and precision, from the automatic up to the extremely uncertain and almost accidental. Unconscious reflex action is explicable as occurring in cases where, between some nerve-fibre bringing an excitement to a centre and some fibre conveying away an impulse, there exists, by the intermediation of nerve-cells, a direct and complete connexion; so that the discharge through the nervous arc occurs with the least hindrance and the greatest rapidity. For reflex actions of the conscious kind, such as the cough and the sneeze exemplify, there are available, as probable instrumentalities, central connexions not quite so perfect. Still less finished connexions will serve for such actions as have been made semi-automatic by habit; like those of the legs in walking, or of the hands in performing familiar movements in response to visual perceptions. And so upwards, through all those gradations of nervous actions which exhibit decreasing degrees of facility.

Observe now the congruity between these results and those reached in the " Special Analysis." On reconsidering the natures of our perceptions of external things, it will be seen that for their essential traits, explanations are supplied by these traits of nervous structure and function. Such components in these perceptions as are invariable, or are repeated in every case, are indissolubly associated in thought —associated in a way that would result from a reflex action established by innumerable repetitions. Thus, between the resistance which a body offers and its occupancy of space, the connexion in consciousness is such that, given the first the second cannot be kept out: the excitement of the one state of consciousness by the other, is as instant and irresistible as that of motion by stimulus in an automatic action, and is explicable as due to a similarly organized nervous connexion—a nervous connexion produced by the experiences, ever recurring through millions of generations, that these two attributes of body invariably co-exist. So, too, with such connexions in thought as that between perception of the nearer side of an object and the idea of a remoter side; that between motion and something which moves; that between a given position as revealed by vision, and the amount of bodily movement required to reach it. All such necessities of thought corresponding to necessary external relations, are accompaniments of reflex discharges through nervous structures so perfectly organized by ancestral and individual experiences, that the channels they open are inevitably taken by the discharges initiated.

Most striking and instructive, however, is the correspondence existing between these facts of nervous structure and function, and the interpretation which was given of our consciousness of space. Grant that what we know psychically as an association of ideas, answers physically to a discharge between two excited nervous elements—grant that the strengthening of this association by repetition, corresponds to the making of the channel for this discharge more permeable—grant that the effect of habit in changing a voluntary conscious act into an act more and more automatic, answers to the formation of a more perfect nervous connexion—grant that the reflex actions thus gradually established in that part of the nervous system devoted to mental functions, are of the same nature as the reflex actions in that part of it by which bodily functions are carried on; and we may see how there has been evolved, and is from moment to moment reproduced, that consolidated conception of space which seems so marvellous. For, in the first place, the visual consciousness of any one point to which the eyes are converged, is automatically connected by infinite repetitions in the individual and his progenitors, with the consciousness accompanying those nervous acts by which the axes and foci of the eyes are adjusted to that point, and, also, when near, with the consciousness of those movements by which the point can be reached; and, in the second place, infinite repetitions have simultaneously established connexions between the nervous adjustments which go along with the consciousness of that point, and the nervous adjustments made in passing through each point on the way to it; so that with the reflex consciousness of the motion required to be gone through in reaching a position on which the eyes are converged, there goes a reflex consciousness of all the intermediate positions. Further, in universal experience, each object looked at, occupying a cluster of positions more or less extensive, has, while exciting the most vivid consciousness of that particular point in it on which the visual axes are converged, also partially excited those nervous agents corresponding to all the other positions it occupies. Whence it has come to happen, that when these other positions are not occupied, yet, by reflex excitement, a distinct consciousness of any one position arouses a multitude of consciousness of the positions which constitute surrounding space. In brief, the laws of nervous organization warrant the inference that there has been evolved, by converse with adjacent space and the objects it contains, an extensive and elaborate plexus, the multitudinous parts of which correspond to the multitudinous positions in adjacent space; and which, in virtue of its extreme definiteness of organization, cannot have one of its parts excited without a reflex excitement of all the rest being produced, so as to generate a simultaneous consciousness of all the positions to which they answer.   As harmonizing with this view, three traits of this consciousness may be named. The first is that the consciousness of the space close to us is far more intimate and detailed than the consciousness of remote space; which would obviously result from this reflex excitement through organic connexions established in experience. The second is that when the eyes are turned in any direction, the space-consciousness is much more minute and complete immediately around that direction than on the outskirts of the field of vision—a fact similarly explicable. And the third is that in the dark, especially when the place is unknown, the ordinary consciousness of space almost disappears, leaving only that part of the consciousness which accompanies freedom to move; while in a known place, as a familiar room, such consciousness of space as remains, accompanies an ideal representation of the objects it contains. Let me add that, while we are thus enabled to understand how the space-consciousness is constituted, we are also furnished with an explanation of such special intuitions as the geometrical axioms; since these are interpretable as indissoluble connexions in consciousness, corresponding to certain reflex actions which occur in the space-plexus when certain data are presented.

Not only, then, do we find entire congruity between the special results synthetically reached and those reached by analysis, but we find that each elucidates the other.

CHAPTER V.

CO-ORDINATION OF GENERAL ANALYSES.

§ 475*i*. The inquiries carried on in the divisions abstracted and compared in the foregoing four chapters, assumed the co-existence and co-operation of subject and object. Avowedly made as provisional at the outset of *First Principles*, and there justified only by a brief survey of the reasons for making it, this assumption was, in Part VII. of this work, returned to for the purpose of finally justifying it. Reverting to the inference originally reached, that justification for this ultimate dictum of consciousness must consist in proof of its congruity with all other dicta, we proceeded to set forth the proof.

The general argument was composed of three portions. The first, dealing with the assumption of metaphysicians, their words, and their reasonings, made it clear that, to whatever school they belong, metaphysicians invariably and inevitably connote, alike by their terms and their arguments, the existence of a *non-ego* independent of the *ego ;* and that thus, while congruity emerges with a realistic conclusion, an absolute and fatal incongruity is involved by any other conclusion. Dealing with the question more specially, the next group of chapters compared the arguments for and against realism in respect to their priority, their simplicity, and their distinctness; with the result of showing that the realistic belief, first in order of genesis, is that on which the idealistic argument stands; that the mental process yielding the realistic belief is relatively brief and simple, and less liable to be vitiated by error than the long and involved process supposed to yield the idealistic belief; and that while the states of consciousness which, as combined, yield the one belief, are of that vivid kind in which most confidence is to be placed, the states of consciousness which yield, or are supposed to yield, the other belief, are of that faint kind in which less confidence is to be placed. And the implication was that while the realistic belief withstands the usual tests of certitude, the opposed belief is triply discredited by them.

After thus broadly distinguishing these antagonist doctrines as the one consistent with itself and with all results otherwise reached, and the other as inconsistent with both, we proceeded to judge between them more definitely by means of a criterion which must be accepted in common by their respective defenders. Having explained that before they can be rightly compared, propositions must be analyzed and reduced to like degrees of simplicity, it was shown that our ultimate ground for accepting a proposition as unquestionably true, is the inability to conceive the negation of it. And having recognized the fact that for every step in an argument this is the ultimate justification, we saw that by no possibility can this test be invalidated; since every step in any argument constituting the supposed invalidation, must assume the test. Hence, as Idealism and Realism both proceed upon the Universal Postulate, the realistic conclusion which, being reached by a single direct act of consciousness, invokes it only once, is of high validity in comparison with the idealistic conclusion, which, reached by many steps and invoking it at every step, is proportionately liable to error from mental *lapsus*.

Such being the negative justification of Realism implied by the logical inferiority of the idealistic argument, we proceeded to that positive justification of it furnished by examination of its psychological nature and genesis. In a chapter on " The Dynamics of Consciousness," we reached the conclusion that we accept, and must accept, those beliefs of which the component ideas cannot be torn asunder. In other words, we saw that a trial of strength which shows certain connexions in consciousnesss to be indissoluble, leaves those connexions out-standing as beliefs which we cannot choose but hold. Hence it became manifest that since, with the states of consciousness constituting perception of an object, there indissolubly coheres a consciousness standing for an existence beyond consciousness, there is, for the indestructible belief thus formed, the highest warrant possible. Such being the psychological nature of the realistic belief, we proceeded, in pursuance of the same method, to trace its psychological genesis. We went on to examine the origins of those indissolubly-coherent aggregates of states of consciousness constituting our conceptions of subject and object. Through three chapters we traced the evolution and separation of states of consciousness into the two great aggregates, primarily distinguished as vivid and faint, and secondarily distinguished in various other ways; each of which is absolutely coherent within itself, and each of which, as yielding us the experience of a *nexus* that remains permanent while the states change, exhibits itself as an independent existence—a self and a not-self.

§ 475*j*. That the Realism emerging from this examination of the way in which our states of consciousness hang together, is congruous with the Realism postulated throughout the preceding divisions of this work scarcely needs saying.

But besides the general harmony, too conspicuous to need indicating, special harmonies which are less conspicuous may be pointed out. The leading truths taught concerning the structure and functions of the nervous system, and concerning the nature and development of intelligence, receive crowning illustrations in the formation of this indestructible consciousness in which Realism abides. The general theory that mental evolution, in common with the vital evolution of which it forms part, is a progressing adjustment of inner relations to outer relations—a widening and improving correspondence between internal changes and external co-existences and sequences—while it necessarily posits subject and object, also implies that, deeper than all special correspondences between related phenomena in the object and connected mental states in the subject, will be that consciousness of these two antithetic wholes of existence, between parts of which the correspondence in every case occurs: experience of their co-existence, being a concomitant of each particular experience, will necessarily be the fundamental experience. Further, from the order of progress of mental faculties, beginning with related sensation and motion, passing to simple perception, then to complex perception, then to concrete reasoning, and finally to abstract reasoning; it must follow that the higher faculties, arising by complications of the lower, and to the last depending upon them, can never rightly yield other than congruous results—can never, when performing their functions normally, give dicta fundamentally at variance with those of the primary faculties they are evolved from. Similarly with the general law of intelligence. We found that establishment of a correspondence between inner and outer relations, implies that " the strength of the tendency which the antecedent of any psychical change has to call up its consequent, is proportionate to the persistence of the union between the external things they symbolize." Now if, to objective relations of all degrees of persistence, there must, to fulfil the law of intelligence, arise subjective relations of all degrees of cohesion; then, since the general relation of subject and object is given along with each correspondence between a particular

73

objective relation and a particular subjective relation, it follows that this general relation between subject and object, more persistent in experience than any particular relation, must have, answering to it, a more coherent relation in consciousness than any other.   In a parallel way, this is an outcome of the law of association as inductively established, or as deductively explained by the formation of nervous connexions proportionate in their definiteness and permeability to the numbers and strengths of the discharges they carry. For if the converse between organism and environment unceasingly discloses some power beyond consciousness, which in every perception and act operates upon the power within consciousness, or is operated upon by it; then the co-existence of subject and object must, by the law of association, either as empirically established or rationally interpreted, produce an answering connexion in consciousness stronger than any other.

So is it, too, with certain other elements of the arguments by which Realism was justified. Examination of the dynamics of consciousness proved that in thinking, continual trials are made of the relative cohesions between states of consciousness; with the result that the most coherently-connected states remain outstanding as beliefs. This result we saw may be interpreted in physiological terms as the issue of a conflict of tendencies among nervous discharges to take various lines; of which tendencies the strongest finally prevails: such strongest being that which takes the most permeable route, and such most permeable route being one that has been made most permeable by the most numerous experiences. Hence the irreversibleness of our belief in a reality beyond consciousness as well as a reality in consciousness.   In like agreement with this principle of nervous evolution, elaborated in the " Physical Synthesis," was that subjectively-established test of belief which we found to be the Universal Postulate. For a proposition of which the negation is inconceivable—a proposition formed of states of consciousness indissolubly connected in a certain order—answers psychologically to a reflex action occurring between the two correlative nerve-agencies: an action such that, the one being excited, excitement of the other follows irresistibly. And since, in conformity with the general theory set forth, those organized connexions of which reflex actions are the functions, have been organized by recurring discharges practically infinite in number; the implication is that such reflex intellectual actions as those which the inconceivability of the negation supposes, answer to the most multitudinous experiences, and are therefore most certain.

So that these agreements, like the preceding agreements, imply the conclusion that the consciousness of subject and object is organically fixed. The belief in an external world is the outcome of reflex intellectual actions established, like all those others which entail forms of thought, during that moulding of the organism to the environment which has been going on through countless millions of years.

CHAPTER VI.

FINAL COMPARISON.

§ 475k. That feeling is a large, if not the larger, factor in determining belief, is shown by the fact that, in controversies concerning even matters the most remote from human interests, men will commit themselves to impossibilities of thought, rather than surrender hypotheses on behalf of which their *amour propre* has been enlisted. They will ask assent to each successive proposition in an argument, on the ground that the contrary cannot be imagined; at the same time that the conclusion they would establish by such argument, is one of which the affirmation is more conspicuously unimaginable.

A striking example of this has of late been furnished by certain mathematicians, in their theories about non-Euclidean spaces. By a chain of reasoning, the existence, or at any rate the possibility, of a fourth dimension in space is held to be proved. Each link in this chain of reasoning consists of premises and inference; the last of which is said to be necessitated by the first. If inquiry is made why, the premises being given, this inference must be admitted; the reply is that, given the premises, the contrary inference is inconceivable. Nevertheless, the conclusion of the entire argument, notwithstanding its inconceivability, is offered for acceptance as a legitimate conclusion. A fourth dimension in space can be conceived neither as existing nor as possible; and yet the test of inconceivability is here disregarded as of no moment, though assent to each step in the argument is regarded as imperative because negation of it is inconceivable. An instance even more extreme in its incongruity, is furnished by the reasons assigned for asserting the possible untruth, under certain conditions, of the Euclidean doctrine concerning parallel lines. Setting out with data which cannot be conceived, the argument proceeds by steps which are to be admitted because the negations of them cannot be conceived, and reaches a conclusion which is held to be proved, though it cannot be conceived. Let there be postulated the existence of intelligent beings in space of two dimensions; then, and then, and then, &c.; therefore — Such is the form of the demonstration. But saying nothing about the inconceivability of beings in space of two dimensions only, there is the preceding inconceivability of space of two dimensions only, itself. No consciousness of such space, in the absence of a third dimension, can be framed. A mathematician once instanced to me the surface of a solid as exemplifying such space. But how is the surface of a solid to be conceived apart from the solid? —which implies a third dimension. Not even the attempt to think of a plane without thickness, can be made without the thought of thickness being involved in the hypothetical exclusion of it: the third dimension persistently intrudes. If I am asked to admit that though space of two dimensions without a third cannot be conceived, yet the absence of a third may be postulated as possible; then, at the first step in the argument, and at each succeeding step, I use the same licence, and say that though the reverse inference to that drawn cannot be conceived, yet the reverse inference may be postulated as possible, and, postulating it as possible, I decline to accept the inference offered: the argument is brought to a stand. Either the impossibility of framing a proposition in thought must be held a valid reason for rejecting it, or it must not. But whichever alternative is accepted must be adhered to. Reasoning which now assumes the validity of this test and now its invalidity, is suicidal.*

I am led to make this seemingly-irrelevant criticism by the suspicion that metaphysical opponents will perhaps deny a proposition which I was about to lay down as beyond question. I purposed setting out by saying that the aggregate of ideas and feelings composing consciousness, either forms the totality of existence or it does not, when I was arrested by the thought that those who deny other immediate dicta of consciousness may with equal propriety deny this. If in some instances hypotheses which cannot be framed in thought are posited and argued from, such hypotheses may be posited and argued from in this instance too. Beliefs entailed by mental necessities, if rejected in other cases, may as well be rejected in this case.

Nevertheless I shall here assume, as the only possible alternatives, that there is existence beyond consciousness, or that there is no existence beyond consciousness. Let us consider the implications of each alternative; taking the last first.

§ 475*l*. Of the proposition that there is no existence beyond consciousness, the first implication is that consciousness is unlimited in extension. For a limit which consciousness cannot transcend, implies an existence which imposes the limit; and this must either be an existence be-

---

* Making these inconceivable assumptions may have, as is alleged, advantages as a method of inquiry. By ascertaining what impossible conclusions arise when certain data of consciousness are supposed absent, it may be shown what truths are necessarily involved in the constitution of consciousness. Discovering what happens when operations with symbols answering to three dimensions are complicated by the introduction of a symbol standing for a hypothetical fourth, may help to elucidate the laws of relation among the symbols which answer to the three. But admission of this may go along with denial that the conclusions drawn have either actual or possible correspondences in existence beyond consciousness.

yond consciousness, which is contrary to the hypothesis, or an existence within consciousness other than itself, which is also contrary to the hypothesis. Something which restrains consciousness to a certain sphere, whether it be internal or external, must be something other than consciousness—must be something co-existing, which is contrary to the hypothesis. Hence consciousness being unrestrained in its sphere becomes infinite in space.

A further implication is that consciousness is infinite in time. To conceive any limit to consciousness in the past, is to conceive either that preceding this limit there was some other actual existence at the moment when consciousness commenced, which would be contrary to the hypothesis, or that there was some potential existence which then became actual, which potential existence, if not regarded as other existence (which again would be contrary to the hypothesis), must have been the same existence in another form.

In the absence of any other existence limiting it in time and space, consciousness must be absolute or unconditioned. No cause existing beyond it, all cause exists within it—everything within it is self-determined. To say that there are conditions which determine anything within it, is to say that there is existence independent of it, which is contrary to the hypothesis. Hence, any state of consciousness, as a pain, is self-produced, and continues only in virtue of conditions which consciousness itself imposes. The ending of any state, say a pleasure, is caused solely by the operation of consciousness on itself. Any thought framed thus or thus, may be framed with equal facility in any other way; since to say that there is anything which determines it in one way rather than another, implies some extrinsic power which is, or has been, operative on consciousness, which again is contrary to the hypothesis.

In brief, then, if there is no existence beyond consciousness—if there is no other being either of the same kind or of another kind; then consciousness, eternally existing, is at once creator and created. It always has been, is, and will be, the sum of all causes and effects, omnipotent and omnipresent.

Further, it may be noted that in the implied absence of any limit to consciousness, there cannot be framed even the hypothesis of any other existence; seeing that the framing of such hypothesis implies the conception of a limit to consciousness beyond which there may be this other existence, and if consciousness is unlimited, this conception becomes impossible, because there is no limit beyond which other existence may be conceived. So that under such conditions, the question of objective existence as distinguished from subjective existence is rigorously excluded. The metaphysical problem cannot even be entertained.

§ 475*m*. Take, now, the alternative, that there is existence beyond consciousness. If consciousness is not the whole of existence, several implications arise.

This other existence must be entirely inert, or partly inert and partly active, or entirely active. If it is entirely inert, then its relation to consciousness can be such only as to exclude consciousness from a region of being it would otherwise fill. In this case consciousness, though not unlimited, remains, within its limits, absolute: in the absence of any other energy, its actions are in all respects self-determined. If, on the other hand, this other existence is either partially active or wholly active, then consciousness is not only restricted in its sphere, but is liable to be acted upon: the energy manifesting itself in consciousness, co-exists with another energy capable of working changes in it and being changed by it. For if these two energies do not stand in such relation as to affect one another, then each is to the other practically non-existent; and we are brought again to the condition in which consciousness becomes, within its sphere, absolute.

But now if these two existences, both seats of energy, co-exist in such wise as to affect one another, there is necessarily implied some place where the action of one upon the other occurs, and where, consequently, they bound one another. The conception of the two as separate energies, implies some kind of limit at which the one ceases and the other begins. In what way this limit is constituted does not here concern us.* It suffices, for the purpose of the argument, to point out that unless consciousness is everywhere shut off from other existence by that which is, relatively to itself, an impassable limit, then the implication is that, transcending the limit, it can include within itself the extra conscious existence; which is contrary to the hypothesis.

The presence of some bound where the one existence ceases and the other begins, implies either unlikeness between the two existences or breach of continuity; but whichever alternative be assumed, it equally results that the existence outside the limit becomes by contrast unconscious. To suppose that something beyond consciousness can be present in consciousness as a part of it, is to suppose that consciousness has gone beyond its limits and incorporated this something, which is contrary to the hypothesis. Necessarily, therefore, with the admission of a limit to consciousness, there goes the admission that whatever lies beyond it is antithetically opposed as something into which consciousness cannot enter, and as thus, by the exclusion of consciousness from it, rendered, relatively to consciousness, unconscious. Though existence beyond consciousness may be as a whole of the same nature, or though parts of it may be of the same nature, yet the occurrence of a breach of continuity prevents such outer consciousness from being present in consciousness as such.

But now, such being the relations between the two ex-

---

* I say this lest it should be assumed that limitation in space is alleged.

istences, what must be the nature of their intercourse? Where the one energy acts on the other (we will for convenience call them outer and inner, though this is not necessary to the argument), the cause and the effect must differ; since the effect, being a product of the co-operation of the two energies, cannot be like either. To say that an outer cause produces an inner effect identical with itself, is to say that the inner existence is acted upon without either acting or re-acting; which is practically to say that it has no attribute by which existence is distinguished from non-existence. As the resultant of two forces differs from both, every product arising in consciousness from co-operation of the inner and outer energies, or parts of them, can be like neither of its factors. So is it, too, respecting any *nexus* among the causes in the one and any *nexus* among the effects in the other. To say that the inner relations of effects can be identical with the outer relations of causes, is to say that while the outer causes are transformed in working the inner effects, yet the order among them undergoes no transformation; and this is to say either that there is no inner order, or that the inner order is inoperative. If the inner existence has no order, then it has no parts distinguishable in either space or time; in which case its existence is indistinguishable from non-existence. If, while it is admitted that the inner existence has some order, it is held that this order is not a factor which, co-operating with the outer order, produces a resultant order; then the implication is that there is a kind of order which is indistinguishable in its effects from no order. But unless this implication is accepted, it must be admitted that whatever inner order exists, must, by its co-operation, modify the impressed outer order: the inner order of effects must be made to differ from the outer order of causes.

Thus, then, rejecting as we are compelled to do the hypothesis that consciousness is the sole existence (since as we see this cannot without suicide entertain the metaphysical problem), and accepting the alternative that there is existence other than consciousness, we find that the conclusions reached are inevitable. If we exclude the hypothesis that both the existences are inert (in which case the existence of either would be to the other the same as its non-existence); and if we exclude the hypothesis that the inner existence is inert and the outer active (which would imply that the inner existence has not that trait by which it knows itself as consciousness); and if we exclude the hypothesis that the inner existence is active and the outer inert (which, save by the presence of limits, would leave the inner existence in every respect self-determined or absolute); and if we posit the remaining hypothesis, that both inner and outer existences are active; there necessarily emerge the conclusions, first that, by the intercourse of the two, the existence of each is implied, and second that causes and their connexions in the one must differ from effects and their connexions in the other. The two necessities are co-equal.

For if it be said that an effect wrought by the one on the other is not like its cause in the other, it is simultaneously said that there is a cause in the other. If it be said that no connexion between the effects in the one can be like the connexion between the causes in the other, it is simultaneously said that there is a connexion between the causes in the other. That is to say, while to the inner existence the outer existence is represented by its effects, but cannot be presented in its nature; yet the representation of it by its effects, necessarily implies its co-existence.

§ 475*n*. This argument, of course, sets out with certain fundamental data of consciousness. There are involved the ideas of limit, of difference, of likeness, of inclusion and exclusion, of cause and effect. There are taken for granted the necessary dependences of certain conclusions on certain premises. Of mutually-exclusive alternatives it is assumed that acceptance of the one necessitates

rejection of the other. It may be contended, and rightly
contended, that these primary intuitions, reduced to their
lowest terms, themselves imply the co-existence of subject
and object. But, as said at the outset (*First Principles*,
§ 39), the intellect can no more stir without the aid
of certain consolidated conceptions, than the body can
stir without the aid of its limbs. The validity of these
conceptions cannot, therefore, be shown by any argument;
since, from step to step, such argument takes for granted
their validity. If subject and object exist, then, necessarily,
intelligence is based on the relation between them; and if
so, it can use no argument to show the existence of the
object, which does not directly or indirectly imply the existence of the object. If, as repeatedly pointed out, the
proof of any truth is the affiliation of it on some more
general truth, and this again on some truth still more
general, until the most general truth is reached; then the
most general truth cannot be proved. We can do no more
than show that this ultimate dictum of consciousness, together with all those derivative dicta constituting our indestructible conceptions, everywhere harmonizes with all
dicta otherwise arrived at.

The foregoing argument, then, simply brings out the
facts that, of the two alternatives that there is existence
beyond consciousness, and that there is no existence beyond
consciousness, the first is in all ways congruous with other
deliverances of consciousness, and the last is in all ways
incongruous with them. The last, implying that consciousness is eternal, omnipresent, and omnipotent, also implies
that the hypothesis of other existence being of necessity
excluded, the metaphysical problem cannot arise: to suppose
that the question of subject and object can be entertained,
is to suppose the hypothesis untrue. The first, implying that
consciousness is an existence limited and circumscribed by
other existence, while it implies that co-existence of subject
and object which all our intellectual operations pre-suppose,

and renders the fabric of our conclusions consistent, yields the further conclusion that the outer reality, though present to the inner reality as existing, cannot be known in its nature.

Thus we are brought again, by another route, to the doctrine of Transfigured Realism. We are shown that, while the opposed doctrines are consistent neither within themselves nor with other beliefs, this doctrine is internally consistent and consistent externally with our beliefs at large.

Here, however, we are chiefly concerned to observe its consistency with the several groups of conclusions reached in the successive parts of this work.

§ 475*o*. As already shown, the conception of Mind as consisting, in common with Life at large, of definitely combined heterogeneous changes in correspondence with external co-existences and sequences, necessarily posits the relation of subject and object. The interpretation of reflex action, instinct, reason, feeling, and will, as factors in the adjustment of inner relations to outer relations, unavoidably pre-supposes an external reality, as well as an internal reality. And the reasoning used to show that the nervous system, and therefore the consciousness accompanying its actions, is evolved through the converse of organism and environment, cannot be carried out without assuming organism and environment.

With scarcely less clearness is the realistic assumption involved by those analyses which reduce consciousness to its lowest terms. The decomposition of complex ideas into simpler ones, and of these again into simpler, until there are reached, as the simplest, the relations of unlikeness and sequence; everywhere takes for granted the existence of an external distribution which the internal distribution represents. When, for instance, there are analyzed certain forms of consciousness in the *ego*, as Space and Time, the analysis pre-supposes certain forms in the *non-ego*, which, if not copied by those in the *ego*, are symbolized by them.

But while throughout both syntheses and analyses, Realism is at every step a necessary implication, there is not necessarily implied Crude Realism. Contrariwise, the argument everywhere harmonizes with, and in some places involves, Transfigured Realism. The conclusion that every nervous discharge consists of successive pulses, making it clear that the discharges being like one another cannot be like the initiating stimuli which are unlike one another, we found to agree with the induction that feelings are relative to the size, nature, state, and part of the organism affected; and both of them we find congruous with that *à priori* inference reached above, that during the converse between including and included existences, outer causes and inner effects cannot be identical in nature. So, too, the truths of nervous structure, implying that the internal *nexus* of nervous changes cannot be like the external *nexus* of actions to which these nervous changes are adjusted, agreeing as it did with the induction that the relations in consciousness, varying with the dimensions, structure, and position of the organism, cannot be like those dependences in the environment to which they refer, agrees also with the above *à priori* inference, that the distribution of effects in a limited existence must be unlike the distribution of causes in the existence limiting it. Thus, whether presented under its most abstract form as above, or under a more concrete form as before, the doctrine of Transfigured Realism, which is but another aspect of the doctrine of the Unknowable, harmonizes with the results of both syntheses and analyses; since, while they imply that inner thoughts answer to outer things, in such wise that cohesions in the one correspond to persistences in the other, they do not imply that the correspondence is anything more than symbolic.

Not only is the actuality of subject and object an implication which everywhere emerges, but the genesis of the notion of subject and object is congruously explained. As already said, if the faculties of the subject have been moulded by converse with the object, the existence of the object is necessarily given in the constitution of these faculties of the subject which have been moulded upon it. Inevitably, too, an explanation of consciousness will be possible if the generating object is postulated; while no explanation of consciousness will be possible in the absence of the generating object. The rise of the cognition that the two are independent is also explicable. Whether we consider from a personal point of view that process of self-interpretation which, as a primary result, evolves the notions of subject and object (as we did when watching how the vivid and faint aggregates segregate); or whether we consider the process vicariously and under its most abstract form, as we have done above, by observing what must happen to an active existence circumscribed by another active existence; we see that there unavoidably arises a distinction between that set of manifestations which, being controllable by an energy ever welling up within, are grouped together as an *ego*, and that set of manifestations which, not being thus controllable, originate the consciousness of an outer energy or *non-ego*.

Once more we are shown why, though consciousness of an existence beyond consciousness is inexpugnable, yet this extra-conscious existence not only remains inconceivable in nature, but the nature of its connexion with consciousness cannot be truly conceived. Carrying on its operations in terms of its own states and the relations among them, consciousness cannot frame in thought a relation of which one term is beyond consciousness. And yet, compelled as it is to recognize objective existence, it can never cease its efforts to make objective existence one term of a relation in consciousness. Even restrained by its limits, but ever trying to exceed them, consciousness cannot but use the forms of its activity in figuring to itself that which cannot be brought within these forms; and is obliged by these forms to think of the relation of subject and object as like relations lying within itself. But since one term of such relation lies outside of it, neither the term nor the relation can be completed in thought. Yet the form of thought has to be filled up; and the only possibility is a symbolical filling-up of it—ending an unfinished relation by an unknown term. To this conclusion we are brought whether we contemplate subject and object under their most abstract forms, as included and including existences; or whether we contemplate them under their concrete forms, as we did throughout the discussion which ended in the doctrine of Transfigured Realism.

§ 475*p*. And then, to round off this exhibition of congruities, we may note that arrival at the doctrine of Transfigured Realism, is a last step in that general process by which Mind is made a differentiated and integrated division of the totality of being.

Regarding Evolution as all-comprehensive, and regarding every consciousness as an individualized part of the Universal Power, we have to observe how, at its highest stage, consciousness exhibits the traits of advanced evolution, not only in other ways but also by becoming most distinctly marked off from surrounding existence. In the *Principles of Biology*, § 53, we saw that during evolution, physically considered, organisms are more and more decidedly differentiated from their environments in respect of structure, form, composition, specific gravity, temperature, and self-mobility. In the foregoing parts of this work it has been shown that in the course of evolution, psychically considered, the aggregate of states and changes constituting consciousness, while augmenting in quantity, while growing more heterogeneous in its components, while integrating into a more coherent whole, while acquiring increased definiteness in the kinds and relations of its parts, becomes by these traits contrasted more markedly with surrounding activities. And here it remains to be shown that it also becomes divided from them by a sharper line of demarkation.

For a long time after there is consciousness there is no self-consciousness. The states and changes of consciousness are not known to themselves as constituting a separate entity. Even in low states of human evolution, self-consciousness is very incomplete: that circumscription of consciousness which is implied by the pronoun " I," is for a long time imperfect in the child, who continues to speak of himself objectively. In the savage, too, there exists no such conception of his consciousness as that which is familiar to the civilized. The part of him which answers to what we call mind, he thinks of as a duplicate of his body, and thinks of it as no less material. Even as this becomes step by step de-materialized, it continues to be thought of as pervading him all through, and like him in aspect. And there are long absent from his language all words by which mental phenomena, considered as such, are expressed. This incomplete differentiation of consciousness from material existence, is well shown in him by the belief that the virtue of a foe may be acquired by eating his flesh; and again, by the belief that a name, which in reality exists only as an idea in the minds of those who know it, has an objective existence and is a part of the owner's being. Under another form this confusion is shown us in the notion which long prevailed among civilized peoples, and is exemplified in mediæval drawings, that vision is effected by something proceeding from the eye to the object; and that thus consciousness, in a way, extends as far as the object. And the incomplete differentiation of subject and object thus markedly exemplified in lower stages of intelligence, is exemplified among ourselves less markedly by Crude Realism. The beliefs that a noise exists objectively as such, that sourness, as tasted, inheres in vinegar, and so throughout, similarly show us a border-region within which subject and object are confounded. What exist in consciousness as sen-

79

sations are identified with properties in outer objects. Most clearly is this seen in the ordinary conception of mechanical force, which, present to consciousness under the form of effort, is supposed to exist beyond consciousness under the same form: the Earth's action on a falling body is conceived as a pull.

But now Transfigured Realism completes the differentiation of subject and object, by definitely separating that which belongs to the one from that which belongs to the other. It does not, with Idealism, say that the object exists only as perceived—does not abolish the line of demarkation between subject and object by bringing the object within consciousness; but it admits the independent existence of the object as unperceived. It does not, with Crude Realism, hold that, apart from a perceiving consciousness, the object possesses those attributes by which it is distinguished in perception—does not ascribe to the object something which belongs to the subject. Asserting an impassable limit between the two, it recognizes an external independent existence which is the cause of changes in consciousness, while the effects it works in consciousness constitute the perception of it; and it infers that the knowledge constituted by these effects cannot be a knowledge of that which causes them, but can only imply its existence.

May it not, then, be said that in thus interpreting itself, subjective existence makes definite that differentiation from objective existence, which has been going on from the beginning of mental evolution?

PART IX.

COROLLARIES.

CHAPTER I.

§ 476. The foregoing divisions of this work have had for their subject-matter the principles of Psychology, considered as the science of Mind in general. Though numerous special facts have been cited, and illustrations have been culled now from the mental phenomena seen in animals and now from those which men exhibit, yet the aim throughout has been to establish truths of universal application—to formulate the laws of psychical action at large, without reference to the particular forms of it displayed in this or that creature and this or that faculty.

But the field of General Psychology having been explored, there opens before us the far more extensive field of Special Psychology. After the task of arriving at universal principles by induction from particular cases, and the deductive verification of these principles, there comes the task of explaining by them the multitudinous particular cases which have not been recognized in the process of generalization. The nature of each mental power, considered as a distinguishable group of activities displayed in common by many animals, is a question in Special Psychology least removed from the questions of General Psychology. The mental constitution of each animal, considered as an aggregate of such powers adjusted in their kinds and degrees to the mode of life, is a more special question—one the remoteness of which from questions of General Psychology is conspicuous. And then among still more special questions are those presented by individual peculiarities, and by the variations which the life of each individual displays.

§ 477. Of the vast field of research included within these bounds, we need here examine but a small part. Having presently to follow out Evolution under those higher forms which societies present, the special psychology of Man, considered as the unit of which societies are composed, must be briefly outlined—or rather, such part of his special psychology as stands in direct relation to sociological phenomena.

It is manifest that the ability of men to co-operate in any degree as members of a society, pre-supposes certain intellectual faculties and certain emotions. It is manifest that the efficiency of their co-operation will, other things equal, be determined by the amounts and proportions in which they possess these required mental powers. It is also manifest that, by continuing to co-operate under the conditions furnished by any social state, the amounts and proportions of these mental powers may be modified, and some modified form of co-operation may hence result; which again reacting on the nature is itself again reacted upon. Hence, in preparation for the study of social evolution, there have to be dealt with various questions respecting the faculties it brings into play, and respecting the modes in which these are developed during continued social life.

§ 478. In the group of corollaries here to be gathered together, sundry of the facts and inferences already used in the development of general principles will naturally recur— not, however, under the same aspects as before, but under aspects somewhat more specific and under relations to one another more or less new.

I may further explain that while the aim will be to give an adequate account of those human faculties which take part as factors in social phenomena, it will not be possible to limit ourselves absolutely to the manifestations of these faculties in human beings. Without glancing at the manifestations of some of them in minds of inferior types, we cannot understand their essential natures, or the modes in which social life affects them.

To re-assure the reader, already wearied with multitudinous explanations, I may add that the needful statements will be comparatively succinct. After the full development of general principles in the foregoing divisions, the applications of them to be now made will be understood without much detail.

CHAPTER II.

§ 479. Before dealing, even briefly, with special mental faculties in a systematic way, we must class them. Classification is here more difficult than usual; and cannot, indeed, be effected in anything more than a vague way. Observe the obstacles.

Though a chemist may in a few cases be uncertain what group an element belongs to, as, for instance, whether selenium is metallic or non-metallic, yet generally his divisions are precise: the things he deals with admit of sharp separations. If we arrange animals in classes, the difficulties that occasionally present themselves do not hinder us in marking out the great divisions and sub-divisions. Evolution of organisms tends ever to produce more pronounced partings—alike between the great groups, the sub-groups, the sub-sub-groups, &c.; so that, using the analogy of a tree, each branch, bearing its secondary and tertiary branches down to the ultimate twigs, is always quite distinct from its neighbours. Occasionally it may not be at a glance obvious which of two adjacent branches a certain twig belongs to; but a nearer examination resolves the doubt completely.   But now, carrying further the tree-analogy, let us suppose that along with this continual divergence and re-divergence of the branches, there had gone on a continual inosculation. Suppose that

510

from the twigs of each branch, as it diverged, there were sent out processes to join the twigs of a neighbouring branch; and that then, from these two branches thereafter growing in this linked manner, there were sent out processes to join other similarly-linked branches; and so on perpetually. It is clear that in this case definite classification would be impossible.

Such a mode of development rudely symbolizes the development of the great nervous centres. There is similarly an integration proceeding *pari passu* with a differentiation. But the development of the functions necessarily follows the same course as the development of the structures. Hence it happens that these functions, which are what we call faculties or mental powers, are but imperfectly distinguished from one another; and there cannot be made a classification of them like that which we make of separable external objects. We may indeed recognize broad contrasts; as, in the branched inosculating structure described, we could say of a certain part whether it belonged to the right side or the left, the upper or the lower. But the perpetual inosculation and reinosculation forbid anything quite specific.

Duly recognizing the fact that the unspecific classification which remains possible is good so far as it goes, and, indeed, needful; and duly recognizing the fact that no kind of classification can be specific; there is a classification to be otherwise made, which we shall here find of great use. Carrying further the analogy employed, let us suppose that our symbolic tree added, year by year, to its periphery, a new stratum of divergent branches with their inosculating processes, and that the lateral communications thus established became continually wider; so that while in the innermost stratum adjacent pairs of branches only were connected, in the next above it pairs of pairs were connected, and above these, pairs of such clusters, and so on continually. Then the structures contained in this aggregate would be classifiable severally as belonging to the first, second, third, or fourth stratum; and, if each stratum had some function in relation to the rest, it would be possible to classify the functions as severally of the first, second, third, or fourth order.

Returning to the structure of the great nervous centre in which the higher mental faculties are seated, we may recognize the propriety of grouping them according as they are removed in the first, second, third, fourth, &c., degree from those simple sense-faculties which are the roots common to them all. Such a mode of classification harmonizes with the results of both analysis and synthesis. It is one which the Doctrine of Evolution indirectly implies; and we shall find it very convenient.

Such difficulty as the reader finds in interpreting this analogical statement, will perhaps disappear on passing, as we will now do, to a direct examination of the facts. These will give meaning to the symbolic illustration at the same time that they are elucidated by it.

§ 480. I need not do more than recall the fact dwelt on in the chapter on the "Composition of Mind," that the primary division of mental elements is into Feelings and the Relations between Feelings (commonly called Cognitions). Nor need I dwell on the fact there indicated that though this is the most strongly-marked distinction, it is not an absolute distinction. While, however, we are compelled to admit at the first step, that mental faculties can be but imperfectly marked off from one another, we are able to perceive a broad contrast between those modes of consciousness in which the sentient states themselves predominantly occupy it, and those in which it is predominantly occupied by the relations among them—a broad contrast between FEELINGS and COGNITIONS.*

Proceeding to sub-divide these two great classes, we find

* The classification which here follows was originally appended to a criticism on Professor Bain's work, *The Emotions and the Will.*

that, to take first the Cognitions, these are divisible in a general way into four great sub-classes.

Presentative cognitions ; or those in which consciousness is occupied in localizing a sensation impressed on the organism—occupied, that is, with the relation between this presented mental state and those other presented mental states which make up the consciousness of the part affected: as on cutting one's finger.

Presentative-representative cognitions ; or those in which consciousness is occupied with the relation between a sensation or group of sensations and the representations of those various other sensations that accompany it in experience. This is what we commonly call perception—an act in which, along with certain impressions presented to consciousness, there arise in consciousness the ideas of certain other impressions ordinarily connected with the presented ones: as when its visible form and colour, lead us to mentally endow an orange with all its other attributes.

Representative cognitions ; or those in which consciousness is occupied with the relations among ideas or represented sensations; as in all acts of recollection.

Re-representative cognitions ; or those in which the occupation of consciousness is not by representations of special relations, that have before been presented to consciousness; but those in which such represented special relations are thought of merely as comprehended in a general relation. Here the concrete relations once experienced are, in so far as they become objects of consciousness at all, only incidentally represented, along with the abstract relation which formulates them. The ideas resulting from this abstraction, do not themselves represent actual experiences; but are symbols which stand for groups of such actual experiences— represent aggregates of representations. And thus they may be called re-representative cognitions. It is clear that the process of re-representation is carried to higher stages, as the thought becomes more abstract.

Passing now to the second great class, which we distinguish as FEELINGS, we find that these are divisible into four parallel sub-classes.

Presentative feelings, ordinarily called sensations, are those mental states in which, instead of regarding a corporeal impression as of this or that kind, or as located here or there, we contemplate it in itself as pleasure or pain: as when inhaling a perfume.

Presentative-representative feelings, embracing a great part of what we commonly call emotions, are those in which a sensation, or group of sensations, or group of sensations and ideas, arouses a vast aggregation of represented sensations; partly of individual experience, but chiefly deeper than individual experience, and, consequently, indefinite. The emotion of terror may serve as an example. Along with certain impressions made on the eyes or ears, or both, are recalled into consciousness many of the pains to which such impressions have before been the antecedents; and when the relation between such impressions and such pains has been habitual in the race, the definite ideas of the pains which individual experience has given, are accompanied by the indefinite pains that result from inherited experience—vague feelings which we may call organic representations.

Representative feelings, comprehending the ideas of the feelings above classed, when they are called up apart from the appropriate external excitements. The feelings so represented may either be simple ones of the kinds first named, as tastes, colours, sounds, &c.; or they may be involved ones of the kinds last named. Instances of these are the feelings with which the descriptive poet writes, and which are aroused in the minds of his readers.

Re-representative feelings, under which head are included those more complex sentient states that are less the direct results of external excitements than the indirect or reflex results of them. The love of property is a feeling of this kind. It is awakened not by the presence of any special object, but by ownable objects at large; and it is not from the mere presence of such objects, but from a certain ideal relation to them, that it arises. It consists, not of the represented advantages of possessing this or that, but of the represented advantages of possession in general—is not made up of certain concrete representations, but of the abstracts of many concrete representations; and so is re-representative. The higher sentiments, as that of justice, are still more completely of this nature. Here the sentient state is compounded out of sentient states that are themselves wholly, or almost wholly, re-representative.

Critical examination of these groups proves them to be but indefinitely distinguishable. That impossibility of sharp separation which even the two primary groups present, is presented still more obviously by the secondary groups; and becomes more conspicuous as we ascend to the highest of these. If we set out with the simplest sensation or presentative feeling, we cannot free it from representative accompaniments: these are involved both in the identification of it as such or such, and in the localization of it in Time and Space. On passing to Perception proper, we meet countless gradations in which the quantity of represented elements bears an increasing ratio to the quantity of presented elements. When, having dropped all presented elements, we enter the region of purely-representative cognitions, we rise by degrees to greater heights of re-representation. Similarly with the Feelings. The quantity of representative feeling which accompanies a simple presentative feeling is indefinitely variable—witness the contrast between the touch of a stone and the odour of hay, one of which recalls other feelings in but inappreciable amounts, and the other of which may produce a decided wave of pleasurable emotion. And in the region of feelings that contain no presentative element, there is a gradual passage to those in which the representativeness reaches its extreme.

But while fully recognizing the fact that consciousness is

an entangled *plexus* which cannot be cut into parts without more or less arbitrariness; and while fully recognizing the consequent fact that the classification here outlined is open to criticisms like those above passed on classifications otherwise framed; it is to be observed that the classification according to degree of representativeness, applicable alike to Cognitions and Feelings, is especially adapted to our present purpose. Note the several reasons.

§ 481. In the first place, it answers as a measure of Evolution, considered under its widest aspects.

Degree of representativeness implies proportionate degree of *integration*. The number of represented states connected in thought with a certain presented state, increases with the development of perception. According to the number of perceptions integrated into a generalization, is the validity of that generalization, other things equal. According to the number of small generalizations (which are severally representative) that are integrated into a wide generalization (which is re-representative) is the increase in the breadth of thought. Throughout, therefore, the degree of representativeness is a measure of the degree of unification of knowledge.

Again, representativeness and *definiteness* vary, other things equal, in the same ratio; for all indefiniteness of thought is failure of representation. If a child confounds its p's and its q's, or if a sign-painter, as sometimes happens, puts the thick stroke of the M or the W where the thin stroke should be, the implication is that the mental representation of a form previously presented, is but vague. While an artist who sketches a portrait from memory, proves that he represents to himself the face very vividly. Similarly, on analyzing errors in calculation or in reasoning, we find they arise from failures of representation: the relations among the states of consciousness were not seen because the consciousness was indefinite.

Representativeness is also a measure of *complexity*. Observe some of the gradations. Here is a stupid dog which knows its master only my smelling at him. Here is an intelligent dog which so remembers how its master's many visible attributes are combined, as to distinguish him by sight from other persons. Here is a physician who, beyond this identification, recognizes the marks of a disease; and not only sees in thought his patient's viscera, but also where and what the lesion is. On comparing these cases it will be clear that the increasing representativeness of the consciousness goes along with its increasing complexity. Moreover, representativeness measures not only the complexity shown by involution of kindred elements, as in the mathematician who from truths respecting special curves passes to truths holding of groups of curves, and then to others holding of groups of such groups; but it also measures that complexity which the increasing *heterogeneity* of the elements implies. Witness the advance from a rustic's conception of the Earth to that which a travelled geologist has reached.

That the like holds of the Feelings—that in them, too, increasing integration, increasing definiteness, and increasing heterogeneity of composition are alike measured by the extent to which representation and re-representation have been carried, will be manifest on reconsidering the above definitions.

§ 482. When, after observing how degree of representativeness measures degree of evolution as defined under its most general form, we observe how it measures degree of mental evolution, as effected in the ways we have traced, we see more clearly still its fitness as a general standard.

It is quite evident that the growth of perception involves representation of sensations; that the growth of simple reasoning involves representation of perceptions; and that the growth of complex reasoning involves representa-

tion of the results of simple reasoning. So that the remoteness from sensation necessarily increases with the
intellectual elevation. And if the genesis of the emotions
has gone on after the manner described in this work, then,
obviously, the steps have been from simple sensations to
sensations combined with represented sensations, then to
represented sensations organized into groups, then to
representations of these representative groups: each higher
degree of representation being made possible only by a
previous lower degree.

Let us look at the matter in the concrete—let us compare
the mental activities of the child, the savage, and the civilized man in his various grades of culture. An infant
gazing, grasping all it can, and putting to its mouth whatever it lays hold of, shows us a consciousness in which presented feelings greatly predominate. An urchin, pulling to
pieces his toys, building card-houses, whipping his top,
gathering flowers and pebbles and shells, passes an intellectual life that is mainly perceptive—presented feelings are
here being associated with represented feelings, forming
knowledge of the properties and actions of things around;
and what goes on of higher representation, as in that dramatizing to which dolls and sets of miniature tea-things
minister, is limited to actions observed in the household.
In the boy and in the savage there is greater excursiveness
of representation; but still, representation that passes not
much beyond those wider concrete experiences which larger
spheres of activity have disclosed. Adventures, triumphs of
strength and skill—these furnish subject-matter for the
talk of the uncivilized man and the air-castles of the youth:
representations are practically limited to the transactions of
individuals. Only as maturity is approached do we find in
a few of the civilized such higher degree of representation,
here passing into re-representation, as that which groups
particular modes of human action under general truths.
When, rising to intellectual activity of high type, we take

for example a statesman, we find that he is habitually absorbed in highly-representative thought. What answer to give a despatch implies the imagination of numerous interests and influences; in the drawing up of a measure, representations of the balance of parties, of popular opinion, of press-criticism, affect the decision; and a speech justifying the measure, specifies evils and benefits and difficulties, each of which is a re-representation of many grouped results of involved observations.

Throughout the other half of the nature we may trace kindred contrasts. With sensational pleasures and pains there go, in the infant, little else but vague feelings of delight and anger and fear—emotions rising but little above direct representations of bodily sensations, and which we see exhibited by inferior types of creatures. More complex emotions, as love of applause and love of property, become active in childhood: these are of the re-representative order. Afterwards we begin to see those higher emotions into which sympathy enters: regard for the welfare of others, usually shown but little in early life, is more frequently manifested. In some such stage as this the lowest type of man remains permanently. Re-representative emotions rarely in him rise beyond a quite rudimentary sentiment of justice. But in the civilized man, or at any rate in the superior form of civilized man, a desire for the public good, sometimes impelling too much personal sacrifice, becomes a frequent trait. Here the highly-re-representative thoughts are productive of highly-re-representative emotions. Disregarding those simple surrounding things which almost exclusively interest the vulgar, the minds that are most developed emotionally, like those that are most developed intellectually, are filled with imaginations in which the degree of re-representation reaches its extreme.

§ 483. Throughout the succeeding chapters, then, in which we have to draw from general principles the special corollaries concerning human nature as socially evolved, degree of representativeness will be our standard of degree of evolution.

In the next chapter, we will thus measure the leading traits of intellectual development, as it affects, and is affected by, civilization. In the subsequent chapters we will similarly deal with the accompanying emotional development.

CHAPTER III.

§ 484. During early stages of human progress, the circumstances under which wandering families and small aggregations of families live, furnish experiences comparatively limited in their numbers and kinds; and consequently there can be no considerable exercise of faculties which take cognizance of the *general truths* displayed throughout many special truths.

Suppose perpetual repetition of the same experience; then the power of representation is limited to reproduction of this experience in idea. Given two often-repeated different experiences, and it thereupon becomes possible to discern in the representations of them what they have in common: to do which, however, implies that the representative faculty can hold the two representations before consciousness; and the ability to do this can arise only after multitudinous recurrences. In like manner it is clear that only after there have been received many experiences which differ in their kinds but present some relation in common, can the first step be taken towards the conception of a truth higher in generality than these different experiences themselves.

I say advisedly the first step, because no single series of such comparisons yields the consciousness of a truth one degree more general. It requires that there shall be other sets of different special experiences, throughout which other constant relations are discerned, before such a conception becomes possible; since such a conception cannot else be dissociated from a particular set of different experiences, and regarded as a truth belonging to a class of truths several-ly presented in other sets.

Each increment of this advance implies a great increase in power of representation. Clearly, too, the habit of repre-senting truths low in their degree of generality, must be long continued, and the correlative nervous structures well de-veloped, before many general truths of this order can be so represented as to make discernible what still more general truth is common to them; since this implies a representa-tion of representations.

It follows, therefore, that in the course of human progress general ideas can arise only as fast as social conditions render experiences more multitudinous and varied; while at the same time it is to be observed that these social conditions themselves pre-suppose some general ideas. Each step towards more general ideas is instrumental in bringing about better and wider social co-operations: so rendering the ex-periences still more numerous and varied, more complex, and derived from a wider area. And then, when the cor-relative experiences have become organized, there arises the possibility of ideas yet higher in generality, and a further social evolution.

§ 485. Small power of representation implies inability to recognize processess that are slow in completing themselves: *long sequences* are unperceived.

The lowest men, identifying intervals only by the migra-tions of animals and the flowerings of plants, and unable even to count high enough to number time by moons any considerable distance back, have no means of reckoning sequences longer than those of the seasons. Nor, indeed, do the lives they lead furnish any motives for reckoning them. Only by becoming settled—only by aggregating into communities capable of accumulating traditional experiences, and presently of keeping records, can men gain opportunities of establishing the connexions between antecedents and consequents widely separated in time: be they those which occur in surrounding nature, in individual life, or in social affairs.

Here, then, as before, the increasing representativeness of thought implied in mentally grasping natural processes that complete themselves in long periods, can arise only by degrees as civilization advances—the growing faculty and the favouring conditions perpetually acting and reacting. Until after a considerable gathering-up of deliberate observations there can be no conception of the astronomical year as a definite, regularly-recurring period. Until after enumeration has become easy, and the social state such that registers of some kind are preserved, there can be reached no definite conceptions of intervals including many years—even the duration of a human life not being previously knowable.

How the lengths of sequences foreseen are dependent on the lengths of recorded sequences; how both are dependent on long continuance of favourable social conditions, making possible both the records and the faculties that can grasp the phenomena recorded; we see best in Science, and more especially in Astronomy. And what holds in this holds in principle throughout.

Hence it inevitably happens that the primitive man has but little *foresight;* and shows no tendency to provide for remote contingencies. Until a developing society has facilitated such registration of events as makes remote contingencies recognizable; until the society has become so settled that measures taken to meet remote contingencies are not thwarted; there cannot be cultivated the power of conceiving remote results with the vividness required to prompt measures for meeting them. That representativeness of thought which makes possible the bringing-together a present cause with an effect far distant in time, can be only little by little increased, along with the increasing facilities given by a settled society of joining such cause and effect in experience. Only little by little, therefore, can anticipations of the future come to have effects in checking the immediate impulses.

§ 486. Experiences made ever more numerous, more varied, more heterogeneous, more involved, as by degrees civilization supplies them and develops the faculties for appreciating them, tend ever to widen the possibilities of thought and diminish the rigidity of belief: *modifiability of belief* increases.

As said in § 253, " mental evolution, both intellectual and emotional, may be measured by the degree of remoteness from primitive reflex action." In reflex action, which is the action of nervous structures that effect few, simple, and often-repeated co-ordinations, the sequent nervous state follows irresistibly the antecedent nervous state; and does this not only for the reason that the discharge follows a perfectly-permeable channel, but also for the reason that no alternative channel exists. From this stage, in which the psychical life is automatically restrained within the narrowest limits, up through higher stages in which increasing nervous complexities give increasing varieties of actions and possibilities of new combinations, the process continues the same; and it continues the same as we advance from the savage to the civilized man. For where the life furnishes relatively few and little-varied experiences—where the restricted sphere in which it is passed yields no sign of the multitudinous combinations of phenomena that occur elsewhere; the thought follows irresistibly one or other of the few channels which the experiences have made for it—cannot be determined in some other direction for want of some other channel. But as fast as advancing civilization brings more numerous experiences to each man, as well as accumulations of other men's experiences, past and present, the ever-multiplying connexions of ideas that result imply ever-multiplying possibilities of thought. The convictions throughout a wide range of cases are rendered less fixed. Other causes than those which are usual become conceivable; other effects can be imagined; and hence there comes an increasing modifiability of opinion. This modifiability of opinion reaches its extreme in those most highly-cultured whose multitudinous experiences include many experiences of errors discovered; and whose representativeness of thought is so far reaching that they habitually call to mind the various possibilities of error, as constituting a general reason for seeking new evidence and subjecting their conclusions to revision.

If we glance over the series of contrasted modes of thinking which civilization presents, beginning with the savage who, seized by the fancy that something is a charm or an omen, thereafter continues firmly fixed in that belief, and ending with the man of science whose convictions, firm where he is conscious of long-accumulated evidence having no exception, are plastic where the evidence though abundant is not yet overwhelming; we see how an increase in freedom of thought goes along with that higher representativeness accompanying further mental evolution.

§ 487. Along with the relative simplicity, relative poverty, and relative rigidity, which characterize thought in its less-developed phases, there goes a relative limitation to concrete conceptions: *abstract conceptions* are impossible.

On reconsidering what has been said respecting the necessary order of the ascending steps, from few and small groups of experiences to the groups of such groups in which are discerned truths of wide generality, and so on to larger groups; it will be seen that where the experiences are simple and little varied, the terms of thought must be

specific things and actions. Only as fast as general facts
presented in common by many special facts, come to be
recognized, can there arise conceptions having proportionate
abstractness—conceptions having the peculiarity that the
matter of thought is no longer any one object, or any one
action, but a trait common to many. With some object or
action remembered as exemplifying an attribute or relation,
there is joined the consciousness of a heterogeneous assemblage throughout which it also occurs: the result being
that this attribute or relation tends to be dissociated in
consciousness from each member of the assemblage. Such
conceptions of one degree of abstractness having become
familiar, there arises the possibility of re-abstraction—the
possibility of recognizing more-abstract truths common to
many of these less-abstract truths. Each further step of
this kind, which, as we see, implies a higher degree of
representation and re-representation, is a further emancipa-
tion from the primordial concreteness of consciousness.
The terms of thought are no longer particular things and
particular acts performed by them; but there are more and
more distinctly conceived the general characters of things
and classes of things, considered apart from the things
themselves; and there are more and more distinctly conceived the general forces displayed, considered apart from
the particular actions.

After a certain stage in this progress there become possible the conceptions of a *property* and of a *cause*, which at
first are impossible. Until many special properties have
been abstracted from groups of things displaying them, no
such thing as the conception of a property in general, considered apart from special properties, can be reached; and
only after many special causes have been separated in
thought from the classes of actions exemplifying them, can
there be formed any notion of cause in general.

It will be manifest, therefore, that primitive thinking,
which for each concrete consequent assigns a concrete

antecedent (if it assigns any) does this not by choice but by necessity. There must be accumulation of experiences more numerous, more varied, more heterogeneous—there must be a correlative gradual increase of organized faculty and corresponding representativeness of thought, before there can be reached even the lower orders of those conceptions we distinguish as scientific. Similarly, it is manifest that the conceptions we distinguish as religious, necessarily pass through parallel gradations. From the demon, thought of by the savage under a form equally concrete with that of the enemy he fights, up to that most abstract consciousness of Universal Power, to which a scattered few have reached, there is a progress made possible only by that development of faculty which advancing civilization has produced.

§ 488. Experiences such as those received by the primitive man, furnish but few data for the conception of *uniformity;* whether as displayed in things or in relations. The notion of likeness, though to us seeming so simple a notion, is one gradually reached by that process of abstraction which accompanies increasing representativeness of thought; and the daily impressions which the savage gets, yield the elements of the notion very imperfectly and in but few cases.

Of all the objects around—trees, stones, hills, pieces of water, clouds, &c.—most differ widely in size, or shape, or colour, or in all these; and few approach complete likeness so nearly as to make discrimination difficult. Even between animals of the same species the differences are usually discernible enough; and even where the individuals have the greatest degree of likeness, it rarely happens that, whether alive or dead, they are presented in just the same attitudes. Among odours, tastes, colours, and the sounds made by living creatures, there are, indeed, close approximations; but there is rarely indistinguishableness. It is only along with a gradual development of the arts, accompanying ascending stages of civilization, that there come frequent experiences of perfectly straight lines admitting of complete apposition; bringing the perceptions of equality and inequality.

Still more devoid is savage life of the experiences which generate the conception of uniformity of succession. The sequences observed from hour to hour and day to day, seem anything but uniform: difference is a far more conspicuous trait among them. Though by stones thrown and arrows shot, certain uniformities of sequence are presented—though after ascent there is descent, and after motion there is rest; yet in no two cases are the relations of phenomena alike: the heights reached, the curves described, and the times taken, obviously disagree. And since, as above shown, a general relation becomes thinkable apart from the many special relations displaying it, only as the faculty of abstraction develops, it is only as the experiences cultivate this faculty that uniformities of sequence, even of simple kinds, become recognizable as uniformities. To sequences of longer durations and to those having more involved antecedents and consequents, the conception cannot be extended until much later. Save in these few mechanical motions, there is but little regularity among the events experienced. The animals chased do not behave twice in just the same ways. Individuals of the tribe conduct themselves more or less diversely under like conditions; and each is more or less variable. Though each kind of plant yields its fruit in successive years at times not differing greatly, yet in the absence of an astronomical measure of the seasons, such regularity as it displays is not distinctly appreciable. And the astronomical sequences themselves, though exhibiting great regularity to the civilized races who have registered and analyzed the movements of the heavenly bodies, do not exhibit it to the uncivilized: such likenesses of daily motions as are conspicuous, being obscured by unlikenesses. So that if we contemplate primitive human life as a whole, we see that multiformity of sequence rather than uniformity of sequence is the notion which it tends to generate.

When, after glancing at these original circumstances of the race, we turn to the circumstances brought about by civilization, we see that only as fast as the practice of the arts develops the idea of *measure*, can the consciousness of uniformity become clear. For only after the use of instruments for measuring lengths had made familiar the abstract ideas of equality and inequality; and only after the use of rude appliances for measuring intervals of time had given distinct ideas of equal and unequal durations; and only after the use of the balance had made definite the consciousness of equal and unequal weights; did there come into existence the materials for that conception of uniformity of actions and sequences which now seems to us so natural.

And if particular uniformities and classes of uniformities can be disentangled only as, along with progressing civilization and progressing arts, there come multiplying generalizations and abstractions, with developing faculties for grasping them; then the conception of uniformity in general, which is an abstraction from many particular uniformities, remains for a long time an impossible one.

Thus the belief in an unchanging order—the belief in *law*, now spreading among the more cultivated throughout the civilized world, is a belief of which the primitive man is absolutely incapable. Not simply does he lack the experiences that give materials for the conception, but he lacks the power of framing the conception: he is unable to think even of a single law, much less of law in general. The needful representativeness of thought is to be acquired only by the inheritance of accumulated increments of faculty successively organized; and it is even now possessed in a high degree only by a very small minority.

§ 489. Progress in *definiteness* of thought is one of the concomitants of that progressing representativeness which makes possible increasing generality, increasing abstractness, and the resulting conceptions of constant relations of coexistence and sequence.

Those conditions furnished by advancing civilization which make possible the notion of uniformity, simultaneously make possible the notion of *exactness*. Until measures of Space, Time, and Force, come to be used, there is nothing to cultivate a consciousness of definite agreement. Likenesses as perceived by the primitive man, scarcely ever reaching to the perfect equality which the arts enable us to produce, the ideas of exactness and inexactness do not get clearly contrasted. This which holds among compared attributes, holds still more among compared relations. In the absence of appliances for measuring Time and Force, nothing like specific connexions can be established among causes and effects. The only specific connexions observable are those among the attributes of each species of animal; and even these present variations which conflict with the conception of preciseness.

Hence the primitive man has little experience which cultivates the consciousness of what we call *truth*. How closely allied this is to the consciousness which the practice of the arts cultivates, is implied even in language. We speak of a true surface as well as of a true statement. Exactness describes perfection in a mechanical fit, as well as perfect agreement between the results of calculations. Straight, and direct, and upright, are words applicable to business and conduct as well as to sensible objects; and crooked designates the policy that deceives, no less than an irregular line. The general notions of agreement and disagreement, apply equally to two lines compared in their lengths and to two accounts of an event; and hence, in the absence of experiences that yield this general notion, accuracy of thought and precision of statement are not possible. There can exist neither the habit of expressing things definitely, nor the habit of testing assertions, nor a due sense of the contrast between fact and fiction.

§ 490. Credulity is an inevitable concomitant of this primitive mental state: *scepticism* and *criticism* cannot become habitual. While there are no clear general conceptions and no clear abstract conceptions, and while the ideas of uniformity, of law, of cause, of truth, are but rudimentary, none but vague notions of probability and improbability exist. Such notions can be evolved only *pari passu* with the evolution of the notions we have just considered.

For, until multiplied experiences have made familiar certain generalities of relation, there can be nothing in thought with which any anomalous relation alleged can conflict. Only as fast as conceptions of uniformity and law are acquired, can there come to be contrasted conceptions of things at variance with uniformity and law. Until the consciousness of cause gains distinctness, there can be no distinct antithesis in thought between events that have known causes and events that have not known causes—that which is natural and that which is afterwards regarded as supernatural, are believed with equal readiness.

Criticism then, even of that spontaneous kind which distinguishes the obviously-true from the obviously-untrue, becomes habitual only as fast as the intellectual powers in general develop; while, conversely, the development of the intellectual powers implies the aid of criticism. And if the habit of spontaneous criticism can be established only as the representativeness of thought increases, still later must it be before there is reached the attitude of conscious and deliberate criticism; since this involves re-represented experiences not only of uniformity, law, cause, &c., but also of many errors that have been made and of the methodical examinations required to disclose them.

§ 491. That in the lower stages of mental evolution *imagination* is feeble, and that it strengthens with each increment of intellectual progress, has been already said in saying that each increment of intellectual progress implies an increase in representativeness of thought. Here, however, this truth must be stated in more familiar terms, because there is a current notion that the less-advanced races and societies are imaginative in a greater degree than the more-advanced. One of those confusions of thought which itself illustrates deficient power of representation, is shown in the belief that superstition implies active imagination, and that the decline of superstition results when the flights of imagination become restrained.

This confusion of thought has been fostered by the habitual antithesis of prose and poetry, fact and fiction. Most of the literature which has much currency, being made up of statements known to be not actually true; and this literature, presenting fictitious personages, adventures, &c., being thus distinguished as avowedly imaginative; there has arisen an association between the idea of imagination and the idea unreality: the implication being that the imagination is powerful where the unreality is great; and consequently that people evolving and believing conceptions the most remote from truth, are thereby shown to be the most imaginative people. After what has been said above, however, it will be manifest that the mental evolution which accompanies civilization, makes imagination more vivid, more exact, more comprehensive, and more excursive. As already shown, that habit of thinking in terms of concrete objects and acts which primitive superstitions show us, is a necessary accompaniment of low mental development; and as we have just seen, the credulity implied by such superstitions can decrease only as fast as the experiences are organized into conceptions more numerous, more general, more abstract, more accurate—conceptions in which the quantity of things imaged, or imagined, is greater, and the representation of them relatively clear.

Acceptance of a proposition at variance with conspicuous fact, implies either so faint a mental image of the asserted

relation or so faint a mental image of the known relation
with which it is at variance, that the incongruity is not perceived. If, for instance, a cabman, after the habit of his
class, instead of driving along two long main streets at right
angles to one another, drives along a rectangular zig-zag
having the general direction of a diagonal; his erroneous
belief that this is the shorter route, implies that he so feebly
imagines the space-relations as not to see that the sum of
one set of short lines in the zig-zag must be equal to one of
the long lines, while the sum of the other set of short lines
in the zig-zag must be equal to the other of the long lines.
His delusion is not the result of imagination but of want of
imagination. And so throughout. By a superstitious mind
the marvellous things listened to are so vaguely imagined,
that the contradictions involved are not perceived; but just
in proportion as the objects and acts are imagined clearly in
all their characters, qualitative and quantitative, it becomes
difficult to believe as occurring, that which is contrary to
experience—the superstition is rejected.

§ 492. One further trait of developing intellectual power
seems worth adding. In continuation of the foregoing section let me point out a distinction of considerable moment
—that existing between *reminiscent imagination* and *constructive imagination*.

Recurring to the doctrine that degree of intellectual
evolution may be measured by degree of remoteness from
reflex action; and remembering how in reflex action the
combinations of psychical states are limited to repetitions of
those which the organized connexions permit; it will be seen
that in primitive men, imagination can rarely go beyond
reminiscence, and then to but a small extent. When the
only channels of thought are those established by experiences comparatively simple and of few kinds, the representations can be little more than repetitions of the pre-
sentations in their original order. But as fast as the

experiences increase in number, complexity, and variety; and as fast as there develop the faculties for grasping the representations of them in all their width, and multiplicity, and diversity; so fast does thought become less restricted to the established channels. When consciousness is habitually occupied with greatly-involved aggregates of ideas which cohere with other such aggregates in ways that are very various and not very strong, there arises a possibility of combining them in ways not given experience. Gaining greater freedom as it reaches the advanced stages of complexity and multiformity, thought acquires an excursiveness such that with the aid of slight suggestions—slight impulses from accidental circumstances—its highly-composite states enter into combinations never before formed; and so there result conceptions which we call *original*.

During the earlier stages of human evolution, then, ibagination, being almost-exclusively reminiscent, is almost incapable of evolving new ideas. In that sphere which answers to literature, its activity is limited to the narrating of past events; and generation after generation passes without a discovery or an invention. Along with advance in civilization, original thoughts occur with increasing frequency. Literature and art are no longer wholly reminiscent; knowledge ceasing to consist entirely of statements received from ancestors, grows by the addition of new truths reached through original imaginations; and industry, from appliances once transmitted unchanged age after age, advances to appliances that are with ever-growing abundance framed in correspondence with conceptions that never before existed.

From reminiscent imagination, then, which is an earlier and less-developed faculty, we pass in the most civilized to constructive imagination—or rather, in a scattered few of the most civilized. This, which is the highest intellectual faculty, underlies every high order of intellectual achievement. And here, indeed, we may see how erroneous is another of the current notions about imagination. Instead of constructive imagination being, as commonly supposed, an endowment peculiar to the poet and the writer of fiction, it is questionable whether the man of science, truly so called, does not possess even more of it. The greater part of that imagination displayed in describing scenes and narrating adventures, whether in verse or prose, is reminiscent imagination—unusually vivid, perhaps, and distinguished by its emotional accompaniment; but still having little more of the constructive character than is implied in kaleidoscopic re-arrangements of objects and actions. Only on rising into that range where, beyond the mere outsides of things and persons and deeds, there are represented the peculiarities of character and combinations of ever-varying feelings whence the manifestations come, is the imagination exercised constructive in a high degree. And the constructiveness of this imagination, though widely different in kind, is probably not greater in degree than that through which the cardinal truths of science are discovered—the representations and re-representations involved in the discovery of these, being still more remote from sensible experiences.

§ 493. Intellectual evolution, as it goes on in the human race along with social evolution, of which it is at once a cause and a consequence, is thus, under all its aspects, a progress in representativeness of thought. By consisting of representations that are more extended, more definite, more varied, more involved, the conceptions of developed intelligence are distinguished from those of undeveloped intelligence. And it is because they have this as their common character, that there exists among them throughout all their ascending stages, the *consensus* we have traced.

Only as social progress brings more numerous and more heterogeneous experiences, can general ideas be evolved out of special ideas, and the faculty of thinking them acquired. Constant relations of phenomena in time, observable by the savage only in sequences that are quick, cannot be established in respect of slow sequences until society has become settled: until then there cannot be exercised that representativeness of thought required to grasp long periods and the connexions of phenomena presented in them. Widening experiences, producing more abundant and more varied associations of ideas, diminish the rigidity of belief by multiplying the possibilities of thought; and this increasing plasticity of thought that accompanies increasing representativeness, continues throughout civilization to make beliefs more modifiable—so furthering other changes, mental and social. Advance in representativeness of thought makes possible advance in abstractness: particular properties and particular relations become thinkable apart from the things displaying them; afterwards the conceptions of property in general and relation in general become thinkable; and as the conceptions of property in general and relation in general become clear, there results the power of thinking of phenomena after the scientific manner, as products of forces acting under conditions. Hand in hand with abstractness of thought goes recognition of uniformities—these being recognizable only when essential relations are abstracted from their non-essential accompaniments; and as fast as recognized uniformities multiply, the conception of uniformity itself, leading to the conception of universal law, becomes possible. The habit of disentangling likenesses of connexion from among disguising phenomena, brings an appreciation of exact agreement—the notions of uniformity and of conformity act and react; and so there develops the idea of truth along with the idea of correspondence. Until fact, considered as coincidence between a relation stated and a relation found to exist, has become clearly distinguished from fiction, in which coincidence has been either disproved or not shown; and until there has arisen the implied practice of making comparisons to test alleged coincidence; there can be no established habit of doubting: criticism and scepticism cannot exist in any clear forms until the abstract ideas of accuracy and truth have been reached; so that credulity can diminish only as intellectual development reaches considerable heights. This progress in representativeness of thought, which brings with it conceptions more general and more abstract, which opens the way to conceptions of uniformity and law, which simultaneously raises up ideas of exact and ascertained fact, which so makes possible the practice of deliberate examination and verification, and which at the same time helps to change belief that is sudden and fixed into belief less quickly formed and more modifiable; is a development of what we commonly call imagination. While throughout the lower grades of human intelligence, the concrete objects and acts within a narrow range of experience are reproduced in thought, and the imagination is thus almost exclusively reminiscent, that development of the conceptions which we have traced, implying a continually-wider excursiveness of thoughts more numerous, more heterogeneous, more involved, and bound together more variously and less coherently, makes possible new combinations of thoughts: imagination rises into the constructive form, and there is an increasing originality which tells at once on the industrial arts, on science, and on literature.

This *consensus* throughout the development of the conceptions, is, indeed, an organic *consensus*. There is among them an inter-dependence analogous to that existing among the functions of the viscera; no one of which can be efficiently performed without the rest being efficiently performed. How necessary is this *consensus*, we may, indeed, see in the less-cultivated of our own society; and especially in women of the inferior ranks. The united traits distinguishing them are—that they quickly form very positive beliefs which are difficult to change; that their thoughts are full of special, and mainly personal, experiences, with but few general truths, and no truths of high generality; that any abstract conception expressed to them they can never detach from a concrete case; that they are inexact alike in processes and statements, and are even averse to precision; that they go on doing things in the ways they were taught, never imagining better methods, however obvious; that such a thing as the framing of an hypothesis, and reasoning upon it as an hypothesis, is incomprehensible to them; and that thus it is impossible for them deliberately to suspend judgment, and to balance evidence. Thus the intellectual traits which in the primitive man are the results not of limited experiences only but of correspondingly-undeveloped faculties, may be traced among ourselves in those cases where the life, relatively meagre in its experiences, has not cultivated these faculties up to the capacity of the type.

CHAPTER IV.

LANGUAGE OF THE EMOTIONS.

§ 494. Before sketching the emotional development which, like the intellectual development sketched in the last chapter, accompanies social evolution, we must consider the ways in which human beings influence one another. Beyond those effects on one another's intellects which signs and words consciously used enable them to produce, there are the effects, much deeper in origin, much more powerful, and in a sense more important, which they unconsciously produce on one another's feelings by the physical manifestations that accompany feelings. The first class of effects, wrought through language properly so called, does not here concern us; but the second class of effects, wrought through what is metaphorically called the language of the emotions, must be briefly explained.

Already among the Data of Psychology, in chapters on "Nervous Stimulation and Nervous Discharge" and on "Æstho-Physiology," the foundations were laid for the needful interpretations. The principles there expressed generally have here to be applied specially.*

* The conception set forth in this chapter goes back, however, to a much earlier date than the first part of this work. It is indirectly implied in an Essay on "Personal Beauty," first published in 1853; and also in one on "Gracefulness" in the same year. It is clearly indicated in § 200 of the First Edition of this work, published in 1855. In Essays on the "Origin

§ 495. Every feeling, peripheral or central—sensational or emotional—is the concomitant of a nervous disturbance and resulting nervous discharge, that has on the body both a special effect and a general effect.

As before explained, the general effect is this. The molecular motion disengaged in any nerve-centre by any stimulus, tends ever to flow along lines of least resistance throughout the nervous system, exciting other nerve-centres, and setting up other discharges. The feelings of all orders, moderate as well as strong, which from instant to instant arise in consciousness, are the correlatives of nerve-waves continually being generated and continually reverberating throughout the nervous system—the perpetual nervous discharge constituted by these perpetually-generated waves, affecting both the viscera and the muscles, voluntary and involuntary.

At the same time, every particular kind of feeling, sensational or emotional, being located in a specialized nervous structure that has relations to special parts of the body, tends to produce on the body an effect that is special. The speciality may be very simple and constant, as in a sneeze; or it may be much involved and variable within wide limits, as in the actions showing anger. But all qualifications being made, it is undeniable that there is a certain specialization of the discharge, giving some distinctiveness to the bodily changes by which each feeling is accompanied.

Hence, in studying emotional language, we have to recognize two classes of effects—those of the *diffused* discharge, and those of the *restricted* discharge. And further, this last has to be distinguished into the *undirected* and the *directed*—that which takes place without motive, and

and Function of Music," and on the "Physiology of Laughter," published in 1857 and in 1860 respectively, special applications of it are worked out. Here, in returning to the conception, I have developed it into a more systematic form, and given it sundry extensions.

that which is shown in the muscular actions guided by motive.

§ 496. The diffused discharge accompanying feeling of every kind, produces on the body an effect that is indicative of feeling simply, irrespective of kind—the effect, namely, of muscular excitement.   From the shrinking caused in a sleeping person by a touch, up to the contortions of agony and the caperings of delight, there is a recognized relation between the quantity of feeling, pleasurable or painful, and the amount of motion generated.   Neglecting for the present their differences, we see that, because of the diffused nervous discharge they all involve, the feelings have in common the character that they cause bodily action which is violent in proportion as they are intense.   We have the set teeth, distorted features, and clenched hands accompanying bodily pain, as well as those accompanying rage.   There is a tearing of the hair from fury as well as from despair. There are the dancings of joy, as well as the stampings of anger.   There is the restlessness of moral distress, and there is the inability to sit still which ecstasy produces.   How essential is this general relation, we see on remembering that it is displayed throughout the whole animal kingdom. By the violence of its motions in struggling or running, we judge that an animal is under strong feeling of some kind; be it bodily suffering, or anger, or terror, or be it, as where the motions are superfluous bounds and scourings around, a pleasurable feeling.

Among the muscles habitually excited by the diffused discharge, are those of the vocal organs—both the respiratory muscles and the muscles which strain the larynx, &c.   Hence the fact that feeling in general, irrespective of its kind, is usually indicated by sounds that are loud in proportion as it is strong.   The screams which accompany bodily suffering are indistinguishable from those which accompany suffering of mind; and there are screams of passion, as well as screams of delight. Anger shouts, as well as joy; and often the noises made by children at play, leave parents in doubt whether pleasure or pain is the cause. In conformity with this same law it results that the sounds which go along with feeling, differ from the ordinary sounds not only in loudness but in pitch—departing from the medium tones more widely in proportion as the feeling increases. Here, too, it is to be observed that the relationship is displayed among animals. The sounds they make are always signs of feeling, pleasurable or painful, and similarly vary in intensity and pitch with the feeling.

§ 497. While the most conspicuous trait of the diffused discharge accompanying feeling of any kind, is that it produces contraction proportionate in amount to the feeling, a less conspicuous trait is that, other things equal, it affects muscles in the inverse order of their sizes and the weights of the parts to which they are attached; and by so doing yields an additional indication of its quantity. Supposing a feeble wave of nervous excitement to be propagated uniformly throughout the nervous system, the part of it discharged on the muscles will show its effects most where the amount of inertia to be overcome is least. Muscles which are large, and which can show states of contraction into which they are thrown only by moving limbs or other heavy masses, will yield no signs; while small muscles, and those which can move without overcoming great resistances, will visibly respond to this feeble wave. Hence must result a certain general order in the excitation of muscles, serving to mark the strength of the nervous discharge and of the feeling accompanying it.

Let us first observe how the animals with which we are most familiar illustrate this truth. In a dog standing still, the muscles that move the tail from side to side are among those which can produce perceptible motion with the least resistance overcome; and hence a slight lateral motion of the tail is the most visible indication of a slight pleasurable feeling. In the cat, too, the relative mobility of the tail enables it to yield early indications of rising feeling—the more or less marked elevation of it being a sign of pleasure, and the lashing from side to side a sign of anger. In the horse we see that the putting-back of the ears, which are among the most-easily-movable parts, is an early mark of irritation: presently, perhaps, to be followed by a kick. Similarly with the motions of the tail in a small bird, and in the raising of its crest by a parrot.

In man this general law is more variously illustrated. Primarily, it is because the muscles of the face are relatively small, and are attached to easily-moved parts, that the face is so good an index of the amount of feeling—its indications being made unusually legible by the partial or complete absence of hair. Observe the facts. Apart from qualitative differences in the contractions of facial muscles, we infer from quantitative differences, differences in amounts of feeling. A face perfectly quiescent we regard as signifying absence of feeling; supposing we have no reason to suspect the concealment arising from intentional arrest of the natural motions. A very slight contraction of those muscles which wrinkle the outer angles of the eyes, joined perhaps with a just-perceptible motion of the muscles which elongate the mouth, implies a faint wave of pleasurable feeling, due, it may be, to a passing thought. Let the gratification augment, and the smile becomes conspicuous; and if it continues to increase the mouth opens, the muscles of the larynx and vocal chords contract, and the relatively-large muscles controlling respiration being brought into play, there results a laugh. If the excitement grows greater yet, there is still to be traced in the effects of the rising nervous discharge, the same general order: the motions of the head and those of the hands, which are easily made, come before those of the legs and trunk, which require more force to produce them. So that the amount of pleasurable feeling, irrespective of its kind, comes to be indicated not only by the quantity of muscular contraction, but also by its distribution.   It is so, too, with painful feeling. Passing over for the present unlikeness in the combinations of contractions, which as we shall see has another cause, the marks of pain which the face yields show us parallel gradations. A slight knitting of the brows is recognized as a sign of annoyance. Strengthening into a frown, it is understood to show positive vexation. Joined presently with contortions of the mouth, and perhaps those actions of the temporal muscles which cause setting of the teeth, it implies anger. And then, though the vocal and respiratory muscles are acted on in a way different from that in which they are acted on by pleasurable feeling, yet the law is the same; for they betray stronger excitements, by the motions of larger masses. When at length fury is reached, the effects produced upon the limbs and body in general, maintain the parallelism. With other forms of painful feeling it is substantially the same. Be it in the rise from a twinge up to acute bodily agony, or be it in the gradations between regret and violent grief, we see that, beginning with the small facial muscles, sensational and emotional sufferings affect progressively more numerous muscles and larger muscles; ending, perhaps, by exciting hysterical or sardonic laughter and violent contortions.

A verification of this general principle is reached on observing that it explains another set of indications, not in the least explicable on the current supposition that those muscles in the face which betray feeling are specially-provided " muscles of expression." I refer to the indications of mental states furnished by actions of hands and feet. Beating the " devil's tattoo " with the fingers on the table, is a recognized mark of impatience; and often a state of pleasurable feeling rising just above equanimity, is betrayed by a motion of the fingers similar in a kind but more gentle. Again, picking and pulling something held in the

hands, such as a glove, often betrays an agitation otherwise not conspicuous. The snapping of the fingers, too,
is an easy muscular action often indicating a flow of good
spirits which for the moment finds no other outlet in action. And again we trace this relation in the motions of the
feet. Swinging the loose foot when the legs are crossed,
sometimes expresses general good humour, and sometimes
impatience—impatience which, rising into vexation, is
shown by a rapid tapping of the toe on the floor. In all
these cases of feeling betrayed by the motions of the extremities, there holds this same common principle, that the
muscles moved with least resistance overcome are the first
to betray rising excitement.

§ 498. From the diffused or unrestricted discharges, let
us pass to the restricted discharges. The special effects
these produce are partly due to the relations established in
the course of evolution between particular feelings and particular sets of muscles habitually brought into play for the
satisfaction of them, and partly due to the kindred relations
between the muscular actions and the conscious motives
existing at the moment.

It is by the restricted discharge consequent on the inherited nervo-muscular connexions, that the natural language of one leading class of feelings is made different from
that of another leading class. For the restricted discharge
which indicates any particular feeling externally, is a discharge partially excited those muscles which that feeling employs during positive action. In § 213 it was
pointed out that the emotional state prompting an action
of any kind, is a partial excitement of the feelings accompanying an action of that kind; and it was argued that
this is shown by the natural language of the feelings.
" Fear, when strong, expresses itself in cries, in efforts to
escape, in palpitations, in tremblings; and these are just
the manifestations that go along with an actual suffering

of the evil feared. The destructive passion is shown in a general tension of the muscular system, in gnashing of teeth and protrusion of the claws, in dilated eyes and nostrils, in growls; and these are weaker forms of the actions that accompany the killing of prey." Here it remains to specify the connexions thus indicated, more fully; and to point out the ways in which the expression of passions in human beings is explained by them.

Throughout the animal kingdom, non-pleasurable feelings are most frequently and most variously excited during antagonism. Among inferior types of creatures antagonism habitually implies combat, with all its struggles and pains. Though in man there are many sources of non-pleasurable feelings other than antagonism, and though antagonism itself ends in combat only when it rises to an extreme, yet as among inferior ancestral types antagonism is the commonest and most conspicuous accompaniment of non-pleasurable feeling, and continues to be very generally an accompaniment in the human race, there is organically established a relation between non-pleasurable feeling and the muscular actions which antagonism habitually causes. Hence those external concomitants of non-pleasurable feeling which constitute what we call its expression, result from incipient muscular contractions of the kinds accompanying actual combat.

But how does this explain the first and most general mark of non-pleasurable feeling—a frown? What have antagonism and combat to do with that corrugation of the brow which, when slight, may indicate a trifling ache or a small vexation, and when decided, may have for its cause bodily agony, or extreme grief, or violent anger? The reply is not obvious, and yet when found, is satisfactory.

If you want to see a distant object in bright sunshine, you are aided by putting your hand above your eyes; and in the tropics, this shading of the eyes to gain distinctness of vision is far more needful than here. In the absence of shade yielded by the hand or by a hat, the effort to see clearly in broad sunshine is always accompanied by a contraction of those muscles of the forehead which cause the eyebrows to be lowered and protruded; so making them serve as much as possible the same purpose that the hand serves. The use of a sliding hood to a telescope, to shield the object-glass from lateral light, and especially from the rays of the Sun, illustrates the use of the contracted eyebrows when vision is impeded by a glare. Now if we bear in mind that during the combats of superior animals, which have various movements of attack and defence, success largely depends on quickness and clearness of vision —if we remember that the skill of a fencer is shown partly in his power of instantly detecting the sign of a movement about to be made, so that he may be prepared to guard against it or to take advantage of it, and that in animals, as for example in cocks fighting, the intentness with which they watch each other shows how much depends on promptly anticipating one another's motions; it will be manifest that a slight improvement of vision, obtained by keeping the Sun's rays out of the eyes, may often be of great importance, and where the combatants are nearly equal, may determine the victory. There is, indeed, no need to infer this *à priori*, for we have *à posteriori* proof: in prize fights it is a recognized disadvantage to have the Sun in front. Hence, we may infer that during the evolution of those types from which Man more immediately inherits, it must have happened that individuals in whom the nervous discharge accompanying the excitement of combat, caused an unusual contraction of these corrugating muscles of the forehead, would, other things equal, be the more likely to conquer and to leave posterity—survival of the fittest tending in their posterity to establish and increase this peculiarity. Support for this inference may be found in the fact that the male of the most formidable anthropoid ape, which has canine teeth nearly equal to those of a tiger, with jaws and temporal muscles to match, is remarkable for an enormous supra-orbital ridge of bone, over which, when angry, he is said to draw the hair-covered skin: so producing a formidable frown—that is, an efficient shade. But why should this mark of anger be also a mark of pain, physical or moral? May we not in reply say that since pains, physical and moral, are throughout the lives of inferior animals as well as the life of Man, inextricably entangled with the other accompaniments of combat, their physiological effects become entangled with the physiological effects of combat; so that the pain, no less than the anger, comes to excite sundry of those muscular actions which originally established themselves by conducing to success in combat? The laws of association will, I think, justify this conclusion.

Another trait of anger, the physiological meaning of which is not at once obvious, is dilatation of the nostrils. But since combat implies great exertion; and since great exertion entails a need for rapid aëration of the blood; and since this requires not only that the lungs shall be made active but also that the air-passages shall be well opened; it must happen that such a distribution of the nervous discharge as specially acted on the dilators of the nostrils, would give an advantage; and would, other things equal, be developed by survival of the fittest. The usefulness of such a nervo-muscular relation we shall see clearly on remembering that when, during combat, the mouth is filled up by a part of an antagonist's body that has been seized, the nostrils become the only air-passages available, and dilatation of them especially useful.

That setting and grinding the teeth and retracting the lips are marks of anger established in this way, needs scarcely be pointed out; for these obviously result from excitations smaller in degree but like in kind with those by which in inferior animals, and sometimes in men, combat is actually carried on. And the like is true of the clenching of the hands.

§ 499. That the vocal expressions of destructive passion are similarly explicable, will not be difficult to show. We have seen that before it has risen to a great height, the diffused discharge excites, among other small muscles, those which strain the vocal apparatus; and further that in proportion as the discharge strengthens, the sounds become not only louder but more divergent from the medium pitch. Given these as tendencies necessarily resulting from the nervo-muscular structure, and they will be modified and developed in such ways as conduce to self-preservation. Hence the explanation of a growl. In such a creature as the dog, that has to defend himself against others of his own race, suppose only the automatic tendency to produce a sound along with a rising emotion; then an individual in which the nervous discharge so affected the vocal muscles as to strain the larynx to a tone of unusually low pitch, and which so aroused in an approaching dog the association established in experience between hearing a deep tone and receiving injury from a furious antagonist, would produce alarm in the approaching dog. By so keeping off other dogs, especially when prey was being devoured, the individual would profit; the tendency and ability to produce a tone of low pitch on such occasions would be increased in posterity; and the growl would become an established and well-understood sign of anger—eventually even being used consciously as a threat.

In Man, kindred relations obviously hold. We have the words " growling " and " grumbling " commonly used to describe the vocal expression of more or less decided anger. Oaths, when uttered with much depth of passion, are uttered in the deepest bass. A curse, muttered between set teeth, is always in a low pitch. And in masses of people indignation habitually vents itself in groans.

That anger also expresses itself vocally in screaming notes, is doubtless true. As already said, a rising tide of feeling, causing increased muscular strain, may adjust the vocal apparatus to tones increasingly higher or increasingly lower—either of these implying muscular strain that is greater as departure from the medium tones is wider. Hence either extreme of pitch is apt to be produced; and often there is a sudden change from the one to the other.* Possibly the reason why anger that is beginning uses the lower tones, and when it becomes violent uses tones of high pitch, is that tones much below the middle voice are made with less effort than tones much above it; and that hence, implying as they do a greater excess of nervous discharge, the higher tones are natural to the stronger passion. An additional reason for suspecting this is that the like antithesis holds with other feelings—that while a groan implies bodily pain or moral pain which is not intense, intensity of either is implied by a shriek or a scream.

Kindred interpretations may be given to the phenomena of *timbre*, which further complicate the vocal manifestations of feeling. The quality of voice which characterizes an unexcited state, is that produced by vocal chords in a state of comparative relaxation; and the more sonorous character of the tones expressing much feeling, ending at length in that metallic ring which indicates great passion, implies increasing strain of the vocal chords.

* How nearly allied in origin and effect are these opposite divergences from the middle voice, is curiously shown in the fact that the emphatic syllable in a sentence, or that which most strongly expresses the emotional comment on the proposition, is indicated by either the lowest or the highest tone of the cadence. And it is interesting to observe that it is the oppositeness of choice in this respect, that causes the most marked contrast between the Scotch cadence and the English cadence. The fact may be exemplified by the very propositions which state it; thus—in English we *áscend* to the emphatic syllable. Aye, but in Scotch we just *déscend* to the emphatic syllable. Here if the two sentences be read, the one with a sudden rise of tone at the accented syllable, followed by a gradual fall, and the other with a sudden fall of tone at the accented syllable, followed by a gradual rise, the characteristic contrast in mode of speech will be perceived, and it will be perceived also how either divergence from the middle note of the voice serves to indicate the attitude of the feelings in respect to the thought expressed.

§ 500. Joined with these various characters of emotional language as physiologically caused, first by the diffused nervous discharges and second by the restricted nervous discharges that are not consciously directed, there are some produced by restricted nervous discharges directed by deliberate motives. These often complicate the emotional manifestations, and make the interpretation of them difficult. I refer more particularly to those restraints intentionally put on the actions of the external organs, for the purpose of hiding or disguising the feelings. The secondary feelings prompting this concealment, have a natural language of their own; which in some cases is easily read even by those of ordinary intelligence, and is read by those of quick insight in cases where it is comparatively unobtrusive.

Some of the most common are those in which the hands play a part. Often an agitation not clearly shown in the face is betrayed by fumbling movements of the fingers—perhaps in twisting and untwisting the corner of an apron. Or again, a state of *mauvaise honte*, otherwise tolerably-well concealed, is indicated by an obvious difficulty in finding fit positions for the hands. Similarly, pain or anger, the ordinary signs of which are consciously suppressed, may be indicated by a clenching of the fingers. In the movements of the face itself there occur some modifications of like origin. That compression of the lips which often goes along with anger not of a violent kind, probably originates in an effort to check the retraction of the lips and showing of the teeth, which is the spontaneous and original action in rising anger. And further, it seems not unlikely that those twitchings of the facial muscles which sometimes betray agitation, result from momentary failures in the endeavour to check muscular actions appropriate to the passing feelings. One form of this secondary natural language of a feeling, arising from efforts to conceal its primary natural language, we have in certain relations

82

between the positions of the eyes and of the head. When glancing at some adjacent object, the required adjustment of the eyes (supposing the object to be on one side) is made partly by turning the head and partly by turning the eyes: the amounts of lateral motion given to the two, maintaining a tolerably-regular ratio. Conformity to this ratio therefore becomes an accompaniment of unconcealed curiosity. Now when there is a desire to see something on one side of the visual field without being supposed to see it, the tendency is to check the conspicuous movement of the head, and to make the required adjustment entirely with the eyes; which are, therefore, drawn very much to one side. Hence when the eyes are turned to one side while the face is not turned to the same side, we get the natural language of what is called slyness.[*]

§ 501. One further set of complications I have left thus far unnamed; both because they would have confused the exposition had they been earlier noticed, and because, having a widely-different origin, they come under a different and almost-opposite law. I refer to the effects wrought by ·feelings on the vascular system, on the consequent supply of blood to the nervous centres, and on the resulting genesis of nervous energy. In many cases the secondary effects thus produced counteract the primary effects above described; and not unfrequently invert them.

The restraining action of the *vagus* nerve on the heart, appears to be the chief cause of these complications. When there is a very intense feeling, bodily or mental, painful or pleasurable—the over-irritated *vagus* arrests the

---

[*] Many illustrations of this are afforded by portraits of the period of the Restoration and after. There had grown up among portrait painters a desire to avoid formality, and an endeavour to get picturesqueness by an unsymmetrical distribution—especially in the attitudes of head and eyes. But not recognizing this law of the normal unsymmetry, they habitually chose distributions which give the sly expression.

heart's action and causes fainting. Here we see that in consequence of the sudden stoppage in the current of blood through the brain, and sudden cessation of nervous discharges, the muscles relax and the body falls: the feeling, instead of causing increased muscular action, paralyzes the muscles entirely. This interpretation of the extreme case being borne in mind, the interpretation of other cases becomes easy. When strong feeling acting through the *vagus,* does not absolutely stop the heart, but only makes its beats slower or feebler or both, there will result muscular prostration that is greater or less according as this effect on the heart is greater or less. And so there must come a conflict between the direct stimulation of the muscular system by a discharge that increases as the feeling increases, and the indirect relaxation of it caused by enfeeblement of the circulation through the nervous centres and through the muscles themselves.

Two classes of external manifestations are thus explained. The first and simplest is diminished strength. The prostration of great grief, the enervation attending utter despair, the almost entire helplessness which extreme fear produces, are examples of this effect. It is an effect shown by loss of power in the vocal muscles as well as by more general loss of power. For while during stages in which they have not too much retarded the heart's action, these passions are expressed in screams as well as in gesticulations, when prostration of the heart has been caused, there is feebleness of voice as well as general loss of power. The other class of manifestations, often simultaneous with this, we have in the tremblings which violent emotions bring on. That the general cause of this trait is the same, we shall see on remembering that trembling is a mark of failing nervous discharge brought about in other ways. Habitually the hand loses its steadiness in the latter part of life when the energies are failing. After a debilitating illness it is more or less shaky. In the drunkard the chronic nervous prostration due to over-stimulation, is similarly shown by the spilling of his drink as he carries it to his lips. Palsy is a still more conspicuous effect of like kind, similarly resulting from failure of nervous discharge. Why this failure in its various degrees produces these various amounts of trembling and shaking, is easy to see. The attitude of an extended limb is maintained by the contractions of muscles that pull against one another more or less directly. If the opposing muscles are simultaneously supplied with waves of molecular motion with such rapidity that each wave comes before the effect of the last has ceased, the limb is kept steady. But if the genesis of nervous energy so far fails that the successive waves do not reach all the muscles with regularity, but now one gets a deficient supply and now another, their respective states of contraction become variable—a flexor not duly antagonized by an extensor, causes motion one way, and then the extensor receiving a renewed discharge causes motion the other way; whence result oscillations that are great in proportion as the breaks in the nervous discharges are long. At the same time the vocal organs may be affected in the same way: the balanced antagonism of their muscles being interfered with, the voice becomes tremulous. Hence, then, this common trait of passions that reach a high degree of intensity. Rage causes shaking as well as fear—the vocal organs, like the hands, often becoming unsteady under both passions. There is a trembling of great anxiety and expectation; and the voice may grow tremulous with great joy or with a strong wave of the tender emotion. Hence the dramatic expressiveness of the *vibrato* in singing—an expressiveness such that singers are prone to use it with undue frequency.

And here we may remark that in consequence of this double mode of action of strong feelings, there is often a mixture of the two sets of effects on the muscular system—

some effects that imply increased contractions going along with other effects that imply decreased contractions. The unsteadiness of strong passion may be joined with violent exertion; and, as we see in the *vibrato* tones, there may go partial failure in the muscular balance of the vocal organs at the same time that the muscles are being contracted to that great extent required for the production of loud sounds.

Influences of one other order which strong feelings have on the vascular system, must be noticed. I refer to those shown by changes of colour—by blushing and growing pale. While waves of nervous energy are being propagated throughout the rest of the nervous system, they are being sent along the vaso-motor nerves, which, therefore, are apt to produce on the blood-vessels effects that vary with the variations of the feelings. The calibre of each artery is changed in opposite ways by discharges from two sources— some being brought through the fibre that comes from the cerebro-spinal system and some being brought through the fibre that comes from the sympathetic system; and the calibre is also changed by the pressure of the current which the heart's contractions send through the artery. Hence the waves of nervous influence that are the correlatives of feelings, may alter the diameters of the arteries in sundry ways, according as they affect most one or other of these sets of fibres, and according as they excite or prostrate the heart—now causing that blushing which dilatation of the small arteries involves, and now the sudden paleness due to constriction of them, or else to failure in the supply of blood. Hence the reason why, not only in different persons but in the same person at different moments, a passion may be shown now by redness and now by pallor.

§ 502. To go further into these manifestations of emotion would be at variance with the purpose of the chapter. Illustrations enough have been given to make comprehensible the doctrine which here concerns us.

We have seen that in virtue of the general law of nervo-motor action, every feeling has for its primary concomitant a diffused nervous discharge, which excites the muscles at large, including those that move the vocal organs, in a degree proportionate to the strength of the feeling; and that therefore muscular activity increasing in amount becomes the natural language of feeling increasing in amount —be the nature of the feeling what it may.   A secondary concomitant of feeling in general as it rises in intensity, we have seen to be an excitement by the diffused discharge, first of the small muscles attached to easily-moved parts, afterwards of more numerous and larger muscles moving heavier parts, and eventually of the whole body. From which we get a further natural measure of feeling, apart from kind.   Passing from the diffused discharges to the restricted discharges, we have noted how there has been established in the course of evolution, a connexion between the nervous plexuses in which any feeling is localized and the sets of muscles habitually brought into play for the satisfaction of the feeling. Whence it happens that the rise of this feeling shows itself by a partial contraction of these muscles; causing those external appearances called the natural language of the feeling.   We further observed that among these restricted discharges, some which are consciously directed, often further complicate the appearances by super-posing on the primary effects certain secondary effects, resulting from the endeavour to conceal the primary ones—secondary effects which, however, themselves constitute a natural language of suppressed feeling, admitting of partial interpretation.   Lastly, we saw that since, when feeling is excessive, the nervous discharge affects the vascular system, there comes into play an indirect cause of depressed muscular action, tending to neutralize the direct cause of excited muscular action—the joint operation of these antagonist causes producing a mixture of effects, of which now some predominate and now others.

There is no foundation, then, for the current notion that there are designed arrangements for the expression of feeling. The Hypothesis of Evolution yields us here, as elsewhere, an adequate solution of the facts. Deep down in the nervo-muscular structures, as they have been evolved by converse between the organism and its environment, are to be found the causes of all these manifestations. By combination, in ever-varying degrees and proportions, of the discharges that are general, that are special, that are consciously-directed, &c., there arise highly-complicated results, differing more or less for each individual, and for each of his constitutional states. We infer *à priori* what we find *à posteriori*—changing sets of appearances having certain characters in common, joined with sets of appearances that have less in common and are more variable.

Finding thus that in the nature of things there have grown up these connexions between internal feelings and external manifestations, we may now go on to inquire what has hence resulted during the intercourse of individuals with one another.

CHAPTER V.

SOCIALITY AND SYMPATHY.

§ 503. If we study the habits of animals of different kinds, with the view of learning what makes the individuals of some species live separately and those of other species live together, we discover two sets of causes uniting or conflicting in various ways and degrees. There are two most general functions, self-maintenance and race-maintenance, to which all more special functions are subservient. Each of these has a share in determining whether the habits shall be solitary or gregarious, or partly the one and partly the other. For according to the circumstances of the species in respect to food, and in respect to rearing of offspring, advantage is gained here by the one habit, here by the other, and here by some alternation of the two. A few instances will make this clear.

An animal of a predatory kind, which has prey that can be caught and killed without help, profits by living alone: especially if its prey is much scattered, and is secured by stealthy approach or by lying in ambush. Gregariousness would here be a positive disadvantage. Hence the tendency of large carnivores, and also of small carnivores that have feeble and widely-distributed prey, to lead solitary lives. Others there are, however, as the wolves and their allies, which, having large prey, profit by co-operation; and gregariousness becomes, in part, their habit. Among herbivorous animals, gregariousness is general for the reason that the distribution of food is not such as would make dispersion decidedly advantageous, while certain benefits arise from living together: more especially the benefit that the eyes and ears of all members of a herd are available for detecting danger; and hence, on the approach of an enemy, each member of the herd has a greater chance of being alarmed in time to escape than if it were alone. Obviously, then, under such conditions as to food, any variety of a herbivorous species which had a tendency for its members to feed within sight of one another, would be the more likely to survive, and gregariousness would be increased and established.

Birds furnish familiar illustrations both of the genesis of these habits as conducing to self-maintenance, and also of the genesis of them as conducing to race-maintenance. Note first the contrasts brought about by differences in kind and distribution of food.   The eagles and hawks are solitary in their habits; so too are the owls; so too are the herons during their feeding times. A moment's thought will show that no one of these species would gain anything by hunting in concert; but, contrariwise, would lose a great deal. On the other hand, among birds living on seeds and on insects, which are so distributed that each bird would get little or no more by wholly separating itself from others, we see a tendency to gregariousness. This tendency is not uniform, however—some species showing it all the year through, and others showing it during one part of the year only. The difference is traceable to the requirements of the species in respect to race-maintenance.   For consider the contrast between the rooks, which are gregarious all the year round, and the smaller birds which, though gregarious in winter, are dispersed during the breeding season. Observe, especially, the contrast in this respect between the rooks and an allied family—the starlings. Rooks being birds of considerable strength and powers of fighting, are in little danger from hawks: probably the most power-ful hawk is no match for several rooks. Hence concealment of their nests by rooks from birds of prey is not necessary. The only requisite is that their nests shall be beyond reach of ground-enemies; so that they are quite safe on the tops of trees, though quite visible. Contrariwise, with small birds having hawks for enemies, concealment of the nest is essential; and obviously were a number of small birds to build close together, the needful concealment would be impossible. Hence the dispersion habitual with them during the breeding season. Hence the contrast between the rooks which do not disperse to breed and the starlings which do, but which flock together and often associate with their kindred the rooks in the winter.

Not to trace further this complicated group of phenomena, it will be manifest enough for our present purpose, that in each species the size, strength, means of defence, kind of food, distribution of food, manner of rearing offspring, &c., must variously co-operate and conflict to determine how far a gregarious life is beneficial, and how far a solitary life.

§ 504. Recognizing the truth that sociality, while in some cases negatived by the wants of the species, becomes in other cases naturally established as furthering the preservation of the species, we have now to consider what mental traits accompany sociality—what feeling it implies and cultivates.

Sociality can begin only where, through some slight variation, there is less tendency than usual for the individuals to disperse widely. The offspring of the same parents, naturally kept together during their early days, may have their proneness to stay together maintained for a longer time —they may tend to part only at a somewhat later age. If the family profits by this slight modification, dispersion will in subsequent generations be more and more postponed, until it ceases entirely. That slight variations of mental

nature sufficient to initiate this process may be fairly assumed, all our domestic animals show us: differences in their
characters and likings are conspicuous.

Sociality having thus commenced, and survival of the
fittest tending ever to maintain and increase it, it will be
further strengthened by the inherited effects of habit. The
perception of kindred beings, perpetually seen, heard, and
smelt, will come to form a predominant part of consciousness—so predominant a part that absence of it will inevitably cause discomfort. We have but to observe how
the caged bird wants to escape, and how the dog, melancholy
while chained up, is in ecstasies when liberated, to be reminded that every kind of perceptive activity habitual to a
race implies a correlative desire, and a correlative discomfort
if that desire is not satisfied. Even during an individual
life, as men around us continually show, a trick or habit of
quite a special and trivial kind comes to have a corresponding longing which is with difficulty resisted. Clearly, then,
in a species to which gregariousness is advantageous, the
desire to be together will, generation after generation, be
fostered by the habit of being together. How strong this
desire does become we see in domestic animals. Horses
left alone are often depressed in consequence, and show
themselves eager for companionship. A lost sheep is manifestly unhappy until it again finds the flock. The strength
of the desire is, indeed, such that in the absence of members
of their own species, gregarious animals will form com-
panionships with members of other species.

Without further evidence we may safely infer that
among creatures led step by step into gregariousness, there
will little by little be established a pleasure in being
together—a pleasure in the consciousness of one another's
presence—a pleasure simpler than, and quite distinct from,
those higher ones which it makes possible. It is a pleasure
of like grade with that displayed by the dog on getting off
the high road into a field, where the mere sight of grass

and contact of the feet with it produce a delight showing itself in scouring around. In the one case, as in the other, there is a set of nervous structures correlated with a set of external conditions. The presence of the external conditions is needful for the exercise of the structures. In the absence of the conditions there arises a craving, and, when the conditions are supplied, a corresponding gratification.

§ 505. From the mental states produced in a gregarious animal by the *presence* of others like itself, we pass to the mental states produced in it by the *actions* of others like itself. The transition is insensible; for consciousness of the presence rarely exists apart from consciousness of the actions. Here, however, we may limit ourselves to actions that have marked significance.

As indicated above, an advantage gained by gregariousness which is probably the first, and remains among many creatures the most important, is the comparative safety secured by earlier detection of enemies. The emotion of fear expresses itself in movements of escape, preceded and accompanied, it may be, by sounds of some kind. Members of a herd simultaneously alarmed by a distant moving object or by some noise it makes—simultaneously making the movements and sounds accompanying alarm—severally see and hear these as being made by the rest at the same time that they are themselves making them, and at the same time that there is present the feeling which prompts them. Frequent repetition inevitably establishes an association between the consciousness of fear and the consciousness of these signs of fear in others—the sounds and movements cannot be perceived without there being aroused the feeling habitually joined with them when they were before perceived. Hence it inevitably happens that what is called the natural language of fear becomes, in a gregarious race, the means of exciting fear in those to whom no fearful object is perceptible. The alarmed members of a flock,

seen and heard by the rest, excite in the rest the emotion
they are displaying; and the rest, prompted by the emotion
thus sympathetically excited, begin to make like movements
and sounds.   Evidently the process thus initiated
must, by inheritance of the effects of habit, furthered by
survival of the fittest, render organic a quick and complete
sympathy of this simple kind.   Eventually a mere hearing
of the sound of alarm peculiar to the species, will by itself
arouse the emotion of alarm.   For the meaning of this sound
becomes known not only in the way pointed out but in another way.   Each is conscious of the sound made by itself
when in fear; and the hearing of a like sound, tending to
recall the sound made by itself, tends to arouse the accompanying feeling.

Hence the panics so conspicuous among gregarious crea-
tures.   Motions alone often suffice.   A flock of birds towards
which a man approaches will quietly watch for a while;
but when one flies, those near it, excited by its movements
of escape, fly also; and in a moment the rest are in the air.
The same happens with sheep.   Long they stand stupidly
gazing, but when one runs, all run; and so strong is the
sympathetic tendency among them that they will severally
go through the same movement at the same spot—leaping
where there is nothing to be leapt over.   Commonly along
with these motions of alarm there are sounds of alarm,
which may similarly be observed to spread.   Rooks on the
ground no sooner hear the loud caw of one that suddenly
rises, than they join in chorus as they rise.

§ 506. Beyond sympathetic fear, thus readily established
in gregarious animals because from hour to hour causes
of fear act in common on many, and because the signs of
fear are so conspicuous, there are sympathetic feelings of
other kinds established after a kindred manner.   Creatures
living together are simultaneously affected by surrounding
conditions of a favourable kind; are therefore liable to

be simultaneously thrown into pleasurable states; are therefore habitually witnesses of the sounds and movements accompanying such states, in others as well as in themselves;
and hence, in a way like that above explained, are apt to
have pleasurable feelings sympathetically excited.

Lambs in the spring show us that the friskiness of one
is a cause of friskiness in those near it—if one leaps, others
leap. Among horses, pleasurable excitement spreads, as
every hunting-field shows. A pack of dogs, too, takes
up the cry when a leader begins to give tongue. In the
poultry-yard kindred facts may be noticed. Early in the
day that quacking of the ducks which is significant of satisfaction, comes and goes in chorus: when one sets the example, the rest follow. The like happens with geese and
with fowls. Gregarious birds in a wild state furnish further
illustrations. In a rookery the cawing rises into bursts of
many voices, and then almost dying away, again suddenly
spreads sympathetically; and the like holds with the scream-
ings of parrots and macaws.

This sympathy is most variously exhibited by that most
intelligent of the gregarious animals which come under
daily observation—the dog. Beyond sympathetic cries of
excitement among dogs when chasing their prey in company,
there is the sympathetic barking which every quarrel in the
streets sets up, and which, under another form, is sometimes
so annoying in the night; and there is also the sympathetic
howling to be heard from dogs kept together in a kennel.
Here, again, the feelings that are communicated from one
to another, are feelings often simultaneously produced in
many by a common cause. Able, however, as the dog is to
perceive more complex and less conspicuous marks of feeling,
it displays a degree and variety of sympathy considerably
beyond this. Having long had men as well as members of
their own species for companions, dogs have acquired
tendencies to be sympathetically excited by manifestations
of human feeling. I do not refer simply to the fact that

sometimes a dog will howl sympathetically when he hears singing, and will even occasionally follow the voice up the gamut; for this is but a slight modification of the effect produced in him by the sounds other dogs make. But I refer to the fact that some dogs are sympathetically affected by the silent manifestations of pain and pleasure in those they are attached to—will stand with drooping tail and grave wistful gaze when the face and attitude of a master show depression, and will display joy on seeing a smile.

§ 507. Here we are naturally introduced to the truth that the degree and range of sympathy depend on the clearness and extent of representation. A sympathetic feeling is one that is not immediately excited by the natural cause of such a feeling, but one that is mediately excited by the presentation of signs habitually associated with such a feeling. Consequently, it pre-supposes ability to perceive and combine these signs, as well as ability to represent their implications, external or internal, or both. So that there can be sympathy only in proportion as there is power of representation.

For this reason it is that among inferior gregarious animals the range of sympathy is so narrow. The signs of pleasure when it becomes great, and the signs of fear, which is the most common pain, alone arouse in them fellow-feelings. With other emotions there is no sympathy; either because the signs of them are comparatively inconspicuous, or because the causes of them do not act simultaneously on all. A ewe that has lost her lamb, does not by her manifestations of feeling excite like feelings in other ewes; first, for the reason that her bleat does not differ much from the bleat caused by simple discomfort; second, for the reason that other ewes have not habitually had such slight modifications of bleat associated in themselves with the pains produced by loss of offspring; and third, for the reason that what other manifestations come from the bereaved ewe in the shape of motions and facial modifications, are inappreciable to the rest, and could not be mentally combined even if they were appreciable. There have neither been the requisite experiences, nor does there exist such power of representation as could combine the experiences, did they exist into the needful antecedent to the feeling.

Hence increase of intelligence is one condition, though by no means the sole condition, to increase in extent of sympathy. Because they lack intelligence, herbivorous creatures, though their habits in scarcely any ways check the growth of sympathy, nevertheless remain unsympathetic in all directions save those above described. While the dog, trained by the habits of his species in the perception of more complex and varied appearances, has gained a considerably-greater breadth of sympathy, notwithstanding that restraint which the predatory life puts on its extension.

§ 508. One further group of general considerations must be set down. The genesis of sympathy implying in the first place the presence of other beings, and implying in the second place subjection to influences simultaneously operating on these other beings, and calling forth marks of feeling from them; it results that sympathy is cultivated by all relations among individuals which fulfil these conditions. Of such relations we have thus far recognized but one—the relation which gregariousness implies. But there are two others—the sexual relation and the parental relation. These co-operate in various degrees; and the most marked effects are produced where they both act along with simple sociality. A paragraph may be given to each.

The sexual relation can be expected to further the development of sympathy in a considerable degree, only if it has considerable permanence. Where the rearing of offspring is so carried on as to keep the parents together during the interval required for bringing up a single brood, and still more where it is so carried on as to keep them together during the rearing of successive broods, there are maintained the conditions under which arise certain sympathetic excitations beyond those entailed by gregariousness alone. As, in their common relation to progeny, parents are liable to have certain pleasurable and painful feelings frequently called out from them by the same cause at the same time in marked ways, they will become sympathetic in respect of such feelings; and in so far as such feelings are in part made up of more general feelings, expressed by more general signs, they will become relatively sympathetic in respect of the more general feelings.   Birds furnish instances of the fulfilment of these conditions followed by production of these results. The contrast between polygamous birds, the males of which take no shares in rearing the offspring, and monogamous birds, the males of which take large shares in rearing them, supplies significant evidence. Where the male joins in feeding the young after they are hatched, as among our hedge birds, there is sympathy in fear, when the offspring are in danger; and probably in other feelings not so conspicuous. Among the martins and swifts, the male often feeds the female during incubation; and here we perceive in the simultaneous twittering of groups sitting on the eaves, or in the simultaneous screaming as they fly about together in the evening, that there is a more active sympathy than among barn-door fowls. Most marked, however, is the contrast in the poultry-yard between fowls and pigeons. The same pair of pigeons brings up successive broods, the female while sitting is fed by the male, and the male takes an unusual share in feeding the young: furnishing them with partially-macerated food from his crop. Here, and especially among the variety named doves, the sympathy is so great as to furnish familiar metaphors.

Fellow-feeling is also cultivated in each parent by its direct relations to progeny. Feeling having this origin is so intimately mingled with the parental feeling, which is a primitive and much simpler one, that the two cannot be

83

clearly distinguished. But since parent and offspring are by their intimate relation often exposed to common causes of pleasure and pain, there must be a special exercise of sympathy between them, or rather, of sympathy in the parent towards the offspring; for the offspring, being but partially developed, cannot so interpret the natural language as to make the effects reciprocal. It will habitually happen that the signs of satisfaction consequent on abundance of food, will be shown by offspring and parent together, as well as kindred signs consequent on genial warmth; and the marks of discomfort, say from inclemency, as well as those of alarm from danger, will be frequently simultaneous. Hence there are furnished the conditions under which specialities of sympathy can arise.

These brief indications of an extensive class of facts, will make it adequately clear that there are three causes of sympathy, due respectively to the three relations—between members of a species, between male and female, and between parent and offspring. Co-operating as these causes do in various ways and degrees, according as the circumstances of the species determine one or other set of habits as most conducive to survival, it is inferable that where the circumstances allow co-operation of all the causes, the effects are likely to be the greatest. Among inferior animals, co-operation of all the causes is not frequent: rooks supplying us with one of the few instances easily observable. And even where all the causes co-operate the effect producible depends on the accompanying degree of intelligence; since the capacity for being sympathetically affected, implies the capacity for having an ideal feeling of some kind aroused by perception of the sounds and motions implying a real feeling of the same kind in another.

§ 509. It is only when we come to the highest races of creatures that this last condition is largely fulfilled. Merely noting that among the lower primates, where considerable intelligence goes along with sociality and prolonged care of offspring by the females, sympathy is shown in various ways, we may now limit our attention to the human race. Here we have all three direct causes of sympathy in action, along with the co-essential condition—elevated intelligence.

The lowest types of mankind, exhibiting fellow-feeling in the least-decided and least-varied ways, are those least subject to these co-operating causes, and fulfilling in the least degree the needful condition. Among the Andamanese, there is no permanent marriage: a mother, as soon as her child is born, is left unhelped by the father to rear it; and hence there is wanting that culture of sympathy resulting from the direct paternal relation, as well as that resulting from the joint interest of parents in offspring. Similarly, where polyandry prevails, and paternity is uncertain or wholly unknown, there is not likely to be so active a sympathy of men towards children as where the monogamous relation makes filiation clear. Moreover, between the parents themselves polyandry is less favourable to culture of the sympathies than is monogamy. And when we remember that along with these inferior forms of domestic relations, the social relations are little more than rudimentary, while the intelligence is not great, we have no difficulty in seeing why among the lowest races the sympathies are weak and narrow.

Conversely, the races that have become most sympathetic are those in which monogamy has been long established; those in which the co-operation of parents for rearing children is continued to a comparatively-late period in the lives of children; those in which social development has made the contact of citizens with one another constant, much closer, and more varied; and those in which representativeness of thought has been gradually increased as society has gradually advanced.

And here we are led to remark that the relatively-slow development of sympathy during civilization, notwithstanding the high degree of sociality and the favourable domestic relations, has been in a considerable degree due to the slow development of representative power. The gratuitous infliction of pain, of which so much went on in the past and of which so much goes on now, obviously implies feeble representation of pain in the minds of those who inflict it. Did the signs of the pains they give arouse in them ideal pains of any vividness, they would be deterred. And those in whom the strong language of physical suffering excites so faint a representation of the suffering, cannot be expected to have any sympathy with feelings of which the natural language is complex and not conspicuous.

§ 510. But though inadequacy of intelligence involves limitation of sympathy, and explains absence of sympathy with feelings that are slight in degree and show themselves in obscure or involved ways, it does not by itself explain absence of sympathy in those cases just named, where strong feelings are expressed in conspicuous ways. For this absence of sympathy there is a cause of another order, which it is important ever to remember.

The human race, though a gregarious race, has ever been, and still is, a predatory race. From the beginning, the preservation of each society has depended on fulfilment of two sets of conditions, which, generally considered, are antagonistic. On the one hand, by destructive activities, offensive and defensive, each society has had to maintain itself in the face of external inimical agencies, partly animal but mainly human; and this has required the natures of its members to continue such that the destructive activities are not painful to them, but on the whole pleasurable: it has been necessary that their sympathies with pain should not prevent the infliction of pain. On the other hand, for the furtherance of co-operation between members of the society, and for such maintenance of the domestic relations as insures rearing of offspring, a certain

amount of fellow-feeling has been needful; and no great
social advance has been possible without an increase of this
fellow-feeling. If the members of a tribe cared no more
about one another's welfare than they cared about the welfare of their foes, there could be none of that mutual trust
and mutual aid required for progress; since the sub-division
of functions implied by social evolution, is but another name
for mutual aid, which can exist only through mutual trust.
So that while the external activities of each society have
tended to maintain an unsympathetic nature, its internal
activities have demanded sympathy and have tended to
make the nature more sympathetic. Noting, as we pass,
the fact that under such conditions as have hitherto existed,
either set of conflicting activities carried to excess has been
fatal—the one by fostering too much in each individual
the anti-social character, and the other by rendering the
society incapable of successfully resisting aggression; we
have here to remark the compromise established in the
moral natures of individuals, in adjustment to these opposite
requirements.

The compromise is shown in a specialization of the sympathies. Fellow-feeling has been continually repressed in
those directions where social safety has involved the disregard of it; while it has been allowed to grow in those
directions where it has either positively conduced to the
welfare of the society or has not hindered it. The possibility of such a specialization is not at first obvious; but a
few illustrations will show its occurrence to be in conformity
with known biological principles.

That adaptation by which actions at first disagreeable and
even painful are rendered by repetition less disagreeable or
painful, is familiar to us both in its bodily and mental forms.
We know that a sensitive skin frayed by much friction,
becomes thickened and callous if the friction is often repeated; and we know that use eventually makes easy the
endurance of a misfortune that seemed at first too great to

bear. These instances will call to mind the wide applications of this general principle. In the case we are considering its application is obvious. Where the circumstances are such as frequently excite a sympathetic pain, that pain will become less and less excitable sympathetically by those circumstances—there will result in that direction a moral callousness. This is sufficiently shown by the example which surgeons furnish. Though, when he first sees an operation, a student not unfrequently faints from sympathetic pain, he becomes gradually less sensitive; so that he is enabled by and by to perform an operation himself, if not without pain, still with a greatly-diminished amount of it. And the surgeon further shows us how very special this limitation of sympathy may be; since, while ceasing to be so sympathetic as the student in respect of these directly-inflicted physical pains, he retains an equal sympathy, or gains a greater sympathy, with his patients in respect of their general sufferings.

Here, then, is an explanation of the fact that men may be cruel in some directions and kind in others. We are enabled to see how it happens that the shooting of game and the chasing of foxes, is enjoyed by men who are not only tender in their domestic relations but generous and just, even to an unusal degree, in their social relations. And it ceases to seem strange that an old soldier who delights in recollections of battles, nevertheless shows kindness in his dealings with those around him. Sundry of the anomalies in the manifestations of sympathy which are thus made comprehensible, may be fitly grouped together.

§ 511. And first let us return for a moment to that seemingly-anomalous absence of sympathy with feeling that is expressed in very strong natural language.

There is a double reason why men may remain relatively unsympathetic in respect of sufferings they entail on their fellow-citizens, while they show sympathy in certain other directions. That suppression of sympathy with directly-inflicted pain, which throughout civilization has been necessitated by the antagonistic relations of societies to one another, has inevitably affected the relations between members of the same society. Antagonism with a fellow-citizen is so near akin to antagonism with a foreign foe, that a mental structure adjusted to the last inevitably comes into play in the first. Men cannot be kept unsympathetic towards external enemies without being kept unsympathetic towards internal enemies—to all those, that is, who stand to them as opponents. The further reason for absence of sympathy in these cases, is that establishment of it implies simultaneous exposure to a common influence; and this does not habitually happen where pain is being inflicted. The giver and the receiver of pain have not at the same time the same feeling expressing itself in the same natural language. The only feeling which is in many cases common to the two, is anger, and this is very apt to be sympathetically increased: the natural language of anger in either of them obviously tends to increase anger in the other —so long, at least, as it does not induce fear.

And now we see the reason for that marked contrast which exists between the universally-quick sympathy with pleasure, when strongly manifested, and the less-quick, and by no means universal, sympathy with pain when strongly manifested. For in multitudinous cases the causes of pleasure act on many simultaneously, and call forth from them in one another's presence the natural language of pleasure. Throughout another large class of cases the receipt of pleasure by each, though not simultaneous with its receipt by others, is not at variance with its receipt by others. In the social state, therefore, sympathy with pleasurable feeling is enabled to develop with but little check. Hence the infectiousness of laughter, which is the natural language common to pleasures of many kinds when raised to great heights. The consciousness of pleasure in each, while venting itself in this natural language, has been so habitually accompanied by witnessing this natural language in others, that the connexion between the feeling and the language has become organic. Quite early in life, sympathy shows itself in this direction irresistibly; as, I suppose, almost everyone will perceive on being reminded of occasions during childhood, when, in the midst of tears, he was compelled to laugh by the laughter of those around him—much to his vexation.

Sundry other specialities of sympathy might here be enlarged upon; as that which causes a thrill of dread on seeing some one at the edge of a precipice; as that whence come involuntary movements of the arms on seeing a horse fall in the street; as that which, among hysterical subjects, brings on a paroxysm in one who witnesses it in another; or as that which shows itself in religious enthusiasms; but it is unnecessary for present purposes to dwell upon these. One special sympathy worth noting because of its anomalousness, is sympathy in yawning. It is true that among gregarious creatures, the physiological state which yawning implies, is likely to be experienced in common, and therefore the feeling which produces a yawn to be accompanied by the sight of yawning in others; and it is true that along with this fulfilment of the conditions needful for the development of sympathy, there goes nothing to impede its development; but the strength of the sympathy seems greater than is thus to be explained. My chief reason, however, for drawing attention to this particular case, is that it illustrates very clearly the nature of sympathetic actions, and also the way in which they pass from their original presentative phase into a higher or representative phase. For, in the first place, we have the fact that on seeing another person yawn, there can be perceived the rise of the feeling which precedes a spontaneous yawn in one's self; which feeling, thus sympathetically induced, is followed by the sympathetic yawn. And in the second place,

we have the fact that the mere mention of yawning, or a
mental picture of the act of yawning, will often arouse the
feeling and produce the yawn. Here there is unquestionably a genesis by representation of a sympathetic feeling
so strong that it passes into action. We have but to bear
in mind that this implies a representation vivid enough
actually to excite an associated sensation, to see very clearly
the representative origin of sympathy. And if we draw
the obvious corollary that in proportion as more-varied and
more-complex states of consciousness can be represented
with like vividness, like effects must arise in respect of
more-varied and more-complex manifestations of feeling in
others; we shall see that sympathy must grow wider and
more intense in proportion as the representative faculty increases in power.

§ 512. The cardinal facts which it has been the aim of
this chapter to bring to view, and which we must carry with
us as aids to the interpretation of emotional development,
and to the subsequent interpretation of the sociological phenomena accompanying emotional development, are these.

Creatures whose conditions of existence in relation to food
or shelter or enemies are such as make it conducive to their
preservation that they should live more or less constantly
and closely in presence of one another, inevitably acquire
through inherited habit, aided by survival of the fittest, a
sociality that increases up to that point at which some
counteracting disadvantage checks it.

Along with the establishment of a social instinct—an instinct finding its satisfaction in the presence of those conditions with which gratifications in general are associated in
experience—there goes the possibility of sympathy in respect of such feelings as are liable to be aroused in common
among the associated individuals, and produce motions and
sounds sufficiently simple, conspicuous, and distinctive.

Limited as the development of sympathy is in gregarious

creatures of low intelligence, to few feelings, primitive, powerful, and clearly displayed, it is furthered as we ascend by every increment of intelligence which serves to increase the discrimination among perceived sounds and motions; by every increment of intelligence shown in greater combination of elements in a perception; and by every increment of intelligence which enhances the vividness of representation, the variety of representation, and the grasp of representation.

When to the general sociality of gregarious creatures there come to be added the special socialities of a permanent sexual relation and of a double parental relation, sympathy develpos more rapidly. In proportion as these relations are enduring and close, there is an increased number and variety of occasions on which the individuals held in them are affected in common by the same causes, and show in common the same outward signs; whence it results both that the sympathetic excitations are more frequent, and that they extend to more numerous feelings. The implication is that the sympathies will become the widest and the strongest where the three forms of sociality coexist along with high intelligence, and where there are no conditions which necessitate repression of the sympathies.

The human race is that in which we may observe in the concrete the truths just expressed in the abstract. Along with but a partially-established relation between the sexes, along with a parental relation which, on the man's side at least, is vague or not persistent, along with a weak cohesion of but few families, and along with a relatively-small power of representation, the lowest types show us a moral nature in which fellow-feeling, relatively feeble where it is shown, is not shown at all in its higher ranges. During the progress from these types up to the highest types yet evolved, sympathy and sociality under its three forms, have been acting and reacting, each as cause and consequence —greater sympathy making possible greater sociality, public and domestic, and greater sociality serving further to cultivate sympathy. All along, however, this moral evolution, negatively restrained at each stage by defect of intelligence, has been positively restrained by the predatory activities —partly those necessitated by the destruction of inferior creatures, but chiefly those necessitated by the antagonisms of societies. And the effect has been so to specialize the sympathies that they have become comparatively strong where these repressive causes have not acted, and have remained comparatively weak where they have acted. While, however, the predatory activities have not prevented the development of sympathy in the directions open to it, they have retarded it throughout its entire range. For that indifference to the giving of positive pain to others which they necessitate, goes along with indifference to that negative pain in others which absence of pleasure implies; and is therefore at variance with the sympathetic pleasure obtained by giving pleasure.

One general inference may be added. The evolution of those highest social sentiments which have sympathy for their root, has not only been all along checked by those activities which the struggle for existence between tribes and between nations has necessitated; but only when the struggle for existence has ceased to go on under the form of war, can these highest social sentiments attain their full development.

CHAPTER VI.

§ 513. When adopting a classification of Cognitions and of Feelings based on their degrees of representativeness (§ 480), it was pointed out that no more by this than by any other mode of classification can states of consciousness be sharply divided into groups. Nothing more is possible than the arrangement of them into groups that graduate one into another, but yet as wholes are broadly distinguishable.

Bearing in mind this qualification, the word Sentiments, as used in this and succeeding chapters, must be taken to comprehend those highest orders of feelings which are entirely re-representative. Though Sentiments are not thus ordinarily defined, yet the feelings habitually called Sentiments are thus definable. That remoteness from sensations and appetites, and from the ideas of such sensations and appetites, which is the common trait of the feelings we call Sentiments, is a remoteness implied by the fact that they are neither presentative states nor representations of such states; but consist of the multitudinous representations of such representations confusedly massed with one another, and with kindred feelings still more vague, organically associated by ancestral experience.

The nature of a sentiment as distinguished from a feeling of an inferior order, will be best seen on considering the marked contrast between that sentiment which grows up between the sexes and that simple instinct with which it is connected. The two are capable of existing quite apart; and while the elements of the instinct are necessarily presentative, or representative, or both, the elements of the sentiment are almost wholly re-representative. Though presentation or representation of another person is needful to initiate the sentiment, and to re-excite it when it recurs in consciousness, yet the sentiment itself is quite separate from the exciting presentation or representation. The body of the sentiment, consisting of that part which is due to inherited nervous organization, admits of no analysis by introspection: its components have not been put together within the experiences of the individual. But there is a part of the sentiment, giving some form to this vague body of it, which obviously consists of representations of certain agreeable feelings that have, on successive occasions, been caused by the presence and actions of the person exciting the feeling. Appearance, movements, manner, voice, expression of face, &c., severally suggestive of pleasurable past relations with human beings, become recollections repeatedly dwelt on in connexion with a particular human being, and by association fused into an aggregate of pleasurable recollections; and as this aggregate grows by accumulation it becomes vague in proportion as it becomes massive. The more multitudinous the component recollections the less possible is it to bring them severally into distinct consciousness; and yet the more voluminous is the consciousness which union of them produces. And on observing how the individually-experienced feelings are thus compounded into an incipient sentiment, it will be readily seen how there has been evolved the inherited sentiment which forms the still-vaguer part of the total emotion.

Carrying with us these conceptions of the re-representative feelings or sentiments, and of the way in which they have arisen, let us now consider one order of them—those which are immediately related to personal welfare.

§ 514. All persons in some degree, and in a great degree persons having imaginations mainly reminiscent, like revisiting the scenes of past pleasures. Unless early life was full of unhappiness, it is delightful to see again the place where early life was passed. As, ordinarily, no special beauty or interestingness of the locality can directly cause the delight, it is obviously caused by the faint revival of those multitudinous enjoyments with which the various objects were associated in boyish experiences. Though particular occurrences of a pleasure-giving kind may be brought to mind by particular spots in the locality, yet the emotion as a whole is not due to this or that memory, but to memories too numerous to be individually discriminated: many of them, indeed, being so faint that they cannot be definitely recalled, but exist only as dim traces of pleasure.

This evolution of a special re-representative feeling or sentiment towards a special place, conveniently illustrates the distinction between sentiments generated in the individual, and sentiments generated in the race. For while attachment to a particular locality, though it pre-supposes an inherited receptivity, is yet obviously organized out of experiences which the individual alone received, there are other sentiments organized out of experiences which, being the same for ancestry as for self, are cumulative in successive generations; and are therefore inherited in such developed forms as to show themselves in advance of individual experiences.

Such inherited sentiments may be looked for wherever the conditions of life have been such as to make certain kinds of acts and certain kinds of relations to surrounding things, living and not-living, habitual sources of gratification to generation after generation. And we may expect to find such sentiments strong in proportion as these acts and relations are connected with enjoyments frequently, directly, and clearly. Observation confirms this inference; as we shall see on passing to the several egoistic sentiments here to be dealt with.

§ 515. The prehension of food, and especially the prehension of living food or prey caught only after effort, is closely associated with the satisfaction of appetite; and hence the mere act of prehension, arousing ideal gratifications that are among the strongest a predatory creature's life furnishes, becomes gratifying as an excitant of these ideal gratifications. Every dog shows this when he tugs at something you hold, of which he has seized the other end—scampering off with it in triumph if he can pull it from your hands; or again when, after mimic chase of it, he surrenders with reluctance the stick he has brought back to you: often yielding only to force. Here, apart from any liking for the thing held in the jaws, there is a marked satisfaction in that simplest form of possession which is most directly related to the satisfaction of hunger. Puss, too, playing with a mouse she has caught, letting it escape from between her paws and catching it afresh, exhibits along with this artificial gratification of the instinct of the chase, a gratification in the act of taking possession and re-taking possession.

In these cases this gratification, primarily presentative and exciting representations of connected pleasures, barely passes into the phase of simple representation: forming, as it does, part of the stimulus to pursuit. Nothing is contained in the consciousness beyond either a presentation or representation of the act of seizing and holding a particular object—the consciousness of holding in general is not distinguished from that of prehension by the jaws and feet. We trace, however, in the dog, a further step towards the love of possession properly so called. When he secretes a portion of food, covering it over to make it invisible, there is a representation of future satisfaction to be obtained from the food: perhaps, also, some idea that the food may, if not hidden, be taken by another animal. Here the relation to the hidden food becomes completely representative; and though possession is probably conceived only in terms of that prehension which precedes eating, yet there is a first step towards a less-concrete consciousness of possession. The state of mind must have something in common with that of the North American Indian or the trapper who makes a *cache*—though doubtless lacking its generalized elements. That in the dog consciousness of possession rises to a considerable height, is further shown by the way in which he will guard his master's property; not simply at home, but even when left in charge of it away from home. Indeed, there seems in this case to be a sympathetic excitement of the feeling in respect to objects that are not sources of gratification to the dog himself, but only to his master.

When we see in the dog so considerable an evolution of this feeling which finds satisfaction in possession, and see that much of this evolution must have taken place since the dog has been domesticated, we cannot doubt that in man, with his higher intelligence and greatly-extended power of representation, the more-developed sentiment of possession has similarly been produced by the accumulated and inherited effects of experiences. How the feeling has grown into that re-representative form which constitutes it a sentiment, and how the sentiment has become more highly re-representative during civilization, a glance at the facts will make clear.

If we contrast the life of a primitive man with that of an intelligent inferior animal, we perceive that along with man's higher and more-varied powers of prehension and manipulation, and along with the more numerous things which he is thereby enabled to use, or to make, for satisfying his desires, there goes an increase in the variety of objects associated in his experience with enjoyment. It is not now food alone the possession of which is antecedent to gratification; but also the rude weapons and tools which aid in procuring and preparing food—the spears, clubs, boomerangs, the flint-knives, scrapers, &c. There are included, too, the skins useful for keeping off the cold, and such materials as may be employed for building rude shel-

ters from the wind and rain. Nor are these the only things
he finds conducive to one or other kind of pleasure. There
are the brightly-coloured or curiously-formed natural products which excite his rudimentary æsthetic sense, and
which, when worn, draw admiration from others; and there
are the pigments with which, in satisfaction of the same
sense, he daubs his skin. Objects of divers kinds, strongly
contrasted in their characters, thus come to be associated
in his experience with various satisfactions. Possession in
one or other form, if not by holding then by keeping
within his hut, or in such relation to him as to be always
available, is, however, the constant antecedent to each of
these various satisfactions. But this possession, having become habitual in respect to objects of various natures, ad-
ministering in many ways to satisfactions of sundry orders,
has, *pari passu*, ceased to be connected in experience with
any particular kind of object or any particular kind of satisfaction. The holding possession has come to be associated
in consciousness with multitudinous unlike pleasures given
by multitudinous unlike things; and the gaining possession
has come to be a pleasurable act because it produces a
partial excitement of all these past pleasures of many kinds
massed together, obscuring one another, and not individually
recallable, but forming a voluminous vague feeling—a feeling that has become a sentiment proper, since it has become
re-representative.

With progress in civilization is reached a higher re-representativeness, corresponding to the greater remoteness of the
satisfactions provided for, and the greater indirectness of the
ways in which they are furthered. Not food, and tools, and
clothing, and decorations only, gratify the love of acquisition; but also the tract of the Earth's surface from which
these are obtained—land becomes something to be possessed. Still more re-representative does the feeling
grow when it finds satisfaction, not through that highly-
imaginative kind of possession of a material something

84

which land-owning constitutes (so remote from the primary seizing and grasping), but when there exists no distinct materiality in the thing possessed—when it is simply a claim. Beginning with a bank-note, visible and tangible, but of no value except for what it represents; passing to a bank-account, in which the possession is represented by figures stating a credit-balance, but where a money-equivalent may usually be had on application; and coming to documents representing holdings in foreign government debts, where there is nothing but a lien on certain supposed property, held by persons unknown, in a region never visited; we see that the sentiment of possession eventually becomes re-representative in a very high degree—is highly generalized, and dissociated very remotely from actual objects.

To prevent a misapprehension, it should be added that the love of acquiring and possessing is not to be wholly identified with the love of property under that developed form finally reached; since the conception of property is completed only when there is a consciousness of a definite limitation to possession, and this consciousness requires the co-operation of another sentiment to be hereafter described.

§ 516. A child over whose mouth a hand is placed, shows a strong tendency to resist, often accompanied by marks of anger. On recalling his experiences, every one may perceive that an arrest of respiration by some external agency, instantly produces an intolerable consciousness of oppression —a consciousness arising far in advance of the oppression due to actual want of breath. The breath may be voluntarily held for some time with equanimity; but the representation of a coming inability to breathe causes agitation of an agonizing kind. Evidently we have here a representative feeling due to experiences, mainly inherited and organic but partly individual, of sufferings from prolonged arrest of respiration. And this feeling may be considered as the first, simplest, and most powerful form of the general feeling produced by whatever restrains the bodily actions.

For this feeling has an element in common with that which results when the movements of the limbs are prevented. Even animals oppose attempts to hold their legs fast, or otherwise stop their motions. Quite apart from direct pain, or negatived gratification, a dog, when it finds that it is being held fast, betrays a strong desire to liberate itself. And in a man the consciousness of ability to move freely is so essential to equanimity, that the slightest attempt to interfere with it by laying hold of him excites quick resentment.

This resentment serves by its strength to measure the latent power of that feeling which is satisfied by unrestrained liberty of motion—latent power, I say, because the satisfaction of it being ordinarily complete from instant to instant, the feeling does not ordinarily obtrude itself in consciousness. Only after denial of it has produced pain, and freedom of movement has been recovered, does there arise a positive gratification.

Clearly this feeling is re-representative. The emotional pain caused by bodily restraint, does not consist of the represented loss of a pleasure about to be obtained. Interference arouses it when there is no immediate good to be pursued, and even when there is no desire to move. The consciousness of an imposed inability to act, is a consciousness containing dimly-represented denials, not of one kind of gratification but of all kinds of gratifications. Power to use the limbs and senses unimpeded, is associated in individual life with every kind of pleasure; and it is similarly associated in the lives of all ancestry, human and prehuman. The body of the sentiment, therefore, is a vague and voluminous feeling produced by experiences organized and inherited throughout the whole past, to which a more definite, but still very general, form is given by the individual experiences received from moment to moment

from birth upwards. And hence in the agitation excited
by arrest of motions, there is a multitudinous re-representation of denials of all kinds, the individualities of which
are mostly quite lost; while in the joy of liberty regained
there are massed together the potentialities of gratifications
in general.

Penal systems of all nations recognize the fact that imprisonment with unshackled limbs, causes less emotional
pain than imprisonment with limbs shackled. Probably
there are two causes of this difference. By restored mobility of the limbs some gratifications are made possible;
and the denial of activity is not so vividly suggested by a
locked door as it is by tied hands. Here the sentiment, so
painfully excited by imprisonment and pleasurably excited
by release, is more highly representative; since it contains
no presentative element even as an initiator—the initial
consciousness is now the idea of inability to get out; and by
this representation there is excited the re-representation,
mostly vague but in part specific, of pleasures craved and no
longer possible.

Following the same lines we may see that when the
restraint is still less strict and definite, as in the condition
of slavery, the painful excitement of the sentiment is further
diminished; and such excitement of it as arises is re-
representative in a more decided degree. For, assuming
him to be tolerably well treated, the slave has the amount
of freedom required for satisfying his desires as well as most
of the poorer members of the human race satisfy them; and
generally he has not to put out effort so great as that which
the free man puts out. Only by representation of those
activities and those successes which complete freedom would
make possible, but which slavery prevents, is he made
aware of the evil he suffers. A considerable reach of representative power is needful for anything like a vivid consciousness of this evil; and hence the fact shown us by the
less-developed human races, that if the physical comforts

are secured and the treatment is mild, slavery is borne with equanimity. Only when there exists that higher power of representation common to the more-evolved races, do we meet with that sullen discontent and restlessness caused by the consciousness of remote benefits that are forbidden and of remote ills that may have to be borne. Only then does the love of freedom reach that highly-re-representative form in which imaginations of the distant and indirect evils of restraint constitute the promptings to rebel; and in which the consciousness of having no one to hinder any activities that may be desired, constitutes the delight in liberty.

A re-representativeness yet more elevated, characterizes the sentiment as we pass through ascending gradations of political freedom. The successive oppositions to irresponsible government, show an increasing consciousness of the ways in which class-power tends, by class-legislation, to restrict the actions of the ruled more than the actions of the rulers. With greater grasp of imagination there comes a more vivid realization of the many evils hence arising; ending in a more decided repugnance to those social relations whence they are seen to grow. The sentiment prompting resistance to restraint, gains in comprehensiveness and sensitiveness—is more and more easily excited by whatever indirectly threatens restraint. And gradually moulding political arrangements into harmony with itself, it finally delights to contemplate ideal social relations under which no citizen shall have privileges that trench upon the claims of others. Here the sentiment reaches so highly re-representative a phase that all ideas of concrete advantages are merged in the abstract satisfaction derived from securities against every possible interference with the pursuit of his ends by each citizen. It needs but to observe how, at a public meeting or on other kindred occasion, any assumption of individual supremacy, or breach of regulations established to maintain equality of privilege, is at once resented, although no one may be able to point out any way in which he can be personally injured or even personally interfered with, to see how far-reaching and how susceptible has now become this most-highly-re-representative of all the sentiments—a sentiment having for its function the maintenance of those conditions which make complete life possible.

It must be added, however, that as in the last case, so here, this primarily-egoistic sentiment attains that final form just described, only by the aid of an altruistic sentiment; the co-operation of which will be indicated in a subsequent chapter.

§ 517. One who fails in some simple mechanical action feels vexation at his own inability—a vexation arising quite apart from any importance of the end missed. Contrariwise, a feat of skill achieved causes an emotional satisfaction, irrespective of the concrete result considered in itself—is just the same whether some ulterior purpose is or is not aided. These opposite feelings are experienced when there are no witnesses to the failures or successes. A careless step leading to accident, or some bungling manipulation, causes self-condemnation with its accompanying feeling of annoyance, though no one is by; and though no one is by, a successful leap over an obstacle, a skilful shot at a bird, or the landing of a fish under difficulties, excites a wave of self-satisfaction. The like holds when the failures and achievements are purely mental. "What a fool I am!" is a common exclamation on discovering some intellectual blunder; and the vexation accompanying the discovery is felt when no word is uttered and when no one else is aware of the error. On the other hand, a glow of pleasure follows the solution of a puzzling question, even though the question be not worth solving. In the search for a forgotten name both effects are illustrated. Inability to remember it is a source of vexation; and when at length it is remembered there comes self-gratulation: each feeling being experienced without regard to any advantage gained by finding the name.

These emotions must inevitably be evolved along with increasing power of representation. A successful bodily or mental act, while it secures the gratification sought, vaguely revives the consciousness of kindred acts that have been followed by kindred gratifications. Each other kind of success, bodily or mental, is similarly associated in thought, not only with the immediate result, but with like results before achieved in like ways. Thus successful action in general, comes to be associated in consciousness with pleasure in general: both the two consciousnesses being re-representative. For the general consciousness of successful action is constituted not by the thought of any one successful act, nor by the representation of many previous successful acts of the same kind, but is one in which representations of past successful acts of multitudinous kinds are represented; and at the same time the accompanying consciousness of pleasure achieved by successful action, is one in which many kinds of represented pleasures are re-represented as components of a vague whole. Hence it happens that each success tends to arouse ideas of one's past self as acting successfully and thereby achieving satisfaction; and thus is produced the sentiment of self-estimation, which, when it rises to a considerable height, we call pride.

That continuous successes tend to bring about an habitual self-exaltation, and that a painful want of confidence follows perpetual failures, are familiar truths clearly implying that the sentiment of pride and the sentiment of humility are thus fostered in the individual. And seeing this, we cannot fail to see that they are thus evolved in the race. We may see also that, like the other egoistic sentiments we have considered, these sentiments have as their function the adjustment of conduct to surrounding conditions. Proper self-estimation is needful for due regulation of our efforts in relation to their ends. Under-estimation of self involves the letting-slip of advantages that might have been gained. Over-estimation of self prompts attempts which fail from want of due capacity. In either case there is an average of evil experienced—benefit missed or effort thrown away. Hence this egoistic sentiment which we describe as a consciousness of personal worth, serves as a balance to the ambitious. And the experiences of each individual are continually tending to adjust its amount to the requirements of his nature.

§ 518. To pursue this synthesis in other directions would delay us too much; else something might be said of the modifications and the combinations af these ogoistic sentiments. For, as will be manifest when we consider the genesis of them, their limits are by no means definite. Within each there are qualitative differences dependent on the circumstances arousing it, and very generally they are excited together in different ways and degrees.

Here I will draw attention only to one other egoistic sentiment; and I do this chiefly because of its mysterious nature. It is a pleasurably-painful sentiment, of which it is difficult to identify the nature, and still more difficult to trace the genesis. I refer to what is sometimes called " the luxury of grief."

The interpretation of this feeling implied by another name given to it—self-pity, does not seem to me a satisfactory one; because pity, under the form alone applying in this case, is itself difficult to interpret, as we shall presently see. After having discovered why pity itself, unaccompanied by any prompted activity, may become a source of pleasurable pain, it has to be shown that the interpretation applies when self is the object of the pity: the last solution depends upon the first, which is not yet found. I do not say that the hypothesis may not be a partially-true one; but only that the explanation is not ultimate, and that there are probably other components in the consciousness.

It seems possible that this sentiment, which makes a sufferer wish to be alone with his grief, and makes him resist all distraction from it, may arise from dwelling on the contrast between his own worth as he estimates it and the treatment he has received—either from his fellow-beings or from a power which he is prone to think of anthropomorphically. If he feels that he has deserved much while he has received little, and still more if instead of good there has come evil, the consciousness of this evil is qualified by the consciousness of worth, made pleasurably dominant by the contrast. One who contemplates his affliction as undeserved, necessarily contemplates his own merit as either going unrewarded, or as bringing punishment instead of reward: there is an idea of much withheld, and a feeling of implied superiority to those who withhold it.

If this is so, the sentiment ought not to exist where the evil suffered is one recognized by the sufferer as nothing more than is deserved. Probably few, if any, ever do recognize this; and from those few we are unlikely to get the desired information. That this explanation is the true one, I feel by no means clear. I throw it out simply as a suggestion: confessing that this peculiar emotion is one which neither analysis nor synthesis enables me clearly to understand.

CHAPTER VII.

EGO-ALTRUISTIC SENTIMENTS.

§ 519. To prevent a misapprehension apt to arise, let me, before going further in explaining the genesis of sentiments by accumulation of the effects of experience, define the word experience as here used. In its ordinary acceptation, experience connotes definite perceptions, the terms of which stand in observed relations; and is not taken to include connexions formed in the mind between states that occur together, when the relations between them, causal or other, are not consciously identified. But a reference to such chapters in the Special Synthesis as those on Reflex Action, Instinct, Memory, &c., or to chapters in the Physical Synthesis on the Genesis of Nervous Systems, Simple, Compound, and Doubly-Compound, will remind the reader that the effects of experience as there and everywhere else understood in this work, are the effects produced by the occurrence together of nervous states, with their accompanying states of consciousness when these exist; whether the relations between the states are or are not observed. Throughout the earlier stages of mental evolution, indeed, there cannot be that recognition of a relation which experience, in its limited meaning, implies. Habitual converse with the environment produces its effects without the recipient knowing them in the full sense of knowing; for there has not yet been evolved that notion of self which is essential to conscious experience.

Here the truth especially to be noted is, that this registration of unconscious experience continues after conscious experience has become distinct and even dominant. Along with the narrow stream of clear ideas definitely related, forming our conscious experience, there flow far more voluminous currents of connected impressions of all degrees of indistinctness, in an order that presents all gradations of vagueness. Only a certain central thread of consciousness consists of perceptions and thoughts; and in proportion to their remoteness from this central thread, the elements of consciousness are more and more loosely connected with one another and with the central thread: the incoherence reaching its extreme at the outskirts of consciousness (§ 180). Yet all these states and their connexions are in a sense present to us; and are producing effects proportionate to their strengths. Hence, when often repeated though never distinctly thought about, the relations among them become well established. On examining consciousness, we find ourselves possessed of much positive knowledge gathered without observing it (as instance our remembrance of the position on the page, of some striking sentence in a book) and of a still larger amount of indefinite knowledge—beliefs which possess us, though we cannot say why.

In this voluminous, heterogeneous, and only partially-definite region of consciousness, are formed those associations of complex states which, perpetually repeated, produce what we call sentiments. The genesis of emotions is distinguished from the genesis of ideas in this; that whereas the ideas, always contained in the narrow, central part of consciousness, are composed of simple elements definitely related, and (in the case of general ideas) constantly related; emotions are composed of greatly-involved assemblages of the outlying elements of consciousness, which are never twice quite the same, and which stand in relations that are never twice quite the same. In the building-up of an idea the successive experiences, be they of sounds, colours, touches, tastes, or be they of the special objects that combine many of these into groups, have so much in common that each, when it occurs, can be definitely thought of as like those which preceded it. But in the building-up of an emotion, the successive experiences so far differ that each of them, when it occurs, suggests past experiences which are not specifically similar, but have only a general similarity; and, at the same time, it suggests benefits or evils in past experience which likewise are various in their special natures, though they have a certain community of nature. Hence it results that the consciousness aroused is a multitudinous, confused consciousness; in which, along with a certain kind of combination among the impressions received from without, there is a vague cloud of ideal combinations akin to it, and a vague mass of ideal feelings of pleasure or pain that were associated with such combinations.

Carrying with us this general conception of the way in which mental states in the large, outlying, vaguer region of consciousness, become connected by repetition without our being aware of it, we shall render it a definite conception on observing what happens in cases readily recallable. From our past lives we may draw abundant proofs that feelings grow up without reference to recognized causes and consequences, and without our being able at once to say how we have got them; though analysis shows that they have been formed out of connected experiences. The familiar fact to which, I suppose, almost every one can testify, that a kind of jam which was, during childhood, repeatedly taken after medicine, may be rendered by simple association of feelings, so nauseous that it cannot be tolerated in after-life, illustrates clearly enough the way in which repugnances are frequently established, without any idea of causal connexion; or rather, in spite of the knowledge that there is no causal connexion. Similarly with pleasurable emotions. The cawing of rooks is not in itself an agreeable sound: musically considered, it is very much the contrary.

Yet the cawing of rooks usually produces pleasurable feelings—feelings which many suppose to result from the quality of the sound itself. Only the few who are given to self-analysis are aware that the cawing of rooks is agreeable to them because it has been connected with countless of their greatest gratifications—with the gathering of wild flowers in childhood; with Saturday-afternoon excursions in school-boy days; with midsummer-holidays in the country, when books were thrown aside and lessons were replaced by games and adventures in the field; with fresh, sunny mornings in after-years, when a walking excursion was an immense relief from toil. As it is, this sonud, though not causally related to all these multitudinous and varied past delights, but only often associated with them, rouses a dim consciousness of these delights; just as the voice of an old friend unexpectedly coming into the house, suddenly raises a wave of that feeling which has resulted from the pleasures of past companionship.

And now having made this further explanation of the way in which feelings are evolved by the organization of experiences, let me resume the interpretation at the point reached with the close of the last chapter. From the egoistic sentiments we pass now to the ego-altruistic sentiments. By this name I mean sentiments which, while implying self-gratification, also imply gratification in others: the representation of this gratification in others being a source of pleasure not intrinsically, but because of ulterior benefits to self which experience associates with it.

§ 520.* An infant in arms, that is old enough vaguely to recognize objects around, smiles in response to the laughing face and soft caressing voice of its mother. Let there come some one who, putting on an angry face, speaks to it in loud,

* This section, and a portion of the preceding section, originally formed parts of an article published in the *Fortnightly Review* for April 1, 1871, under the title of "Morals and Moral Sentiments."

harsh tones. The smile disappears, the features contract into
an expression of pain, and, beginning to cry, it turns away
its head and makes such movements of escape as are possible. What is the meaning of these facts? Why does not
the frown make it smile and the mother's laugh make it
weep? There is but one answer. Already in its developing
brain there are coming into play the structures through
which one cluster of visual and auditory impressions excites
pleasurable feelings, and the structures through which
another cluster of visual and auditory impressions excites
painful feelings. The relation between a ferocious expression
of face and the evils that may follow perception of it, is no
more known to the infant, than there is known to the young
bird just out of its nest, a connexion between possible death
and the sight of a man coming towards it; and as certainly
in the one case as in the other, the alarm felt is due to a
partially-established nervous structure. Why does this
partially-established nervous structure betray its presence
thus early in the human being? Simply because, in the
past experiences of the race, smiles and gentle tones in
those around have been habitual accompaniments of
pleasurable feelings; while pains of many kinds, immediate and remote, have been continually associated with
the impressions received from knit brows and set teeth
and grating voice. Much deeper down than the history of
mankind must we go to find the beginnings of these connexions. The appearances and sounds which excite in the
infant a vague dread, indicate danger; and do so because
they are the physiological accompaniments of destructive
action—some of them common to man and inferior mammals, and consequently understood by inferior mammals, as
every puppy shows us. What we call the natural language
of anger, is due to a partial contraction of those muscles
which actual combat would call into play; and all marks of
irritation, down to that passing shade over the brow which
accompanies slight annoyance, are incipient stages of these

same contractions. Conversely with the natural language of pleasure, and of that state of mind which we call amicable feeling: this, too, has a physiological interpretation (see §§ 497-499).

The children in the nursery yield us a further lesson. What have the experiences of each one of these been doing in aid of the emotional development we are considering? While its limbs have been growing more agile by exercise, its manipulative skill increasing by practice, its perceptions of objects growing by use quicker, more accurate, more comprehensive; the associations between these two sets of impressions received from persons around, and the pleasures and pains received along with them, or after them, have been strengthened by frequent repetition, and their adjustments made better. The dim pain and the vague delight which the infant felt, have, in the urchin, severally taken shapes of some definiteness. The angry voice of a nursemaid no longer arouses only a formless feeling of dread, but also a specific idea of the slap that may follow. The frown on the face of a bigger brother, along with the primitive, indefinable sense of ill, excites the sense of ills that are definable in thought as kicks, and cuffs, and pullings of hair, and losses of toys. The faces of parents, looking now sunny, now gloomy, have grown to be respectively associated with multitudinous forms of gratification and multitudinous forms of discomfort or privation. Hence these appearances and sounds which imply amity or enmity in those around, become symbolic of happiness and misery; so that eventually, perception of the one set or the other, even when it is slightly marked, can scarcely occur without raising a wave of pleasurable feeling or of painful feeling. The body of this wave is still substantially of the same nature as it was at first; for though in each of these multitudinous experiences a special set of facial and vocal signs has been connected with a special set of pleasures or pains, yet since these pleasures or pains have been immensely varied in their kinds and combinations, and since the signs that preceded them were in no two cases quite alike, it follows that to the last the consciousness produced remains as vague as it is voluminous. The myriads of partially-aroused ideas resulting from past experiences are massed together and superposed, so as to form an aggregate in which nothing is distinct, but which has the character of being pleasurable or painful according to the nature of its original components: the chief difference between this developed feeling and the feeling aroused in the infant being, that on the bright or dark background forming the body of it, may now be sketched out in thought the particular pleasures or pains which the particular circumstances suggest as likely.

What must be the working of this process under the conditions of aboriginal life? The emotions given to the young savage by the natural language of love and hate in the members of his tribe, gain first a partial definiteness in respect to his intercourse with his family and playmates; and he learns by experience the utility, in so far as his own ends are concerned, of avoiding courses which call from others manifestations of anger, and taking courses which call from them manifestations of pleasure. Not that he consciously generalizes. He does not at that age—probably not at any age—formulate his experiences in the general principle that it is well for him to do things which win smiles from others, and to avoid doing things which cause frowns. What happens is, that having, in the way shown, inherited this connexion between the perception of anger in others and the feeling of dread, and having discovered that particular acts of his bring on this anger, he cannot subsequently think of committing one of these acts without thinking of the resulting anger, and feeling more or less of the resulting dread. He has no thought of the goodness or badness of the act itself: the deterrent is the mainly-vague, but partially-definite, fear of evil that may follow. So understood, the deterring emotion is one developed out of experiences of utility—using that word in its ethical sense; and if we ask why this dreaded anger is called forth from others, we shall habitually find that it is because the forbidden act entails pain somewhere—is negatived by utility.　　On passing to injunctions current in the tribe, we see no less clearly how these emotions produced by approbation and reprobation come to be connected in experience with actions that are beneficial to the tribe, and actions that are detrimental to the tribe; and how there consequently grow up incentives to the one class of actions and prejudices against the other class. From early boyhood the young savage hears recounted the daring deeds of his chief—hears them in words of praise, and sees all faces glowing with admiration. From time to time, also, he listens while some one's cowardice is described in tones of scorn, with contemptuous metaphors, and sees him meet with derision whenever he appears. That is to say, one of the things that comes to be strongly associated in his mind with smiling faces, which are symbolical of pleasure in general, is courage; and one of the things that comes to be associated in his mind with frowns and other marks of enmity, which form a symbol of unhappiness, is cowardice. These feelings are not formed in him because he has reasoned his way to the truth that courage is useful to his tribe, and, by implication, to himself, or to the truth that cowardice is a cause of evil. In adult life he may perhaps see this; but he certainly does not see it at the time when bravery is thus associated in his consciousness with all that is good, and cowardice with all that is bad. Similarly, there are produced in him feelings of inclination or repugnance towards other lines of conduct that have become established or interdicted, because they are beneficial or injurious to the tribe; though neither the young nor the old know why they have become established or interdicted. Instance the praiseworthiness of wife-stealing, and the viciousness of marrying within the tribe.

85

We may now ascend a stage to an order of incentives and restraints derived from these. The primitive belief is that every dead man becomes a demon who remains somewhere at hand, and may at any moment return to give aid or do mischief. Hence among other agents whose approbation or reprobation are contemplated by the savage as consequences of his conduct, are the spirits of his ancestors. When a child, he is told of their deeds, now in triumphant tones, now in whispers of horror; and the instilled conviction that they may inflict some vaguely-imagined but fearful evil, or give some great help, becomes a powerful incentive or deterrent. Especially does this happen when the narrative is of a chief distinguished for his strength, his ferocity, his persistence in that revenge which the experiences of the savage make him regard as beneficial and virtuous. The consciousness that such a chief, dreaded by neighbouring tribes, and dreaded, too, by members of his own tribe, may reappear and punish those who have disregarded his injunctions, becomes a powerful motive. But it is clear, in the first place, that the imagined anger and the imagined satisfaction of this deified chief are simply transfigured forms of the anger and satisfaction displayed by those around; and that the feelings accompanying such imaginations have the same original root in the experiences which have associated an average of painful results with the manifestation of another's anger, and an average of pleasurable results with the manifestation of another's satisfaction. And it is clear, in the second place, that the actions thus forbidden and encouraged must be mostly actions that are respectively detrimental and beneficial to the tribe; since the successful chief, usually a better judge than the rest, has pursued the welfare of his tribe in pursuing his own welfare. Hence experiences of utility, consciously or unconsciously organized, underlie his injunctions; and the sentiments which prompt obedience are, though very indirectly and without the knowledge of those who feel them, referable to experiences of utility.

This transfigured form of restraint, differing at first but little from the original form, admits of immense development. Accumulating traditions, growing in grandeur as they are repeated from generation to generation, make more and more superhuman the early-recorded hero of the race. His powers of inflicting punishment and giving happiness become ever greater, more multitudinous, and more varied; so that the dread of divine displeasure and the desire to obtain divine approbation, acquire a certain largeness and generality. Still the conceptions remain anthropomorphic. The revengeful deity continues to be thought of as displaying human emotions in human ways. Moreover, the sentiments of right and duty, so far as they have become developed, refer mainly if not wholly to divine commands and interdicts; and have little reference to the natures of the acts commanded or interdicted. In the intended offering-up of Isaac, in the sacrifice of Jephthah's daughter, and in the hewing to pieces of Agag, as much as in the countless atrocities committed from religious motives by early historic races in general, we see that the morality and immorality of actions, as we understand them, are at first unrecognized; and that the feelings, chiefly of dread, which serve in place of them, are feelings felt towards the unseen beings supposed to issue commands and interdicts.

§ 521. Much of what passes as religious sentiment, is thus but a more highly re-representative form of that ego-altruistic sentiment which mainly guides men in their behaviour to one another. By implying its close kinship to worldliness, Leigh Hunt's happy phrase " other-worldliness," vividly suggests the truth that the feeling by which religious observance was almost wholly prompted in the past and is mainly prompted now, is a feeling in which the representation of divine approval goes along with a representation of general future happiness to be secured by that approval—a feeling which is vague in proportion to its high representativeness, but is nevertheless composed of elements originally furnished by experiences of gratification.

Let us mark carefully, too, this fact, that the consciousnesses of right and wrong, as they exist among the uncivilized and semi-civilized, and even to a great extent among those who are at present most civilized, originate in the ego-altruistic sentiments. If we glance back at past beliefs and their correlative feelings, as shown in Dante's poem, in the mystery-plays of the middle ages, in St. Bartholomew massacres, in burnings for heresy, we get proof that in comparatively-modern times right and wrong meant little else than subordination and insubordination—to a divine ruler primarily, and under him to a human ruler. Down to our own day this conception largely prevails, and is even embodied in elaborate ethical works: instance the *Essays on the Principles of Morality*, by Jonathan Dymond; which recognizes no ground of moral obligation save the will of God as expressed in the current creed. Indeed while sermons set forth the torments of the damned and the joys of the blessed as the chief deterrents and incentives, and while we have prepared for us printed instructions " how to make the best of both worlds," it cannot be denied that the feelings which impel and restrain men are still largely composed of elements like those operative on the savage—the dread, partly vague, partly specific, associated with the idea of reprobation, human and divine, and the sense of satisfaction, partly vague, partly specific, associated with the idea of approbation, human and divine.

Neither in the religious nor in the ethical sentiments, as thus developed to the ego-altruistic stage only, is there involved a consciousness, pleasurable or painful, caused by contemplation of acts considered in their intrinsic natures, apart from any consequences to self, immediate or remote.

§ 522. For this reason it is that the standards of right

and wrong have been, and still are, so unlike in different societies. Obviously, while the incentive and deterrent emotions have no other exciting causes than the real or ideal manifestations of approbation and disapprobation, human or divine, the notions of right and wrong with their corresponding sentiments, must depend on the theological traditions and the social circumstances. If the god of the race is represented as insisting on the extermination of enemies, and as being offended by mercy shown to them—if, as must hence happen, revenge comes to be associated in consciousness with the thought of divine pleasure and consequent rewards to be received, while forgiveness goes along with the thought of divine anger and pains that will follow it; then revenge and forgiveness become in consciousness respectively pleasurable and painful in their total results, or right and wrong. Similarly with the sentiments referring to acts that excite human approbation and disapprobation. Usages, no matter of what kind, which circumstances have established, so that conformity to them brings approval from those around while nonconformity brings frowns and blaming words, become sanctified. The aggregates of ideal pleasures and the aggregates of ideal pains which these opposite behaviours of fellow-men severally suggest, are associated with fulfilment and neglect; and hence fulfilment and neglect come to be thought of with liking and repugnance, and called proper and improper.

Evidently, then, the regulative sentiments of ego-altruistic nature, are, in their relations to concrete action, as variable as are the kinds of conduct conducive to social well-being under different social conditions. The needs of a small tribe that has to exist amid tribes daily threatening to destroy it, are widely different from the needs of a semi-civilized society, which, though warlike, has grown by the development of industry; and the needs of this, again, are widely different from those of a society like our own, in which the predatory activities have greatly decreased, the required subordination of ranks has become less, and rigidity of custom is no longer so necessary; and to such various needs, more or less unlike in every race and every age, the ego-altruistic sentiments continually adjust themselves— adjust themselves as the higher sentiments, standing related to conduct in the abstract, cannot adjust themselves. The ego-altruistic sentiments are the chief regulative agents in those transitional stages during which predominance of the highest sentiments would be fatal, because inconsistent with the conditions.

Nevertheless, the ego-altruistic sentiments have important components that are constant; and there are certain permanent feelings of right and wrong into which they enter. Pleasurably excited as they are by the display of approval, it must happen that a kind of conduct which calls forth marks of approval among all races and in all times, will be felt as right, irrespective of the people and the age; and *vice versâ*. A causeless insult, for example, is condemned everywhere in the world. The particular act or speech which is insulting varies with local circumstances. To spit in his face is the complimentary salute to a stranger among certain Nile tribes, and to omit returning this salute in kind would be a disrespect causing reprobation; while, among most peoples, the implications and accompanying feelings are just the opposite. So, too, in some societies to call a man a brother-in-law is an indignity, prompting resentful words and actions; while in other societies, naming one whom you are introducing as your brother-in-law implies a complimentary appreciation rather than otherwise. But though in these cases there is absolute disagreement as to what are insulting deeds and words, there is agreement in the feeling that to give offence without provocation is improper, and that it is proper to do that which conduces to friendly relations. It is thus throughout. The ego-altruistic sentiments, while inconstant in respect of the special characters of the acts exciting them, are constant in respect of the general characters of these acts, as being acts which, in their respective times and places, call forth from others signs of friendship or of enmity.

§ 523. One other aspect of the subject is worth dwelling on a moment, both as in itself interesting and as yielding a verification of the foregoing interpretations. I refer to the feeling of shame and its manifestations.

If there needs any further proof that the ego-altruistic sentiments are constituted as alleged, it will be found in the fact that shame, produced by representation of the contempt of others, is the same in its essential nature whether this imagined contempt is excited by a wrong thing really done or by a wrong thing supposed to be done. Children often furnish evidence of this substantial identity—showing us that a blush is as apt to arise in the innocent to whom guilt is ascribed as in the actually guilty.

It is true that the two states of feeling excited in these antithetical cases, must differ somewhat by the presence of a consciousness of guilt in the one case and its absence in the other; but the similarity, if not the identity, of the physiological manifestations, shows how substantially alike the two states of consciousness are. It is true also that in the majority of persons, believing in future rewards and punishments, the two consciousnesses differ by the presence in the one, and absence from the other, of a consolatory belief in ultimate rectification; though this is pretty clearly a secondary phase of the feeling—as is also implied by the order of the bodily effects. But the recognition of both these qualifying differences, serves but to make clear how relatively slight they are, and how substantially this painful form of ego-altruistic sentiment consists of a voluminous and vague re-representation of the mental attitudes of others, and the general unhappiness associated in thought with such mental attitudes.

And here we may see how far men at present are from

that highest moral state, in which the supreme and most powerful sentiments are those called forth by contemplation of conduct itself, and not by contemplation of other persons' opinions of conduct. In the average mind the pain constituted by consciousness of having done something intrinsically wrong, bears but a small ratio to the pain constituted by the consciousness of others' reprobation: even though this reprobation is excited by something not intrinsically wrong. Consider how difficult it would be to get a lady to wheel a costermonger's barrow down Regent-street, and how easily she may be led to say a malicious thing about some lady she is jealous of—contrast the intense repugnance to the one act, which is not in itself reprehensible, with the feeble repugnance to the other act, which is in itself reprehensible; and then infer how great is the evolution of the moral sentiments yet required to bring human nature into complete fitness for the social state.

CHAPTER VIII.

ALTRUISTIC * SENTIMENTS.

§ 524. The inferior regulative sentiments dealt with under the title of ego-altruistic, we find have the character that the actions exciting them, agreeably or disagreeably, are very inconstant in their concrete forms. Though in all societies and all stages of progress there are some kinds of behaviour, as those by which associates are intentionally pleased or are gratuitously irritated, which call forth marks of approbation and reprobation, serving to excite these ego-altruistic sentiments; yet there are also many kinds of behaviour not directly pleasing or irritating to others, but which have been made indirectly pleasing or irritating to them by the traditions and habits of their society, to which the ego-altruistic sentiments respond—actions which, in different times and places, are often exactly opposite. Hence it has been argued that the genesis of emotions after the manner described, can never result in

---

* I gladly adopt this word, for which we are indebted to M. Comte. Not long since, some critic, condemning it as new-fangled, asked why we should not be content with such good old-fashioned words as benevolent and beneficent. There is a quite-sufficient reason. Altruism and altruistic, suggesting by their forms as well as by their meanings the antithesis of egoism and egoistic, bring quickly and clearly into thought the opposition, in a way that benevolence or beneficence and its derivatives do not, because the antitheses are not directly implied by them. This superior suggestiveness greatly facilitates the communication of ethical ideas.

any settled and universal sentiments responding to intrinsic right and wrong.

The implication of this criticism is, that because in human customs and the correlative feelings, there has been and is so much variability, there can be no constancy. It is tacitly concluded that in the nature of things, there is nothing which makes one kind of conduct rather than another adapted to social life—everything is indeterminate. To infer that no settled sentiments can ever be generated by the process described, is to assume that there are no settled conditions to social welfare. Clearly if the temporary forms of conduct needful, initiate temporary ideas of right and wrong with responsive excitements of the sentiments, it is to be inferred that the permanent forms of conduct needful, will initiate permanent ideas of right and wrong with responsive excitements of the sentiments; and hence to question the genesis of these sentiments is to doubt the existence of these forms.

That there are such permanent forms of conduct, no one can deny who compares the law-books of all races which have outgrown the purely-predatory life. This variability of sentiment is but the concomitant of the transition from the aboriginal type of society fitted for destructive activities, to the civilized type of society fitted for peaceful activities. All along there has been going on a compromise between conflicting requirements, and a corresponding compromise between conflicting sentiments. The conditions are perpetually being partially changed, the corresponding habits modified, and the sentiments re-adjusted. Hence all this inconsistency. But just as fast as the peaceful activities become more dominant, just so fast do the conditions under which the peaceful activities are to be harmoniously carried on become more imperative, just so fast do the corresponding ideas become clear and the corresponding sentiments strong. And these ideas and sentiments must eventually grow uniform and permanent, for the reason that the conditions to complete social life are uniform and permanent.

§ 525. The industrial *régime* is distinguished from the predatory *régime* in this, that mutual dependence becomes great and direct while mutual antagonism becomes small and indirect. In a predatory society, feelings gratified by the ill-being of others (enemies) are habitually exercised, along with feelings gratified by the well-being of others (friends); whereas in an industrial society, feelings gratified by the ill-being of others, not being kept in extreme and constant activity, do not antagonize and repress the feelings gratified by the well-being of others. And since, as a society advances in organization, the inter-dependence of its parts increases, and the well-being of each is more bound up with the well-being of all, it results that the growth of feelings which find satisfaction in the well-being of all, is the growth of feelings adjusted to a fundamental unchanging condition to social welfare.

The feelings thus described we have here to deal with as the altruistic sentiments. They arise along with the ego-altruistic sentiments, from which they are not sharply marked off—as, indeed, if evolved, they could not be. Let us observe the process of differentiation.

§ 526. When impressed by the appearances and sounds constituting the natural language of any feeling in another being, the aggregate of feelings aroused by the associations which experience has established, mainly in the race but partly in the individual, form two groups that may be variously proportioned to one another; but of which neither commonly exist wholly unaccompanied by the other. The manifestations of the feeling tend to excite a kindred feeling in the observer; and they simultaneously tend to excite in the observer, feelings compounded out of experiences of pleasures and pains to himself, such as are apt to follow these manifestations. As shown in the chapter on " Sociality and Sympathy," intelligent creatures that live in presence of one another, and are exposed to like causes of pleasure and pain, acquire capacities for participating in one another's pleasures and pains. And we have seen in the chapter just closed, that in creatures living together and liable to receive pleasures and pains from one another's acts, prompted by amity or enmity, there are evolved emotions responding to manifestations of amity or enmity. That is to say, these last, or ego-altruistic sentiments, which have for their components representations of feelings likely to be under-gone by self, and the first, or altruistic sentiments, which have for their components representations of feelings that are being actually undergone by another, are simul-taneously aroused; and in the absence of counteracting causes might be expected to develop *pari passu*. There is nothing in the intrinsic natures of the unselfish emotions, which makes their evolution more difficult than is the evolu-tion of the selfish emotions, excited by the same manifes-tations. How is it, then, that the ego-altruistic sentiments may become so active, while the altruistic sentiments remain almost dormant?

The reply has already been indicated at the close of the chapter on " Sociality and Sympathy." Some instances were there given showing that the emotions, as with the sensations, frequent repetition of a painful stimulus brings about a remedial callousness. And we saw that con-sequently, if the conditions of existence are such as to neces-sitate frequent sympathetic excitements of a painful kind, the pains sympathetically excited will become gradually less, and there will result indifference. Further, it was pointed out that during the struggle for existence among societies, originally very intense and even now by no means ended, the conditions have been such as to make imperative the readiness to inflict pain, and have correspondingly re-pressed fellow-feeling. It may here be added that beyond this checking of the sympathies which the antagonisms of societies have necessitated and still necessitate, there has been a checking of them consequent on the struggle for existence within each society. Not only does this struggle for existence involve the necessity that personal ends must be pursued with little regard to the evils entailed on unsuccessful competitors; but it also involves the necessity that there shall be not too keen a sympathy with that diffused suffering inevitably accompanying this industrial battle. Clearly if there were so quick a sympathy for this suffering as to make it felt in anything like its real greatness and intensity, life would be rendered intolerable to all. Familiarity with the marks of misery, necessarily produces (or rather maintains) a proportionate indifference; and this is as inevitable a concomitant of the bloodless competition among members of a society, as it is an inevitable concomitant of the bloody competition between societies.

Coming to the fact which here especially concerns us, we may now see why it happens that out of the various feelings produced in each by the expressions of feelings in others, the ego-altruistic may develop to a great height while the altruistic remain comparatively undeveloped. For under past conditions to social existence, the welfare of society and of each individual, have not necessitated any repression of the ego-altruistic feelings; but, contrariwise, the pleasure of the individual and the well-being of society have both demanded the growth of these feelings. Love of fame has been a main stimulus to military achievement, and therefore to national self-preservation. Desire for approbation, by smoothing the intercourse of individuals, has tended greatly to facilitate co-operation. Dread of reproach, both by checking cowardice in battle and by restraining misbehaviour in social life, has tended to public and private advantage. Only when he so eagerly pursues the applause of others as to sacrifice immediate welfare, does the individual find his desire for this indirect representative gratification kept in check by a desire for some direct presentative gratification. Thus the ego-altruistic sentiments have been greatly fostered and but little repressed. And for this reason the dominant tendency has become such that on witnessing any display of feeling in another, the observer has a quick and large rush of that consciousness in which represented results to self take the leading place, while representation of the feeling that prompts the display is but feeble, or is even absent.

§ 527. Of the two groups of feelings which thus become differentiated, the altruistic, to which we are now turning our attention, are all sympathetic excitements of egoistic feelings; and they vary in their characters according to the characters of the egoistic feelings sympathetically excited.

Certain altruistic feelings thus produced do not come within the definition of sentiments, as above given. When a yawn produces a sympathetic yawn, when the sight of one who is sick at sea increases the tendency to sickness in the observer, when a thrill in the limbs is felt on seeing another person at the edge of a precipice, or when, on witnessing an operation, an assistant undergoes such agitation as to faint, the excitement is in some of the cases wholly, and in others cases partly, a sympathetic excitement of sensations —the content of consciousness is representative simply, and not re-representative.

An altruistic feeling becomes re-representative, or a sentiment proper, only when the feeling sympathized with is an emotion; and, as we shall see, the more-developed forms of altruistic feeling are entirely of this kind. Nevertheless, we must here recognize the fact that no line can be drawn between the two—that in the simplest cases there is sympathy in sensation, that very generally there is sympathy in sensation and in the emotion accompanying it (for in the subject of a sensation strong enough to excite sympathy, there is usually an emotional accompaniment), and that we pass gradually up to that higher stage at which the sympathy is with feelings containing no presentative elements.

This qualification being borne in mind, we may now consider in succession the leading forms of altruistic sentiment.

§ 528. Very much of the feeling ordinarily classed as generosity is ego-altruistic. The state of consciousness which accompanies performance of an act beneficial to another, is usually mixed; and often the pleasure given is represented less vividly than are the recipient's feeling towards the giver and the approval of spectators. The sentiment of generosity proper, is, however, unmixed in those cases where the benefaction is anonymous: provided, also, that there is no contemplation of a reward to be reaped hereafter. These conditions being fulfilled, the benefaction clearly implies a vivid representation of the pleasurable feelings, (usually themselves representative) which the recipient will have.

Unmixed generosity thus constituted, has two distinguishable degrees. In the lower form of it, the represented gratification of another is strong enough to prompt the act conducing to that gratification, providing the act entails no considerable sacrifice in the shape of trouble taken or selfish gratification relinquished. Mostly, unmixed generosity does not go beyond this; since benefaction of the kind described, usually takes the form of pecuniary aid from one able to give it with little if any inconvenience. Only in the comparatively-rare cases where the anonymous benefaction is from one who can ill afford the money or the labour required, does generosity rise to that highest form in which altruistic gratification out-balances egoistic gratification.

Generosity being a relatively-simple altruistic sentiment (or at least that generosity which gives pleasure of a sensuous kind), it is shown in some measure, and occasionally to a considerable degree, during early stages of human evolution. Though, in the conduct of savages, what seem to be generous acts are usually caused by desires for applause, yet, occasionally, an unselfish pursuit of another's welfare appears undeniable; though even here we may observe that it goes along with strong attachment, like that of a dog to his master, and is therefore to be distinguished from the generosity shown when there is no close personal relation. Admitting, however, that while much mingled with lower sentiments, generosity early displays itself slightly and erratically; we may safely say that it becomes marked and frequent only as fast as civilization develops the sympathies. Contrasting the philanthrophy of modern times with the very little answering to it in ancient times, suffices to show this.

§ 529. The last comparison introduces us to a closely-allied altruistic sentiment, the development of which, indeed, it illustrates better than it does the development of generosity: I mean the sentiment of pity. Pleasure that is constituted by representation of pleasure in another, being the feeling which prompts generous actions; the feeling which prompts endeavours to mitigate pain, is a pain constituted by representation of pain in another. As already explained, this sentiment is necessarily repressed during phases predatory activity; and is even, to a considerable degree, kept in check by industrial competition. Always, indeed, domestic life has afforded some scope for it —joining its exercise with that of the sexual and parental feelings. But pity proper, or the altruistic sentiment which prompts the relief of suffering in others, though there exists no connexion personal or social with those others, nor is felt any liking for them, is a sentiment that takes a considerable development only as fast as diminution of the predatory activities allows.

Sympathy with pain, produces in conduct modifications of several kinds. In the first place, it puts a check on the

intentional infliction of pain. Various degrees of this effect
are observable. Supposing no animosity is felt, the hurting
another by accident arouses a genuine feeling of regret in
all adults save the very brutal: representation of the physical pain produced, is sufficiently vivid in nearly all civilized
persons to make them avoid producing it. Where there
exists a higher degree of representative power, there is a
reluctance to inflict emotional pain. The disagreeable state
of mind that would be excited in another by a sharp word
or harsh act, is imagined with such clearness that the
imagination serves partially or wholly as a deterrent. And
in sympathetic persons, representation of the annoyance to
be given is so vivid that it often prevents them from doing
or saying unpleasant things which they see ought to be done
or said: the sentiment of pity checks the infliction of pain,
even unduly.

In another class of cases, pity modifies conduct by prompting efforts to assuage pain that is already being borne—
pain arising from disease, or from accident, or from the
cruelty of enemies, or even from the anger of the pitying
person himself. The sympathy thus exhibited with pain,
sensational or emotional, may, however, lead to two opposite
courses, according as the individual sympathetically affected
has a small or a great amount of representative power. If
he is not highly imaginative, he may, and often does, rid
himself of the disagreeable consciousness by getting out of
sight or hearing; and even if highly imaginative, he is
prompted to do this when no remedial measures can be
taken. But if his imagination is vivid, and if he also sees
that the suffering can be diminished by his aid, then he
cannot escape from his disagreeable consciousness by going
away; since the representated pain continues with him, impelling him to return and assist.

And here we see how altruistic sentiment under this
form, as under other forms, becomes high in proportion as it
becomes re-representative. It fulfils its function far more

effectually when it is excitable not by actual manifestations
of pain only, but also by ideas of those manifestations.

Here, too, is a fit place for remarking that higher representative power does not involve greater commiseration, unless there have been received painful experiences like, or
akin to, those which are witnessed. An important truth implied in all these interpretations is, that every altruistic feeling needs the corresponding egoistic feeling as an indispensable factor; since unless a sensation or emotion has been felt,
it cannot be sympathetically excited. For this reason strong
persons, though they may be essentially-sympathetic in their
natures, cannot adequately enter into the feelings of the
weak. Never having been nervous or sensitive, they are unable to conceive the sufferings which chronic invalids experience from small perturbing causes. Hence the frequent
remark that the healthy, after having once been seriously ill,
become much kinder to those who are ill than they were
before. They have now had the egoistic feelings which,
being sympathetically excited, produce the appropriate
altruistic feelings.

§ 530. From the simpler forms of altruistic sentiment, we
pass now to the most complex form of it—the sentiment of
justice. This sentiment evidently does not consist of representations of simple pleasures or pains experienced by
others; but it consists of representations of those emotions
which others feel, when actually or prospectively allowed or
forbidden the activities by which pleasures are to be gained
or pains escaped. The sentiment of justice is thus constituted by representation of a feeling that is itself highly re-
representative.

The feeling thus represented, or sympathetically excited
as we say, is that which, under the head of egoistic sentiments, was described as the love of personal freedom. It
is the feeling which delights in surrounding conditions
that put no restraint on the activities—the feeling which is

pained, even in inferior natures, by whatever shackles the limbs or arrests locomotion, and which, in superior natures, is pained by whatever indirectly impedes the activities, and even by whatever threatens to impede them. This sentiment, primarily serving to maintain intact the sphere required by the individual for the due exercise of his powers and fulfilment of his desires, secondarily serves, when sympathetically excited, to cause respect for the like spheres of other individuals—serves also, by its sympathetic excitement, to prompt defence of others when their spheres of action are invaded. Evidently, in proportion as the sentiment under its egoistic form becomes more highly re-representative, so as to be excitable by more indirect and remote invasions of liberty, it simultaneously becomes under its altruistic form more appreciative of the liberty of others,—more respectful of others' like claims, and desirous not to trench on others' equal rights. Here, as in every case, there can be no altruistic feeling but what arises by sympathetic excitement of a corresponding egoistic feeling; and hence there can never be a sense of justice to others when there is not a sense of justice to self, at least equally great. The last, however, does not necessarily involve the first as its complement; for, in the absence of sympathy, the last may exist without the first. But sympathy remaining constant, the egoistic and altruistic forms of the sentiment of justice will develop together; and the egoistic form of the sentiment remaining constant, the altruistic form of it will vary with the degree of sympathy.   Societies, past and present, supply ample evidence of these relations. At the one extreme, we have the familiar truth that the type of nature which readily submits to slavery, is a type of nature equally ready to play the tyrant when occasion serves. At the other extreme, we have the fact, well illustrated in our own society, that along with the increasing tendency to resist aggression, there goes a diminishing tendency on the part of those in power to aggress. In England, the same nature which in the classes ruled has more and more asserted liberty, has in the ruling classes more and more respected liberty. There has been an increasing readiness to yield, partly because of an increasing sympathy with the feeling prompting the demand.

The limit toward which this highest altruistic sentiment advances, is tolerably clear. Its egoistic factor, finding satisfaction in surrounding conditions which put no immediate or remote restraint on the activities; and its other factor, sympathy, by which it is made altruistic, ever tending as it grows more sensitive and comprehensive to excite a vivid fellow-feeling with this love of unrestrained activity in others; it results that the advance is towards a state in which, while each citizen will tolerate no other restriction on his freedom, he will tolerate that restriction on it which the like claims of fellow-citizens involve. Nay more—he will not simply tolerate this restriction, but will spontaneously recognize it and assert it—will be sympathetically anxious for each other citizen's due sphere of action as for his own; and will defend it against invasion while he refrains from invading it himself. This is manifestly the condition of equilibrium which the egoistic sentiment and the altruistic sentiment co-operate to produce.

§ 531. And now mark how erroneous is the belief that evolution of mind by the accumulated and inherited effects of experiences, cannot result in permanent and universal moral sentiments, with their correlative moral principles. While, as we have seen, the ego-altruistic sentiments adjust themselves to the various modes of conduct required by social circumstances in each place and age, the altruistic sentiments adjust themselves to the modes of conduct that are permanently beneficial, because conforming to the conditions needful for the highest welfare of individuals in the associated state. The conflict that has hitherto gone on in every society between the predatory life and the industrial life, has necessitated a corresponding conflict between modes of feeling appropriate to the two; and there have similarly been necessitated conflicting standards of right. But now that the pain-inflicting activities are less habitual, and the repression of the sympathies less constant, the altruistic sentiments, which find their satisfaction in conduct that is regardful of others and so conduces to harmonious cooperation, are becoming stronger. The sacredness of life, of liberty, of property, are more and more vividly felt as civilization advances. Among all the higher races that have long been subject to social discipline, there is approximate agreement on these points, in so far as the intercourse between fellow-citizens is concerned. And even during the antagonisms of war, the predatory activities are now exercised under considerable limitations: the lives, and persons, and goods, of non-combatants, and even of combatants, are much more respected.

Along with evolution of the altruistic sentiments thus caused, there goes evolution of the ideas and principles answering to them. And here we may observe the relation which this view bears to current ethical theories, and especially to the Doctrine of Utility. Before pointing out how far the Evolution-theory of moral feelings and conceptions, harmonizes with that implied by the Doctrine of Utility, and how far it differs from it, something must be said respecting the meaning of the word Utility. Conveniently comprehensive as is this word, it has inconvenient and misleading implications. It vividly suggests uses, and means, and proximate ends; while it but faintly suggests the pleasures, positive or negative, which are the ultimate ends, and which, in ethical discussions, are alone considered. Further, it implies conscious recognition of means and ends —implies the deliberate taking of some course to gain a perceived benefit; and ignores the multitudinous cases in which actions are determined and made habitual by experiences of pleasurable or painful results, without any conscious generalizing of these experiences. When, however, the word Utility has been cleared of misleading associations, and its meaning adequately extended, we see that the Doctrine of Utility may be harmonized with the Evolution-theory of moral feelings and ideas, provided it recognizes the accumulated effects of inherited experiences; and that thus even sympathy, and the sentiments resulting from sympathy, may be interpreted as caused by experiences of utility.

Supposing all thoughts of rewards and punishments, immediate or remote, to be left out of consideration, any one who hesitates to inflict a pain because of the vivid representation of that pain which arises in him, is restrained not by any sense of obligation, nor by any formulated doctrine of utility, but by the association established in his consciousness. And it is clear that if, after repeated experiences of the moral discomfort he has felt from witnessing the evils indirectly caused by certain of his acts, he is led to check himself when again tempted to those acts, the restraint is of like nature. Conversely with the pleasure-giving acts: repetitions of kind deeds, and experiences of the sympathetic gratifications that follow, tend continually to make stronger the association between such deeds and feelings of happiness. Eventually these experiences may be consciously generalized, and there may result a deliberate pursuit of sympathetic gratifications. There may also come to be distinctly recognized the truths that the remoter results of cruel deeds and kind deeds are respectively detrimental and beneficial—that due regard for others is conducive to ultimate personal welfare, and disregard of others to ultimate personal disaster; and then there may become current such summations of experience as " honesty is the best policy." But such intellectual recognitions of utility do not precede and cause the moral sentiments. The moral sentiments precede such recognitions of utility, and make them possible. The pleasures and pains that follow sympathetic and unsympathetic actions, have first to be

slowly associated with these actions, and the resulting incentives and deterrents frequently obeyed, before there can
arise the perceptions that sympathetic and unsympathetic
actions are remotely beneficial or detrimental to the actor;
and there must be a still longer and still wider registration
and comparison of experiences, before there can arise the
perceptions that they are socially beneficial and detrimental.
When, however, the ultimate effects, personal and social,
have gained general recognition, are expressed in current
maxims, and lead to injunctions having the religious sanction, the sentiments that prompt sympathetic actions and
check unsympathetic ones, are immensely strengthened by
their alliances. Approbation and reprobation, divine and
human, come to be associated in thought with sympathetic and unsympathetic actions respectively. The commands of the creed, the legal penalties, the code of social
conduct, unitedly enforce them; and every child as it grows
up, daily has impressed on it by the words and faces and
voices of those around, the authority of these highest principles of conduct.

And now we may see why there arises a belief in the
special sacredness of these highest principles, and a sense of
the supreme authority of the altruistic sentiments answering
to them. Many of the actions which, in early social states,
received the religious sanction and gained public approbation, had the drawback that such sympathies as existed were
outraged, and there was hence an imperfect satisfaction.
Whereas these altruistic actions, while similarly having the
religious sanction and gaining public approbation, bring a
sympathetic consciousness of pleasure given or of pain prevented; and, beyond this, bring a sympathetic consciousness of human welfare at large, as being furthered by making
altruistic actions habitual. Both this special and this general sympathetic consciousness, become stronger and wider in
proportion as the power of mental representation increases,
and the imagination of consequences, immediate and remote,

grows more vivid and comprehensive. Until at length the altruistic sentiments begin to call in question the authority of the ego-altruistic sentiments, which once ruled unchallenged. They prompt resistance to laws that do not fulfil the conception of justice, encourage men to brave the frowns of their fellows by pursuing courses at variance with old but injurious customs, and even cause dissent from the current religion: either to the extent of disbelief in those alleged divine attributes and acts not approved by this supreme moral arbiter, or to the extent of entire rejection of a creed which ascribes such attributes and acts.

§ 532. Did it seem needful, a section might here be given to a yet more complicated altruistic sentiment—that of mercy. The state of consciousness thus named, is one in which the execution of an act prompted by the sentiment of justice, is prevented by an out-balancing pity—by a representation of the suffering to be inflicted. Here we have two altruistic sentiments in antagonism; and it is interesting to observe how, occasionally, there arises a painful hesitation between their two dictates, each of which would seem morally imperative in the absence of the other. The anxiety to avoid giving pain prompts one course; and an opposite course is prompted by the sentiment responding to those supreme principles of equity which cannot be relaxed without danger.

Dwelling no further on this sentiment, I will devote a brief space to one other belonging to the group; and I do so mainly because it has, in common with a kindred sentiment commented on in a previous chapter, a quality difficult to understand—I refer to what we may call, by analogy, the luxury of pity.

For there is often an element in pity distinct from the elements already dealt with, and not to be referred to the same causes. Under its primary form, pity implies simply the representation of a pain, sensational or emotional, experienced by another; and its function as so constituted, appears to be merely that of preventing the infliction of pain, or prompting efforts to assuage pain when it has been inflicted. In this process there is implied nothing approaching to pleasure—relief from pain is all the pitying person gains by gaining it for the person pitied. But in a certain phase of pity the pain has a pleasurable accompaniment; and the pleasurable pain, or painful pleasure, continues even where nothing is done, or can be done, towards mitigating the suffering. The contemplation of the suffering exercises a kind of fascination—continues when away from the sufferer, and sometimes so occupies the imagination as to exclude other thoughts. There arises a seemingly-abnormal desire to dwell on that which is intrinsically painful—a desire strong enough to cause resistance to any distraction: a resistance like that which the luxury of grief causes. How does there originate this pleasurable element in the feeling? Why is there not in this case, as in other cases, a readiness, and even an eagerness, to exclude a painful emotion? Clearly we have here some mode of consciousness which the foregoing explanations overlook.

I see but a single possible solution of the mystery. This pleasurable feeling which joins itself with the sentiment of pity, is not one that has arisen through the inherited effects of experiences, but belongs to a quite different group, traceable to the survival of the fittest simply—to the natural selection of incidental variations. In this group are included all the bodily appetites, together with those simpler instincts, sexual and parental, by which every race is maintained; and which must exist before the higher processes of mental evolution can commence. The parental instinct is that member of this group with which, I think, the feeling we are considering is allied: not, of course, the parental instinct under its concrete aspect, but the parental instinct in its intrinsic nature.

We commonly suppose that the parental instinct is shown

only in a creature's attachment to his or her own offspring. But a moment's thought shows this to be too narrow a conception. In cases of adoption, the feeling goes out towards offspring of others; and the habitual conduct of adults towards children not their own, proves clearly that the feeling is excitable apart from parenthood. Even animals show us this fact. Adoption is by no means uncommon; and sometimes there is adoption of young belonging to another species. Thus the instinct is not adequately defined as that which attaches a creature to its young: though most frequently and most strongly displayed in this relation, it is not exclusively so displayed. How, then, shall we describe it in such way as to include all its manifestations? What is the common trait of the objects which excite it? The common trait is always relative weakness or helplessness. Equally in the little girl with her doll, in the lady with her lap-dog, in the cat that has adopted a puppy, and in the hen that is anxious about the ducklings she has hatched, the feeling arises in presence of something feeble and dependent to be taken care of.

On comparing young creatures of all classes, we see that the clusters of special attributes by which they impress their respective parents, are extremely various. The one thing constant in all such clusters of attributes is the incapacity indicated: smallness joined, usually, with relative inactivity, being the chief indications of incapacity. May we not infer, then, that the instinct which is constant in parents stands related to the trait which is constant in offspring? And if so—if love of the helpless is that which essentially constitutes the feeling, then it becomes clear how, through association of ideas, manifestations of helplessness in beings other than offspring tend to excite it. Not simply the young of the same species and the young of other species will be its objects; but weakly creatures in general, and creatures that have been made weakly by accident, by disease, or by ill-treatment.

This love of the helpless seems to me the chief root of that which Dr. Bain names the tender emotion. Deep down as it is in the natures of highly-developed beings in general, and playing so dominant a part as it does in their adult lives, it is liable to be excited by a variety of properties and relations suggestive of the things which primarily excite it. And so not only does the sight or the thought of one who fails to cope with his surroundings call it out, but it is called out by any of the traits which commonly go along with helplessness, as primarily and habitually displayed in offspring. Even mere smallness in an inanimate object will cause a slight wave of it; as you may perceive in the expression, " dear little thing," applied by a lady to some art-product or ornament that is much less than others of its kind. And sundry of the physical attributes which Dr. Bain names as arousing it, probably do so because they are in some way like attributes of the infant. Similarly, when the relation to another person is one of yielding aid, or one in which there is a desire to aid, the parallelism to the relation between parent and offspring brings into consciousness more or less of the same feeling. This is conspicuously the case in the emotion that grows up in a man towards a woman. That relative weakness, which in the woman appeals for protection, satisfies in the man the desire for something to protect; and this satisfied desire forms a large component of the tender emotion produced in him by the relation. What is the nature of the reciprocal emotion, I, of course, cannot say; but it must differ in some measure as being a feeling entertained by the weaker towards the stronger, though it may be the same as being a feeling entertained towards one who is prized and possessed, actually or representatively.

Returning to the mysterious sentiment here to be considered, we get a possible explanation of it. All those cases where the luxury of pity is experienced, are cases where the person pitied has been brought by illness or by misfortune of some kind to a state which excites this love of the helpless. Hence the painful consciousness which sympathy produces, is combined with the pleasurable consciousness constituted by the tender emotion. Verification of this view is afforded by sundry interpretations it yields. Though the saying that "pity is akin to love" is not true literally, since in their intrinsic natures the two are quite unlike, yet that the two are so associated that pity tends to excite love, is a truth forming part of the general truth above set forth. That pleasure is found in reading a melancholy story or witnessing a tragic drama, is also a fact which ceases to appear strange. And we get a key to the seeming anomaly, that very often one who confers benefits feels more affection for the person benefited than the person benefited feels for him.

It is to be observed, finally, that a reciprocal excitement between sympathy and the tender emotion, must be recognized as habitually complicating altruistic sentiments of all kinds. Wherever there exists the tender emotion, the sympathies are more easily excited; and wherever sympathy, pleasurable or painful, has been aroused, more or less of the tender emotion is awakened along with it. This communion arises inevitably. In the parental instinct, with the actions it prompts, we have the primordial altruism; while in sympathy, with the actions it prompts, we have the developed altruism; and naturally the two forms of altruism become connected. Remote as are their roots, they grow inextricably entangled, because the circumstances which arouse them have in common the relation of benefactor to beneficiary.

CHAPTER IX.

ÆSTHETIC SENTIMENTS.

§ 533. Many years ago I met with a quotation from a German author to the effect that the æsthetic sentiments originate from the play-impulse. I do not remember the name of the author; and if any reasons were given for this statement, or any inferences drawn from it, I cannot recall them. But the statement itself has remained with me, as being one which, if not literally true, is yet the adumbration of a truth.

The activities we call play are united with the æsthetic activities, by the trait that neither subserve, in any direct way, the processes conducive to life. The bodily powers, the intellectual faculties, the instincts, appetites, passions, and even those highest feelings we have lately dealt with, have maintenance of the organic equilibrium of the individual, or else maintenance of the species, as their immediate or remote ends. Arrest one of the viscera, and the vital actions quickly cease; prevent a limb from moving, and the ability to meet surrounding circumstances is seriously interfered with; destroy a sense-organ, paralyze a perceptive power, derange the reason, and there comes more or less failure in that adjustment of conduct to conditions by which life is preserved; and if those egoistic sentiments which prompt care of property and liberty, or those ego-altruistic and altruistic ones which regulate conduct towards others, do not act, impediments to complete life are caused by absence of means or by the alienation of fellow-men. But while the primary actions of the faculties, bodily and mental, with their accompanying gratifications, are thus obviously related to proximate ends that imply ulterior benefits, those actions of them which constitute play, and those which yield the æsthetic gratifications, do not refer to ulterior benefits—the proximate ends are the only ends. It is, indeed, true that activities of these orders may bring the ulterior benefits of increased power in the faculties exercised; and that thus the life as a whole may be afterwards furthered. But this effect is one that pairs off with the like effect produced by the primary actions of the faculties—leaving the difference just where it was. From the primary action of a faculty there results the immediate normal gratification, *plus* the maintained or increased ability due to exercise, *plus* the objective end achieved or requirement fulfilled. But from this secondary action of a faculty exhibited in play or in an æsthetic pursuit, there results only the immediate gratification *plus* the maintained or increased ability.

Before dealing with the æsthetic sentiments as thus distinguished and thus classed, we must go a little deeper,— asking whence arises the play-impulse, and how there finally comes that supplementary activity of the higher faculties which the Fine Arts imply.

§ 534. Inferior kinds of animals have in common the trait, that all their forces are expended in fulfilling functions essential to the maintenance of life. They are unceasingly occupied in searching for food, in escaping from enemies, in forming places of shelter, and in making preparations for progeny. But as we ascend to animals or high types, having faculties more efficient and more numerous, we begin to find that time and strength are not wholly absorbed in providing for immediate needs. Better nutrition, gained by superiority, occasionally yields a surplus of vigour. The appetites being satisfied, there is no craving which directs the overflowing energies to the pursuit of more prey, or to the satisfaction of some pressing want. The greater variety of faculty commonly joined with this greater efficiency of faculty, has a kindred result. When there have been developed many powers adjusted to many requirements, they cannot all act at once: now the circumstances call these into exercise and now those; and some of them occasionally remain unexercised for considerable periods. Thus it happens that in the more-evolved creatures, there often recurs an energy somewhat in excess of immediate needs, and there comes also such rest, now of this faculty and now of that, as permits the bringing of it up to a state of high efficiency by the repair which follows waste.

In the chapter on "Æstho-Physiology" (§ 50) it was pointed out that "nerve-centres disintegrated by action, are perpetually re-integrating themselves, and again becoming fit for action." It was further pointed out that "in proportion as any part of a nerve-centre has been for a long time unused—in proportion, that is, as repair of it has gone on day after day and night after night unhindered by appreciable waste, it must be brought to a state of more than ordinary instability—a state of excessive readiness to decompose and discharge. What must happen? In common with all other parts, it is exposed to the reverberations which from instant to instant fill the nervous system. Its extreme instability must render it unusually sensitive to these reverberations—unusually ready to undergo change, to yield up molecular motion, and to become the seat of the concomitant ideal feeling. * * * Here we have the interpretation of what are called *desires*. Desires are ideal feelings that arise when the real feelings to which they correspond have not been experienced for some time."

Every one of the mental powers, then, being subject to this law, that its organ when dormant for an interval longer than ordinary becomes unusually ready to act—unusually ready to have its correlative feelings aroused, giving an unusual readiness to enter upon all the correlative activities; it happens that a simulation of those activities is easily fallen into, when circumstances offer it in place of the real activities. Hence play of all kinds—hence this tendency to superfluous and useless exercise of faculties that have been quiescent. Hence, too, the fact that these uncalled-for exertions are most displayed by those faculties which take the most prominent parts in the creature's life. Observe how this holds from the simplest faculties upwards.

A rat, with incisors that grow continuously in adaptation to the incessant wear they undergo, and with a correlative desire to use these incisors, will, if caged, occupy itself in gnawing anything it can get hold of. A cat, with claws and appended muscles adjusted to daily action in catching prey, but now leading a life that is but in a small degree predatory, has a craving to exercise these parts; and may be seen to satisfy the craving by stretching out her legs, protruding her claws, and pulling at some such surface as the covering of a chair or the bark of a tree. And still more interestingly in the giraffe, which when free is all day long using its tongue to pull down branches of trees, there arises, when in confinement, so great a need for some kindred exercise that it perpetually grasps with its tongue such parts of the top of its house as can be laid hold of—so wearing out the upper angles of doors, &c. · This useless activity of unused organs, which in these cases hardly rises to what we call play, passes into play ordinarily so called where there is a more manifest union of feeling with the action. Play is equally an artificial exercise of powers which, in default of their natural exercise, become so ready to discharge that they relieve themselves by simulated actions in place of real actions. For dogs and other predatory creatures show us unmistakably that their play consists of mimic chase and mimic fighting—they pursue

one another, they try to overthrow one another, they bite
one another as much as they dare. And so with the kitten
running after a cotton-ball, making it roll and again catching
it, crouching as though in ambush and then leaping on it,
we see that the whole sport is a dramatizing of the pursuit
of prey—an ideal satisfaction for the destructive instincts in
the absence of real satisfaction for them.   It is
the same with human beings. The plays of children—
nursing dolls, giving tea-parties, and so on, are dramatiz-
ings of adult activities. The sports of boys, chasing one
another, wrestling, making prisoners, obviously gratify in a
partial way the predatory instincts. And if we consider
even their games of skill, as well as the games of skill
practised by adults, we find that, significantly enough,
the essential element running through them has the same
origin. For no matter what the game, the satisfaction is in
achieving victory—in getting the better of an antagonist.
This love of conquest, so dominant in all creatures because
it is the correlative of success in the struggle for existence,
gets gratification from a victory at chess in the absence of
ruder victories. Nay, we may even see that playful conversation is characterized by the same element. In banter, in
repartee, in " chaff," the almost-constant trait is some display of relative superiority—the detection of a weakness, a
mistake, an absurdity, on the part of another. Through
a wit-combat there runs the effort to obtain mental
supremacy. That is to say, this activity of the intellectual
faculties in which they are not used for purposes of guidance
in the business of life, is carried on partly for the sake of the
pleasure of the activity itself, and partly for the accompanying satisfaction of certain egoistic feelings which find for the
moment no other sphere.

But now mark that this which holds of the bodily
powers, the destructive instincts, and those emotions
related to them that dominate in life because they are
directly concerned in the struggle by which life is main-

87

tained, holds of all other faculties. Their organs undergoing repair during rest, similarly tend to become more
excitable, to pass into ideal action in the absence of real
action, and readily fall into any artificial mode of exercise
substituted for the natural mode of exercise, when that is not
to be had. The higher but less essential powers, as well as
the lower but more essential powers, thus come to have
activities that are carried on for the sake of the immediate
gratifications derived, without reference to ulterior benefits;
and to such higher powers, æsthetic products yield these
substituted activities, as games yield them to various lower
powers.

§ 535. The general nature and position of the æsthetic
sentiments, thus made dimly comprehensible, will be made
more clearly comprehensible by observing how we distinguish certain modes of feeling as æsthetic rather than others.
Setting out with the simplest sensations, we shall find that
the æsthetic character of a feeling is habitually associated
with separateness from life-serving function.

In scarcely any degree do we ascribe the æsthetic character to sensations of taste. Very many tastes which are
greatly enjoyed do not in the smallest degree suggest ideas
of beauty; and even sweet things, though we may consider them delicious, we do not consider beautiful in the
proper sense of the word. This fact goes along with the
fact that the gustatory gratifications are but rarely separated
from the life-serving functions: they accompany eating and
drinking, and do not ordinarily occur apart from one or
other of them. Take next the pleasures which
odours produce. These, much more separable from life-
serving functions, become pleasures sought for themselves;
and hence they have in some degree the æsthetic character.
A delightful perfume, if it does not give an æsthetic feeling
of a quite distinct kind, gives something nearly approaching
to it: on smelling a flower there may, besides the agreeable

sensation itself, be discerned a secondary vague gratification.   In sensations of colour, which are still
more dissociated from life-serving functions, the æsthetic
element becomes decided. Though the clustered patches of
colour which make up our visual perceptions, severally serve
as signs by which we identify objects and so guide our actions, yet recognitions of colour are not in most cases essential
to our guidance: witness the comparatively-small inconvenience felt by the colour-blind. Hence, though the
faculty which appreciates colour has a life-serving function,
the relation between its activity and its use is not close.
Consequently, the gratification derivable from this activity,
carried on for its own sake, becomes conspicuous: the delight in fine colours is deliberately ministered to, and the idea
of beauty strongly associated with them.   Similarly is it with sounds. The power to perceive and distinguish sounds, primarily aids in adjusting actions to circumstances; but most sounds do not so concern us that we
have to modify our conduct on hearing them. Thus the
actions of the auditory faculty are much dissociated from
life-serving functions; and there arises a wide scope for
pleasures derivable from superfluous actions of the faculty.
These pleasures we class as æsthetic: tones of certain kinds
are regarded as beautiful.

I do not mean that wherever a faculty of sensation has a
sphere of exercise beyond the sphere of useful application,
the sensations brought by non-useful exercise have *necessarily* the æsthetic character; for obviously most of the
olfactory, visual, and auditory sensations gained within such
non-useful spheres of action, are devoid of the æsthetic
character. I mean simply that this separableness from life-
serving function, is one of the *conditions* to the acquirement
of the æsthetic character.

That this is so, we see on passing to the other extreme—
on comparing sentiments instead of sensations. The love
of possession is but little separable from life-serving func-

tion. The motives and deeds which result in acquisition, always have ulterior benefit in view; and cannot well be separated from the thought of ulterior benefit. Here the æsthetic character is entirely absent: neither performer nor observer sees any beauty in the acquisitive activity. This is not because it is a purely-egoistic activity; for there are sentiments and corresponding activities quite as egoistic, and even more egoistic, to which the æsthetic consciousness responds. It needs but to recall the delight with which prowess, in such superfluous combats as tournaments, is seen and read about, to perceive that in this case, though the activity is absolutely egoistic, there is nevertheless aroused an admiration of something described as fine and glorious. So, too, with the display of the purely-egoistic sentiment, pride. The actions in which this is manifested are dissociated very widely from life-serving functions; and there is a certain form of them capable of arousing the æsthetic feeling of grandeur and dignity, both in actor and spectator.

A further proof that the æsthetic consciousness is essentially one in which the actions themselves, apart from ends, form the object-matter, is afforded by the conspicuous fact that many æsthetic feelings arise from contemplation of the attributes and deeds of other persons, real or ideal. In these cases, the consciousness is remote from life-serving function, not simply as is the consciousness accompanying play or the enjoyment of a beautiful colour or tone, but also in the further way that the thing contemplated as a source of pleasure, is not a direct action or affection of self at all, but is a secondary affection of self produced by contempla-tion of acts and characters and feelings known as objective, and present to self only by representation. Here the separateness from life-serving function is extreme; since neither a beneficial end, nor an act conducive to that end, nor a sentiment prompting such act, forms an element in the æsthetic feeling. Imagination of these, or rather of some of them, is all that the subject of the æsthetic feeling experiences.

The above hypothesis respecting the æsthetic feelings is thus fully verified. For, as we before saw that the æsthetic excitement is one arising when there is an exercise of certain faculties for its own sake, apart from ulterior benefits; so, in these cases we see that the conception of *beauty* is distinguished from the conception of *good* in this, that it refers not to ends to be achieved but to activities incidental to the pursuit of ends. In the conception of anything as good or right, and in the correlative sentiment, consciousness is occupied with representations and re-representations, distinct or vague, of happiness, special or general, that will be furthered; but in the conception of a thing as fine, as admirable, as beautiful, as grand, consciousness is not occupied, distinctly or vaguely, with ultimate advantage, but is occupied with the thing itself as a direct source of pleasure. Though in many cases this pleasurable consciousness has originally grown out of the representations of benefits to be gained, yet it has come to be a pleasurable consciousness in the object or act apart from anything beyond; and in so doing has passed into the class of feelings which includes at the one extreme the sportive activities and at the other extreme the æsthetic sentiments.

§ 536. To deal fully with the psychology of æsthetics is out of the question. Its phenomena are extremely involved, and to treat them adequately would require many chapters. Here, in addition to the above general conceptions, I will set down only such hints as seem needful for rightly developing them.

Under the head of æsthetic feelings we include states of consciousness of all orders of complexity, some of which, originating in purely-physical conditions, are merely perfected modes of sensation, while others, such as the delight in contemplating a noble action of a fictitious character, are

re-representative in an extreme degree. Simple sensations
of all kinds that have the æsthetic quality, probably have
it when the physical causes are such as bring the sensory
apparatus into the most effectual unimpeded action. There
is good evidence that it is so with auditory sensations.*
Sounds of fine *timbre*, and harmonies of sounds, have in
common the character that they result from vibrations so
related, as to cause in the auditory apparatus the least
conflict of actions and the greatest amount of co-operation
—thus producing the largest total of normal excitement in
the nerve-elements affected. It seems not improbable that
the feeling of beauty in colour has the same origin. Indeed
where harmony of colours is the source of pleasure, we get
clear indication that it has. Here, then, recognizing as the
primary requirement that the activity shall not be one of a
directly life-serving kind, we conclude that it rises to the
æsthetic form in proportion as it is great in amount and is
without the drawback of any such units of painful feeling
as result from discordant actions of aërial waves or of
ethereal waves: such units of painful feeling being the
accompaniments of excesses of function in certain of the
nerve-elements.

There is, however, a secondary pleasure given by these
simple feelings, as by all other feelings of a normal kind.
As was hinted in § 128, and as was more fully explained
in § 261, " while Pleasures and Pains are partly constituted of those local and conspicuous elements of feeling
directly aroused by special stimuli, they are largely, if not
mainly, composed of secondary elements of feeling aroused
indirectly by diffused stimulation of the nervous system."
From this it is a corollary that a sensorial stimulation such
as is produced by a fine colour or a sweet tone, implying
as we here infer a large amount of normal action of the
parts concerned, without any drawback from excessive ac-

* On this point, see an instructive essay by Mr. James Sully in the
Fortnightly Review for April, 1872.

tion, and thus involving a powerful diffused discharge of which no component is in excess, will tend to arouse a secondary vague pleasure. Æsthetic feelings in general are largely composed of the undefinable consciousness hence arising.

There is an allied but more special component in this feeling of beauty yielded by sensation. A good deal of the agreeable consciousness which a fine colour excites, is traceable to associations established in experience. Throughout our lives, reds, blues, purples, greens, &c., have been connected with flowers, sunny days, picturesque scenes, and the gratifications received along with impressions from them. Turning from natural to artificial spheres, it equally holds that on festive occasions, pleasant excitements have been joined with perceptions of bright colours. The result is that the diffused discharge produced by a bright colour, which if general would cause vague pleasure, causes a stronger and more definite pleasure by taking such directions as to awaken these aggregates of agreeable recollections.   Similarly with sweet sounds. Many of these, experience associates with human intercourse of a pleasure-giving kind. While the tones of anger and of brutality are harsh and coarse, the tones of sympathy and refinement are relatively gentle and of agreeable *timbre*. That is to say, the *timbre* associated in experience with the receipt of gratifications, has acquired a pleasure-giving quality; and consequently the tones which in music have an allied *timbre* become pleasure-giving, and are called beautiful. Not that this is the sole cause of their pleasure-giving quality. As above implied, there is a primary physical cause; and the fact that great delight results from harmony, which is not explicable by association, shows that the physical cause is a dominant one. Still, on recalling those tones of instruments which approach the tones of the human voice, and observing that they seem beautiful in proportion to their approach, we see that this secondary æsthetic element is important.   A like added source of æsthetic pleasure may be identified in olfactory sensations.   Most sweet odours are pleasurable not intrinsically only, but by association.   The scents of flowers are connected with enjoyments in the fields and strolls in charming gardens.   It needs but to remember the wave of agreeable feeling raised by the smell of hay, the intrinsic sweetness of which is but moderate, to perceive how largely the dim revival of past joys, felt during many midsummer days, enters into the delight given.   Indeed, it is even possible in some cases to discriminate between the immediate and the remote sources of the pleasure.   The perfume of musk or sandal-wood, however much it may be liked, excites none of that vague feeling of the romantic or poetical which the perfume of a lily of the valley excites: this last having associations of a poetical class, which the others have not.

§ 537. When we rise from simple sensations to combinations of them, of kinds that awaken ideas and feelings of beauty, we may, I think, discern the same general and special truths. The primitive source of æsthetic pleasure, is that character in the combination which makes it such as to exercise the faculties affected in the most complete ways, with the fewest drawbacks from excess of exercise. Joined to this comes, as before, a secondary source of pleasure—the diffusion of a normal stimulus in large amount, awaking a glow of agreeable feeling, faint and undefinable. And, as before, a third source of pleasure is the partial revival by this discharge of the various special gratifications connected in experience with combinations of the kind presented. Let us pause a moment before each of these. Illustrations of the primary cause will be furnished us by combinations of movements, combinations of forms, combinations of lights, shades, and colours, and combinations of tones.

Movements of the body pleasurable to self, and associated with the consciousness of gracefulness (as in skating), are movements of a kind that bring many muscles into moderate harmonious action and strain none. An awkward motion is one that implies sudden change of direction, angularity, destruction of much momentum, excess of muscular effort; whereas a motion called graceful—a motion in curved lines, flowing one into another without break, is a motion in which little momentum is destroyed, no undue exertion thrown on any muscle, no power lost. And while in the actor the æsthetic consciousness is mainly constituted by this feeling of moderate but efficient muscular action without check, without strain, without loss, the consciousness of gracefulness in the observer, arises in large measure from sympathy with the feelings implied by such motions.* Turning to forms, we observe that the delight in flowing outlines rather than in outlines which are angular, is partly due to that more harmonious unstrained action of the ocular muscles, implied by perception of such outlines: there is no jar from sudden stoppage of motion and change of direction, such as results on carrying the eye along a zig-zag line. Here again, then, we have a feeling accompanying an activity that is full, but contains no element of pain from excess. In the more complex combinations, including many forms presented together, it is relatively difficult to trace out the principle; but I see sundry reasons for suspecting that beautiful arrangements of forms, are those which effectually exercise the largest numbers of the structural elements concerned in perception, while over-taxing the fewest of them. Similarly with the complex visual wholes presented by actual objects, or by pictorial representations of objects, with all their lights and shades and colours. The requirements for harmony, for subordination, and for proportion—the demand for a variety

* For particulars see Essay on "Gracefulness."

sufficient to prevent monotony, but not a variety which too much distracts the attention, may be regarded as all implied by the principle that many elements of perceptive faculty must be called into play, while none are over-exerted: there must be a great body of the feeling arising from their moderate action, without the deduction of any pain from extreme action. The pleasure excited by sequences of sounds, such as form musical phrases and cadences, though not mainly due to this cause, is partly due to it. Song differs from speech by using a much wider range of tones, and so exercising many auditory agents in succession; not over-taxing any one in the way that monotonous speech over-taxes it. The like holds in respect to variations of strength. To be artistic, that is, to excite the feeling of beauty effectually, the notes must not be all *forte* or all *piano;* and the execution is the finer the more numerous the gradations—supposing these are such as to satisfy other requirements. So is it too with contrasts in emphasis, with rhythm, and with *timbre.* Due regard being paid to meaning, the rendering is the better the more heterogeneous it is; and, other things equal, its greater heterogeneity implies greater variety of excitements in the percipient, and avoidance of that over-excitement of some perceptive agency which uniformity implies.

Of the supplementary pleasures of perception above named, that which arises from the diffused nervous discharge proceeding from perceptive faculties normally exercised, needs no further illustration. But something must be added in elucidation of the third kind of æsthetic pleasure accompanying perceptive activity—that more special kind which results from the special associations formed in experience.

The feelings from time to time received along with perceptions of graceful movements were mostly agreeable. The persons who exhibited such movements were usually the cultivated, and those whose behaviour yielded gratification. The occasions have usually been festive ones—balls, private dances, and the like. And the places with which graceful motions are associated, such as theatres and the houses of friends, are places where enjoyments of various kinds have been received. Hence the diffused excitation that follows the perception of graceful movements, becomes one by which pleasures derived from these sources are ideally revived in a confused way.   With beautiful forms much the same happens. Persons having figures that satisfy the æsthetic requirements, are more frequently than not, connected in experience with agreeable recollections. So, too, are the fine shapes of art-products—architectural, plastic, pictorial: the occasions on which these have been contemplated have mostly been occasions of happiness, social or other. This is a reason why the æsthetic pleasure derived from form, though not great in the uncultured, becomes relatively voluminous in the cultured, by wealth of association.   When from simple forms we pass to complex combinations of them with colours, and lights, and shades, as for instance in landscape, this indirect source of æsthetic gratification becomes distinguishable as a large one. The connexion between perception of a grand view and the multitudinous agreeable feelings brought by freedom and relaxation, mostly experienced at the same time, is too clear to permit doubt that a considerable part of the delight given, is caused by this partial revival of many past joys —some within individual experience, and some deeper than individual experience. (See § 214.) And then, in the pleasure derived from a skilful representation of a landscape, we have a still more remote result of these associations. For beyond the direct æsthetic satisfaction given by the picture, there is this dim consciousness of enjoyments that have accompanied the actual presence of scenes like the one represented.   Once more, it is to be observed that the like holds of the melodic element in music. The expressiveness of musical cadences depends on their relations to cadences of the human voice under emotion. When the emotion suggested by a cadence is a joyous one, opportunity is given for pleasurable sympathy; and when a painful emotion is suggested, there comes an opportunity for the pleasurable pain of pity. Song is distinguished from speech, by various traits that result from idealization of the traits of strong feeling as vocally expressed. And the indirect æsthetic pleasure which melody yields, is due to this derived power of exciting the feelings connected in experience with such traits.*

§ 538. Here we find ourselves passing unawares into that higher region of æsthetic feeling, where the states of consciousness are exclusively re-representative. From the æsthetic in sensation, which is presentative, but with added representative elements; and from the æsthetic in perception, which is also presentative, but with added representative elements of more involved kinds; we rise now to the æsthetic in those states of consciousness that are reached *through* sensations and perceptions. As just admitted, we verge into these in taking count of the remoter mental states aroused by landscape and by music. But there are certain æsthetic sentiments dissociated much more decidedly from the lower modes of consciousness. I refer to the æsthetic sentiments excited by the literature of imagination.

Recognizing the simple æsthetic pleasures derivable from rhythm and euphony, which are explicable in ways above indicated, the feelings of beauty yielded by poetry, are feelings remotely re-representative; not only in the sense that they are initiated by ideas or representations, but also in the sense that the sentiments indirectly aroused are re-representative, often in a high degree. And in prose fiction, where the vehicle used yields no appreciable sensuous gratification, this re-representativeness of the feelings awakened is complete. A condition to æsthetic pleasure in these

---

* For details see Essay on " The Origin and Function of Music."

higher ranges of it, as in the lower, is that there shall be excited great masses and varieties of the elements out of which the emotions are compounded, while none of them shall be excited in undue degrees. A large volume of emotion without painful intensity in any part, is the effect which a successful drama, or poem, or novel, produces. It is true that success is often measured by the intensity of the resulting feeling—especially pitiful feeling; though even here the effect may be lost if this feeling is over-taxed by too continuous an appeal. But noting such cases, it must still be held that æsthetic pleasure, properly so called, is the highest when the emotional consciousness has not only breadth and mass, but a variety such as leaves behind no satiety or exhaustion.

The like may be said of æsthetic sentiments excited by actions pictorially set forth instead of verbally described. For beyond the æsthetic pleasures derivable from a picture considered simply under its technical character, as giving the direct and indirect gratifications of sensation and perception harmoniously co-operating, there is the æsthetic pleasure derivable from a re-representative consciousness of the feelings implied by the action. And here, as before, the requisite is that these feelings shall have in them as much as may be of the moderate, mingled with as little as may be of the violent; and that where, as often happens, a sympathetic pain is aroused, it shall be that form of pity having a dominant pleasurable element.

§ 539. Yet one other question may be briefly discussed—the measure of height in æsthetic feeling. Two modes of estimation may be adopted, which, as we shall see, substantially correspond in their results.

Subject always to the cardinal requirement that the feeling is one not immediately aiding any life-serving function, it follows from what has been said, that the highest æsthetic feeling is one having the greatest volume, produced by due exercise of the greatest number of powers without undue exercise of any. Again, from the general doctrine of mental evolution, it is a corollary that the highest æsthetic feeling is one resulting from the full but not excessive exercise of the most complex emotional faculty. That these two standards harmonize is not at once manifest; but a little thought will show that in most cases, though not in all cases, their dicta agree. For, on the one hand, a large quantity of feeling no component of which rises to painful intensity, can be obtained only by the simultaneous action of many powers; and, on the other hand, many powers can be brought into simultaneous action only through the instrumentality of a complex faculty. A truth pervading the interpretations of this work, is that each higher faculty arises as a means of co-ordinating the actions of various lower faculties—duly adjusting and balancing their functions. The activity of a high or complex faculty is therefore, by implication, an activity of the many subordinate faculties it co-ordinates. Using the standard of measure thus jointly indicated, the hierarchy of the æsthetic feelings will stand thus.

Lowest are the pleasures derivable from simple sensation, as of sweet odours, beautiful colours, fine tones; and somewhat higher come the feelings produced by harmonies of tones and harmonies of colours.

Next above these must be ranged those pleasurable feelings that go along with perceptions more or less complex, of forms, of combined lights and shades, of successive cadences and chords; rising to a greater height where these are joined into elaborate combinations of forms and colours, and elaborate structures of melody and harmony: all these ascending stages evidently fulfilling at once the requirements of greater complexity and greater volume.

Much higher, however, stand the æsthetic sentiments strictly so called, which contain no presentative elements. In the above two lower orders of the feelings we class as æsthetic, the presentative elements are essential and the representative elements incidental. But in the highest order of æsthetic feeling, the presentative elements are incidental and the representative elements essential. The impressions of form and colour yielded by a picture, the cadences and chords of an air or chorus, and still more the verbal symbols, oral or written, by which a description of something beautiful or grand is conveyed, are here simply the agents through which certain emotions are ideally excited. Thus, the feeling produced is high, alike in its remoteness from simple sensation, in its complexity as containing an immense variety of those elements of which emotions are composed, and in its volume as being a faint reproduction of the enormous aggregate of such elements massed together in the course of evolution. Moreover it is to be observed that among these highest æsthetic feelings themselves, a like gradation holds: those which originate by excitement of the altruistic sentiments, being higher than those which originate by excitement of the ego-altruistic and egoistic sentiments—obviously higher in their degrees of representativeness and of complexity, if not at present in their volume.

Of course, the most perfect form of æsthetic excitement is reached when these three orders of sensational, perceptional, and emotional gratification are given, by the fullest actions of the respective faculties, with the least deduction caused by painful excess of action. Such an æsthetic excitement is rarely experienced, for the reason that works of art rarely possess all the required characters. Very generally a rendering that is artistic in one respect, goes along with a rendering that is in other respects inartistic. And where the *technique* is satisfactory, it does not commonly happen that the emotion appealed to is of a high order. Measuring æsthetic sentiments and the correlative works of art by the above standards, we find ourselves compelled to relegate to a comparatively-inferior place, much that now stands highest. Beginning with the epic of the Greeks and

their representations in sculpture of kindred stories, which
appeal to feelings of egoistic and ego-altruistic kinds; passing through middle-age literature, similarly pervaded by
inferior sentiments, and through the pictures of the old
masters, which by the ideas and feelings they excite very
rarely compensate for the disagreeable shocks they give to
perceptions cultivated by the study of appearances; down to
many admired works of modern art, which, good in *technique*, are low in the emotions they express and arouse, such
as the battle-scenes of Vernet and the pieces of Gerôme,
which alternate between the sensual and the sanguinary—
we see that in one or other of the required attributes,
they nearly all fall short of the forms of art corresponding
to the highest forms of æsthetic feeling.

§ 540. The results of this rapid survey of a large subject,
demanding more time and space than I can give to it, may
be briefly summed up thus.

The æsthetic feelings and sentiments are not, as our
words and phrases lead us to suppose, feelings and sentiments that essentially differ in origin and nature from the
rest. They are nothing else than particular modes of excitement of the faculties, sensational, perceptional, and emotional—faculties which, otherwise excited, produce those
other modes of consciousness constituting our ordinary impressions, ideas, and feelings. The same agencies are in
action; and the only difference is in the attitude of consciousness towards its resulting states.

Throughout the whole range of sensations, perceptions,
and emotions which we do not class as æsthetic, the states of
consciousness serve simply as aids and stimuli to guidance
and action. They are transitory, or if they persist in consciousness some time, they do not monopolize the attention: that which monopolizes the attention is something
ulterior, to the effecting of which they are instrumental.
But in the states of mind we class as æsthetic, the opposite

attitude is maintained towards the sensations, perceptions, and emotions. These are no longer links in the chain of states which prompt and guide conduct. Instead of being allowed to disappear with merely passing recognitions, they are kept in consciousness and dwelt upon: their natures being such that their continued presence in consciousness is agreeable.

Before this action of the faculties can arise, it is necessary that the needs to be satisfied through the agency of sensational, perceptional, and emotional excitements shall not be urgent. So long as there exist strong cravings arising from bodily wants and unsatisfied lower instincts, consciousness is not allowed to dwell on these states that accompany the actions of the higher faculties: the cravings continually exclude them.

This is another mode of stating the truth with which we set out, that activities of this order begin to show themselves only when there is reached an organization so superior, that the energies have not to be wholly expended in the fulfilment of material requirements from hour to hour. Along with occasional surplus nutrition, and along with that variety of faculty existing in creatures to which surplus nutrition is frequent, there occur the conditions making it possible for the states of consciousness accompanying the actions of the higher faculties, to become states sought for their own sakes, apart from ends: whence arises play.

Gratifications that accompany actions performed without reference to ends, will mostly be those which accompany actions predominating in the creature's life. And hence this first form of them called play, is shown in the superfluous activity of the sensori-motor apparatus and if those destructive instincts which habitually guide its actions. When they are established, the higher orders of co-ordinating powers also come to have their superfluous activities and corresponding pleasures, in games and other exercises somewhat more remote from the destructive activities. But,

88

as we see in the mimetic dances and accompanying chants of savages, which begin to put on a little of the character called æsthetic, there is still a great predominance of these substituted gratifications of feelings adapted to a predatory life. And even on reaching those more-developed æsthetic products and correlative feelings which ancient civilizations yielded, we find a like prevailing trait.

When, however, a long discipline of social life, decreasingly predatory and increasingly peaceful, has allowed the sympathies and resulting altruistic sentiments to develop, these, too, begin to demand spheres of superfluous activity. Fine Art of all kinds takes forms more and more in harmony with these sentiments. Especially in the literature of imagination we may now see how much less appeal there is to the egoistic and ego-altruistic sentiments, and how much more to the altruistic sentiments—a trait likely to go on growing.

A final remark worth making is, that the æsthetic activities in general may be expected to play an increasing part in human life as evolution advances. Greater economization of energy, resulting from superiority of organization, will have in the future effects like those it has had in the past. The order of activities to which the æsthetic belong, having been already initiated by this economization, will hereafter be extended by it: the economization being achieved both directly through the improvement of the human structure itself, and indirectly through the improvement of all appliances, mechanical, social, and other. A growing surplus of energy will bring a growing proportion of the æsthetic activities and gratifications; and while the forms of art will be such as yield pleasurable exercise to the simpler faculties, they will in a greater degree than now appeal to the higher emotions.

APPENDIX.

OUR SPACE-CONSCIOUSNESS—A REPLY.

Since the second edition of this work was published, there have come, from adherents of Kant, some criticisms on the doctrine contained in §§ 326—335. They have adopted a common controversial practice, of which the formula is—When you cannot meet an issue that has been raised, raise a new issue. Instead of defending the Kantian doctrine against my attack they have made a counter-attack. I set forth six objections. Besides showing that on the very first page of the *Critique of Pure Reason*, Kant so changes the meaning of a word as to vitiate the rest of his argument; and besides showing the untruth of his assertion, currently accepted, that Space is a form of sense-intuition at large (for it is a form only of the intuitions derived through touch and sight); I have pointed out that the Kantian hypothesis involves four impossibilities of thought (*Prin. of Psy.*, § 399).

Though it would, I think, be time enough to answer my critics after my criticisms have been answered, or, at any rate, after some attempt has been made to answer them; yet it appears needful without waiting longer, to rebut the arguments used against me. By nine out of ten, absence of reply is supposed to prove inability to reply. Hence I have decided to pause a moment for the purpose of showing that while there has been no defence against my attack, the counter-attacks fail.

Of such counter-attacks the most elaborate is that made by Prof. Watson, of the Queen's University, Canada, in *Kant and his English Critics;* and as I am not aware that any arguments have been used by others which he has not used, I may fitly limit my attention to the chapters in which he seeks to refute my views. Had I any wish to avoid joining issue on essential points, I should, indeed, have valid reasons for doing so, of which here are some.

When dealing with the beliefs held by me concerning certain of our ultimate consciousnesses, and more especially our consciousness of Space, Prof. Watson says, on p. 262, that he confines himself "mainly to the third chapter of the second part of Mr. Spencer's *First Principles:*" the word "mainly," not implying that he takes account of other works of mine, but merely that he takes account of other passages in *First Principles.* Now in the chapter he professedly criticises, there is a foot-note stating that the justification for the doctrine there briefly set forth as part of a general argument, will be found in the *Principles of Psychology*, where the full exposition of it occupies a chapter—or rather two chapters; for the chapter on "The Conception of Body as presenting Statical Attributes," contains the first part of the argument which is brought to a conclusion in the next chapter on "The Conception of Space." This full exposition occupying 42 pages, Prof. Watson deliberately ignores: preferring to base his criticism on a brief summary occupying 3 pages, which does not profess to contain the justification, but only the conclusion! An author dealt with after this fashion would, I think, be warranted in disregarding the attack.

Moreover I might, with good ground, conclude that it is useless to discuss a philosophical question with one who professes to have a consciousness of something which I find it impossible to frame any consciousness of. If two contestants give different meanings to the words and phrases used, and, still more, if one sees a meaning where the other sees none, there is no chance of an agreement between them. Prof. Watson says,—"In intelligent experience space and time are not posterior, but prior, to co-existing and successive objects, as undifferentiated space is prior to positions—*i. e.*, limitations of space " (p. 273). Now when I look into my consciousness to find the something described as undifferentiated space, or space as preceding in order of existence all positions, I find nothing whatever answering to it. Unless I suppose that Prof. Watson is using words to which he attaches no ideas, I must suppose that he can think of this undifferentiated space in which there are no positions; and as I am utterly incapable of doing this, there does not exist between us that common ground which is needful before argument can be carried on to any purpose. Were I to use the phrase "undifferentiated space," as defined by Prof. Watson, I should be using what is, to my mind, though not it seems to his, one of those eviscerated phrases which will no more help to lay hold of a truth than a stuffed greyhound will catch a hare.

Again, there is the question of a criterion of truth, in the absence of which, as accepted by both of two disputants, an argument may be stopped at any point, or its conclusion rejected, by simple denial. I have myself propounded and defended such a criterion ; and though there have been criticisms on my argument, I have not yet met with any other proposed criterion. The assumption seems to be that discussion may profitably be carried on while the parties to it have not come to an agreement respecting the character of a proposition which must be accepted, as distinguished from one which may be denied. Prof. Watson discusses the universal postulate, and raises various objections, concerning the validity of which I need here say nothing. I have merely to point out that he proposes no criterion in its stead. If, of two who were negotiating a commercial transaction, one offered security and asked for security in return, while the other, objecting to the security offered, declined to make any arrangements by which evasion of the contract should be guarded against, the first of the two would very properly drop the negotiation. And, in like manner, I might properly decline discussion with one who refused to abide by a proposed guarantee of validity, and failed to offer one himself.

Yet another justification for passing over Prof. Watson's criticisms would be that he refuses to recognize, as a possible problem, the problem I deal with; since by assuming that knowledge has at the beginning the same characters which it has at the end, he tacitly denies the process of development. He says:—" Individual feelings, however numerous, cannot possibly account for the knowledge of extended things or of extension, since such feelings are assumed to be destitute of that universality which is the condition of any knowledge whatever " (p. 272). Does Prof. Watson think that at the moment the newly-born infant first closes its lips round the nipple, it knows its sensations in connexion with their respective universals? If he does not think this, then he must admit that in the infant what he calls knowledge slowly emerges out of something which does not answer to his definition of knowledge. If, however, he has the courage of his opinions, and affirms that consciousness of "that universality which is the condition of any knowledge whatever " precedes in the infant the reception of its first sensations; then, as I say, no good can come of an argument between one who proposes to trace the genesis of intelligence, and one who holds that intelligence did not acquire by degrees the structure which we recognize in it, but had such structure at the outset.

This tacit assumption that what we now distinguish as thought, has always had the traits which are conspicuous in it, and this tacit ignoring of the very hypothesis to be discussed, that these traits have arisen in the course of a slow genesis, crop up continually throughout Prof. Watson's criticisms. For example, he says:—" It is not possible to be conscious of events as uniformly sequent, without being conscious of substances as dependent upon and influencing each other; or, to take experience at an earlier stage, it is not possible to think of events as following upon each other in time, apart from the thought of things as co-existing in space" (p. 270). This is an implied repetition of the Kantian dogma respecting forms of intuition, which is true only of certain classes of intuitions. For, as I have elsewhere shown (*Prin. of Psy.*, § 399), neither sounds nor odours have space for their form of intuition. If Prof. Watson does not perceive that were he without the knowledge obtained through touch and vision, he could be conscious of successive sounds "apart from the thought of things as co-existing in space;" and if he does not perceive that even now he can be thus conscious of a melody which persists in intruding upon consciousness; then he affords further evidence that our two consciousnesses differ so much that comparison of experiences can lead to no definite result.

Contending that the consciousness of space is inseparable from the first experiences of things in space, Prof. Watson says:—"We are told of 'impressions of resistance,' and of 'muscular adjustments.' Now, an impression of resistance is not a mere feeling, but the conception of an object as resisting, and such a conception involves a construction of reality by relations of thought. Similarly, 'muscular adjustments' presuppose a knowledge of the muscular system, or, at least, of the body as it exists for common consciousness and, here again, relations of thought are inconsistently attributed to mere feeling" (p. 275). As before, we see that Kant's defenders insist on carrying with them the contents of developed consciousness when interpreting undeveloped consciousness; or, in other words, tacitly deny the possibility of a consciousness which does not contain the chief components of consciousness as it exists in ourselves. As already shown, their method of studying the evolution of thought is that of assuming that thought is complete in essentials at the outset; and, pursuing this method, they do not admit the original separability of states of consciousness which are extremely coherent, though even in ourselves it is still possible to separate them. For an impression of resistance is a feeling quite distinguishable from the perception or idea of a thing producing it, and may be conceived as occurring in a revolutionary consciousness without any idea of a causing object. Hamilton, while recognizing the distinction between sensation and perception, says the two always co-exist, though in inverse intensities. As I have pointed out (*Prin. of Psy.*, § 353), the law, rightly stated, is that sensation and perception tend to "exclude each other with degrees of stringency which vary inversely:" the illustration which here concerns us being that the sensation of resistance, when it rises to great intensity, monopolizes consciousness. After pressing the finger gently against an angle, and noting that the shape of the angle is the subject of thought, and after observing that as the pressure increases the sensation more and more solicits attention, until when the pressure becomes extreme the sensation alone is attended to, any one may perceive that, even in the developed consciousness, the subjective state produced is separable in thought from the objective producer; and may then conceive an undeveloped consciousness, not yet made coherent by organization of experiences, in which a presentation of the one may occur without idea of the other.

Thus, as I have said, the conditions to be observed in carrying on profitable discussion are so inadequately fulfilled, that entrance into it might be held useless. But though, for the reasons that Prof. Watson ignores the specific statement of the views he combats, and that he misconceives the problem I have proposed to deal with, and that he professes to have ideas which I cannot frame, and that he neither accepts my criterion of truth nor proposes one of his own—though I might, for these reasons, fitly decline all controversy as futile; yet, as I have said, readers unaware of these reasons will, I doubt not, in this case as in other such cases, conclude that arguments which have not been refuted are valid arguments. I therefore feel it necessary to show that they are not valid.

Past culture, and in great measure the culture received at present, has not familiarized men with the idea of transformation. Only in our own times have the world, and man, and the products of human activity, come to be contemplated as results of a continuous becoming; and even still, this way of looking at things is alien to the minds of all but a few—alien in the sense that it is not constant enough to affect their thinking. One consequence is an inability to believe that something now known as having certain conspicuous traits, can ever have existed under a form in which no such traits were discernible. The difficulty felt is like that felt by the old biologists when they adopted the theory of *emboîtement*—the theory that in the germ of every living creature, the future adult exists in little; and that within this exist the immeasurably more minute forms of adults which will eventually descend from it; and so on *ad infinitum :* the reason for accepting this theory being that it was impossible to understand how a complex structure like that of the human body, could have arisen out of something which had no structure. An analogous difficulty is at present felt by the disciples of Kant. These cannot imagine how it is possible that our space consciousness can have arisen out of that which was not originally a space consciousness. Yet a cursory survey shows that each of the sciences yields examples of transitions which connect, by insensible gradations, things having apparently no kinship whatever.

Mathematics furnishes us with one. A circle and a straight line seem absolutely unrelated; and yet we may pass from the one to the other by an unbroken movement. Cut a cone at right angles to its axis, and the result is a circle. Incline the cutting plane in the slightest degree, and the circle becomes an ellipse. Increase the inclination, and the ellipse grows more excentric, until it passes into an hyperbola as the parallelism to the side becomes complete. Further rotation of the plane turns the parabola into an hyperbola, which changes its form with every change of position of the plane; until, when the plane, emerging from the opposite side of the cone, becomes a tangent plane, the two sides of the hyperbola coalesce, and become a straight line. Though the transition may be more simply made, yet this best shows the variety of figures which are united as members of a continuous series.

Take next a case from Physics. To one of the uneducated, and, indeed, to one whose knowledge is limited to that given by ordinary education, nothing could seem more absurd than the assertion that heat and motion are but different forms of the same thing. Motion, he would say, rapid or slow as you may make it, must ever remain motion; and heat, increase or decrease its intensity in whatever degree you please, must always remain heat. Nevertheless, their reciprocal convertibility is a proved truth. When a bullet placed on an anvil is struck by a hammer, what disappears as arrested motion of the hammer reappears as increased heat of the lead. When steam is let into a cylinder, the heat it loses as it expands is transformed into the motion of its own mass and sundry masses of iron. Though molecular motion is intrinsically of the same nature as molar motion, yet the unaggregated form in which it exists in the one case affects our senses in so utterly different a manner from the aggregated form in which it exists in the other case, that it appears to common sense inconceivable that the two are but different modes of one.

Chemistry furnishes countless instances of transformations from which qualities that appear radically different result. Here is a piece of phosphorus, semi-transparent, waxy-looking, luminous in the dark, showing a powerful affinity for oxygen, burning flesh which it touches, and hence acting as a poison when swallowed. Expose it for a certain time to the temperature of 230° while oxygen is excluded, and all is changed. It has become brick-coloured, perfectly opaque, non-luminous, chemically inert, and may be swallowed in large quantities with impunity. Having neither lost nor gained in weight, nor in any way changed its ultimate nature, it has yet by re-arrange-ment of its molecules acquired different, and indeed opposite, properties. To which add that when subjected to the fit condi-tions it re-acquires the original properties.

Biology is rich in examples. One who, lacking entirely the ideas insensibly taken in during ordinary life, was brought suddenly face to face with the facts, would find it incredible that hair and nerve, tooth and eye, had all arisen by insensible steps out of the same originally-uniformed dermal tissue. If he contemplated the parts which carry on the pulmonic circulation as they exist in man or any other mammal, he would conclude that their connexion is necessary, and must have existed from the beginning: arguing, as he might, that the right auricle and ventricle would be useless in the absence of lungs, and that the lungs would be useless without the right auricle and ventricle. " See," he might say, " if we stop the breath the heart soon ceases to pulsate, and if the heart stops the breathing quickly comes to an end. Clearly, then, the two must have co-existed as such from the beginning. Their interdependent functions constitute a *form* of physiological action." Yet the investigations of biologists show that no such arrangement originally existed, but that this reciprocal dependence has been established by degrees.

Nor does Psychology itself fail to yield undeniable instances of transformation allied to those which the Kantists hold to be impossible. An example is furnished by rapidly-recurring sensations of light. Every child, at some stage or other of mental development, observes that on whirling round a stick, of which the end is burning or red-hot, an apparent circle of light is produced: by a succession of sensations there is produced what appears to be a continuous sensation. The direct verdict of consciousness is that there exists a luminous circle ; whereas we know that at any moment light exists only at one very small part of the circle. An illusion of like nature, but less easily shown to be one, is supplied by various flames which appear steady and persistent, but each of which consists of a series of small explosions : a fact demonstrated in singing flames. In these there are simultaneously produced a con-tinuous impression of light and a continuous impression of sound, by impressions which are in both cases discontinuous. This example, which singing flames furnish, introduces us to the example furnished by musical sounds in general. These show us clearly how a state of consciousness which seems perfectly simple and perfectly homogeneous, may be neither the one nor the other. The crack of a whip or the tap of one's nail on the table, seems quite unrelated to a musical tone ; save in the respect that both are sounds. To those who have not experimented on the matter, nothing can seem more obvious than that, however short the length into which you cut a tone, it will still retain its quality as tone; and, conversely, that by no possibility can a musical tone be produced from separate sharp cracks. Yet both of these conclusions are false. The rotating instruments of Hooke and of Savart, by which separate sharp cracks can be made with increasing rapidity, prove incontestably that brief unmusical noises may be so arranged as to constitute a long musical sound; and that musical sound, smooth and continuous though it seems, really results from successive impacts of aerial waves, which yield separate impressions to the nerves.

But the Kantists, bent on maintaining that supernaturalness of mind which is implied by the hypothesis of pre-determined forms of thought, and therefore profoundly averse to that evolutionary view which contemplates mind as having had a genesis conforming to laws like those conformed to by the genesis of the body, ignore these significant facts furnished by various orders of phenomena, and ignore even the significant facts furnished by psychology itself. They are positive that a certain kind of consciousness which, in the developed mind, seems continuous and homogeneous, must always have had the traits of continuity and homogeneity—cannot possibly have been composed out of units of thought which were different and discontinuous. But the reader who is not bound by a foregone conclusion, will perhaps be prepared by these illustrations to see that the consciousness of space may have arisen out of components which, considered individually, contain no consciousness of space.

The reader will be still better prepared if, after contemplating these instances of transformations throughout things in general, as well as throughout certain modes of mind, he pauses a moment to contemplate a familiar experience which, in another way, elucidates the process of producing, by composition, mental states that are unlike their components.

When the end of a walking-stick is thrust into clay or other yielding matter, the consciousness of softness presents two significant traits. The first is that though it seems quite simple, it is demonstrably compounded out of elements which, considered separately, are unlike it. One of them is the sensation of slight pressure from the handle of the stick on the palm of the hand. Supposing the limb to be motionless, something hard may be pressed against the end of the stick with such small force as to produce in the palm just the same sensation. Similarly, if we consider by themselves the sensations of muscular tension which occur in the moving arm while the stick is being thrust into the clay, it is clear that, taken by themselves, these do not yield the consciousness of softness: equal feelings of tension and motion might be produced by pushing forward a child's perambulator. But when with the pressure on the palm of the hand and the changing sensations of tension in the arm, is joined the visual perception of stationariness in the mass, a consciousness of softness arises : there results a knowledge which, by the unanalytical intelligence, is taken to be simply and directly yielded, instead of being, as we see, complex and inferential.

The other trait of this cognition is its apparent externality. Anyone who accepted his experiences uncritically, would say that the softness was felt by him at the place of its existence; and if you pointed out that this could not be, since the stick is senseless matter, you would simply puzzle him by the conflict between reason and perception. But to one who can rightly interpret it, the experience shows that this feeling of softness at the end of the stick is not only compounded of mental states unlike it, but that though the soft object is remote from the organs of sense, its softness appears directly present to them.

And now, carrying with us these general truths, (1) that a consciousness which appears to be simple, continuous, and undecomposable, may nevertheless consist of multitudinous units, (2) that by the compounding of consciousnesses, now of the same kind and now of different kinds, a consciousness quite unlike, in apparent character, may be produced; and (3) that by a seeming extradition of sensations, perception may have its bounds apparently extended to places beyond the organism ; let us consider how far, by their help, we are enabled to conceive the space-consciousness as a product of evolution.

It is clear that as the apparently continuous and homogeneous consciousness of sound is constituted by separate units, so may be the apparently continuous and homogeneous consciousness of space; and we have, in fact, more easily accessible evidence that it is so constituted, since it is readily decomposable into relations of positions.

But if the consciousness of a relation of positions as tactually disclosed, contains certain elements which are separable from space-implications, and would be cognizable were space unknown—if it contains two sensations of touch with an intervening sensation of changing muscular tension ; then, as in other cases above instanced, there may be produced by union of these components, a state of consciousness unlike any of them—a state in which they become so fused, and their respective natures so masked, that the resulting relation of positions appears to be *sui generis*—seems as unlike the sensations it is formed of, as the transparent liquid sulphuret of carbon is unlike the opaque and solid sulphur and carbon which form it by their union.

And then, passing from the primordial relations of position as known by touch to the relations as known by sight, which experience discloses as their equivalents, we may observe, in the third place, that in virtue of the extradition of sensations so clearly illustrated when the walking-stick is thrust into the clay, we are made to feel as though the relations of position at a distance are present to a consciousness which extends to them. Whence also it follows that by the fusion of an infinity of such relations, which are simultaneously presented to us because the multitudinous retinal elements can receive simultaneous impressions, there is produced our aggregate space-consciousness.

And now, possessed by these preliminary conceptions, let us consider more closely the process of genesis as we may conceive it to have taken place in a developing consciousness.

Wholly to divest ourselves of that space-knowledge, the great body of which lies latent in our inherited nervous structures, and the finished form of which is produced by personal experiences, is of course impossible. All we can do is so to place ourselves as to exclude the space-knowledge accompanying acts of vision, and to reduce to a minimum the space-knowledge which tactual exploration yields; and having done this to suppress as much as possible the ideas of past experiences. These ends may be best compassed by being led blindfold into the middle of a large, entirely unknown, and absolutely dark room : the blindfolding being desirable to prevent perception of the positions of the walls on entering, and such revelation of them as is yielded by light through crevices. After being left alone it will be found that in the absence of any space-suggestions implied by visual and tactual perceptions, or those ideas of them which knowledge of the room would give, much of the space-consciousness is lost. So little space-consciousness remains that there is almost a sense of imprisonment—an oppressive feeling of being shut in by the darkness. What components of presentative consciousness continue distinct ? Primarily those sensations of changing muscular tension which accompany movements of the limbs, and which, in the absence of space-knowledge, are still known as continuous slight efforts, varying according to the muscles contracted and the degrees of their contraction ; and there is experience of the ability to produce and reproduce those slight serial feelings without check—an experience which we ordinarily identify with freedom of movement. If the observer proceeds to grope about until he touches an article of furniture, he finds that one of these series of muscular feelings previously known only with indefinite beginnings and endings, is sharply cut short by the occurrence of a vivid feeling of another kind— a sensation of touch. On moving his hand along the edge of, say, a table from the corner first touched to another corner, he may perceive that in the absence of any space-interpretation he would still be conscious of a series of muscular tensions, a simultaneous series of touches, and, in this double series, two sharp marks caused by the corners; as also of reversed series when his hand was moved the other way. And he may see that such experiences would be receivable and distinguishable if no space-knowledge existed; as would also the experiences in which a series of muscular tensions was cut short at either end by a touch without any intervening sensations of touch : the cases being those in which the hand was moved, not over a surface or edge but from one projecting point to another. Amid these varied experiences there is one thing constant. The muscular strains forming the series may be strong or weak; they may form a short series or a long one; they may come from these muscles or those; the touch may be slight or strong; may be received by this part of the body or that. But in every case there is a reversible series of sensations of tension sharply marked off at either end by a sensation of touch.

What in other cases happens when among many experiences one element is constant while all others are variable? The variable elements, ever conflicting, continually cancel one another; while the constant element becomes more distinct. Hence, then, there arises an established association between two separate touches and an intervening series of strains—a general experience abstracted from particular experiences. And it may be perceived that the abstraction might be made by a developing intelligence before there existed any space-knowledge of two positions and the interval.

When, by groping about the table, some article, say a small book, is laid hold of, there comes a further experience. Two sharp sensations of touch are simultaneously received from two angles. Whereas two such sensations were, before, separated by serial feelings of effort occupying an interval of time, now they are not thus separated. Or, to speak in terms of a rudimentary consciousness, not yet containing the abstract idea of time, in the first case there come between the two feelings certain others unlike them, while in the second case there are no such others : the two exist in consciousness together. Though, literally, they may not be equally present, yet the transitions from the one to the other are so rapid that they appear present at once. A further fact is disclosed. While the sensations from the angles of the book are simultaneously received, it is found on experiment that they may, like those from the angles of the table, be also received in succession with an intervening reversible series of sensations of touch and tension, or of tension only: these two experiences are discovered to be equivalents. That is to say, the time-element, or that which answers to the time-element, disappears; and two consciousnesses which are connected by a reversible series of muscular tensions are proved to be identifiable with two consciousnesses which coexist. Though in a developed intelligence the two positions are thought of as having a space-interval, and the potential series of sensations uniting them is thought of as motion, yet it is clear that, apart from the thoughts of space and motion, the experiences described may be distinguished and classified, and there may be reached that consciousness of co-existence out of which the consciousness of space is to be built.

Sundry other experiences are to be named which aid in developing the consciousness of tactually-known space. Sensations of touch from comparatively remote points, say, on the surface of a wall, may be simultaneously received at the extremities of the outstretched arms; and may then, as before, be united by long change of feelings of touch and tension. The hands and feet may be similarly used to achieve parallel results. And often-repeated experiences, yielded by the same environing objects, reveal such approximate constancy in the serial feelings between particular sensations of touch, that it comes to be known at about what points in such series these last will occur. There is so constituted a knowledge of the whereabouts of surrounding things, given in terms of serial sensations—a knowledge which implies ability to carry on some converse with things in space, without any greater knowledge of space than is implied by knowledge of co-existing things. Self-exploration of the body and limbs affords further components. Here the part touching and the part touched yield simultaneous sensations, giving a kindred, though different, experience of co-existence. Moreover, it is found that two sensations originated on the skin may be brought into relation in consciousness either by the passage of the finger from the one to the other, or by laying the whole hand upon the surface between them: another way in which the equivalence between certain co-existing sensations and certain serial sensations is established.

This consciousness of space acquired tactually, is of course vastly extended and transfigured when there is added the visually-acquired consciousness of space. The retina is a tract of multitudinous separate sensitive agents which, by the focalized rays cast upon it, is enabled to touch the images of surrounding objects, as the skin touches the objects themselves. It has the immense advantages that while mediately touching one object, or part of an object, with absolute distinctness, it mediately touches a multitude of others with considerable distinctness; and so brings all of them into relations of co-existence, while touch can bring only a few into such relations. Moreover, by those focal adjustments which produce distinct images at different distances, the consciousness of co-existence is extended from objects on the same plane to objects on planes at all distances; whence results that consciousness of space of three dimensions, in yielding which vision so immensely transcends touch. At the same time, the relations of co-existent positions previously known only in term of serial tensions and touches, come to be known also in terms of visual impressions and the serial strains of ocular muscles. When looking at the small book, as when grasping it, there is practically a simultaneous consciousness of the angles, while there is the power of directing the eye, as of moving the fingers, from angle to angle, and perceiving that the impressions of the angles are in each case united by a double series of sensations: the equivalence between the two double series being such that the one being given the other is known. What next happens? The same two occupied positions produce, now a pair of consciousnesses through touch and now a pair through vision, and these two pairs being united by different sets of serial sensations, these different sets tend to cancel one another: become known as non-essential elements in the experience of the relation between the different positions. Once more the two positions, being occupied at one time by these objects and at another time by those, come to be dissociated from all particular objects occupying them, and conceived in themselves, apart from the objects; just as the relation between them comes to be conceived apart from the serial sensations, tactual or visual, experienced in establishing it. Hence eventually arises a consciousness of two positions in space and an interval between them—a consciousness freed from all sensory elements. This purified consciousness of co-existing positions having been reached, the building up of the consciousness of space at large becomes easy to understand. And then, further, it becomes easy to understand how the space-knowledge gained through vision, being at once relatively extensive, relatively exact, and apparently effortless, is habitually used instead of the space knowledge gained through touch. The symbols which our eyes yield are so immeasurably more convenient and copious than those which our hand yield, and the substitution of the first for the last has grown into so irresistible a habit, that thought is carried on in the substituted symbols almost to the exclusion of the original ones, and without recognition of the truth that they derive their meanings from the original ones. Whoever will observe that, while running his eyes over these printed marks, he practically ignores the equivalent oral articulations into which he is internally rendering them; and if he will further observe in how vague a way he imagines the objects and acts for which these words stand; and if he will then remember that this partial substitution of printed marks for the things they remotely signify has taken place in the course of a few years; he will have no difficulty in conceiving how the substitution of that knowledge of space expressed in visual language for that knowledge of space expressed in tactual language, which has been taking place through the whole series of ancestral beings, has become organic. When he recollects, too, that words much used seem to have absorbed some of the natures of the things they stand for, so that the uneducated think there are real connections between the two; he is helped to perceive how these visual space-impressions have absorbed the meanings of the tactual space-impressions they are equivalent to, and have come to have meanings which appear to be independent. While at the same time it becomes comprehensible that, from this compounding of elements of consciousness of sundry kinds, there eventually emerges this kind of consciousness which seems unlike in quality to any of them; as we have already seen happens in other cases, with things material and mental.

To the last, however, our developed consciousness of space yields up its original components when analyzed. As distinguished from body, it presents itself as possibility of movement; its parts are reached by movements; its amounts are measured by movements. A prisoner in the dark learns the size of his cell by muscular motions, which are severally ended by touches; and the consciousness that he has but little space is the consciousness that he has but little freedom of motion. Even in a lighted room, when shut up, the consciousness of space is, for the time being, practically restricted to the sphere of potential movement within the walls. Moreover, our visual consciousness of space is given in terms of the muscular movements which adjust the axes and foci of the eyes and turn them about. Lastly, when there is any doubt about visually-perceived space relations, they are brought to the test of comparison with tactually-perceived space relations; and, as in the case of optical illusions, the verdict of these last, received through muscular motions and touches, is held to be conclusive. That is, muscular motions and touches are the ultimate components of the space-consciousness: all other components being but symbols of them.

These last paragraphs prepare the way for a final reply—the reply, namely, that all the truth there is in the doctrine of forms of intuition is not only congruous with the hypothesis of evolution, but is inevitably implied by it, and is implied under a comprehensible shape instead of under an incomprehensible shape. For the inherited structures of the organism presuppose actions, bodily and mental, to be performed by them; and their respective adjustments constitute the predetermined forms of such actions.

The first elucidation of this general truth may be given as a reply to a possible argument. Some pages back, when dealing with the statement that consciousness of the object touched is necessarily given along with the sensation of touch, and when pointing out that if the sensation caused by pressure against the object becomes intense it excludes all thought of the object, I passed over a rejoinder that might be made, because I intended to deal with it here: the rejoinder that though, when a sensation of pressure becomes intense, thought of the external object causing it may cease, yet there remains a consciousness of the position of the part in which the sensation exists. This is certainly true in the adult, and doubtless it soon becomes true in the infant. But already, before individual experiences are received, there exist the nerves supplying the parts affected, and the nervous centres with which they are connected; and already, therefore, in these inherited structures, evolved during converse between organism and environment through countless ancestral lives, there pre-exists a potential knowledge of position: infinitely numerous past experiences have so moulded the nervous organization that the sensation excites the correlated consciousness of the spot affected. Several kinds of evidence yield indirect verifications of this view. We have, in the first place, the fact that the apprehension of position is definite or vague according as the part is well or ill placed for purposes of exploration. Knowledge of the point at which a finger has been touched is far more precise than knowledge of the point at which the back has been touched. In the second place we have the fact that more exact and detailed knowledge of the positions of parts that are touched, is acquired when an unusual amount of exploration is carried on by the part; as in the fingers of a blind man, who becomes able to read by touch. In the third place the fact that when a limb has been amputated, irritations set up in the remains of the nerves are referred to those remoter parts of the limb which no longer exist, joined with the fact, of which I have personal experience, that under certain abnormal conditions irritation of the end of one finger produces a sensation localized in the end of another finger, show that such consciousness of space as is implied by consciousness of places in the body, depends on the presence of those channels which convey impressions from the periphery of the nervous system to its centre. And once more, the fact that consciousness of position is determined by the inherited distribution of the nerves is conclusively shown by the well-known behaviour of a decapitated frog in using its limbs to push away a scalpel from a point that is touched.

Evidently these facts, along with numerous kindred facts, fall into their places as results which the process of evolution has necessitated; and they carry with them the implication that, in superior creatures, inheriting the effects of infinite experiences, some potential consciousness of space precedes experiences of things in space. Just as before birth the stomach implies food to be by-and-by swallowed, just as the lungs presuppose an environing air to be presently breathed, just as the lenses of the eye presuppose light-reflecting objects which are to have their images cast on the retina, just as the hand foretells a surrounding world full of things to be grasped; so do the nerve-centres which are to co-ordinate the actions of senses and limbs, contain partially-organized adjustments to the external relations of phenomena; and so do certain of them contain structures in which there lies latent the apprehension of space-relations—structures requiring but a little exercise to complete them, and to change the vague potential consciousnesses of positions into definite consciousnesses. Obviously, too, there exist, partially-developed in these nerve-centres, certain universal necessities of action corresponding to certain universal necessities of relation: latent axioms, the truth of which is apprehended the moment their terms are clearly recognized. As, in the course of converse with the environment, a limb, habitually bent in a certain way, acquires a structure which prevents it from bending in an opposite way; so, perpetual converse with space-relations having a fixed order, results in the formation of nervous structures which will act only in a corresponding order: thought in an opposite direction becomes impossible.

And here, indeed, we see that not only the Kantian hypothesis, but also the Experience-hypothesis in its original form, is found wanting when brought face to face with the facts of nervous organization. What is the meaning of the brain? What are the meanings of the various ganglia at its base, their entering nerve-trunks, their commissures, their connexions with the cerebellum and the superjacent hemispheres? Is not the conclusion irresistible that these imply potentialities of established, or partially established, nervous actions, with the corresponding established, or partially established, modes of consciousness? If in the drum of the ear, the attached ossicles, the cochlea, the semi-circular canals, &c., we recognize appliances for reception of sounds, various in *timbre*, pitch, and loudness; then it is absurd not to recognize the correlative nervous centres as appliances for the apprehension of those sounds in their various qualities and relations; and it is similarly absurd not to recognize other parts of the brain as severally organized for the apprehension of other groups of related phenomena—organized most elaborately in those cases where the continually-inherited results of experiences have been most frequent and uniform, as in the relations of space. And on remembering that the potentialities of those modes of mind which we distinguish as emotions evidently exist in the infant, which now shows signs of anger, now of fear, now of pleasure, it becomes a still more irresistible implication that all the other modes of mind are potentially present as correlatives of structures more or less developed; and emerge from their vague forms into definite forms as fast as the structures evolve, in the same way that the fumblings of the hands grow into definite prehensions as the muscles and nerves of the hands become better organized.

The above sketch, which presents in a briefer and partly different way the arguments contained in the chapters on "The Perception of Space" and "The Perception of Body as presenting Statical Attributes," must of course be taken as a rude and simplified account of a process which is extremely involved. Further, it must be acknowledged that as we can never wholly free ourselves from our developed space consciousness, it is difficult, when tracing out its genesis, to avoid including, at each stage of explanation, nothing beyond that which has been previously explained. We have to contemplate the process of genesis as vicariously undergone; and have to verify the successive stages by reference to our own analyzed experiences.

Even, however, were the developed consciousness of space so organically inwoven with every perception and thought as to disable us from even partially separating it, we might still be right in believing that it has been developed. For there are phenomena of consciousness which we cannot represent to ourselves as taking place, and yet which we know with perfect certainty do take place. We have an instance in the commencement and growth of consciousness in general. One who watches the early vague gropings of an infant which has "no speculation" in its eyes, must admit that there does not yet exist in it any appreciable amount of mind. Joining the testimony of parents with the implication of universal experience, he sees it to be an inevitable conclusion that he himself was once without any such coherent consciousness as that which he calls thought. Yet, if he attempts to go back to this stage, and imagine his mental state when he had no power to recognize things, he finds himself unable to do so. He is obliged to carry with him his mental habits, and to read into his earliest preceptions those processes of perception which have become confirmed. But this fact that in thinking about the genesis of his intelligence he cannot free himself from his intelligence, does not make him question the truth that he was once without intelligence. Similarly, then, with that consciousness of space which forms a part of his mental possessions.

Of course, the interpretation takes for granted the existence of objective space, or rather of some matrix of phenomena to which our consciousness of space corresponds. Manifestly, the hypothesis that a form of intuition is generated by converse with a form of things, necessarily postulates the existence of a form of things. With this admission, however, may be joined the assertion that the Kantian hypothesis tacitly, though unavowedly and inconsistently, makes the same assumption. When Kant said that "Space is *nothing else* than . . . . the subjective condition of the sensibility," he by implication, proved that in his mind there existed the thought of it as *something else.* If the consciousness of space is exclusively "the subjective condition of the sensibility," how could there have been suggested the thought of space as a "something else," the existence of which had to be denied?

It must also be pointed out that since, on the evolution hypothesis, that consciousness of space which we have lies latent in the inherited nervous system, and since, along with those first excitations of the nervous system which yield rudimentary perceptions of external objects, there are produced those first excitations of it which yield the rudimentary consciousness of the space in which the objects exist; it must necessarily happen that space will appear to be given along with these rudimentary perceptions as their form. There will necessarily very soon result something like that inseparability which the Kantists allege. Hence we cannot expect completely to decompose into its elements the space-consciousness *as it exists in ourselves.* We can expect only, as above said, to trace the synthesis of it vicariously —to see whether, in conformity with the known laws of mental growth, we cannot put together the experiences out of which it has been evolved.

Much more might be added; but if what has been said above does not carry conviction, neither would anything further. With those who have not yet thought about the question at issue, and with those whose judgments are in suspense concerning it, the foregoing arguments may have weight; but they are unlikely to weigh with those who have espoused transcendentalism. Though, when that original form of the experience-hypothesis which ascribes all mind to the experiences of the individual is replaced by this developed form, which ascribes mind in chief measure to the inherited effects of the experiences of all antecedent individuals, we are enabled to understand how forms of intuition are produced by the moulding of thought during converse with things, the solution is, as already said, unacceptable by the neo-Kantists. Implying the production of mind by natural evolution instead of by supernatural endowment, it is at variance with that conception of the universe with which supernaturalism is bound up.

To suppose that the neo-Kantists and the English Hegelians are likely to abandon their views, is to suppose that they are likely to abandon their theology; for on looking round it is obvious that those who, among ourselves, defend these doctrines of German thinkers, are mostly those who regard them as a stronghold against the assaults of modern science. In dealing with antagonists whose reasons cannot be met, they find it convenient to draw them into a region where reason is asphyxiated. What safer refuge can there be for incredible dogmas than behind unthinkable propositions? If we accept the proposition that space is "nothing but" a form of thought, to conceive which we must unite in consciousness the idea of self and the idea of space, as the one containing the other—a mental feat never performed by Kant nor any one else; then, much more readily may we accept the proposition that the Power manifested in thirty millions of suns with their attendant groups of worlds, made a bargain with Abraham for allegiance in return for territory, and demanded his foreskin as a sign of subjection.

Here, so far as I am concerned, the matter must rest. Controversies in general are of little use, and they are especially futile where there can be no agreement respecting the test of truth. It is useless to argue unless such a test is agreed upon; and it is impossible for my opponents to accept my test (the inconceivableness of the negation), since, did they accept it, their doctrine would disappear at the first step.

SUBJECT - INDEX.

(For this Index the Author is indebted to F. HOWARD COLLINS, Esq., of Edgbaston, Birmingham.)

and relations between feelings, I, 168–72; cohesion of feelings, I, 172–5, II, 505g; and definiteness, I, 175–7, II, 505g, 505r; compound clustering of feelings, I, 177–9, II, 505g, 505k; limitation and coherence of feelings, I, 179–81, II, 505g, 505k; composition of vivid and faint feelings, I, 181–3, 185; composition of, and compounding of feelings, I, 183–6; conformity to laws of evolution, I, 186–90; nervous structure and composition of, I, 190–2, II, 505i; differentiation from intellect, I, 192; interpretation and evolution, I, 291, 614; definition of life, I, 292–4, II, 505m; not assimilable to motion I, 403; Carpenter on evolution of, I, 501a; material and mental evolution, I, 507, II, 505o; the physical problem, I, 508–10; evolution of, résumé, I, 614–6, 627–8, II, 505m–p; materialism, I, 616–24; congruity of data and inductions, II, 505e–l; relation of object and subject and conception of, II, 505ss; final differentiation of transfigured realism, II, 505vv–xx; classification of elements, II, 512–6; (see also Life).

Mollusca: self-mobility, I, 3, 6, 10; nervous structure, I, 15; and centralization, I, 31; sense of touch I, 359; reflex action, I, 427, 428.

Molecules (see Motion, molecular).

Morphia, action of, I, 605, 634.

Morphology (see Nervous System).

Motion: nervous system development, I, 3, 4–6, 13; its size, I, 6–12, 13; summary of nerve function in terms of, I, 64–7; symbolical conception only, I, 158; effect of varying, in object and subject, I, 201–3, 205; illusiveness of, I, 261; ciliary and vital correspondence, I, 297–9: increase in organic sensibility and, I, 354–7; co-ordination of correspondences, I, 371, 372, 374; not assimilable to mind, I, 403; growth of intelligence, I, 425; materialism, I, 616–24; ultimate nature of mind, I, 624–7; relation to sound and reasoning, II, 66; perception of statical attributes, II, 159–61, 161–3, 171–2, 176, 183; perception of space, II, 188, 195–7, 269: of time, II, 214; ideas of space and time, II, 216–8, 218–20; their development, II, 220–5; and

concurrent evolution, II, 225–30; perception of, II, 231, 505u, 505z; resistance and cognition of, II, 235, 236; cognition of extension, II, 267; subjective and objective rest, II, 277; likeness of perception, II, 282; Berkeley's conception, II, 321, 322; necessary propositions illustrated, II, 448; symbolization, II, 477; result of emotion, II, 541; relation to quantity of feeling, II, 542–5, 556; sentiment of restrained, II, 584–8; æsthetics and grace of, II, 639, 640; convertibility to heat, II, 656.

Motion, molecular: nervous reservoirs of, I, 35, 44; the stimulus of afferent nerves, I, 47; nervous differentiation, liberation, and conduction, I, 49–52, II, 505f; nervous co-operation and liberation of, I, 52–4; relation to nerve centres and connections, I, 54–6, II, 505f; conditions for nervous action, I, 76–8; time and nerve transmission, I, 81–5; intermittent nerve discharge, I, 81, 152; molecular complexity and absorption of, I, 83; nerve impressibility, I, 85–8; also stimulation and discharges, I, 95, II, 540; relation of nervous action to feeling, I, 107; duration of feeling, I, 108; actual and ideal forms of feelings, I, 124; origin of desires, I, 125–7, II, 629; unit of consciousness, I, 152–4, 184; rhythm, I, 156; subjective nature of feeling, I, 207; revivability of feelings, I, 238; reflex action, I, 427; genesis of will, I, 496–9; the physical problem, I, 508–10; nerve genesis, I, 511–4, 519, II, 505o; improvement of nerve communication, I, 515–9, 519–20, II, 505o; contractility of *cœlenterata*, I, 521–4; genesis of ganglia, I, 524–7; ganglia and nerve fibre connections, I, 527–30; size of organism and nervous system evolution, I, 530; rudimentary vision and muscular contraction, I, 533–7, II, 203; advantages from ocular development, I, 537–9; genesis of compound nervous co-ordination, I, 543–6; laws of association, I, 577–9; intellectual development, I, 582; nervous symbolization, I, 585–7; mental effects of age, I, 587–9.

" Murder will out," the proposition, II, 398.

Muscle : self-mobility and nervous

68-71, 77; of heat, I, 71, 73, 77, II, 505j; quantity of blood and activity of, I, 72-4; also quality, I, 74-5; effect of carbonic acid and urea, I, 75; molecular motion, and conditions of action, I, 76-8; similar effect of varied stimulation, I, 79, II, 505j; intermittent nerve discharge, I, 80, 152; time of nerve transmission, I, 81-5, 95; nerve force not allied to electricity, I, 83-5; duration of effect in nerve, I, 83-5; enfeeblement from action, I, 85-8, 95; rhythm of waste and repair, I, 88-91, 95, 125; multiplication of effects, I, 91-3; universal nerve discharge, I, 93-4, 95, 114; summary of discharge and stimulation, I, 95; anæsthetics, I, 103, 198, 610-12, 631-5; relation to feeling, I, 97-100, 103-7, 127, 128, II, 505r, 505y; psychical and physical correlation, I, 115-20, 128; origin of desires, I, 125-7, II, 629; unit of consciousness, I, 154; structure and composition of mind, I, 190-2, II, 505i; subjective nature of feeling, II, 206; relativity of relations between feelings, I, 224; revivability of feelings, I, 238; and of relations between, I, 248; associability of feelings, I, 257-8, II, 505i, 505k; and of relations between, I, 270; evolution, I, 388; of *radiata* and *articulata*, I, 396; reflex action, I, 427, 430, II, 505aa, 505ii; instinct, I, 432-4, 436-40; organic memory, I, 452; intelligence and degree of evolution, I, 463-5; experience and transcendental hypotheses, I, 468-71; the physical problem I, 508-10; nerve genesis, I, 511-4, 519, II, 505o; improvement of communication, I, 515-9, 519-20, II, 505y-cc; isomerism and nerve currents, I, 520; action of muscles, I, 520a-522; Balfour on evolution, I, 520b; genesis of ganglia, I, 524-7, II, 505p; ganglia and nerve fibre connections, I, 527-30; size of organism and genesis of, I, 530; light and rudimentary vision, I, 532; visual and muscular co-ordination, I, 533-7, 548-51, II, 203; advantages from ocular development, I, 537-9; central ganglion development, I, 539-41, II, 505p; structural intercalations of visual and muscular co-ordination, I, 551-3, 554, 556; genesis of compound co-ordination, I,

543-6; and doubly compound, I, 546, II, 505p; doubly compound co-ordination in space and time, I, 553-7; involved nature of its genesis, I, 557; perceptual evolution, I, 559-62; its structure and function, I, 562-4; structure and function of ideas, I, 564-8; of emotions, I, 568-71; phrenology and localization, I, 572-6; traits of intellectual development, I, 580-2, II, 505x; symbolization of nervous fluid and current, I, 585-7; variations from age, I, 587-9, 592; from bodily constitution, I, 589-91, 591-2; daily constitutional variation, I, 592-4; variation from increased special function, I, 594-6; intellectual effect of emotion, I, 596-8; pleasures, pains, and nerve pressure, I, 598-603, 610, II, 636; emotional effect of nervous debility, I, 604-5; cerebral vascular congestion, I, 606-8; vascular derangement and insanity, I, 608; co-operative causes of variation, I, 612; *résumé* of mental evolution, I, 614-6, 627-8, II, 505m-p, 505x; sensations of touch and pressure, II, 158; ideas of space, time, and motion, II, 220-5; their concurrent evolution, II, 225-30; impressions of coextension, II, 268-9; physiological and psychological generalizations, II, 302; experience hypothesis and inconceivability of negation, II, 419, 426; congruity of data and inductions, II, 505e-l; co-ordination of syntheses, II, 505m-p; congruity of syntheses, data, and inductions, II, 505p-s; congruity of analyses and syntheses, II, 505w-cc; congruity with realism, II, 505ff-ii; relation of object to subject, II, 505ss.

Object (*see* Subject).

Odour (*see* Smell).

Opium: effect on feelings, I, 103, 606; and dreams, I, 213, 217; revivability of feelings, I, 237; and of relations, I, 248; temporary insanity, I, 610; action of anæsthetics, I, 631-5; space perception and dreams from, II, 199-201.

Optic nerves, &c. (*see* Eye).

Otolites, function, I, 36, 38.

Oxygen, dependence of nervous activity on, I, 75, 77.